PROFESSIONAL PRACTICE FOR

Interior Designers

PROFESSIONAL PRACTICE FOR
Interior Designers

Fifth Edition

Christine M Piotrowski, FASID, IIDA

Published by John Wiley & Sons, Inc., Hoboken, New Jersey.
Published simultaneously in Canada.

For general information about our other products and services, please contact our Customer Care Department within the United States at (800) 762-2974, outside the United States at (317) 572-3993 or fax (317) 572-4002.

Wiley publishes in a variety of print and electronic formats and by print-on-demand. Some material included with standard print versions of this book may not be included in e-books or in print-on-demand. If this book refers to media such as a CD or DVD that is not included in the version you purchased, you may download this material at http://booksupport.wiley.com. For more information about Wiley products, visit www.wiley.com.

Library of Congress Cataloging-in-Publication Data

Piotrowski, Christine M., 1947–
     Professional practice for interior designers / Christine M. Piotrowski, FASID, IIDA. — Fifth Edition.
        1 online resource.
     Includes index.
     Description based on print version record and CIP data provided by publisher; resource not viewed.
        ISBN 978-1-118-09079-4 (cloth); ISBN 978-1-118-41595-5 (ebk);
        ISBN 978-1-118-41906-9 (ebk)
        1. Interior decoration firms—United States—Management.   2. Design services—United States—Marketing.   3. Interior decoration—Practice—United States.   I. Title.
NK2116.2
747.068—dc23
                                                                                    2012044646
     978-1-118-09079-4

Printed in the United States of America
  10   9   8   7   6   5   4   3   2

For my parents, Martha and Casmer:
I am sorry you are not here to share this with me.

CONTENTS

Part of the education of an interior designer consists of learning about the business practices of the profession. Students cannot assume that a business's success results solely from the innate creativity of the designers who own or work for a firm. It also comes from the quality of the professional practices of those involved in the business.

Regardless of the size of firm or design specialty, professional interior designers must understand and conduct themselves as businesspeople. Clients expect interior designers to be responsible for their decisions and practice. They expect excellence not only in creative work but in business conduct as well. This naturally results in an interior designer's ever-increasing need for comprehensive knowledge of business.

As a design professional, manager, educator, and business owner, I have long believed in the importance of effective business practices for this profession. I have seen where good business practices have led to success. I have seen where poor business practices have led to frustration for business owners. My interests in trying to help students and professionals become better in their business led to the publication of the first edition of this book.

I have consistently updated this book to offer a comprehensive resource that provides a solid background in business practices for students. Educators should not feel that they must try to cover everything, and students should not feel overwhelmed by the contents. Educators can easily tailor their classes around the contents to meet the instructor's desired focus and an institution's priorities.

Its comprehensive content also makes it a practical choice for practitioners wanting to start or grow their own business. There are many chapters that are generally of greater concern to a business owner than a student, just as there are some chapters that will be of greater interest to students than professionals. For both professionals and students, *Professional Practice for Interior Designers* remains one of the primary references for the NCIDQ examination concerning many aspects of business practice.

The profession of interior design continues to be transformed. Concerns for legal and ethical business operations, sustainable design practice, the impact of technology, new ways of collaborating with industry cohorts, and generational changes in the client marketplace have all had an impact on business practice. These issues and others of importance are included in this new edition.

Changes in the outline of chapters, and content additions and deletions, were undertaken after receiving input from a variety of educators and professionals. Current information on business in general and interior design business in particular was also obtained by a review of relevant literature to gauge impact on practice. An extensive review and revision of all the text and examples was undertaken to update content. The material in the chapters was carefully reviewed to eliminate duplication of material, and this has, in some cases, led to a reorganization of topics.

Distinctive features of the fifth edition include the following:

1. Based on recommendations by educators, the material most applicable to what is commonly covered in a business practices class is grouped together at the beginning of the book.

2. The exception to this is that all the career chapters are grouped together at the end of the book.

3. New topics important to practice in the 21st century have been included throughout the book so that it continues to be a comprehensive text on interior design business practices. Those new sections are highlighted later in this preface.

4. Chapters most applicable to organizing and managing a practice now appear together. They follow a logical sequence of topics, from developing the business idea, to business plan and structure, to finances, marketing, and employee issues.

5. Each chapter begins with a list of critical issues to help the student study for exams; instructors can use these for class discussion or written assignments.

6. A box titled "NCIDQ Component" indicates the chapters or parts of chapters covering material that might be part of the examination.

7. Additional "What Would You Do?" scenarios have been added at the end of the chapter.

8. Important terms have been listed at the end of each chapter.

9. A list of Web sites relevant to the chapter content has been added at the end of each chapter.

10. The text remains easy to read, with many bulleted lists highlighting key points.

11. Icons are placed in the margins, showing where related content appears on the companion Web site, www.wiley.com/go/ppid.

So that readers can see where new sections and topics have been added, those items are italicized in the following discussion about the changes in the text.

Chapters 1 and 2 provide a comprehensive overview of the profession. Topics include why the study of business practices is important, the definition of a profession, the NCIDQ examination, professional association requirements, and the importance of licensing. *A new section in Chapter 1 provides an overview of the business of interior design and how that relates to students and the study of professional practice. New sections have been added to discuss professional responsibility in a changing world, the value of interior design, and social responsibility.*

Chapters 3 and 4 remain at the beginning of the book to highlight the importance of ethical and legal practice. The "What Would You Do?" discussion items at the end of Chapter 3 have been expanded. *Information on cyber law and copyright now appears in Chapter 4.*

Based on recommendations by educators, Chapter 5 provides a presentation of how and where designers work. This was done to give an overview of the "working world" of the design practitioner. *A new section called "Expectations" discusses what the employer views as keys to what it will be looking for in a new employee.*

The next four chapters cover critical information concerning how design firms earn revenue. Chapter 6 covers fees and project compensation methods;

Chapter 7 details design contracts specifically related to design services; Chapter 8 details product pricing of goods; and Chapter 9 outlines important information about sales law and warranties related to selling merchandise. *New information has been added concerning proper signatures on contracts, strategies for avoiding contract disputes, and using small claims courts.*

The chapters concerning business project management begin with a discussion of trade sources in Chapter 10. The business side of project management is detailed in Chapter 11 with *new material added concerning research—especially evidence-based design—as a project benefit, project delivery methods, selecting project teams, integrated design, and building information modeling.* After careful review and updating, *a new section discussing sustainable product specifications and an explanation of construction agreements were added to Chapter* 12. Chapters 13 and 14 have been updated and revised.

Chapter 15 and the next five chapters focus on the development and management of a design practice. After thoroughly reviewing and updating existing material, a few chapters have been reorganized for clarity and new information added sparingly. However, *important discussions on the triple bottom line, benchmarking, and green office management have been added.*

The former two chapters on accounting were combined into Chapter 21. Material has been reorganized to better delineate the flow of the accounting process for interior designers. In particular, the first part of the chapter should make it easier for students to understand the importance of the forms and processes necessary to manage the firm's finances.

Chapters 22 through 26 form a group on marketing and selling. It is hoped that the reorganization of topics in the first three chapters will not only be conducive to a better understanding of the importance of marketing for the continued health of a design firm, but also act as a discussion of strategies and tools to make that happen. *New material has been added concerning specializing in green design, the changing demographics of clients, social media marketing, and the buyer decision-making process.* A revision of the previous discussions on etiquette is included, as professionals still deem it a necessary topic.

Chapter 27 combines the previous edition's two chapters on employee management. This reorganization and revision is expected to make this information more logically sequenced. Although brand new material was not deemed necessary, the chapter was thoroughly reviewed and modified for current practices.

As previously mentioned, the last three chapters group the information concerning career decisions and the job search. This was done because many educators report that these chapters are often covered together. Materials in all the chapters were carefully reviewed and revised based on current practice. Emphasis was placed on the digital job search and tools. Chapter 30 highlights the job interview and the transition from student to professional. *It also includes a new section concerning on-the-job strategies to assist emerging professionals and practitioners make the best of their current job situation.*

There is an extensive and updated list of references covering the topics in this book. Additional updated references to articles and other resources (including Web sites of organizations and sources of information useful to the reader) appear again in this edition.

Ancillary materials, including business forms, brief articles, and additional references, is available on this book's companion Web site (www.wiley .com/go/ppid) whether readers purchase an electronic version or printed version of the text. The forms are PDFs so that they can be used in class.

A revised Instructor's Manual—available only to educators—can be obtained online by contacting the publisher. The Instructor's Manual includes a detailed table of contents that will help an instructor transition from the fourth to the fifth edition. As with previous Instructor's Manuals, a test bank and discussion items are provided for each chapter. A series of Power Point slides are available to instructors for the first time as a teaching resource.

Since its first publication in 1990, this book has become the leading choice of educators for use in teaching an interior design business practices class in colleges and universities throughout the world. Educators often cite it for its clear writing style and content based on realistic practice situations. I am very proud and humbled by the extent of its adoption and practical use.

Visit the companion Web site:
www.wiley.com/go/ppid
for additional learning resources

ACKNOWLEDGMENTS

I owe a great measure of gratitude to the many designers, organizations, and educators that have contributed to this and previous editions of this book. Their unselfish sharing of information, business forms, and editorial comment has helped continue to enrich this book.

Thank you to those who shared documents in this edition: Charlene Conrad, IDC, IDNS; Juliana Catlin, FASID; Phyllis Moore, FASID; Suzan Globus, FASID; Michael Thomas, FASID; Greta Guelich, ASID; Debra May Himes, ASID; James Tigges, ASID, IIDA; Allyson Calvert, ASID; Kathleen Chaffee, Hickory Business Furniture; Leonard Alverado, Contract Office Group; Jain Malkin, CID; Fred Messner, IIDA; Sally Thompson, ASID; and Merritt Menefee, IIDA. I also want to thank the American Society of Interior Designers, International Interior Design Association, and National Council for Interior Design Qualification for their contributions and continued support.

Numerous educators have provided insights and comments that have helped in the revision of this book. They are too numerous to mention, but I want specifically to thank Liz Thompson of the Art Institute of Pittsburg; Robert Krikac from Washington State University; Cindy Stedman from the Art Institute of Phoenix; Carl Clark from Northern Arizona University; Dr. Carol Morrow from the Art Institute of Phoenix; Robin Wagner from Marymount University; Christine Kennedy of the Art Institute of Michigan; Tom Witt from Arizona State University; and Renee Hern of the International Academy of Design and Technology in Nashville, TN.

Many other interior design practitioners and organizations have provided information and documents in previous editions. I do not want to let their contributions to this text to go unnoticed; however, the list has become too long to include. My thanks to you all, nonetheless, is heartfelt. I do want to specifically thank a few for their tremendous support over the years: Dave Petroff, IIDA; Beth Harmon-Vaughn, FIIDA; Carl Clark, FASID; and Michael Thomas, FASID.

I would like to give a special thank-you to everyone at John Wiley & Sons who has supported this project over many years. In particular, thanks to Michael New, Editorial Assistant, and other editorial and production assistants; and Amanda Miller, Vice President and Publisher, my first editor at John Wiley & Sons. A very special thank-you to Paul Drougas, my editor and good friend, for your patience, support, and understanding during a trying time to complete this book.

I owe a great measure of gratitude to my family and great friends who have supported me in this edition and all the previous editions of this book. I especially want to thank Gail Schabow, Greta Guelich, and Mary Knott for holding me up when I wasn't sure this would ever come about.

Lastly, I want to thank the readers who have continued to find this book an important resource for the operation of their businesses and as a learning tool for students. Your continued support and praise has been humbling and inspiring.

Christine M. Piotrowski

PROFESSIONAL PRACTICE FOR

Interior Designers

CHAPTER 1

Interior Design as a Profession

After completing this chapter you should be able to:

- Discuss why the study of professional practices is important to any entry-level designer.
- Explain how interior design is different from decorating as if you were talking to a client.
- Identify the characteristics of a profession.
- Explain how these characteristics relate to the practice of interior design.
- Understand the history of the profession in order to learn about the professional practice of interior design.
- Explain how the Great Depression of 1929 affected the interior design professional.
- Name the organizations that became the American Society of Interior Designers and International Interior Design Association.
- Identify key changes that led to the increasing professionalism of interior design.
- Compare the practices of residential interior design and commercial interior design.
- Explain how the section on the business of interior design affects your understanding of the profession as a whole.
- Discuss how interior design provides value to a residential client and a small business owner.

The stereotype of the interior design profession has been of someone who understands how to use color and can rearrange furniture. This is, as you already know, not the full story of what an interior design professional is or does.

Interior design is a complex process and it requires learning much more than the color wheel. The body of knowledge and skills needed by professionals is extensive, and the work of the interior designer—regardless of specialty—is demanding as well as exciting. The professional interior designer's solutions have to meet functional needs of the client, as well as result in a pleasing environment. The individuals who design interiors must be sure that their designs meet building, fire safety, and accessibility codes. Interior design solutions must also meet sustainable design criteria required by the owners.

A professional interior designer must be willing to accept the legal and ethical consequences of his or her actions. Those actions impact the general public, clients, and other practitioners. Local laws (including professional regulation, where it exists) can impact the work of the professional interior designer. The profession of interior design is also a business. The management and efficient operation of a business are critical to the successful ongoing life of an interior design practice.

Society tends to grant professionals higher status, money, and respect, yet these do not come automatically upon attaining the educational criteria required of the profession. They come to the individual who has the attitude of service, commitment, and knowledge that is expected of the professional. This is no less true for an interior design professional than any of the "traditional" professions.

This chapter, to use a design metaphor, is a foundation of information important to the overall study of the profession and how it functions as a business. The professional practice of interior design requires attention to the business procedures, strategies, and protocols that any business must use for the business to be successful, profitable, and long lasting. Designing interiors is not only an enjoyable way to make a living, but also an awesome responsibility.

WHY STUDY PROFESSIONAL PRACTICE?

The profession of interior design is incredibly fascinating. Practitioners have the opportunity to design the interiors of multimillion-dollar houses or help a family have a more pleasing and nurturing home environment. Practitioners also have the opportunity to help a small business or huge corporation provide an interior environment that positively influences their clients and employees and helps the business achieve greater functionality and success.

The profession of interior design is also a business, so knowledge and application of business practice concepts are essential. A designer who is bad at business subconsciously hints to clients that they can take advantage of the designer by arguing and second-guessing the designer's decisions. Furthermore, if the firm is not successful as a business, if it does not sustain profitability, it makes no difference how creative the practitioners might be: The poorly run business is likely to fail.

Interior design is much more than a way to express creativity. It is an endeavor that must recognize the importance of ethical conduct. It is about being socially responsible and realizing that, in today's world, the interior design profession has a global reach. It's not just about "us" in the United States, it's about all of "us" on this planet. It is not a hobby; it is not the quick, do-it-yourself situation portrayed on cable TV.

An interior design firm must make a profit—or at least hopes to consistently make a profit. Studying and applying business practices to the management of the firm helps the owner have a greater chance of achieving a profit. If the business owner is to allow his or her company to grow to the extent that he or she would like it to grow, the owner must understand all the aspects of professional practice.

As an employee, you will be held accountable for the ongoing success of an interior design firm. You have a responsibility to work productively and bill those hours, or otherwise professionally and effectively complete your job tasks. You need to have some awareness of the expense it takes to operate a practice so that you do not waste company resources.

Students must master a basic understanding of business practices. Although a business practices class may come late in the curriculum, that placement does not make it any less important. I believe it is one of the two most important classes in a student's curriculum, even if it's not the most important to you individually. Without an understanding of the professional practice of interior design, as a student, emerging professional, or employee, your success will be limited.

Finally, many topics in this book are topics important to the National Council for Interior Design Qualification (NCIDQ) examination. Business topics are also common parts of other certification or licensing programs, as they are expected to be within curriculums accredited by the Council for Interior Design Accreditation (CIDA). If business were not important to the profession, these groups would not include business practices topics in their certification/accreditation requirements.

An interior design firm owner once told me that he wants to hire individuals who want his job. That doesn't happen without knowing how to run a business.

DEFINING THE PROFESSION

Compared to many other professions, such as teaching and medicine, interior design is a relatively young. The use of the term *interior design* did not appear in general usage until after World War II, and the profession defined by any term did not really exist much before the 1900s. Individuals and organizations involved in the interior design profession work tirelessly to help the profession gain recognition in the minds of the public, as well as among practitioners and allied professionals.

What constitutes interior design has been debated and nurtured for many decades. Much of the public believes that "people who decorate interiors are interior decorators." They often do not understand that there is a difference between decoration and design. The words of an article by Charlotte S. Jensen, FASID, then president of the NCIDQ board, still ring true: "Interior design is not the same as decoration. . . . Decoration is the furnishing or adorning a space with fashionable or beautiful things. Decoration, although a valuable and important element of an interior, is not solely concerned with human interaction or human behavior. Interior design is all about human behavior and human interaction."[1] And much more, many would say.

The most commonly quoted and utilized definition of *interior design* comes from the NCIDQ. This definition, offered in part with the complete version presented in the appendix, has been acknowledged and supported by the interior design professional associations:

> Interior design is a multifaceted profession in which creative and technical solutions are applied within a structure to achieve a built interior environment. These solutions are functional, enhance the quality of life and culture of the occupants, and are aesthetically attractive. Designs are created in response to and coordinated with the building shell, and acknowledge the physical location and social context of the project. Designs must adhere to code and regulatory requirements, and encourage the principles of environmental sustainability. The interior design process follows a systematic and coordinated methodology, including research, analysis and integration of knowledge into the creative process, whereby the needs and resources of the client are satisfied to produce an interior space that fulfills the project goals.[2]

Another excellent definition comes from outside the profession. According to the U.S. Department of Labor, Bureau of Labor Statistics, interior designers "plan, design and furnish interiors of residential, commercial or industrial buildings. Formulate design which is practical, aesthetic, and conducive to intended purposes, such as raising productivity, selling merchandise, or improving life style."[3]

As you can see from these, interior design is much more than the stereotypical idea of picking out colors and fabrics. The responsibilities and skills required also go beyond those of the individual who has a flair for decorating.

WHAT IS A PROFESSION?

A profession is much more than the words in a definition provided by interested groups. According to one dictionary, a *profession* is "a paid occupation, especially one that involves prolonged training and a formal qualification."[4] Johnson writes, "As defined by sociologists, a profession is an occupation that is based on theoretical and practical knowledge and training in a particular field. . . . Professions tend to be credentialed and regulated in relation to certain standards of performance and ethics, which makes them more autonomous and independent than other occupations."[5]

Some argue that interior design is not really a profession. This has often occurred when discussions with state legislatures concerning regulation of interior design or use of the title "interior designer" take place. Yet the interior design profession meets the standards set for defining a profession.

The profession of interior design, as we know it today, is guided by all the points noted by both of these authors and as further clarified by the definitions. If the measure of a profession involves the criteria offered by the preceding material, then interior design is a profession that has evolved and continues to evolve. Gordon Marshall writes, "A profession includes some central regulatory body to ensure the standard of performance of individual members; a code of conduct; careful management of knowledge in relation to the expertise which constitutes the basis of the profession's activities; and lastly, control of number, selection, and training of new entrants."[6]

A professional does not emerge merely as a consequence of learning the technical principles required in the profession. Becoming a professional also requires an attitude of dedicated commitment to the work one does and to the advancement of the profession. Understanding what it takes to organize and maintain an interior design practice follows an understanding of the roots and contemporary concerns of the profession. In the 21st century, having talent as a designer is not enough to survive the ups and downs of the economic roller coaster.

How would you define the interior design profession?

PROFESSIONAL RESPONSIBILITY IN A CHANGING WORLD

Have you ever had the opportunity to stand below the soaring branches of a sequoia tree? I had a chance to do this when I visited Sequoia National Park in California several years ago. These magnificent redwoods can grow to more than 200 feet tall and live for more than 2000 years! I visited a site within the park where trees had been harvested in the late 1800s. The base of the trunk is huge. You don't just walk up to the remaining stump and sit down. I walked up stairs to the top of a stump that was more than 10 feet above the ground. The surface size of that stump, as I recall, was about the size of a two-car garage.

It turns out that the wood of the sequoia tree—a species of redwood—although resistant to fire and decay, is very brittle, making it unsuitable for building. The wood was mostly used at the turn of the century for fence posts, grape stakes, and shingles. What a waste of a piece of our magnificent natural world!

Why is this story offered in a book about interior design professional practice?

Our industry uses huge amounts of natural resources in the creation of the products we specify for homes and businesses. The use of these materials has led to the depletion of many resources and threatens others. Construction and remodeling contribute to landfills at alarming levels. According to the U.S. Green Building Council (USGBC), "commercial construction projects generate up to 2.5 pounds of solid waste per square foot of floor space."[7] The math means that a 10,000-square-foot building could produce up to 12.5 tons of waste! That is a lot of wasted resources going to the landfill.

The choices we make when we specify goods and design solutions for the client can have profound future effects. Removing and disposing of carpeting that still has some useful life is a poor choice if there is a place in your community that can utilize this material. Exotic woods like rosewood are beautiful—yet rosewood forests are being depleted, and should you choose to specify this exotic wood, you must be sure it is coming from a legal source. Consider the specification of paints made with volatile organic compounds that harm users of the space as well as the contractors doing the work. I know of a painter who worked in the construction industry for more than 30 years. He told me he now has only one lung, in large part because of the volatile materials he breathed those many years.

Of course, the interest in sustainable design and the willingness of clients and designers to embrace this concept in interiors varies widely. Often at issue is the assumed versus actual additional cost of specifying environmentally friendly or green products. A client who has serious allergies or respiratory problems suffers allergic reactions to the chemicals in many floor coverings, furniture products, and various textiles. Naturally, this type of client easily sees the benefits of green products. Commercial clients may see that the benefits of "going green" are worth an additional cost, but many are still reluctant to spend the extra money. However, design projects using green products and designing a project using the USBGC's LEED® guidelines continue to gain momentum.

What we do as professionals—the specification of interior spaces and products—affects both the environment and the users of spaces. It behooves interior designers to learn more about sustainable design and how to mitigate environmental damage and support users' health. Interior designers who wish to market or encourage the use of green design concepts must become thoroughly educated on the benefits to clients of using green products.

Another important issue for interior designers relates to the aging population—or should I say the aging of our client base? Baby boomers—those born between 1946 and 1964—began turning 60 in 2006. The group called "matures," who were born between 1901 and 1945, represent another large proportion of our population of consumers. The issues of designing a home environment, as well as almost all types of commercial spaces, that are friendly to the senior user are critical.

As an interior designer, you need to realize an important fact about these older age groups: Most do not think of themselves as "old," nor do they like being treated as old. It is not the interior designer's responsibility to think of consumers in the older age groups either as being "old" or being less able to take care of themselves. It is, however, the interior designer's responsibility to help create a home or working environment that is satisfying, safe, and functional for the users.

Interior designers have a professional responsibility to learn about and apply design concepts that can make a home or business environment safe for all ages and abilities. Universal design concepts come to us as second nature now, as many no doubt like the extra size of an accessible toilet facility or the ease of using a ramp instead of stairs. Designers who are young themselves must learn about the older client and also the diplomacy involved in specifying products that will enhance the environment of their older adult clients.

You no doubt have heard of the term "aging in place." In relation to the interior design of the home, this refers to a concept of designing or remodeling a residence so that the occupants can remain in their private residence rather than moving to some sort of senior living facility or apartment. Many changes to a residence that will help support or accommodate the inevitable physical changes to residents can be easily incorporated, whether by client choice or simple design specifications.

The concepts of safe and accessible interior design apply to both residential and commercial interiors, and thus should be part of the practice of all interior designers. In a commercial facility, we are guided by accessibility codes that require certain things to be designed into the space to make sure the space is accessible to all users. In a home—especially with younger home owners—many accessibility and safety issues might not be acknowledged until someone breaks a leg skiing and must cope with designs that are incompatible with someone on crutches or must use a wheelchair.

These issues also have become a business choice for many. Some designers have chosen to increase work with clients in senior care and assisted-living facilities. Just as we realize we must abide by accessibility codes in a commercial space, so too should interior designers now look toward simply deciding to meet client needs and demands for the design of LEED®-certified buildings and aging-in-place products and planning concepts.

Sustainable design, universal design, and design for an aging population are as much a way of thinking and a professional responsibility as design specialties. "If not now, when?" was asked about other important topics years ago. It is also asked now: When will you learn more about topics that affect the profession and interior design practice and lead to professional responsibility in a changing world?

The practice of interior design is a continually growing and changing profession. Interior designers must continually keep informed and up to date on critical issues that will likely affect their business in the present or the near future. Our professional responsibility in a changing world will likely take the interior design professional to places he or she never envisioned.

HISTORICAL OVERVIEW

History classes cover important material on furniture and architecture, but many do not discuss how the interior design profession arose and evolved. This brief section provides some context for that history.

Before the 20th century, interior decoration was the responsibility of artisans, craftsmen, painters, sculptors, and early architects. Shopkeepers were called *ensembliers* or *ateliers* in Europe. According to John Pile, Charles Percier (1764–1838) and Pierre-François-Léonard Fontaine (1762–1853) are thought by many to be the first professional interior designers. "Percier and Fontaine conceived of interior spaces developed under their full control in the manner of modern interior designers."[8]

Elsie de Wolfe (1865–1950) was among the first individuals to bring the concept of professionalism to interior decoration in the United States. It was approximately during her career that the term *interior decoration* began to be used. Born in New York City and a member of the upper class, de Wolfe began her career as a professional interior decorator in 1904, when she was 39 years old. Her first commission, in 1905, was for the design of the Colony Club in New York City. Among de Wolfe's clients were such notable figures as Henry C. Frick and Anne Pierpont Morgan. Because these early decorators often had a wealthy clientele, the term *society decorator* was often associated with them.

De Wolfe also wrote one of the earliest books about interior decoration, *The House in Good Taste*, in which she related her philosophy of decoration for homes. This book, which was republished in 2004, gives a fascinating glimpse into early interior decoration. She also is credited with being responsible for another milestone in the profession: receiving a fee for her design services rather than a commission on the sale of furniture.[9] De Wolfe's success inspired other women to enter the profession. It was one of the few acceptable professions for women at the turn of the century.

In approximately 1904, formal educational preparation was offered at the New York School of Applied and Fine Arts—founded as the Chase School. (This school is now known as Parsons, The New School for Design, located in New York City.) A few courses were offered in art or home economics programs in other schools, but formal training in interior decoration was not easy to obtain. Individuals who could not avail themselves of formal courses generally learned from magazines of the time, such as *House Beautiful* or *House & Garden*.

Postwar prosperity after World War I saw an increased interest in, and employment of, the interior decoration professional. In 1924, Eleanor McMillen opened McMillen Inc., claiming to be the first full-service interior decorating firm in the United States.[10] This prosperity led to an increasing number of professionals with specialized knowledge in different types of interiors beyond residential interior decoration. By the late 1920s, many local "Decorators' Clubs" had been started in various parts of the country. The Decorators Club located in New York is credited with being one of the first, if not the first, such organization.[11]

Furniture manufacturers in the 1920s were producing fine-quality furniture in places such as Grand Rapids, Michigan, and High Point, North Carolina. Department stores used a display technique called a *vignette* to help the middle-class consumer visualize a room of furniture and thus encouraged consumers to utilize better-quality design in their homes.[12] (*Vignette*, as used in the interior design profession, means a display of furniture and furnishings that simulates an actual room.) Magazines continued to be used by the masses of consumers to appreciate quality interior decoration done by professionals and primarily available only to the wealthy.

The Great Depression of the 1930s had a profound influence on the furniture industry and thus the interiors profession. It had a disastrous effect on the ability of the middle class to purchase furniture. Yet the leading society decorators remained relatively unaffected by the depression, as their wealthy clients could still afford to purchase quality goods. The society decorators, however, were purchasing goods from Europe rather than using American-made goods. This had a further, and decidedly negative, impact on American manufacturers.

Grand Rapids, Michigan, was the site of one of the earliest and largest to-the-trade-only semiannual furniture markets. At the time, Grand Rapids was one of the largest manufacturing centers in the United States. The Grand

Grand Rapids Furniture Exposition, as it was officially called, was first held in December 1878.[13] The market was held in January and June for 87 years. Local manufacturers displayed their products, educational programs were held, and manufacturers from other locations rented storefronts to show their goods.

The leaders of the Grand Rapids manufacturing center in the 1930s needed to bring the decorators to Grand Rapids so that they could see the quality of American-made furniture. With William R. Moore of Chicago, they put together a conference to organize a national professional organization. The conference was held during July 1931, in Grand Rapids, and speakers such as Frank Lloyd Wright were scheduled to appear in order to entice decorators to the conference. The decorators were invited to the various manufacturing plants and showrooms to see the furniture firsthand. By the end of the conference, the American Institute of Interior Decorators (AIID)—the precursor to the American Society of Interior Designers (ASID)—had been founded, with William R. Moore as its first national president.

World War II led to new manufacturing techniques that changed furniture and design styles. The modernism of the Bauhaus school—originally located in Germany—greatly influenced the design of buildings and interiors in the United States. Consumers had larger disposable incomes and were willing to buy again. It was during the 1940s that the term *decorator* began to lose favor in the industry. It was also at this time that educational standards and the number of programs offered grew, as interest in the profession increased. Massive growth in industrialism after the war also boosted the building, furniture, and interiors industries.

After World War II, nonresidential design became an increasingly important aspect of the profession for many reasons. The evolution of giant corporations was one factor. Curtain wall construction, suspended ceilings, and changes in construction to allow for vast, open interior spaces in office buildings all affected the design–build industry. Changes in the philosophy of the workplace created new furniture concepts, such as that of the "office landscape." As companies embraced this planning philosophy, new specialists in space planning, lighting design, and acoustics became part of the profession.

Women were making an impact on the commercial design industry as well. Dorothy Draper (1889–1969) is credited with being the first woman interior decorator who specialized in commercial interiors.[14] Florence Knoll established the Knoll Planning Group in the 1940s. This design company's focus was on commercial interior design.[15]

New design concepts, as well as other issues, created tension and arguments over educational requirements and admission to professional associations for interior designers. A renewed debate ensued over the words "decorator" versus "designer." As educational programs developed, curriculums varied, resulting in uneven preparation. It was recognized that education needed to be more stringent, with formalized preparation that went beyond aesthetics. The growing complexity of the work of the interior designer led to professional associations formalizing requirements for membership.

New pressures and responsibilities will continue to affect all practitioners, businesses, and even students of interior design. This short history provides a context for the development of the interior design profession and is meant to give readers an appreciation of the roots of the profession called interior design. Table 1-1 summarizes its chronological development. This table is also included on the Wiley companion Web site as item 1-1. Additional history of the associations is presented later in Chapter 2.

The profession thrives during economic booms and, like every industry, redefines itself when the economy is slow. Regardless of the impact of the

TABLE 1-1.

Highlighted chronology of the growth of the interior design profession

1878	First-of-its-kind semiannual furniture market. Held in Grand Rapids, Michigan.
1904	First real use of term *interior decoration*. First courses in interior decoration offered at the New York School of Applied and Fine Arts.
1905	Elsie de Wolfe obtains her first commission as an interior decorator. She is credited with being the first interior decorator.
1913	Elsie de Wolfe publishes the first true book on interior decoration, *The House in Good Taste*.
1920s	Greater effort is made by department stores to market home furnishings. Manufacturing centers of home furnishings begin to develop. Art Deco period creates greater interest in interior decoration of homes and offices. Dorothy Draper credited with being the first woman interior decorator to specialize in commercial interiors. Decorator clubs begin forming in larger cities. Design education strengthened in many parts of the country.
1931	Grand Rapids furniture show. Meeting to create a national professional organization. In July, American Institute of Interior Decorators (AIID) is founded; William R. Moore elected first national president of AIID.
1936	AIID's name changed to American Institute of Decorators (AID).
1940s	Post-World War II industrialism encourages new technologies in furniture manufacturing. Industrialism produces increased need for, and importance of, nonresidential interior design.
1950s	Development of open landscape planning concept in Germany by Quickborner Team.
1951	First time a state considers legislation to license interior design.
1957	National Society for Interior Designers (NSID) founded from a splinter group of the New York AID chapter.
1961	AID changes its name to American Institute of Interior Designers (AIID).
1963	National Office Furnishings Association (NOFA) creates NOFA-d (NOFA-designers), a professional group for interior designers who work for office furnishings dealers. Interior Design Educators Council (IDEC) founded to advance the needs of educators of interior design.
1967	NOFA and NOFA-d change names to NOPA and NOPA-d, respectively, when NOFA merges with stationery and supplies dealers to form National Office Products Association.
1968	Introduction of "Action Office," designed by Robert Probst for Herman Miller, Inc. First true open-office furniture product.
1969	Institute of Business Designers (IBD) incorporated. NOPA-d is parent organization.
1970	Charles Gelber elected first national president of IBD. Foundation for Interior Design Education Research (FIDER) is founded. Is responsible for reviewing and accrediting undergraduate and graduate interior design programs.
1974	National Council for Interior Design Qualification (NCIDQ) incorporated. Charged with the development and administration of a common qualification examination. Louis Tregre, FAID, serves as first president of NCIDQ.
1975	American Society of Interior Designers (ASID) formed from the merger of AID and NSID. Norman de Haan is first national ASID president.
1976	The first Canadian provincial associations—Interior Designers of Ontario and the Interior Designers of British Columbia—were admitted as members of NCIDQ.
1982	Alabama becomes first state with title registration legislation for interior design.
1988	First major discussion of 1995 Hypotheses, the document that begins a discussion of unification of interior design professional associations.
1992	Passage of Americans with Disabilities Act (ADA), which establishes accessibility standards for all public buildings.
1993	U.S. Green Building Council formed to promote sustainable design.

(Continued)

TABLE 1-1.

(*Continued*)

1994	Unification of IBD, ISID, and CFID to form International Interior Design Association (IIDA). The existing code councils form the International Code Council (ICC) to develop a new universal standard of building codes.
1995	First International Code from the ICC is published.
1996	Federal government officially recognizes interior design as a profession.
1990s	Numerous states pass title, practice, or certification legislation.
2000	ASID and IIDA leadership begins discussions concerning potential merger. Talks discontinued in 2002.
2002	ASID and the Government Services Administration (GSA) sign an agreement to promote interior design excellence in federal buildings.
2003	InformDesign® is initiated as a Web site to locate and make available research on interior design practices.
2006	The Council on Interior Design Accreditation (CIDA) replaces FIDER as the accrediting group for interior design education.
2010	Update and revision of the Interior Design Body of Knowledge.
2011	Regulation and licensing continue to be sought after for the profession.

economy, interior design professionals and students will be faced with continuous change in the profession. Finding one's way by gaining education, experience, and competency to work as a professional interior designer in the 21st century includes achieving knowledge and skills in professional practice.

INTERIOR DESIGN DIVISIONS

The line between residential and commercial interior design as "divisions" of the profession has blurred due to changes in lifestyle and work style throughout the world.[16] Many of those who think of themselves as residential designers occasionally do some small offices or other types of commercial spaces. Of course, those who are primarily commercial designers also occasionally design a client's residence.

The practices of many in the profession beg the question, "Are there really two classic divisions to the interior design profession?" We have always thought that there were "residential" interior designers and "commercial" interior designers. Residential designers focus exclusively on the interiors of private residences, especially single-family dwellings, as well as other types of dwellings such as condominiums, townhouses, mobile homes, and apartments. Commercial interior designers focus on one or more types of spaces used for business and government, such as offices, stores, hotels, restaurants, schools, airports, hospitals, and so on.

Some refer to commercial interior design as nonresidential or contract interior design. The term *contract design* comes from the fact that many years ago, commercial projects more frequently were executed based on contracts for services. Of course, both residential and commercial projects are undertaken after a contract for services has been executed. In this book, I have labeled anyone who works with public spaces a *commercial interior designer*.

Perhaps it is time to consider that, regardless of the type of space, the process of design follows the same path. To put it very simply, information must be gathered concerning the client's needs (programming); ideas must be generated to potentially solve those concerns (schematic design); those ideas are further developed into detailed and accurate drawings or documents (design development); additional drawings and documents are created to ensure that the project is constructed and installed properly (construction documents); specifications for the goods and materials needed are processed and managed, as is the installation or finishing of all those interior goods (construction administration); and numerous business practice issues must be managed and practiced.

In the 21st century, it is not as important to define a division as it is to define the profession. The definition of interior design provided in an earlier section does not differentiate any particular number or types of divisions of interior design. Perhaps it is time to recognize that neither is a less or more important part of the profession.

INTERIOR DESIGN VALUE

"I don't understand why you charge so much!"

Most interior designers have, at one time or another, heard this comment from clients. Many professionals are still stumped as to how to respond to this statement. After all these years, professionals and the profession still must combat the undervaluing of interior design services.

Unfortunately, many clients still view interior design services as "fun" and "easy" and more "creative" than business. Because they do not see or designers do not communicate how interior design can be of value to them, many question the designer's suggestions and fees. Too many clients still do not understand why professional interior designers should be compensated for their services or even respected like other professional service providers.

To some degree it might be argued that we ourselves have been responsible for this misconception. Interior designers can be bad businesspeople: giving away design ideas at initial meetings; being unconcerned about costs in running a business; and (frankly) letting the designer's ego get in the way of solving the client's problem. These kinds of behavior do not identify good businesspeople. The media contribute to this undervaluing of design as well, too often portraying interior design as easy or frivolous. And with so many people offering design and decorating services—many for free—why should clients value interior design?

Part of the problem arises because interior design is an intangible: it doesn't exist until after it is done. The only way that the clients can judge the quality of what they hope they will get is by seeing photos or drawings of work that the designer has done for someone else. They can feel a product; they can get comparisons online. Frequently the basis for judging the quality of what they will get from an interior designer is personal aesthetics—and that is very subjective.

As competition increases, designers have become more aware that they are not solely in the business of creating wonderfully aesthetic and functional interiors. Clients, including residential clients, are very interested in how the work of the interior designer will benefit them. Sometimes this is primarily a financial consideration. Sometimes this results in an interior that soothes the soul or creates a low carbon footprint, or provides a healthy place for the inhabitants. Interior designers can bring order out of chaos. They can bring psychological comfort to those traumatized by serious health issues. They can bring joy to children in a play area. And these do have value.

Thus, the interior designer must communicate his or her value and worth to a project on the basis of factors beyond how nice it will look at the end and the discount the client will get on furniture. The designer brings value because of his or her professional education, knowledge of how to make a space work better, be healthier, improve the users' comfort in the space, and, yes, look better.

The value of interior design also increases in the minds of clients as they see that the design community is committed to community service. Providing their problem-solving skills to nonprofit organizations like the Ronald McDonald House shows the community that interior designers are not just interested in making money by selling expensive furniture. It shows the community that interior designers are interested in the community at large.

It is hard to argue the fact that most individuals who choose interior design as a profession do so to apply their creative and aesthetic skills and talents to interior spaces. Consequently, those projects arguably improve the aesthetics of residences and various commercial facilities. Nevertheless, the true value of interior design goes way beyond these traditional views. As interior designers know well, the colors chosen for an interior can create excitement or calm. The fabric chosen can reduce maintenance issues or explode them. The products themselves, if not chosen wisely, can sabotage basic safety in an emergency or emit poisonous and harmful fumes.

An individual I once worked with, at an office furnishings dealership, introduced the design department to a client by saying "and this is the icing on the cake—the design department." Interior design is much more than icing, regardless of the space. The designer brings value to the client through his or her knowledge, experience, and skills gained through educational training and work experience. As you will read in depth in Chapter 2, these elements are critical keys to the advancement of the individual and the profession.

THE BUSINESS OF INTERIOR DESIGN

Not all designers get to work on multimillion-dollar residences, mega-hotels, or the latest celebrity chef's restaurant. The vast majority of interior designers work on smaller projects of various kinds. They help a family get a new home ready for occupancy and enjoyment. They remodel a franchise motel/hotel along the freeway. They give new life to a restaurant that needs a fresh look. They help seniors adjust their home environment to be more ergonomically friendly. Quite honestly, they might also simply specify new wall treatments, a few pieces of furniture, and stage a house for resale.

Interior design is all of these things and many more. It touches people in all walks of life and all economic positions. Also, it is a global profession: Interiors play a significant part in helping businesses succeed and people to feel comfortable in their homes throughout the world.

It is important for the student and emerging professional interior designer to understand what it is like in the real world. This section has been added to the chapter to present some basic yet very important information to help readers understand that interior design is a business as well as a creative opportunity.

For a business to exist and (we hope) succeed, it must have at least three elements. First, it has to have people who are committed to operating and participating in the business. Second, it must have customers or clients who will purchase whatever the business provides in terms of services and possibly products. Third, it must have adequate financial resources for operation.

People

An interior design business starts with the owner committed to doing design work the way he or she thinks is right. The owner should have experience in the field before opening the doors. Many students think that once they have graduated from a program, they are automatically ready to open their own offices. Some do. Many fail and end up working for someone else.

When you read Chapter 15 and the other chapters dealing with creating a design business, you will gain a deeper appreciation for what it is to be the owner of a design firm—even one whose only employee is the owner. There is a lot more to it than having a diploma, passing a licensing exam, and setting up an office.

There is risk involved in opening a business: financial risk, legal risk, and even risk in hiring employees. Employees—the people of the firm—must work as a team and must work in accordance with the rules the owner has set up. If you work for a sole practitioner or any small design firm, your willingness and ability to be a team player are crucial. Each individual in the company has a role on the team. Sometimes that role is not very glamorous. Not everything about interior design is glamorous.

As an employee, you need to remember that the firm does not belong to you. The owner, not you, makes decisions concerning how to go about doing a design project. The owners may veto work that you have spent hours doing with a wave of the hand. Guess what? It's their prerogative to do so, because it's their names on the door. Their risk is paramount to yours.

As the new person in the office, it is wise for you to keep your eyes and ears open; listen and observe what is going on. Each office has its way of doing things, and you need to learn those processes. Become a team player, and your experience opportunities will grow, just as your experience as a professional interior designer will grow.

Clients

You will read in Chapters 23 and 24 about marketing strategies and methods. Your boss will spend a great deal of time cultivating business and projects for the firm. Certainly some client opportunities walk in the door because of a referral or something the client saw on the Internet or in a magazine. Those are part of the strategies and methods that the owner must use to cultivate clients.

Design firms work very hard to create an image that they hope will appeal to potential clients. That image is commonly referred to as the company's *brand*. A design firm's brand is the combination of images and encounters that the customer perceives, accepts, and experiences with a company providing services and (depending on the company) selling products. You and your work express that brand to clients.

Clients have an impression of what it is like to work with an interior designer. That impression has been fostered by what clients see in the media, movies, and previous experiences with designers or others in the design–build industry. For many, the reality of working with you or others in the studio will be different from what their reference impression is. That is why your boss, your professors, and this textbook stress the importance of professionalism.

The more professional you are in your interactions with clients, coworkers, vendors, and others who come in contact with the firm, the stronger the firm's brand will grow.

Financial Resources

Marketing brings in clients with projects. Those projects bring in the funds to pay salaries and operate the business. Our industry and profession have suffered through recessions as well as exceptional economic times. But the financial resources needed to operate the practice are never easy to obtain and retain. When your boss is concerned about someone in the office using the telephone or Internet for personal use, she is probably remembering that those personal calls cost the company—not the user—money.

A firm makes money by charging design fees for services and perhaps by selling merchandise to clients. Design services have a cost to the company, as well as representing revenue. The biggest cost to the firm for providing design services is the salary of the designer. As you will read in Chapter 27, salary is not the only part of the employee cost of providing design services.

There are other costs involved in those services. The company has to pay utility bills, buy supplies like pens and ink for the printer, and pay monthly Web fees. These operating expenses are deducted from the revenue that is obtained from clients. Only after the expenses are paid does the firm make a potential profit. And when there is no profit, there are no funds for the owner to provide benefits to employees.

You might not think it's important to understand accounting, but it is. Chapter 21 on basic accounting will not teach you how to be an accountant or how to keep the financial records, but it will help you understand the important point that revenue and profit are not the same thing. Just because the company has sold a sofa or charged a design fee does not mean it has made a profit and can now give you a raise.

Profit only results after all the expenses of the company are subtracted from revenue. So, when it costs your boss more to operate the company than the amount of revenue the company brings in, a loss occurs. Too many months of operating at a loss means the owner might have to let you go and even close the doors.

As a final note, the business of interior design, which is the professional practice of interior design, goes way beyond just design. It is important for the student, the emerging professional, and the experienced interior designer to understand ethics, legal issues, contract creation, and appropriate ways to be compensated for work. It is also critical to be a good project manager, as any project (regardless of size) has many components to be controlled. It is also important for anyone in the interior design profession to understand basic accounting, marketing strategies, and how to organize a practice, operate that business, and hire and manage employees. All of these topics and more are presented in this textbook.

The "real world" of interior design is at times glamorous. Yet it is also many hours of paperwork to create specifications, prepare drawings, resolve problems with vendors, track missing furniture, and more problems that you probably don't want to read about right now! Mostly, it is an opportunity to create places for people to come home to and be safe and comfortable; to encourage recovery from illness; to enjoy a special event or vacation; and so on. It is a great way to work and make a living. Very few interior designers who have worked for several years would say differently in good times—or bad!

Interior Design Economic Snapshot

The economic impact of interior design is hard to judge, because so many businesses are single owners. These businesses stay under the radar of most agencies that gather information on industry. Like many businesses, interior design booms when construction and the general economy boom and falls when a recession hits.

One place to find the impact of interior design on the economy is the U.S. Bureau of Labor Statistics (BLS). It publishes a report on occupational outlook that pinpoints various occupations, including interior design. Look for the *Occupational Outlook Handbook* on www.bls.gov/ooh/arts-and-design. It is also referred to as SOC Code 27-1025. This report gives information on overall job outlook for the next 10 years, information on median pay, and other important general information for anyone looking at interior design as a career.

According to the latest report, the BLS suggests that interior design employment will grow over the next 10 years; it reports that in 2010, the number of those employed as interior designers was 56,500 and that the number is expected to hit 67,400 in 2020. The median wage in 2010 was reported as $46,280.* Additional information on salaries in interior design is provided in Chapter 30.

Median wage information on many cities can be accessed from the U.S. Department of Labor site www.careeronestop.org. This site allows you to compare wage information by state. You need to click the tab "Arts, Design, Entertainment, Sports and Media" to find the information on interior design. There is other information on that site related to job search.

The American Society of Interior Designers prepares an annual report titled the *Environmental Scanning Report*. This report looks at the economy, demographics, and other topics more specific to interior design. It is available online to members and may be available to nonmembers by contacting the national office (www.asid.org). Another worthwhile report from ASID is *The Interior Design Profession: Facts and Figures*, updated in 2012. There is a charge for this report, but it is well worth the cost, as it provides information on numbers of designers, firms, design specialties, and other interesting information. Readers may also want to check with the International Interior Design Association or other professional associations for additional reports on economic and demographic topics.

Interior Design magazine annually provides interesting statistical information on very large ("giant") interior design firms. This information gives a glimpse of the economic impact of the interior design profession. The January 2012 issue reported group earnings at $2.4 billion in fees.** This represented an increase since the previous report. Data are also provided on median salary rates ($65,000 for "designer"). It also reported that hires were up for this report, but still lower than prerecession numbers.

The *Interior Design* magazine report also provides information on the amount of fees earned by specialties, including residential and the largest firms that do foreign projects. Remember that salary rates in this report are for the 100 largest design firms participating in this annual report; they may not reflect salary rates in your area. Note also that these types of data reports lag approximately one year from when the data were obtained. In other words, a report published in 2012 is based on data from 2011.

*U.S. Department of Labor, Bureau of Labor Statistics, "Occupational Employment Statistics: 27-1025 Interior Designers" (as of August 2012). Available at www.bls.gov/oes
**Ron Marans, "Giants 100: Back to Business," *Interior Design* (Jan. 2012), pp. 84–98.

WEB SITES RELEVANT TO THIS CHAPTER

www.asid.org American Society of Interior Designers

www.interiordesigncanada.org Interior Designers of Canada

www.iida.org International Interior Design Association

www.bls.gov U.S. Bureau of Labor Statistics

www.careeronestop.org CareerOneStop is sponsored by the U.S. Department of Labor

www.ncidq.org National Council for Interior Design Qualification

KEY TERMS

ateliers

Brand

Commercial interior design

Contract design

Ensembliers

Interior design

Profession

Residential interior design

Stakeholders

Vignette

KEY NAMES

Elsie de Wolfe

Dorothy Draper

Florence Knoll

Eleanor McMillen

William R. Moore

ORGANIZATIONS

American Institute of Decorators (AID)

American Institute of Interior Decorators (AIID)

American Institute of Interior Designers (AID)

American Society of Interior Designers (ASID)

Council for Interior Design Accreditation (CIDA) (formerly FIDER)

Institute of Business Designers (IBD)

Interior Design Educators Council (IDEC)

International Interior Design Association (IIDA)

International Society of Interior Designers (ISID)

National Council for Interior Design Qualification (NCIDQ)

National Office Products Association (NOPA)

National Society of Interior Designers (NSID)

WHAT WOULD YOU DO?

Each chapter concludes with several situations that may or may not involve ethical behavior or other professional choices and challenges. These scenarios can be discussed individually or in groups. As you read these scenarios, consider ethics, good business practice, and overall professional conduct. The code of ethics from ASID or IIDA may apply to some situations.

1. It came to Phyllis's attention that her boss was considering hiring a designer—Jane Doe. Phyllis knew Jane because they worked together at a different design firm a few years ago. Phyllis knew that Jane had been fired because the other employer discovered Jane falsifying several types of client documents in connection with projects. Jane found out this information from someone at that previous firm after Phyllis had left the firm.

2. Alex has been designing hospitality spaces in the East for six years. She has become increasingly interested in sustainable design and is planning to become LEED® certified. A former client, Robert Smith, has contacted her about the design of his second home in Wyoming. Because Alex started in design at a residential furniture store/studio, she feels very comfortable in doing the project.

   Mr. Smith wants to use green products, but is concerned about the extra costs. He heard from a friend that "green stuff costs a lot of green." The client wants Alex to do the interior planning and specification and to use green products if they do not cost too much. He is also reluctant to pay the fees that Alex plans to charge to cover her travel. He suddenly says, "Let's reduce your carbon footprint by not having you travel to the job site at all."

3. John graduated from an accredited four-year program in interior design and has been working as a residential interior designer for four years. A past client asks John to design a 25-unit assisted-living facility that would include 6 units to house nursing care patients. John has no experience per se in the design of medical facilities. Should John take on this project?

4. Roberta owns a design studio and specializes in the design of high-end residential projects. She has recently lost two projects to a competitor where a former employee now works. One of those projects was for a former client couple, who are building a very large penthouse in Manhattan.

   Roberta is quite upset about losing the project for the former clients. She thought they had gotten along very well and doesn't understand why the clients would go to someone else. She calls the former clients to ask why they went with a different designer. Feeling that she got an unsatisfactory answer, Roberta now plans to ask vendors about the designer who was given the contract by her former clients.

REFERENCES

1. Jensen, September 2001, p. 91.
2. NCIDQ, www.ncidq.org/about_us/definition, 2004.
3. U.S. Department of Labor, Bureau of Labor Statistics Web site, www.bls.gov
4. *Concise Oxford American Dictionary*, 2006, p. 706.
5. Johnson, 1995, p. 216.
6. Marshall, 1998, p. 527.
7. USGBC, 2006, p. 11.
8. Pile, 2005, p. 180.
9. Campbell and Seebohm, 1992, p. 70.
10. Abercrombie, December 1999, p. 148.
11. Abercrombie, December 1999, p. 146.
12. Pile, 2005, p. 317.
13. Carron, 1998, p. 72.
14. Tate and Smith, 1986, p. 322.
15. Russell, 1992, p. 11.
16. Martin and Guerin, 2006, p. 90.

CHAPTER 2

Professional Advancement

After completing this chapter you should be able to:

- Explain the three Es and how they relate to the interior design profession.
- Discuss why advanced education may be important for some interior designers.
- Explain why continuing education is important for all interior designers.
- Discuss how an internship program can be beneficial for a student.
- Discuss how the interior design profession protects the health, life safety, and welfare (HSW) of clients and the general public.
- Explain why it is important for the National Council for Interior Design Qualification to be an independent organization.
- Explain the responsibility of NCIDQ and why you believe (or don't believe) this examination is important to the profession.
- Compare a practice act to a title act regarding a practitioner's qualifications and impact on the public.
- Explain the responsibility of the interior design professional associations to their members and the general public.
- Discuss the pros and cons of affiliating with a design professional association.
- Name three ways in which you will give back to the profession after you begin practice.
- Discuss why an interior designer should consider public service through pro bono work or other contributions.

NCIDQ COMPONENT

Based on best information available, some material in this chapter might appear as part of the NCIDQ examination. The reader should not depend solely on this text for study material. See the sections on licensing and registration.

As discussed in Chapter 1, a professional must attain certain standards recognized by those in the profession. Interior design professionals and educators often talk about the "three Es" as a necessary part of the practice of interior design: education, experience, and examination. Although entry into the interior design profession may come in many ways today, the principles of the three Es remain valid.

Professional interior design in the 21st century requires educational preparation in a wide variety of courses specifically within the body of knowledge for interior design. Educational standards have become progressively more stringent, with advances in technology, regulations, and safety of clients and the users of spaces moving to the forefront. Individuals in interior design must realize that educational preparation does not end at graduation. It should continue with professional seminars and workshops for updating and expansion of the professional practitioner's knowledge and skills.

Work experience through internships and/or entry-level positions in the design industry helps designers see the "real world." Practitioners gain experience on the job in a wide variety of settings and design specialties. It is through work experience in design that professionals gain valuable familiarity in working with clients and the industry.

Professions seek to further qualify what it means to be a professional by expecting or requiring an examination that tests a would-be practitioner's basic competency. An examination after completion of education and some period of work experience seeks to test a practitioner's knowledge and skills in the body of knowledge recognized as necessary for practice of the profession.

Of course, not everyone who has something to do with the planning and design of an interior has received formal education and training and has been certified by examination. The "on-the-job" entry route is still an option for many individuals. However, with the ever-increasing legal responsibility inherent in the design of any size or kind of interior, obtaining educational training in design is a minimal achievement for individuals involved in the profession of interior design.

This chapter focuses on the elements of the profession that relate to the movement of an individual from student to entry-level practitioner. This chapter also discusses the widely recognized credentials of a professional interior designer. A discussion of the qualifying examination that has been established as the benchmark for licensing and for professional-level association membership is included. It is important to review licensing and title registration issues as they affect the profession. This too is discussed, albeit in broad strokes, as the particular regulations vary from jurisdiction to jurisdiction.

Finally, the discussion of the major professional associations will help readers appreciate the breadth of design specialties within the profession. The association section begins with a brief history of the major associations, an outline of which appeared in Chapter 1.

EDUCATIONAL PREPARATION

Regardless of whether someone wishes to design residences or become involved in designing any type of commercial interior space, strong educational preparation should be considered mandatory. Owners and users of interior spaces who hire professional help expect the interior designer to have the knowledge and skills to perform the required work with more in mind than aesthetics.

To encompass the range of knowledge and skills development required today, interior design programs are interdisciplinary, drawing from the arts, architecture, and human ecology. It is also important for students to have coursework in business and the liberal arts. Depending on the location of the program and the educational institution, the professional and technical coursework will have a slightly different focus.

The Council for Interior Design Accreditation (CIDA), with assistance from the National Council on Interior Design Qualification (NCIDQ) and the Interior Design Educators Council (IDEC), and funding from the Interior Designers of Canada, American Society of Interior Designers, and the International Interior Design Association, has helped to research the common body of knowledge and skills needed by competent professional interior designers. The complete listing of the elements of this body of knowledge is available at the Web site www.idbok.org.

Whether a two-year program at a community college, a three- to four-year program at a professional school or university, or a "two plus two" program where a student begins at a community college and finishes a bachelor's degree at a university, in-depth educational preparation is imperative. In some cases, advanced education is important for an individual's career choice. Teaching requires educational preparation beyond the bachelor's degree. Some specialized areas such as lighting design also benefit from advanced education.

Regardless of the level of degree sought, professional educational training in interior design must provide the student with the theory and skills of the profession, as well as with the general education required in the 21st century. The focus of that training must also meet the student's interests, abilities, and career goals.

Advanced Education

Many designers seek postgraduate education in interior design, architecture, and business, to name just a few broad areas. Sometimes designers obtain additional education in order to increase their technical skills and to allow themselves an opportunity to advance within the firm in which they work. Sometimes they seek additional education in order to retrain for a new area of expertise, such as lighting design, or to move into management.

Design professionals who seek an advanced degree most often obtain a master's degree. A master's degree involves advanced studies or research work. Master's-degree work commonly requires a minimum of 30 semester credit hours, with actual degree requirements being prescribed by the institution. A graduate student's work culminates in a graphic or written thesis, depending on his or her academic focus and the requirements of the institution.

Individuals who are particularly interested in teaching at the college level or are interested in research topics may choose to obtain a doctorate rather than a master's degree. Doctoral studies are more extensive than master's, with additional numbers of credit hours and research requirements. Research studies conclude with the production of a doctoral dissertation that presents research conclusions.

Curriculum Accreditation

Design education strengthened throughout the 20th century. An increasing number of formal college course and programs in interior decoration became available across the country. The profession became more formalized and began to change its image from that of the untrained decorator to that of the trained professional.

Yet, these new educational programs caused concerns about educational requirements and programs that evolved during the 1940s and 1950s. The professional organizations supported the creation of an accrediting agency to help standardize interior design education. In 1970, the Foundation for Interior Design Education Research (FIDER) was founded to provide voluntary accreditation. In 2006, the FIDER board voted to rename the organization the Council for Interior Design Accreditation (CIDA). This nonprofit organization, recognized by the Council on Higher Education Accreditation (CHEA), is considered the reliable authority on the equality of postsecondary interior design education in North America. Accreditation of a program indicates to the student that the curriculum meets educational standards that are accepted and supported by the profession of interior design.

The CIDA "has been passionately committed to the ongoing enrichment of the interior design profession through identifying, developing and promoting quality standards for the education of entry-level interior designers."* The council continues to develop and evaluate educational standards in interior design programs as a means of granting accreditation. These standards are reviewed from time to time, and the full details of the updated standards are available on the Web site, www.accredit-id.org/resources. A brief description of the standards are provided in item 2-1 on the companion Web site.

Currently, CIDA accredits a single type of program of interior design education, the professional-level program. The program must result in a minimum of a bachelor's degree and must include classes in the arts and sciences, as well as courses specific to interior design and other specific standards detailed in the *Professional Standards* document available from CIDA.

Accreditation of an interior design program is a voluntary process of self-study and measurement of the curriculum against the CIDA standards. This self-study investigates the quality of programs as meeting the needs of professionals in the current market. After the self-study, a group of site visitors conducts reviews of materials and discussions with faculty, students, and administrators. Accreditation is not forever; a program must be reevaluated every six years.

Interior design curriculums also use another tool to help determine accreditation and overall course offerings. A research study, entitled *Interior Design Profession's Body of Knowledge* (currently prepared by Dr. Denise Guerin and Dr. Caren Martin at the University of Minnesota) and supported by the professional associations, is periodically prepared to investigate the knowledge areas of interior design professionals. A copy of this report can be downloaded from www.idbok.org. The latest version, published in 2010, looks carefully at how interior design's body of knowledge relates to the areas of health, safety, and welfare.

*Council for Interior Design Accreditation, 2006, *Accreditation Manual*, p. 1–1.

INTERNSHIPS

A very important part of educational preparation in interior design is an internship. An *internship* is a supervised work experience within an interior design firm or other appropriate company within the industry. Internships are generally a part of the required curriculum. It is an intensive work experience providing students the opportunity to work in the real world before starting a full-time job. Internships help students see how all the coursework that they have taken relates to the work done in the real world. In addition, internships give students some work experience that they can include on their resumés.

Most internship opportunities are with interior design and architectural firms. The experience might be with a small residential firm, a furniture store, large or small interior design practices, or the design departments within architectural firms. The interests of some students may also lead them to valuable internship experiences at other businesses in the design–build industry, such as with contractors and vendors.

The length of the internship will vary with the requirements of the academic program and the employer. An internship should last at least six to eight weeks, full-time, to allow the student to obtain the greatest exposure to tasks performed in the firm.

Ideally, an internship should include as many actual tasks and activities as possible in the chosen work environment. The student should discuss the types of work experiences that will be provided during the internship. In some situations, the supervising faculty member will already have discussed this issue with the employer, so work tasks will already have been generally determined. However, not all internship locations include all the tasks that might be of interest to the student. For example, few internship positions allow students to work directly with a client.

Sometimes students get their expectations of what they will do during an internship confused with the reality of the internship. As I have told my students in the past, you get the internship (or job) because of what you are learning in school. However, the employer is uncertain of your ability and must be shown on the job what you can do—usually in a gradual way.

Of course, the internship experience is different for everyone. Certainly, some internship positions give a supervised intern responsibility for project work. Often these spots are in firms that go through extensive, competitive application processes for any interns, as they often also hire the student upon graduation. Most locations gradually involve students in assisting with parts of projects, doing such things as researching products or drafting parts of plans or other design documents from sketches by more senior designers. They may have the intern attend meetings with clients to silently observe and take notes, and/or perform other tasks that are all part of the professional experience; however, all the intern's work is supervised, and firms rarely give the intern final decision-making tasks.

It is very important for each student to carefully consider what he or she hopes to gain from the internship. The focus should not be on whether you are being paid; the focus should be on what you will learn. This helps the faculty supervisor connect students to the types of firms that most closely match student interest and ability with what the firm needs. For example, having a student do an internship at a firm that primarily designs small commercial spaces when the student is really interested in residential design is clearly a mismatch.

It is also important to note that the student is expected to meet the general policies of the design firm. That will mean meeting a business dress code, arriving on time, keeping track of time worked on various tasks, attending appropriate meetings, and observing any other business regulations applicable to any employee. Students should remember that the internship is in a way an "audition" for a job. The student "hat" and attitude should be checked at the door before entering. This is a time to be sure you act as if you are a professional interior designer, as many firms hire interns at the conclusion of their internship term or after graduation.

The Interior Design Experience Program

A work experience program established by NCIDQ, called the Interior Design Experience Program (IDEP), provides structured, diversified, and monitored experience in interior design after graduation. It is not the same thing as an internship. The IDEP experience provides a useful way for participants to assess their skills and gain valuable experience that is often helpful to them in passing the NCIDQ examination.

IDEP is a voluntary program in most jurisdictions. However, a state or provincial board may require enrollment in IDEP for work-experience requirements for licensing/registration. As always, designers should be aware of any requirements by a regulatory board in the area in which they wish to work, in this instance specifically as to IDEP participation.

Very briefly, here is how the IDEP program works. After finding a job in interior design, a participant secures a supervisor at that place of employment who is an NCIDQ certificate holder or licensed/registered interior designer or architect. The supervisor supports the entry-level professional by assessing skills and promoting development of the individual's experience in the scope of work expected at the firm.

Participants are also required to have a mentor who also is an NCIDQ certificate holder or is a licensed/registered interior designer or architect. This mentor might be in the same firm or work for some other firm. The mentor is someone who does not supervise the individual (if the mentor is within the firm), but can provide career advice during the IDEP experience. Participants are required to track their structured work experiences with a log book provided by NCIDQ. The participant, supervisor, and mentor review and check off progress on the requirements. NCIDQ recognizes that an individual participant may have more than one supervisor, place of employment, or mentor during the time frame of the IDEP work experience.

It takes two to three years to complete IDEP, depending on the student's education level and hours worked. Participants do not have to work full time or with only one employer.

Detailed information on how to apply for the IDEP experience, eligibility, fees, and other answers to other questions can be obtained from www.NCIDQ.org.

LIFELONG LEARNING

Regardless of the type of interior design one practices, professionals must be ready to embrace lifelong learning. Technical updating in this age of technology is a paramount need for most designers. Others may want access to topics related to a specific design specialty. Business owners often seek professional education on business practices. Like all other professionals, interior designers should seek out continuing lifelong learning opportunities.

Many professionals do not desire the depth of study that is required when taking additional college courses, or to obtain an advanced degree. Professional education via seminars, workshops, lectures, correspondence courses, online seminars, webinars, and intensive professional studies can successfully meet individual needs. These continuing education offerings are available in almost every topic and area of the profession.

Educational programs that provide *continuing education units (CEU)* furnish short-term coursework in a wide variety of topical-interest areas. This is the most common way for professionals to obtain lifelong learning opportunities. CEU classes provide a means for professional interior designers to remain current in the practice of interior design. Courses that provide CEU credits are those that have been approved by a reviewing body. Not all seminars and workshops provide approved CEU credits.

Continuing education is also very important because several states that have passed licensing or title registration acts require continuing education for maintaining registration. Professional associations also require continuing education for their members. The exact requirements vary, and it is the individual's responsibly to understand any licensing board or organizational requirements. In most cases, these entities will require approved CEU credits.

Continuing education courses are held for anywhere from one or two hours to perhaps a full day, and a participant will earn one-tenth of an hour of credit (0.1) for each hour of the class. These courses and workshops are also developed to be of differing difficulty. A course may be very basic in nature, meaning that anyone is likely to gain from taking the course. Advanced courses generally expect that participants have some to fairly extensive knowledge in the subject matter.

Educators, interior design practitioners, and other experts in many fields teach continuing education courses. Participants should investigate the provider of the program to understand the speaker's expertise in the topic.

Programs that are available for approved CEU credits are reviewed by volunteer experts in the design subject matter and selected by the authorizing organization. The organization that approves CEU credit courses for interior designers is the Interior Design Continuing Education Council (IDCEC), an organization that coordinates professional education specifically for ASID, IIDA, IDC, and some other professional organizations in design. Non-IDCEC-approved courses might not be acceptable to state regulatory agencies or professional organizations to meet continuing education requirements.

The review process conducted by IDCEC assures that teachers and speakers are qualified to present courses, that the course content meets minimum standards approved by the core professional organizations, and that the presenters' teaching methodologies are appropriate for the subject matter, level, and content. This is especially important for required courses that cover content on health, safety, and welfare topics. According to IDCEC, these courses must have a minimum of 75 percent of their content focused on such topics as codes (to receive a Health/Safety designation), or a minimum of 75 percent on such issues as ethics or psychological well-being of clients (to receive a Welfare designation). Other topics can also receive CEU credit and are usually categorized as general design knowledge.[1]

Each association provides a number of CEU classes each year, and others are available at conferences such as NeoCon. Reciprocity exists among many of the professional associations, so that an ASID member, for example, can take a class sponsored by IIDA or possibly another association. There are also numerous sources for webinars provided by associations, vendors, and independent providers. Not all are approved for CEU credit, but they do provide professional education content.

Lifelong education comes in other forms as well. Here are a few examples:

- In-house learning opportunities where senior designers provide educational information to staff members.
- Distance learning classes offered on a wide variety of topics from colleges and universities around the world.
- The research and preparation time required to prepare a seminar or to write an article.
- Entering design competitions that require a new design, such as the design of rugs or a speculative interior, rather than one done for a previous client.
- Community service participation (discussed later in this chapter).

NCIDQ EXAMINATION

As we saw in Chapter 1, a professional competency examination is one of the criteria of a profession. Before looking at the current testing examination from the National Council for Interior Design Qualification, it is helpful to briefly look back at how examination for interior designers developed.

The early professional organizations, such as the National Society for Interior Designers (NSID), favored licensing to restrict practice to qualified professionals, whereas others favored qualifying examinations. An examination was devised by the American Institute of Decorators (AID), and in the 1960s prospective members of AID had to pass the examination for professional membership. Because of philosophical differences, NSID designed and utilized its own qualifying exam.

All through the 1960s, discussions occurred regarding educational training and testing procedures for qualification. The NCIDQ was organized in 1972 and became an independent corporation in 1974. It is concerned with maintaining standards of practice through the testing of members of the profession and the establishment of requirements for legal qualifications for licensing and title registration.

During those formative years, an examination that both organizations could use was developed. The examination developed by Louis Tregre in the 1960s for AID became the basis of the exam later devised and administered by NCIDQ. Tregre was elected the first president of the NCIDQ board in 1974 and remained in that post for 12 years.

In the interior design profession, the accepted examination is the one administered by NCIDQ. It is accepted by the major professional associations in the United States and Canada, as well as the Interior Design Educators Council and the Council for Interior Design Accreditation. The NCIDQ examination is also the primary examination in those U.S. states and Canadian provinces that have licensing, certification, or other registration statutes.

NCIDQ is not a professional association in the same way as ASID or IIDA. No individual memberships exist within NCIDQ. Membership resides with state and provincial member boards representing jurisdictions that regulate the interior design profession. Individuals are certificate holders, meaning that they have successfully completed all the requirements of the examination. Certificate holders are not allowed to place the NCIDQ acronym on their business cards or other marketing materials, as they would another professional or educational appellation. Each certificate holder receives a unique number, however, and may place this number along with "NCIDQ" on his or her marketing materials (e.g., "NCIDQ Certificate number 12345"). Placing something like "Jim Jones, NCIDQ" on a business card is an incorrect use.

NCIDQ conducts ongoing research to evaluate and analyze candidate performance, educational and professional practice skill, and knowledge requirements, along with methods to promote public protection by the interior design profession. Major research studies began in 1998 to gather the most up-to-date information about the practice of interior design as a basis for revision of the NCIDQ examination. A similar study is conducted approximately every five years to ensure that the content of the examination parallels the body of knowledge and skills currently required in the profession.

NCIDQ also provides other services to the profession. It can provide research and expertise to assist jurisdictions with the development of licensing laws. It also provides webinars and IDCEC-approved continuing education monographs that are individual learning opportunities focused on health, safety, and welfare topics.

The Examination Overview

The NCIDQ examination is given at examination centers throughout the United States and Canada. When a designer has achieved the minimum combination of education and work experience, the designer contacts the NCIDQ office for application materials. In some states, such as Texas, candidates must apply to the state regulatory board in order to take the examination.

Eligibility requirements involve a combination of years of education in interior design and a period of work experience. The eligibility requirements discussed here were accurate at the time this book was published. Because eligibility requirements can change, the reader should review NCIDQ's current requirements via the Web site or telephone discussions.

Acceptable work experience can be full- or part-time. NCIDQ recommends that the work experience be under the direct supervision of an NCIDQ certificate holder, a registered interior designer, or an architect who offers interior design services. The information on the Interior Design Experience Program is very important as it relates to work experience: Individuals without a baccalaureate degree would be required to have a larger number of hours of work experience. For the most current eligibility requirements, contact NCIDQ or review exam eligibility criteria on the NCIDQ Web site: wwe.ncidq.org/exam/eligibility requirements.

The examination is given over two consecutive days every six months. It is divided into three sections, with two sections given on Friday and the third on Saturday. A candidate may take all three sections of the exam at one time, or may elect to take individual sections or combinations of sections at different times. Only sections of the examination that are not passed must be taken again. NCIDQ requires that a candidate pass all three sections within a five-year time frame; if the candidate cannot, he or she must retake the sections not passed previously.

The first two sections, given on Friday, are two multiple-choice, computer-graded tests. The third section, given on Saturday only, is the practicum section; this section generally takes all day. Computer-delivered exams may be available, although most candidates use the paper-and-pencil method for exam taking.

The exams are based on content areas typical of interior design practice. Those content areas, as reported on the NCIDQ Web site, are building systems, codes, construction standards, contract administration, design application, professional practice, and project coordination.

Exam questions are focused on application of knowledge and skills, not simply recall of facts. Many questions incorporate drawings, pictures, symbols, and textual formats that are typical in the interior design profession, requiring candidates to recall, apply, and analyze information. A brief description of the three exam sections follows. Note that these descriptions may vary based on whether the candidate takes a computer-based test or a paper-and-pencil-based test. The descriptions are for the paper-and-pencil-based test.

Section I. This is a multiple-choice test consisting of 150 questions; candidates are given 3½ hours to complete the section. It addresses the areas of codes, building systems, construction standards, and contract administration.

Section II. This is also a 150-question, multiple-choice test addressing design application, project coordination, and professional practice. The candidate again has 3½ hours to complete the section.

Section III. This is the practicum section of the exam. It requires that candidates produce design solutions. Design skills are tested in space planning, lighting design, life safety, millwork design, and areas concerned with egress, codes, and universal design. All candidates at any one testing session are given the same problem.

Candidates can obtain information concerning availability of preparatory exam materials, sample tests, reference lists, and tips on how to study for the exam by visiting the NCIDQ Web site. Third-party exam prep materials may also be available, and other reference materials that can be found online. The STEP program for study and preparation previously offered by ASID may not be available when you read this text. Contact ASID for information about the current availability of this study program.

LICENSING AND REGISTRATION

Regardless of the profession, professionals are predominately licensed or registered by a state or provincial regulatory body. In the case of interior design, licensing or registration is done to recognize the minimum standards and qualifications of those who wish to engage in the interior design profession within a jurisdiction. It is important to understand that although local design practitioners spearhead licensing and registration efforts, licensing and registration standards are established by state and provincial legislation.

Licensing and registration efforts have been a part of the profession's activities since 1951, when the Southern California chapter of AID attempted to get a bill passed in the state legislature. Professionals, with the assistance of local licensing coalitions, continue to pursue licensing legislation or regulation on a state-by-state basis. Professional associations provide coalitions with information, but do not advocate legislation that would limit who may practice in the interior design industry.

Several terms relating to this topic are used frequently. Here we define them and then discuss them in detail. The distinctions are important.

- *Licensing:* most frequently associated with a state or province whose legislation defines who may practice interior design—much like a state law defines who may practice medicine.

- *Practice acts* are a type of licensing in which guidelines are established concerning what an individual can or cannot do in the practice of a profession in a particular state.

- *Title acts* are concerned with limiting the use of certain professional titles, such as *interior designer, registered interior designer,* or *certified interior designer.*

- *Registration* or *certification* is most frequently associated with legislation that defines who may use a certain title, such as *registered interior designer.*

- *Self-certification:* similar to a title act, but use of the title is controlled by an independent organization; the jurisdiction has very little control. California is the only state with self-certification.

- *Permitting statutes:* allow interior designers to submit plans for building permits. There is no jurisdictional oversight. Colorado is the only state with a permitting statute.

In most cases, the purpose of licensing legislation is to ensure the *health, life safety, and welfare* (HSW) of the public that hires interior designers, as well as the general public that uses interiors designed by a professional interior designer. Licensing and registration laws help the general public determine what level of professional is appropriate for their needs. For example, not all projects require the preparation of working drawings, and thus the client may not need a licensed professional to do the work.

These laws are enacted to establish minimum standards of competency of any individual who wishes to practice or engage in interior design activities as defined by the legislation within the jurisdiction. Legislation does not regulate the creative activity of interior design.

Where licensing legislation exists, an added tool of enforcement and redress exists for clients. Because legislation seeks to ensure that only competent practitioners offer design services or call themselves by a regulated title, a client can ask the jurisdiction's board of registration to investigate, and even fine and/or discipline the designer, if something goes wrong.

The two most common types of legislation are title acts and practice acts. Title acts restrict the use of the designated title to only those who meet the qualifications of the state title act. Interior designers who meet these qualifications must also register with a state agency or board. An individual who does not meet the qualifications of the title act may not use the title, for example, *interior designer* in any of his or her business dealings. With title registration, the title of *interior designer* connotes to the public that the individual has met the highest standards of the profession and can thus provide the most competent service to the consumer. These standards are related to education, experience, adherence to a code of conduct, and passing a qualifying examination.

Practice acts are much more stringent, as they limit what an individual can or cannot do in the practice of a profession in a particular jurisdiction. If a jurisdiction has a practice act, individuals cannot engage in any of the activities defined by the act unless they meet the qualifications established by a state board and become licensed.

Practice acts are commonly legislated for professions that have an impact on the health and safety of the public. Lawyers, doctors, architects, and engineers have had to meet state practice act regulations for many years. Practice acts definitely limit who may practice a profession, and they usually require that individuals meet very stringent qualification criteria. When a person enters into a contractual relationship with an unlicensed professional, the contract may or may not be enforceable, depending on the statutes in the individual states.

Those working under the supervision of a licensed interior designer in a jurisdiction with a practice act do not themselves need to be licensed. However, when a designer decides to work for himself or herself or has his or her own business, then the designer must become licensed. In some states, those who only design residences are exempt from licensing requirements.

States generally have a board of technical registration or state board of registration—or some other titled group operated by the state—to oversee professional registration of any kind. A state board also oversees contractors, architects, and many other professions. The intent of legislation, however, is to indicate to the consumer which individuals have met the specific criteria related to education and work experience, indicating that those individuals have acquired professional competence in the field. Licensing or title registration legislation also provides a definitive measure of experience and educational preparation for those who practice interior design. Licensing protects the consumer from unregulated practice by those who do not have proper educational background, training, and experience in the profession of interior design.

Those who have been actively engaged in bringing licensing legislation to their states would all agree that it has not been an easy task—nor will it be in the future. Despite the frustration of many years of struggling with legislators and those who would rather that interior design not be licensed, many states have passed some type of interior design legislation. In 1982, Alabama became the first state to pass a title registration act. In 2001, Alabama successfully converted its title act to a practice act to become the sixth jurisdiction (at the time of this writing) to have a practice act. The companion Web site includes a list of jurisdictions with legislation (item 2-2) and a map showing interior design laws in North America (item 2-3). Many other states are working on legislation for either title registration or practice acts.

Readers may wish to contact their state coalition or the Government and Public Affairs Department of ASID, the Legislative Issues Committee of IIDA, or the national offices of other professional associations for information on legislation within their jurisdiction.

Whether one works toward licensing through title registration or practice acts, interior design professionals and students must be prepared to accept the ethical and legal responsibilities that such recognition brings. Chapter 3 discusses the ethics and codes of conduct, and Chapter 4 discusses the many legal responsibilities that a practitioner faces.

Other Professional Certifications

There are other professional certifications that might be of interest to interior designers. Complete information regarding the qualification and application procedures for these certifications can be obtained from these organizations' national offices or Web sites. Other certification programs for builders and contractors may be appropriate for the interior designer based on education, experience, and business/professional goals.

American Academy of Health Care Designers (AAHID). This professional certification is specifically for those designers who have become specialized in healthcare interior design. Use of the AAHID appellation means the individual has achieved specific experience, passed the NCIDQ examination, and provided other evidence of his or her interior design experience in healthcare facilities. Contact www.AAHID.org for complete qualifications and testing information.

Certified Aging-in-Place Specialist (CAPS). Administered through the National Association of Home Builders (NAHB), for individuals who have achieved additional business, technical, and customer service skills necessary for working in the aging-in-place segment of the industry. Contact www.nhab.org for qualifications and testing information.

Certified Kitchen Designer (CKD) or Certified Bathroom Designer (CBD). Administered through the National Kitchen and Bath Association (NKBA), for individuals who have demonstrated extensive experience and specialized education in the design of kitchens and bathrooms. Contact www.nkba.org for qualifications and testing information.

Leadership in Energy and Environmental Design (LEED®). LEED® certifications are administered by the U.S. Green Building Council for those designers interested in and dedicated to sustainable design. Several certifications are available for interior designers, based on specialty: LEED-AP ID+C, for interior design of commercial spaces; LEED-AP BD+C, for building design and construction; LEED AP Homes, for designers involved in the design of green homes; and LEED Green Associate, for those interested in green building practices but engaged in a nontechnical field. Other LEED-AP certifications exist for areas less related to interiors. Contact www.usgbc.org.

Lighting Certified professional (LC). This certification is granted by the National Council on Qualifications for the Lighting Professions (NCQLP). Indicates a specific and high level of expertise and knowledge concerning lighting techniques, principles, design, and compliance. Contact www.ncqlp.org for qualifications and testing information.

PROFESSIONAL ASSOCIATIONS

Professional associations have existed, in one form or another, since the early days of the interior design profession. This section begins with a brief history of professional associations for interior designers.

In some ways, the large associations that we know today began as local clubs focusing on the needs of decorators within a small geographic area. By the late 1920s, many local decorators' clubs had been started. The New York Decorators' Club is credited with being one of the first.

In many respects these early clubs functioned more as social clubs than as groups focusing on professional education and standards. Standards for membership existed, but they varied from one group to another.

The first national association was the American Institute of Interior Decorators (AIID), established as part of the proceedings of the 1931 furniture market and show in Grand Rapids, Michigan. William R. Moore was elected the first AIID national president. In 1936, the organization moved its headquarters from Chicago to New York City and changed its name to the American Institute of Decorators (AID). Over the years, education and work experience requirements for membership changed and became more stringent.

In 1957, a group belonging to the New York branch of AID broke off and formed the National Society for Interior Designers (NSID). For many years, disagreements over qualifications, testing, and terminology continued between the two organizations. In 1961, the American Institute of Decorators became the American Institute of Interior Designers (AID). Finally, in 1975, the American Institute of Interior Designers and the National Society for Interior Designers overcame their differences and merged into one national organization, the American Society of Interior Designers (ASID). Norman de Haan, FASID, took office as the first ASID national president. Today there are nearly 30,000 members of ASID in chapters in the United States and Canada.

In the late 1960s, the Institute of Business Designers (IBD) was incorporated to meet the needs of the commercial/contract designer. Charles Gelber was elected the first IBD president in 1970. IBD was conceived in 1963 by members of the National Office Furnishings Association (NOFA), who were concerned about the quality of interior design service in office furnishings dealerships. In 1963, NOFA-d (NOFA-designers) was formed to accommodate interior designers who were working for office furnishings dealers.

During the late 1980s and early 1990s, the professional associations discussed unifying into one national organization. Although this effort did not bear fruit, in 1994 the members of IBD, the International Society of Interior Designers (ISID), and the Council for Federal Interior Designers (CFID) agreed to unify and created the International Interior Design Association (IIDA).

Why Join a Professional Association?

There are many reasons one might decide to become a member of one of the professional associations. In fact, some professionals belong to more than one association, as each can bring different benefits or professional advantages to a member. I have always encouraged students and professionals to find the association that best meets their needs and become involved as much as they can.

A large number of professionals feel that the greatest tangible benefit of professional association membership is the privilege of placing the association appellation after the member's name. It is not the primary benefit; it is only one benefit. Although the tangible benefits are important, sometimes the intangible ones bring the greatest satisfaction and growth to members. Some of the intangible benefits most noted by members are:

Interaction with colleagues. Friendships established with colleagues within the chapter and around the country or the globe are enriching personally and professionally. Designers are proud of the professional and personal friendships that they have formed through association activities.

Educational opportunities. Professional associations at the national and chapter levels provide continuing education seminars and workshops to assist members in advancing their knowledge in all areas of the profession. Chapter meetings, newsletters, national conferences, research studies, and online discussion groups are also important educational benefits.

Involvement that brings valuable personal enrichment. Volunteering for a chapter committee or board provides opportunities to meet members as well as to contribute personally to the chapter in a very important way.

Pride in accomplishment. It is important to have a sense of pride in having achieved the educational, experience, and testing milestones indicating that one has reached the highest level in one's profession.

Recognition. Consumers and allied professionals recognize the dedication and credentials of the interior designer who is affiliated with professional associations. To many others, peer recognition as a member of an association is gratifying.

These are just some of the intangible benefits of membership. You may think of others that are just as important.

Members of associations are pleased to discover and take advantage of numerous tangible benefits as well. For example, attending a chapter meeting might be a social opportunity for the sole practitioner or, more likely, an educational opportunity with a speaker. Many other tangible benefits are available, although they vary by the organization. Those shown in Table 2-1 are the most common.

The remainder of this section briefly describes the major professional associations. The reader can obtain a great deal of information about membership, benefits, and activities from association Web sites—including online membership applications. Of course, you can also contact the national or provincial offices (listed in the Internet Resources) for more specific details about the association.

The two largest professional associations for interior design are ASID and IIDA. Of course, there are other groups that have a focused membership and mission for their members. Several of these are listed in Table 2-2 later in this chapter.

American Society of Interior Designers (ASID)

The largest of the interior design professional associations, with approximately 30,000 members in 48 chapters in the United States and Canada, is ASID. Members are engaged in both residential and commercial interior design, and include students and industry partners. "ASID is a community of people driven by a common love for design and committed to the belief that interior design, as a service to people, is a powerful, multifaceted profession that can positively change people's lives."[2]

TABLE 2-1.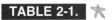

Tangible member benefits of interior design professional associations

Association leadership. Membership offers an opportunity to be involved in the growth of the profession through officer positions at the chapter and national levels.

Leadership training. Association chapter and national board members and officers receive training to assist them in accomplishing their association responsibilities. Much of this training can be directly applied to an individual's work experience as well.

Chapter participation and networking. By participating in chapter committees and events, members meet colleagues for opportunities for leadership growth, friendships, and collaborative work.

Mailings. Associations provide mailings to members that keep them informed of the associations' activities as well as of external influences on the profession. Mailings might take the form of member magazines, supplemental newsletters and news bulletins, chapter newsletters, and conference reports.

Practice aids. A number of associations provide sample contracts, business forms, marketing tools, reference books, and other useful aids for members to use in their practice in order to become better professionals.

Government affairs. The associations maintain contact with federal, state, and/or provincial government agencies that may have an effect on the right to practice. Members are kept informed of any pending legislation that might affect design practice.

Group insurance. It is possible for members to take advantage of group insurance rates for a variety of personal and business insurance needs.

Business services. Discounts and special pricing are available from some associations for car rentals, telephone service, express shipping, credit cards, and other similar business services.

Magazine subscriptions. Members might receive a limited number of complimentary subscriptions to trade magazines.

Design competitions. Professional prestige can be achieved through juried national competitions for projects, research, and writing.

Industry liaison. Members receive technical information from industry suppliers.

Continuing education. Members can find out where continuing education sessions are being held throughout the country via their association's Web site.

World Wide Web. Members can obtain information from association national offices, be informed of association business and issues affecting the members, and even conduct online chats with the national office or other members. Chapters may also offer marketing programs in which a member may link his or her Web site to the chapter's Web site.

ASID provides many membership benefits, including:

- Chapter meetings and activities
- *ASID ICON*, a member magazine providing articles of interest to interior designers
- A national conference held in conjunction with NeoCon, a major trade show
- Various electronic newsletters and communications
- Educational programs such as webinars and the Distinguished Speakers Program
- Many other programs, documents, and activities for the support of the association, its members, and the profession

There are several membership categories in ASID for interested individuals and industry partners. The current requirements for each category are available on the ASID Web site under the "Membership Information" tab. Membership applications for all levels and information about fees and dues are also on the Web site. A few highlights of those requirements follow.

The highest level of membership is *professional*. Members in this category have satisfied rigorous standards of education, work experience, and testing in order to qualify as professional-level members. A key component of obtaining professional-level membership in ASID is passage of the NCIDQ examination. Only professional-level members may use the appellation *ASID* after their names and in advertising (e.g., Mary Jones, ASID).

Another level of membership is *allied*. Allied members are practicing interior designers and must meet the same general membership requirements as for professional membership. However, an allied member has not as yet satisfactorily completed the NCIDQ exam. As of 2011, allied members are able to use the appellation *Allied ASID* after their names (e.g., Mary Smith, Allied ASID).

Professional and allied practitioner members of ASID are required to complete 10 contact hours (equal to 1.0 CEUs) every two years. This is a self-reporting requirement. Failure to comply with the CEU requirement makes the member subject to a termination of Society membership.

Students who are enrolled in interior design programs may become *student* members of an ASID chapter at their school or join as independent student members if the school does not have a chapter. The program requires at least 40 semester credit hours or 60 quarter credit hours of design-related classwork. Students receive mailings from the national office and have the opportunity to participate in the local professional chapter. Student members who are in good standing through graduation may apply for allied membership immediately upon graduation. Student members may use the membership appellation *Student Member, ASID* after their names (e.g., John Jones, Student Member ASID).

Industry partner (IP) memberships are available for those who represent suppliers to the interior design industry, as well as manufacturers. Industry partners have the opportunity to interact with designers and vice versa at events such as chapter meetings or events that the IP member hosts. Industry partner members often also provide generous financial backing to the profession through sponsorship of continuing education classes, chapter activities, and design competitions.

There are three categories of membership for *educators*. The different categories relate to working experience at an accredited university or school. Full details on membership qualifications for educators are available on the ASID Web site. Passage of the NCIDQ examination is only required for full-time educators or department chairs.

It is important to note that when an individual applies for any level of membership, by signing the application, he or she agrees to abide by the association's bylaws and code of ethics. Incorrect use of the appellation on business cards and in advertising is one issue addressed in the code of ethics. Of course, there are many other serious issues, and ethics are discussed in detail in Chapter 3.

International Interior Design Association (IIDA)

The IIDA "works to advance the value of the interior design and its practitioners as well as to cultivate leadership within the profession."[3] The IIDA has approximately 13,000 members in 31 chapters around the world, working in all areas of residential and commercial interior design. Members practice in 10 specialty practice forums that help provide specialized information. Members can select one or more of these forums, but may be required to pay fees for joining more than two forums.

IIDA provides several membership benefits, including:

- Chapter meetings and activities
- A national conference held in conjunction with NeoCon
- The national news magazine called *perspective*
- Various electronic newsletters and communications
- Educational programs such as webinars and speaker-led presentations
- Many other programs and activities helpful to the membership

There are several membership categories in IIDA for interested individuals and industry partners. The current requirements for each category are available on the IIDA Web site under the "Membership" tab. Membership applications for all levels and information about fees and dues are also on the Web site. A few highlights of those requirements follow.

Professional membership is the highest category of membership in IIDA. It is reserved for those members whose work experience, educational background, and successful completion of the NCIDQ examination permit them to apply for this membership category. Architects who are actively designing interiors might also be eligible for this category. Only professional members may use the appellation *IIDA* after their names (e.g., Jane Smith, IIDA).

Associate members are actively engaged in the profession of interior design. Associate members have met the same educational requirements as professional members, but have not completed the NCIDQ examination. These members may use the appellation *Associate IIDA* after their names for marketing purposes (e.g., William Smith, Associate IIDA).

Professional and associate members are required to complete 1.0 CEUs every two years.

Student memberships at a national level are available to students who are enrolled in a recognized design school or college program. Student members receive many benefits, such as receiving the *perspective* magazine and eligibility for design competitions. Students who maintain their student membership in good standing through graduation may apply for allied membership immediately upon graduation.

Industry members are those who are interested in and supportive of interior design but who are not practicing designers. These members include manufacturers, individual representatives, design centers, and schools.

Another membership category is called *affiliate* membership. These members are individuals who are involved in an area related to interior design, such as graphic design, lighting design, or landscape architecture, but do not qualify for professional membership.

The *educator* membership category is for full-time educators; depending on qualifications, the educator may become either a professional or an associate member. Educator members are also required to complete 1.0 CEU credits or 10 hours of continuing education every two years and may elect two specialty forums.

There are other membership categories for which some designers or those affiliated with the interior design industry may be eligible. A review of the "Membership" tab at www.iida will fully inform readers on those categories.

As with ASID, by signing the application for any level of membership, the individual agrees to abide by IIDA's bylaws and code of ethics.

International Federation of Interior Architects/Designers (IFI)

This professional association was founded in 1963 in Denmark. "IFI is the sole international federating body for Interior Architecture/Design organizations and acts as a global forum for the exchange and development of knowledge and experience, in worldwide education, research and practice."[4] Its headquarters are located in Montreal, Quebec, Canada.

The IFI supports interior architects/designers on an international network. It represents designers, educators, and others in the international community. It is also is a member of the International Design Alliance (IDA). That group combines IFI, the International Council of Society of Industrial Design (ICSID), and the International Council of Graphic Design Associations (ICOGRADA) to further cooperative multidisciplinary work.[5]

There are several membership levels in IFI, the highest being *professional*. The professional level of membership has requirements that are similar to those of professional membership in ASID, IIDA, or IDC, but requirements do vary somewhat. You can find out more about IFI and its specific membership requirements by contacting its national office or searching www.ifiworld.org.

Interior Designers of Canada (IDC)

The Interior Designers of Canada (IDC), founded in 1972, is the national professional association in Canada. IDC works in coordination with eight provincial associations:

- Interior Designers Institute of British Columbia (www.idibc.org)
- Registered Interior Designers of Alberta (www.idalberta.com)
- Interior Designers Association of Saskatchewan (www.idas.ca)
- Professional Interior Designers Institute of Manitoba (www.pidim.ca)
- Association of Registered Interior Designers of Ontario (www.arido.ca)
- Association of Registered Interior Designers of New Brunswick (www.aridnb.ca)
- Association of Interior Designers of Nova Scotia (www.idns.ca)
- Association of Professional Interior Designers of Quebec (www.apdiq.com)

The IDC is "the national advocacy association for the interior design associations"[6] in Canada. It works with its eight provincial association members to advance the interior design profession and design education in Canada. Its members work in all specialties of interior design and design education. Members of IDC must hold the highest level of membership in their provincial association and must pass the international NCIDQ qualification examination.

IDC offers its members conferences, a newsletter, and education and learning opportunities through continuing education classes and programs. IDC also serves as the primary representative of the Canadian interior design profession to the Canadian federal government. It supports forums related to government relations, the environment, and cross-disciplinary collaboration, and also offers assistance to members who are working in the global market.

The eight provincial associations have individual membership categories and requirements. The reader should contact the appropriate provincial association for information. There is a direct link to those associations on the website www.idcanada.org.

Interior Design Educators Council (IDEC)

Full-time educators felt that it was necessary to establish an organization that specifically met their needs. Thus, in 1963 educators formed the Interior Design Educators Council (IDEC).[7]

The IDEC mission is the advancement of interior design education, scholarship, and service.[8] Most members of IDEC are full-time faculty members. Full-time interior design educators who have also received appropriate interior design education and have professional work experience may become professional-level members. Many are also professional or educator members of ASID, IIDA, and other associations.

IDEC is responsible for the publication of the *Journal of Interior Design*, a refereed journal. It is the only scholarly journal of the profession. The journal provides a mechanism for research materials to be widely distributed to educators and interested professionals.

For information on the complete requirements for membership in IDEC, visit www.idec.org.

SOCIAL RESPONSIBILITY

The services of an interior designer have an impact on facilities of all kinds, from private residences to the wide variety of commercial and public spaces.

TABLE 2-2.

Other professional organizations

There are several other professional organizations that might be available to interior designers based on their professional interests. Complete information regarding the qualification and application procedures of these associations can be obtained from the organizations' national offices or Web sites.
American Institute of Architects (AIA). The professional organization for architects. Interior designers may be eligible for affiliated membership. (www.aia.org)
Building Office and Management Association (BOMA). Members are owners and managers of office buildings. Interior designers who design large corporate office facilities often are members. (www.boma.org)
National Association of Home Builders (NAHB). NAHB represents members of the building industry concerning public policy on a wide variety of home construction issues. (www.nahb.org)
Construction Specifications Institute (CSI). Members are those involved in creating and building any type of building structure. (www.csinet.org)
International Facility Management Association (IFMA). This organization is for those actively engaged in corporate facility management and planning. (www.ifma.org)
Institute of Store Planners (ISP). The ISP is for professionals specializing in the design of retail stores and shopping centers. (www.ispo.org)
National Kitchen and Bath Association (NKBA). This organization is for those interested in specializing in kitchen or bath design. (www.nkba.org)
U.S. Green Building Council (USGBC). This organization represents designers and others in the built-environment industry who design and promote buildings that are environmentally healthy. They administer the examinations for LEED® certification for architects and interior designers in commercial and residential design. (www.usgbc.org)
Canada Green Building Council (CaGBC). A national organization to support sustainable design in Canada. (www.CaGBC.org)
Many other organizations are listed in the "Internet Resources" section of the Reference List.

There are all sorts of nonprofits and public places that can use the expertise of the designer to enhance and enrich the interiors.

Interior designers can also affect the communities they live in, through services that use their skills and problem-solving ability but not necessarily their creative expressions. Service on community boards, such as design review boards, historic sites, sustainable initiatives councils, community development boards, and many other city or county boards, can be a particularly good use of the designer's volunteer time. Local government depends on volunteers to take part in these commissions to help city management make living in a city or town better for the whole of the community. These commissions are formed without regard to political leanings; rather, they seek individuals with a willingness to serve in a neutral capacity.

You may have heard the term *pro bono*, which means providing something at no charge. Interior designers often provide their services at no charge to a community, church group, or nonprofit organization such as Habitat for Humanity. Pro bono work can be personally rewarding, in addition to helping these groups obtain top-notch design services for little or no expense.

Most of the professional associations' chapters yearly "adopt" a community service organization as a way for members to give back as a group, providing their professional skills—or just their time—for the public good. Perhaps it is remodeling the local Ronald McDonald House, or a battered women's shelter, or another of countless charity and community programs. Of course, nonaffiliated interior designers also participate in these types of programs, likewise bringing design skills and interests to serve the community.

If you have an interest in a particular type of nonprofit organization, your public service will provide you with enriching opportunities to help your community and beyond. Not only are you helping out these nonprofits, but you are also going to have the opportunity to meet many new people you might otherwise never meet. Just as you are encouraged to join and participate in a professional association, it is beneficial for you to participate in some sort of public service role.

Interior designers are frequently asked to speak to students in design programs. Lectures, guest critiques, tours of the designer's office facilities, and helping to arrange tours of significant design projects in the area are all examples of this important type of service. Personally speaking, it is very rewarding to speak to students. When you have the opportunity, please say yes—enthusiastically! Professionals need only contact liaisons at the interior design programs in their area to find out how they can contribute in this way.

Professionals can also assist in the education of students by:

- Hosting interns and serving as IDEP supervisors
- Jurying student design competitions
- Participating on an advisory board for an interior design program
- Serving as part-time adjunct faculty

Active involvement in the local chapter by volunteering for a chapter committee, or even serving on the governing board, is very rewarding. Chapters have numerous activities run by committees of volunteers. There are never enough volunteers to help put on those activities and meetings for the members.

Time is precious to many practitioners, and for some, community service can't be accomplished by being actively involved in the ways just discussed. Monetary contributions through gifts, grants, trusts, special awards, and other methods of financial support of the profession provide another avenue for designer community involvement. Association foundations accept many forms of financial support to help further the profession. Some of these include supporting students and design education and research through grants and awards for professional contributions.

The satisfaction of being involved in interior design is in itself very rewarding, and should go beyond seeking awards and accolades for one's creative work. That satisfaction grows immensely when one contributes in any way to the community and society in general.

WEB SITES RELEVANT TO THIS CHAPTER

www.aahid.org American Academy of Health Care Designers

www.aia.org American Institute of Architects

www.asid.org American Society of Interior Designers

www.boma.org Building Office Managers Association

www.CaGBC.org Canadian Green Building Council

www.csinet.org Construction Specifications Institute

www.accredit-id.org Council for Interior Design Accreditation

www.idbok.org Interior Design Body of Knowledge

www.idec.org Interior Design Educators Council

www.idcanda.org Interior Designers of Canada

www.ifma.org International Facility Managers Association

www.ifiworld.org International Federation of Interior Architects/Designers

www.iida.org International Interior Design Association

www.ispo.org Institute of Store Planners

www.nhab.org National Association of Home Builders

www.ncidq.org National Council for Interior Design Qualification

www.ncqlp.org National Council on Qualifications for the Lighting Professions

www.nkba.org National Kitchen and Bath Association

KEY TERMS

Certification

Continuing education unit (CEU)

Interior Design Experience Program (IDEP)

Internship

Licensing

Permitting statute

Practice acts

Pro bono

Registration

Social responsibility

The three Es

Title acts

ORGANIZATIONS

American Institute of Decorators (AID)

American Institute of Interior Decorators (AIID)

American Society of Interior Designers (ASID)

Council for Interior Design Accreditation (CIDA) (formerly FIDER)

Institute of Business Designers (IBD)

Interior Design Continuing Education Council (IDCEC)

Interior Design Educators Council (IDEC)

Interior Designers of Canada (IDC)

International Federation of Interior Architects/Designers (IFI)

International Interior Design Association (IIDA)

International Society of Interior Designers (ISID)

National Council for Interior Design Qualification (NCIDQ)

National Society of Interior Designers (NSID)

WHAT WOULD YOU DO?

1. Elizabeth graduated from an accredited four-year program in interior design and has been working in the industry for three years at an office furnishings dealership. She has been in one of the professional associations since being a student and has recently taken the NCIDQ examination. Through a relative, Elizabeth had the opportunity to meet one of the state legislators who will be on the committee to review her state coalition's interior design legislative proposal. This legislator expressed to Elizabeth her skepticism about the necessity for legislation of "decorating." As if you were Elizabeth, frame a response to this legislator on why interior design legislation is necessary to protect the public.

2. Andrew's client, the Peters family, was unhappy with his performance in the design of the Peters' summer cabin. He was constantly making changes in the design, causing cost overruns and delays in completion. Andrew blamed the problems on suppliers and contractors. The Peters family hired an attorney to investigate this allegation and it was found that Andrew's errors were the cause of the problems—not other companies. The client contacted the professional association to which Andrew claimed to belong and decided to file an ethics complaint. Andrew said that they had no standing to file an ethics complaint because he was never a member of the association and had, in fact, no knowledge of the codes of ethics.

3. Carl Jones of Jones Interior Design has been designing hospitality spaces in the Midwest for three years. One of those clients has decided to open a restaurant in a suburb of Las Vegas. The restaurant will be more than 75,000 square feet, and the owner wants to include a small casino area off the lobby. The owner is looking for a design concept reminiscent of the Old West casinos, so he has hired an architect from Colorado to do the structural design. The client wants Jones Interior Design to do the interior planning and specification, but the architect wants to do the interiors himself.

   Carl Jones is not registered in the Midwestern state where his business is located. He has told the client that he really would like to be involved in the project in Nevada, but he isn't licensed to do work there. The client is insisting that Carl's company do the interior and says he doesn't understand why Carl is reluctant.

REFERENCES

1. IDCEC *Presenter's Guide for Interior Design Continuing Education*, 2011, p. 11.
2. ASID Web site, 2012, www.asid.org
3. IIDA Web site, 2006, www.iida.org
4. IFI Web site, www.ifiworld.org
5. IFI Web site, www.ifiworld.org
6. IDC Web page, www.idcanada.org/english/about-us
7. IDEC, 2000, www.idec.org
8. IDEC Web site, 2011, www.idec.org/who

CHAPTER 3

Ethics and Professional Conduct

After completing this chapter you should be able to:

- Explain the importance of ethical standards.
- Explain a conflict of interest that might exist between you and your client or between you and a colleague.
- Explain why a conflict of interest can be damaging to your professional activities.
- Discuss at least two fiduciary duties you have to your employer and your client.
- Explain the different kinds of ethical situations in business discussed in the chapter and provide examples of each.
- Differentiate and explain an example of proprietary and nonproprietary employer information.
- Explain how someone's unethical behavior can affect others working in your market location.
- Discuss whether commissions or kickbacks are permissible based on the ASID or IIDA code of conduct.
- Discuss why ethical behavior is important for anyone working in the interior design profession, regardless of association affiliation.
- Explain the purpose of ethical standards and codes of conduct in this profession.
- Discuss what you should do if you discover that a colleague has breached or behaved in contradiction to the code of conduct of one of the professional associations.
- Name the three specific reasons discussed in the text why people behave unethically. Discuss how these actions negatively affect dealing with clients.

NCIDQ COMPONENT

Based on best information available, some material in this chapter might appear as part of the NCIDQ examination. The reader should not depend solely on this text for study material.

Interior designers on occasion will come to an ethics crossroad: One path leads to behavior that is expected of a professional; on the other path are temptations that lead to behavior contrary to ethical standards. Perhaps the temptations result from an omission rather than outright commission, yet the unethical behavior occurs. The decision has consequences for the individual, his or her company and client, and the profession as a whole.

Although the unethical behavior of an interior designer is very unlikely to garner headlines, ethical standards are just as important in the interior design profession as in any other. The expectations and demands for ethical professional behavior in interior design increase as our world continues to become more complex.

If we expect other professionals who affect our lives to behave ethically, interior designers must be held to the same standards. Thus, it is imperative that ethical behavior be treated as more than just a brief discussion in class while students anticipate getting into "more important" subjects.

This chapter presents an overview of ethics concepts and issues as they relate to the professional practice of interior design. It is only a beginning, and I hope that readers—whether students or professionals—will seek additional information and guidance related to this important topic from an association chapter or an organization. Questions are raised through examples and the What Would You Do? case materials at the end of each chapter, so that readers have opportunities to think about and discuss ethical solutions to the examples. It is hoped that, in this way, readers will begin to connect the code of ethics to situations that they might encounter in the profession.

ETHICAL STANDARDS

As discussed in Chapter 1, one of the characteristics of a true profession is that the profession and its members are guided by a set of *ethical standards*. These ethical standards define what is right and wrong in relation to the professional behavior of the members and the general practice of the profession.

Ethical standards and behavior have always been a concern of the interior design profession and professional associations. Adherence to the "Code of Ethics and Professional Practice" was expected of members of the AID in its earliest years.[1] In fact, the *AID Code of Ethics and Professional Practice* was published in a professional practice manual at least as early as 1961.[2]

Establishment of ethical standards is not limited to associations that expect ethical behavior of their members. Jurisdictions that pass legislation for title registration, practice acts, or other legal recognition often include ethical standards and usually disciplinary standards for those who violate the statutes. Furthermore, those in the profession—regardless of association, legislative edict, or choice to be part of this profession—should feel an obligation to behave in an ethical manner and abide by an ethical standard.

Ethical standards and behavior affect interior designers in many ways. Naturally, they have an impact on the relationships between the designer and his or her client. However, serious ethical situations may arise between the designer and those with whom the designer must work in the interest of the client: contractors, vendors, craftspeople, and others in the trade and the wider design–build industry.

Many situations involving ethical standards and behavior affect the business of design: the creation of contracts, marketing activities, budgeting, employee management, and financial activities are only a few. The interior design professional also owes a duty of ethical behavior toward others in the profession, whether they are other employees, the employer, or colleagues at other design firms.

The teaching and discussion of ethics and an enforceable code of ethics from professional associations provide definable and enforceable standards for this profession. However, a code of ethics cannot by itself produce ethical behavior. Ethical behavior must come from individual designers themselves in their daily dealings with clients, peers, the public, and allied professionals.

ETHICS IN THE BUSINESS ENVIRONMENT

If a design business operates within the law, is it also operating within an ethical business environment? You could reverse that and ask: If a company operates ethically, is it also operating within the law? Most people believe that ethics involves "doing the right thing." Operating within the law, to most people, means abiding by the legal statutes that apply to the business. Sometimes these concepts overlap, but they are not identical.

A little later in this chapter you will read the codes of ethics from ASID and IIDA. You will clearly see that specific parts of the codes overlap with legal issues. For example, clause 2.1 in the ASID code of ethics says, "Members shall comply with all federal, state and local laws, rules, regulations and codes governing business procedures and the practice of interior design in the jurisdiction in which they practice."[3] IIDA's code of ethics has a similar clause (3.1). Thus, legal behavior in practice goes hand in hand with ethical behavior in the profession.

Ethics Definitions

Following are a few definitions of *ethics* from a variety of sources.

Ethics are "moral principles that govern a person's or group's behavior; the moral correctness of specified conduct."*

"Ethical standards are not the standards of the law. In fact, they are a higher standard. Sometimes referred to as normative standards in philosophy, ethical standards are the generally accepted rules of conduct that govern society. . . . Ethics consists of those unwritten rules we have developed for our interactions with each other."**

"Ethics in a business context; a consensus of what constitutes right or wrong behavior in the world of business and the application of moral principles to situations that arise in a business setting."***

Oxford American College Dictionary, 2002, p. 463.
**Jennings, 2006, p. 3.
***Miller and Jentz, 2006, p. 47.

The preceding definitions provide a variety of meanings, and you might find others if you do an online search. However, they will have similar qualities and views.

The news headlines continually give us lessons in ethical behavior—or, rather, the lack of it. Politicians, business leaders, corporations, sports figures, and practitioners in almost every walk of life test how far ethical behavior can be stretched before someone notices and takes action. Unfortunately, this also holds for interior designers. As a result, the teaching and discussion of ethics in interior design is very important.

Making ethical decisions in the general business environment often comes down to making choices that have something to do with conflict of interest, competition, misuse of proprietary information, and employee theft.[4] Of course, other problems can also cause ethical dilemmas. These four are discussed because they represent major ethical issues in business and also can affect the interior designer as an individual or the individual's design business.

According to *Black's Law Dictionary, conflict of interest* is "a real or seeming incompatibility between one's private interests and one's public or fiduciary duties."[5] *Fiduciary duties*, by the way, are responsibilities assumed when one person acts in a position of trust or confidence for someone else. For example, when a supplier offers a *personal* advantage to a designer for specifying a certain product, the designer who accepts the offer acts in a manner that is a conflict of interest. Putting personal gain above the good of the person or the organization that the designer is supposed to represent is an example of unethical behavior.

Consider this scenario: Marty is the design director for an interior design firm that specializes in healthcare facilities. His firm is considering responding to a request for proposal (RFP) for the redesign of the emergency services area of a major hospital. Marty's wife, Jane, works at the hospital and is on the selection committee that will review the RFPs from responding firms. The committee she is on also makes the recommendation for which design firm to hire. Marty's employer knows this and wants to proceed with the RFP. What do you think Marty should do?

In many instances, conflict of interest hinges on some sort of monetary issue or motive. An example is asking for a special price from a vendor in exchange for a promise of future business. Another is charging a client "a little extra" for a product and keeping that extra money for oneself rather than turning it over to the design firm. Yet another might be consistently recommending to clients a specific vendor who happens to be a relative of the designer.

Issues related to competition also can involve ethical consequences. The free-market system creates rivalry between businesses—in other words, competition. When there are many businesses that offer the same or similar services or products, the competition can be intense. In slow economic times, competition can become extreme. When it does, business owners, managers, and some employees may stretch ethical boundaries in order to win customers. Maybe a designer who works on commission asks for a special discount (without passing it on to the client). Perhaps a vendor offers a special discount to a designer in order to have its product specified.

Many interior designers feel that there is not much of a problem with competition in interior design. However, this is not really true. All design firms are in competition with each other, in one way or another. Architectural firms, retail stores, and vendors who sell directly to the client are also competitors of interior designers. In a practical sense, they are not likely to be pursuing the exact same clients, but some are. And when the economy is slow, even more designers are competing for the same clients. Regardless of the size of the interior design firm and how well the local economy is doing, plenty of competition exists among interior design firms.

When competition is fierce, temptations to bend ethical and even legal rules can and do arise. Many respond to this by saying "What goes around comes around," meaning that if someone yields to the temptations of unfair competitive practice, eventually it will catch up with him or her. For example, a designer who does not obtain the contractor's license required by local laws to sell certain products will one day be reported to the registrar of contractors and possibly put out of business.

Of course, an ethical crossroad concerning a competitive market can be arrived at from another direction. Rather than designers disregarding competitive ethics, clients can put designers into a position that tests the interior designers' ethics. Some clients shop around for design ideas and prices, which in some ways is fine. Sometimes, however, a client who has a contract with designer A takes drawings prepared by designer A to designer B so as to get a lower price on merchandise specified for the project. What is designer B to do?

Another issue that has an impact on ethics in business is the misuse of propriety information. *Proprietary information* comprises a wide variety of data or information, graphics, or designs that belong to a particular person or business. In working with clients, the interior designer learns all sorts of private, propriety information about the client (and the client's business if the job is a commercial project). Residential clients are no different, in that they expect the interior designer to keep confidential the information he or she learns about the family in the course of the project.

A client's own proprietary information, such as trade secrets about a product or unique information about the operations of the business, might be exposed during the process of space-planning of a facility. Financial information that could be of use to a competitor of the client will likely be shared with the designer, at least to some degree. When doing design work for the government or even some private businesses, the designer might be required to sign a nondisclosure agreement.

Even one's employers own all sorts of propriety information that employees will learn and must keep in confidence. Financial data, client lists, and discounting policies are a few examples. Firms try to combat this issue by having employees sign nondisclosure agreements, which means that employees are not allowed to take proprietary information with them upon termination or voluntary separation. Such information may range from binders of information provided to employees to design work done by the employee.

Whether the proprietary information belongs to the design firm or a client, the owner of the proprietary information would not want an interior designer—or anyone else—to divulge the information to competitors or to the public. If the employee shares that information with someone outside the firm, the employer could both fire and/or sue him or her. This behavior can also result in an ethics complaint against the designer.

In the general business environment, colleagues have obligations to each other. Students occasionally complain to professors about someone "stealing" design ideas or saying that student A did the work actually turned in by student B. Unfortunately, this type of behavior also happens in the professional world. When two or more employees are vying for a promotion or a raise, taking credit for someone else's work might occur. It is simply not appropriate ethical and professional behavior.

Employee theft is another problem in the general business environment that can also affect interior design firms. Technically, taking home office supplies that are provided by the employer for personal use is employee theft, though it is rare indeed for any employer to press charges against an employee for taking home a few pens or a half-used pad of paper. But employees have taken money, goods from the sales floor or warehouse, and even office equipment—all of which are of greater value to the company. Perhaps a designer "borrows" a lamp for his home, and "forgets" to sign it out on approval; or a designer makes a copy of a software specification template so that she can use it for a personal business. Theft by employees does occur, although one must hope that it is not a great problem in interior design offices. What would you do if you knew that a colleague had made a copy of some software to use while he was moonlighting in his spare time?

Why do some people behave unethically? According to Brown and Sukys, it is because people (1) are motivated by self-interest, (2) are careless, and (3) see no harm in the behavior.[6] When someone places his or her own interests before those of others, he or she may be behaving unethically. Consider the case of a design student who includes work in her portfolio that has been done by someone else but represents to a potential employer as her own. In reality she cannot do that quality of work, so she has put self-interest first. The employer at some point will figure out that something is not right.

People become careless about ethical behavior when they get into a habit of being unethical. Perhaps a designer has gotten away with overbilling clients for services. Maybe a designer consistently overorders upholstery fabrics by a few yards and charges the extra yardage to the client—not to ensure that the amount will be enough for the project, but to warehouse the extra fabric or use it to make throw pillows for other clients.

The "But everybody does it" and "I see no harm in ____" excuses are another reason why people behave unethically. For instance, many designers could say, "Everybody uses down payments from one client to pay for orders for another client." Nevertheless, this practice is unethical and can be illegal if the state that designer works in requires that down payments be held in escrow and used only for the client who made the down payment (see Chapter 8 for a further discussion of this). Just because "everybody does it" does not make it right. Harm is created for every designer with this kind of thinking.

Commissions and Kickbacks

It is not uncommon for interior designers to receive a commission from some vendors when the client purchases products directly from the vendor. These commissions constitute additional revenue to the interior designer. This type of commission is not usually very large and is paid to the designer only if the client actually orders from the vendor.

These commissions raise ethical debates and ethical problems. Is the interior designer required to tell the client about these commissions? According to the codes of ethics from both ASID and IIDA, it is necessary to disclose all forms of compensation to the client. Some interior designers debate whether their colleagues should accept these commissions at all.

A clear conflict of interest and unethical situation occur when a designer receives a kickback. According to the Cornell Law School Web site, *kickbacks* "entail the return of a certain amount of money from seller to buyer as a result of a collusive agreement."* Kickbacks are clearly improper and are not the same as the commissions described in the previous paragraph. An example of a kickback is when a vendor gives a special discount to one designer for specifying or bidding on a project but not to other designers who are also bidding on the job. Another example of a kickback is when someone gives a payment of some kind as a very special inducement to favor the specification of one product over another. It is important to note that the discounts or commissions that vendors regularly give to interior designers are not illegal or unethical. It becomes unethical only when the special price is given for special treatment, such as in the preceding examples.

In commercial interior design, a practice that might be considered unethical, but can also be an appropriate business practice, is buying a job. Some firms lower their price drastically on services or bids on goods in order to be awarded a project. *Buying a job* refers to the practice of pricing the goods or fees at an unusually low level in order to make the sale. Some feel it is unethical because it sets a price with which other firms cannot compete. Others argue that setting a very low price is merely a marketing and business tool to enter a market, to obtain a specific type of work, or for other reasons that are legal and essentially ethical. However, how would you feel if you owned a firm and discovered that you had lost three recent projects to a firm that did not charge a design fee and offered to sell the merchandise to the client at a very substantial discount?

*Cornell Law School, www.law.cornell.edu/wex/kickbacks

These issues provide a background for looking more closely at professional conduct and ethical behavior in the interior design profession. The demand for ethical behavior does not apply only to interior designers who have joined one of the professional associations. Rather, ethical behavior should be practiced by anyone involved in this profession and in business in general. It is important to note that ethical conduct may be legally required of those in jurisdictions with practice or title act legislation. The legislation defining the practice, title, or certification parameters almost uniformly includes an ethics portion.

PROFESSIONAL CONDUCT

Samantha goes to the home of a new client. The client shows her boards and plans that obviously were not prepared by the client, although no designer name is on the boards. Samantha would really like to do this project, because the client is a well-known celebrity and her company needs the business.

If you were the interior designer who had originally prepared the drawings and boards given to Samantha, what would you want her to do? What would you want her to say to the client?

It is argued that we learn our values and morals as we grow up and that our ethics spring from those years of learning. Value systems and moral conduct as a professional should, then, be ingrained from what we have learned from parents, relatives, teachers, clergy, and friends. As professionals, how we conduct our business relationships with clients, colleagues, and cohorts can have a positive or negative impact on everyone in the profession.

A professional is expected to provide competent services in a manner considered customary by those in the profession as well as those who utilize those professional services. Professional conduct also means that those entering the profession must abide by standards accepted by others in the profession.

A starting point for that professional conduct lies within the associations. Regardless of the type of business, professional organizations expect their members to behave and conduct business in a manner that reflects positively upon all the members—and even nonmembers—of the association. Remember that when a designer at any level signs the application for membership in a professional association, the applicant is agreeing to abide by the association's code of ethics.

Choosing not to belong to an association, however, does not mean that someone in a profession can ignore ethics. Licensing and registration legislation almost invariably includes some reference to ethical behavior or discussion of disciplinary procedures for nonprofessional behavior.

The codes of ethics of the professional associations deal with enforceable ethical standards of practice and provide philosophical comments concerning the professional conduct of members. This discussion of *codes of conduct* (sets of ethical principles) and codes of ethics uses those from ASID and IIDA, because these two organizations represent the majority of professional association memberships in interior design. Readers can easily research codes of ethics or conduct from other associations or jurisdictional licensing boards by using the Internet.

The ASID Code of Ethics and Professional Conduct (see Figure 3-1) contains standards related to five areas of responsibility: (1) to the public, (2) to the client, (3) to other interior designers and colleagues, (4) to the profession, and (5) to the employer. The IIDA Code of Ethics (see Figure 3-2) consists of four sections: the designer's responsibility (1) to the public, (2) to the client, (3) to other designers and colleagues, and (4) to the association and interior design profession.

ASID Code of Ethics and Professional Conduct

AMERICAN
SOCIETY OF
INTERIOR
DESIGNERS

1.0 PREAMBLE

Members of the American Society of Interior Designers are required to conduct their professional practice in a manner that respects the interests of the general public, their clients, fellow professional designers, as well as suppliers of goods and services to the profession. It is the individual responsibility of every member of the Society to uphold this Code of Ethics and Professional Conduct and the Bylaws of the Society.

2.0 RESPONSIBILITY TO THE PUBLIC

2.1 Members shall comply with all federal, state and local laws, rules, regulations and codes governing business procedures and the practice of interior design in the jurisdictions in which they practice ("Applicable Laws").

2.2 Members shall not seal or sign drawings, specifications, or other interior design documents except where the member or the member's firm has prepared, supervised or professionally reviewed and approved such documents, as allowed by Applicable Laws.

2.3 Members shall at all times consider the health, safety and welfare of the public in spaces they design. Members agree, whenever possible, to notify property managers, landlords, and/or public officials of conditions within a built environment that endanger the health, safety and/or welfare of occupants.

2.4 Members shall not engage in any form of false or misleading advertising or promotional activities.

2.5 Members shall neither offer, nor make any payments or gifts to any public official, nor take any other action, with the intent of unduly influencing the official's judgment in connection with an existing or prospective project in which the members are interested.

2.6 Members shall not assist or abet improper or illegal conduct of anyone in connection with a project.

3.0 RESPONSIBILITY TO THE CLIENT

3.1 Members' contracts with a client shall clearly set forth the scope and nature of the project involved, the services to be performed and the method of compensation for those services.

3.2 Members may offer professional services to a client for any form of legal compensation.

3.3 Members shall not undertake any professional responsibility unless they are, by training and experience, competent to adequately perform the work required.

3.4 Members shall fully disclose to a client all compensation which the Member shall receive in connection with the project and shall not accept any form of undisclosed compensation from any person or firm with whom the member deals in connection with the project.

3.5 Members shall not divulge any confidential information about the client or the client's project, or utilize photographs of the project except as is expressly allowed by agreement between the Member and client.

3.6 Members shall be candid and truthful in all their professional communications.

3.7 Members shall act with fiscal responsibility in the best interest of their clients and shall maintain sound business relationships with suppliers, industry and trades.

FIGURE 3-1.

ASID Code of Ethics. (Reprinted with permission of A.S.I.D. (American Society of Interior Designers), Government and Public Affairs, Washington, DC.)

4.0 RESPONSIBILITY TO OTHER INTERIOR DESIGNERS AND COLLEAGUES

4.1 Members shall not interfere with another interior designer's existing contractual relationship with a client.

4.2 Members shall not initiate, or participate in, any discussion or activity which might be reasonably expected to result in an injury to another interior designer's reputation or business relationships.

4.3 Members may, when requested and it does not present a conflict of interest, render a second opinion to a client, or serve as an expert witness in a judicial or arbitration proceeding.

4.4 Members shall not endorse the application for ASID membership and/or certification, registration or licensing of an individual known to be unqualified with respect to education, training, experience or character, nor shall a Member knowingly misrepresent the experience, professional expertise or moral character of that individual.

4.5 Subject to the provisions of section six, members shall only take credit for work that has actually been created by that Member or the Member's firm, and under the Member's supervision.

4.6 Members shall respect the confidentiality of sensitive information obtained in the course of their professional activities.

5.0 RESPONSIBILITY TO THE PROFESSION

5.1 Members agree to maintain standards of professional and personal conduct that will reflect in a responsible manner on the Society and the profession.

5.2 Members shall seek to continually upgrade their professional knowledge and competency with respect to the interior design profession.

5.3 Members agree, whenever possible, to encourage and contribute to the sharing of knowledge and information between interior designers and other allied professional disciplines, industry and the public.

6.0 RESPONSIBILITY TO THE EMPLOYER

6.1 Members leaving an employer's service shall not take drawings, designs, photographs, data, reports, notes, client lists, or other materials relating to work performed in the employer's service except with permission of the employer.

6.2 Members shall not divulge any confidential information obtained during the course of their employment about the client or the client's project.

7.0 ENFORCEMENT

7.1 The Society shall follow standard procedures for the enforcement of this Code of Ethics and Professional Conduct as approved by the Society's Board of Directors.

7.2 Members having a reasonable belief, based upon substantial information, that another member has acted in violation of this Code of Ethics and Professional Conduct, shall report such information in accordance with accepted procedures.

7.3 Any deviation from this Code of Ethics and Professional Conduct, or any action taken by a Member which is detrimental to the Society and the profession as a whole shall be deemed unprofessional conduct subject to discipline by the Society's Board of Directors.

(Adopted by the National Board 10/10)

Information concerning how to file an ethics complaint—which is part of the Code of Ethics document—can be obtained from www.asid.org.

FIGURE 3-1.

(*Continued*)

INTERNATIONAL
INTERIOR DESIGN
ASSOCIATION

Policy D.8:	Code of Ethics and Professional Conduct
Purpose:	To establish minimum standards of behavior and conduct for Professional and Associate Members of the Association
Intent:	To provide the public, legislators, and the profession of Interior Design with standards of conduct and behavior for Professional Interior Designers

1.0 PREAMBLE

Professional and Associate Members of the International Interior Design Association shall conduct their interior design practice in a manner that will encourage the respect of clients, fellow interior designers, the interior design industry and the general public. It is the individual responsibility of every Professional and Associate Member of IIDA to abide by the Code of Professional Ethics and Conduct, Bylaws, Policies and Position Statements of the Association.

2.0 DEFINITIONS

The terms used in this Code shall be defined in the same manner in which they are defined in the Bylaws, Policies and Position Statements of the Association.

3.0 RESPONSIBILITY TO THE PUBLIC

3.1 In performing professional services, Professional and Associate Members shall exercise reasonable care and competence, and shall conform to existing laws, regulations and codes governing the profession of interior design as established by the state or other jurisdiction in which they conduct business.

3.2 In performing professional services, Professional and Associate Members shall at all times consider the health, safety, and welfare of the public.

3.3 In performing professional services, Professional and Associate Members shall not knowingly violate the law, or counsel or assist clients in conduct they know, or reasonably should know, is illegal.

3.4 Professional and Associate Members shall not permit their name or signature to be used in conjunction with a design or project for which interior design services are not to be, or were not, performed under their immediate direction and control.

3.5 Professional and Associate Members shall not engage in any form of false or misleading advertising or promotional activities and shall not imply, through advertising or other means, that staff members or employees of their firms are Professional or Associate Member unless such is the fact.

3.6 Professional and Associate Members shall not make misleading, deceptive or false statements or claims about their professional qualifications, experience, or performance.

3.7 Professional and Associate Members shall not, by affirmative act or failure to act, engage in any conduct involving fraud, deceit, misrepresentation or dishonesty in professional or business activity.

3.8 In performing professional services, Professional and Associate Members shall refuse to consent to any decision by their clients or employers which violates any applicable law or regulation, and which, in the Professional and Associates Members' judgment, will create a significant risk to public health and safety.

FIGURE 3-2.

IIDA Code of Ethics. This version is applicable to interior design practitioners only. (Reprinted with permission of International Interior Design Association, Chicago, IL.)

3.9 Professional and Associate Members shall not attempt to obtain a contract to provide interior design services through any unlawful means.

3.10 Professional and Associate Members shall not assist any person seeking to obtain a contract to provide interior design services through any unlawful means.

4.0 RESPONSIBILITY TO THE CLIENT

4.1 Professional and Associate Members shall undertake to perform professional services only when they, together with their consultants, are qualified by education, training or experience to perform the services required.

4.2 Before accepting an assignment, Professional and Associate Members shall reasonably inform the client of the scope and nature of the project involved, the interior design services to be performed, and the method of remuneration for those services. Professional and Associate Members shall not materially change the scope of a project without the client's consent.

4.3 Prior to an engagement, Professional and Associate Members shall disclose, in writing, to an employer or client, any direct or indirect financial interest that they may have that could affect their impartiality in specifying project-related goods or services, and shall not knowingly assume or accept any position in which their personal interests conflict with their professional duty. If the employer or client objects to such financial or other interest, Professional and Associate Members shall either terminate such interest, or withdraw from such engagement.

4.4 Professional and Associate Members shall not reveal any information about a client, a client's intention(s), or a client's production method(s) which they have been asked to maintain in confidence, or which they should reasonably recognize as likely, if disclosed, to affect the interests of their client adversely. Notwithstanding the above, however, Professional and Associate Members may reveal such information to the extent they reasonably believe is necessary (1) to stop any act which creates a significant risk to public health and safety and which the Professional or Associate Member is unable to prevent in any other manner; or (2) to prevent any violation of applicable law.

5.0 RESPONSIBILITY TO OTHER INTERIOR DESIGNERS AND COLLEAGUES

5.1 Professional and Associate Members shall pursue their professional activities with honesty, integrity and fairness, and with respect for other designers' or colleagues' contractual and professional relationships.

5.2 Professional and Associate Members shall not accept instruction from their clients which knowingly involves plagiarism, nor shall they consciously plagiarize another's work.

5.3 Professional and Associate Members shall not endorse the application for membership in the Association of an individual known to be unqualified with respect to education, training or experience; nor shall they knowingly misrepresent the experience, professional expertise, or moral character of that individual.

5.4 Professional and Associate Members shall only take credit for work that has actually been created by the Member or the Member's firm or under the Member's immediate direction and control.

6.0 RESPONSIBILITY TO THE ASSOCIATION AND INTERIOR DESIGN PROFESSION

6.1 Professional and Associate Members agree to maintain standards of professional and personal conduct that will reflect in a responsible manner on the profession.

6.2 Professional and Associate Members shall seek to continually upgrade their professional knowledge and competency with respect to the interior design profession.

FIGURE 3-2.

(*Continued*)

6.3   Professional and Associate Members shall, wherever possible, encourage and contribute to the sharing of knowledge and information among interior designers, the interior design industry, and the general public.

6.4   Professional and Associate Members shall offer support, encouragement, and information to students of interior design.

6.5   Professional and Associate Members shall, when representing the interior design profession, act in a manner that is in the best interest of the profession.

6.6   Professional and Associate Members may only use the IIDA appellation in accordance with current Association policy.

6.7   Professional and Associate Members shall not knowingly make false statements or fail to disclose any material fact requested in connection with their applications for membership in the Association.

                                                                    03/01

FIGURE 3-2.

(*Continued*)

These rules of conduct exist for members of the organizations. They have no actual impact on interior designers who are not members of one of the organizations. They can serve, however, as a guide to nonaffiliated interior designers and those in the design–build industry. An ethical charge cannot be brought against an unaffiliated designer, although a wronged party could file civil suits or other charges with the appropriate boards within a jurisdiction.

Members must keep codes of conduct in mind and observe them when they deal with other designers, whether or not the other designers are members of one of the organizations; with their clients; with others in the industry; and with the public in general. Just because someone who is practicing interior design or interior decoration is not a member of one of the associations does not mean that the individual can behave unethically.

The examples mentioned in this chapter pose serious ethical problems. However, they do not encompass the most common ethical problems that have found their way into the national associations' ethics committees for disciplinary hearings, according to the interior design professional associations. Some broad examples of ethics complaints filed with the ASID national office and provided by ASID appear in the following list. Note that these are not listed in the order from most often reported to least often reported; nor do they represent all the issues that relate to ethics complaints.

- The use and misuse of copyrighted images via the Internet, and other Internet misuse issues
- Complaints dealing with financial compensation, such as overbilling
- Communications issues, such as purposely avoiding or not returning client communications
- Using an unclear or nonspecific contract
- Not performing in the best interest of the client
- Withholding merchandise that is paid in full
- Contract alteration as the job progresses without prior client approval

Professional conduct and professional responsibility are interwoven in the overall practice of interior design. Designers do not necessarily give conscious thought to whether a daily activity that is part of working on a project for a client is done ethically or in a manner prescribed by the profession. Sometimes, though, a designer comes to an ethical crossroads and chooses to behave in a manner that contradicts a code of ethics or even the person's personal moral compass. When this happens, it hurts the individual, to be sure—tomorrow if not today—and it hurts everyone else and the profession in general.

Item 3-1 on the companion Web site is a design contract that involves an interesting ethical situation and will challenge your understanding of the professional code of conduct in interior design.

DISCIPLINARY PROCEDURES

Ethics complaints received by the professional associations have been on the rise, as clients learn that they have this recourse against designers who they feel have not treated the client fairly. What happens when a client or someone else decides to file an ethics complaint? This brief discussion will provide readers with a general overview of the process, although disciplinary procedures may vary slightly from the information according to the association or jurisdiction involved.

The individual against whom a complaint is made must be a member of one of the professional associations. A client cannot expect an association to discipline someone who is not a member of that association. However, clients may have recourse even with nonaffiliated designers: if the laws exist, they may file a complaint with a licensing board or a consumer protection agency in their state.

The complainant—let us say a client—must file the complaint in writing, explaining the details and facts of the situation. The letter is sent to the national or chapter office of the appropriate association. The complainant should include supplemental information with this originating letter. Sometimes clients who are unfamiliar with the process may be asked to supply supplemental documentation, if they wish, after the initial contact is made with the association.

An appropriate party, such as an attorney, designated staff member, or chapter ethics committee, may review the information to make an initial determination of whether a violation has actually occurred. This is done because many disputes concerning design do not constitute a violation of ethical conduct (for example, the client is upset because the design is not what the client generally expected).

If a determination is made that more detailed review and consideration are warranted, the member is notified. A copy of the complaint is sent to the designer, and the designer is given an opportunity to respond within a specified period of time. All the materials from the complainant and the designer are then sent to the association's ethics committee. Although the makeup of the ethics committee varies by association, it generally consists of three or more professional-level members. Sometimes the ethics committee may request additional information from one or both parties.

What happens after the review by the ethics committee? If the ethics committee determines that an ethics violation has not occurred, the association will so notify both parties in writing. When the ethics committee determines that a violation may very well have occurred, the complaint may be reviewed by another committee—although this step varies by association—before going to the association's disciplinary committee. If the complaint is forwarded to a disciplinary committee, each party to the complaint is permitted to provide testimony, bring witnesses, and/or provide additional documentation before the disciplinary committee.

In some cases, one or both sides may wish to submit additional material. If so, that submitting party must also send a copy of these supplements to the other party prior to the hearing. At the time of the disciplinary committee hearing, the parties may also have legal counsel present. The disciplinary committee then determines if the facts provided by each party truly indicate that the designer charged by the complainant has violated the association's code of ethics. The committee may take several courses of action, from dismissing the case to terminating the designer's membership in the association.

Disciplinary hearings are not courts of law and have no legal bearing on either party. A client may, however, also decide that the designer's actions are legally actionable and may file a civil claim (see Chapter 4). A disciplinary committee functions to investigate allegations of unethical behavior by members of the association. It has no authority over nonmembers who may have behaved unethically.

Actions taken to the disciplinary committee are no light matter. The names of those members whose memberships have been revoked by the disciplinary committee might appear in the association's newsletters. Although this may be personally embarrassing to the member whose name appears in print, it also serves to advise all members that the association will enforce the code of ethics.

WEB SITES RELEVANT TO THIS CHAPTER

www.asid.org American Society of Interior Designers

www.idcanada.org Interior Designers of Canada

www.iida.org International Interior Design Association

KEY TERMS

Codes of conduct	Ethics
Commissions	Fiduciary duties
Conflict of interest	Kickback
Disciplinary procedures	Proprietary information
Ethical standards	

WHAT WOULD YOU DO?

1. John has been running radio ads that give the impression that he and all his staff are professional-level members of one of the associations. John is a residential designer and his clients are obtained primarily by referrals from past clients. Only one staff member is a member of one of the associations and that person is a professional-level member. John lost his membership through an ethics violation three years ago.

2. Gray designed a doctor's suite, providing space-planning services, finish specifications throughout the suite, and specifications of furniture items for the waiting room and the offices. The client approved samples and furniture items from a sample board. Gray only charged the client for design services and the furniture items. He did not sell the client the architectural finishes, nor was he responsible for the construction work. The project is now at the stage of installation of the finishes. The client is upset that the colors and materials for the walls and floors do not look like what he expected and is also upset that the whole project is six weeks behind schedule.

3. During her initial marketing presentation, Mary makes it clear to the client that she is experienced in handling complex restaurant designs. Her marketing materials show photos of restaurants in other cities—none of which were designed by Mary. In fact, Mary has no experience in this area. Mary was awarded the project and has already made numerous errors in the floor plans.

4. Katie has been working for a design firm for five years and has gained much experience in a design specialty area. She became a bit disgruntled because she did not receive a raise and promotion recently. Katie has been approached by other design firms in the past year. After finally deciding to look for another job, she takes plans of projects she has been involved in and includes them in her portfolio for the job interviews, without permission of her current employer.

5. Richard works at GBS Interiors. He has been hinting to some vendors that he was responsible for three or four major model home designs, but that his boss is taking all the credit. Richard feels that because all the boss did was meet with the client to show ideas that Richard had developed, the projects are really his own.

6. Don was very excited that the primary home magazine in his city was interested in publishing photos and a story about a large residential project Don completed a few months ago for a high-profile celebrity. Before the photo shoot by the magazine, a reporter interviewed Don about the project and what it was like to work with the client. Don had never had any work featured in print before and was very energized during the interview, giving the reporter all kinds of interesting information about the project and the client. The reporter—uncharacteristically—asked if Don was a member of any professional association and Don said yes, though he did not clarify that he was in fact an Allied member. When the photographer and the editor arrived to shoot the house, the client indicated that although Don had "been involved," the client's designer from another city had actually been the primary designer. The client also was now a little uncomfortable with a photographer taking pictures of the interior: He had not realized that a photographer was going to be coming to the house. The client thought that the photos would come from the designer in the other city who had already had photos taken of the house.

REFERENCES

1. Allwork, 1961, p. 13.
2. Allwork, 1961, p. 13.
3. ASID, *Code of Ethics and Professional Conduct*, 2011. Available from www.asid.org
4. Ivancevich et al., 1994, p. 97.
5. *Black's Law Dictionary*, 7th ed., Bryan A. Garner, ed., 1999, p. 295.
6. Brown and Sukys, 1997, p. 8.

CHAPTER 4

Legal Responsibilities

After completing this chapter you should be able to:

- Identify where the laws that govern business and personal behavior originate.
- Explain how an interior design business meets its legal obligations in the business environment, citing specific examples.
- Compare the differences (in a general sense) between criminal and tort law.
- Discuss how the interior designer must protect himself or herself in relation to cyber law.
- Explain what must be proved to show that an interior designer was negligent.
- Analyze a situation and determine if the interior designer was negligent.
- Explain the concept of assumption of risk as it applies to an interior design project.
- Discuss how a client might contribute to an event that the client later claims was professional negligence by the interior designer.
- Compare statements that are misrepresentation versus statements that are considered salesperson's puffing.
- Explain the difference between the unintentional and intentional torts as discussed in this chapter.
- Discuss how intentional torts against a person relate to the practice of interior design.
- Discuss the basic process of protecting a designer's copyright for design drawings and documents.
- Explain why the design work of an employee is not owned by the employee.
- Compare copyright protection for a sole practitioner versus an employee of a design firm.
- Compare the intent of the building code, fire safety code, and barrier-free regulations.

> **NCIDQ COMPONENT**
>
> *Based on best information available, some material in this chapter might appear as part of the NCIDQ examination. The reader should not depend solely on this text for study material. See the sections on general legal responsibilities.*

Rarely do we hear about interior designers being sued by clients, yet lawsuits do occur in this profession. Only a small number of disputes and problems that occur in the interior design profession actually make it to a court. Perhaps it is a dispute about the quality of work done by a contractor hired by the designer. Or a client might sue a designer because the designer did not complete the project according to the provisions of state law—specifically, a state home improvement act.

It is critical to understand that there are a great number of ways interior designers might be involved in a legal action, either against them or by them. Even the smallest design project involves activities and responsibilities that can be the basis of potential legal actions against the designer. This chapter follows the chapter on ethics because so many legal issues are also ethical concerns.

For example, not holding a proper license in the jurisdiction can result in a lawsuit concerning the work, a fine from the state, and an ethics hearing should the client complain to the designer's professional association. A designer's strong negative comments to a prospective client about a designer at another firm that cost the second designer the project can be both a legal and ethical dilemma for the first designer.

Legal responsibility is not a matter of choice in the 21st century; it is a fact of professional life. Interior designers are legally liable for the work they or members of their staff do, and thus they can be sued. This exposure includes the planning, specification, and execution of the design and design documents.

It is the responsibility of the professional designer to be aware of the legal responsibilities that affect his or her practice. It is not necessary to become a lawyer, but it is necessary to understand all the ramifications of engaging in a professional practice so as to avoid legal problems.

This chapter provides an overview of legal responsibilities that can affect the practice of interior design. The chapter begins with an overview of the legal environment in interior design practice and continues with a focus on tort-law issues of negligence.

The examples given in this chapter are simple illustrations to help clarify the legal concepts discussed. In reality, a great many factors are always involved in the determination of the actual guilt or innocence of persons in situations similar to the examples given here. These chapters do not constitute legal advice. The information provided should not be used as a substitute for any discussion with an attorney.

THE LEGAL ENVIRONMENT OF INTERIOR DESIGN PRACTICE

Legal responsibility in interior design practice is woven into every aspect of practice. It is also intertwined with ethical conduct. As you read this chapter and the others that include information about legal responsibilities, you will see clearly how true this is.

There are a diverse and large number of statutes and rulings that have an impact on businesses; Table 4-1 lists the sources of most of them. State statutes requiring a resale license for businesses that sell merchandise are one example. Federal laws concerning what can and cannot be asked on job applications and during interviews are another example. Disputes between the client and the designer are affected not only by what is in the contract, but also by the statutes within the jurisdiction. What obligations a designer might have should a product that he or she specifies for a project fail is defined in the uniform laws. Ownership of items of intellectual property, such as the drawings the designer creates for the project, falls under federal laws. These are only a few examples of the numerous ways laws affect business.

Business practice accountability does not suddenly heighten when licensing or registration legislation is enacted in a jurisdiction. Any size or type of practice has to meet its obligations in the business environment, starting when someone begins the business and continuing until the owner closes or sells the firm. However, business owners are not the only parties who must adhere to legal precepts. Legal responsibility holds employers and employees responsible for their actions and interactions with clients, vendors, and others.

By far, the kinds of cases that most commonly involve interior designers are based on negligence or breach of contract. *Negligence liability*, often referred to as *professional negligence*, legally means that the designer has failed to use the due care normally expected of a professional in carrying out his or her design responsibilities. *Breach-of-contract liability* refers to the designer's failure to complete (or properly meet) the requirements of a contract. Breach of contract is discussed in Chapter 7; negligence is a major portion of the discussion in this chapter.

Give Examples

Strict liability refers to liability regardless of who is at fault. Under strict liability, people are responsible for their acts, regardless of their intent or use of reasonable care. For example, a painter has been hired to paint the exterior of a home. The next-door neighbor goes out to inspect her house and finds overspray of the blue paint on the side of her white house. The painter is liable under strict liability.

TABLE 4-1.

Where do our laws come from?

Laws that govern business and personal behavior come from several sources.

Constitutional law. The highest level of law in the United States is expressed in the U.S. Constitution.

State constitutional law. Each state and commonwealth also has a constitution that is the supreme law in that state, although a state constitution cannot supersede U.S. constitutional law.

Statutory law. Created by governmental entities such as the U.S. Congress and state legislatures. A state statute applies only within that state, whereas a federal statute applies to all states.

Ordinances. Local governments create ordinances governing such things as zoning, building codes, and traffic (among others). An ordinance applies only to the municipality or county that enacted it.

Administrative law. The source of administrative law is the rules and decisions of agencies of federal, state, and local governments. For example, the Department of Justice enforces laws concerning accessibility.

Case law, also called *common law*. When a case is decided in court, that ruling enforces, changes, or adds to case law. Case law is what governs areas of law not regulated by statute or administrative law.

Uniform laws. A national conference of commissioners develops and suggests laws for adoption by the states, to try to bring consistency to the numerous versions of laws on similar subjects passed by individual states. The Uniform Commercial Code, discussed in Chapter 9, is an example.

Although strict liability issues can be raised concerning an interior designer's performance, like the painter in the example, to an interior designer, this tort is most related to product liability and product specification. It is discussed in detail in Chapter 9 on sales law and warranties.

Business legal responsibility begins as the business begins. A new practice must be created in accordance with laws existing in the jurisdiction. This means filing forms for business-entity creation and licensure with state and local government agencies. Obtaining a resale tax license for firms planning on selling merchandise to clients is one example. Meeting regulations concerning the practice of interior design is another, as is obtaining a contractor's license to allow the designer to sell and supervise the installation or construction of interior finishes. Information concerning these areas of legal responsibility is discussed in Chapter 19.

Interior design professionals enter into many kinds of contracts in the course of operating their practices. The primary contract, of course, is with the client, describing the services to be performed for a project and the payment arrangements. A second type of contract is for the sale of goods to clients. Some employers use employment contracts to define the responsibilities of employees. When a firm buys goods for a client, the firm enters into a contract each time a purchase order for goods or a service in the name of the client is created. The primary discussion of contracts is in Chapters 7 and 9.

Employers have a duty and responsibility to employees to treat them fairly and provide them with a safe work environment that is free from harassment and discrimination. The employee also has duties and responsibilities to the employer. An employer's responsibility begins with the hiring process, in knowing that certain types of information and questions are not permitted in employment advertisements, on employment applications, or during interviews. The responsibility continues throughout the working association, encompassing wages, benefits, promotions, and recommendations, as well as discharge when the firm no longer requires or desires the employee's services. An employee is expected to follow the legal direction of the employer to accomplish the tasks that the employee has been hired to perform. Issues of employment law are covered in Chapters 27 and 29.

Interior designers might also occasionally be asked by a client (or others) to provide advice or an interpretation of what someone else has done. Care must be taken in such situations, as there can be serious legal and ethical consequences for the designer who is asked to render advice. In some instances, the opinion asked for might be related to an issue that is in fact within the expertise of the designer. But if the advice requested is outside the designer's expertise, he or she should diplomatically suggest that the client seek that opinion from a different source, such as an architect, or engineer, or even an attorney.

Some highly experienced designers are called upon to provide expert witness testimony in court actions. Designers who serve in the role of expert witness not only have very specialized design experience, but also have good reputations and are highly regarded by others in the profession. They must also be confident and skillful communicators, as testifying in court or at arbitration meetings can be stressful. This role should be undertaken only by an interior designer who has many years of experience and absolute comfort in rendering that type of advice.

I hope that this brief overview helps readers recognize that interior design practice involves more than creative problem solving and creation of aesthetic and functional interiors. Students beginning their pursuit of a career must realize that their design efforts place them in a position of responsibility to their clients that goes beyond designing an aesthetically pleasing environment. As practitioners, they will also take on many areas of legal responsibility to clients, colleagues, employees, the profession, and others with whom they will come into contact.

Cyber Law: A Brief Introduction

Cyber law—that is, law dealing with utilization of the Internet and computers—is constantly being created and changed to deal with the business environment. The use of e-mail in business also has an indirect impact related to the scope of cyber law. It should be no surprise to readers that interior design practitioners utilize the Internet and cyberspace for many operational procedures. Using this technology in a legal way is imperative for all interior designers.

Much traditional law can be applied to communications and transactions conducted in cyberspace (using the Internet and World Wide Web). Nevertheless, confusion abounds as to the application of law to electronic communications. If you send a contract via e-mail, that contract is a legitimate offer. If you promise to do something in an e-mail, that promise can be held to be a contract offer.* As discussed in Chapter 9, your name at the end of an e-mail is considered an electronic signature and can also create a binding agreement as to what is said in the e-mail. Thus, care must be taken in writing e-mails, as messages will likely be retained by the receiver and can potentially be used as evidence in a dispute.

Interior designers and trade sources might wish to use the Internet to broadcast a message to potential clients or buyers. Readers have most likely received e-mail messages from businesses with which they have done business—and from many others who have sent unsolicited e-mails. Unsolicited mailing on the Internet is essentially the same thing to the receiver as the "junk mail" sent through the Post Office. It is, of course, more commonly known as *spam*. To cut down on spamming, numerous states have passed laws limiting unsolicited e-mailing. A federal law, titled the Federal CAN-SPAM Act (enacted in 2003 and revised in 2008), imposes several conditions on anyone who sends e-mails for commercial purposes. These rules are provided to protect recipients from unwanted, unsolicited, and continuing e-mail marketing proposals. E-mail marketing is routinely done by small and big companies alike, but the practitioner who uses e-marketing tools must be sure that it is done within legal guidelines.

This brief discussion is intended to alert readers to the consequences of using the Internet in an inappropriate manner. Additional information concerning business and cyberspace is presented in Chapter 9.

*Miller and Jentz, 2006, p. 307.

CRIMINAL VERSUS TORT LAW

Our laws are also classified into criminal laws and tort laws. A criminal offense, referred to as a *crime*, is an offense that is regulated by a *statute*. These statutes are created to protect the public at large and are considered wrongs against all of society. The punishment for the criminal act defined in the statute is imprisonment and/or a fine.

We are all familiar with the concept that an individual person can commit and be punished for a crime. A legal entity can also commit a crime. Businesses, whether proprietorships, partnerships, or corporations, are legal entities (technically, they have the legal status of persons). Thus, the business and its owners/officers can be accused of and tried for crimes. For example, executives from corporations have been tried and found guilty of insider trading, bank fraud, obstruction of justice, and many other widely publicized activities.

Tort law comes into play when a person commits a wrong against another and causes injury to the other person or entity. Torts are not legislated by statute and thus are considered civil matters. The injured person—called a *plaintiff*—commonly sues the party who harmed him or her (the *defendant* or *respondent*). Most legal problems that interior designers experience involve some aspect of tort law; only rarely are they involved in criminal law issues regarding their practice.

A tort issue might be unintentional, which is commonly called *negligence;* or intentional, which means that the harm was committed consciously or deliberately. Negligence and several intentional torts are discussed in detail in later sections of this chapter.

Because the intentional tort act is against one person (or entity) by another, a tort is a civil action, in which the person harmed sues, in a civil court, the person who has done the harm. When we think of "harm," we normally think of someone suffering a physical injury. In tort law, however, harm can be to property, to a person's reputation, to a person's physical being, or even to a person's business.

The injured person may seek various remedies for the damages caused. A remedy might be monetary, performance of the task at issue, or even stopping performance, to cite a few types. For example, a client might sue an interior designer to provide a complete set of the drawings that were agreed to in a contract. Some torts, such as assault and battery, are also criminal acts if there are statutes defining them as such.

NEGLIGENCE

Did you realize that transposing numbers on your purchase order so that the wrong product is shipped is a form of negligence? Perhaps a client tells you not to design a commercial space to meet code. If you bow to your client's demands, your actions could also be considered negligence. These two simple examples are illustrations of acts of commission and omission that can lead to a negligent performance. These examples in themselves, however, are not negligence.

Negligence is an unintentional misdeed that occurs because of omission or commission in the activities and responsibilities of a person engaged in—for our purposes in this text—interior design. "Negligence is the failure to exercise the standard of care that a reasonable person would exercise in similar circumstances."[1] Not shoveling snow off your sidewalk, so that pedestrians might slip and fall, is a form of negligence.

You have no doubt heard the term *professional negligence*. In this case, someone in a profession, such as interior design, architecture, medicine, or so on, has committed (or omitted) the act at issue. The negligence refers to the performance (or lack of performance) of standard duties and responsibilities of someone in the profession. Professional negligence indicates that the designer in some way was negligent in his or her conduct while executing a project.

The negligent act must be the cause of harm that actually occurs to a person or his or her property. Negligence is unintentional: the designer did not think that any wrongful or harmful consequences would occur from the action and did not want them to occur. The person accused of negligence creates a risk, that risk creates the environment for the tort of negligence, and harm occurs because of that risk. The risk in these instances is such that a reasonable person could have and would have anticipated it and prevented it. If there is no creation of risk, there cannot be negligence.

Anyone can be involved in a situation that results in negligence. It does not have to be a catastrophic situation. Simply designing a project that greatly exceeds the client's stated budget could be construed as negligence. Selling and installing a carpet that the designer knows does not meet fire-code is negligence. Supplying a dresser whose drawers do not have stops and can thus cause injury may be negligence.

A large number of relatively unintentional acts related to an interior designer's everyday responsibilities can be considered professional negligence. Let us look specifically at the factors that must be proven in order to show negligence and how they relate to an interior design practice. If these factors do not exist, then it is most likely that the courts will say that negligence has not occurred.

Duty of Care

Everyone has a duty to use reasonable care in his or her interactions with others. For a professional, that duty extends into using reasonable care in his or her dealings and actions as a professional working for others and in the interests of clients.

This duty extends not only to resulting physical harm, but also to economic harm. A business that cannot open on time due to problems in the design project might have a negligence cause of action against the designer. Staying within the budget stated by the client is a duty owed to the client. The concept of duty of care is very important to the notion of negligence.

Breach of Duty

Other criteria for deciding whether negligence has actually occurred concern whether a duty owed to others was really breached. A breach of duty results when a designer fails to act in a way that is considered reasonable for the professional designer.

The reasonable person standard, in terms of interior design practice, means that the actions considered a breach are things that others in the profession would not have done in the given situation. A breach of duty can occur through knowingly specifying the wrong carpet for the client (intentional); or an omission, such as not stopping the work when the designer sees that the carpet being installed is incorrect (carelessness). The benchmark of reasonableness is sometimes hard to define, so expert witnesses are often used to help the court determine what is reasonable for an interior designer concerning the case in question.

Causation

Another important element that must be proved to show negligence is that the action or omission caused the injury or harm. Legal cause is called *proximate cause*. Proximate cause exists when "a connection between an act and a injury is strong enough to justify imposing liability."[2] In other words, if the injury occurs exclusively because of the designer's act, then there is, in all likelihood, negligence.

Because causation is not always easy to determine, the courts often use the "but-for" test to determine causation in fact: "But for the wrongful act, the injury would not have occurred." How foreseeable one act is over another is determined by the courts and is not easy to establish. For the designer to be held liable, actual cause between the act and the harm created must be present.

Injury or Harm

A tort of negligence does not exist unless there is some legally recognizable loss, harm, wrong, or invasion to a plaintiff. Injury must occur in order for the plaintiff to recover compensation. Remember that harm can also be economic harm; harm does not have to be an injury to a person for this element to exist. Plaintiffs in tort cases seek compensation for damages from the defendant; they usually do not seek to imprison the defendant.

Principal Defenses to Negligence Charges

For an act to be considered negligent, the four elements (criteria) just discussed must all be proven. Beyond proving that one or more of these factors did not exist or were not the responsibility of the defendant, there are some additional defenses for negligence claims. The first is called assumption of risk. In *assumption of risk*, the plaintiff who knowingly and willingly enters into a risky situation cannot recover damages if harm or injury occurs. For example, if a client agrees to purchase a residential-grade carpet, knowing it will not provide the wear required in his or her commercial installation, the designer cannot be found negligent.

Another defense to negligence is *contributory negligence*. In this defense, it must be shown that both sides have been negligent and that injury has resulted. This comes from the idea that each person should look out for his or her own interests and safety. Many states have, however, modified this defense to a defense called *comparative negligence*. In this instance, it is recognized that both parties are in some way at fault, and thus their level of negligence is compared and determined. The courts determine the degree of fault by each side and grant damages related to it. Comparative negligence often softens the effects of contributory negligence.

INTENTIONAL TORTS

Negligent acts are considered unintentional torts. There are several other torts that are considered intentional, meaning that a plaintiff has committed the acts on purpose and with knowledge that they were wrongful. Some of these acts occur against a person and others against property. Some of these torts may occur in situations that could arise with an interior designer or the design business.

Against a Person

Intentional torts against a person must show intent; that is, the person must have consciously performed the act and must have known or have been substantially certain that the act would harm another person.

- *False imprisonment* is the intentional confinement of a person for an appreciable duration of time without justification. Perhaps an employee or showroom owner believes that a customer has tried to shoplift an item. If the customer has not taken anything, but is nevertheless detained, he or she might sue for false imprisonment. In many jurisdictions, *shoplifting* does not occur until the person has walked out the door of the business with goods that have not been properly paid for.

- *Defamation* is wrongful harm to a person's good reputation. If the defamation is in writing, it is called *libel;* if it is oral, it is *slander*. To be defamatory, statements must be made to, or read or heard by, a third party. Some harm must result from the statements made in order for them to be considered to be defamation by a court.

- *Invasion of privacy* protects everyone's right to freedom from others' prying eyes. This might occur if a designer photographs a client's interiors and subsequently publishes them in the designer's marketing materials without the client's permission. Disclosure of personal information about clients can also be an invasion of privacy.

- *Fraud* (also called *misrepresentation*). When a designer intentionally misrepresents facts to deceive a client and thereby receives personal gain, fraud has been committed. The common test in this situation is misrepresenting facts. Factual deception in order to obtain personal gain is a form of misrepresentation. An expression of personal opinion is not considered misrepresentation unless the person is considered an expert in the subject matter.

- Related to misrepresentation is something often called *puffing*. The use of puffing, or offering personal opinions about intangible qualifiers of a product or a service, is not usually considered fraud unless the seller represents as fact something that he or she knows is not true.

- *Wrongful interference*. In our context, this involves one business intentionally meddling with another business. If a designer lures a client away from another design firm, this tort has potentially occurred. Quite often this type of tort is also a violation of ethical conduct.

- *Assault* occurs when a person intentionally performs an act so that another person has a feeling of apprehension or fear of harm or physical injury. Actual contact or physical harm is not necessary for an assault to occur; causing another to be apprehensive is enough.

- *Battery* occurs when there is intentional touching or other physical contact by one person upon another without the contacted person's consent or without any justification.

Against Property

The three torts against property are conversion, trespass to land and personal property, and nuisance. Although each may be a problem to the interior designer, the torts of conversion and trespass to personal property are potentially the most damaging.

- *Conversion* occurs when someone takes the property of another. In criminal law, this is commonly called stealing or theft. Perhaps a client asks for a "loan" of a piece of furniture but does not pay for it. Until the client pays for the item, it rightfully belongs to the designer.

- *Trespass to land* occurs when a person enters onto or causes something to happen to land that does not belong to him or her. Care must be taken and permission granted by neighbors when remodeling work, for example, might damage a neighboring property.

- *Trespass to personal property* occurs when a person either injures the personal property of another or interferes with the owner's right to exclusive possession or use of the personal property. This can include the taking or misuse of personal information.
- *Nuisance.* "A nuisance is an improper activity that interferes with another's enjoyment or use of his or her property."[3] The designer and the client can be sued by a neighbor if the noise and dust from a remodeling project interfere with the neighbor's enjoyment of his or her home.

These brief descriptions are provided for the reader's basic understanding and are not to be construed as complete legal definitions. As with many things in the law, circumstances, facts, and interpretation by a judge and court affect the decision as to true legal wrongdoing.

INTELLECTUAL PROPERTY—COPYRIGHT

The client hires the interior designer to create a floor plan or perhaps a custom piece of furniture. The interior designer routinely conveys the ideas in his or her head into the "reality" of a drawing so that the floor plan or custom furniture item can be executed. Who owns that drawing: the interior designer or the client?

The interior designer hopes that these drawings of intangibles will become reality, that is, a completed interior or a product. There will be instances in which the designer will wish to legally protect these design ideas so that they cannot be duplicated or copied without permission and fair compensation. In some cases, the client may also desire that these designs not be duplicated.

The section of law that deals with the protection of these creative achievements is called *intellectual property law;* specifically, the protections are referred to as copyright, trademark, or patent. Primarily federal statutes govern intellectual property law. Creative work such as design drawings, fine art, CD-ROMs and DVDs, photography, furniture designs, and writings such as this textbook are examples of items that are considered *intellectual property* because they are essentially intangible.

- *Copyright* is the method by which written, artistic, and graphic forms of intellectual property (such as books and design drawings) are legally protected.
- A *trademark* protects words and/or symbols specific to a person or a business (such as a company logo) that are very creative and out of the ordinary.
- *Patent* law protects the original design of tangible objects such as a piece of furniture.

Because trademark protection focuses on symbols and designs that are seldom the responsibility of the interior designer, the process for obtaining trademark protection is not discussed in this section. The process of obtaining a patent is quite complex. Readers who may want information on this process or the process of protecting a trademark can obtain detailed information from the U.S. Patent and Trademark Office at www.uspto.gov.

Copyright Overview

The actual law that protects copyright at this time is the Federal Copyright Act of 1976. In fact, the U.S. Constitution, in Article 1, section 8, also addresses intellectual property law. The rights to a copyright last for a substantial period of time, but the length of that time can vary depending on whether the work has been published. Note that *publication* occurs when the creator somehow distributes the work to others for review without restriction of use by the creator.

Any written or graphic work that was created on or after January 1, 1978, is protected by copyright for the life of the author or designer, plus 70 years for an individual. If the work was created by an employee, the copyright, which belongs to the employer, lasts for 95 years from the date of publication or 120 years from the date of creation, whichever comes first. The difference between works created as an individual and as an employee is discussed later in this section.

The design idea itself cannot be copyrighted. It is the expression of the idea as a written, graphic, or artistic work that is protected. In other words, the idea must be put into a physical, tangible form (such as a floor plan, a sketch, or the written word) before it can be copyrighted. That expression must be in some way original as well, though it does not have to be unique.

The tangible medium need not be in final form for copyright protection to exist. Copyright protection extends to a designer's floor plan scribbled on a napkin when the designer and client met about the project. Thus, floor plans for a prototype fast-food restaurant would be copyrightable, but the *idea* for that restaurant would not be. The idea for a custom-made dining room table is not eligible for patent or copyright protection until the design of that table has been put down on paper.

The copyright begins at the moment at which the interior designer begins the act of completing the work. This means that the moment the interior designer begins drafting the working drawings, sketches, or specifications, the legal protection of the work begins. Thus, common law provides the creator of an artistic work with automatic protection—to a limited degree.

As mentioned earlier, the life of the copyright is affected by when the work was published. If the interior designer gives a sketch to a client before attaching a copyright notice or in some other way restricting the use (perhaps the designer says "for review only" on the drawing), then the work has been "published" and is considered to be in the public domain. The creator no longer owns the work and it can be used by anyone in any way without compensation to the creator.

To protect the designer's ideas, all plans and copies should include a copyright notice. The work must bear a copyright notification prior to its being "published" (distributed) and must be registered with the Copyright Office in order to receive full, legal statutory protection. Including at least the three following items provides a measure of protection, but not the right to sue for infringement. Placing these three elements on a drawing, sample board, or specification sheet does not fully protect the work, or initiate copyright protection, unless the work is registered with the U.S. Copyright Office. Notice serves to protect what the claimant publishes.

So what exactly are a copyright "notice" and "publication"? *Copyright notification* must contain the following elements:

1. The word *copyright*, or the abbreviation *copr*, or the copyright symbol (©)
2. The year of publication
3. The name of the copyright claimant

For example, on a set of drawings, the notice should look like this: "© by Tracy & Jones Interiors, 2010," or Copyright by Tracey & Jones Interiors, 2010." For a sole practitioner, it might read: "Copyright by Fraser McKain, 2012," or "© 2012 Fraser McKain."

The unauthorized use of copyrighted materials is called *infringement*. This can best be explained by an example. Michael Smith Interiors has prepared a set of working drawings for the interior of a prototype fast-food restaurant in a specific location. The drawings contain a copyright notice. If the owner of the fast-food restaurant later duplicates the restaurant in another location, using those plans without consent of and compensation to the design firm, the restaurant owner has infringed on the copyright.

On the other side of this issue, infringement also occurs if a designer uses a design created by someone else to create a "custom-made" piece of furniture. Even making very small changes, such as using a different finish, can be construed as infringement. Assuming that the original designer copyrighted or even obtained a patent on the design, the second interior designer has infringed on the original designer's copyright when he or she "knocks off" or imitates the original design. Of course, this is neither legal nor ethical. Numerous court cases have been heard about just such an issue.

The Foundation for Design Integrity (FDI) represents numerous manufacturers and designers and aids them in protection of their product designs and litigation for design infringement by other designers. However, these efforts are aimed primarily at patent infringement, not copyright or trademark infringement. For more information on FDI, you may wish to view its Web site: www.ffdi.org.

Placing a copyright notice on design documents is needed for legal protection. In addition, interior designers should include a clause in their design contracts concerning copyright and ownership of documents. Courts have upheld the contention that work commissioned by a client from a designer belongs to the designer or company, even if there are no clauses in the design contract giving ownership to the designer or company. Full statutory protection, however, is afforded only when the work contains the proper notification and meets registration and publication requirements.

Copyright Registration

To gain complete legal protection that allows the copyright holder to file a lawsuit against an infringer, the designs must be registered with the federal government through the U.S. Copyright Office. To register a copyrightable item, the creator must obtain the proper forms from the Copyright Office. The "VA" form is used for graphic or visual works, and the "TX" form is used for books, articles, and other general written works. Forms can be downloaded from the Internet at www.copyright.gov. A sample of the Form VA is included on the companion Web site as item 4-1.

An original form, not a photocopy of the form, must be accompanied by one copy of the work if the work is unpublished and by two copies of the work if it has already been published. Instructions on the Web site inform submitters how to do this. The copy of the work must be a "best-edition" copy. Because originals cannot be readily submitted, properly prepared photocopies, photographs of the work, or plots of floor plans may suffice. What constitutes a best-edition copy, however, is up to the Copyright Office. A fee is charged to process the copyright.

It is not necessary to send each project under a separate copyright form. A bulk of work, called a *collection*, may be submitted at one time. A collection can constitute any work that has been created within the same year, as long as all the work is of the same basic type and is submissible with the same form.

For full statutory and actual damages to be awarded, registration must exist either before the work is published or under specific circumstances thereafter. If the work is registered within three months of first publication, the copyright holder is still able to claim statutory and actual damages. If the work is registered up to five years after first publication, there is a presumption of a valid copyright. After five years, the claimant has to prove that he or she is the original author. In these instances, the copyright claimant may be awarded actual damages, but not statutory damages or attorney's fees and costs.

Statutory damages refer to amounts determined by the court for each infringement. *Actual damages* are damages that the copyright holder suffers as a result of the infringement. Actual damages may include payment of design fees, profits the designer may have lost, and profits the infringer may have made by the infringement.

Copyright and Employees

Copyright ownership is different for individuals who are employees. When a design work is created by an employee of a firm in the course of employment, the copyright belongs to the employer, not the employee, under the concept of work for hire and shop right. The concept of *work for hire* is that an employee who creates something within the scope of normal work responsibilities relinquishes copyright ownership of the design to the employer. *Shop right* means that the employer holds the exclusive rights to anything the employee produces as part of his or her normally expected work.

Any design that an employee creates as part of his or her normal responsibilities, and for clients of the employer, belongs to the employer, not the employee. Those drawings are also sometimes called *work product*, as the work is a product of the employer even though it is actually produced by an employee. Legally and ethically, the employee cannot take the project work he or she has done as an employee and show it as his or her own without also showing that the work was created while he or she was an employee. Taking work you have done as an employee and showing it as your own without permission of the employer is a legal and ethical breach.

What if the employee creates an item that can be patented? The shop-right doctrine applied to patents says that employers hold a nonexclusive free license to any creation or invention of tangible products an employee designs that result as a part of employment.[4] "The theory is that because such inventions are developed with the employer's funds or property, the employer should at least be able to use them."[5]

The employee is still the patent holder, however. An example is a situation in which an interior designer creates a computer program that provides a new way to handle the firm's data processing, and the program is (for whatever reason) sold to a local software company. If the program is created on company time, the employer has an interest that allows it to use the program without paying royalties to the employee.

This distinction is important because designers, being creative and thoughtful people, often dabble in works that stretch their job responsibilities in different ways. Generally, designs created on the employee's own time, using his or her own materials and facilities, belong to the employee, unless there is a statement to the contrary in an employment agreement.

Sometimes a small firm may hire an independent contractor—a nonemployee—to prepare drawings for a project. In such a case the hiring firm would own the work only if the independent contractor signed an agreement that the drawings are "works for hire." Otherwise, the independent contractor—the creator of the finished drawings—retains ownership. Chapter 27 fully discusses the distinctions between an employee and an independent contractor.

Interior designers frequently hire photographers—who are independent contractors—to shoot photos of completed projects. The interior designer usually wishes to use those photos in some sort of marketing effort. Of course, the interior designer has paid the photographer to take the pictures, but who owns the rights to use the photos? The answer to this question depends on the contract between the designer and the photographer.

The photographer owns the copyright to the images taken for the designer unless the photographer's contract specifically states that he or she has given up those rights. If the photographer has not given up rights in whole or part, the interior designer must obtain permission (and may have to pay a fee) for each use of any of those photos. The photographer's contract can assign certain rights of use to the interior designer as part of the fee, but this generally does not include ownership. Interior designers need to negotiate the use and rights to photos taken of their projects so that they are legally using images taken by someone else.

An interior designer or firm may not always be concerned about copyrighting all the design documents that leave the office. Depending on the practice and projects, however, there may be instances in which certain projects or parts of projects would require this protection. Knowing how to prepare documents for legal protection is very important. Including a clause in the design contract related to "design ownership" or "copyright permission" will also aid in legally protecting the designer.

CODE COMPLIANCE

It does not matter what type of design specialty a practitioner focuses on; compliance with codes is an important professional responsibility of all interior designers. Code compliance is not only a design responsibility, but also a legal responsibility, and thus merits this brief discussion in this chapter.

Codes affect many aspects of the commercial designer's work. However, residential designers hired to design spaces in high-rise buildings and high-rise condominiums must also meet many of the same codes as interior designers in commercial specializations. Of course, other building code requirements must be met by the residential designer for any type of residential property.

This section only highlights key code concepts. Studio and codes classes added to the curriculum of interior design programs over the years have influenced the reduction of this section. However, no interior designer today can ignore code compliance. An excellent reference for the interior designer who has not had a recent codes class is *The Code Guidebook for Interiors* by Sharon Koomen Harmon and Katherine E. Kennon.[6]

Codes are systematic bodies of law created by federal, state, and local jurisdictions to ensure safety. For the most part, codes originate from independent agencies and are adopted and modified by federal, state, and local jurisdictions.

Building codes primarily regulate structural and mechanical features of buildings. They define minimum standards for the design, construction, and quality of materials, based on the use, type, and occupancy of the building. Public safety is a key purpose of building code requirements. Issues of egress, accessibility, and some architectural finishes are also included. The International Building Codes (IBC) is a set of model building codes first approved in

2000 by a joint commission and adopted by most jurisdictions. Readers should check to determine which building codes have been adopted in their area.

Fire safety codes and regulations exist to provide a reasonable measure of safety in a building from fire, explosions, and other comparable emergencies. A fire safety code is used along with a building code in most jurisdictions. The intent of these codes is to prevent a fire whenever possible or control a fire should one start. Fire prevention is facilitated by the regulation of hazards and the kinds of materials—both construction and furnishings—that can be used in buildings. Fire safety control is further facilitated by the requirement of sprinklers, fire doors, and the like. The International Fire Code (IFC) from the International Code Council (ICC) and the Uniform Fire Code (UFC) from the National Fire Protection Association (NFPA) are standards that may be adopted in any jurisdiction.

The *Life Safety Code*—also called *NFPA 101*—concentrates on fire safety and evacuation issues in an attempt to lessen the danger to life from fire, smoke, and hazardous fumes and gases.

Several codes, first adopted in specific areas of the country and later adopted by other jurisdictions, deal with architectural finishes and furniture items. Not all of these codes are applicable in all areas, so the designer must understand which codes are valid for the project area under design. Remember that the code applies to the project site, not the interior designer's office location.

Barrier-free codes relate to making all buildings—public and private—accessible to those who are handicapped or have disabilities. These requirements were established by the U.S. federal government in the Americans with Disabilities Act (ADA), first enacted in January 1992. Barrier-free codes have a limited, if any, application to most private residences. The ADA is actually civil rights legislation, not a building code. Until a state or a local jurisdiction creates enforcement statutes or incorporates the ADA regulations into its building code, a complainant must file a civil rights action in federal court.

ADA regulations do not apply in the Canadian provinces or other nations, of course. However, the international community has adopted many types of accessibility standards to meet the needs of various populations.

WEB SITES RELEVANT TO THIS CHAPTER

www.ffdi.org Foundation for Design Integrity

www.loc.gov Library of Congress

www.nolo.com Publisher of numerous legal references

www.copyright.gov U.S. Copyright Office

www.doj.gov U.S. Department of Justice

www.uspto.gov U.S. Patent and Trademark Office

KEY TERMS

Administrative law	Constitutional law
Assumption of risk	Contributory negligence
Barrier-free regulations	Conversion
Breach of contract	Copyright notice
Building codes	Copyright notification
Case law/common law	Crime
Codes	Cyber law

Defamation	Professional negligence
Duty of reasonable care	Proximate cause
False imprisonment	Publication
Fire safety codes	Puffing
Fraud	Shop right
Infringement	Slander
Intellectual property	Spam
Intentional torts	Statutes
Invasion of privacy	Statutory law
Legal injury or harm	Strict liability
Libel	Tort
Misrepresentation	Trademark
Negligence	Uniform laws
Ordinances	Work for hire
Patent	Work product
Plaintiff	

WHAT WOULD YOU DO?

1. Alice was the project interior designer for an assisted-living facility. The project involved specification of all the architectural finishes for common and public areas, using as many sustainable products as the budget would allow. The project also included setting up a program of finishes that the residents could choose for their apartments. The owner wanted to use low-VOC flooring materials in the apartments.

   Alice marketed herself as an experienced residential designer and talked about some of the homes and apartments she had done for seniors. About six months after the installation was completed, the staff noticed an increase in the number of residents who were stumbling—and some falling—while walking down the corridors and in the dining room. A doctor thought it was due to the pattern and style of the carpeting. It was a medium-sized pattern that was slightly sculpted. Could Alice and her design firm be liable in any way for this sudden increase in the number of falls?

2. David and Monica have finally made some inroads with a client who is opening a series of small retail stores in two European countries. The client is comfortable with the design firm, but David and Monica have had problems getting approvals on drawings from the foreign building officials. Exasperated, David implies that he will provide furniture for the home of one of the officials after the approvals are finalized.

3. Your firm prepared design drawings to explain to a client what an outdoor gazebo at a restaurant would look like. There were no notations on the drawings that they were for design only and not for construction. The client gave those drawings to a carpenter who was doing work on the interior of this new restaurant. The carpenter constructed the gazebo using only the design drawings. At an opening-night party, a large number of people gathered within the gazebo, and someone was injured when one of the railings gave way. The injured

person and the client named you in a lawsuit because you designed the gazebo.

4. George prepares drawings for a custom table for a client and hires a cabinetmaker to build the table. The drawings provided to the cabinetmaker had the proper notices concerning copyright. The cabinetmaker not only produces the table for George, but also begins to produce the same design for other interior designers.

George learns through a colleague that his table is being marketed and that, in fact, the colleague had specified and sold four of the tables to the colleague's client.

REFERENCES

1. Miller and Jentz, 2006, p. 123.
2. Miller and Jentz, 2006, p. 127
3. Jentz et al., 1987, p. 55.
4. Garner, 1999, p. 1384.
5. Elias, 1999, p. 288.
6. Harmon and Kennon, 2011.

CHAPTER 5

Where Do Designers Work?

Spend 2-4 minutes here

Do you know what type of interior design work you plan to do when you graduate? Do you have your heart set on designing mansions in Beverly Hills, or perhaps penthouses in Manhattan? Perhaps you already know you want to design in health care, or hospitality. Do you see yourself in a neighborhood design studio, or working for one of the interior design "giants" in a major metropolitan city?

One of the fascinating aspects of the interior design profession is the variety of ways in which an individual can work in the field. Although many designers engage in residential design, working in a commercial specialty is attractive for many others. It is also fairly common for some designers to occasionally be "switch hitters," designing both residences and commercial spaces.

Interior designers also work in different ways. That is, some are fully involved with clients and a project from programming through contract documents. Some prefer the technical side of design rather than working directly with clients. And there are those who enjoy client interaction so much that they move from performing space-planning tasks to selling and representation positions with stores or even manufacturers.

This edition has been modified to bring the discussions of where and how designers work to the beginning of the book. This was suggested by educators who feel that students need to understand the different ways an interior designer works, as well as the multitude of possible career specialties. The chapter discussing career options has been relocated to the end of the book and now accompanies the chapters on resumés and interviews. The chapter on personal goal setting has also been moved toward the end, thereby consolidating the material on job search in one location.

HOW DO DESIGNERS WORK?

There are many different ways to work in the interior design field. Some of these will appeal to your creative side and some to technical prowess. These descriptions begin our clarification of the wide variety of career opportunities in the interior design profession. The following is a basic description of the ways designers work.

"On-the-Boards" Responsibility

The term *on the boards* is an old one used by many interior designers to refer to the traditional tasks of doing a project. Being on the boards means that the designer spends a significant amount of time preparing space plans, construction drawings, and other design documents utilizing a drafting board. Of course, today the on-the-boards designer is working with a computer rather than paper-and-pencil drawing and drafting.

On-the-boards designers are involved in all phases of a design project and are responsible for preparing the plans, specifications, and all the other documents needed to design a project. This designer can be involved in any of the specialty areas of design. Another term for this type of specialty is *designer/specifier*, a term that also refers to interior designers who prepare all the design elements of a project and specify the needed products, but rarely sell merchandise.

An interior designer in this situation could be working in an independent design firm, an architectural office, or several other environments not focused on selling products. That being said, many designers who sell products may also be on the boards, as they must prepare plans and other documents in order to sell merchandise. These designers are paid a salary.

Selling Responsibility

Many positions in interior design require a certain amount of selling responsibility. In fact, it might be argued that *all* positions require the ability to sell. Selling responsibility starts with the job interview with an employer. Designers must then "sell" themselves to prospective clients as they attempt to be hired by the client. Selling also occurs as designers sell their design ideas to the client as the project progresses.

For some, selling becomes the major responsibility, overshadowing planning and design tasks. Many designers who work in retail specialty stores (such as lighting fixture stores, department stores, and office furnishings dealerships) find that the ability to sell is primary to preparing plans and specifications. Depending on the role one is hired for, this may also be true for an employee of a residential furniture store. In many cases, designers working in a store environment may be limited as to what they may sell to the client based on the products carried or featured by that store.

Selling responsibility positions are usually compensated by a commission on each sale rather than a salary. A *salary* is a fixed payment per hour, week, or month, whereas a commission is a flexible amount based in some way on the amount and dollar value of products sold. You will read more about these compensation terms in Chapter 27.

Freelance Consulting

Designers who have gained experience in interior design may decide to become freelance designers/consultants. It could be argued that a sole practitioner designer is a freelance designer. For our purposes, however, this discussion refers to designers who work irregular hours, not necessarily full time, and not directly for end-user clients such as a home owner or commercial space owner.

A freelancer might work in one or more specialty areas of interior design. He or she might provide CAD services to designers who do not do their own computer drafting. He or she might provide consulting to designers concerning lighting design, or commercial kitchen design, or other highly technical design areas.

Freelancers contract with the designer/client for whom they will do work and are not considered employees of the design firm. Their compensation could be an hourly, daily, or per-job fee. Depending on experience, such a designer might work for more than one client at the same time and even do more than one kind of project at a time. For example, a CAD consultant might be doing plans for more than one interior designer, and the projects involved might be a mix of residential and commercial projects.

This type of freelance consultant enjoys variety and does not want to work full time. The Internet allows freelancers to work on a global basis if they so choose. It is unusual for the freelance consultant to have employees. Drawbacks include an irregular income, as work comes at an unsteady pace. These individuals must also pay their own working benefits, taxes on income, and have the self-discipline to work to the extent required for each consulting job.

Management

Interior designers also work as managers in design industry businesses. An individual might be the design director with an interior design or architectural office, supervising a design staff. She might be the manager of the design staff in a furniture store, or the manager of a specialty store. She might have a management position as a project manager for a construction company or development company. These are only a few examples of management positions.

The person who is considering management positions in interior design will be required to have extensive experience in one or more specialty areas of interior design. A business background based on experience in the profession, along with educational background in management, is also helpful—if not required—for these positions.

Managers supervise the design staff, assign the work in the office, prepare reports to ownership, and meet with clients. Design office managers are often involved in marketing to obtain new clients. Depending on the size of the firm and design staff, the manager may find it necessary to limit his or her personal design involvement in projects. The larger the firm is, the more the manager will need to attend to various administrative activities rather than being involved in creative work.

These brief descriptions paint a broad-stroke picture of how interior designers may work. The next section on work environments is an overview of where interior designers work. Numerous types of career options are discussed in detail in Chapter 28.

GLOBAL DESIGN WORK

Interior design is certainly a global profession. Computers and the Internet have expanded the reach of designers throughout the world. Virtual communications make it easy to hold meetings, transmit drawings and other documents, and manage projects on a global market net. In some cases, firms enter into joint ventures to design international projects. Larger firms and existing international firms continue to obtain international projects. Of course, international firms may also form joint ventures with U.S. firms here in the United States.

Certainly, the downturn in the U.S. economy has enticed interior design firms to seek out global design work. However, West Coast design firms have, for many years, responded to project possibilities in the Pacific Rim countries; many large, multidisciplinary firms have actively obtained international design work for many years. The small interior design firm that has visions of international work must enter this arena with caution and care.

Working globally is not for everyone anchored in the United States. It can be expensive and financially risky. Here are some of the issues to be considered:

- *Travel*. Travel expenses must be absorbed when marketing to foreign clients. Travel time—a major component of global design—cannot be charged at the same rate as design time.

- *Staff.* When U.S. staff work on an international project, staff must be taught protocol, language, and etiquette. Staffing an office in another country also adds financial costs and risks for a firm.
- *Fees.* Fees might not be as generous as they first seem when all the expenses of working on an overseas project are totaled up.
- *Collaboration on site.* Collaboration with a local foreign design firm—though it offers many advantages—is another project expense that can lower the profitability of doing an international project.
- *Regulations differences.* Codes and regulations can be different from U.S. codes. Projects must be designed in accordance with those international codes, whether national or local or both. Each country will have different regulations that have an impact on many aspects of an interiors project.

Ease of communication based on language skills is a paramount issue. International design work requires staff members to have (or quickly acquire) applicable language skills. Being able to communicate in one or more languages gives a firm engaging in global design a definite advantage. However, language skills are only part of the challenge; an understanding of cultural differences and customs is also critical. International work thus requires the firm to build relationships and embrace those international differences. Table 5-1 lists some key international etiquette points.

If you are an interior designer looking for a position with a design firm that does international work, you must prepare yourself for that experience. Learn at least one non-English language fluently; two is even better. Naturally, target those language skills to the area of the globe you feel you would most like to work. Learn about customs, religious practices, and politics of other countries. In some cases, you might be able to learn about these issues from a

---

TABLE 5-1.

International etiquette

If you wish to conduct business outside North America, it is critical to be sensitive to cultural differences and etiquette issues in the countries to which you may travel. Working internationally will require that you make it a point to read up on the country's differences in etiquette and cultural differences that will affect business dealings and design decisions.
A smile is universal.
A gesture of greeting might be a slight bow, a hug, the shaking of hands and a bow, or some other manner of greeting. Whether you shake hands or bow can literally mean the difference between having a positive encounter or causing an international incident.
Though clients may speak English, they may choose at some point to conduct business in their own language.
Treat business cards from others with respect; don't write on them, for example, as this can be perceived as an insult.
Punctuality is generally appreciated, but not necessarily the norm in all countries. Make sure you understand this issue if you are working with international clients.
Respect the cultural differences of the country in which you are traveling. Do not expect the client to conduct himself or herself as a North American client would.
Before traveling to a foreign country, investigate how you will be expected to dress and what types of apparel are appropriate. This is particularly an issue for women traveling to many countries.
Respect their culture and customs, and they will respect you.
A few books specifically on international etiquette are included in the references.

faculty member at a community college or university. You might also find a "mentor" of sorts affiliated with a local cultural group, such as an Italian-American club. And, of course, focus on doing your assigned design work with the utmost care and concern.

For the design firm, building a reputation at home for best practices and excellent design work is critical to being considered for foreign work. U.S. design firms often obtain international projects when a project done in the United States belongs to clients who have an international presence. Excellent design work for this type of client is a great way to open the door for international projects. "Maintaining a solid reputation and level of trust with established clients who are expanding into foreign markets can bring global opportunities."[1]

As with deciding to enter any new market or specialty, it is vital for the firm to carefully consider why it wants to pursue an international clientele or a specific project overseas. Research must be performed on issues such as those mentioned earlier, and possible quite a few others. International work also requires collaboration on a high level. For interior designers, that collaboration starts with the architectural firms that are likely to hold the prime contract. Collaboration will also include working with local sources and resources on the site. If your firm is not part of a strong team whose members cooperate with each other, then international work may not be for you.

TYPES OF WORK ENVIRONMENTS

I have always been fascinated by the realization that interior designers can work in so many settings and do so many different kinds of jobs. Students need to recognize the opportunities that exist beyond the stereotypical work in "a residential store" or a "commercial design office." This section begins with the most typical starting locations for entry-level interior designers. Positions that require experience or perhaps additional education are discussed at the end.

These descriptions are very general and actual experiences and settings will vary. Size of the firm, geographic location, design specialty, and business philosophy of ownership all affect the work environment and experience.

Independent Design Firm

An *independent* design firm is one that has no affiliation with a particular product and may not have any products displayed for sale in its office or studio. It is very common for interior designers to start their businesses working alone with no full-time employees; these would be considered independent interior design firms.

Some, however, have a limited amount of showroom space. It is common for many independent design firms to sell merchandise to supplement revenue, in addition to providing design services. Because such a firm is independent, it may specify any products that are available in the marketplace.

An independent design firm may be a one-person design studio or a large firm that has dozens of employees. In a small firm, the owner always takes the lead in developing relationships with clients and marketing in general. Yet it is also common for designers in some small firms to be expected to obtain new clients, and manage projects with minimum assistance from the owner. The owner of the smaller firm also does a lot of project work in addition to managing the firm.

The larger firms will have various management and staff levels. Client contact is usually the responsibility of the owner, the senior designers, or possibly a marketing manager. Senior designers are primarily responsible for managing projects, and they often supervise a team of designers and support personnel during the course of the project. In some firms, there are also individuals who have many specialized job functions, such as specification writers and renderers, who can free the project designers from such activities.

The firm may specialize in some type of interior or design a combination of types of spaces. The projects obtained by independent design firms frequently require that the designer travel extensively, as the firm's work comes from all over the country, if not the world. This is especially true for the very specialized firm. Design employees are paid a salary and possibly a commission or bonus for product sales.

Residential Furniture Stores

Entry-level designers who begin their careers in a residential retail furniture store generally do so as an assistant to one of the senior designers. Assistants learn the business and gain experience with clients as they help senior designers with product specifications, drafting, sample boards, and specifications, along with many other activities. Direct client interaction occurs as the assistant gains experience and confidence.

The experienced designer works with the client in either the store or the client's home. Projects might involve designing a single space or designing and specifying items for an entire home. The designer is encouraged to sell what the store carries in inventory, but may be allowed to sell other items as well. Most often, the design service is free or offered at nominal cost, because the expense of the designer's service is covered through the sale of goods at retail.

Designers are often required to meet sales quotas and most often are paid on a commission basis rather than a salary. Entry-level individuals are more often paid a salary, though they might receive a small commission. Depending on the store's management philosophy, it might take an entry-level person from two to four years to be promoted out of the assistant's position.

Office Furnishings Dealer

An office furnishings *dealer* is, in a sense, a retail showroom for commercial furniture products. Office furnishings dealers primarily design office complexes, though some also design other kinds of commercial interiors. They will have showroom displays and an inventory to back up what is displayed. Many office furnishings dealers have certain exclusive products that they expect designers to specify most often.

An office furnishings dealer rarely sells products at suggested retail. More often, products are sold at a discount from suggested retail or at a markup on cost. Outside salespeople are largely responsible for selling furniture products, while the design staff provides planning services. Design services are billed to clients as would many other types of design studios.

Office furnishings dealerships can provide excellent entry-level opportunities for those interested in commercial interior design. It often takes at least two years to advance to a position of project responsibility. The pay is usually a salary for the designers, who might also be eligible for commission on certain items.

Becoming a member of the sales staff at an office furnishings dealership is another option for interior designers. Salespeople's primary responsibility is to sell furniture and other products. They are usually not required to be designers, although many were at one time, and are generally not required to do any interior design planning. Sales staff must generate new business and are paid a commission on the furniture products they sell.

Retail Specialty Store

A specialty store is a retail store selling a particular type of product other than furniture to the end user. Design services, if offered, are complimentary. Specialty stores are excellent opportunities for the entry-level designer to gain sales experience and product knowledge. Depending on the product, the staff will receive training related to the products. However, some specialty stores, such as art galleries or antique stores, may require staff to have specialized knowledge prior to hiring. Designers are commonly paid a small salary plus a commission.

Architectural Office

Many architectural offices have interior design divisions, providing yet another setting for the interior designer. These designers work primarily on projects in partnership with the architects as part of a design team. The work might involve residential or commercial projects, or both, depending on the nature of the architectural practice.

Interior design employees in this setting will be required to have very good space-planning and technical skills, design creativity, and skill with the production of construction drawings and documents; the use of CAD is critical in this practice setting. Compensation is salary based.

Department Store

Department stores often have interior design staff. The size and complexity of the design studio will depend on the size of the store. Working for a department store is very similar to working for a retail furniture store. A designer might sell one item or a range of products. Often, however, the designer is limited to selling what the department store carries. Department stores may also have a studio that focuses on commercial projects, in addition to residential. Some department stores offer a limited range of design services through the drapery or floorings departments. There may also be an opportunity to become a furniture sales associate whose primary responsibility is selling rather than design. Generally, design services are offered free to the client. The designer is generally paid only a commission on sales.

Developers

Interesting positions are available with real estate developers and construction companies. One of the most common is a designer working for a residential homebuilder. The designer assists new buyers with finish selections. The common job title for this position is *colorizer*. Although each homebuilder has a group of standard materials that are calculated into the purchase price, the buyer may upgrade to more expensive materials. These designers earn a commission when the buyer upgrades any of the materials.

Developers or construction companies might hire designers as project managers or as marketing specialists. Positions are also available for designers who help create the basic floor plans of a new development, prepare renderings of the various models, and perhaps design the model homes.

Manufacturer

Companies that manufacture furniture, furnishings, and equipment (FF&E) products use interior designers in many ways. A designer might work in a manufacturer's showrooms, assisting the interior designers and other allied professionals who come to the showroom. A few manufacturers have staff designers at a factory location to aid other designers and architects in planning and specifying the company's products.

An interior designer with a minimum of three years' experience in the business might be hired as part of the sales representative group. Sales representatives (also called *reps*) are almost always paid a commission rather than a salary. These individuals call on design firms and large clients that are considering use of the company's products. Becoming part of the product design staff is a less frequent but still possible option. Depending on the product, the company may require that the designer have an industrial design background rather than an interior design background.

A designer who works for a manufacturer often has the opportunity to travel throughout the United States, and possibly to work outside the country. Many of the major manufacturers have showrooms in foreign countries. Designers who do design layout work as employees of a manufacturer also have an opportunity to travel within the United States. Compensation depends on the actual job. Showroom sales positions and sales reps are commission based; designers are paid a salary.

Corporations

Many large corporations have in-house interior designers or facility planners. Corporate designers might be in charge of the complete design process for departments and facilities, or might work with outside designers in the design of corporate facilities. Responsibility might involve designing the chief executive officer's office as well as any group of offices or spaces within the facility.

Hotel chains, for example, have in-house designers who work with architects and franchise owners in the design or remodeling of their facilities. Interior designers can also become employees of many other kinds of commercial businesses, such as hospitals, restaurants, and retail stores. In some situations, the designers might travel to various company locations. Designers who work in a corporate environment are paid a salary or possibly an hourly wage.

Government

The federal government's General Services Administration (GSA) is responsible for employing interior designers to perform design work for government agencies. The designer is commonly limited to designing with the products currently on the GSA purchasing schedule, although some projects allow additional flexibility in product specification. Willingness to travel is necessary, as the GSA designer designs facilities potentially anywhere in the country. The salary, which is based on the individual's "GS" rating, is sometimes a bit higher than an entry-level salary in the private sector, and the government, of course, offers excellent benefits.

Some state and city government agencies have salaried interior designers and architects. These professionals function in much the same way as designers who work for the federal government. Not all state governments have design employees, though, because many states have laws forbidding state agencies from performing work that competes with private-sector companies and workers. Compensation is salary based. States and cities also tend to have very good benefits packages.

Universities and Colleges

Most universities, colleges, and community colleges have a facilities planning office. This office works with outside architects, interior designers, and the school staff to develop new building designs and remodel existing structures. A few of the largest universities retain design staff as employees. Educational design work is challenging, because most projects must be designed as economically as possible while still providing interesting and functional environments. Compensation is by salary and the employee benefits are also very good.

Independent Organizations

Numerous independent organizations employ individuals as interior designers or utilize the employee's skills acquired in an interior design career for other management or administrative work in the agency. A very few examples include the U.S. Green Building Council (USGBC), Construction Specifications Institute (CSI), National Association of Home Builders (NAHB), and professional associations such as ASID, IIDA, IFMA, and NCIDQ.

EXPECTATIONS

As an employee, you are no doubt looking for opportunities that will challenge you to use the design education you have recently completed. Truthfully, your new bosses probably want to challenge you—and get the best possible work out of their new employee investment—but they will not quite be ready to give you the "keys to the Mercedes." That simply means although you showed them enough skills, knowledge, and enthusiasm to be hired to work at ABC Design Studio, they are not ready to let you loose on clients or major projects. You have to pay your dues, and I don't mean to a professional association.

Your boss will be assigning you work responsibilities that might even seem beneath your skill level. Just about everybody who has graduated from an intense interior design program has thought to themselves in those first weeks, "I didn't go to school to file price lists and brochures or clean up sample books!" There is actually method to this task: it is an excellent way for the novice to learn sources . . . and filing these things keeps the studio looking organized.

While projects are being processed, interior design work in most studios and offices is intensely busy. The owner and senior designers are pushing to prepare whatever design documents are needed for the projects on the schedule board. Often decisions on specifications for the wide range of products used in a residential or commercial project have to be made quickly.

The time to gradually chill out while plans are sketched, finalized, and specifications selected, as you may have experienced in school, just doesn't exist in the real world. The time to agonize over the floor plan, or color scheme, or selections is speeded up sometimes exponentially from the academic environment.

A firm owner told me a story about a very talented recent graduate. This relatively new employee came up to one of the senior designers and said, "How about this carpet for Mr. Brown's house?" The senior designer looked at the novice blankly and said, "That project was presented two weeks ago." After a discussion with the employee, the owner decided to let that person go. The office is not going to slow down to your pace. You are going to have to learn to work at the office's pace. That includes being very conscious of time management.

It is perfectly reasonable for you to expect that the boss or senior designers will spend time training you in the way the office does projects. However, because of the speed at which design work must be done, sometimes those experienced individuals don't give much thought to their training responsibilities. You need to ask questions, ask to be involved, ask how you can help. When you are new, asking questions is not going to be considered a bad thing. Sitting around reading trade magazines waiting for someone to involve you only makes you look like you are not interested in working.

Each office has its own particular way of doing things. Many novice designers have found out that those ways are different from how they were taught. It's not that you were taught the wrong information or wrong skills. It's just that practicing designers learn shortcuts or techniques that are difficult to incorporate into an educational program.

As an entry-level interior designer, it is important to understand that job opportunities will not be available to you unless you have the skills and knowledge gained in an academic program. Nevertheless, you still have a lot to learn about doing projects, professionalism, and meeting responsibilities related to working directly with clients. Although you may be impatient to be given responsibility for designing a project, it is important for you to understand that the time spent in learning on the job is necessary to help prevent you from making mistakes that can hurt both your short-term and your long-term career.

WEB SITES RELEVANT TO THIS CHAPTER

www.asid.org/education American Society of Interior Designers

www.careeronestop.org Careeronestop—U.S. Department of Labor

www.interiordesigncanada.org Interior Designers of Canada

www.iida.org International Interior Design Association

KEY TERMS

Commercial interior design

Contract interior design

Independent design firm

On the boards

Residential interior design

WHAT WOULD YOU DO?

1. Marilyn had been working very hard for the past nine weeks with a very difficult client, Mr. Norton, owner and developer of a facility for Alzheimer patients. He constantly challenges her suggestions. These client challenges have already caused four major changes in the specifications of products and three changes in the equipment plans for the common areas of the facility. His primary argument is that Marilyn is overspecifying materials, using "expensive" products when cheaper ones would do—at least as far as he is concerned.

   "You have not even come close to staying within the budget we discussed at the beginning of this project. I insist that you find something besides that expensive cubicle curtain and drapery fabric and find me a cheaper chair for the dining room," complains Mr. Norton. "It's not that the cubicle curtain and drapery fabric is expensive, but it must meet a certain level of code compliance, which this one does. Less expensive chairs will not hold up to the special needs of the residents who need an armchair," responds Marilyn. "I don't care about that!" Mr. Norton explodes.

2. Judy's uncle mentioned to a friend of his that Judy had recently started work at a residential interior design studio only a month after

graduation. This friend thought that hiring Judy would be a great way to get some design ideas "on the cheap." The friend's project involved the remodeling of his kitchen and family room. Judy was excited about doing a project like this and jumped at the opportunity. She did not mention the project to her boss, as she felt that it did not need to involve the employer. Judy plans to do the project in her spare time and charge the client an hourly fee paid directly to Judy.

3. Mary is inspecting a job site designed by her firm. She notices that the wallpaper installer is using the wrong wall covering in the family room. She calls her boss about the mistake, but is interrupted by the client, who has questions about other areas of the project. A few days later, Mary finds that the wrong paper was installed in the family room.

4. Cassidy works for a small interior design firm that specializes in public facilities such as courts and city halls. She and other members of the design firm were involved in the design of a series of courtrooms for a county courthouse in another state. The purchasing agent for the county directed Cassidy and her team to design the courtrooms using a specific type of seating that the chief judge preferred. The project was large enough that the furniture items had to be presented as a competitive bid rather than a direct purchase.

   Knowing that the chief judge and purchasing agent wanted a specific seating unit for the jury boxes and other nonbench seating, Cassidy contacts the rep from the chair company and asks him to help her write up the bid specifications so that the only chair that can be bid is the one desired by the chief judge. When the bids are released to vendors, two firms challenge the bid documents as unfair.

REFERENCE

1. Schrank, Fall 2012, p. 25.

Project Compensation and Design Fees

After completing this chapter you should be able to:

- Calculate a billing rate based on the DPE.
- Discuss several factors that affect which fee method is used for a particular project.
- Compare the pros and cons of the hourly fee method to the cost plus percentage markup method.
- Calculate the billing rate based on a designer's salary rate.
- List and compare other fee methods discussed in this chapter.
- Prepare an estimate of fees based on information provided.
- Determine which fee method to utilize based on a specific project description.
- Discuss how to use the value-oriented fee method.
- Compare and contrast the hourly rate method with the fixed-fee method of compensation for a small residential project.
- Compare and contrast the fixed-fee method of compensation with a markup percentage from cost.
- Explain how to control indirect job costs and keep them from negatively affecting overall fee profitability.

NCIDQ COMPONENT

Based on best information available, some material in this chapter might appear as part of the NCIDQ examination. The reader should not depend solely on this text for study material. See the sections on calculating/estimating fees; possibly fee methods.

Income for a design firm comes from the fees the designer charges for services. Some firms also sell merchandise, and income from merchandise sales also results in income for the firm. Design services fees—the focus of this chapter—when not combined with merchandise sales, must cover the cost of the designer's time or salary expense and overhead expenses, such as electricity, cost of drafting paper, and telephone calls. Those fees must also provide a margin of profit.

It can be argued that charging a professional fee (rather than selling merchandise) is one additional factor in "professionalizing" the profession. Some might argue that it does not take an educated, certified, licensed individual to sell desks or sofas. The changing opportunities for clients to purchase goods from sources other than an interior designer have meant that the designer must be sure his or her time spent on design concepts is compensated.

There is no one way to charge for services that will satisfy all situations and all types of interior design practice. Each firm must decide which fee method is appropriate for its purposes. Many factors will affect this decision. The methods used by local competition may force the design firm into using certain fee methods, if clients have become used to specific practices. The type of design in which the designer chooses to specialize may dictate that the firm must use one fee method rather than others. The designer's own experience and knowledge may direct the designer to use a particular fee method.

The variety of fee methods available allows the professional to choose a method with which he or she is comfortable and appropriate for the job. A professional can customize how he or she charges clients to suit the client's needs and the specific project. However, the different fee methods can create confusion. Inconsistency can be a problem if the designer is working with clients who talk to each other a lot, as is often the case in residential interior design practice.

This chapter emphasizes fee methods related to compensation for interior design service as might be used by a designer or a firm. However, fee methods used alone or in combination with service fees are also discussed. Pricing methods for the sale of goods are discussed in Chapter 8.

CALCULATING THE BILLING RATE

John charges $125 per hour regardless of who in his firm works on the project. At her firm, Susan determines a fixed fee that she relates to the salary of each employee team member on the project. At his company, Otto insists on a flat consultation fee of $750 for a two-hour meeting. Each of these examples—which are all fictitious—shows that designers charge in many different ways. And each is in some way determined by the billing rate of each design staff member.

The *billing rate* is a dollar amount charged for each design professional, staff member, or (in some cases) the type of service provided. Most typically, the billing rate is expressed as an hourly rate. Some situations might call for a day rate, in which case the billing rate is for a full day's work rather than per hour. A billing rate is used to calculate fixed fees and in most other types of fee methods as well.

The billing rate begins with the salary rate of the employee. However, the salary rate alone does not cover all the overhead expenses and profit that must be considered in determining a billing rate. Thus, the billing rate is actually calculated based on the firm's *multiple* (also called a *multiplier*).

A multiple is calculated to include overhead and profit. For some fee methods, especially the fixed-fee and square-footage methods, the billing rate is primary to the determination of the total fee. In other methods, such as cost plus or percentage off retail, it has an indirect bearing on the fee itself. The salary rate is multiplied by the multiple to establish the individual's billing rate.

Traditionally, the most commonly used multiple is 3.0. No one seems to know where this factor came from. It might be interpreted as meaning that one part is equal to the salary rate, one part covers overhead burden, and one part allows for profit. This is not necessarily accurate, as overhead can be greater or less than that "one part." Rarely does a firm make a profit of one third or roughly 30 percent.

A method commonly used in interior design and architectural offices is to determine the multiple of direct personnel expense. The *direct personnel expense* (*DPE*) is a number that includes the employee's salary and costs of employee benefits such as unemployment taxes, medical insurance, and paid holidays. Calculation of the DPE is the most accurate way to determine a firm's multiple.

It is not simply a combination of the salary and benefits. The DPE, to be accurate, must include direct and overhead expenses as well as profit; otherwise, the fee multiple will not be adequate to result in profitability. Direct expenses, by the way, are those that are directly related to a specific project. Overhead expenses are those that relate to the general operations of the business. See Chapter 21 for more information on these and other accounting terms. For example, on average, the cost of employee fringe benefits can add 25 to 60 percent to the cost of the employee. Sixty percent is quite high and is probably reached only in the largest multidisciplinary firms. Even a 25 percent factor for a small firm can make a serious dent in a firm's profitability if not factored into the fee.

Too often, the small firm owner or sole practitioner forgets that any benefits provided to employees—even themselves—add expenses that reduce profits. Many new owners of an interior design firm are very surprised to find that they made a net profit of only 2 to 4 percent—if they see any net profit at all—because they have not carefully considered their expenses of operating the firm when determining their compensation. Net profit rates of around 10 to 15 percent are more common, especially in firms that carefully control costs and accurately translate profit plans into billing rates.

A multiplier based on the DPE is a factor that is based on the direct labor expense plus the cost of employee benefits. This discussion follows the numbers shown in Table 6-1.

All of this information can be obtained easily from the financial records of the design firm. First, the total annual salary of all employees is determined. Then, the total of employee fringe benefits expenses are found, such as for unemployment taxes, workers' compensation, medical and/or life insurance, FICA, sick leave, pension plans, and paid holidays. Table 27-3 in Chapter 27 provides examples of common employee benefits. Next, the owner must determine the total of overhead expenses for the year. Adding these three items together gives the total annual expenses for the firm. At this point, the owner should include a factor for a profit goal. In Table 6-1, we have added a percentage that would give a reasonable profit goal of 20 percent.

The total net revenue shown in the example is revenue that does not include any sale of furniture. It is solely related to the offering of design services. In this situation, the revenues are realized when designers work on design projects; thus, it is necessary to determine a factor for direct labor. Because it is very difficult for all professional staff to work at 100 percent billable time, and little of the support staff's time is billable, it is necessary to create a multiplier based on DPE to be accurate.

This is done by the calculations shown in the remainder of Table 6-1. Assuming that only 70 percent of possible work time is billable (referred to as a *utilization rate*), then $70,000 would be direct labor. A 70 percent utilization rate is reasonable if the designer also has nonbillable responsibilities such as marketing, administration, and employee supervision. Designers whose primary responsibility is to be fully engaged in designing projects are expected to have a utilization rate closer to 100 percent. The remaining salary expense is indirect labor: that salary expense that cannot be billed to clients. The amount of payroll taxes, fringe benefits, and overhead expenses is restated in the lower portion of the table for clarification.

Employees whose time is billable are the professional design staff. The time of secretaries, office assistants, and bookkeepers is generally not billable

TABLE 6-1.

Example of how to calculate the billing rate based on DPE

Direct Personnel Expense and Fee Multiple	
Total annual salaries	$100,000
Total fringe benefits	20,000
Total overhead expenses	32,000
Total Expenses	**$152,000**
Total profit goal (20% of revenue)	38,000
Total Net Revenue (income goal for year)	**$190,000**
Direct labor $100,000 × 0.70	$70,000
Indirect Expenses:	
Indirect labor $100,000 × 0.30	30,000
Payroll taxes and benefits	20,000
Overhead expenses	32,000
Total of indirect salary and expenses	82,000
Total of Direct Salaries and Indirect Expenses	**$152,000**
The DPE multiplier would be:	
Direct salary divided by direct salary: $70,000 divided by $70,000	1.00
Total indirect expenses divided by direct salary: $82,000 divided by $70,000	1.17
Adding profit: $38,000 divided by $70,000	0.54
Total DPE multiplier	2.71

to the client. However, the time that a secretary spends preparing specifications and certain other written documentation specifically needed as part of a project *can* be billed if the owner so chooses. However, it is not very common for design firms to charge for this time.

The net multiplier is calculated against the salary rates to get the billing rates. For example, if the senior designer is paid $42.50 per hour, her billing rate would be $113.82, rounded to $114 per hour. An entry-level design assistant who is paid $20 per hour could be billed at $54.20 or $55 per hour. Note that at the time of this writing, actual billing rates vary widely from those used in these examples. These numbers are provided merely for you to see how the calculation is accomplished.

When the owner is determining the expense portion of the billing-rate multiple, there is another concept that he or she should consider. As the business expands, the cost of direct expenses will expand as more revenue is generated. For example, additional supplies may be needed, and extra telephone charges may be incurred that were not estimated. In addition, staff overtime, paid when staff must stay after normal business hours in order to complete projects, adds to overall utility bills. This extra work could also mean additional work for support personnel. Calculating these extra overhead expenses into the multiplier may not be an easy thing to do, but recognition of their impact should be taken into consideration or reduced profit margins will surely result.

Billing rates also can be used to determine if the fixed-fee and the percentage-rate methods yield sufficient income. The fee divided by the billing-rate multiple will give the amount of salary dollars that the owner can use for that project at the profit margin that is normally maintained. This method helps the owner determine if the amount of salary dollars available is sufficient to cover the expenses and desired profit for the project. If it is determined that the project cannot be done for that amount, then the owner can either reject the project or try a different fee method or a combination of methods to ensure that there will be proper compensation.

Billing Rate Based on Salary

There is another way to determine a billing rate rather than one based on the DPE. It is not as accurate, but it will yield a reasonable rate to cover expenses and still provide a profit margin.

The calculation begins with an individual's annual salary. Then a factor for fringe benefits is determined. A fairly common factor is between 25 and 30 percent of salary. However, that varies greatly based on the actual array of fringe benefits and their cost. Next, the designer must determine how many weeks per year he or she is expecting to work and divides this into the salary expense. Not every sole practitioner, for example, chooses to work 50 weeks out of the year. A further calculation of the number of expected billable hours is needed in this method. That factor varies widely based on the individual and how carefully the designer or firm keeps track of billable time. A positive standard is to assume that, on average, a design staff member should be billing a minimum of 75 percent of his or her time per week. A multiplier is determined and an hourly billing rate results from the calculations as follows:

Annual salary	$50,000
Fringe benefits (30% of salary)	15,000
	$65,000/50 weeks = $1300 per week
Average of 40-hour week with 75% billable on average	$1300/30 hrs = $43.34

A multiplier of 3 would result in a $130 per hour billing rate (rounded for simplicity).

This method does not accurately reflect how overhead expenses affect the multiplier. A sole practitioner working out of a home office will have far fewer overhead expenses than the same designer who works from a commercial office space with support staff. Office-space rent, utilities, and extras can add up to substantial overhead expense.

Another factor is the number of billable hours. Many designers do not charge for all their time, because they also earn revenue from the sale of goods. Even more important is that many small business practitioners fail to accurately track their time working on projects versus taking care of administrative responsibilities.

Although it might seem that this method of determining an hourly fee is simpler than using the DPE calculations shown in Table 6-1, the DPE method is recommended because it is more accurate.

WHICH COMPENSATION METHOD?

Professionals have many choices as to exactly how they are going to determine which fee method is appropriate for their business. Fee methods vary depending on the nature of the project, the client, shifts in competition, and other personal and business reasons.

No one method is better than any other all the time, although interior designers tend to use one or two methods most of the time. Often this is because they have successfully used that method with many clients.

Several factors must be considered when determining which compensation method to use and estimating the amount to charge. Following are a few important considerations. A discussion of estimating factors is provided in the next section of this chapter.

Scope of services. The scope of services has the most impact on what method to use and the amount of the fee that will be negotiated. The scope affects the amount of time and work required and even the skill level of the designers. More can go wrong with a complex project that requires a large number of services. Thus, contingency planning in the selection of fee methods and amounts is necessary for a large, complex project.

Residential projects. Residential interior designers tend to earn the majority of their revenue from selling merchandise, rather than fees only. Critical to this is ensuring that the expenses of operating the business have been considered in the determination of the pricing method used and the pricing itself. Sometimes a separate fee is charged for design consultation. There are, of course, residential designers who do not sell furniture and other furnishings at all and charge clients based on fees for services.

Commercial projects. Commercial designers predominately charge a fee for the services they perform, and less frequently sell merchandise. They use a variety of methods to calculate fees, but commonly use an hourly fee, a fixed-fee method, or the square-footage method; other methods are certainly used, but less frequently. The fixed-fee method has become more popular than the hourly rate because clients get concerned about the "meter always running" when an hourly rate is used.

The designer's experience. The less experience the interior designer has with a particular type of project, the longer (logically) it will take to execute the project. In this case, an hourly fee might be fair to the designer but not the client. There is a learning curve with every project. Clients do not like having to teach the designer about their type of project. They do not like to pay for that learning curve. Clients like to hire experts.

The client's experience with an interior designer. Clients who have had no previous experience working with an interior designer require more of the designer's time and patience, and more education and "hand-holding." These clients ask more questions, want more choices, and deliberate more before they make decisions. They also change their minds more often and generally challenge the interior designer more frequently. The client who has previously worked with a designer will, for the most part, be just the opposite. Projects generally take longer to complete for the client who has not previously worked with a designer.

Size and complexity of the project. It is easy to understand that the larger and more complex the project is, the more time the designer will have to spend on the project. Complexity is a project-specific and often arbitrary issue. For example, certainly the interior design of a hospital is complex, but so too can be the design of a large residence with multiple finish treatments and custom cabinets, or the design of a multilevel condominium in a high-rise. In contrast, there are some projects that are large in terms of square footage but do not require a lot of unique designs, such as a hotel.

The fee method to use depends on all the factors just discussed, as well as many others that are particular to the design firm. The owner must consider competition, the desire to do a particular project, the design firm's cash-flow situation, and many other factors every time the client wants to know "How much will this cost?" Now let us look specifically at the typical fee methods used in the professional practice of interior design.

ESTIMATING DESIGN FEES

Accurately and profitably estimating design fees for a project is never easy. Many factors can and do influence which fee method to use, the amount of time involved, and the resulting fee to charge the client that yields both revenue and profit.

Regardless of the fee method, the key to profitability is proper estimation of the design fees. Several issues to consider that affect the design fee are shown in Table 6-2. Two key issues are (1) understanding the scope of services to be provided and (2) carefully calculating costs to ensure that the fee method both satisfactorily covers the costs of executing the project and provides a profit margin. These both have a significant impact on the fee estimate and potential profitability of the project.

The first step must be a detailed analysis of the tasks included in the scope of services. Of course the tasks themselves must be determined, but it is crucial also to determine how much time each design task will take. Firms use estimating sheets, such as item 6-1 on the companion Web site, to assist them in calculating what has to be done and how long it will take. The designer's experience in doing similar projects helps the designer create an estimate of how much time the project will take once he or she determines what has to be done.

Interior design projects include expenses beyond the time involved. Financial expenses include items such as supplies to execute a project, telephone and cell phone costs, and other overhead expenses that are necessary for

TABLE 6-2.

Factors that affect fee estimates

Scope of services
Estimates of direct expense items
Overhead expenses
Experience of design staff
Existing office schedule
Project location versus design firm location
Client familiarity with design process
Client expectations
Client budget expectations
Need for meetings with consultants such as architects, contractors, and lighting designers
Jurisdictional limitations—codes, license requirements
Competition—are other designers being interviewed?
Research time for codes or other special issues
Research for product specification
Custom design of products and millwork
Preparation of formal bid specifications versus equipment lists
Extent of design drawings/construction drawings required

Note that this list is not all-inclusive but represents major impacts on fee estimate.

execution of the work. Salaries for the support personnel needed to assist the interior designer with many phases of the project are another factor. Naturally, these are just a few of the expenses associated with completion of an interior design project. Somehow they must be included in the estimate for design work. These important factors are discussed in detail in Chapter 21.

The other items in Table 6-2 must also be factored into the fee estimate. A client who has never worked with an interior designer before is likely to take longer to make decisions. If consultations with a consultant such as a lighting designer are required, these meetings must be factored into the design fee. A client budget that is too low and is accompanied by high expectations likely will require extra resource research time and meetings with the client. Furthermore, the knowledge that the client is interviewing two, three, or even several other firms will definitely influence the final fee estimate.

With this information in hand, the designer can apply one or more fee methods to the project to determine which method provides the greatest profit. Projects requiring a lot of meetings, drafting, and specification writing are best charged at an hourly fee. Projects that have a lot of similar design decisions (multiple spaces like hotels and hospitals) might work out better if the designer uses a fixed fee or a percentage of cost. Computer simulations can be set up to compare costs and revenue generation based on the fee method that a firm generally uses. These simulations help the designer determine which fee method will generate the greatest profit for a particular job.

What method will be used to charge for design services and produce an appropriate level of revenue is the responsibility of the business owner. Planning for a profitable business begins with understanding the financial side of the business. If a designer is clear about the expenses of operating the particular practice, then the designer has taken the first step toward determining a reasonable fee and maintaining a profitable and successful design practice.

INDIRECT JOB COSTS

It is not easy to estimate design fees that both cover expenses and return a profit. Several things can reduce profitability of a design project. Some of these *indirect job costs*—charges that add to project costs but are not associated with normal service expenses—can be mitigated through carefully drafted contract clauses and contingency allowances. Obviously, it is very important to control these indirect costs to maintain business profitability.

Following is a brief discussion of the most common and costly indirect job cost factors:

Lack of experience. Designers may venture into projects with which they have minimal experience. This lack of experience can mean time and cost overruns as well as a disgruntled client.

The indecisive client. Clients who cannot make up their minds can have a very negative effect on the fee estimates for the project. Experienced interior designers learn to recognize the indecisive client during the initial interviews and take that into consideration when quoting a fee. The designer must diplomatically find ways to urge clients to make up their minds and move on with the project.

Scope creep. When client-initiated changes and/or additions to the project occur, a situation called *scope creep* exists. For example, perhaps the client changes her mind about some portion of the project, which necessitates extra planning or drafting. Another common example is when the client requests design work for other parts of the space that originally were not part of the project. Because they were not part of the original scope of services, the designer is entitled to additional fees. Avoid this problem by including contract clauses that clearly define the original scope and charge for extra services or extra areas.

Overtime. If the design firm must pay overtime salary to any of its staff, the gross margin of the project and potential profitability will decrease. Careful supervision of projects by the design director or project designers will help to hold down the amount of overtime needed for projects.

Unexpected technical or professional consultation. Designers are often asked to do projects that require the preparation of construction documents. Most jurisdictions have strict regulations as to who may prepare construction documents, resulting in extra consultation fees by an architect or engineer.

Clients purchasing independently rather than through the designer. Interior designers who sell merchandise must protect themselves from the client who uses them for ideas but buys from some other source. The key protection in this event is gained through providing appropriate clauses in the design contract that spell out purchasing arrangements. Chapter 7 discusses these clauses.

Jobsite challenges. Clients may make changes during construction without informing the interior designer, causing all manner of problems with delivery and installation of merchandise. The structure itself can cause problems—such as the presence of an unexpected thermostat or electrical switch—hampering the installation of merchandise.

Unexpected delivery issues. Furniture items that are difficult to deliver may cause extra and unanticipated charges that reduce the designer's profit margin. Furniture may arrive as scheduled but prior to site availability. If the design firm does not have a warehouse to hold merchandise until it is ready to be delivered, extra cost will be incurred for storing and later delivering it to the jobsite. This extra cost may be the responsibility of the design firm, as it is in charge of project management and should have anticipated the delays.

All of these examples involve factors and occurrences that require extra design time or in some other respect affect the design firm's expected revenue. All too frequently these factors have not been calculated properly or otherwise considered in the fee and contract. The extra costs in some of these examples may be passed on to the client, if the proper clauses are in the design contract, which we will discuss in Chapter 7. Unfortunately, many of the extra costs discussed in this section are often the responsibility of the design firm.

METHODS FOR SETTING DESIGN FEES

You must consider a great number of factors when determining which fee method to use for each design project. No one method works for all projects for any one design firm, and there is no one fee method that can be guaranteed to work best all the time for a particular type of project. This section discusses the typical methods of setting design fees. Table 6-3 discusses several differences between residential and commercial projects that can affect the choice of fee method and the amount of the fee.

TABLE 6-3.

Factors that affect commercial versus residential fees

Commercial projects

Are often large, starting at about 3000 to 5000 square feet.

Are very complex because of their size.

Require a considerable amount of coordination between the designer and other project stakeholders—the architect, contractors, and engineers.

Often can take numerous months or even years to complete.

Can also go through many changes, even during the design stages. Clients may add employees or change functional requirements during the course of the project.

May experience code changes, resulting in needed design modifications.

Can have construction and product cost increases due to long completion time, which can affect the fee estimate.

Require an emphasis on time management, time keeping, scheduling, and project management.

Commercial clients

Generally make decisions quickly—they do not like to waste time.

Often will agree to the products presented at the earliest schematic and design development meetings.

Select fewer items that are custom-made, instead approving products available in manufacturers' catalogs.

Agree to using products from a limited number of sources, since pricing advantages result from the economy of single-source purchasing.

Residential projects

Vast majority of projects are portions of a home, townhouse, or other private living space with various sizes of project space.

Many projects are complete single-family residence, although that varies with experience level of the designer.

Are most often single-family residences (SFR) from 2000 to 5000 square feet, with some projects 10,000 to 15,000 square feet.

Are often very complicated due to multiple architectural finishes, custom cabinets, and numerous other details.

Can be built in about six to nine months (barring weather or construction delays), though it can take longer for larger, more complex residential construction projects.

Often require revision of plans and extra research or "shopping" for the products that will go into the project if client is indecisive.

Can exceed delivery and completion expectations due to custom-manufactured items.

Require coordination with architects, contractors, and subcontractors.

Can also be affected by cost overruns if client makes changes.

Residential clients

Often take longer to make up their minds concerning the decisions that must be made. Need assurance and servicing, described by professionals as "hand-holding," that can take considerable extra time.

Often insist on many more moments and hours of communication with the designer on what sometimes seem minor issues.

Are often reluctant to pay a reasonable fee for services when the designer also sells merchandise to the client.

Clients have often "shopped" the designer utilizing Internet searches.

Generational factors impact buyer behavior, decision making, and interests in specific types of products.

Based on surveys that I have taken, the most common methods of charging design fees are: hourly rate, fixed fee, and markup from cost. This discussion focuses on those methods, but also addresses other common methods.

Hourly Fee Method

Regardless of a practitioner's experience, an interior design project is time-intensive. Everyone is granted the same 24 hours in a day, and an individual can do only so much in any one hour of that day. Of course, the more experienced person is likely to be able to do more with an hour than a less experienced person. Thus, the more experienced the individual, the higher the hourly rate, because that experience has worth and value.

The *hourly fee* is very common. Clients are familiar with this method, as many other professionals (such as accountants, attorneys, and other service providers) charge by the hour. Quite simply, the service provider is paid an amount for each hour or part of an hour that work is done on behalf of the client. The interior designer needs to determine an hourly rate, as many other fee methods are based on this figure.

Hourly rates vary considerably around the country and even within the same city. Those in residential or commercial practice often use the hourly rate. It is a very satisfactory way of ensuring that the firm will be compensated for all the work it does for a client. Not all clients will quickly agree to be charged an hourly rate, however (see Table 6-4).

Many clients are reluctant to agree to an hourly fee, since the meter, metaphorically speaking, is always running. The longer the designer works on the project, the higher the charges will be. The client is often afraid to allow the designer this much freedom in setting a fee schedule based solely on time. Clients are often afraid that the designer will take extra time so that he or she can increase the fee. Of course, this would be an unethical thing to do. Many firms get around this objection by setting a *not-to-exceed limit* in the contract. It can be argued that this is another way of establishing a fixed fee, as the designer cannot charge more than the not-to-exceed limit.

Hourly billing rates are commonly charged in three ways:

1. Based on the professional level of the employees, with principals and senior designers charged at a higher rate than less experienced designers.

2. An hourly billing rate as an average of all the rates of the various levels of design staff. A disadvantage of this method is that senior designers will not be charged at a rate that is commensurate with experience, while less experienced designers are charged at a rate that exceeds their expertise level.

3. By the kind of service rather than the personnel used. Generally using the project process as a guide, services are grouped based on criteria such as design skill needed to complete the service. Common groupings are: design (or creative) service (the highest level of service); documentation and drafting, which require some design skill and knowledge; and supervision and/or miscellaneous time, which would be the lowest level of service. A drawback of this method is that commensurate fees will not be charged for experienced designers, especially for design/creative services.

An hourly rate can also be calculated to create a *daily rate*. A daily rate might be used for travel to market with the client, out-of-town meetings with the architect and/or client, or any other services that can be accomplished in

---

TABLE 6-4.

When to use the hourly fee method

1. For the initial consultation if the designer decides to charge for that initial meeting
2. Specific project consultations on small-scale projects
3. Whenever the scope of the project is unclear, making it difficult to use any other fee method
4. When the project involves a great deal of consultation time with architects, contractors, and subcontractors
5. When the designer perceives that the client will have difficulty in making up his or her mind
6. To cover travel time to the job site, to markets, or for other travel time
7. When it is necessary to prepare working drawings and specification documents
8. Whenever it is difficult to estimate the total amount of time needed to complete a job, for example, a law office in which each partner wishes to have his or her office designed in a very individual manner

only a day or a few days. The daily rate is rarely used for creative services. The amount of hours that constitute a "day" does vary, with six to eight hours common calculators. The day rate often is larger than the number of hours times the DPE multiplier, but that also varies with the designer.

To be accurate in determining the hourly rate, the DPE formula discussed earlier in this chapter should be utilized. Salary surveys can provide some guidance, but are not always reliable for your particular location.

Fixed-Fee Method

Many designers and their clients have become increasingly satisfied with the fixed-fee method of compensation for interior design services. The *fixed-fee method*, also called the *flat-fee*, *lump-sum*, or *stipulated-sum* method, requires the interior designer to calculate a fee that will cover all the work and expenses required in the project scope of services, knowing that the fee cannot be increased beyond the fixed amount. It is common to add a reasonable additional amount to cover contingencies. The estimated fee is usually charged to the client whether the amount of time estimated is correct or not.

This fee method appeals to clients who are most concerned about the bottom line. Designers who wish to use this fee method should have a database of previous projects that will help them determine the approximate average times and expenses needed to execute various kinds of projects. This fee method is not recommended for the inexperienced designer, as she or he will not have a good idea or history as to how long it will take to complete projects.

The fixed-fee amount must be carefully considered. If the firm's owner has estimated badly and the time involved in completing a project exceeds the estimated fee, the firm cannot be compensated for the extra time. If the firm has estimated too high and the project does not require the full amount of estimated time, the firm is not obligated to refund any of the fee to the client. Of course, it is improper to overinflate the fixed fee as a way of seeking to obtain a huge profit at the client's expense. The fixed fee includes charges for all services and expenses other than those that the firm charges as reimbursable expenses.

To use this method, it is important for you to have a thorough understanding of the services that must be performed. The client's budget also is critical, as an unclear budget or a very low budget means that the designer will need more time to research sources for products and potentially will have to do more revision to the plans. You must also have a feeling for the client's decision-making ability, to predict if the client will be difficult or easy to work with. Problems with this fee method can arise if the client does not understand the time element so that all phases of the project can be satisfactorily accomplished within the fee estimate.

The fixed-fee method, which can be used for both residential and commercial projects, is a satisfactory method of charging fees when:

1. The scope of work for the project is easy to determine and not expected to change.

2. The amount of supervision on the job site is limited or can easily be controlled by the designer.

3. It is easy to determine the time and requirements of the project.

4. The designer has a significant amount of experience with the type of project and scope of services required so that the fee estimate is clear-cut.

5. The client is not purchasing goods from the designer. This allows the designer to utilize goods that he or she might not normally use, as the designer is not selling the goods. For the client, this may mean that the goods specified may be at a lower cost than those the designer usually sells.

6. Whenever a large amount of the same item is to be purchased. This is often the case for projects such as restaurants and office complexes, in which standardized products are specified; little additional time is required for such projects after the final product selections are made.

Cost Plus Percentage Markup Method

A compensation method that many interior designers utilize when they also sell merchandise to the client is the *cost plus percentage markup* method. The client agrees to pay a specific markup on the actual cost of the merchandise and other items that the designer sells to the client. Increasingly, this method has been combined with the hourly method for design consultation. In this situation, the client obtains a better price on merchandise when he or she buys from the designer, because the designer passes on all the discounts that suppliers provide, arriving at a competitively low cost.

The cost plus percentage markup is more commonly used in residential design, but can also be effective for commercial projects. It can be the least remunerative method, if a very small markup is added to the net price or the client does not buy any merchandise from the designer. It can also be quite profitable, though, as long as sufficient product is sold to the client and the markup percentage has been carefully calculated. It is critical, for designers who do not charge a design fee for services, that the percentage be carefully considered and sufficient to create an appropriate amount of revenue and remain competitive.

The key in using this fee method is to charge an adequate percentage. There is no average markup, as each firm decides what percentage to use based on business needs, competition, and what the client is willing to pay. Residential designers might charge from 10 percent to more than 30 percent markup. When commercial interior designers use this method, the percentage is generally quite low, due to the competition for the sale of goods in the commercial area of interior design.

The cost plus percentage markup method works well for firms as long as:

1. The budget is not reduced at the last moment.
2. The client does not use a lot of existing furniture in the new project.
3. The client does not decide to hold off purchasing any of the merchandise until a later time, thereby reducing the amount of revenues the firm may collect.
4. The client does not decide to purchase items from someone other than the designer.

Another segment of the interior design industry that uses the cost plus percentage markup method consists of design firms that are just getting started. Many new design firms offer this method of compensation as a way of competing with larger, more established firms.

Remember that the markup amount is not really "profit" in and of itself: It also must cover the designer's costs of doing business and direct costs of doing the project. Any firm that is considering the use of this method should use it in conjunction with some other fee method to be sure the firm receives a reasonable gross margin to cover costs and obtain a profit.

Square-Foot Method

Another method that requires a good history with projects is the *square-foot method*. The fee is determined by a rate per square foot times the amount of square footage of the project being designed. Commonly used in commercial design and by some designers in residential practice, the square-foot method can be a profitable way of determining the design fee. There are no industry-standard square-foot fees, so the designer must have some experience with similar projects to establish an appropriate rate.

An owner who has never used the square-foot method for determining fees can gather data on several completed projects (for example, similar-size doctors' suites or real estate offices). The actual design fee charged for these projects is divided by the square footage of the project, which provides a historical view of the per-square-foot cost of the design work. Consideration for the scope of services, expenses, and profit margin are then placed into the mix to determine the square-foot fee.

Fee amounts will vary based on the type of project and the scope of services. It is obvious that a more complex project will take more time, so the square-foot rate for such a project should be higher. In addition, regional factors, the design firm's experience, and local competition may drive rates up or down.

Value-Oriented Method

A fee method that has become increasingly accepted in recent years is one based on value. It is not so much a method as a concept that affects the fee amount.

The experienced interior designer brings value to the project based on his or her experience with the type of project and scope of services. A designer with several years' experience doing hospitality projects, for example, should be able to bring greater value and be worth more to the client than a designer with very little experience who wants the same job.

The *value-oriented*, or *value-based*, method is based on the concept that the design firm prices services based on the value or quality of the services rather than focusing solely on the cost of doing those services. This fee method will only work for a design firm whose services have additional value in the marketplace. It is critical for readers to understand that although the designer grasps the value of his particular services versus those of other designers, the client may not share this view. It is the client's/buyer's view of value that counts.

The perception of most clients is that all designers do the same thing and provide the same services. With the value-oriented fee method, the designer must show the client how his services are valuable to the client and superior to those of competing designers. The designer must show also how he differs from the competition and is thus worth the fees requested. If the client perceives that what one design firm offers has greater value than what other design firms offer, the more valued firm will win the contract.

In many cases, this perceived value means that the design firm can charge a premium for its services. Firms with a lot of experience are expected to do a better job. For example, a designer who has specialized in residences for 10 years has a far greater expertise in that type of facility than someone starting out or who has never designed a private residence. The first firm will try to show the client that experience has value and that this value should be compensated accordingly.

Clients who are unfamiliar with or do not appreciate the time and subtleties involved in completing a project react favorably to the value-oriented method. The fee is based on the designer's ability to meet the client's expectation and experience in doing the work, rather than on the time it will take to complete the project. When the designer can clearly differentiate how she can be of value to the client, and can demonstrate that her experiences and ability warrant this consideration, this fee method should be considered.

Percentage of Merchandise and Product Services Method

A fee method primarily used by commercial interior designers is called the *percentage of merchandise and product services method*. This fee method is similar to the architect's percentage of construction cost method. It is very similar in concept to the cost plus percentage markup method.

In this case, interior designers determine the design fee based on a negotiated percentage of the cost of the goods and installation (and possibly some portion of the construction) that will be involved in the project. Firms that do not intend to sell merchandise to the client frequently use this fee method. Because residential designers more often sell merchandise in addition to providing design services, it is not very common for residential designers.

The final fee amount results from the percentage that was negotiated multiplied by the budgeted or final costs of the project. This might include the furniture, wall coverings, floor coverings, ceiling and window treatments, lighting fixtures, accessories, built-in cabinets, and even general construction costs.

The percentage rate varies with the size and complexity of the project. The larger the project is, the smaller the fee percentage will be. The more complex the project is, the greater the fee percentage will be. For example, a large project like a hotel, with a large dollar volume but a potentially small number of design decisions, would require a smaller percentage fee than a group of individually designed executive offices requiring a great deal of time.

There are some disadvantages for the designer that must be weighed carefully:

- The amount of revenue for the designer is reduced when the client purchases cheaper goods than those specified.
- A measure of distrust may arise if the client feels the designer is specifying more expensive goods to increase the overall price.
- The designer may also have reduced revenues when third-party vendors try to "buy the job" at a very low price.
- Clients may suspect the designer of double-dipping, that is, of earning revenue from the design and specification of the products and also from selling the merchandise.

Because the project fee is based on cost, the client may actually save money if any extra discounts are provided on merchandise that the client purchases. Thus, budgets must be carefully considered to ensure that the project is done as required and that the designer is compensated fairly. This method should be used cautiously and only in combination with another method that will ensure fair compensation for design time and services.

Retail Method

In the *retail method*, the design firm charges the client the retail price suggested by the manufacturer or supplier. If the manufacturer does not provide a suggested retail price, then the design firm marks up the merchandise from the net or cost price to achieve the retail price. Because both the suggested retail price and the markup percentage commonly used are 100 percent, the retail method provides a high gross profit margin for the firm. Although the most common markup is 100 percent, when selling to the consumer the markup can be higher.

Residential design firms that are not retail stores sometimes use the retail method instead of cost plus a markup. Of course, retail furniture and merchandise stores use the retail method when selling directly to the consumer. In concept, the markup amount of at least 100 percent is sufficient to cover all direct and overhead expenses and provide a profit margin.

There are some key issues when using the retail method:

- It might *not* be suitable when a great deal of planning, drafting, specification writing, or supervision work is required.
- There is no guarantee that the client will purchase merchandise from the designer, which means that the designer will not be fully compensated for time spent working on the project.
- The retail method is used less often today because designers have become more willing to quote a design fee for services.

Clients are becoming accustomed to the concept of paying for the professional services that an interior designer can offer, and thus are willing to pay the separate design fees. In addition, clients are far more willing to shop around for a good price on both products and services. This has led many designers to use a method for generating revenue other than the retail method.

Discounting or Percentage off Retail Method

The *percentage off retail* method is another common method of fee setting that is directly related to the purchase of goods. Stores and showrooms that have an inventory of merchandise offer those items at a percentage off retail in order to gain a competitive edge over stores that are strictly retail priced. They might do this because the firm expects that the volume of merchandise purchased by the client will offset the design services costs. Office furnishings dealers frequently use this method.

In this method, the design firm reduces the selling price of the merchandise by some percentage off the suggested retail price, rather than marking up merchandise from cost. Care must be taken when the design firm determines what that discount will be, as the resulting difference between the selling price and the net price (the gross margin) must allow for a profit and cover overhead costs. The larger the discount, the smaller the gross profit margin will be, so less will remain to pay expenses and maintain profits.

Office furnishings dealers have found that this method does not always cover the cost of design services. This has become even more true recently because of the rash of deep discounting on many projects and the highly competitive market in office furnishings. Because of these deep discounts (discussed in Chapter 8), dealers have been forced to charge design fees, such as an hourly fee, to make sure the designer's time is covered and compensated.

Consultation Fee

Mr. Jackson knew he should have some help with his small office suite because it was important to him to have a very professional look to his office. Through client contacts, he was able to purchase furniture. He asked Dianne Dawson, an interior designer one of his clients knew, if she would provide ideas on what he could do himself. They negotiated and she agreed to provide four hours of consultation at a flat fee.

In some situations, such as the preceding example, a client may want some ideas from a designer but does not need complete design services. The interior designer would then charge the client a fee for the consultation. In such an arrangement, the designer provides ideas but generally does not execute plans or other documents. The consultation is generally limited to a maximum of a few hours, though any arrangement that the designer wishes to develop is possible.

Goods are generally not sold under a consultation arrangement. Of course, the client may later decide that he or she does need the full services and/or purchasing ability of the interior designer. Generally, when the interior designer later takes on a more complete design contract, he or she subtracts any consultation fee already paid from the project amount, although this is not standard.

Combination Method

In many cases, using only one of the described fee methods does not provide sufficient compensation to cover all the expenses and desired profit margin for the firm. Thus, many firms use a combination of two different fee methods to meet their revenue needs.

Because projects involve a variety of activities, it is defensible for the firm to charge the client a variety of fees. For example, consider a project that involves a lot of the designer's time in meetings with the client, contractors, and the architect for specifying interior finish materials but not a large dollar amount for the actual materials to be purchased. The designer might find that adequate compensation can be reached with an hourly charge for meetings, travel, and on-site supervision in combination with either a cost plus percentage markup or percentage discount from retail for the merchandise sold. If properly considered, a combination of design fee methods can provide excellent compensation to the designer at a fair price to the client.

The two methods most commonly combined are cost plus percentage markup with a fixed fee and cost plus percentage markup with an hourly fee. Both residential and commercial interior designers might use either of these methods when they sell merchandise in addition to providing design services.

Some clients object to these combination fees, especially when a service fee is combined with product markup. Many clients see the markup (or the consultation fee) as double-dipping. It behooves the designer to explain that the fixed fee (or hourly fee) is calculated to provide only a portion of the revenues needed to cover labor, expenses, and profit and that the client is also obtaining the goods at a substantial discount.

An important issue when the fee is an hourly rate/markup combination is the determination of which services will be charged at the hourly rate and which will be considered included in the markup of the merchandise. Designers who use this combination feel that they are more likely to cover all or most of the time that they actually work on the project. This does not always happen with a combination of the fixed-fee and cost plus percentage markup methods.

The danger in using either of these combinations is that the designer may rely on the client's purchase of goods to generate needed revenue. However, if the client purchases from some other source, delays purchasing, or buys goods at a lower price, the designer will receive less income than estimated. Safeguards can be incorporated into the design contract in the event that some of these problems occur. They are discussed in Chapter 7.

The designer can negotiate a reasonable and fair fee by using any of the fee methods described in this section. Considerations for each situation as to what is most appropriate for the designer, the client, and the project always affect the selection of fee method. There comes a time when any interior designer feels that he or she wants to charge more, whether in consideration of the competition or for personal needs. Table 6-5 provides some pointers concerning obtaining higher design fees.

TABLE 6-5.

Strategies to increase your design fees

Know what the market charges. You must know what the market charges for services similar to yours. If you are charging too little in comparison to others, a potential client may think you are not very good. If you are charging more than the market, the client will want to know why you feel you are worth more. Remember that those with little experience will never be considered of the same value as those with a great deal of experience.

Establish and maintain your reputation. Always work honestly and ethically. Your reputation often precedes you to new clients, and a good reputation can even have a status or prestige effect on a client, thus positioning you for higher fees. Don't do anything that harms your reputation.

Provide excellent customer service. Be sure you understand what level of service is expected by your clients, and provide an even greater level than their expectation.

Your value relates to what the client values. The client must feel that what you provide has value to them, regardless of your reputation, background, or experience. If they do not see the value, they will be reluctant to hire you.

Build a good relationship. Interior design—especially residential—is a highly relationship-affected profession. Many times designers get hired because of the impression that is projected at the initial meeting and the relationship that is built as the project progresses.

Offer services that few others propose. Find a niche that is needed and not being serviced in your market or some other market. Then become very good at it. The more expertise you have in a specialty or when you are the first to offer something new, the more you can charge.

Pinpoint your value-adds. Determine what you can do better than other designers. You have to have something of value to clients for them to be willing to pay you more.

Add to your personal value. Continually update your knowledge of topics and tasks needed within the profession through continuing education. Obtain state licenses and certificates such as the NCIDQ. Go back and get a degree if necessary to improve your standing in the industry.

Why are you worth more? Have good reasons for why you charge more than others. You can't charge more just because you think you should. You must be able to explain your value to the client. You also need to have good reasons to explain to existing clients why you are raising your rates.

Charge differently. Maybe you have experience or abilities that can allow you to charge in a way that is different from the competition. Instead of charging by the hour, perhaps you can charge for a "menu" of services. This one is tricky, so consider it carefully before plunging in.

WEB SITES RELEVANT TO THIS CHAPTER

www.bls.gov U.S. Bureau of Labor Statistics

www.ftc.gov U.S. Federal Trade Commission

You might also want to check with the various professional associations.

KEY TERMS

Billing rate

Combination fee

Consultation fee

Cost plus percentage markup

Daily rate

Direct personnel expense (DPE)

Double-dipping

Fixed fee

Flat fee

Hourly fee

Indirect job costs - *concept*

Lump sum

Multiple

Not to exceed limit - *guaranteed max*

Percentage of merchandise and product services

Percentage off retail

Retail method

Scope creep

Scope of services

Square-foot method

Value-oriented

WHAT WOULD YOU DO?

1. Margaret is designing the living room, dining room, and kitchen of an apartment space in a high-rise building. As part of her design contract, she included a clause stating that "all products needed for this project will be purchased only through the designer. That merchandise will be sold to the client at cost plus 30 percent." Because all indications led her to believe that the client would be purchasing a substantial amount of items through her firm for the project spaces, Margaret charged only a small consultation fee of $2000.

   The client kept delaying the ordering of several of the items, saying he was short of funds. Margaret found out that the client was purchasing items on his own and warehousing them at his office.

2. Arthur takes Jane to lunch to discuss a design project they are both working on. During the lunch meeting, Arthur, who is the senior project designer on this project, repeatedly touches Jane's hand and shoulder as they talk about the project. He also suggests that it will be necessary for them to travel to the job site to meet with the client's construction project manager. Arthur makes some veiled suggestions to Jane that if she is "nice" to him, he will get her a raise after the project is completed.

3. The practice of Shape/Box Interiors focuses on hospitality projects. Due to the nature of these projects, the designers often need to spend a large amount of time in the preparation of contract documents and specifications for rooms that are basically the same items, though in various color schemes. Many of Shape/Box Interiors' clients purchase the needed merchandise directly from vendors rather than the interior designer. The designer generally charges a per-square-foot fee for the specification, but is wondering if other fee methods would be more lucrative.

4. Alice designed the interiors of a six-unit apartment complex for a client who planned to lease the spaces to students. The property is located a short walk from campus and he decided to rent the apartments furnished. Students began moving into the apartments the day after the furniture was delivered.

   The final walk-through with her client occurred on Tuesday. Alice had her client sign off on the punch list, which indicated that everything was delivered as required. There were no notations related to any damages or missing items. Alice bills the client for the remainder of design services and all the products that had not previously been billed. However, the client refuses to pay this final invoice, as he claims that some merchandise was damaged and a few items were not what was agreed to.

CHAPTER 7

Preparing Design Contracts

After completing this chapter you should be able to:

- List and explain the basic requirements (or elements) needed to create a valid contract for services.
- Describe an offer and a counteroffer and explain what happens when a client makes a counteroffer.
- Explain the concept of contractual capacity.
- Explain what kinds of consideration can be used in a design contract.
- Compare and contrast a letter of agreement and a contract.
- Explain the difference between a proposal and a contract.
- Discuss the benefits of a written contract over oral agreements.
- List and describe the five items that must be included in a design contract for it to be enforceable.
- Describe how the Statute of Frauds affects contracts for services.
- Explain why it is important for the contract to clearly state the client's name and address and include a description of the project at the beginning of the contract.
- Discuss strategies for ensuring that the appropriate clauses are included in a contract for interior design services.
- Explain why a detailed scope of services is so important in a contract.
- Analyze a contract for services and determine its flaws.
- Explain charges for third parties, publishing rights, ownership of documents, and arbitration.
- Explain why it is important for the firm's name to be on the signature box of a design contract.
- Discuss the concepts of assignment and delegation.
- Explain how the designer's signature should appear on the contract and why its format is so important.
- Explain why an electronic signature is a good or bad idea.
- List and explain the forms of performance that signify completion or breach of a contract.
- Discuss strategies for mitigating disputes.
- Explain how a designer might be able to use small claims court to settle disputes.

NCIDQ COMPONENT

Based on best information available, some material in this chapter might appear as part of the NCIDQ examination. The reader should not depend solely on this text for study material.

Designers enter into many contracts: with clients, with vendors, with crafts-people, and even with other designers. Sometimes they should have entered into a contract but did not. Too often, when this happens, a dispute occurs between the parties, as each claims he or she did not get what was agreed to verbally. Interior design contractual relationships should never be taken lightly. Serious consequences occur when promises made in a contract are not fulfilled.

It is imperative that designers take care in the preparation of their contracts. They must carefully compose and organize the various clauses to protect themselves and ensure that the work outlined can be accomplished. In addition, in a contract for design services, it is the interior designer's responsibility to fulfill the contract. A common issue in ethics complaints surrounds contract disputes.

In this chapter, we review the basic ingredients of a contract and contract law as they relate to a contract for services or a combination of services and goods. In Chapter 9 we discuss the specific differences concerning contracts for the sale of goods. The counsel of an attorney is strongly recommended for obtaining a complete explanation of the legal considerations of contracts. *The information in this chapter is general in nature and should not be construed as legal advice.*

DEFINITION AND BASIC ELEMENTS OF A CONTRACT

A contract to provide interior design services is like most other contracts. It is made to explain what both the designer and the client will do. Because the designer prepares the contract, it outlines what compensation is expected from the client. These are just basic items of what is included in an interior design contract. But what is a *contract* in a legal sense?

Offering services and developing a design contract in order to work with a client are serious matters. What is included and even the wording are also very important. Simply describing what will be done and how much it will cost the client for the designer to perform those services does not by itself create a legally enforceable contract should a dispute occur. Other terms must be included so that the interior designer has the force of law on her or his side.

So then, what technically is a contract? A *contract* is a promise or agreement that is made between two or more parties to perform or not perform some act. A legally enforceable contract must have these basic elements:

1. *Offer.* One party (the interior designer) proposes to do something or not to do something for another party (the client).
2. *Acceptance.* The client agrees to accept the offer and is bound by the exact terms set up in the offer.
3. *Contractual capacity.* Both the interior designer and the client must have the legal ability to enter into the contract.

[handwritten margin note: Termination Clause- smaller font on back]

4. *Consideration*. Something of value must be exchanged as it relates to the contract. It must be legally sufficient for a court to take it seriously.

5. *Mutual assent*. The giving of the offer and acceptance of the offer must be done willingly.

6. *Legality*. The contract must exist to support the performance of some legal act.

Let us now look at each of these elements in detail.

Offer

A contractual *offer* is made by the *offeror*—the party who makes the offer (for our purposes, the interior designer). In legal terminology, the client is referred to as the *offeree*. For example, Julie prepares a contract for the interior design of a retail store. Thus, Julie—the offeror—makes an offer to her client, Heavenly Jewels, owned by Rita Jones and Sara Barrow—the offeree.

Everything that the designer puts in the contract must be included only with serious thought and intent. Contractual statements are in effect promises. There can be very serious legal consequences if the designer is unable to achieve or neglects to have someone else achieve what was in the contract. Forgetting to put something into a contract can also have serious consequences. For example, if Julie's contract with Heavenly Jewels requires a fee of $25,000, but in the terms of the contract, Julie neglects to require a retainer, Julie cannot later ask the client to pay a retainer, since that was not part of the original offer.

A contract can and should include a time limit. Time limits encourage action by the client. The time period of the offer begins when the offeree receives the offer, not when the offer is prepared or mailed by the offeror. If no time limit is stated in the offer, the time limit terminates at the end of a reasonable period, based on consideration of the circumstances of the offer. This matter is discussed further later in this chapter.

A legal offer must express serious intent; not be ambiguous or vague; must be fully communicated to the offeree; and must include the offeror's ability to terminate the contract. Let's look at each of these.

Merely expressing an opinion is not a valid form of serious intention. For example, if Julie says to her client, "The project can probably be completed in about five days," her client cannot sue if it actually takes ten days, because "five days" is an opinion, not a promise. However, even though an opinion is not legally binding, ill will is likely to occur when the project is not completed as mentioned in the opinion.

Problems commonly occur with contracts when the offer is vague. The terms of the offer must be definite enough for a court to determine whether the contract has been fulfilled or not. A statement such as "select all finishes" can leave the firm responsible for selecting interior and exterior finishes when the firm only planned on selecting interior finishes. Designers often mistakenly include a vague description of the scope of the job, such as "design your house" when the job really involves the furniture and finish selections for the family room and kitchen. This vagueness can leave the designer responsible for services related to other parts of the house, probably without additional compensation.

The third element of a legal offer is that the offer must be fully communicated or explained to the offeree so that the offeree knows of the existence of the offer. For example, unless the client knows that out-of-town travel expenses

[Handwritten margin notes:]
1. Time limit
2. clear intent
3. fully communicated; has exclusions
※ additional services
4. Termination clause

are over and above the design fees, the client is not expected to pay these expenses. The designer cannot expect the client to do something or pay for something that was not disclosed and explained in the contract offer.

The last element in a legal offer concerns the ability of the offeror (the designer) to terminate the offer or the acceptance of the offer. Generally, an offer can be terminated only if the designer withdraws the offer before the client accepts it. A designer may wish to withdraw the offer because of an error. For example, Peter discovers that he miscalculated his design fee for a project. If he completes the work for the stated fee of $21,000, he will actually lose $6000. Peter wants to rescind the offer, because he cannot afford to lose that much money. Peter can rescind the offer only if the client has not already agreed to the offer. Another example relates to the time frame of the offer: If the designer's proposal states that the price for the services is good for 10 days but the client responds on the 15th day, the designer is not obligated to provide the services at the stated price.

When a client responds to the original offer with some sort of modification or change, that modification effectively terminates the original offer. This is called a *counteroffer*. For example, if Heavenly Jewels tells Julie, "Your design fee is out of the question. I am prepared to pay only $5000 for these services," the offer of $5000 is now a counteroffer. The designer is now in a position to either accept or reject this counteroffer. This also means that Julie's negotiation skills are needed as she discusses the original fee and counteroffer.

An offer can be terminated if the client rejects the offer, effectively ending the negotiation for that project contract. Should this happen, there is no obligation on either side to fulfill the contract. Should the client later wish to accept the offer, the designer can refuse, accept, or modify the original offer. This is because the client's initial refusal of the offer terminates the original offer. But if the client says something like, "Is this the best price you can give me on design fee?" this does not constitute rejection of the offer.

There is another important point to discuss concerning contract offers. Interior designers are often invited to bid on design projects or sales of goods. An invitation to bid or to negotiate is not an offer, but merely shows a willingness on the part of the client to enter into discussions with the designer about a potential contract. For example, Steve is asked to respond to a proposal by the City of Phoenix on the specification of new furnishings for the mayor's office. The request for proposal (RFP) from the city of Phoenix is not a contract offer, but an announcement that a project exists.

Acceptance

Rita Jones and Sara Barrow, owners of Heavenly Jewels, read the contract prepared by Julie and indicate that everything is fine with them. Each of the owners signs the agreement and they are happy to learn that Julie can begin the project in only a few days. Because the client agrees to the terms of the offer, acceptance has been given. "In order to exercise the power of acceptance effectively, the offeree must accept unequivocally. If the acceptance is subject to new conditions, or if the terms of the acceptance change the original offer, the acceptance may be considered a counteroffer that implicitly rejects the original offer."[1]

Unequivocal acceptance is referred to as the *mirror image rule* of acceptance in law textbooks. When someone accepts a contract proposal and does not make changes, he or she has "mirrored" the offer. If Rita and Sara had asked for some changes in the agreement—a new charge for a lighting designer, for example—then the original offer was not accepted and agreement was not reached. (Instead, the client made a counteroffer.)

Interior designers are often anxious to begin working on a project even though the client has not yet returned the signed agreement. Perhaps they have a "good feeling" that the client will sign. However, the interior designer should never begin work without a signed agreement.

Just because the client seems inclined to go ahead does not mean that the client has agreed to the contract. Silence should not be construed as acceptance unless the client has received a benefit from services that the designer has provided. In such a case the courts will likely rule that the client has accepted the contract. For example, the designer has sketched some layouts for the remodeled kitchen and given the sketches to the client. Because the client has received those sketches, the court could rule that the client has received a benefit and is liable for the costs involved in creating the sketches even if the client has not yet signed the agreement.

Interior designers should be very careful about beginning any type of work on a project for which the client has not returned a signed design contract. Good intentions or enthusiasm by the interior designer are often not rewarded by the unscrupulous client.

Finally, acceptance must be made within the time limit set in the terms of the offer. If no definite terms are stated, acceptance must be made within a reasonable time frame, considering the conditions of the offer and the subject of the offer.

Contractual Capacity

Contractual capacity relates to the full legal competency and authority of the parties. Both parties in a contract must have the legal capacity or authority to enter into a contract. It is very important for the interior designer to be sure this is so. For example, Harold, the owner of HRH Interiors, obtains a signature on a contract from the office manager of a physician's office. The doctor refuses to pay the first invoice for the design fee, because the office manager did not have the legal authority to sign the contract.

In residential design, the interior designer normally deals with a legally competent adult who is head of a household or a spouse. As an added protection—which in some states is an absolute necessity—both the husband and wife or the other owners of the residence should sign the contract. It is not uncommon for a divorce or breakup of the family to occur while a project is under way. Signatures of all the owners of the property obligate all the owners to the contract.

In commercial interior design, the designer often deals with people other than the actual owner of the business or the chairperson of the board of the corporation. As indicated in the example with HRH interiors, not everyone who seems to have an authoritative job title has contractual capacity. Julie had both Rita and Sara sign the contract for the design work for Heavenly Jewels, because she knew that they were partners in the business.

Consideration

Consideration is the legal term for the "price" that the offeree "pays" to the offeror for the offeror's fulfilling the promise made in the contract. In an interior design contract, the consideration is the design fees that the client must pay for the services agreed to by the client. The consideration must be sufficient to be fair. What was the consideration that Julie was negotiating with Rita and Sara for Heavenly Jewels?

Consideration can be money, property, services, or anything else of value that is legal. For example, a designer might barter or agree to provide interior design services to his or her accountant in exchange for accounting services. An interior designer might also accept a piece of property, such as a painting from a gallery, for interior design services provided to the gallery. Of course, money is the primary type of consideration.

Considerations are negotiated for actions that take place in the future or in the present, not in the past. Let's say that a design contract says, for example, that the designer will provide detailed construction drawings suitable for obtaining a building permit. Later the designer tells the client that he or she must pay the designer an additional $1000 for those drawings. The client is not obligated to pay, because the design firm is already legally obligated to supply those drawings at the originally agreed-to fee.

A promise to give consideration for something that has already occurred or that the designer is already obligated to do is not binding. If the client says, "Because you did such a great job in finishing the office installation on time, I will give you a $500 bonus," the client is not legally obligated to pay the bonus; that would be consideration for something that happened in the past.

Mutual Assent

The legal concept of *mutual assent* means that the parties to a contract must be willing and free to enter into the contractual offer and acceptance. Sometimes a contract that is made by two parties who have the full legal competency to make a valid contract may not be enforceable because the reality of the assent by one or another of the parties is called into question.

Roger keeps insisting that Mr. and Mrs. O'Neil sign the agreement to order the new appliances for their kitchen. He repeatedly mentions that the price on the refrigerator is going up "very soon." He cannot order the item until they sign the agreement. Mrs. O'Neil has her heart set on the refrigerator, and finally her husband signs the agreement. Not completely happy about the pressure that Roger used, Mr. O'Neil calls someone he knows who has access to the refrigerator vendor and finds out that the price is not expected to increase for at least two months.

Roger's insistence that the client sign the agreement while effectively threatening an impending price increase that he knows not to be true is an example of the lack of mutual assent. Our example is also a case in point for *undue influence*, where one party exerts so much influence on the other party that the other party is virtually unable to exercise his or her own free will.

Other occurrences that a judge may consider to constitute a lack of mutual assent happen because of (1) a mistake (this must relate to a mistake by one or another of the parties with regard to the facts of the terms of the contract, not an error of judgment or quality), (2) fraudulent misrepresentation (the terms of the agreement have been intentionally presented with incorrect information, in an attempt to deceive the other party), or (3) duress (this negates a contract if the offeree is forced by certain kinds of threats to agree to the contract). If any one of these occurrences is proven to exist for either party, then the contract is not valid.

Legality

A design contract must describe and concern only legal acts. In addition, designers who belong to a professional association or who are licensed or regulated by a state agency must abide by these legal obligations or face ethics disciplinary hearings.

An *illegal contract* is any contract that, if performed, would constitute an act against legal statute, would break tort law, or in any way would be opposed to the public good. It is highly unlikely that an interior designer's design contract would run afoul of the concept of legality unless the interior designer entered into a contract in restraint of trade.

Contracts in *restraint of trade* are intentionally made to be detrimental to the public good, and generally have an effect on the potential for fair competition in a given market. For example, if two or more interior design firms in a market area in which they are the only source for furniture get together and agree to sell merchandise at the same markup, they would be guilty of collusion, and their agreement would be in restraint of trade. If one subsequently lowered prices and the other sued, saying they had an agreement, the lawsuit would be thrown out, and both firms would likely be charged with a crime.

Some contracts in restraint of trade are actually legal, however. Certain clauses in employment contracts that restrain the activities of former employees can be legal, if the restrictions relating to noncompetition are reasonable. This is discussed in Chapter 27.

These elements are primary to the formation of a contract for such services as might be offered by an interior designer. The interpretation of these elements and the enforcement of contracts is governed by common law. When a designer sells goods to a client, the Uniform Commercial Code governs sales contracts. These contracts are discussed in Chapter 9.

Common Contracts in Interior Design Practice

A contract for the performance of interior design services or the sale of merchandise are not the only contracts commonly part of the practice. Some of the most common are listed here.

- Employment
  - Basic employment agreement
  - Independent contractor agreement
  - Consulting agreement
  - Confidentiality agreement
- Leases
  - To obtain equipment
  - To obtain office/studio space
  - To provide furniture to clients
- General business
  - Construction contract
  - Partnership agreement
  - Joint venture agreement
  - For special services such as attorney and accountant
- Sales
  - Purchase order to vendors
  - Sales agreement with clients

LETTER OF AGREEMENT OR CONTRACT?

For some clients, the idea of signing a "contract" produces fear. Interior designers for many years have used a different term for the agreement between interior designer and client for services: they call it a letter of agreement. A *letter of agreement* is a contract that is less formal in content and terminology and looks more like a letter. Nevertheless, if it meets the criteria discussed in this chapter, it is a contract and affords the designer the same legal consideration for enforcement as a contract.

It is really only a semantic difference as to what the agreement is called. Many residential interior designers prefer to use the terminology "letter of agreement," whereas the term *contract* is more commonly used for commercial projects. Unfortunately, with the increasing litigation in the industry, letters of agreement are not very simple anymore. It is up to the designer to decide whether the term *contract* or *letter of agreement* is more appropriate to his or her interior design practice. Whatever terminology is used, it is critical to include clauses that protect the designer in case of a dispute. This chapter generally uses the term *contract*.

Format examples of both a letter of agreement and a contract are shown in this chapter. *Do not use any sample contract provided in this chapter without review by an attorney for appropriateness and applicability to the designer.*

The letter of agreement in Figure 7-1 shows an outline indicating basic information that should be incorporated. Item 7-1 on the companion Web site is a completed version of Figure 7-1.

PROPOSALS VERSUS CONTRACTS

Have not agreed yet

A *proposal* is defined in the dictionary as "a plan or suggestion put forward for consideration or discussion by others."[2] A contract, in simple terms, is an agreement between two parties to do or not do something. The contract contains statements concerning consideration along with the offer of what will be done. A proposal is more commonly thought of as the foundation for preparing the contract rather than as the actual contract.

Although in some respects a proposal and a contract provide similar information, they serve different purposes. Generally, in architecture and interior design, a proposal sets forth what is to be done based on information provided by the client through a written document or obtained from the client through other means. It states the designer's understanding of the needs and explains how the design firm will approach the solution. A contract also generally explains the scope of work, but details more information on fees, and includes clauses that are uncommon to a proposal (such as photographic rights, among others).

The term *proposal* can have other meanings. Designers sometimes use the term *proposal* instead of *contract* or *letter of agreement*. To some clients, "proposal" sounds less legally threatening than "contract." Still, because it can be considered an offer from the designer to the buyer, a proposal can serve as a contract if signed by the client. This often depends on the complexity of the project.

Some designers use the term *proposal* to define what will be purchased for a client. If the client agrees with the proposal, the designer will then move forward with ordering those items.

Another common use of the term *proposal* is in the request for proposals (RFP) commonly used in commercial interior design. In this context, the proposal is a response to a request issued by a client for specific information concerning a proposed project. It is not a contract in this context. In this circumstance, the proposal is more a marketing tool than an agreement to begin design work. A detailed discussion of the request for proposal document is included in Chapter 24.

Addresses
Date
Dear Ms. Jones:

It was a pleasure meeting with you on Monday to discuss your design project. This letter of agreement outlines the services, fees, and other responsibilities of this firm.

My understanding is that the spaces to be included in this project are to remodel your kitchen and family room and the design of a custom entertainment center for the master bedroom. It is also my understanding that you will be purchasing all new kitchen appliances and furniture for the family room. It is not expected that I will be selling you the products as part of this agreement. If you choose to purchase products from me, a supplemental agreement will be prepared.

The approach to this project will be the following:
[The interior designer outlines the scope of services in a logical sequence.]

Compensation

The client agrees to pay the interior designer a fee of:
[The fees and expenses to be reimbursed must be clearly described and explained. If it is expected that any other consultants will be needed for the project, a statement must include their fees/costs as well.]

Payment

[This section details how the client will pay any retainers and how the client will be billed for services performed. It is always a good idea to include a late payment clause to help ensure prompt payment.]

Other Terms Applicable to the Project

[This section details any additional terms concerning such things as responsibility of the designer, supervision, additional work, termination, and other clauses deemed appropriate by your attorney and you.]

In Conclusion

[Clauses in this section may be different depending on advice of your attorney, but the following are common:]

The designer and the client agree that this letter constitutes the complete agreement between the designer and the client. Both parties also agree that disputes are to be handled by a third-party arbitrator.

Your authorized signature on a copy of this agreement and a check for the retainer are necessary before we can begin the services described.

We thank you for the opportunity to submit this agreement.

_____   _____

XYZ Design, LLC   Ms. Jones
Jane Doe, Designer

_____   _____

Date   Date

FIGURE 7-1.

Sample letter of agreement. Items in italics are explanatory comments, not language that would be included in an actual letter of agreement.

CONTRACT FORM AND THE STATUTE OF FRAUDS

Sadly, it is not unusual for interior designers to begin projects for clients without a written contract or agreement. For example, John Smith, an interior designer who owns S.I.D. Interior Design Group, meets with his client, Paul Drummond, and says to him, "My fee for the feasibility study of your restaurant

Common Law

will be $8000." Drummond asks him a few questions and then says, "That will be fine. When can you start?" Have Smith and Drummond entered into a contract for services?

On the face of what we know, yes, because an oral agreement for services has been made by Smith and Drummond. An *oral agreement*, fairly obviously, means an agreement made without any writing. An oral understanding or agreement, however, is not good professional practice in this age of increased litigation and ethical disputes.

An oral contract can be legal, except in some specific instances that require a written contract. Proceeding to design a project on the basis of an oral agreement leaves the designer subject to many potential misunderstandings and disputes. Having a written agreement, whether it is required by statute or not, is simply a professional way of working.

Yet, there remain many interior designers who believe an oral agreement is the best way to work with a client. Perhaps the designer doesn't want to lose the job because she feels the client will be threatened or insulted by the contract. Or perhaps the designer knows the person or the person's reputation and figures it is not necessary to have a written agreement. Whatever the reason, it is simply not a good idea to proceed on the basis of an oral agreement.

As the old saying goes, "An oral contract is as good as the paper it is written on." Some designers have worked for many years "on a handshake" and have never had any problems. Others work with some clients without contracts and use written agreements with other clients. Notwithstanding good luck and familiar clients, an oral contract leaves more room for dispute and misunderstanding. It is simply not good professional practice in the 21st century.

A written agreement is the strongest evidence a designer has to show that a contract for services exists between the client and the designer. A court always prefers written evidence over someone's word when it is determining the facts. Although an oral agreement might be considered legal by many judges, a written contract indicates definite parameters that a judge can use to make a determination should a dispute occur. Although it is true that an occasional client's feelings may be bruised by the offer of a contract, it is better to lose an occasional client than to experience costly and time-consuming contractual disputes. A written contract helps protect the designer; it also helps to protect the client if the designer fails to fulfill his or her obligations to the client.

Because it is harder to determine performance or lack of performance when only an oral agreement exists, there is more opportunity for fraud and perjury when disputes occur. Laws or statutes prohibiting fraud and perjury in relation to oral contracts are enacted to reduce the opportunity for fraud when two parties enter into some sort of agreement. These statutes prescribe when a contract must be in writing and the form of that contract.

The Statute of Frauds is standardized law included in the Uniform Commercial Code that all states have adopted. In addition, each state has its own Statute of Frauds to clarify issues the state feels are important to that jurisdiction. Of the six types of contracts that must be in writing, three relate to the interior designer: (1) contracts that cannot be completed within one year of their origination, (2) contracts for the sale of goods, and (3) contracts for the sale of real estate. There are other situations in which the contract must be in writing, but these do not apply to the work of an interior designer. Additional information on the Statute of Frauds with reference to the sale of goods and agreements for the sale of goods is presented in Chapter 9.

so bored

Contract Performance That Will Take More than One Year

The Statute of Frauds requires that a contract for services that cannot be fulfilled in one year be in writing. These large-scale, complex projects should never be undertaken without a written contract. Good business practices dictate that any project that will take less than one year should also be in writing, but this is not legally required by the Statute of Frauds. The time period begins one day after the contract is agreed to by both parties.

Contract for Sale of Goods

Interior designers often take orders for furniture and furnishings without obtaining any written agreement from the client. Many of these same designers sometimes find themselves owning furniture and furnishings that their clients have refused to accept.

The Statute of Frauds requires that a written contract or agreement be in existence for the sale of any goods for an amount over $500. Changes in the UCC have raised the minimum to $5000. However, because not all jurisdictions have adopted this higher number, the designer should check with his or her accountant or attorney to be sure what the minimum is in the designer's area.

This sales agreement need not be as formal a contract as those for services. The writing should state quantity, provide a description, and set out the terms of the agreement; it must be signed by the party or parties involved. The agreement can be very informal or completed on an appropriately designed sales agreement form (illustrated in Chapter 13). The written contract or agreement provides more authority for the designer to obligate the client to pay for the goods.

Contract for the Sale of Real Estate

At one time or another, almost everyone becomes involved in the sale of real estate. The interior designer might purchase an office or studio location rather than lease office space. Of course, he or she will also likely purchase a private residence. A contract for the sale of *real estate*, which is any land and buildings, plants, trees, or anything else affixed to the land, must always be in writing. Any oral contract for this kind of transaction is not binding on either party.

DEVELOPING THE DESIGN CONTRACT

Gathering of the information needed to develop a design contract begins at the time of the initial meeting with the client. Only rarely will you be able to offer a complete contract to the client at this initial meeting. You should also not be overeager to quote specific design fees at the initial meeting. You should consider your fees after you have the information you need to make that determination. The initial meeting is to get to know the client and the project, and for the client(s) to get to know you. What is critical here is to gather the information you need to write your design contract.

Table 7-1 lists some of the questions that must be answered before a design contract is drafted. To enhance the quality of the contract, it is important that questions such as those in the table are answered before the contract is prepared.

Designers regularly use questionnaires or other forms to help them obtain the necessary information from the client (see Figure 7-2). Depending on the exact nature of the project, other stakeholders, such as an architect, engineer, and employees for commercial projects, may provide additional information

TABLE 7-1.

Typical questions used as the basis of design contract preparation

Who are the owners?
What is the exact location of project?
What spaces will be involved in the project?
Is the project new construction or a remodeling project?
What is the square footage of the project?
Does the owner occupy or lease the building?
Will designer/client CAD networking be required?
What is the budget? Is it realistic for the proposed project?
Has a credit check been initiated?
What is the targeted completion date? Is it realistic?
Are architectural floor plans available, or will the space need to be site-measured?
Have you worked with this client before?
Has the client worked with a designer before?
Will presentation graphics, such as perspectives, be required? What media is appropriate?
Does the current design staff have the time and experience to do this project?
Will consultants or additional staff be required in order to do this project?
If it is a remodeling project, what code requirements must be researched and met?
If it is new construction, who is the architect?
Does the designer have the licenses required to perform remodeling design work?
Who and how will the contractors be selected?
What kind of presentation will be required at preliminary and final meetings?
Will sample and image presentation boards be required?
If it is new construction, what code requirements must be researched and met?
Who will obtain permits?
How much demolition is expected?
How much supervision must be done on site?
Will the project go out to bid, or has a purchasing agreement already been established?
Will the project be completed all at once or be done in stages?
What portion of the construction or interiors project will be handled by the client?
Does the client require moving services, or will the client take care of this himself or herself?
How much existing furniture will be used?
Who is responsible for production of construction documents?
What styles of new furniture are preferred?
Are new architectural finishes to be selected?
Are custom cabinets, custom furniture items, or treatments expected?
Are office systems furniture (or other furniture) evaluations required prior to specifications?
Will art, graphics, accessories, interior plantscaping be required?

Note: This list, of course, is not all-inclusive.

necessary for the interior designer to complete the contract and subsequent project requirements. Figure 7-2 has been included on the companion Web site as Item 7-2.

It is unfortunate that interior designers are sometimes tempted to work with a client on a project when their capabilities to do the project are questionable. The designer should not enter into a design contract for a project if the designer is not competent and capable of performing the work required. Errors can be costly in terms of both finances and reputation. If the project is something the designer wants to do in order to gain experience, the designer might consider setting up a joint venture with an experienced designer. Otherwise, the designer should steer clear of working on any project or in any area in which his or her skills are marginal.

Project Information

Date of contact: _____

Project #: _____

Designer: _____

Appointment date: _____

Appointment time: _____

☐ Existing clients   ☐ New clients

Move-in date: _____

Client: _____

Project Location: _____

Address: _____

Address: _____

Phone: _____

Phone: _____

Cell: _____

Cell: _____

Email: _____

Email: _____

Project area involved:

Budget:

Site conditions:
☐ New construction
☐ Renovation
☐ Renovation—finishes only
☐ Movable FF&E only
☐ Other: _____

Architect: _____

Scope of Services:
(Attach Fee Estimate Form)

© Christine M. Piotrowski, 2012

FIGURE 7-2.

A type of form that designers can use to obtain detailed information about the design project in order to prepare the design contract.

Expected Deliverables:
- ☐ Design concept statement
- ☐ Programming report
- ☐ Presentation documents
    - Specify in Notes
- ☐ Purchase proposals

- ☐ Full construction documents
- ☐ Partial construction documents
    - specify in Notes
- ☐ Bid documents
- ☐ Other

Expected Staffing
- ☐ Principal
- ☐ Senior designer
- ☐ Project manager
- ☐ Design assistant
- ☐ Consultant:
- ☐ Consultant:

- ☐ Clerical
- ☐ Warehouse service
- ☐ Other

Reimbursable expenses:
- ☐ Travel: airfare, hotel per diem:
- ☐ Ground transportation
- ☐ Misc. travel
- ☐ Printing/copying documents
- ☐ Other

Notes:

FIGURE 7-2.

(*Continued*)

CONTENT FORMALITIES

An enforceable written contract does not have to be full of legalese and confusing language. So, then, what does *writing* mean? The written contract should be intelligible and readable and printed on the design firm's stationery. It can be in letter form, a memo, or even written on a napkin or an envelope (although these latter are not recommended). It can even be a telegram or electronic document.

There is no ideal way to write a design contract that will cover all the contingencies of how you offer your services. With the assistance of your attorney, you will probably develop a variety of contracts. These different contracts should focus on the various kinds of business in which the design firm is engaged. ASID and the AIA have standardized contracts that have been carefully developed based on input from interior designers and attorneys who specialize in contract law. Members of the professional organizations can obtain copies of these standardized contracts from the national office. In some cases, these documents are available to nonmembers as well.

Interior designers often send purchase orders via fax or e-mail. Commercial clients might utilize an electronic signature feature on contracts and agreements if that is acceptable to the interior designer. Electronic transaction laws help clarify that a paper-and-pen record is not always required if a properly executed electronic record is produced. However, care must be taken when accepting an electronically signed agreement for services or products, as not all states have passed legislation permitting this type of agreement. It is important to discuss this matter with your attorney.

The Uniform Electronic Transaction Act of 1999 (UETA) and the Electronic Signatures in Global and National Commerce Act of 2001 (ESIGN) are model laws adopted by most of the states that help to enforce contracts transmitted electronically.[3] The Uniform Commercial Code (UCC) discusses the use of electronic contracts for the sale of goods (see Chapter 9).

A written agreement concerning interior design services—and indeed, almost all forms of contracts—must provide enough information to signify that an agreement has been made between the parties. To be more specific, to be fully enforceable a contract must include the following information:

- Date
- Parties involved
- What services are to be provided
- How fees are to be charged and the terms of payment
- Signatures of the parties, especially the party being charged—the client

The next section of this chapter discusses each of these elements, as well as other terms that are often appropriate. Remember that this chapter discusses contracts for design services. Contracts for the sale of goods are covered in Chapter 9.

INTERIOR DESIGN CONTRACTS: CONTENT AND FORM

Clients have high expectations of interior designer performance regardless of the type or size of the project. A design contract for services serves as an effective promise of what the interior designer will do for the client. Carefully prepared contracts start with understanding the parts and pieces of what is commonly included.

This important section provides explanations of common clauses supplemented by examples that help the reader see these clauses in context of different types of projects. It is not possible to offer samples to satisfy every situation. Also, these sample contracts and clauses should not be used without examination by and the advice of the practitioner's attorney, to be sure the language suits the needs of the particular firm and project.

It is fairly obvious that a connection exists between the client and the interior designer to complete a project. In legal terminology, that connection is referred to as an agency relationship. In common law, an *agency relationship* arises when one person or entity agrees to represent or do business for another person or entity. Agency relationships exist between an interior designer and the client when the designer provides design services to the client and when the interior designer places orders for merchandise for the client that are purchased directly through the interior designer's company.

It is important for the designer to be sure that the contract for services spells out the scope of the designer's authority as an agent for the client. In many respects, this is accomplished primarily through the scope-of-services clauses in the contract and appropriate clauses suggested by the designer's attorney.

TABLE 7-2.

A checklist of typical types of clauses found in design contracts

1. Date
2. Client's name and address
3. Detailed description of project areas involved
4. Detailed scope of services to be provided
5. Detailed purchasing arrangements
6. Price guarantees
7. Method and payment of compensation
8. Reimbursements for out-of-pocket expenses
9. Charges for extra services
10. Designer responsibility disclaimer
11. Charges and responsibilities of third parties
12. Photographic and publishing rights
13. Termination of contract
14. Responsibilities of the client
15. Assignment and delegation
16. Ownership of documents
17. Time frame of the contract
18. Matters of arbitration
19. Mutual understanding and legality
20. Conditions and amount of retainer
21. Signatures

Handwritten margin notes:

Design Fees:
- Hourly
- Fixed
- Hourly w/ gauranteed max
- Square Footage Fee

→ by activity, not by person

Scope of services must be clear

Providing the drawings and specifications as spelled out in the contract is an example of the designer fulfilling his or her role in the agency relationship. Ordering merchandise that has not been approved by the client is an example of the designer failing in his or her relationship as an agent for the client.

Both residential and commercial contracts contain the same basic parts. Table 7-2 lists the items commonly found in a contract for interior design services. Some projects do not require all of these clauses; in contrast, a very complex project may require the inclusion of clauses not shown in the figure or discussed in this chapter. We will discuss each item in the list as it relates to residential and commercial projects, noting any differences between the two.

Here are a few additional tips before we discuss each typical clause in detail:

- Use clear, plain language and short sentences if possible.
- Be specific and provide sufficient detail. Ambiguity causes disputes.
- Be sure you spell the client's names/company names correctly.
- Be prepared to discuss why each clause was included.
- Be clear about what you are and are not responsible for.
- Base the types of clauses on type of project, client, and necessity.

Refer to Figures 7-3 through 7-5 for sample contracts. Note that Figure 7-4 has been included on the companion Web site as Item 7-3.

August 31, 20XX
Mr. and Mrs. Michael Hamilton
1479 E. Stanford Drive
Hazelton, Rhode Island

Dear Mr. and Mrs. Hamilton:

This letter will confirm our agreement concerning the professional services we will provide for your residence at 1479 E. Stanford Drive, Hazelton, Rhode Island. It is understood that the project specifically involves the living room, dining room, family room, and kitchen.
    We will provide the following services:

A. Design Concept Services

   1. Measure the existing spaces and prepare sketches or take photos of the existing interior.

   2. Discuss your specific needs and preferences.

   3. Prepare conceptual furniture floor plans.

   4. Make preliminary selections and color schemes for new furniture items to be purchased, as well as selections for walls, floors, and window treatments.

   5. Prepare a preliminary budget for the project.

   6. Review all of the above with you.

B. Purchasing Services

   1. Upon approval of the preliminary selections mentioned above, we will prepare finalized specifications and pricing proposals.

   2. It is understood that all items specified by the interior designer will be purchased only through the interior designer, should you wish to purchase them.

   3. All items to be purchased will be detailed as a specification and will require your signed authorization, as well as 90% of the total price for each item prior to placing the order. The balance, including applicable taxes, shipping, and handling fees, is due upon delivery.

   4. The price for each item shall be the regular or normal wholesale or cost price to the interior designer plus _____% purchase fee plus shipping and handling fees at actual cost. The fee is in addition to Design Concept and Supervision fees, to be described below.

   5. As might be necessary, the designer will provide counsel and guidance in the selection of necessary contractors to perform the required work. Client will enter into any contract for these services directly with the contractor(s).

   6. Periodic visits to the residence will be made to observe that the work is being done in accordance with standard acceptable practice. Constant on-site observations are not part of the designer's responsibilities.

C. Compensation

The fee for the concept and supervision services described will be $_____. Additional services requested by you that are beyond the scope of services outlined in this agreement will be billed separately at $_____ per hour.

Billing for services shall be in the following manner:

20% upon signing the contract (retainer)

40% at the end of the preliminary review meeting

30% when construction and furniture orders are placed

10% upon completion of the project

FIGURE 7-3.

A sample design contract for a residential project.

All payments are due ten days after receipt of invoice.

The above fee does not include client-approved expenses for long-distance telephone calls, out-of-town travel to shop for resources, and special renderings. These charges, if required, will be billed separately at our actual cost plus 10%.

D. Other Matters

1. The drawings and specifications are intended for design concept only and cannot be used for construction or architectural purposes.

2. The designer does not accept any responsibility for the design of structural, electrical, plumbing, heating, or other mechanical systems that exist or might be needed for the project.

3. The drawings and documents prepared by the interior designer remain the property of the design firm and cannot be used by you for any purpose other than the completion of the project by the interior designer.

4. We will perform the services described in good faith but cannot be responsible for the performance, quality, or timely completion of work by others. Further, we shall not be responsible for any changes to the project that the client(s) or contractor(s) make without informing the designer.

5. You are expected to grant reasonable access to the premises for the designer and the designer's agents, as well as to contractors required to perform the agreed-upon work. By signing this proposal, you understand that the peace and privacy of your home may be disrupted for the time required to perform the work.

6. This proposal may be terminated for any reason by either the client or the designer, provided that ten days' written notice has been given. In the event of termination by the client, the client will pay the designer for all work done and expenses due up to the date of termination.

7. Upon completion of the project, the designer may require permission to photograph the project for the firm's records. The interior designer shall not use the photographs for promotional purposes without the permission of the client.

8. This agreement is the complete statement of understanding between the interior designer and the client. No other agreements have been made other than those stated in this agreement. This agreement can only be modified in writing, signed by both parties.

It will be our pleasure to begin your project as soon as we have received a copy of this proposal signed by both of you and a check for the retainer. We appreciate your selection of our firm for your interiors project and look forward to working with you.

Sincerely yours,

EastCoast Interiors, Inc.

Betsy Smith,

_____

(Owner)

_____
Date

_____
Michael Hamilton

_____
Betty Hamilton

FIGURE 7-3.

(*Continued*)

January 30, 20xx

John Smith, Chief Executive Officer

Smith Serve, Inc.

1776 N. Adams

Boston, MA

Dear Mr. Smith:

We are pleased to submit the following proposal of professional interior design services for the space planning and interior design of your new office in Amherst, Massachusetts at [insert project address]

Scope of Service

A. Programming and Schematic Design

  1. Meet with you and/or selected members of your staff to determine all requirements that will affect the space planning and interior design of your project.

  2. Obtain floor plans from the architect.

  3. Inventory existing equipment that might be used in the new space plan.

  4. Conduct interviews with staff to determine equipment needs and adjacency requirements.

  5. Determine project objectives as well as budget considerations.

  6. Review all programming findings with your project committee.

  7. Prepare preliminary schematic layouts.

  8. Develop preliminary furniture, color, and materials selections.

  9. Review schematic layouts, selections, and sketches with your project committee.

B. Design Development

  1. Finalize space plans showing locations of walls, furniture, and built-in equipment.

  2. Finalize selections of all materials, finishes, and treatment for furniture, walls, flooring, windows, and ceilings.

  3. Provide 3-dimensional drawings of typical work stations.

  4. Provide 3-dimensional sketches of lobby and employee "think tank" space.

  5. Finalize lighting specifications with lighting consultant.

  6. Prepare a budget of all interior furnishings.

  7. Present plans and product specifications for your approval.

C. Contract Documents Phase

  1. After final approval of all space plans, furniture layouts, and product selections, prepare appropriate working drawings and documents for the construction of the space and installation of the interiors. This will include dimensioned floor plans, furniture plans, electrical location plans, reflected ceiling plans, and cabinet shop drawings as needed.

  2. Prepare bid specifications for furniture and other movable equipment.

  3. Consult with you on developing the qualified bidder's list.

FIGURE 7-4.

An example of a design contract for a commercial project with an extensive scope of services.

4. Provide information for the preparation of bid specifications for floors, walls, windows, ceilings, and lighting fixture materials or products (bid specification to be written by your facilities department).

5. Coordinate with your facilities department to develop complete set of bid documents.

D. Contract Administration Phase

1. Assist you in obtaining competitive bids for furnishings and equipment.

2. Assist you in coordinating the schedule for delivery and installation of the work.

3. Make periodic visits to the job site to ensure that the work is progressing according to the specifications in the bid documents.

4. Supervise installation of furniture and movable equipment covered in the bid documents.

5. Upon completion of the installation, the designer shall prepare a punch list of items needing attention by the designer or vendors. This will be reviewed with you prior to transmittal to appropriate parties.

Terms of Compensation

For the interior design and consultation services outlined above, you will be billed a fee of $_____ payable according to the following:

You will be invoiced monthly for actual hours worked. Payment is due within ten (10) days of receipt of invoice. A late payment charge of 1-1/2% per month (18% per annum) will be added to invoices thirty (30) days past due. Note that a retainer is required to begin work. The amount is detailed later in this proposal.

The total fee is based on a maximum of two revisions after each client review. Work required or requested beyond the two revisions will be charged at the described hourly fees, but will be in addition to the maximum estimate.

Additional services not outlined in this proposal but requested by you or required after client approval results in changes in the project will be billed separately at an hourly rate of [insert rate].

Fees include provision of six sets of contract documents for the client's use. It is understood that your company is responsible for reproduction of all sets of contract documents required for the bidding process.

Reimbursable Expenses

Reimbursable expenses are in addition to the charges detailed above. Such expenses as out-of-town travel and living expenses, long-distance telephone charges, special renderings, mock-ups, and reproduction costs other than those detailed shall be billed at actual cost to the designer.

Out-of-town travel in the interest of the project shall only be made with proper notification and approval of the client. At this time, it is estimated that a minimum of four site visits will be necessary during the progress of the project.

General Conditions

1. The designer shall not be responsible for the quality, workmanship, or appearance of products should you purchase products other than those specified.

2. The designer is not responsible if you, architect, or contractor(s) make changes to the project without notification to the designer.

FIGURE 7-4.

(*Continued*)

3. The designer or representatives of the designer reserves the right to photograph the project upon completion in order to provide a record of the project. The design firm shall have the right to use these photographs for business purposes.

4. This contract does not include provision for fees by third-party consultants required to complete the project. Contracts for these services will be negotiated separately and their contract negotiations must be completed within twenty (20) days after the date of execution of this contract.

5. You shall make provision for the design firm and/or its agents to have access to the project site as needed for the completion of the project in a timely fashion.

6. This proposal may be terminated by either party upon seven (7) days written notice. In the event of termination by you, you shall pay the designer for all services performed and reimbursable expenses due up to the date of termination.

7. Drawings, specifications, and sample boards, as instruments of service, are the property of the designer. The designer reserves the exclusive copyright to these items and provides them to you for your use on this project only. Any reproduction or reuse of the drawings, specifications, and sample boards without the prior written consent of the designer is not permitted.

8. The timely completion of this project and the fees quoted are based on this signed return of this proposal to the designer within ten (10) calendar days.

9. Any controversy or claims arising out of or relating to this project or breach thereof shall be subject to review and settled by arbitration in Massachusetts. Arbitration shall be in accordance with the rules of the American Arbitration Association. The decisions of the arbitrator shall be final and binding on both parties.

10. This contract represents the complete understanding between the designer and the client. Changes and modifications must be made in writing and signed by both parties.

Approval of this proposal is signified by your signature in the space below. Work will begin on your project when the designer receives a signed copy of this proposal along with a check for a retainer of [insert retainer amount].

We would like to thank you for the opportunity to submit this proposal for professional interior design services. We look forward to a set of challenges which we pledge to meet with our best professional efforts and attention.

Sincerely,

Authorized:

Columbia Interior Design, Inc.

_____

Smith Services

_____

(Design Director)

_____

(By)

_____

(Date)

_____

(Title)

_____

(Date)

FIGURE 7-4.

(*Continued*)

ASID Document ID123

RESIDENTIAL INTERIOR DESIGN
SERVICES AGREEMENT

This **AGREEMENT** is

made this _____ day of _____ in the year of Two Thousand and _____

BETWEEN the **CLIENT**:
(name and address)

---

and the **DESIGNER**:
(name and address)

The **CLIENT** and the **DESIGNER** agree as follows:

The Project pertains to the following areas within Client's residence located at

_____ :

(List areas below:)

ID123-1996   1

FIGURE 7-5.

ASID document ID 122: Residential Design Services Agreement (fixed fee). (Reprinted with permission of American Society of Interior Designers, Washington, DC)

INTERIOR DESIGN SERVICES

1. <u>Design Concept Services</u>

1.1 In this phase of the Project, Designer shall, as and where appropriate, perform the following:

    A. Determine Client's design preferences and requirements.

    B. Conduct an initial design study.

    C. Prepare drawings and other materials to generally illustrate Designer's suggested interior design concepts, to include color schemes, interior finishes, wall coverings, floor coverings, ceiling treatments, lighting treatments and window treatments.

    D. Prepare layout showing location of movable furniture and furnishings.

    E. Prepare schematic plans for recommended cabinet work, interior built-ins and other interior decorative details ("Interior Installations").

1.2 Prior to commencing Design Concept Services, Designer shall receive an Initial Design Fee of _____ dollars ($_____). This non-refundable Design Fee is payable upon signing this Agreement and is in addition to all other compensation payable to Designer under this Agreement. Not more than_____ (____) revisions to the Design Concept will be prepared by Designer without additional charges. Additional revisions will be billed to Client as Additional Services.

2. <u>Interior Specifications and Purchasing Services</u>

2.1 Upon Client's approval of the Design Concepts, Designer will, as and where appropriate:

    A. Select and/or specially design required Interior Installations and all required items of movable furniture, furnishings, light fixtures, hardware, fixtures, accessories and the like ("Merchandise").

    B. Prepare and submit for Client's approval Proposals for completion of Interior Installations and purchase of Merchandise.

    ID123-1996 2

FIGURE 7-5.

(Continued)

2.2 Merchandise and Interior Installations specified by Designer shall, if Client wishes to purchase them, be purchased solely through Designer. Designer may, at times, request Client to engage others to provide Interior Installations, pursuant to the arrangements set forth in the Project Review services described in paragraph 3 of this Agreement.

2.3 Merchandise and Interior Installations to be purchased through Designer will be specified in a written "Proposal" prepared by Designer and submitted in each instance for Client's written approval. Each Proposal will describe the item and its price to Client (F.O.B. point of origin). The price of each item to Client ("Client Price") shall be the amount charged to Designer by the supplier of such item ("Supplier Price"), plus Designer's fee equal to _____ percent (____%) of the Supplier Price (exclusive of any freight, delivery or like charges or applicable tax).

2.4 No item can be ordered by Designer until the Proposal has been approved by Client, in writing, and returned to Designer with Designer's required initial payment equal to _____ percent (____%) of the Client Price. The balance of the Client Price, together with delivery, shipping, handling charges and applicable taxes, is payable when the item is ready for delivery to and/or installation at Client's residence, or to a subsequent supplier for further work upon rendition of Designer's invoice. Proposals for fabrics, wall coverings, accessories, antiques, and items purchased at auction or at retail stores require full payment at time of signed Proposal.

3. Project Review

3.1 If the nature of the Project requires engagement by Client of any contractors to perform work based upon Designer's concepts, drawings or interior design specifications not otherwise provided for in the Interior Specifications and Purchasing Services, Client will enter into contracts directly with the concerned contractor. Client shall provide Designer with copies of all contracts and invoices submitted to Client by the contractors.

3.2 Designer will make periodic visits to the Project site as Designer may consider appropriate to observe the work of these contractors to determine whether the contractors' work is proceeding in general conformity with Designer's concepts. Constant observation of work at the Project site is not a part of Designer's duties. Designer is not responsible for the performance, quality, timely completion or delivery of any work, materials or equipment furnished by contractors pursuant to direct contracts with Client.

3.3 Designer shall be entitled to receive a fee equal to _____ percent (___%) of the amount to be paid by Client to each contractor performing any work based upon Designer's concepts, drawings, specifications ("Project Review Fees").

ID123-1996 **3**

FIGURE 7-5.

(Continued)

3.4 The Project Review Fees shall be payable by Client to Designer as follows:

4. MISCELLANEOUS

4.1 Should Designer agree to perform any design service not described above, such "Additional Service" will be invoiced to Client at the following hourly rates:

Design Principal	$_____
Project Designer	$_____
Staff Designer	$_____
Draftsman	$_____
Other employees	$_____

Hourly charges will be invoiced to Client _____ and are payable upon receipt of invoice.

4.2 Disbursements incurred by Designer in the interest of the Project shall be reimbursed by Client to Designer upon receipt of Designer's invoices, which are rendered _____. Reimbursements shall include, among other things, costs of local and long distance travel, long distance telephone calls, duplication of plans, drawings and specifications, messenger services and the like.

4.3 Designer's drawings and specifications are conceptual in nature and intended to set forth design intent only. They are not to be used for architectural or engineering purposes. Designer does not provide architectural or engineering services.

4.4 Designer's services shall not include undertaking any responsibility for the design or modification of the design of any structural, heating, air-conditioning, plumbing, electrical, ventilation or other mechanical systems installed or to be installed at the Project.

4.5 Should the nature of Designer's design concepts require the services of any other design professional, such professional shall be engaged directly by Client pursuant to separate agreement as may be mutually acceptable to Client and such other design professional.

4.6 As Designer requires a record of Designer's design projects, Client will permit Designer or Designer's representatives to photograph the Project upon completion of the Project. Designer will be entitled to use photographs for Designer's business purposes but shall not disclose Project location or Client's name without Client's prior written consent.

ID123-1996   **4**

FIGURE 7-5.

(Continued)

4.7   All concepts, drawings and specifications prepared by Designer's firm ("Project Documents") and all copyrights and other proprietary rights applicable thereto remain at all times Designer's property. Project Documents may not be used by Client for any purpose other than completion of Project by Designer.

4.8   Designer cannot guarantee that actual prices for Merchandise and/or Interior Installations or other costs or services as presented to Client will not vary either by item or in the aggregate from any Client proposed budget.

4.9   This Agreement may be terminated by either party upon the other party's default in performance, provided that termination may not be effected unless written notice specifying nature and extent of default is given to the concerned party and such party fails to cure such default in performance within _____ (____) days from date of receipt of such notice. Termination shall be without prejudice to any and all other rights and remedies of Designer, and Client shall remain liable for all outstanding obligations owed by Client to Designer and for all items of Merchandise, Interior Installations and other services on order as of the termination date.

4.10   In addition to all other legal rights, Designer shall be entitled to withhold delivery of any item of Merchandise or the further performance of Interior Installations or any other services, should Client fail to timely make any payments due Designer.

4.11   Any controversy or claim arising out of or relating to this Agreement, or the breach thereof, shall be decided by arbitration only in the _____ in accordance with the Commercial Arbitration Rules of the American Arbitration Association then in effect, and judgment upon the award rendered by the arbitrator(s) may be entered in any court having jurisdiction thereof.

4.12   Client will provide Designer with access to the Project and all information Designer may need to complete the Project. It is Client's responsibility to obtain all approvals required by any governmental agency or otherwise in connection with this Project.

4.13   Any sales tax applicable to Design Fees, and/or Merchandise purchased from Designer, and/or Interior Installations completed by Designer shall be the responsibility of Client.

4.14   Neither Client nor Designer may assign their respective interests in this Agreement without the written consent of the other.

4.15   The laws of the State of _____ shall govern this Agreement.

4.16   Any provision of this Agreement held to be void or unenforceable under any law shall be deemed stricken, and all remaining provisions shall continue to be valid and binding upon both Designer and Client.

4.17   This Agreement is a complete statement of Designer's and Client's understanding. No representations or agreements have been made other than those contained in this Agreement. This Agreement can be modified only by a writing signed by both Designer and Client.

ID123-1996   **5**

FIGURE 7-5.

(Continued)

5. ADDITIONAL TERMS

CLIENT:

_____

_____

DESIGNER:

_____

_____

ID123-1996   6

FIGURE 7-5.

(_Continued_)

These items are discussed in the typical order in which they would appear in a contract.

1. *Date.* Contracts must be dated with the day, month, and year.

2. *Client's name and address.* The name of the client and the client's billing address are identified at the beginning of the contract. In residential design, it is important for both the husband's and wife's (or partners') names to be on the contract and for both to sign the contract. This obligates each in the event of divorce, separation, or death of either of the partners.

   In commercial design, the name of the person having the authority to contract for the business should be listed. That is the person who should sign the contract. The address of the home office is listed when the business has several locations, unless someone at a branch location has the authority to sign the contract.

3. *Detailed description of project areas involved.* The areas involved in the contract should be detailed. This clarification helps to avoid confusion and arguments over extra charges or threats of breach. In a residential project, this may mean including a clause as broad as "your residence at 1234 Hummingbird Lane," which means the designer is responsible for the scope of services to be defined in the contract for the entire house. If the services relate only to the living room, the contract should state this.

   A contract for a commercial project often must be even more specific. If the address of the project is different from the main office, that fact should be noted and the project address listed. It may be necessary to list the specific area by department or room and even the amount of square footage. "The main dining room, foyer, and meeting rooms, but excluding the kitchen of your restaurant at the Harbor Hotel, San Diego" is a clear definition of what rooms in what building are covered by the contract. Saying "your restaurant at the Harbor Hotel" leaves the designer open to a lot of unplanned additional design.

   Should the client want additional areas to be included beyond what was originally described, the designer can prepare a secondary contract or addendum to cover these areas, the services desired, and the additional fees.

4. *Detailed scope of services.* A detailed scope of services leaves little room for disagreements about what is to be done. Using the accepted outline of project phases will create an outline that is easier for the client to understand. Refer to Table 7-3 and Chapter 10 for detailed samples of the range of services that might be required of either a residential or commercial project.

   When a detailed scope of services is identified, there is less opportunity for scope-creep issues to arise. Clients are reluctant to add services they feel the designer should have included in the first place once the project has begun. Designers also should want to be compensated for services the client asks for after the project begins. See item number 9 for further discussion of this issue.

   On-site supervision causes considerable misunderstandings between designer and client. It is important for the designer to be very clear as to the extent of on-site supervision and what the designer can and cannot do during this phase of the project.

TABLE 7-3.

A detailed list of common services for a scope-of-services specification

Scope of Services

Programming Phase

Interview client to determine user needs and goals.
Evaluate existing job site or review any drawings for new construction.
Inventory and evaluate existing furniture that might be used in the project.
Obtain scaled floor plans of the project space from the client (the architect or landlord).
Measure job site to obtain necessary dimensions of site.
Determine style, color, etc. preferences.
Meet with landlord (if needed) concerning building standards and regulations.
Ascertain potential building code, life safety code, and barrier-free regulations as might affect the project.
Evaluate special needs such as sustainability, functional restrictions, and aging in place.
Develop project schedule.
Develop project budget.
Coordinate (if needed) with appropriate consultants.
Determine feasibility of meeting the client's requirements.
Determine and inform the client of any restraints that will affect the feasibility of the project.
Prepare final design program.

Schematic Design

Develop spatial and communication adjacencies.
Develop preliminary space utilization plans.
Prepare preliminary furniture plans.
Prepare preliminary selections of interior architectural finishes.
Prepare preliminary furniture, furnishings, and equipment selections.
Review applicable building, life safety, and accessibility codes, and apply as required.
Make preliminary color selections.
Refine budgets.
Prepare design drawings, such as perspectives, elevations, etc., as needed.
Meet with consultants, such as architect, contractors, or others as required.

Design Development

Finalize relationship diagrams or charts.
Complete space plans and layouts.
Complete furniture, furnishings, and equipment plans.
Complete working drawings concerning custom furniture, cabinets, or architectural treatments.
Determine specifications of architectural finishes.
Prepare specifications of furniture, furnishings, and equipment.
Prepare other drawings, such as lighting plans, elevations, and sections, etc., as required.
Prepare presentation boards or other presentation media.
Prepare presentation graphics, such as renderings of perspectives, isometrics, or axonometric drawings.
Prepare a budget of expected costs for all construction and furnishings, as specified.

Contract Documents

Prepare working drawings and schedules for the construction and/or installation of the space.
Prepare written specifications to accompany working drawings, schedules, and furniture, furnishings, and equipment.
Prepare furniture and equipment installation drawings.
Obtain approvals and permits from jurisdictional agencies.
Provide or assist client with the preparation of bid documents.
Qualify vendors, suppliers, and subcontractors.
Assist client in obtaining competitive bids for all phases of the project.
Provide guidance in the selection of necessary contractors.
Assist client with owner-contractor contacts.
Coordinate with project stakeholders such as architect and contractors.

(Continued)

TABLE 7-3.

(*Continued*)

Contract Administration
Assist with securing of bids and pricing.
Provide project management supervision of the job site during construction/installation.
Procure furniture and furnishings by submitting purchase orders to suppliers and installers.
Assist in the procurement of furniture and furnishings through bid administration.
Make periodic visits to the jobsite to ensure the work is being done in accordance with the contract documents and specifications.
Supervise installation of furniture, furnishings, and equipment.
Maintain project management and schedule records.
Assist in determination of substantial completion, payments to vendors, and securing releases.
Prepare as-built drawings if necessary.
Provide or coordinate FF&E product maintenance information to client.
Prepare and administer postoccupancy evaluations.

Note: This list suggests a wide range of services and is not meant to be all-inclusive.

Designers must also be careful when using words such as *supervise* or *manage* in relation to the installation of interior finishing materials or any actual construction. All states require that licensed contractors perform construction supervision, and many states also require that only licensed contractors supervise the installation of interior architectural finishing materials. Additional information on this topic appears in Chapter 10.

5. *Detailed purchasing arrangements.* A clause should be included in the design services contract to inform the client of the conditions under which the design firm will be selling any products to the client. This information introduces the client to the design firm's policies concerning the ordering of goods for clients. However, it is not necessary to spell out all the conditions related to sales of goods here, as those conditions will be made in the separate sales contracts.

The minimal information that should be covered in this clause is how the client will be charged for furniture and furnishings; the terms of payment; penalties for cancellation of orders; the design firm's responsibilities regarding warranties of goods sold; charges for installation, freight, sales tax, and delivery costs; and whether there is a late payment penalty on the sale of goods. Detailed confirmation proposals signed by the client should be part of these policies. This paperwork item is discussed in Chapter 13.

An additional clause or statement should have specific language regarding what happens if the client purchases the goods specified from someone other than the designer. If goods are purchased from someone else, the designer will not receive compensation, unless the contract specifies otherwise.

As part of completing the installation of certain types of goods, such as carpeting and wall treatments, it is necessary to procure outside sources or contractors to perform these services. In some cases, the interior designer will want the client to hire these outside contractors directly, rather than having to do so himself or herself. This section of the contract should inform the client as to expectations and requirements in this regard. Once again, this service might require the interior designer to have a license from the appropriate jurisdiction, as discussed in Chapter 10.

6. *Price guarantees*. An important clause that ASID recommends deals with price guarantees. Interior design projects often last many months, and may extend through a year or more. It is quite possible for the prices for products and services to increase as the project moves from conceptualization through design development and final client approvals. Although the designer is responsible for maintaining a tight control on the budget and for keeping the client informed of any price increases, a price guarantee clause helps to provide some protection for the designer if the actual bid prices of construction and goods increase over time.

7. *Method and payment of compensation*. This is one of the truly critical clauses, as it helps a judge determine valid consideration for services rendered. The compensation section is the most common changeable part in standardized contracts. Table 7-4 provides examples of wording for three common compensation methods. An interior design firm is likely to have two or more different standard methods of explaining compensation, as it is rare for a firm to charge the same way for all projects.

TABLE 7-4.

Sample compensation clauses for three different ways of charging design fees

Hourly Fee

1. For the design services as described, you will be charged on an hourly fee basis of _____ per hour. You will be invoiced monthly for all hours actually worked.
2. Compensation for the design services described will be billed:

_____ per hour for Principals
_____ per hour for Senior Designers
_____ per hour for Project Managers
_____ per hour for Designers
_____ per hour for Design Assistants
_____ per hour for Draftspersons/CAD

Fixed-Fee Method

1. The design fixed fee for this project will be _____. You will be billed as follows:
   20 percent upon signing of contract as a retainer
   20 percent at the end of the preliminary review meeting
   40 percent at the completion of the preparation of drawings and specifications
   10 percent when construction begins and purchase orders are placed
   10 percent upon completion of the project
2. The design fee for basic services will be _____. You will be billed as follows:
   _____ Percent upon signing of contract as a retainer
   _____ Percent upon completion of Programming
   _____ Percent upon completion of Schematic Design
   _____ Percent upon completion of Design Development
   _____ Percent upon completion of Construction Documents
   _____ Percent upon completion of the project

Cost Plus Percentage Markup

1. Design Consultation
   The designer will be compensated for consultation services as described under the scope of services on an hourly basis at the rate of _____ per hour. Client will be invoiced on a monthly basis. Upon signing this agreement, the client shall provide _____ as a nonrefundable retainer for design consultation services. (Note that a flat fee could be substituted for an hourly rate.)

(Continued)

TABLE 7-4.

(*Continued*)

2. Purchasing Services
   The designer will be compensated at a cost plus percentage of markup on a basis of a _____ mark-up percentage of cost of furniture, furnishings, and equipment specified. Cost will be defined as the Designer's cost as stated by the manufacturer or supplier's invoice. The client will be required to pay an initial payment of _____ of the expected invoice cost prior to orders actually being placed with the supplier. The balance will be due upon delivery.
   Products specified shall be purchased only through the interior designer.
   (There are many other ways of stating the purchasing services section of a contract.)

Note that these examples may not include all the phrases or clauses you may wish to include in your agreements/contracts. Actual wording should be reviewed with your attorney.

Your contract should also specify payment terms, including how the client will be billed and whether there will be any penalties for late payment. Such clauses as "payments are due upon receipt," "payment is due upon receipt of invoice," or possibly "payments are due within 10 days" are needed to clarify how quickly the designer expects the client to send payment. Late-payment penalties are common in business and provide your only recourse should the client not pay on time. Discuss this clause with your attorney to ensure that it conforms to the laws of the jurisdiction.

8. *Reimbursements for out-of-pocket expenses.* Out-of-pocket expenses, more commonly referred to as *reimbursable expenses*, are those expenses that are not part of the design contract but that are made in the interest of completing the project. These expenses are something that the client should pay for but are often charged separately from the design fee. Some designers refer to these charges as *disbursements*. Note that some firms do not charge for reimbursable expenses, but instead calculate them as overhead expenses when determining the fee.

   A few examples include:

   • Travel by the interior designer to an out-of-state jobsite
   • Long-distance telephone calls
   • Postage
   • Printing of plans and drawings
   • Express shipping of plans to contractors or others
   • Overtime
   • The cost of renderings, models, and mock-ups

   Travel, whether to meet with clients or others involved in the project, to get to the jobsite, or even to take the client to showrooms at a distant location, is the most expensive type of reimbursable. *Per diem* ("for each day") refers to a fixed dollar amount that is allowed to cover hotel, meals, and transportation costs for client-approved travel.

   Most firms charge reimbursable expenses at actual cost. Some, however, add a service charge to the expense. If a service charge will be added, this should be clearly stated in the contract. Many firms only put a clause concerning reimbursable expenses in the contract if they anticipate out-of-town travel, the need for renderings or models, or an unusually high amount of other kinds of expenses.

9. *Charges for extra services.* "While you are working here, can you also redesign the master bath?" There is always the chance that the client will ask you to design additional areas or provide services beyond those described in the contract. Certainly discuss this additional work, but never work on additional spaces or provide additional services until an addendum or memorandum to the original contract has been executed.

This clause protects the designer from having to perform extra design services for free. It also informs the client as to how other work can be added to the contract or done at the same time, and how the client will be charged for the additional work. Many designers who use an hourly rate charge extra services at a higher rate than stated in the original contract.

What should you do if the client makes changes to the project after certain phases of work have been completed? Another clause in this section spells out extra charges to be incurred if this happens. For example, if the designer has already received approval for the overall space plan and the client subsequently requests changes, the designer should be compensated for the additional work. This clause covers extra work required by the client, not work needed due to a mistake or omission by the designer, so compensation for redoing the work is appropriate.

10. *Designer responsibility disclaimer.* This section describes any portions of the project for which the designer cannot claim responsibility or be held liable. For example, perhaps the client wants another company to plan the lighting for the interior. This clause clarifies that the design firm claims no responsibility for the lighting design. A disclaimer clause informs the client that the interior designer is not responsible for errors made by others.

Many times the interior designer notes that there are certain services he or she cannot render or limitations on the work that the designer can do on a project. Here are several examples:

- The interior designer might not be permitted to prepare construction drawings. Errors should be the responsibility of those who do prepare the drawings.

- If the client purchases products other than those specified, the designer should not be responsible for the quality, workmanship, or performance of those products.

- When the owner, architect, or contractor makes changes to the project or site without the designer's consent or knowledge, the designer cannot be held responsible for the effects of such changes on product orders or installation of items that were the responsibility of the designer.

These examples highlight only a few of the situations that can affect the work of the interior designer for which he or she cannot be held responsible—assuming the clause is included in the contract.

11. *Charges and responsibilities of third parties.* You might think of this clause as a companion to the disclaimer clause regarding designer responsibility. When a *third-party* consultant is required for a project, such as a commercial kitchen consultant for a restaurant, these charges should be billed directly to the client by the third party rather than by the interior designer. Short meetings with consultants are

ordinarily included as part of the project, but the work any consultants may have to do for the project should be considered a separate service. The designer should still charge for the time that he or she spends with the third party.

12. *Photographic and publishing rights.* A portfolio of projects is an important marketing tool for all design firms. Although it is unlikely that every project will be photographed, it should be standard practice to include a clause in all contracts permitting the designer to photograph projects. Clients should be informed up front how the designer intends to use the photographs of the project for publication. Some clients may object to allowing this kind of intrusion. In some commercial installations, it may be against company policy because of security reasons. When clients object to having their living or working quarters photographed, the designer may be able to get permission if he or she does not publish the name of the client. Remember that releases must also be obtained from any recognizable people in the photographs, even if the owner of the space has given permission to photograph the interior.

13. *Termination of contract.* A termination clause is included to ensure compensation for services rendered in the event that the project ends for some reason *other than* by the designer's wishes. For example, if the client runs out of money, cannot take the space, and must end the project, it is important for the designer to be paid for design work that has already been done. Without this kind of clause, it is more difficult for the designer to collect any fees. One example of wording is: "In the event the project is terminated through no fault of the designer, the designer will be compensated for all work actually performed." Other wording may be recommended by the firm's attorney to meet specific needs of the firm.

14. *Responsibilities of the client.* Certain tasks in some projects might have to be the responsibility of the client. For example, providing approvals expeditiously is a client responsibility. It might be necessary for the client to obtain permits and approvals. The client must provide reasonable access to the jobsite and provide a place to receive, unpack, and store products prior to installation on the jobsite. For a commercial project, it is also necessary for the owner of the building or site to designate an employee as a liaison between the designer and the owner.

15. *Assignment and delegation.* Sometimes an unforeseen event prevents the designer (or even the client) from fulfilling the contract. For example, the designer/owner of a sole proprietorship might become ill, or the client may sell the property to someone else while the project is being designed. When unforeseen incidents occur, it might be necessary to turn over the work on and/or responsibility for the project to someone else. If the rights in a contract are transferred to another party, it is called *assignment*; if they are given to someone else, it is called *delegation*.[4] The assignment and delegation clause requires that the assignment or delegation of responsibility of either party to another cannot be done without written notice to and consent by the other party. Such clauses are highly recommended.

16. *Ownership of documents*. As you will recall from the discussion of copyright in Chapter 4, design ideas executed as drawings and specifications belong to the interior designer and are provided for use to the client. Many clients do not understand why they do not own the drawings, since they are paying for the production of the drawings. Your answer relates to copyright, and a copyright notice should appear on all drawings.

   A sample clause might read: "Documents and specifications are provided for the fair use by the client in completing the project as listed within this contract. Documents and specifications remain the property of the designer and cannot be used or reused without permission of the designer." This will clarify the issue. This clause also helps prevent the drawings from being copied or imitated without the designer receiving fair compensation.

17. *Time frame of the contract*. The time frame of or time limit on a contract is an important part of the offer. A time limit on acceptance of the contract is important to be sure the project can be completed by a move-in date. A sample clause is: "To complete the project as specified in the scope of services, the signed contract must be received by the designer no later than June 20, 20xx." This should help clients to make up their minds quickly as to whether they will engage the designer.

   When a project is expected to last longer than one year, the designer should consider renegotiating a portion of the fee for the long-term completion. Of course, this should be taken into consideration when the contract is first drawn up. This type of clause often comes into play when the designer is on retainer for an extended period of time. In this relationship or situation, design work may be scattered over time, and it may be necessary for the design firm to renegotiate a fair increase in its fees every so often.

18. *Matters of arbitration*. Although no one wants to think that a disagreement will occur during a project, something might happen to disturb the designer–client relationship. All contracts should include a clause specifying arbitration as the means of resolving contractual conflicts and disputes that cannot be resolved privately between the designer and the client. *Arbitration* means that rather than going to court, an arbitrator (a disinterested third party) will be called in to listen to the arguments of both sides and then render an opinion as to what must be done. Both client and designer must agree beforehand to abide by the arbitrator's decision.

19. *Mutual understanding and legality*. It is important for designers to add a clause specifically stating that the contract, as written, is the full and complete mutual understanding of the terms and conditions of the agreement. If this clause is included and a claim is later made that there were other arrangements and understandings, the later claim is unlikely to be upheld by a court. For example, a client claims that the designer made some verbal comment that created an addition to the contract or superseded the original intent of the contract. Such a claim will in all likelihood be dismissed because of

the inclusion of this clause. This positive protection for the designer is only one reason why changes to the project that the client requests or that the designer finds are needed should be made in writing as an addendum to the original contract. An example of this clause is found in Figure 7-3.

Along with this clause, the contract should note that the laws of a specific state or province govern the agreement and its interpretation. The specific state or province generally is the one in which the design firm is located, as that is the legal location of the business.

20. *Conditions and amount of retainer.* A *retainer* is an amount of money paid by the client to the designer for professional services that will be done in the future. The retainer is applied by the designer to the total fee of the project as work progresses. In some ways, the retainer acts as "earnest money" from the client, showing the client's good faith in proceeding with the project. If a retainer is expected, the amount and when it is due must be spelled out in the contract. It is also a good idea for the designer to explain briefly how the retainer will be applied to the total fee. Typically, the retainer clause appears at the end of the contract.

    A deposit (or down payment) is similar to a retainer, but it is usually applied toward the purchase of furniture and furnishings. Refer to Chapter 8 for additional information on down payments and deposits.

21. *Signatures.* Space should be provided for the client to sign and date acceptance. Should there be more than one responsible client—such as husband and wife—then both should sign the contract. According to contract law, the person being charged—the client—must sign the contract for it to be enforceable. See the feature box on signatures for more information.

The information and clauses discussed in this section are those that are typically included in contracts or agreements for interior design services. Each contract must be developed to suit the individual project. Certain clauses are considered "boilerplate," meaning that they are very standard and apply to any kind of project. Two examples are the clauses concerning ownership of documents and arbitration. A design firm can create standard contracts and clauses to cover almost all contingencies, and then parts can be "cut and pasted" to make the final contract.

Table 7-5 lists several standard contracts available from ASID that might be suitable for your project. These standardized contracts can be obtained by ordering online from the national office. These contracts may meet the conditions of many normal projects. Space is provided to type in standard information, such as the designer's name and address, and some can be imprinted with the design firm's name. Whatever the final form of the contract is, it should be periodically reviewed by the firm's attorney to be sure that the contract meets the requirements of the firm's individual practice.

TABLE 7-5.

Standard contracts available from ASID

ID 120–1996 Option 1 Residential Contract This form is intended to be used by those setting forth their own description of design services to be rendered and the corresponding compensation method. This document does not contain a description of design services or compensation arrangements.

ID 121–1996 Option 2 Residential Contract The compensation basis in this agreement has language consisting of (a) A fixed initial Design Fee and No Fee Charged on Purchases; or (b) A Fixed Initial Design Fee and Fees Charged on Purchases.

ID 122–1996 Option 3 Residential Contract The compensation basis in this agreement has language consisting of (a) A Fixed Fee and a Fee Charged on Purchases.

ID 123–1996 Option 4 Residential Contract The compensation basis in this agreement has language consisting of (a) Cost plus on purchases, with a fixed initial design fee for design concept services and a percentage of contractor's fees for project review; or (b) Hourly fees for design concept services, with an initial design fee and a percentage of contractor's fees for project review.

ID 124–1996 Option 5 Residential Contract The compensation basis in this agreement has language consisting of (a) Cost plus on purchases, with a fixed initial design fee for design concept services and hourly fees for project review services; or (b) Hourly fees for design concept services, with an initial design fee and hourly fees for project review services.

ID 125–1996 Option 6 Residential Contract The compensation basis in this agreement has language consisting of (a) A presented price for purchases, with a fixed initial design fee for design concept services and a percentage of contractor's fees for project review services; or (b) Hourly fees for design concept services, with initial design fee and hourly fees for project review services.

ID 126–1996 Option 7 Residential Contract The compensation basis in this agreement has language consisting of (a) A presented price for purchases, with a fixed initial design fee for design concept services and hourly fees for project review services; or (b) Hourly fees for design concept services, with initial design fee and hourly fees for project review services.

ID 301–2008 Option 1 Commercial Contract The compensation basis in this agreement is based on a Fixed Design Fee.

ID 302–2008 Option 2 Commercial Contract The compensation basis in this agreement is an hourly design fee.

ID 303–2008 Option 3 Commercial Contract The compensation basis in this agreement is based on (a) Hourly charges for project program services; (b) A percentage of interior construction costs; and (c) A percentage of the vendor costs for project furniture, furnishings, and equipment.

Note that all contracts are sold in paper form only. Information on ordering is available at www.asid.org. Used with permission, ASID Headquarters.

Signatures

When a business contract is put into writing, it must be signed for the acceptance to be formalized. The person or entity that must sign the contract is the party to be charged—the client. By signing, the client indicates acceptance and his or her intention to go through with the contract. If more than one person or entity is responsible on the contract, all should sign. For example, two partners in a small office project should both sign. As was discussed in the sections on the basic elements of contracts, signatories must have legal authority to sign. A secretary generally does not have that legal authority.

The client will expect the designer making the offer through the contract to sign the contract. Technically, because the designer made the offer, the designer is bound to fulfill the contract whether or not he or she signs the contract.* It is a measure of good faith for the designer to sign the contract. Many advise that the designer not sign before the client, as this creates a situation in which the designer is bound by the terms as written while the client is not yet obligated.

A signature is usually done by hand. Other forms of signature are also recognized depending on the jurisdiction. In this electronic age, electronically generated signatures are generally legal (see Chapter 9). The validity of electronic signatures for contracts varies by jurisdiction and you should know what is correct in the jurisdiction for your place of business.

It is critical, when a designer signs a business contract such as a design contract, that the designer sign that contract in the name of the company. For example, as shown in Figure 7-4, the company's legal name is Columbia Interior Design, Inc. The designer should place his or her signature and title beneath that of "Columbia Interior Design, Inc." as shown in the figure. By signing in the name of the company, the business owner may enhance protection of personal assets and personal liability. However, whether the designer signs his or her name or the name of the business, the designer has created an obligation. By placing only his or her name on the contract, without the name of the business above the designer's signature, the designer assumes greater personal liability.

A business owner should check with an attorney to be sure he or she understands the obligations related to signatures in the jurisdiction of the business.

*Brown and Sukys, 1997, pp. 171–172.

PERFORMANCE AND BREACH

As we have already discussed, when the interior designer and client have come to agreement about the terms in the contract offered by the designer, and have appropriately signed a document, a legal contract exists. Each is legally bound to fulfill the agreed-upon terms of that contract. This completion of the acts called for in the contract is called *performance*. A contract terminates—or, using the legal term, *discharges*—when both parties perform the acts or activities promised in the terms of the contract. Only after that performance happens does the agreement come to a conclusion. When performance doesn't happen, the contract remains open. Depending on the seriousness of the lack of performance, the party that feels it has not gotten the deal it bargained for might consider suing the other.

For example, you have agreed to prepare a set of construction documents so that the client can obtain a building permit for some nonstructural remodeling of the kitchen, The client has agreed to pay you $5000 for those drawings. If your client cannot obtain the building permit because of errors in your drawings, there is a problem with your contractual performance.

When there is disagreement as to whether the terms of a contract have been fulfilled, it is wise to begin resolution with a discussion to clarify the disagreement, to determine whether performance has occurred. Disagreements commonly occur when the contract insufficiently specifies the required services. That is why it is so important to clarify the scope of services and other considerations in a written agreement.

In contract law, there are three types of performance: (1) complete; (2) substantial; and (3) inferior, or performance far below what is considered reasonable. For *complete performance* to occur, the terms expressed in the contract must be fully accomplished in the manner in which they are specified in the contract. Here is an example of incomplete performance: Alice's design contract for the project has as one of its terms the provision that "the designer will provide two computer-generated color renderings of the dining room." The contract is not complete if she does not provide these renderings. This is true even if all other terms in the contract have been fulfilled. In this case, the client has grounds to sue for breach of contract, if he or she so chooses.

Because it is sometimes impossible to satisfy a party's idea of complete performance, the courts hold that performance is complete if it is done so as to be substantially complete. *Substantial completion* means that the performance cannot vary greatly from what has been spelled out in the contract. If, in the preceding example, the designer provides two black-and-white computer-generated renderings of the dining room, the court might rule that the terms have been performed substantially and that the client must pay the designer for the services performed. However, it is also likely that the judge would rule that the designer must reduce or refund a portion of the fee, because the designer did not provide what was called for in the contract. Note that substitution of a different medium, such as markers for computer printing, technically constitutes a breach of contract and could result in a refund to the client for the difference between what was promised versus what was delivered.

In our example, should the designer provide only pencil or ink sketches of the areas, rather than the computer-generated color renderings, it could be argued that what was provided was inferior. *Inferior performance* is work that varies quite considerably from what is specified in the contract. Inferior performance causes a material (major) breach of contract and excuses the non-breaching party from fulfilling his or her obligations in relation to the contract. When a material breach occurs, the nonbreaching party would not have to pay agreed-upon fees and would likely be entitled to damages.

You have probably heard the term "breach of contract" somewhere before you began reading this chapter. A *breach of contract* occurs when one of the parties of the contract does not perform his or her duties as spelled out in the terms of the contract—that is, when performance has not occurred. Clients might say that the designer has breached the contract and "you will hear from my lawyer!" This discussion of breach and performance is important so that you do not find yourself hearing those words.

Here's an example of a potential breach: An interior designer included in the scope of services that he would select and specify all the architectural finishes for an advertising agency office complex. It turned out that the architect made these selections as part of his contract and the client did not tell the interior designer of this change. Was there a breach of the interior designer's contract?

Often the breach is minor, such as when the designer discussed earlier does a black-and-white rendering rather than a color one, or when a designer neglects to provide copies of her invoices to the client as agreed in the contract. When a minor breach occurs, the client is not excused from his or her obligation to the designer, but the client generally does not have to pay until the designer has provided all the services as required or until some other agreement has been worked out. When the breach is material, such as the designer failing to provide accurate drawings as called for in the contract, the client is excused from the contract and may also be entitled to damages. A material breach terminates the agreement. A possible material breach means the designer should talk to an attorney before he or she has to talk to a judge.

A breach of contract may also have occurred if the designer was negligent or performed tasks in what could be considered an unskillful manner. Interior design services must be performed to standards considered reasonable for a professional in this profession. If, for example, drawings are submitted that do not meet code, or the furniture as drawn does not fit into the actual rooms, the client can claim that the designer has breached the contract—and is likely also to charge that the designer is guilty of professional negligence. "Wrongful performance or nonperformance discharges the other party from further obligation and permits that party to bring suit to rescind the contract"[5] or recover monetary damages as compensation.

Compelling performance is, of course, one remedy that may be enforced against the breaching party. Another could be the award of damages. The term *damages* refers to money awarded to the party that has been harmed as a result of the breach. Several types of damages can be awarded. The first is *actual* or *compensatory damages*. This type of damages consists of a sum of money equal to the financial loss that the harmed party has suffered. They are compensatory because they are meant to compensate for the loss. Another type of damages is *incidental*, which are meant to cover expenses that have been paid out by the harmed party. *Consequential damages* might be awarded to cover losses that could have been foreseen by the party who breached the contract. *Nominal damages* may be awarded as a token to indicate that the breaching party has done something wrong but that the harm incurred is not very great.

The most serious kind of damages are *punitive damages*, which are awarded to punish the guilty party for grievous harm caused by the breach of the contract. It is more common for punitive damages to be awarded in tort cases than for breach of contract; they are most likely to be awarded when physical injury or malicious or outrageous conduct has occurred to the harmed party. Readers should note that there are additional kinds of damage awards and may wish to review these in a business law textbook. Although they may apply to an interior design breach-of-contract case, they are less of a factor in the discussion here.

Another type of remedy for a breach of contract is *specific performance*. *Specific performance* is a remedy in which the court orders the breaching party to perform whatever was spelled out in the contract. For example, Phillip was supposed to provide sample boards and renderings suitable for display in the leasing agent's office. As the project progressed, he provided some sample boards, but they did not display well in the office. In fact, materials kept falling off the boards. If this situation went to a judge, in a strict sense, he or she could require Phillip to provide boards and renderings suitable for display in order to specifically perform this clause in the design contract.

The nonbreaching party generally is satisfied with specific performance, as it requires that what has been bargained for actually be done. It is usually demanded only if the monetary damages are insufficient to satisfy the non-breaching party. However, courts are reluctant to order specific performance of service contracts, because such application requires that the courts force someone to perform a specific service.[6]

A breach of a contract can occur easily, especially if the designer has not been careful in the preparation of the contract or agreement terms. It can also occur when the designer is not fully capable of performing the services spelled out in the scope of services.

Performing to completion all provisions of the design contract is the natural desire of the interior designer and the client. Doing so is always the goal.

Small Claims Court

Sometimes the designer may feel it will be necessary to sue the client over non-payment of the designer's invoices. A potential remedy called the small claims court system may be available in the jurisdiction. The *small claims court* is for civil actions and, as the title indicates, for situations in which the damages being sought are a small amount. The upper limit on this amount varies from state to state, so no absolute dollar amount can be given here, but a figure of $5000 or less gives you an idea of the amount of the claims generally heard in a small claims court.

When you use the small claims court remedy for a dispute with your client, you generally agree to forego any right to larger damage awards and further suits. Due to the nature of these courts, the plaintiff (the designer) generally argues his or her case without the presence of an attorney. The case is heard before a magistrate or a judge; only rarely is a jury involved. The magistrate will make the decision. If the decision does not go the plaintiff's way, it cannot be appealed. If the plaintiff wins the decision, it is still up to the plaintiff to collect from the defendant in the manner set out in the laws of the jurisdiction.

Detailed information about how the small claims court system works in the reader's jurisdiction can be found by online research using the state attorney general's site or other government sites of the jurisdiction.

TERMINATION BY AGREEMENT

Adam had been working on the plans for a small doctor's office for six weeks. The drawings were ready to review with the client for final approval. At this point the National Guard called Adam up for service, making him unable to finish the project. He met with the client and introduced another designer who would take over for Adam. The client, however, was unwilling to have the other designer take over, as he had a good personal relationship with Adam. The client sent a letter terminating the contract with Adam's design firm.

Contracts can be terminated by agreement. Adam's design firm wanted to continue, but the client was adamant about terminating the agreement. The client did pay the firm's fees due up to the point of the last meeting with Adam. As we noted in a preceding section, in which we discussed the termination of a contract, the designer can seek to protect himself or herself if something occurs that is not the designer's fault. However, it is not necessary for there to be such a clause in the contract for the contract to be terminated by agreement.

It is possible for a contract to be terminated at any time if both parties agree to the termination. If there is no termination clause in the original contract, it will be necessary to draw up a second contract dealing with the terms of the termination, as a protection for both parties. An oral agreement to terminate a contract is not advisable. All terminations by agreement, regardless of who initiates the termination, should be spelled out in writing.

AVOIDING CONTRACT DISPUTES

It is never easy to handle disputes with clients over terms in a contract or performance of a design contract. Simply having a dispute can be stressful even when the designer can resolve the problem relatively quickly. Nevertheless, despite best efforts, disputes do occur.

One way to avoid contract disputes is be completely clear in the design contract and in all other communications with the client—and others involved in the project. Clarity right from the initial interview about how you work and what will happen during the project is very important in avoiding disputes. Some designers like to use industry jargon so that they sound more like "experts." Some clients who don't know what you are talking about may not ask for explanations. This can easily lead to misunderstandings. If you need to use industry language, be sure you explain as you go along.

Another important protection is to have an appropriate level of detail in your contract. Your attorney will advise you on this matter. The scope of services must be detailed and clear enough so there is no question about what you are going to do. How you are going to charge also must be absolutely clear. Clarity in your contracts and communications with clients is a huge factor in avoiding disputes. What are you hiding, anyway?

Avoiding disputes also means keeping promises. What you have put in the contract is your promise. What you say in e-mails are promises. What you communicate on the phone are also promises. Keeping your promises is a professional responsibility and another important way to avoid disputes.

Another thing to do to avoid disputes is to learn to watch for warning signs. Many clients who are upset will tell you. They may, in fact, yell and scream at you. Certainly screaming back will do no good. Most people have trouble with confrontation. You need to neutralize them with calm questions, demonstrating to the other person that you are trying to understand what has gotten him or her upset. Acknowledge that they are upset and show that you are trying to understand and resolve the problem. Fighting back or caving in just to make peace doesn't get you anywhere. Fighting back only intensifies their anger, and caving in most likely will just weaken your position.

Then again, there are clients who "tell" you they are upset by not communicating with you. Have you ever heard "I'm so upset I don't want to talk about it!" from a friend or relative? How can you do anything if they will not tell you what is wrong? Clients who don't return your calls, never seem to be available, or just don't want to talk about something are likely giving you a warning sign that something is bothering them. Clients who don't want to talk to you about the problem are also difficult because they are giving you no way to figure out what is wrong. Noncommunicative clients should be questioned carefully, though you will have to exhibit a lot of patience waiting for them to respond.

Another good tactic is to diplomatically mention right at the beginning of the project that your experience has shown that something almost inevitably happens along the way that will cause a problem or a misunderstanding. Maybe a product they have fallen in love with is discontinued before it can be ordered, or a contractor fails to complete work on time. Maybe a code is changed and the city inspector now wants things done according to the new code. To avoid disputes, you can simply assure the client that you will take care of the problems. That's what they're paying you for, isn't it?

Yet another way to avoid disputes is to tell clients that you want them to ask questions because you want to know what they are thinking. Their questions—along with your good communications—will help avoid disputes and problems. There are always those clients who bombard you with questions and e-mails and expect instantaneous responses. There are plenty of interior designers who would probably say that telling the client to ask plenty of questions is the last thing they really want the client to do! If you explain up front the process and the ground rules for communication (e.g., "It usually takes me two to three days to return an e-mail"), it will help with the client who wants to be too involved and asks "too many" questions.

When a problem occurs, check up on the situation immediately and determine what options exist to solve the problem. Then suggest one or two options that are workable. Document the problem and your solutions. Don't avoid the documentation. You can be sure that the client is saving all the e-mails you send during the course of the project, so take care what you say in e-mails and do what you say you will do. And for heaven's sake, don't stop responding to the client or start blocking e-mails. That is a giant ethical issue that can also cause you massive legal problems.

WEB SITES RELEVANT TO THIS CHAPTER

www.asid.org American Society of Interior Designers

www.law.cornell.edu Cornell Law School

www.nolo.com Nolo—publisher of legal information

You might also want to check the Web sites of other law schools.

KEY TERMS

Acceptance

Agency relationship

Arbitration

Assignment

Breach of contract

Compensatory damages

Complete performance

Consideration

Contract

Contractual capacity

Counteroffer

Damages

Delegation

Disbursements

Electronic Signatures in Global and
National Commerce Act (ESIGN)

Inferior performance

Legality

Letter of agreement

Mirror image rule

Mutual assent

Mutual understanding

Offer

Offeree

Offeror

Oral agreement

Per diem

Performance

Proposal

Punitive damages

Reimbursable expenses

Restraint of trade

Retainer

Scope creep

Signature

Small claims court

Specific performance

Substantial completion

Statute of Frauds

Third party

Uniform Electronic Transaction Act
(UETA)

WHAT WOULD YOU DO?

1. William met with his client, Andy, at a coffee shop after they had toured a spec office space that Andy wanted to acquire for his accounting practice. During their discussions at the coffee shop, William made notes about the project scope and wrote down an estimate for design fees for services only. William always dates his notes, so the date of the meeting was already attached to the notes. After reading these notes, Andy signed and dated the paper and said, "You've got a deal! When can you start?" Two months into the project, Andy begins to have second thoughts and claims that there is no contract between him and William. He refuses to pay invoices, does not return phone calls or e-mails, and even threatens to sue.

2. Suzanne returns from an initial interview with a client and is directed to prepare a contract for the interior design of a large, high-end residence. Part of the project responsibilities would involve working with the architect and general contractor. The home is for a sports figure who met briefly with Suzanne and said he was leaving the rest of the particulars to his agent and girlfriend. What kinds of issues should Suzanne cover in the contract, and what problems might occur in this situation? Would you even take this project under the stated conditions?

3. Holly has worked with her client, Alice Greatly, for many years, completing many small projects for Mrs. Greatly's residence.

Mrs. Greatly asked Holly to order $20,000 of furniture for her daughter's home, and Holly, as usual, did not ask Mrs. Greatly to sign an agreement before ordering the furniture. "I wouldn't think of asking Mrs. Greatly for a contract to order anything for her." When the furniture is delivered, the daughter claims that nothing that was delivered is as she expected it. She tells her mother not to pay the bill.

REFERENCES

1. Clarkson et al., 1983, p. 129.
2. *Oxford American College Dictionary*, 2002, p. 1089.
3. Emerson, 2004, p. 126.
4. Conry et al., 1993, p. 227.
5. Brown and Sukys, 1997, p. 197.
6. Jentz et al., 1987, p. 227.

CHAPTER 8

Product Pricing

After completing this chapter you should be able to:

- Discuss the meanings of the different price terms.
- Calculate a discount from retail, a quantity discount, and a multiple discount.
- Explain the purpose of price codes.
- Explain a cash discount and how it benefits the interior designer.
- Calculate a markup from cost and the markup percentage.
- Calculate a gross margin in dollars and the gross margin percentage.
- Discuss how the perception of value affects the price a consumer is willing to pay for products.
- Describe prestige pricing and how it might affect the services of an interior designer.
- Explain the differences between a deposit and a down payment.
- Discuss a retainer and how it differs from a deposit.
- Explain the differences in the freight terms presented in the text.
- Discuss why it is important to include charges for delivery and installation.
- Explain how sales taxes are to be collected and who has the responsibility for paying those amounts.
- Discuss the impact of the Sherman Antitrust Act on the interior design profession.
- Explain how the Robinson-Patman Act affects interior design product pricing.

NCIDQ COMPONENT

Based on best information available, some material in this chapter might appear as part of the NCIDQ examination. The reader should not depend solely on this text for study material.

Designers who specify and sell merchandise must be very careful in calculating prices they quote to clients. Mistakes are costly to the design firm. It can also be costly to the designer if his or her payment is in some way based on selling merchandise. For designers who sell merchandise, care in pricing and in budgeting merchandise is as important as determining how much to charge for a design fee.

Whether the project is a residence or a commercial space, clients are unlikely to pay additional sums to the designer because the designer has made a mistake. In competitive bidding for a commercial project, mistakes in pricing and budgeting can create projects that the client cannot afford to purchase from any supplier (see Chapter 12 for a discussion on competitive bidding). Mistakes in budgeting and pricing for any reason can also leave the designer open to accusations of professional negligence and ethics complaints.

Many factors are involved in determining the price of a product or a service. The *price* is, of course, what something sells for. And, unfortunately for the individual who is new to the interior design profession, there are many different prices with which the interior designer has to deal.

This chapter focuses on explaining the most typical terms associated with product pricing. The ways in which a "price" is determined are explained, and we include examples of how these various prices are calculated. There are, of course, other topics that also affect product pricing and thus must be understood by the student and practitioner. Those covered in this chapter are deposits and down payments, shipping charges, and sales and use taxes.

CATALOG PRICING

Pricing merchandise for a client often begins with a review of the pricing catalog supplied by a vendor. These might be contained within the product catalog or given separately to the designer by the vendor representative.

Although designers use pricing obtained from the Internet, many designers price projects based on catalog pricing obtained from vendors. Designers must be very conscientious about keeping catalogs and price lists up-to-date. Old price lists must be purged from the files to prevent mistakes in pricing. Interior design staff need to verify that the price lists on file are current and accurate. Any failure at this chore can mean that products will be estimated and billed at incorrect lower charges, thus causing a loss to the design firm.

The designer must be very careful in understanding what price list he or she is reading. A *catalog price* list can be designated "suggested retail," "list," "retail," "net," or "wholesale." These different terms have different meanings regarding the price the designer must pay for the goods, and are defined in the next section.

Because many suppliers offer varying discounts based on the volume of purchases, suppliers more frequently provide price lists in terms of list price rather than net price. Such things as purchasing an amount of goods over some specific time period and whether or not the designer will inventory goods are two of the many possible factors that affect discount percentages. This is particularly true of furniture items. Architectural finishes and textiles are generally priced the same to all designers and the price lists for these types of goods are generally net prices.

Receiving a retail or suggested retail price list means the designer must negotiate with the manufacturer's representative for the discount percentage that the design firm may expect to receive when ordering from each vendor. Discounts from vendors range from 10 percent to as much as 50 percent, or possibly even more for a very large order.

If a designer is sent a net price list, this means that the designer can purchase the goods at the price listed in the catalog. This net price list, of course, is the designer's cost price. No further discount should be taken on this price. A selling price determined by quoting or discounting a net price list means that the designer has sold the goods to the client for the same price at which the designer purchased the goods from the supplier.

[Handwritten margin notes:]

net can = wholesale

cost: to designer or end user? avoid the word cost

retail price list is suggested price to charge end user (MSRP)

don't pay retail for a commercial project

furniture net to retail is usually x2 clients should never see net price book

architectural finishes net to retail x 1.2

PRICING TERMS

Marjorie told her client that the price of the products for the real estate office would be $36,140 plus tax and delivery. Marjorie determined this after she was quoted a total cost to her of $27,800 by the two key vendors. The vendor for the desks quoted a net price of $21,000 for the desks; another vendor quoted a 20 percent discount from suggested retail of $8500 (SR), for a cost of $6800 to Marjorie for the chairs. SR for desks would be $42,000 at a 100 percent markup (MU). Her MU on the sale was 30 percent, or $8340.

As this example shows, there are many terms related to pricing in the interior design industry. The designer quotes prices to the client, and a supplier quotes prices to the designer. To add to the possible confusion, some of these pricing terms often mean the same thing. The amount a client pays for a chair is one interpretation of "price"; the amount the designer pays for supplies is another interpretation of "price."

Other terms can also be interpreted as a "price": for example, *fee* is the term commonly used to represent the price of services; *rent* is the price for an office space. Students are familiar with the term *tuition*, which is the price for classes; *interest* is the price one pays for a loan.

You may be familiar with the term *suggested retail price*. This is a price suggested by the supplier for use by the seller; it is also called *list price*. List price is generally accepted as being the same as suggested retail price. Suggested retail price is sometimes indicated by the acronym MSRP, which stands for *manufacturer's suggested retail price*. It is universally accepted to be the price that the consumer or end user pays for any goods purchased from a business. It is important for you to be aware that this price term might apply to the price from the interior designer to the client as well as that from a vendor to the interior designer.

Accurate pricing for design firms that count on product sales for revenues can make the difference between paying bills or losing creditworthiness with suppliers. It is important, therefore, to clarify the different terms that are related to buying and selling merchandise as they apply to the interior design industry.

Pricing from the Supplier to the Interior Designer

In our example at the beginning of this section, two different terms are used to indicate the price to the interior designer for the goods she must order. What were those terms?

In practice, three different terms are commonly used to represent the price that the designer must pay to the supplier for goods: net, wholesale, and cost. The example used the term net price. *Net price* represents a 50 percent reduction (or discount) from the suggested retail price (or list price). Some vendors and designers use the term *wholesale price* to represent net price, such that *net* and *wholesale* mean the same thing. *Wholesale price* can also be defined as a special price, given to a designer by a supplier, which is lower than what it would cost the consumer.

The third term is cost price. *Cost price* is the price that the designer must pay for the goods; it is not always the same as the net or wholesale price. Not all designers have the privilege of purchasing goods at a 50 percent discount from all suppliers.

In our example, the designer only received a 20 percent discount off suggested retail from the chair supplier. These smaller discounts are usually offered to the interior designer who only occasionally buys items from a supplier, rather than being a regular purchaser. A designer who frequently purchases from the same vendor is more likely be given the full 50 percent discount. A major reason why designers are not granted the 50 percent discount from retail is because they do not have quantity purchasing agreements. It should be noted that federal law governs pricing from the supplier to the designer. This point is discussed at the end of this chapter.

Pricing from the Interior Designer to the Client

Selling price is a term many designers use to refer to the actual price at which they sell goods to the client. The client, often referred to as the *consumer* or *end user*, is the person or entity that will end up owning the merchandise. In our example, Marjorie's selling price is $36,140 plus tax and delivery. Because some designers sell goods at a discount (a price lower than suggested retail) and others may occasionally sell goods at a price that is higher than suggested retail, selling price is not always the same thing as suggested retail price and list price.

The selling price to the end user may be different from the list or suggested retail price, because designers may sell merchandise to the consumer or end user at any price they wish. They are not obligated to sell goods at the suggested retail price. In fact, federal laws prohibit manufacturers from requiring merchants to sell goods to the end user at a set price. Manufacturer-required pricing—that is, a requirement that all sellers sell the same goods to all retail buyers at the same exact price—can be considered price fixing. *Price fixing* occurs when two or more businesses agree to sell merchandise or services at the same price. This illegal practice is discussed at the end of this chapter.

We have already used the term *retail price* several times in this section. *Retail price* is a term commonly used in retailing. *Retailing* refers to businesses such as department stores that sell goods to consumers. It is the price at which goods and services are sold to the consumer who is the end user. In retailing, retail price generally is not a price suggested by the manufacturer, but rather a price determined by the retailer.

Because the price to the consumer can be any price that the seller wishes to quote or offer, it is actually legal for "retail" to be higher than the suggested retail price when a seller sells goods to the end user. In this chapter, *retail* is considered to be a suggested retail price and is calculated as a 100 percent markup from net.

It is unknown where all this confusion originated. It is part of the long history of sales transactions over the centuries. Perhaps it is due in part to sellers' desires to keep the prices they pay secret from consumers or manufacturers that are trying to control who can sell their products.

In this chapter, we use the term *selling price* to mean the price quoted to the client and *cost price* to mean the price the designer must pay for the goods. Other terms are also used in the discussion, but are carefully differentiated and defined to prevent confusion.

DISCOUNTS

Interior designers rarely purchase merchandise from vendors at suggested retail. The merchandise they purchase for resale to clients is sold to the designer at a discount. A *discount* is a reduction, usually stated as a percentage, from the suggested retail price. In the earlier example, Marjorie received two different discounts from the two vendors she was utilizing.

The *full discount price* given by most manufacturers is 50 percent off the suggested retail. Remember that this is also called net price and that not all designers receive the full discount of 50 percent.

A manufacturer may decide that a 50 percent discount will be given only to those designers that are stocking dealers or that purchase a certain minimum quantity of goods in a given time period. A *stocking dealer* is a vendor that stocks a certain inventory level of goods at all times. Designers who do not carry inventory but do purchase from a particular manufacturer on a regular basis might also earn the large 50 percent discount.

To protect designers, some manufacturers use code words concerning their prices, or only quote a suggested retail price. They do this to protect designers from clients who try to "shop" the price that the interior designer gives the client.

One common code word is *keystone*, which means a 50 percent discount. A keystone price can also mean a price that is double the wholesale price; this relates to a selling price. Another price code used by some manufacturers is something like "your discount is *5/10*." This code might mean that the designer should take $5.00 off the dollar portion of the quoted price and $0.10 off the cent portion of the quoted price. For example, if the retail price of the goods is $23.50, the designer's price would be $18.40.

On the Internet, many manufacturers do not include pricing information for their products. They present quality specification information to inform the interior designer as well as the client, but sites clearly indicate that the potential buyer must obtain price quotes from resale suppliers. This too is a way to protect the interior designer (and others in the built environment industry).

It is essential for designers to know how to calculate a cost price from a stated discount so that they can determine their selling price to the client. The mathematical formula is provided so that you can see how the cost price is determined from a discount on suggested retail.

A design firm received a 50 percent discount for purchases made from Martin's Paint and Coverings. Wallpaper that has a suggested retail price of $35 per yard would cost the designer $17.50 per yard.

The following formulas might help:

$$\text{Discount in dollars} = \text{Suggested retail price} \times \text{Discount percentage}$$

$$= \$35 \times 0.50 = \$17.50$$

$$\text{Cost} = \text{Suggested retail} - \text{Discount in dollars}$$

$$= \$35 - \$17.50$$

$$\text{Cost} = \$17.50$$

To see the numerical difference resulting from a different discount, another designer receives only a 35 percent discount from suggested retail on the same wall covering:

$$\text{Discount in dollars} = \text{Suggested retail price} \times \text{Discount percentage}$$

$$= \$35 \times 0.35 = \$12.25$$

$$\text{Cost} = \text{Suggested retail} - \text{Discount in dollars}$$

$$= \$35 - \$12.25$$

$$\text{Cost} = \$22.75$$

These same formulas are used whenever a designer calculates discounts to determine cost.

The most common discount used in pricing goods is the basic discount from suggested retail price. However, several other types of discounts are also used in the industry. The most common additional types of discounts are quantity, multiple, trade, cash, and seasonal. Two other types of discounts, called advertising allowances and deep discounts, are specialized discounts available to and utilized by only a few interior design firms.

Quantity Discounts

When an interior designer has the opportunity to sell a large quantity of products to a particular client, the designer will try to negotiate a larger-than-normal discount for the order from the vendor. This is called a *quantity discount*. A quantity discount is one that is greater than the normal 50 percent discount because of the size of the order purchased at one time. For example, if a designer purchased one chair, the discount would probably be 50 percent, if that is the firm's normal discount. If the designer ordered 500 chairs, the manufacturer would most likely give a larger discount—perhaps 55 percent.

Some manufacturers offer a quantity discount for a cumulative number or amount of orders. This means that the special discount is given because of quantity purchases over a given period of time (probably during the previous year or quarter). The discount might increase as the quantity purchases increase. For example, perhaps a designer has more than one project in progress, each of which includes the specification of plumbing fixtures. The plumbing fixture supplier may give a cumulative discount as an incentive or as an acknowledgment of loyalty by the designer. Of course, this type of discount could cause ethical concern on the part of the designer. Realize also that federal laws exist to prevent price discrimination given by manufacturers to designers.

Multiple Discounts

Another type of discount offered for especially large orders is referred to as a multiple discount. *Multiple discounts* are a series of discounts from the suggested retail price. Manufacturers usually give multiple discounts to designers only for exceptionally large orders. Occasionally the design firm may in turn offer a multiple discount to the client because of a very large order.

The written notation for such a discount appears as 50/5 or 50/5/2, or some other combination of numbers. This does not mean that the designer takes 55 percent off the retail price in the first example or 57 percent off in the second. Rather, each discount is taken separately. For example, if the manufacturer offers a 50/5/2 discount on a large purchase of $500,000, the cost to the designer would be figured as:

$$\text{Total retail price} = \$500,000$$
$$\text{Less 50 percent} = -250,000$$
$$\$250,000$$
$$\text{Less 5 percent} = \underline{-12,500}$$
$$= \$237,500$$
$$\text{Less 2 percent} = \underline{-4,750}$$
$$\text{Final Cost} = \$232,750$$

What would the final cost to the designer be if the manufacturer offered a 48/7/3 discount?

Trade Discounts

Trade discounts are discounts given as a courtesy by some retailers and vendors to designers and others in the interior design and built environment trade. The

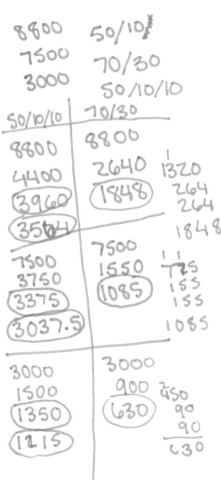

designer intends to resell the items to his or her client. Trade discounts are usually a small percentage off retail, though they can be as much as 50 percent. For example, a retail lighting fixture store offers a 20 percent trade discount to interior designers for resale. When the interior designer resells the lighting fixtures to his client, he will mark up the fixtures as he sees fit. To calculate what the cost price to the designer would be, use the basic discount formula shown at the beginning of this section. Let us look at an example:

$$\text{Discount in dollars} = \$150 \times 0.20$$

$$= \$30.00$$

$$\text{Cost} = \text{Suggested retail} - \text{Discount in dollars}$$

$$= \$150 - \$30.00$$

$$\text{Cost} = \$120.00$$

Cash Discounts

Manufacturers and suppliers often give a special discount called a *cash discount* to interior designers who pay their bills promptly. A notation like "2/10 Net 30" must appear on the invoice if a cash discount is allowed. The notation translates into an additional 2 percent deduction from the cost price if the invoice is paid within 10 days of receipt of the invoice. If the invoice is not paid within 10 days, then the designer must pay the invoice amount within 30 days. The cash discount is also considered by some to be an expression of credit terms. The notation automatically establishes an interest-free credit of 30 days.

The cash discount is taken after all other discounts have been taken. The following example shows how to calculate the final amount or cost that the designer must pay to the vendor. The cost to a firm for an order of goods is $5000. The invoice offers a cash discount of 2/10 Net 30. If the firm pays the invoice within 10 days, it only has to pay $4900.

$$\text{Cash discount} = \text{Cost} \times \text{Percentage}$$

$$= \$5000 \times 0.02$$

$$\text{Cash discount} = \$100$$

$$\text{Amount due} = \text{The original invoice amount minus the amount of}$$

$$\text{the cash discount}$$

$$= \$5000 - 100$$

$$\text{Amount due} = \$4900$$

[Handwritten margin notes: "2% more in 10 days", "aka. terms on a contract", "If it can be bought locally, you probably pay sales tax", "Sales tax vs. Use tax?"]

Seasonal Discounts

Interior design firms that have a showroom to display merchandise available directly to the end user might utilize a seasonal discount. A *seasonal discount* is given to encourage early purchasing of certain goods from vendors. By the way, any interior design business that has a commercial store location is technically called a *retailer*, even if it does not actually sell merchandise at retail.

For example, a designer with a showroom that sells accessories might obtain a seasonal discount from a vendor on holiday accessories. A supplier most often will give a seasonal discount to a designer. Of course, a designer technically may give a seasonal discount to the end user on these special items.

Advertising Allowances

Some suppliers and manufacturers offer an interior designer a special *advertising allowance* if the designer uses their products in promotions and advertising. A small design firm in a Midwestern city might use a carpet company's name in the design firm's advertising, perhaps as a special promotion before the holidays. The carpet company would then give the advertising allowance to the designer to pay for the advertising costs. It is not an extra discount on the purchase of goods for clients.

Deep Discounting

Deep discounting represents an extremely large discount from the suggested retail price for extremely large orders. This last type of discount is a pricing strategy embraced by many manufacturers of commercial furniture in order to obtain very large orders from clients such as major corporations. For example, a manufacturer might offer a deep discount of 75 percent off retail for a $5 million order of systems furniture for a large corporate installation. These deep discounts are offered directly to the end user, bypassing the interior designer or retailer such as an office furnishings dealer. A designer or dealer might, however, receive a small percentage for servicing the job at the local level.

A customer that gets a deep discount once will probably expect it for all purchases thereafter. However, designers and retailers that cannot offer that same price structure argue that deep discounts erode profit margins, hurting many firms that sell commercial goods. Other designers state that this pricing policy affects even those designers who sell goods but who rarely do larger jobs.

Manufacturers counter by saying that deep discounts have become a part of the competitive nature of the industry. They argue that commercial furniture dealers have forgotten that commercial furnishings products are a commodity and that deep discounting is a way of selling that commodity. Many of these representatives feel that deep discounting is a pricing strategy that designers and sellers must understand and learn to accept.

SELLING PRICES

Recall that Marjorie told her client that the price of the products for the real estate office would be $36,140 plus tax and delivery. This amount represents the selling price to the client. In this context, *selling price* is the price at which the designer offers to sell merchandise to the client.

A selling price could be suggested retail, or any other price the designer feels is appropriate, as long as the sale is going to the end user. Designers often sell merchandise to clients at a discount from suggested retail. Others sell merchandise to clients at a markup from the designer's cost price. These practices are found in residential as well as commercial interior design.

The following section discusses selling-price terminology and how to arrive at selling prices. It includes a brief description of gross margin, as this has a definite impact on the selling price, and it concludes with a brief discussion of price value. This is quite important, as clients are very interested in the value of the products they purchase and the price they must pay.

Discounting from Retail *how much off retail*

The selling price based on a discount from retail is calculated in the same way that the discount is calculated to find cost. Any discount amount can be used when the buyer is the end user.

Here is an example on how to calculate a discount from retail: A designer has prepared a specification of products with a total retail price of $6500. The designer has decided to offer the goods to the client at a 25 percent discount; thus, the selling price would be $4875. This selling price is determined in this way:

$$\text{Discount in dollars} = \text{Retail price} \times \text{Discount percentage}$$

$$= \$6500 \times 0.25$$

$$\text{Discount in dollars} = \$1625$$

$$\text{Selling price} = \text{Retail price} - \text{Discount in dollars}$$

$$= \$6500 - \$1625$$

$$\text{Selling price} = \$4875$$

If the product to be sold had a retail price of $350,000 and the designer offered a multiple discount from retail of 30/5, what would the selling price be?

A term used in retail when discounts are taken for promotional sales is *markdown*. A markdown is calculated in the same way as a regular discount. Interior designers do not usually use the term *markdown*. They may, however, refer to a discount as a markdown if they mark down inventory during a clearance sale.

Markup from Cost

A favored method of arriving at a selling price on merchandise is to apply a markup amount to the cost of the merchandise. A *markup* is a percentage amount that is added to the cost of goods to get the selling price. Recall that suggested retail is usually a 100 percent markup from the net price.

When using markup from cost for a selling price, the markup percentage or dollar amount that the designer adds to the cost price can be whatever the designer wishes. Marjorie used a markup from her cost to determine her selling price. Were both items at net?

When the designer knows the cost of the goods, it is necessary for him or her to multiply the cost by the percentage of markup. Let's look at an example other than Marjorie's situation first. An end table costs the designer $250. With a 100 percent markup, the selling price would be $500.

$$\text{Markup in dollars} = \text{Cost price} \times \text{Markup percentage}$$

$$= 250 \times 1.0$$

$$\text{Markup in dollars} = \$250$$

$$\text{Selling price} = \text{Cost} + \text{Markup in dollars}$$

$$= \$250 + \$250$$

$$\text{Selling price} = \$500$$

If the same table were to be sold at only a 50 percent markup, the selling price would be $375.

$$\text{Markup in dollars} = \$250 \times .50$$

$$\text{Markup in dollars} = \$125$$

$$\text{Selling price} = \$250 + \$125$$

$$\text{Selling price} = \$375$$

What numbers from the description of Marjorie's sale would be needed to determine her selling price? What was the amount of markup in dollars? What else does this amount of money represent for Marjorie's company?

There are two ways to find the markup percentage. With one method, you would find the markup percentage based on the retail price of the product. In the other, you would find the markup percentage based on the cost price of the product. For example, the retail price of a table lamp is $350, the cost price is $175, and the markup in dollars is $175. To find the markup percentage based on the retail price, use the following formula:

$$\text{Markup percentage based on retail price} = \text{Markup in dollars} \div \text{Retail price}$$
$$= \$175 \div \$350$$
$$\text{Markup percentage based on retail price} = 50\%$$

The formula for the markup percentage based on the cost price is as follows:

$$\text{Markup percentage based on cost price} = \text{Markup in dollars} \div \text{Cost price}$$
$$= \$175 \div \$175$$
$$\text{Markup percentage based on cost price} = 100\%$$

In practice, most interior designers use the markup percentage based on the cost price, whereas most retailers use the markup percentage based on the retail price as a method of determining the markup percentage.

Gross Margin

Chapter 21 on money management discusses gross margin as the difference between revenue and cost. The concept of gross margin is also important in terms of pricing merchandise. In this case, it is the difference between selling price and cost. The gross margin on the sale of merchandise must be sufficient to pay all overhead expenses, including the designer's draw or salary. Large firms often use the gross margin or gross margin percentage to determine commission on sales.

This example shows the methodology in terming the gross margin percentage and the gross margin expressed in dollars. Both calculations are important, as it is very useful to know the percentage value of the gross margin as well as the actual dollars. Assume that the net price is the designer's cost of $2500 and that the designer's selling price is $3375. The gross margin in dollars is $875 and the gross margin percentage would be 26 percent. It is necessary to calculate the gross margin dollars first:

$$\text{Gross margin dollars} = \text{Selling price} - \text{Cost price}$$
$$= \$3375 - \$2500$$
$$\text{Gross margin dollars} = \$875$$

To calculate the gross margin percentage:

$$\text{Gross margin percentage} = \text{Gross margin in dollars} \div \text{Selling price}$$
$$= \$875 - \$3375$$
$$\text{Gross margin percentage} = \$26 \text{ percent}$$

To calculate the gross margin in dollars and percentage of the sale that Marjorie made to the real estate office:

$$\$36,140 - 27,800 = \$8340$$

$$\$8340 \div 36,140 = 23\%$$

Perceived Price Value

Many things influence the price a person is willing to pay for a product or service. Naturally, one of these is how much the client actually has to pay to obtain the goods or services. One way this is done is by comparison: The buyer compares the price from one provider to that of another provider. You make comparison-pricing decisions when you are considering buying something for yourself. Likewise, as you consider different products for your clients, you are also doing comparison pricing.

The buyer's decision on whether the selling price you are quoting is too high—or even too low—is influenced by another factor called a *reference price*. This is the amount customers internally acknowledge as the price they believe is reasonable. It is influenced by what they previously paid for the same or similar merchandise. It can also be influenced by a friend who told them how much they paid for a similar item or by prices for similar goods advertised in the newspaper or on the Internet.

When the reference is higher than what you are quoting, the price you quote may seem to be a good deal. In contrast, if your price is significantly lower than their reference price, your clients may believe that the product or your service is of inferior quality. Even more disconcerting for a seller is when the reference price is lower than your price. This situation may cause the client to believe that you are overcharging.

Another perceived price concept relates to prestige and status. Products like a Ferrari, diamonds, and antiques, because of their quality, rarity, status, the manufacturer's reputation, and other factors, have attained a special place in the minds of some consumers. Because of this status, certain kinds of goods can be priced substantially higher. "Prestige pricing involves setting a high price so that status-conscious consumers will be attracted to the product and buy it."[1]

For those that sell merchandise, the competition of the marketplace and the demands of the consumer force designers to consistently monitor their pricing policies and strategies to be sure they are competitive. The days of selling every item at more than 100 percent markup are gone for all but a small number of designers.

DEPOSITS, DOWN PAYMENTS, AND RETAINERS

Alice expects her clients to pay a *deposit* of 50 percent of the total purchase price for all goods ordered that are not custom-made before Alice orders the goods. David tells his client, Mr. Robinson, that he requires a *down payment* of $10,000 toward the purchases that David will be making for the Robinson's summer home. The design contract from Miller Interiors to ACD Developers for preparing tenant improvement drawings requires a *retainer* of one-half the total design fee at the time the contract is signed. These three terms have similar meanings, but actually have different legal definitions. Many designers use these terms interchangeably, although they should not. This section explains those differences.

Deposits, down payments, and retainers are all forms of prepayment. Designers require these prepayments from clients before goods are ordered or services are begun. Vendors also require a prepayment from the designer before the designer's order from a vendor is fulfilled.

Prepayments from clients are an important way for the interior designer to determine if the client is really serious about continuing with the project. Someone who is not really interested in the designer's ideas and concepts will be reluctant to pay a deposit or down payment for goods. Likewise, if they are not serious, they are unlikely to pay a retainer for design services.

The term *deposit* has several legal definitions. For our purposes, *deposit* means money that is part of the purchase price, prepaid by the buyer as security in contracts for the sale of goods. In our example at the beginning of this section, Alice required a 50 percent deposit before she would order merchandise. It is common for designers to request that clients provide a deposit at the time an order is taken, in order to process the order. This is especially true if designers must special-order goods for the client. The deposit is credited toward the full purchase price as the contract is fulfilled. If for some reason the contract is not fulfilled, then (depending on the terms of sale) some or all of the deposit will be returned. For example, if the client paid a deposit of $5000 and the merchandise delivered to the client only amounted to $3700, the designer would have to return $1300 if the contract concerning further orders or work was terminated.

Funds collected from clients as deposits generally do not have to be deposited in escrow accounts and do not have to be used solely for the client who has given the deposit. However, the designer should check with his or her accountant to be sure that this is true in his or her state. To ensure that such funds are properly identified, the term *deposit* must be used in contracts and agreements.

A *down payment* is a portion of the total selling price paid at the time something is ordered or to be purchased. As with deposits, designers often use the down payment money as the prepayment required by the supplier. Also as with a deposit, the designer may have to return all or part of the down payment if the client cancels the order.

The term *down payment* does create a problem for designers in several states. Some states require that money collected as a down payment be deposited in a separate escrow account and be used exclusively for the client from whom it has been collected. In other words, David, in our example, must place the down payment of $10,000 in escrow for Mr. Robinson and cannot use those funds to order something for any other client. Check with your tax accountant or attorney to see if your state regulates the use of down payments.

Designers who order from any type of supplier or vendor commonly are required to pay a portion of or the entire price for goods and services up front, at the time the order is placed. This is also called *pro forma credit* (see Chapter 16). Interior designers who have not yet established credit with suppliers must require some prepayment from their clients, which the designers then pass along to the suppliers. Interior designers also seek to establish credit with manufacturers and suppliers so that they do not have to pay anything at the time the order is placed. This gives the design firm more flexibility in its cash management.

A *retainer* is a payment to a professional to cover future services or advice by that professional. Retainers are not prepayments to be applied to the sale of goods; rather, they are for design services or other professional services. In the example at the beginning of the section, Miller Interiors requires a retainer before it will begin the work for ACD Developers. Interior designers and other design professionals in allied areas usually require that clients pay a retainer, to show good faith and serious intentions, before work begins.

Designers can also create an open-ended design contract in which the designer is "on retainer" with a client, similar to when someone "retains" his or her attorney (that is, has an attorney on retainer). This means that the designer is more or less on call to the client whenever the client requires design services.

The fee for those services has already been negotiated. Additional discussion about retainers for design services contracts was presented in Chapter 7.

Federal Laws and Pricing Practices

The Federal Trade Commission (FTC) was established by the federal government in 1914 as an independent agency through the Federal Trade Commission Act. The purpose of this act and the commission is consumer protection, and to prevent unfair or deceptive competition or practices between businesses.

The Sherman Antitrust Act dates to 1890. It prohibits practices by which businesses make agreements in restraint of trade or engage in price-fixing to limit competition. An example of *restraint of trade* is when two or more businesses agree not to sell in each other's territory or to each other's customers. This agreement limits the consumer's options.

Price-fixing is also covered under the Sherman Antitrust Act. *Price-fixing* occurs when two or more businesses agree to sell the same goods to the consumer at the same price. This relates directly to the concept of suggested retail. At one time, certain consumer goods were sold at the same price, dictated by the manufacturers, no matter where someone went to purchase them. Some people even referred to these goods as "fair trade goods." However, enforcement of the Sherman Act negated these "fair trade" pricing polices. Today, all goods sold to the consumer are sold at whatever price any merchant that carries the goods decides to sell them. This means that a suggested retail price by the manufacturer is just that—suggested. The designer can sell the goods at any price that he or she wishes, whether higher or lower than the suggested retail price. If the manufacturer insists that the designer sell the goods to the consumer at a particular price, then the manufacturer is in violation of the Sherman Act.

You may have noticed that certain items in retail stores are the same price regardless of the store. This same price might be right down to the exact manufacturer and product item number. Although this seems to be a violation of the Sherman Act, a true violation exists only if these two stores made an agreement to price exactly the same or if the manufacturer required that the stores price exactly the same. On the face of this, it would seem that the two stores are probably just selling the goods at the suggested retail price.

One of the most important pieces of legislation that the FTC enforces is the Robinson-Patman Act. This legislation makes it illegal for a merchant to charge various merchants different prices for the same goods. Price discrimination "occurs when a seller charges different prices for commodities of like grade and quality."* This price discrimination must effectively lessen competition or create a monopoly. For example, if a manufacturer were selling the same quantity of product to two different design firms, it would have to offer the goods at the same price to both. However, if one firm had a record of purchasing a larger quantity of goods or stocking a quantity of goods, then the manufacturer could sell the goods at different prices to each designer.

Price discrimination only affects sales between merchants. A merchant has the legal right to sell to the consumer at any price that he or she determines. If Wendy Jones Interiors decides to sell a Knoll chair to Mrs. Smith for $1500 and the same chair to Mr. Peters for $100, the designer would not be in violation of any laws, as long as Smith and Peters were the end users.

There are several other pieces of legislation affecting businesses that prevent unlawful business practices; these are related to such things as monopolies, mergers, and labor relations. The ones already discussed, however, have the most relevance to an interior design practice. If you wish to investigate these other pieces of legislation, you might want to start by visiting the Web site of the Federal Trade Commission, www.ftc.gov.

*Emerson, 2004, p. 493.

FREIGHT AND FOB

The actual price of the goods from a vendor to the designer and the selling price of the goods to the client do not constitute the complete price amount. *Freight*, also called *shipping*, is the cost and process involved in the delivery of goods from the manufacturer to the interior designer. Each supplier has different shipping policies. Freight can be quite costly and is something the client is responsible for paying.

Let's look at the process. Most frequently, freight is handled by trucking companies, which are either independently owned or owned by the manufacturer. Goods are sometimes shipped on trains. This is generally done only for very large loads or when the manufacturer sends one of its trucks "piggyback." *Piggyback* means that the truck's trailer is loaded on a train flatcar and is shipped by train to the general destination. The trailer is then removed from the train and is driven to the warehouse or the client's final destination. Small items, like accessories, fabrics, and many wall coverings, are shipped via a parcel delivery service, such as UPS or FedEx.

There are several industry terms relating to freight charges. An important acronym in this industry regarding freight or shipping charges is FOB. According to the Uniform Commercial Code (UCC), *FOB* means "free on board" (also referred to as "freight on board"). Both interpretations mean the same thing. In and of itself, "FOB" means that the manufacturer is responsible for the cost of loading the goods onto a freight truck or train. For our purposes, we will use "free on board," as that is the definition used by the UCC.

If you look in a price list for a desk or other furniture products, you will find the FOB acronym along with either the word "factory" or "destination." These last two terms define which party—the manufacturer or interior designer—is responsible for the freight charges and when ownership of the goods changes hands.

The cost of transporting the goods to the destination is covered in the second part of the notation. If a manufacturer's catalog says *FOB, Factory*, this means that the buyer assumes ownership or title of the goods when they are loaded on the truck at the factory. In this case, the interior designer pays all transportation costs and assumes all risks during transit. If the catalog has the notation *FOB, Destination*, then the manufacturer bears the cost of transportation, retains ownership of the goods, and assumes all risks until the goods reach the destination.

Another notation used by some manufacturers is *FOB, factory—freight prepaid*. What this means is that the manufacturer passes ownership of the goods to the buyer as they leave the factory loading dock, but the manufacturer will pay the freight charges. This is done as a means of reducing the manufacturer's liability during shipping. It is also a convenience to its customers, as the manufacturer absorbs the freight charges. To be clear, the interior designer has ownership and responsibility for damages during transit, but the manufacturer pays the transportation charges to the destination.

Some catalogs specify zone pricing for shipping charges. In *zone pricing*, a manufacturer determines two or more shipping zones based on geographic distances from the factory. Anyone within each zone pays the same amount for shipping, and each zone has a different rate. Shipping charges for locations within each zone are averaged. When a manufacturer uses zone pricing, the seller pays the actual freight and bills the buyer for the zone average charge. For example, a desk company that is located in California uses a zone price for shipping. Assume that the zones have been divided similarly to the way time zones are divided. The cheapest shipping charges will be in the zone that includes California—the point of origin. As the zones progress toward the East Coast, the shipping charges will be higher.

Freight charges are legitimate charges that the client should pay if the goods are not sent prepaid by the supplier. Most interior designers charge clients *actual freight*, which means that the designer bills the client whatever the interior design firm is billed for the transportation of the goods to the designer's warehouse or the jobsite. Some firms add a small service charge to the actual freight charges to cover handling the payment and the necessity of dealing with the freight companies if there are any damages in transit.

Rather than charging actual freight, a firm may determine a freight factor on all items that must be shipped. A *freight factor* is obtained by finding the average and usual freight charges for all the kinds of goods and quantities of goods received FOB, Destination. This factor is added to the selling price or the cost price (as determined by the policies of the firm) of any goods ordered for the client that are shipped to the designer's warehouse.

There are times when an item must be rushed from the supplier to the project. The most common "rush" is shipping textiles for a custom upholstery job to the upholsterer or seating manufacturer. Wall coverings are also a common rush item. Naturally, anything can be needed in a hurry requiring express shipments. These express charges are also legitimate extra charges to the client if, in fact, the rush was not caused by the interior designer's delay. A clause should be included in the contract to cover the cost in the event an express shipment is needed. A few other terms related to the freight process are discussed in Chapters 13 and 14.

DELIVERY AND INSTALLATION CHARGES

Another legitimate charge to clients to complete a project is for needed delivery and installation of products at the jobsite. Although the two terms may seem like the same thing, in reality they are not. *Delivery* means taking tangible goods to the jobsite and placing them in their correct location. *Installation* means that some additional services are involved in the delivery process, such as assembly or construction of the products. An area rug is delivered to the site and placed where the interior designer has specified. Wall-to-wall carpet must be installed to complete a job.

Delivery charges can be either a flat rate, determined by how far away the client is from the warehouse, like the zone shipping pricing discussed earlier, or an hourly charge. Hourly charges are often quoted as door-to-door. *Door-to-door* means that the client is charged from the time the delivery truck leaves the designer's warehouse loading dock to the time it leaves the client's location after the delivery is completed.

The cost of delivery services involves more than transporting a sofa or desk, for example, from a local warehouse to the jobsite. All of these services represent expense items that can either be charged to the client or absorbed by the interior designer:

- Trained personnel are needed to check in the merchandise from the freight company truck.
- Goods must be inspected for damage.
- Transportation costs accrue to move the merchandise to the client's location.
- Depending on the items, the goods will be uncartoned (unpacked).
- Some items require simple assembly.
- The merchandise must be placed in the desired location.

- Delivery services also include removal of any cartoning or packaging materials, and dusting or slight cleaning of the merchandise.
- The delivery personnel or the designer should also explain to the client how to care for the merchandise.
- Responsibility for damages or other loss while the goods are at the warehouse or in transit from the warehouse to the jobsite must be clarified.

Note that some of these items are also discussed in Chapter 14.

Other products require some sort of installation or assembly. Wallpaper, carpet, drapery, and architectural finishes obviously have to be installed. A roll of carpet is not a finished good. Until the carpet has been installed, that item is not complete. The tradespeople and craftspeople who do this work charge for their time and materials to complete the installation. As for architectural finishes, all these installation charges are the liability of the client, and the design firm must remember to pass them on in the pricing of the finishes.

Exactly what constitutes installation services depends on the products being installed. In general, the goods must be delivered to the jobsite, and some type of preparation of the surfaces or area is required prior to installation. In addition, specialized supplies are often required, such as tack strips for carpet, adhesives for wall coverings, and wall anchors for wall-hung furniture items. When the items are installed, initial cleaning or dusting will be needed, and, as with the delivery of simpler items, maintenance and care instruction should be provided by the installer or the designer.

These installation services constitute charges that are required to make a finished product and should be absorbed by the client rather than the design firm. The designer must be familiar with the jobsite so that he or she can explain to the installer, prior to the installation, what services will be required. For example, neglecting to tell the carpet installer that the existing carpet is a glue-down installation (which will require removal of the carpet and preparation of the floor) will result in an improperly quoted price on the installation of the new carpet. In many design firms, this error in pricing comes out of the designer's commission or revenue for the company.

Interior design projects often involve remodeling or renovating existing spaces. The charges to install architectural finishes in these circumstances are often higher than for new construction projects. Designers must charge not only for the installation of the new goods but also for the removal of the old materials and for the preparation of the surfaces for the new goods.

When the designer neglects to add charges for delivery and installation to the estimate and final pricing of the job, the client is under no legal obligation to pay for the work. The work must be completed, however, and this means that the design firm or possibly the vendor will absorb the charges. Thus, care in specification of all architectural finishes, custom cabinets, and any goods requiring installation is critically important.

SALES AND USE TAXES

Almost all jurisdictions require sales tax be collected on goods considered to be tangible personal property sold to clients. *Tangible personal property* is any property that is movable, can be touched, or has physical existence. Sofas, desks, lamps, and draperies are just a few examples. A few states or municipalities require sales tax be collected for professional services; most do not, although that number has grown. Sales taxes that are not collected from the client will nevertheless be collected by the state or city from the interior design firm—along with potential penalty fees.

To sell merchandise to clients, the design firm must obtain a resale license—also called a *resale tax certificate*—from the state sales tax agency, as well as municipal or county agencies (if necessary). Permits must also be obtained if the business is located in another city or states. The resale tax certificate exempts the designer from paying the sales tax at the time he or she orders the merchandise for the client. It is then the designer's responsibility to collect the sales tax from the client and report and pay the collected taxes to these revenue agencies.

Some items that are tangible do not literally become so without some process such as labor to complete the item. Thus, labor, installation, delivery, and freight are subject to various interpretations as to when sales tax must be collected and when they are exempt. A case in point is draperies: In many states, the labor to make the drapery and hang the finished product in the home is taxable, because it is considered a vital part of completing the item. However, the amount a drapery store might charge to rehang a drapery after it has been cleaned is not taxable, as the labor of simply hanging the drapery is considered a service.

Certain kinds of items that are at first considered personal property, in that they are moved from the factory to the jobsite, are legally considered fixtures (sometimes called *capital improvements*). A *fixture* is legally defined as "a thing which was once personal property, but has become attached to real property in such a way that it takes on the characteristics of real property and becomes a part of that real property."[2] Items such as wall-to-wall carpeting, wall coverings, and installed mirrors are a few examples.

Sales tax must be charged if installation of the product causes it to become part of the building or become permanently affixed to the structure in such a way as to make it difficult or impossible to remove it without damaging the structure. When this happens, the product becomes a fixture. In many instances, sales tax is charged on the material and supplies needed to manufacture the finished goods, but not the labor. In some states, as in the drapery example, if the labor to manufacture and install the capital goods is necessary to make the "finished goods," then sales tax must also be charged on the labor.

In most cases, freight and delivery charges are either considered a service and generally are not taxable, or are considered part of doing business and are calculated into the price of the goods. If for some reason a finished good does not exist without these services, the designer may have to collect sales tax. Most often this happens when freight and delivery charges are calculated into the price of the goods; in this instance, sales tax *technically* can be calculated and must be paid to the state or city revenue office. For example, a designer does not call out a delivery charge as part of her sales agreement, but includes the delivery charge in the price of the furniture item. She is thus charging sales tax on delivery, and this sales tax must be paid to the state or other revenue office.

It is important, as with all sales tax collection policies, for the design firm to obtain information from the firm's accountant or the state and city revenue departments regarding the requirements for charging sales tax in all situations.

In general, design fees, such as hourly fees or a flat fee that does not relate to specific purchases of goods, are exempt from sales tax because the design fee is compensation for services. If, however, the design fee is added to the selling price of some goods, then the total price is taxable. For example, the designer does not show a fee for design services as a separate item on his invoice. Instead, he adds a 25 percent charge for design services to the selling price of $5000 for office furniture. The taxable amount would be $6250: $5000 for the tangible goods and $1250 for the design fee. If the design fee was a separate line item, then sales tax would be charged only on the tangible goods. Is it ethical to hide the design fee in the price of the goods?

Use taxes are a bit more complicated, and states have begun to clamp down on use tax reporting. Basically, a *use tax* is a type of tax assessed on tangible items purchased from a state other than where the buyer lives when those items are used by the purchaser in his own state. Some states may also apply a use tax to services. If the buyer does not pay sales taxes on goods purchased from another state, he or she would be liable to pay use taxes in his or her own state.

Here are two examples in which use taxes must be paid. Goods that the design firm purchases from out-of-state suppliers for use in the design firm's business are subject to a use tax if those goods would normally have a sales tax charged against them when bought within the home state. In general, if a firm purchases goods for a client and those goods come from out of state, the firm must collect and pay the use tax on those goods to the state where the design firm resides. In other words, a use tax takes the place of sales tax on goods purchased from out-of-state suppliers. The liability to pay the use tax lies with the buyer, not the seller.

The tax laws from state to state vary tremendously regarding when sales and use taxes must be collected. Some jurisdictions do not require the collection of sales tax at all. It is therefore very important for the firm to understand all the laws of the state in which it does business. What might be taxable for a design firm working out of an office in New York City and selling to a client in New York City might not be taxable in New Jersey. The reader is advised to check with the appropriate state agency where the business is formed and where the firm does business to determine if sales and use taxes must be collected. Much information concerning sales and use taxes can now be obtained on the Internet by searching for the state government departments responsible for collecting these taxes.

The design firm is responsible for recording sales and use taxes and paying the appropriate amounts to the state tax agency on a quarterly basis. It is thus very important for the interior designer and the design firm to fully understand the laws relating to the charging of sales tax on the goods and services they provide where the firm is located. The firm must also keep complete records of items that are exempt from taxes. Wherever the design firm does business, the burden of knowing which items are taxable and which items are not is on the design firm. State tax auditors have the authority to seize the moneys and/or property of the business if they discover that the business has not submitted the proper amount of sales and use taxes.

WEB SITES RELEVANT TO THIS CHAPTER

www.ftc.gov Federal Trade Commission (U.S.)

You might also want to check the Web sites of professional associations.

KEY TERMS

Actual freight	Deep discounting
Advertising allowance	Delivery
Buying the job	Deposit
Cartoning	Discount
Cash discount	Door-to-door
Catalog price	Down payment
Cost price	End user

Fixture

FOB, Destination

FOB, Factory

FOB, factory—freight prepaid

~~Free on board (FOB)~~ *Freight on Board*

Freight

Freight factor

Full discount price

Gross margin

Installation

Keystone

List price

Manufacturer's suggested retail price (MSRP)

Markdown

Markup

Multiple discount

Net price

Piggyback

Prestige pricing

Price

Price-fixing

Pro forma credit *billed before purchase order is processed*

Quantity discount

Reference price

Restraint of trade - *look at pg. 165*

Retainer

Sales tax

Seasonal discount

Selling price

Stocking dealer

Suggested retail price

Tangible personal property

Trade discount

Use tax

Wholesale price

Zone pricing

WHAT WOULD YOU DO?

1. Gayle was asked by her boss, Marcia, to price six sets of tables and chairs from a particular vendor for a client. Gayle looked up the prices in the price catalog and marked up the tables and chairs 100 percent. She then discounted the merchandise 25 percent per Marcia's instructions. The client was thrilled with the price and immediately ordered the merchandise.

   Three weeks later the bookkeeper comments to Marcia that the markup was really very good: "Good job on that sale!" the bookkeeper exclaims. As it turned out, Gayle mistakenly assumed that the pricing in the catalog was a net price, when it was actually a suggested retail price.

2. Jeff has been working on an adaptive-use project in which a former firehouse is being converted into a bed and breakfast. It is in a very nice older neighborhood, but it is not in a historic district. The guest rooms will be on the second floor, which was previously the living quarters, and the public spaces like the lobby and dining/kitchen will be on the first floor.

   Jeff has told the client that in order to meet ADA requirements, one of the guest rooms has to be accessible. The only way to do that is to install an elevator. Jeff has come up with a way to include the elevator in the design, but the client tells Jeff that he will not pay for changes shown on the plan that indicates an accessible guest room, nor will he add an elevator.

   Jeff then changes the plans, which means they no longer meet code. The client subsequently submits the revised drawings to the city for a building permit. (Jeff does not have permitting privileges.) The city refuses to issue a permit based on the drawings. The client threatens to sue Jeff for the delays.

3. Super Interiors always includes a photographic rights clause in its design contracts. The clause states, "Super Interiors reserves the right to photograph all areas of the project throughout the phases of installation and upon final completion of the project." This clause is included in the contract to design various spaces for a mid-sized accounting office.

Six months after the project is completed, the owner of the accounting office designed by Super Interiors sees photographs of his reception room and employee lounge in a magazine. The client's business name was clearly visible in the photograph and was also listed in the caption. The client was both flattered and upset that photos of his office spaces were shown in the magazine. He felt he had not given anyone permission for the photos to be published.

REFERENCES

1. Berkowitz et al., 1994, p. 379.
2. Clarkson, 1983, p. 1203.

CHAPTER 9

The Selling of Goods: The Uniform Commercial Code and Warranties

After completing this chapter you should be able to:

■ Identify the purpose of the Uniform Commercial Code and explain how it affects the practice of interior design.

■ Compare an interior designer as a merchant and as a seller.

■ Describe the rights the seller has when buying goods.

■ Explain the buyer's rights when a consumer purchases goods from an interior designer.

■ Explain if and when electronic agreements are valid for the ordering of goods by the interior designer from a vendor and the purchase of goods by a client.

■ Discuss how the Statute of Frauds affects interior designers.

■ Explain if and when an oral agreement for the sale of goods remains a valid contract.

■ Explain the differences between a sales agreement for the sale of goods and a sales agreement for the sale of services.

■ Explain acceptance as it is regulated by the sale-of-goods laws.

■ Compare a shipment contract to a destination contract.

■ Discuss the intent of product warranties.

■ Compare the warranty of title to the express warranty.

■ Differentiate a statement of express warranty from puffing.

■ Explain the implied warranty of merchantability.

■ Explain why an interior designer is or is not liable if a client is injured by the failure of a product specified by the interior designer.

■ Discuss the difference between a full warranty and a limited warranty.

■ Discuss product liability and professional negligence.

NCIDQ COMPONENT

Based on best information available, some material in this chapter might appear as part of the NCIDQ examination. The reader should not depend solely on this text for study material. See sections on the UCC and buyer's and seller's rights.

As an interior designer, are you aware of the laws that affect your purchases from suppliers and manufacturers? Do you have any idea what the law states about your client's ability to refuse delivery of goods or to cancel an order? These questions and hundreds of others are regulated by common law, along with a uniform set of regulations concerning the law of sales called the Uniform Commercial Code (UCC).

For the majority of members of the interior design profession, selling and ordering of goods for clients are everyday occurrences, yet few have ever heard of the Uniform Commercial Code. It seems that most designers learn about the intricacies of selling and buying goods from experience. This may be fine if you are purchasing a loaf of bread from the grocery store. However, designers who own an interior design practice and make the sale of merchandise their major source of income need more knowledge about the legal rights and responsibilities involved in ordering and selling goods.

Article 2 of the UCC is concerned with the sale of goods. It also covers law concerning the transfer of the title for goods from one party to another. Article 2 *does not* cover sales of services, real estate, or intangible property such as stocks. Should a dispute arise over the sale of goods, the UCC provisions prevail, whereas a dispute over the sale of services would be governed by common law. These laws affect sales between merchants, between merchants and consumers, and between consumers and consumers.

This chapter is not meant to be an in-depth discussion of the UCC, nor should it be considered legal advice. Readers are advised to verify application of the UCC to their jurisdiction and situation. All states have adopted some version of the UCC. However, those versions are not identical in all respects, and interpretations discussed in this chapter may differ in a specific state. Readers are encouraged to investigate the specific interpretations of the UCC by going to the Web site for the National Conference of Commissioners on Uniform State Laws (www.nccusl.com) or their state attorney general's office.

This chapter also provides an overview of warranties and product liability. Designers are liable for the performance of the products that they specify for any project. They can also be held accountable for what they say about products and how the product might perform for the client's situation. These are just two of the issues concerning warranties discussed in this chapter.

HISTORIC OVERVIEW OF THE UCC

Most laws related to commercial business activity, including interior design, originate from the individual states. During the early years of this country, this fact often resulted in the passage of confusing and conflicting laws. As the nation's commercial business activity became more complex, the problems became more acute.

In the late 1800s, the National Conference of Commissioners on Uniform State Laws (NCCUSL) was established to create uniform statutes related to business activities. These statutes, revised over the years, helped to alleviate many of the problems of commercial business. Yet there remained instances in which these uniform statutes overlapped or conflicted. Work was begun in 1945 to revise all the statutes into one uniform document. In 1957, after much effort, the Uniform Commercial Code (UCC) was completed.[1] The purpose of the UCC is to help "state legal relationships of the parties in modern commercial transactions. The Code is designed to help determine the intentions of the parties to a commercial contract and to give force and effect to their agreement."[2]

The UCC consists of nine articles dealing with many aspects of commercial transactions. The article (or section) that is specifically concerned with the normal practices or activities of interior designers is Article 2: Sales.

The UCC has been adopted by all states. Each state might adopt only parts of the UCC at its own discretion. Nevertheless, for practical purposes, readers may assume that all states have adopted these laws. It is the designer's responsibility to understand which UCC sections are in effect in his or her state. Note that the NCCUSL periodically updates the UCC to reflect current commercial transactions and customs. You can go to the Web site of the NCCUSL (www.nccusl.com) to research changes and specific information on the UCC.

UCC DEFINITIONS

Each state may interpret the uniform statutes in Article 2 and other sections of the UCC in ways that meet their individual legislative needs. These localized interpretations generally concern whether the buyer of goods is an end user (consumer) or a merchant. Definitions that clarify common terms are very helpful in understanding the provisions of the UCC: The main ones that we wish to look at here are those for goods, sale, seller, merchant, buyer, and price.

Goods (Section 2–105) are any items that are tangible, have physical existence, and can be moved. This includes custom-made goods. Furniture and accessories are tangible goods. Items such as carpet, wall coverings, and window treatments are goods, because they have physical existence. When these items are permanently attached to a home or a building, they are generally considered to become real property or fixtures. Or are they? The sale of the merchandise itself, from the supplier to the designer and the designer to the client, would be covered by the UCC, because the goods do not become real property until they are "permanently" attached to the home or office. If the client later wants to remove these goods from the home or office and sell them, or even sell the building with the merchandise intact, the sale would be governed by real estate law.

A *sale* (Section 2–106) occurs when the seller transfers title or ownership of the goods to a buyer and the buyer provides some consideration to the seller. For example, Marcia purchased a sofa from Gail, an interior designer. Marcia paid Gail $4000 for that sofa by check. The sofa was delivered to Marcia, and Marcia paid Gail's subsequent invoice for delivery charges after delivery of the sofa. Whenever the designer agrees in good faith to sell a piece of furniture to a client for some amount of money and the client takes delivery of the furniture and sends the designer a check for the agreed-upon price, a sale has occurred. There are, however, some special considerations with regard to when "ownership" actually occurs. This matter is discussed later in this chapter.

In the preceding example, Gail provided goods to her client, Marcia; thus, Gail is a seller. To be clear, a *seller* (Section 2–103) is anyone who sells goods or contracts to sell goods. A manufacturer that sells goods to an interior designer is also considered a seller. When a home owner holds a garage sale, technically that person is a seller. However, both the interior designer and the manufacturer are also considered "merchants." Special conditions govern the sale of goods between merchants.

A *merchant* (Section 2–104) is anyone who is involved with the buying and/or selling of the kinds of goods with which he or she is dealing. Someone who "holds himself or herself out as having knowledge and skill unique to the practices or goods involved in the transaction"[3] is also considered a merchant. Thus, although the interior designer who sells a personally owned stereo to a friend is a seller, if he or she sells a chair to that same friend and that sale occurs through the business, the designer is now considered a merchant. Naturally, manufacturers and suppliers of goods to the interior designer are also considered merchants, as is any retailer selling goods to consumers.

Many interior designers who sell goods never have a showroom, warehouse, or installation crew who are employees of the firm. Nevertheless, any interior designer who purchases goods, whether or not through a firm's inventory account, and resells them to a client so that the purchase and the resale "pass through" the design firm's books, is a merchant.

A person becomes a *buyer* (Section 2–103) when he or she contracts to purchase or purchases some good. Marcia, the client in the preceding example, is a buyer. A buyer also is someone who buys from someone else who is in the business of selling goods; thus, Gail the interior designer is also a buyer. The designer is protected by the same rights as the end user, as long as the purchase is from a seller whose business it is to sell the sofa.

The term *price* (Section 2–304) can be any kind of payment from a buyer to a seller, including money, goods, services, or real property. Therefore, it is possible, for example, for a client to offer to trade his or her own professional services as the price of a sofa.

A term used frequently in this chapter and others in this book is *end user*. Though the term is not officially part of the UCC, it is commonly understood to mean the person who ultimately owns and uses goods. It is defined in this chapter in order to clarify the term.

THE BUYER'S RIGHTS AND OBLIGATIONS

It is important to understand that clients—the buyers of what an interior designer either directly sells or specifies for them—have rights related to that sales transaction. Designers sometimes forget this when a somewhat troublesome client refuses a delivery or says the fabric is the wrong color. Yet, the designer who desires a sales relationship has both a legal and an ethical responsibility to understand buyers' rights.

From a different perspective, interior designers are also buyers when they order merchandise from a vendor for a client. Designers are also buyers when they purchase items needed in the operations of the office, such as a computer or even office supplies. Once again, an understanding of these rights and obligations is important for all interior designers.

To avoid problems, it is critical for the interior designer to describe what is being ordered on the sales agreement in sufficient detail so that the client clearly understands what he or she is purchasing. Because of long lead times for delivery, clients might forget what the product that they approved three months ago looks like. A sales agreement that says "one 96-inch sofa in beige fabric" leaves a lot of room for argument as to whether what is being delivered is what the client ordered. If the sales agreement instead says, "one Michaels Style 234 Breakridge Sofa, 96″ wide by 36″ deep, button tufted, and finished in

#234 Beige velvet," there can be very little disagreement as to what was to be ordered and what was delivered. Details help clarify orders and prevent those arguments. If the seller delivers the goods that are described in the sales contract, the buyer has an obligation to pay for those goods.

The buyer also has a right to inspect the goods before paying for them. Any modification in what has been delivered versus what is described gives the buyer the right to refuse the delivery. If the delivered goods are as described in the sales agreement, they are referred to as *conforming goods*. If the goods are somehow different, they are nonconforming goods. *Nonconforming goods* are simply any goods that are not as described in an order.

If they are nonconforming goods, the buyer (designer or client) has the right to refuse the goods and to not pay for the nonconforming goods. The buyer may also accept any part of the order, reject only the nonconforming goods, or accept the goods even if they are nonconforming.

Designers purchasing goods for a client also have the right to inspect the goods before paying the supplier. Even though it is common for the manufacturer to send a bill for goods prior to the designer receiving the goods, the designer has a right to inspect and verify that the order is correct before becoming obligated to pay for the goods. According to the UCC, this right is absolute for all buyers, except for COD orders (Section 2–606a). This is just one reason that it is very important for the designer to check all deliveries from manufacturers and suppliers.

If the buyer rejects the goods as nonconforming, the buyer must promptly notify the seller of the rejection. A telephone call is notice, but a written notice is more binding, as it is tangible evidence. Written notification, via an e-mail or letter with a full description of the problems, is the best way to provide notice. If the buyer does not provide notice and retains the goods, the seller is justified in expecting the buyer to pay for those goods.

The longer the goods are in the hands of the buyer, the more likely it is that the buyer will be obligated to pay for the goods, even if they are nonconforming: "Inaction results in acceptance."[4] The buyer's failure to inspect and reject the goods within a stated or reasonable time period constitutes acceptance. If the buyer rejects some or all of the goods as nonconforming but uses the goods without prior agreement from the seller, the buyer is taking ownership of the goods and the seller by law may demand that the buyer pay for the goods.

The buyer is also obligated to make payment for the delivered conforming goods in accordance with the terms in the sales agreement. For example, if the terms are cash payment upon delivery, the designer expects the client to pay in cash (or at least with a check). If the terms are for a credit purchase, the buyer is expected to make payment within the time frame indicated in the sales agreement. COD shipments are valid only if COD shipment has been agreed to in the sales contract (Section 2–601).

State laws generally allow buyers a *72-hour right of refusal* concerning any contract signed in the home or other location that is not the seller's place of business. In some states, this is called a *three-day right of cancellation*. This means that even if the goods are as ordered, the buyer has 72 hours in which to return the goods and receive full repayment. In many states, this right of refusal applies only to contracts signed in the buyer's residence. The right-of-refusal allowance for contracts signed in a residence was developed to protect buyers from feeling pressured into purchasing by a seller who has come to the residence. The exact conditions of the right of refusal vary by state and can be researched by visiting the Web site for the office of the state's attorney general.

Although many companies have the philosophy that "the customer is always right," according to sales law this is not necessarily true. Designers who buy and sell goods need to understand not only their rights as sellers but also their rights as buyers.

THE SELLER'S RIGHTS AND OBLIGATIONS

Many laws have been passed to protect consumers from unscrupulous sellers. However, sellers also have rights, as well as obligations to their customers/clients. This section discusses some of those obligations.

A key issue for many designers is the possibility that the buyer/client will cancel an order or want to change the order after it has been placed with a supplier. One of the best ways to avoid at least some of these problems is for the designer to have a well-thought-out, written sales agreement with clear terms and conditions of the sale. (See Chapter 13 for a sample terms and conditions.) One of these clauses stipulates the conditions under which an order can be canceled or changed. Many designers indicate that restocking charges will be assessed if the client cancels an order. This *restocking charge* is considered a fee to cover the paperwork costs that have already been incurred, as well as a small penalty for taking back merchandise that the client does not want. In almost all cases, a manufacturer will charge the designer a restocking charge for canceling an order.

The seller **has** other rights when the buyer refuses to accept the goods or in some other **way** breaches the sales contract. In general, when the buyer breaches the sales contract, the seller is allowed to withhold delivery of the goods.

One common issue arises when the client claims that the items delivered are not those specified in the sales agreement. This disagreement is often caused by the designer using vague descriptions of goods in sales agreements. Frequently, this sort of disagreement concerns a discrepancy between colors and finishes. To avoid this issue, the designer should obtain a cutting of current stock for fabric, or an otherwise appropriate sample for other goods, and have the clients sign or initial that they approve the material in question before the order is ever placed. If the designer can show that the fabric was substantially the correct color (barring anything greater than a dye-lot variation), the buyer would be in breach of contract by refusing acceptance of the order. The designer, on written notification, would have a right to cancel the order and could sue the client for breach of contract. However, if the designer was not justified in canceling the order, the buyer could sue the designer for breach of contract.

It is also common for designers to perform a partial delivery of goods to the client and bill the client for what was delivered. A partial delivery billing is feasible only if it was permitted by the terms and conditions of the sales contract. If a client refuses to pay for the partial delivery, the client breaches the contract. The designer could withhold delivery of the other furniture items until the client pays for the previous delivery.

In some situations, the seller may resort to canceling the contract with the buyer when the buyer breaches the contract (UCC 2–703[f]). A breach may occur when the client refuses to pay for the goods or wrongly refuses delivery of the goods. Canceling the contract requires notification to the client that he or she is in breach and that the client is still obligated to pay for any goods already delivered. Again, it is important to have a cancellation clause in the sales agreement in the first place, to better protect the designer if such a situation

TABLE 9-1.

Tips to help designers avoid problems when selling goods

Fully describe on the sales agreement the goods to be ordered and sold. Include dimensions, finish selection, and/or fabric name and color number for furniture items. Include similar information for other products.
Do not process any purchase orders until the client has signed the sales agreement and has provided the required prepayment.
Be sure to go over the terms and conditions on your sales agreement with each new client and whenever a client orders goods from the firm.
Obtain credit reports on all new clients.
Request textile cuttings of current stock to ensure color matches are correct before finalizing the purchase with the supplier.
If you use faxes or e-mails to order goods, make sure that you receive a report copy of the fax that the supplier has received the purchase order and/or that you print a hard copy of all e-mails that you send or receive concerning purchases, acknowledgments, and quotes.
Obtain client signatures or initials, approving all goods that might be questioned, such as upholstered furniture items.
Make sure that your terms and conditions concerning the client's right to cancel an order are clear and protect the design firm. Be certain that you also explain the client's legal rights to cancel an order.
Work only with manufacturers and suppliers who provide reputable service and goods. Understand the terms and conditions of sale from every supplier with whom the firm does business.
Keep the client informed of the progress of all special orders.
Inspect all merchandise at the time of delivery to the firm's warehouse. Make sure this is done prior to paying the supplier in full.
Insist that the client sign off on all delivered goods. Take care of any discrepancies immediately so that the client has little room to argue for nonpayment.

arises. However, it is advisable to negotiate with the client over the issues rather than immediately resort to canceling future deliveries.

Designers must protect themselves against the possibility of a buyer trying to cancel an order, refuse an order, or refuse to pay for goods. This can be done by being very careful in writing up the descriptions of the goods on the sales order, getting the buyer's signature on the sales order, carefully preparing the purchase order, and checking on the progress of orders. If the delivered goods are as described, the buyer knows what will be ordered, and the buyer knows the terms and conditions of the sale, the buyer has no choice but to pay for the goods. Table 9-1 lists some hints on how to avoid problems in selling goods.

STATUTE OF FRAUDS

State legislatures establish specific requirements for when certain types of contracts must be in writing to be enforceable. The common terminology for such a law is the *Statute of Frauds*. Section 2–201(1) of the UCC discusses the Statute of Frauds as it applies to the sale of goods. This statute clarifies requirements and conditions of when contracts for the sale of goods actually exist and their terms.

A base condition of the Statute of Frauds is that a contract for the sale of goods over $500 must be in writing to be enforceable. Although the base dollar amount is generally considered to be $500, an amendment to the statute in the UCC in 2003 changed the amount to $5000.[5] It is critical that the practitioner contact the attorney general's office within his or her state to clarify this base amount.

Although a valid written contract for the sale of goods does not mean that the designer can force the client to take the goods, it does give the designer the legal right to sue for payment if he or she so chooses. A discussion of how this statute affects design contracts appears in Chapter 7.

The writing for the sale of goods does not have to be a formal single document. Often, orders for goods are a combination of faxes and sales slips or purchase orders. If something is ordered verbally, it should always be followed up by a written sales confirmation. The order should name the parties involved, provide a description of what is to be ordered, and indicate the quantity and price. It should also be signed by the person to be charged. For the ordering of goods, the critical elements are the quantity of what is to be ordered and signature.

There are also specific exceptions to the rule that an agreement for the sale of goods must be in writing. First, between merchants, an oral agreement is valid if one party sends the other party a signed confirmation outlining the details of the agreement. The receiving merchant has 10 days to respond in writing to any conditions or content of the offer with which he or she does not agree. Failure to respond within the 10 days results in the formation of a valid contract.

Second, in some states an oral contract for the special manufacture of goods that are not suitable for anyone else, and whose manufacture has been substantially started, becomes a valid contract. For example, Mary Jones Designs places a telephone order to Smith's Drapery Company for the manufacture of 10 different-sized arched mini blinds at a price of $1800. A month later, after production has been started but not finished, the client cancels the order and Jones calls to cancel the order. If it is unlikely that the blinds can be sold to another client of Smith's Drapery Company, Mary Jones Designs is liable. It is for this reason that designers include in the terms of their confirmations a statement that a restocking charge (of at least 25 to 50 percent) will be charged for any order the client cancels.

Third, in some states, if one party to the contract admits in court or in legal proceedings that a contract does exist, then an oral contract is binding as to what was admitted. For example, Robert Class places a telephone order for 50 yards of Wilton weave carpet from an English mill. The value of the carpet is $6000. The mill ships 500 yards. Class refuses the shipment, and the mill sues. Class admits in court that he ordered 50 yards of carpet. Because Class has admitted that an oral contract did exist, he would be liable to pay for the 50 yards of carpet, but not the mistaken extra yardage.

Finally, an oral agreement is enforceable up to the amount of payment made and accepted or the amount of goods delivered and accepted. For example, if a designer makes a verbal contract to order mini blinds for a client and the client provides the designer with a deposit, the client is liable to pay for and accept the quantity of blinds that the deposit covers. If the designer delivers a portion of the order for the blinds, the client is also liable for the value of the blinds that are delivered.

Interior designers should not agree to sell goods to clients and/or order goods for clients without a sales order or sales confirmation. Remember that this sales agreement must be signed by the client if the designer is to have legal recourse if the client later refuses delivery. Written agreements and follow-up agreements to verbal orders to suppliers are also good practice to protect the interior designer. If the designer fails to send a confirming order to the manufacturer, the manufacturer may not be bound to a sale. And the designer who fails to read an acknowledgment of an oral agreement is obliged to accept whatever the acknowledgment says.

THE SALES CONTRACT

The statutes related to the sale of goods generally follow the principles of contract law, although there are exceptions because the nature of selling and purchasing agreements varies. This is especially true when the selling occurs between merchants.

The buying and selling of goods occurs in person, over the phone, by mail, by fax, and via the Internet. The form of the agreement to buy and sell can thus also take many forms. Section 2–204 states, "A contract for the sale of goods may be made in any manner sufficient to show agreement, including conduct by both parties which recognizes the existence of such a contract."[6] The date of the agreement, description of what is being sold, price, and signature by the person being charged are handled somewhat differently from a contract for the sale of goods. Those differences are discussed throughout this chapter. This section investigates how offer, acceptance, and consideration function in sales law.

Offer (Sections 2–204, 2–205, 2–206, 2–305, 2–308, and 2–311)

Normally, a contract exists when an offer is followed by an acceptance. In sales law, however, the nature of offers and acceptances renders the point at which a contract comes into existence somewhat inexact. Because offers and acceptances in sales contracts are exchanged verbally, through the mail, electronically by e-mail and faxes, and by the behavior of the buyer and seller, it is more difficult to determine exactly when a contract begins to exist. To assist with this problem, the UCC in Section 2–204 states that a contract exists when there is sufficient agreement to an offer so that a contract has been formed. This agreement may be verbal, written, or by the actions of the parties. For example, the price for a sofa in a catalog is an offer. When the designer sends a purchase order for this sofa to the manufacturer, a contract is formed.

In contract law, the terms of the offer and the acceptance must be clearly stated before the contract can become effective. Because of the unusual circumstances surrounding offers and acceptances in sales law, though, the UCC permits an offer to be valid even if one or more terms of the agreement are not stated, provided that the parties intend to go through with the contract and the courts can agree that a contract is intended and can determine a remedy for breach of contract.

Open-Terms Provisions—An Introduction

Even if the designer forgets to put all the pertinent information on the purchase order that is sent to a supplier, in most situations the contract will still be effective. When items are omitted from or left blank on a purchase order, the order is said to have *open terms*. Provisions of the UCC allow the contract to be valid even when some of the terms of the contract are indefinite. Terms include quantity, description, part number, delivery location, payment, and price.

In general, if the terms are incomplete, it is likely that the contract will be valid, as long as it can be shown that both parties intend to fulfill the contract. However, the more terms there are that are left incomplete, the more difficult it will be for the courts to determine if the contract is valid. For example, should a designer order some tables and all the terms needed in the purchase order are present except the finish of the wood, the order would still be valid. However, if the quantity is missing, the order would usually be considered invalid, because the courts cannot determine the full value of the contract in order to establish a remedy. The general rule of thumb regarding open-terms provisions is: If the parties intend for a contract to exist, then one does exist, even if some of the information is missing.

Sally prepared a purchase order for four items from the same manufacturer for her client. She was in a hurry and left out the description of the sofa but included the catalog number, and also forgot the finish code for the coffee table and end tables. Her price for the end tables was also missing. Assuming that only the information mentioned here was on her preprinted purchase order, what other information seems to be missing?

Open-Price Term

It is not a good idea to leave the price off a purchase order to a supplier or to the client. If the price is missing, the other party can cancel the offer or determine a reasonable price. The question here is whether the two parties intend to conclude an agreement in "good faith," which would mean an honest and fair price. For example, if ABC Design Company agrees to furnish drapery tiebacks for a client but forgets to provide a price for those tiebacks, the client can either set a reasonable price for the items or cancel the order for the tiebacks.

The problem with this concept is that most often the price is reasonable only to the person who is setting the price. The interior designer should always be the person who sets the price to the client. Naturally, the interior designer should know what the price will be from the supplier before quoting prices to a client and placing an actual order. Any form or manner in which the interior designer gets a quotation from a supplier should clearly indicate that it is just that—a request for quotation and not an order. In this way, the designer avoids inadvertently ordering goods at a price that is higher than what the client is willing to pay before the client even agrees to purchase the goods.

Open-Payment Term

Another open term that is related to offers is an open-payment term. A *payment term* specifies the way an order or invoice can be paid—cash or check, for example—and when payment is due. If a payment due date for the goods has not been specified, the UCC stipulates that payment is due upon delivery to the buyer or at the time of "receipt of goods." The buyer receives the goods when he or she takes physical possession of the goods. Additionally, if payment terms have not been specified, the payment must be in cash, check, or agreed-upon credit. When the designer (or supplier) includes a phrase such as "Payment due within 10 days of receipt of invoice," the designer effectively gives the buyer 10 days of credit at no cost.

For the client, receipt of goods takes place when the goods are delivered to his or her home or office or when the client leaves the designer's place of business with the goods. According to UCC subsections 2–310(b) and (c), receipt of goods shipped from a manufacturer to the designer occurs when the goods are placed in the hands of the carrier. This is the reason that invoices often arrive before the goods do. However, this means that payment is due before the goods can be inspected. All buyers have the right to inspect the goods before they make payment. These same subsections provide for that right of inspection, but state that the inspection must be done promptly. If the goods are not as ordered, the seller must be notified immediately if the buyer does not want to be bound to pay.

Open-Delivery Term

If the location for the delivery has been omitted, it is customary for delivery to be made at the seller's business location. Neglecting to specify that the goods are to be delivered to the designer's warehouse service facility could result in a freight truck arriving at the designer's home office or wherever his or her place of business is located. In another situation, the goods might remain at the supplier's location, requiring the designer to pick up those goods rather than having the supplier deliver them to a warehouse. In either case, this omission could be quite costly to the designer. It is unlikely that any major manufacturer of goods would not call to check with the designer as to delivery location. However, the manufacturer is not obligated to do so if the delivery location has been omitted from the order.

Interior designers must also be very clear in circumstances where very large shipments or deliveries are due from a supplier. Manufacturers want to ship out goods as soon as they are ready, even if that means making more than one shipment. The UCC gives them that right if agreement as to full or partial shipments was not made in the original order. Section 2–307 states that delivery and payment are due at one time for all the items being sold, unless provisions in the agreement or "circumstances" allow for delivery and payment in lots—meaning partial shipments. The designer should include wording on the purchase order that informs the supplier whether shipment of less than the full order is acceptable.

The designer needs to protect himself or herself concerning partial deliveries to the client as well. For large-sized projects involving multiple items, it is not unusual for the client to want the goods delivered as soon as they arrive. The designer usually prefers to deliver the goods to the client promptly in order to maintain a smooth cash flow. However, if the designer wants to receive payments for goods delivered in lots rather than as a whole, he or she must include a term in the sales contract notifying the buyer of this fact. When several deliveries are made to the client to complete one order, and there is no written term in the contract covering this situation, payment is not required until the entire order has been delivered. It should also be noted that multiple deliveries to the same client are expensive, as the warehouse service will charge for each trip from the warehouse to the jobsite.

Open-Quantity Term

It is critical for the interior designer to include the quantity of each item that is being ordered, both on the supplier's order form and in the client's invoice. It is difficult if not impossible for a court to determine what to do when the quantity of goods has not been specified. Not only does it make it impossible to know if a sufficient "number" of items was delivered, but it is also impossible for the courts to determine what the charges for the items should be.

The Firm Offer

If the merchant makes an offer in writing, whether or not consideration has been given by the buyer or a time limit to the offer has been set, the merchant cannot revoke the offer either during the time limit or for a reasonable length of time. This is referred to as a *firm offer*. It is critical to point out that a firm offer must be in writing and signed by the merchant. This provision protects the buyer—whether that buyer is an interior designer buying from a supplier or a client buying from the interior designer—from quoting one price and then raising the price. For example,

Mary Smith signs a written contract to sell $30,000 of furniture to Susan Rose, but Rose does not sign the agreement and does not provide any deposit. Ten days later, Smith realizes that she made an error in her calculations. If Rose accepts the contract within a reasonable length of time, Smith will lose $2000, since she used a net price list to discount some of the goods. Legally, Smith cannot revoke the offer, as it was a "firm offer" in writing and was signed by her.

The points in this discussion are important to the interior design practice. They show the value of good preparation of paperwork of the specification list, the contract for the client, and purchase orders. Designer omissions can cost time and money. They can even result in lawsuits against the designer.

Acceptance: Sections 2–206 and 2–207

Suppliers and manufacturers generally articulate their terms of sales through catalogs and price lists. Of course, some suppliers for custom goods, for example, discuss terms of sales with designers and prepare a proposal that then outlines the terms of sale. Ordering is based on the terms established in a price list or on a proposal from a supplier. The designer must also be careful to see if a time limit is involved in the offer and order process, as interim price changes can cause the designer to lose money.

When the designer orders from a manufacturer or supplier, if acceptance is not made in the manner specified by the seller, the acceptance can be rejected or considered a counteroffer. However, the law generally considers an acceptance to be valid if it is received within the time limit set, even if it is by a different method of acceptance. Usually the seller wants an oral acceptance, followed by a signed acceptance of the sales proposal. When the supplier sends or otherwise indicates an acceptance to the merchant to buy (receipt of the designer's purchase order), a sales contract has been formed. In general, the acceptance should mirror the offer; that is, if the offer was made via a purchase order sent through the mail, the acceptance should be mailed. If the order was placed via fax, the acceptance should be faxed, and so on.

Although interior designers should place orders with suppliers only after a written purchase order is provided or accompanies a purchase, some designers do not avail themselves of this type of documentation 100 percent of the time. The excuse of being in a rush to order and too busy to follow up is just a cover-up of poor practice. For example, Ralph Brown telephoned in an order for mini blinds and did not follow up with a written confirmation. When the blinds were ready for installation, Brown found that they were the wrong size. The size of the length had been made the size of the width, and vice versa. Brown claimed that the blinds company had made the mistake. The blinds company played a tape recording of the telephone order. It was clear that Brown had given the dimensions incorrectly. He had to pay for the blinds and reorder them, using the correct sizes.

Interior designers establish their terms of sale through their sales agreements and proposals to clients, and acceptance of those agreements is represented by the client's signature on the sales agreement. In the designer/end-user relationship, there are usually few problems or questions related to the existence of the contract. This is because, in everyday practice, the designer prepares a confirmation proposal that states who is being charged; lists the quantities, descriptions, and prices of the items being sold; lists the terms of sale, such as when payment is due; and requires the client's signature on the confirmation. Assuming that price is not an issue, rarely does the client indicate acceptance in any way other than by signing the confirmation.

A key to the agreement between designer and client is the time limit of the offer and whether or not the client has signed the agreement. If the designer's proposal states that the offer is good only for 10 days (or some other time limit), the client must respond within that 10-day period; if he or she does not, the designer does not legally have to honor the original offer. If no time limit is stated, the client has a "reasonable length of time" to respond. For example, a month after receiving the proposal, the client signs and returns the confirmation. However, the price of the goods to the designer has increased during that time. The designer may very well be expected to sell the goods at the quoted price, thus lowering his or her profit margin. Thus, it is important that all offers to sell goods to clients state a time limit for acceptance on the confirmation.

In contract law, a contract exists only if all the terms of the offer are exactly matched by the acceptance. Any differences constitute a counteroffer. In sales law, it is not uncommon with sales between merchants for the terms on the purchase order and the terms of the acknowledgment to contain some differences. In interior design practices, the quantity, description, and price commonly match. Terms such as ship date and general terms of the sale often vary. The UCC allows a contract to be formed when the conditions of the purchase order and the acknowledgment are different, as long as the offeree's response indicates a definite acceptance of the original terms of the offer and there are no conditional terms in the offer or acceptance. For example, designer A sends a purchase order to manufacturer B for some custom-made bedspreads. The purchase order is prepared following the instructions in the catalog. The acknowledgment comes back from B with the statement, "On condition that a 50 percent deposit be submitted within ten days of receipt of acknowledgment. No work will be started until deposit is received." If this term is not stated in the catalog, no contract exists, unless the buyer agrees, because the seller has added a condition to the terms of the offer.

When the differences in terms are minor and neither party objects to the differences, a contract has been formed. If the offer and acceptance are made over the phone, the printed confirmation and acknowledgments are proposals confirming the oral contract—and, again, a contract has been formed, as long as no objections are made, no conditions are placed on the order or acceptance after the original offer is made, and the differences are minor.

What all this means to designers is that they must not only carefully prepare the terms of sale on their purchase orders used to order from suppliers, but also that they must be familiar with the terms and conditions of sale from all the suppliers. What is ordered is usually not the problem in interior design orders. The price, ship dates, warranties, and payment terms are more often the issue. Chapter 13 contains an example of the terms and conditions on the back of a firm's sales order—the document that should be used to clarify what has been ordered for each client (see Figure 13-2).

Should the acknowledgment from the supplier contain discrepancies with regard to quantities, descriptions, and so on, it is important for the designer to make prompt written notification of the errors to the supplier. There are literally only a few days, to a general maximum of 10 days, to catch and correct any errors in an order. Failure to do so means acceptance of the acknowledgment and thus the formation of a contract, and the designer then "owns" the merchandise, even if the error was made by the supplier.

If there are material differences between the designer's purchase order terms and a supplier's acknowledgment terms, the designer may be protected by the UCC constraints against material differences. A *material difference* refers to a substantial or essential change from the original. However, to be protected, the designer is encouraged to object in writing to any terms that are different from his or her own.

Consideration: Section 2–304

Recall from Chapter 7 that *consideration* is the price one pays to another party for fulfilling a contract. Consideration is usually monetary payment by cash, check, or credit. In general, the UCC does not differ from the general contract law precept that consideration must be part of the acceptance. Between designer and client, the consideration is primarily a deposit that is paid when the agreement, which states that the client will pay full value at a later time, is signed. Between designer and supplier, consideration is generally the good-faith credit that the supplier affords to the designer, knowing that the designer will pay the supplier in full after the goods have been shipped.

There are strict rules governing consideration when the buyer or seller attempts to modify the contract. One of the most problematic areas in this regard is that of price increases. For example, after the designer sends the purchase order to the supplier and the supplier acknowledges the order to the designer, but before merchandise has been shipped, the supplier informs the designer that the price will go up 10 percent as a result of an increase in materials price. The designer subsequently notifies the supplier that he or she accepts the increase. Later, the designer changes her mind and says that she will only pay the original price. Whether or not the designer accepts the increase orally or in writing, she is bound by the new price. This is true as long as the supplier can show that the change in price is due to a reason such as a change in availability of materials to manufacture the finished goods, causing an increase in price for the finished goods. If the supplier makes a mistake in its pricing, the attempted modification of the contract is invalid.

Once the terms and conditions are agreed to by the designer and the supplier, modifications agreed to later are binding, if they are reasonable as a result of some occurrence that is beyond the control of the party who is asking for the modifications. If the supplier later tells the designer that the price will be higher and the designer does not agree, the contract is revoked. If the original or modified contract must meet the Statute of Frauds or stipulates that changes must be in writing, these changes must be in writing to be valid.

ELECTRONIC AGREEMENTS AND SIGNATURES

The interior designer's business use of the Internet for buying and selling merchandise is not foreign to most readers. The use of electronic agreements likely began as interior designers ordered merchandise for clients by use of facsimile (fax) machines. Today designers order all manner of merchandise for clients via the Internet, in addition to continued use of faxing. It is thus important to have some understanding of electronic agreements and signatures on electronic documents (including e-mails).

The Uniform Commercial Code and the federal ESIGN Act permit electronic agreements for a contract for the sale of goods. This helps business-to-business ordering of goods, such as a designer ordering goods for a client. (Information on the ESIGN act and other federal law is discussed later in this section.)

It is important for readers to understand that the developing laws and standards concerned with electronic agreements do not, for the most part, deal with the sale of services. An electronically transmitted contract for design services might not be a valid contract in the reader's jurisdiction. Readers should discuss this question with their attorneys before issuing an online contract for design services.

An electronic agreement or contract for the sale of goods must follow the basic elements of any contract. If the contract falls under the Statute of Frauds, the electronic agreement must meet those requirements. Any electronic agreement should include such things as descriptions of what is to be ordered, quantities, and pricing, and must certainly convey the seller's intent to sell and the buyer's intent to buy. What the courts are looking for is evidence that both parties intend to go forward with the terms stated in the electronic contract. It is also critical to the courts that the person signing was the right person to be involved in creating the agreement.

The designer can create a contract to order merchandise from a vendor and then transmit that order or contract to the vendor. The designer might also be able to initiate an order by completing a scanned PDF order form and transmitting that order to the vendor. If the vendor sends it back to the designer with some sort of electronic signature showing acceptance, an agreement is created. The designer can likewise initiate a sales agreement to a client in the same manner.

An important element in an online agreement concerns terms and conditions of sale. Designers need to be sure that they carefully read the terms of sale shown on a vendor's Web site, so that they understand their rights concerning nonconforming goods, returns, damages, and the like. Online buyers also need to understand how goods are to be paid for and refund policies, if any. From the seller's point of view, these same items must be carefully and clearly stated on the Web site. If a designer uses an online sales agreement with a client, those same concerns about terms and conditions of sale must be conveyed to the client.

Of course, an electronic agreement is not a contract signed in the traditional paper-and-pen style. Online purchasing also raises questions about *electronic signatures* (e-signatures). Recall that contracts generally cannot be enforced unless they are signed by the party to be charged—the buyer (interior designer or client) for most of the situations in interior design.

Unfortunately, the law does not clearly define an "electronic signature." A signature can be created digitally using special keys or codes within the system. Readers are no doubt familiar with the use of digitized pads, where you sign your name with a stylus to make a credit card purchase. Sometimes these agreements are converted to PDF documents so that an actual signature can be added. In other cases, people type in their name on a document, perhaps using a script typeface. Even a mark rather than a person's full name may be a signature in the electronic world. The mark must be something that can be identified with the person making the mark; however, the meaning of "mark" is also not clearly defined.

Issues do exist when using a scanned actual signature. A signature that is out in cyber space can be captured by unscrupulous people who use it to forge one's signature. If you are concerned about the possibility of fraud when using online methods and digital signatures, then don't use online contracts. Insist on using paper-and-pencil contracts with original signatures.

An electronic agreement can also come into existence when the ordering party simply clicks a box on the screen that says something like "I agree" or "Accept." This is called a *click-on agreement:* The moment the buyer clicks that box, the legal acceptance needed to form a contract is created. The buyer is bound by the terms of sale, even if the buyer didn't bother to read the terms. That is why it is important for sellers to make the terms available to the buyer and for buyers to seek out that information from the seller.

For the most part, when a disagreement occurs concerning an online sale, courts generally interpret existing contract law and the UCC principles to make their determination. E-contract law is still being created, so the judgments and determination about any particular case in any specific jurisdiction are not predictable with any certainty. Questions concerning online contracts should be directed to the reader's state/provincial attorney general's office, because e-signature laws vary.

Although it is not necessary to follow up an electronic agreement with a paper copy, it is very important to print out and maintain a paper copy of that electronic agreement. In fact, this may be required by laws in the designer's jurisdiction, so always prepare a hard copy of electronic agreements made by fax, e-mail, or other online methods.

In 1999, the U.S. Congress passed the Uniform Electronic Transactions Act (UETA). This law clarifies that an e-signature is valid whether it is digitally recorded, is the name at the end of an e-mail, or is a click-on located in a Web site.[7]

Also in the United States, the Electronic Signatures in Global and National Commerce Act (ESIGN Act) was passed in 2000 to "provide that no contract, record, or signature may be 'denied legal effect' solely because it is in an electronic form."[8] This makes electronic signatures as valid as on-paper signatures in the United States for many types of situations. Not all are covered, so readers are advised to discuss electronic signatures in their jurisdiction with an attorney.

Many other countries also have e-commerce and e-contract laws. Readers in foreign countries should seek information from their country to understand how valid electronic agreements are made.

Many designers still use a freestanding fax machine to send and receive orders, although sending faxes from a computer has gained a lot of support, and it is now possible to send and receive faxes through most computers. To send a fax by computer, it is usually necessary to purchase and install the appropriate software, whether that is part of the computer system's existing programs, or purchased from a third-party software company. Online faxes can also be sent by arrangement with fee-based online fax services. If you need to fax a document such as an order form, you must first scan the document into the computer and then attach it to the fax. In some respects it is similar to sending an e-mail with an attachment.

An important issue in ordering via fax is being sure the designer sends and receives information on the terms and conditions of the sale along with the face page of the actual order. Often, the normal terms and conditions of sale, which are generally on the back of the paper sales order to a client or on the back of the acknowledgment from the supplier, are not faxed. A statement to the effect, "The product is sold subject to the terms and conditions of sale of goods by 'the design firm,' which are available for review upon request,"[9] is necessary to protect the designer and suppliers who use faxes to acknowledge orders. It is the seller's responsibility to make sure that the buyer knows the terms and conditions of the sale, whether these terms are printed in a price list, on the sales agreement, or on an acknowledgment, or are covered by a clause such as the preceding one for a fax.

In general, designers must also be careful about what they promise or even say in e-mails, as the exchange of information via e-mail can also create an electronic agreement or contract. The names included in the end of an e-mail create a formal signature and acceptance. If the client's e-mail simply says "go ahead with the drawings," in this age of electronic agreements, that "go ahead" indicates agreement for work to be done. It also, of course, applies to a designer's promises or comments to vendors and the client. Remember, whether the correspondence is on paper or in some electronic communication, if it includes an offer and acceptance, it in all likelihood creates a contract.

The law covering electronic agreements and electronic signatures is evolving quickly. Not all jurisdictions have adopted the ESIGN Act or the UETA act. Therefore, someone planning to use electronic agreements in business should seek the advice of an attorney. The information overview provided in this section is very broad and should not be construed as legal advice.

SALES ON APPROVAL

A common special sale situation in the interior design profession is the *sale on approval*. In this situation, the client who is not sure about a product takes it to his or her home or business location to see if it is appropriate. If the client subsequently keeps the product, he or she pays for it; otherwise, he or she is obligated to return the product. As with any kind of sale, it is best practice to have the client sign an appropriate document indicating that the item is on approval and the length of time the item can remain in the client's possession.

The UCC imposes a normal condition to the sale on approval that is explained by the following example. Jane Miller finds a sofa on a showroom floor but is not sure that it will go with her decor. She asks if she can try it "on approval." The store allows her five days to decide. If she calls and says that she will keep the sofa before the five days are up, or fails to call before the five days and makes no attempt to return the sofa, the store considers the sofa sold and sends her a bill. If Miller damages the sofa before the five days are up and before she approves the sale, the loss is Miller's. If it is damaged in transit or in some way but through no fault of Miller, the loss is the seller's (Sections 2–326 and 2–327).

TITLE

In legal terms, ownership of goods is called *title*. When goods are bought and sold, ownership of those goods changes from the seller's hands to the buyer's. For a sale to take place, goods must exist and must be identified in the contract. Section 2–401 of the UCC clarifies the law related to the title of goods. Unless otherwise specified and agreed, title passes when possession changes from the seller to the buyer.

Most commonly, title passes at the time and place that physical delivery of the goods is made by the seller to the buyer. This is clear-cut when a sale occurs between the designer and a client. The designer should use a sales confirmation describing what has been sold. If the goods are delivered to the client's home or jobsite, a delivery ticket or other evidence of what has been delivered and accepted should be used. The delivery ticket should also be dated and signed by the client. This provides clear evidence of what has been delivered and that the title has passed to the buyer. The description of the goods on the delivery ticket should mirror what is on the sales confirmation, signed by the client prior to ordering (or turning over) the goods. A signature accepting delivery is very important in case the client does not pay for the goods for any reason. A signed delivery ticket shows acceptance of the delivery and title transfer, and thus responsibility for payment.

When the designer buys from a manufacturer, title often passes by use of a shipment or a destination contract. Under a *shipment contract*, title to the goods passes to the buyer when the manufacturer (seller) places the merchandise into the hands of the shipper. In Chapter 8, the term *FOB, Factory* was defined; with this designation, title passes when the supplier places the goods into the hands of a shipper. Recall that FOB is an abbreviation for "free on board." A price list does not have to specifically say "factory." A shipment contract means from the place the goods are originally shipped. Because title passes to the buyer once the goods are on a shipping vehicle, the buyer is also responsible for the risk of loss during transit. This is discussed in the next section. This is the most common way for title to change hands, unless otherwise noted in the price list, catalog, acknowledgment, or other documentation from the seller.

When the seller uses a *destination contract*, the manufacturer retains title to the goods until they arrive at the buyer's delivery address—the destination of the shipment. The manufacturer thus retains ownership of the goods and subsequent responsibility and risk until the goods are delivered. The manufacturer often places "FOB, Destination" in the catalog to indicate this choice. If the purchase order does not designate a destination, the supplier will instruct the shipper to deliver the goods to the designer's place of business listed on the purchase order.

The reader may be familiar with yet another term of shipment called *cash on delivery (COD)*. Shipments sent COD require that the buyer pay cash (or other approved payment) at the time the merchandise is delivered to the buyer's location.

Some buyers do not require shipping or delivery and take the merchandise right from the studio or showroom. When no delivery is required, the title passes to the buyer when the contract is made. If the buyer refuses delivery or otherwise wants to return the goods, title reverts to the seller.

RISK

Because title can change at differing times, the UCC must address who is liable for the risk of loss during shipping of the goods. It does so in Sections 2–319 through 2–323.

"FOB" and the notation following it indicate who assumes the risk of loss should the goods be damaged in transit. In a shipping contract, the risk of loss is transferred to the buyer when goods are passed to the carrier. If the goods are damaged before they arrive at the buyer's location, it is the buyer's responsibility to recover damages from the carrier. For example, Darby & Smith Designs was expecting a large shipment of furniture for a radio station in Chicago. The truck got into an accident on the freeway, in which all the furniture was damaged. Darby & Smith Designs will have to deal with the shipping company concerning claims for damages.

In destination contracts, the risk for loss is transferred to the buyer when the goods reach the buyer's destination. If the goods have been damaged in transit, it is the seller's responsibility to recover the damages from the carrier. Using the facts from the preceding example, under a destination contract, the manufacturer, not Darby & Smith Designs, must deal with the shipping company concerning claims for the damaged furniture, because the manufacturer retains title to the goods.

When no delivery is required, risk passes in different ways, depending on whether the seller is a merchant. If the seller is a merchant, then risk passes when the buyer receives the goods. If the seller is not a merchant, then risk passes when the seller gives the merchandise to the buyer. This very subtle difference exists only to show that a merchant selling goods has more responsibility concerning the damage of undelivered goods than a non-merchant seller. Additional discussions concerning FOB and shipping can be found in Chapters 8 and 14.

WARRANTIES AND PRODUCT LIABILITY

Another obligation under sales law relates to product warranties and liabilities. When selling products directly to the client—that is, when the interior designer profits from the sale of the goods—the interior designer takes on a certain amount of responsibility for product failures. Interior designers must fully understand the implications of warranties and product liability.

Designers are liable for the performance of the products that they specify in any project. They can also be held accountable for what they say about products and how the product might perform for the client's situation. Products must meet the expectations of reasonable use and fitness for the situation in which they will be used. These concepts relate directly to warranties.

A product that is improperly manufactured or installed can cause physical harm or damage to the client, the client's property, or a guest of the client. Designers are responsible for making sure that the products they specify are of sound quality, are appropriate for the intended use, and are specified and installed in such a way as not to cause injury to the people who will use the products or cause damage to the space in which the products will be installed. These are issues of product liability.

Warranties

Consumers are protected by a large number of regulations and laws that place much of the burden on vendors and designers to provide safe products. The day when the phrase "buyer beware" was standard for consumers has long since passed.

Warranties are one way in which the buyer is protected. *Warranties* place a burden on the seller to ensure that the goods he or she sells meet certain standards. In contract and sales law, a *warranty* is "a promise that something in furtherance of the contract is guaranteed by one of the contractors, especially the seller's promise that the thing being sold is as promised or represented."[10] Buyers regularly ask questions about warranties—or written guarantees—on many of the products that they purchase. Other regulations and laws help to satisfy the customer that what he or she is purchasing meets correct standards of design, manufacturing, and use.

Four important kinds of warranties arising in commercial sales are governed by the UCC:

1. Warranty of title (Section 2–312)
2. Express warranty (Section 2–313)
3. Implied warranty of merchantability (Section 2–314)
4. Implied warranty of fitness for a particular purpose (Section 2–315)

When a designer or a design firm offers a warranty on a product, failure to honor that warranty is a breach of contract duty and gives the client the right to sue. The seller's breach also allows the customer to cancel the order.

Warranty of Title

Warranty of title indicates that the seller has title or legal ownership to the goods and can legally sell them to others. Only the legal owner can sell the goods. Basically, this means that the seller, knowingly or not, is not selling stolen goods or goods that he or she does not have authorization to sell. For example, Jason had a chair in his studio on approval from a vendor for almost a year.

Jason recently sold the chair to a client. If Jason did not subsequently pay the vendor for the chair, he had no warranty of title to sell the chair to his client.

A second function of warranty of title is to protect the buyer from loss if he or she unknowingly buys goods with a lien attached. A *lien* indicates that someone other than the person who has possession of the goods has a security interest in the goods. In the example with Jason, the vendor that actually owned the chair had a security interest in the goods and could have filed a lien against Jason for selling the chair. The buyer of the chair probably did not know that Jason did not actually have title; thus, that buyer would be protected and would be entitled to recover the cost of the chair if the vendor actually filed a lien. However, if the buyer buys the goods knowing that there is a lien against the goods, he or she will not be able to collect from the seller.

A third aspect of warranty of title concerns infringement. This means that the goods do not infringe on any patent, copyright, or trademark claimed by anyone else. For example, a designer created a logo for a client of the design firm in which he works and the copyright is registered by the design firm. However, the client was not shown the design at that time. Six months later, the designer starts his own design practice and contacts the former client about possible work. The client hires the designer to produce a logo and is shown the logo that the designer did for his previous employer. The client buys that design and incorporates it into all of the client's letterhead. The original design firm can sue both the client and the designer for infringement, because the original design firm owned the copyright to the logo.

Express Warranty

Nora's client was very concerned that the wall covering in the locker room of a country club would resist moisture. Nora told the client that the grass cloth was specially treated to resist moisture, so the client gave the go-ahead to order and install the grass cloth. Unfortunately, Nora's statement was untrue.

Promises, claims, descriptions, or affirmations made about a product's performance, quality, or condition that form the "basis of the bargain" are *express warranties*. In effect, the *basis of the bargain* means that the information provided is what primarily influences the buyer's decision. Nora's claim about the moisture resistance of the grass cloth material substantially formed the client's decision to purchase that wall covering.

Interior designers and salespeople, in the course of their discussions with clients about a product's viability, often make statements about what the product can or cannot do. Specific promises or statements by the seller, whether made in writing or orally, can create an express warranty. Care must be taken when making statements about products, as those words can create an express warranty—though not always.

The seller need not use words such as *warranty* or *guarantee* in the sales presentation, nor does he or she even have to intend to make a warranty. The UCC is not entirely clear about how precise these statements have to be and how strongly they must be worded to be taken as warranties, so care must be taken to say exactly what is meant to avoid misunderstandings. Nora's comment that the grass cloth was specially treated created an express warranty. Displaying a sample of the goods that are to be sold also creates express warranties. For example, many designers sell merchandise from a catalog, with the client never seeing the piece before purchase and delivery. The goods delivered must conform to what was displayed in the catalog. Designers who sell goods in this way need to be sure they clarify fabric choices, wood or metal finishes, and so forth on sales orders so that what is actually being ordered is clear to the client.

When a seller's statements are only the seller's opinion or relate only to the worth of the product, generally no express warranty is created. For example, Jimmy says to a client, "This is the best open-office system on the market." This is an expression of opinion, not a statement of fact. This kind of salesmanship is called *puffing*. In contrast, a statement from Jimmy such as "This wood flooring is care-free" is a promise that can be interpreted by the customer as meaning that he or she will not have to wax the floor. In this situation, Jimmy is very likely making an express warranty. Care should always be taken when using words that express quality, because a judge's interpretation of what is said will determine how he or she decides the case.

If the salesperson is believed to be an expert concerning the goods being sold, any statements of opinion are more likely to constitute express warranties. Comments made about a product by a designer who only occasionally sells the product could be considered puffing, whereas statements made by a manufacturer's representative—who is an expert—are more likely to be considered an express warranty.

It is therefore important to be careful when making statements about the quality and performance of a product. If the statement is reasonable and a reasonable person believes the statement, a warranty may be created.

Implied Warranty of Merchantability

The implied warranty of merchantability affects sales made by merchants. When a client purchases goods from an interior designer, the designer is considered a merchant by the UCC. The law states that when a merchant sells goods, it is implied that the seller understands the characteristics of the goods he or she is selling and can thus specify them for proper use. Implied warranties thus exist by the operation of law. In its simplest form, the UCC says that the goods must be "fit for the ordinary purposes for which such goods are used."[11] As long as the merchant is a merchant of the kind of goods in consideration, he or she is held liable. Thus, a desk sold by an interior designer to the owner of a real estate office automatically has an implied warranty of merchantability associated with the desk.

Under this section of the UCC, goods sold must be of fair to average quality and must be comparable in quality to other similar goods. They must be fit for the normal purpose of the good. They must be packaged and labeled adequately, and must conform to the statements made on the packaging or labels. For example, strippable wallpaper must be strippable; fire-retardant fabric must not ignite or burn within the limits stated on the binder; a solid brass headboard must be made of solid brass.

This section of the UCC makes an implied warranty of merchantability applicable to every sale by a merchant. Liability does not disappear, even if the merchant is unaware of any defect in the product. The interior designer most likely will be held liable, along with the manufacturer, when a product fails or causes some injury to a person or property.

Implied Warranty of Fitness for a Particular Purpose

Implied warranty of fitness for a particular purpose affects the goods that any seller—merchant or not—sells to another. When the seller knows the intended purpose for the goods and the buyer must rely on the seller's knowledge to select or recommend goods for the purpose, an implied warranty of fitness for a particular purpose exists.

The seller does not need to know the exact purpose of the purchase. If he or she has a general idea of the purpose, and if the buyer has relied on the seller's knowledge or skill in selecting the goods, an implied warranty of fitness has been created. For example, Mrs. Damon hires John Simmons to redecorate her home. Simmons sells the wall coverings for the kitchen and the bathrooms to Damon. Damon makes it clear to Simmons that the wallpaper in the bathroom must be able to withstand a lot of steam and dampness, as her husband takes long, hot showers. A few weeks after installation, the bathroom wallpaper begins to peel away. Because Simmons knew the purpose of the goods and Damon relied on Simmons's professional knowledge, Simmons has breached the implied warranty of fitness. Of course, the paperhanger, if he or she also knew the purpose of the purchase, may also be held liable for the breach.

Magnuson-Moss Warranty Act

The Magnuson-Moss Warranty Act is a U.S. federal law enacted to make it easier for the consumer to understand what is being warranted in any product sold to end users. Warranties between merchants are regulated by the UCC rules. Oral warranties are not covered by this legislation.

The act does not require that sellers provide a written warranty for goods sold to consumers. It also does not apply to warranties on services. If the cost of the consumer goods is more than $10 and a seller chooses to make an express written warranty, the warranty must be labeled as "full" or "limited." In addition, if the goods have a value of more than $15, the Magnuson-Moss Warranty Act requires that a written warranty be provided to the potential consumer.* In this situation, who warrants the goods, what is covered, any limitations, the legal rights of the consumer, and how those rights can be enforced must all be spelled out.

Full warranties require repair or replacement at no charge to the buyer should the goods be defective. There cannot be a time limit on the replacement. If there is, it is not a full warranty, but rather a limited warranty. When repairs cannot be made in a reasonable time, the product must be replaced or a refund must be given to the consumer. Limited warranties must clearly state what is warranted and the time limit of the warranty.

An excellent resource for information on this act, as well as other federal warranty laws, is the Federal Trade Commission, www.business.ftc.gov.

*Miller and Jentz, 2006, p. 394.

Disclaimers of Warranty

An express warranty can be disclaimed if the manufacturer or seller does not make any express promises or statements of fact relating to or describing the goods. Designers must always be careful about what they say concerning the performance and suitability of products, or other factual statements about the products they specify and/or sell. This is true whether the statements are written or verbal. Saying, "We guarantee that this fabric will not show wear for five years," constitutes an express warranty. A disclaimer to that statement might be this: "We provide no warranty beyond that of the manufacturer, whose tests under normal use in a home indicate that the fabric will show no significant wear for five years."

An implied warranty of merchantability can be verbal, but a disclaimer of warranty must be specific as to disclaiming merchantability and must use the term *merchantability* in the oral or written disclaimer. For example, Michael Cobb of Cobb Designs sells Mr. Smith a budget-priced guest chair to be used as a desk chair based on the needs described by Smith. Cobb verbally informs Smith that he does not warrant merchantability of the chair, as it is not fit for use as a desk chair. Cobb also attaches a note making the same disclaimer to the sales agreement. The chair does not hold up, and Smith wants Cobb to replace it. Because warranty was disclaimed as to merchantability, Cobb is not liable to replace the chair on those grounds.

An implied warranty-of-fitness disclaimer must be in writing and displayed prominently. Using the term *warranty of fitness* in the disclaimer is strongly suggested, though the term *fitness* is not required. For example, a designer sells a client a kitchen stool with a cane seat, which will be used at a kitchen counter. The confirmation says something like, "ABS Designs provides no warranty of fitness beyond that of the manufacturer's for normal, reasonable use." A few weeks after purchase, the client uses the stool to stand on and the cane breaks, resulting in injury to the client. The designer is not liable, because the client was not using the stool in a manner that was normal and reasonable for the product.

Disclaimers of fitness are also written with such words as *as is*. It is common to see retailers label used furniture "as is" to protect themselves against claims regarding used or damaged goods. According to the UCC, however, even new merchandise may be sold labeled "as is" to indicate that no warranty other than what the manufacturer provides exists.

If a client refuses to inspect goods before signing a delivery ticket, there is no implied warranty concerning defects. This is because the client has refused, for whatever reason, to inspect the goods prior to acceptance. If the seller does not ask the buyer to inspect the goods and the goods are damaged or defective, the seller is liable.

Products Liability

As consumers, we expect the products we purchase to be safe and not cause harm. When interior designers purchase products for clients from a manufacturer, they expect the same safety of design and manufacture.

There is an expectation that the products will meet certain minimal standards of materials, workmanship, and design for their intended use. If the products fail, certain express or implied warranties may have been breached. Manufacturers and sellers of products may be liable to end users, bystanders, and other merchants if individuals are physically harmed or if property damage occurs. This is called *products liability*. Products liability includes the areas of tort law related to negligence and strict liability and contract law related to warranty.

Whenever the interior designer specifies a product, if the product fails and causes injury, the designer is almost always named as a defendant in the lawsuit along with the manufacturer. The designer is included in the suit because tort law related to product liability allows anyone involved in the distribution of products to be held liable. It should be remembered that product liability usually covers only reasonable, normal use of a product. If the client uses a product in a way for which it was not designed, the interior designer will most likely not be held liable.

Products Liability and Negligence

In Chapter 4, we defined *negligence* as a failure to use the care that is expected of a reasonable person in the same or similar situation, when this failure to use care results in injury to another person or his or her property. Manufacturers of products must use this same care in the design, materials selection, production, and testing of their products, so that the products will be safe when they are used as intended.

In situations concerning products liability, the plaintiff—the harmed party—must show that the manufacturer did not use due care and that the defective product caused an injury. The plaintiff must also show that he or she used the product as designed and knew the risk of using the product incorrectly. If a guest at a client's house was injured when a chair collapsed, to recover damages he would have to prove that the item was manufactured improperly, that the chair had been sold in a defective condition, and that he had been using the chair for its intended purpose. The designer who specified the chair will likely also be named in the lawsuit.

Designers must take the time to be sure that they specify products that are suitable for a client's use and that the client is warned if the designer feels the client is demanding an unsuitable product. If the designer believes the client wants an unsuitable product, the designer should be willing to refuse the order—after diplomatically suggesting more suitable alternatives. Should this just not be possible, written disclaimers, indicating that warnings have been given and that the designer accepts no responsibility for misuse, should be given to the client, and a copy should be kept on file. This procedure may not eliminate all liability, but it will show a court that a conscientious effort to warn the client was made.

Strict Liability

Strict liability means that "a seller is liable for any and all defective or hazardous products which unduly threaten a consumer's personal safety."[12] It is also a legal doctrine related to negligence regardless of fault. Strict liability specifically related to products exists to protect the consumer from harm as a result of products sold to any consumer. This is true in spite of the seller's intentions or care.

Strict liability is sometimes called *liability without fault*. Generally considered a negligence tort, liability without fault involves some act that in some way departs from the use of reasonable care. For the designer, this liability may arise from putting incorrect information in drawings, documents, and/or specifications that causes injury. For example, if the designer incorrectly labels a material in a construction drawing and the structure later fails, causing injury, the designer is responsible under strict liability.

For strict liability to be applied to a products liability case, the plaintiff must prove the following:

1. The goods were defective when purchased.
2. The seller or manufacturer was in the business of selling the product.
3. The defective goods would be unreasonably dangerous to any user.
4. Physical injury occurred to the plaintiff or to his or her property.
5. At the time of the injury, the goods were in substantially the same condition as when they were purchased.

For example, Mr. Shasta of Shasta Commercial Interiors orders fabric from a textile company that is described as fire retardant for use on restaurant booths. A few months after the fabric is installed, a dropped cigarette smolders and ignites it, causing extensive damage to the restaurant. A strict liability case is brought against the textile company and (probably) the designer.

The plaintiff, Mr. Shasta, must show that the goods were defective at the time of purchase. Further, it must be shown that injury was caused to the premises, that the fabric was dangerous in its use, and that the fabric remained in a basically unchanged condition since purchase. Although most of the liability in this case rests on the manufacturer of the fabric, there is nothing in tort law or in the UCC to prevent the unknowing designer from also being held liable.

Liability Without Fault for Design Defects

Interior designers create many design elements and custom products. Designers also specify and sell products that have been designed and manufactured by others. In both cases, the designer may be liable if the specified product causes injury due to defective design.

For example, Mary Nixon designed and produced the drawings for a custom table desk. The table desk was manufactured according to the specifications and drawings provided by Nixon. After delivery, the client was propped on the front edge of the table desk (although he was not actually sitting on the desk). The desk leg nearest where the client was propped split at the joint, causing the client to fall on his left side and break his left arm. It would appear that there was a design defect in the way the joint between the top of the table leg and the table desktop was designed. This in itself does not mean the designer will be held liable; however, it will affect a court's decision concerning liability.

Interior designers must be careful that the custom treatments and products they create are properly designed and meet performance standards relating to the structural integrity of the design. Those who are unfamiliar with product design should either refrain from creating custom designs themselves, or retain the services of product designers, craftspeople, or other appropriate experts to help in the design of custom goods. Designers also need to be constantly vigilant that the goods from manufacturers that they specify are designed safely and have no history of liability due to design defects.

Warranty Law and Products Liability

Warranty law and products liability are the only portion of products liability related to the UCC. All other law related to products liability is found in tort and contract law. Warranty responsibility and product liability are based on the laws discussed in the previous sections of this chapter. They are mentioned again here in relation to an injury to a third party.

In contract law, the only parties that can claim redress for injuries are the parties to the contract. However, much of what is governed by the UCC also affects third parties who are not signatories to the original contract. The UCC regulations make manufacturers and/or sellers liable for injuries to persons who are not parties to the original contract. For example, Mrs. Johnson hires an interior design company to redecorate her home. Through this company, she has some wall-hung shelves installed in the living room. One day, a bracket pulls out of the wall so that a shelf strikes one of Johnson's guests. The guest sustains a head injury. If it were not for UCC Section 2–318, the guest would not be able to sue the installer for an implied warranty of merchantability—only Johnson could.

However, the UCC is not clear as to how responsible sellers and manufacturers are. It was written with three alternatives, which assign different levels of responsibility. Alternative A is limited to household members and their guests who use or are injured by the goods. Alternative B is broader, not limiting injury to family members or guests; and alternative C is the broadest, protecting anyone who is injured by the defective product. Thus, should someone who is using a product sustain some injury when the product fails, the person has grounds for filing a lawsuit even though he or she did not purchase the product.

WEB SITES RELEVANT TO THIS CHAPTER

www.law.cornell.edu Cornell University Law School

www.nccusl.com National Conference of Commissioners on Uniform State Laws

www.sba.gov U.S. Small Business Administration

You may also want to review sites for other law schools and your state attorney general's office.

KEY TERMS

As is	Price
Basis of the bargain	Products liability
Buyer	Restocking charge
Click-on agreement	Sale
Conforming goods	Sale on approval
Destination contract	Seller
Electronic signature	72-hour right of refusal
End user	Shipment contract
ESIGN Act	Statute of Frauds
Express warranty	Strict liability
Firm offer	Title
Goods	Uniform Commercial Code (UCC)
Merchant	Uniform Electronic Transaction Act
Nonconforming goods	Warranty
Open terms	Warranty of title

WHAT WOULD YOU DO?

1. "I know you are concerned about traffic paths showing up on the carpet because of the traffic with your four children using the family room and play room. This plush carpet will not show traffic paths because it is thicker and denser," the interior designer tells the client. "The color will also help with this concern," the designer continues. Finally convinced by what the designer has said, Mrs. Jones instructs the interior designer to go ahead and order the carpet. Six months after installation and after the client has cleaned the carpet, she calls the designer, complaining about the fact that traffic paths look

unsightly even after cleaning. She demands that the carpet be replaced at no cost to her.

2. Ralph has used a certain vendor for all his lighting specifications for three years. On average, he has ordered more than $200,000 of lighting for the residences and small bed-and-breakfast facilities he usually designs for clients. Recently, a new client was referred to Ralph, who wants Ralph to provide the furniture and all the lighting fixtures for a very large house. Ralph wants to use his "favorite" vendor, as he has gotten a generous commission from the vendor on each order. The client is not pleased with the products that are being specified and repeatedly asks Ralph to choose other items. Ralph insists on the items he has already specified. Unbeknownst to the client, Ralph has already ordered the lighting items although they have not yet been installed.

3. Shelly's job responsibilities included interior design services as well as selling furniture and accessories. Her income was partially dependent upon commission on the sales of furniture, although that commission was not a very high percentage of the sales.

   Mr. Robinson has talked to Shelly two previous times about the layout of his restaurant, and now they are discussing specific products for the interior. "Well, I keep saying that this chair will not hold up for use in a restaurant, even with vinyl fabric for the upholstery. It is just too flimsy. I think you need to move up in price to this chair, which has better-quality construction and nicer fabrics," Shelly says to Mr. Robinson.

   "Well, I don't know. This whole thing is beginning to cost me way more than what I figured and what you estimated when we first sat down to talk about the project. You keep trying to upgrade me on the products. I've checked on the Internet about the less costly chair, and it is supposed to be a commercial-grade chair," Mr. Robinson replies.

   "Look, Mr. Robinson, if you insist on buying the cheaper chair, we will not be responsible if it doesn't hold up," retorts Shelly.

4. Mr. and Mrs. Franklin purchased a dining room suite, including eight chairs, for their new home from interior designer May Jefferson. Jefferson knew that the manufacturer was a reputable company and had used the company's products numerous times. The Franklins liked the style of chair and relied upon Jefferson's expertise in design when they approved the chairs. The Franklins gave a dinner party a short time after the chairs were delivered. One of the guests leaned back on the chair, causing the chair to tilt up and rock on its back legs. One leg cracked, causing the chair to collapse, and the guest broke his arm in the crash. The guest attempted to sue both the manufacturer and the designer.

REFERENCES

1. Stone, 1975, p. 2.
2. Clarkson et al., 1983, p. 9.
3. Miller and Jentz, 2006, p. 331.
4. Quinn, 1999, p. 2/201.

5. National Conference of Commissioners on Uniform State Laws, 2003 Amendments UCC Article 2, summary p. 2. Available at www.nccusl.org.

6. Quinn, 1999, p. 2/201.

7. Miller and Jentz, 2006, p. 316.

8. Ibid., p. 314.

9. Quinn, 1999, 2/201.

10. *Oxford American College Dictionary*, 2002, p. 1594.

11. Quinn, 1991, p. 2.

12. Black, 1990, p. 1422.

CHAPTER 10

Trade Sources

After completing this chapter you should be able to:

- Discuss the importance of trade sources for interior designers.
- Differentiate how the various trade sources work with interior designers.
- Explain the differences between trade markets, showrooms, and manufacturer's representatives.
- Explain what kind of information manufacturers' representatives can provide.
- Explain the importance of attending major trade shows.
- Discuss why trade showrooms are open only to the trade.
- Discuss the difference between the responsibilities of a general contractor and subcontractors.
- Explain the benefits of online trade libraries and sources.
- Discuss the importance of hiring quality trade sources.
- Understand how to establish a vendor account.

NCIDQ COMPONENT

Based on best information available, some material in this chapter might appear as part of the NCIDQ examination. The reader should not depend solely on this text for study material. See the sections on selecting trade sources and vendor accounts.

Many professionals use the opportunity to seek out the best products to specify for a project as a means of creative expression. Sometimes there are too many choices and not enough time to research all the options. Projects with very tight budgets present the opposite problem of not enough choices. Still, the choices are really incalculable, considering the variations on colors, styles, finishes, and other features that go into the design and construction of products.

The manufacturers, suppliers, and tradespeople who provide the various goods and services a designer uses to complete a project are called *trade sources*. Many of these sources sell to or deal only with the design industry, whereas others also sell directly to end users.

Trade sources come from many settings. A trade source may be a manufacturer across the country or in some other part of the world. It might be a local resource, such as the cabinetmaker on whom the designer depends for custom millwork. The local installers of tile, wall coverings, carpet, lighting fixtures, and many other items needed in the interior are other examples of trade sources. Trade source products are also displayed at local trade-only showrooms or at major trade marts in New York City, Chicago, Los Angeles, or many other cities. These examples are merely a few of the many sources that interior designers can use.

You will encounter the word *vendor* often in this chapter and subsequent chapters. A *vendor* is someone who sells products or services either to the end user or to some other person, like the designer. The term encompasses all the sources discussed in this chapter, including the interior designer. Commercial clients are used to working with vendors, whom they classify as anyone from whom they purchase any product or service. Residential clients, in contrast, are used to working with salespeople or designers, and so may not be familiar with the term *vendor*.

For the student, understanding who all the trade sources are and what they offer is a big task. For the professional, it is essential to find the trade sources that complement his or her business ideals.

This chapter tries to help readers sort out the different places designers can go to obtain products and services. In addition to providing goods and services, trade sources provide information to help the designer make choices and even to help the designer's clients make choices.

MANUFACTURERS

The manufacturing of furniture and furnishings products is big business in the 21st century. In the 2012 *Interior Design* magazine "A to Z Index" within the Buyers Guide issue, there were 58 pages listing manufacturers of various kinds of furniture. These do not even touch upon the smaller local manufacturers that exist in every market but do not end up in the Buyers Guide listing. Does this give you some concept of the breadth of trade sources?

Manufacturers of FF&E interiors products serve many roles for the interior designer and can provide:

- Specification information
- Manufacturing criteria
- Maintenance information on their goods
- Product catalogs, price books, and tear sheets
- Samples of textiles and finishes such as woods for desks
- Sample products for a client's inspection
- Special products or semi-custom-designed products

It is important to note that manufacturers are moving away from printed catalogs, tear sheets, and price books. This information is now available on the Internet. Designers may also have to pay for catalog books of textiles more than they once did. For textiles and other fabrics, the designer can request current samples. Some availability of the information may be limited to designers who have set up special accounts with the manufacturer or who receive a code from the representative. This helps ensure that the general public does not have access to the same pricing information given to the trade.

Other sources related to manufacturers are *jobbers*. These trade sources are wholesalers who purchase smaller quantities of goods from manufacturers—usually a specific category of goods—and resell them to the trade. Textiles, accessories, and even furniture can be obtained from jobbers. Because some manufacturers will only sell large quantities, designers can obtain goods from a jobber in the smaller quantity required. Of course, the designer might have to pay a higher price for the goods than if he or she could order directly from the factory.

The designer needs to be sure that he or she understands the terms and conditions of ordering and subsequently selling for each manufacturer. For example, finding out that a company charges a 25 percent fee for using a customer's own material (COM) on seating after the fabric and seating have already been ordered and delivered is poor business practice. The product catalog and sales representatives provide information on how to order and the conditions of sale. Specific questions are directed primarily to a sales representative, although, of course, the designer can contact the factory directly.

A design firm must establish credit with each manufacturer with which it wishes to deal. It is not unusual for many manufacturers to never allow some design firms to order on credit. When that is the case, the designer is required to pay for the goods in full at the time of ordering. Smaller design firms have the hardest time establishing credit and must be prepared to make substantial prepayments when ordering from many manufacturers for the first time.

SALES REPRESENTATIVES

It is most common for interior designers to work with a local or regional representative of a manufacturer. That is not to say that there are not times that the designer must contact someone directly at the factory concerning an order or product specifications. *Representatives*, or *reps*, are the men and women who either work for the manufacturer or represent the manufacturer to the architecture and design (A&D) community.

There are two kinds of reps: independent representatives and factory representatives. *Independent reps* work for themselves or a sales group. Many handle several manufacturers' products. These products may be related (e.g., all are from lighting manufacturers) or, as is more often the case, may be a combination of furniture and other products. *Factory reps* work for one manufacturer as employees of the company. They only represent that manufacturer's products, or possibly only a segment of the manufacturer's product line. Both kinds of representatives are extremely helpful to the interior designer, and most small firms would not survive without their valuable assistance.

Here are just some of the ways a representative can help the designer:

- Quote prices
- Provide product information
- Provide in-depth information on sustainability and green issues
- Make product specifications to the client on the designer's behalf or with the designer
- Provide samples of fabrics, finishes, and even whole products
- Deliver catalogs, price lists, and tear sheets

Some reps bring information and even samples of new merchandise to the attention of designers by having trunk shows. A *trunk show* occurs when a manufacturer's rep invites interior designers to view a small selection of new merchandise. The trunk show got its name from the traveling salesman's traditional use of a trunk to transport the selection of goods that the salesman wished to show retailers at the retailer's store. The trunk show could take place at the designer's studio, or the rep might invite more than one designer to a hotel conference area.

Manufacturers' sales representatives also have a role in generating sales independent of a designer or a dealer. For products generally used in commercial design, reps make calls on potential clients. Leads are generally turned over to dealers or are referred to designers. Sometimes, of course, representatives sell directly to the client, bypassing the designer or vendor.

MARTS, SHOWROOMS, AND MARKET CENTERS

Manufacturers and other trade sources display their products in marts and showrooms. A *mart* is a building in which many firms have separate showrooms or share showroom space. A smaller-sized building consisting predominately of trade showrooms might be called a *trade building*. A *showroom* is the leased or owned space that a manufacturer uses at a market center or other location. The term may also be used in reference to a retail store.

Market centers are concentrations of trade sources in one area of a city. Visiting marts and showrooms in these market centers allows designers the opportunity to see numerous samples of the products that they are specifying. Designers often bring clients to the mart or showroom so that the client can see the items being specified.

The largest marts are located in the major urban areas of cities such as Chicago, New York, Toronto, Dallas, High Point (North Carolina), San Francisco, and Los Angeles. A number of regional marts and trade buildings are located in many other cities in the United States and Canada. The Merchandise Mart in Chicago is still the largest single mart in the United States and holds the largest national trade market. As one would expect, the number of marts and trade buildings fluctuates annually. The annual *Interior Design* magazine Buyers Guide issue lists the locations of major trade showrooms in the United States and Canada.

Marts and trade buildings have building access policies that limit admittance to the trade only. Trade showrooms also have similar access limitations. Special passes obtained by trade members from mart officials are needed to gain entrance to many of the floors in the larger marts. Showrooms generally admit individuals without passes if they have proper credentials that identify them as members of the trade. Proper credentials might include a business license, a tax license, business checking account, association membership card, or other documentation beyond a business card that establishes the individual as a representative of a design business. Admittance to a showroom does not automatically allow the individual to purchase products from the manufacturer.

Student members of ASID and IIDA or other professional organizations are able to get into most showrooms by showing their student membership card. Showrooms, however, have their own policies, and some do not admit anyone unless he or she has an official building pass.

Students visiting a trade showroom should be respectful, courteous, and professional in conduct—and dress. Certainly ask the staff questions and pay attention to their answers. Students who act professional and ask intelligent questions will get positive results from the showrooms. Students should be cautioned not to grab for or ask for every sample, catalog, or brochure. These items are expensive for the manufacturer, so understand when they do not offer these items to students.

Merchandise, if it is priced in the showroom, is often tagged with a suggested retail price or a price code. This is done to protect the designer's profit policies as he or she shows clients the products specified for the project. Occasionally, showrooms have sales in which discontinued items or slightly damaged floor samples are sold to the trade at very good prices.

Trade Shows

An important and enjoyable professional activity for many interior designers is attending a major trade show. *Market* is a term that many interior designers use to mean one of the annual shows that they are going to visit. These annual shows give manufacturers an opportunity to showcase new products and educate various members of the built environment industry about their products. These shows often include seminars, workshops, and continuing education classes.

The largest furniture show in the United States is held at the NeoCon World's Trade Show in Chicago, at the Merchandise Mart. Frequently, more than 30,000 interior designers, architects, facility planners, and related professionals travel to Chicago in June to see the new products. Although contract furniture is highlighted at NeoCon, many residential products, as well as floor coverings, wall coverings, lighting, and accessories, are also displayed. Numerous seminars offering continuing education unit and other learning unit credits are also offered for attendees.

Other large market shows are held in other parts of the country. Here are just a few:

- KBIS Kitchen & Bath Industry Show in April in Chicago
- The International Home Furnishings Market in High Point, North Carolina, during April
- HP Expo Hospitality Design Exposition & Conference in Las Vegas, Nevada, during May
- IIDEX/NeoCon Canada in October
- Greenbuild in changing locations during the fall

The annual January Buyers Guide issue of *Interior Design* magazine has an extensive calendar of industry events to help designers plan their market trips. Specialty shows are also held at these same marts, either just prior to the major market shows or at other times of the year. Most of the smaller regional marts also have shows. These generally attract the local design community.

Market shows like NeoCon Chicago are exciting, energizing events, especially for students who are attending them for the first time. Even professionals approach markets as an endurance contest, hoping their feet will hold up to all the walking! Professionals have learned to bring an abundance of business cards and request materials so that manufacturers can mail their catalogs to the designer. Owners of small design firms who have had problems with getting mailings may want to bring their business license or resale license as well. The major shows generally include presentations and events planned for students. Item 10-1 on the companion site is a list of the major trade shows that are generally held during the year.

LOCAL SHOWROOMS

Many manufacturers locate regional showrooms or showroom/sales offices in cities other than where major marts are located. Some of these are for major furniture manufacturers, like Herman Miller and Knoll International, or various suppliers of interiors products. Several manufacturers may locate within a local trade building, creating a small mart. It is not unusual for these local trade tenants to organize special events like speakers, provide space for professional association offices, and admit students to view products.

Local showrooms generally are also restricted to the trade. These trade showrooms have policies for admittance, pricing, and purchasing similar to those of showrooms in the major marts. Local trade buildings and showrooms increase the opportunity for designers to view more actual products when the designer's office is too far from the major marts. Designers can often place orders directly from small, local showrooms. The usual requirements regarding establishment of credit, prepayment, and other terms of sale apply.

RETAIL SPECIALTY STORES

A retail specialty store is open to the public but is often utilized by the trade, especially when items are needed in a hurry. Retail stores that sell lighting fixtures, accessories, art objects, and furniture pieces can be a convenient resource for the interior designer. They are generally not owned or franchised by any of the manufacturers whose products are displayed.

These stores generate the majority of their revenue from retail sales directly to consumers. Retail specialty stores often give trade discounts to interior designers. These trade discounts are reduced prices given to trade members so that designers can then resell them to their clients. Trade discounts were discussed in Chapter 8.

MANUFACTURER'S DEALERS

Manufacturer's dealers (or just *dealers*) are generally not owned or franchised by a manufacturer; instead, they are privately owned businesses. They are usually retail furniture stores, as opposed to specialty shops. They are called dealers because they have made special arrangements with one or more manufacturers of furniture to feature and sell those products at a higher volume than other products. They frequently stock inventory of considerable size of those specific products. However, they sell a wide variety of products, not just products from one or two manufacturers.

A full-service furniture dealership offers design, sales, and installation services. It may also provide other services, such as installation of flooring and wall coverings. Thus, it can help a client through the entire design process, from programming to completion. This sometimes is referred to as *turnkey design*. In architecture, turnkey projects commonly include financing assistance and perhaps even property acquisition, as well as design services. Dealers often become involved in bidding on projects specified by other dealers or outside interior design and architectural firms. Smaller dealerships may operate a bit more like retail stores.

The term *manufacturer's dealer* is most associated with office furnishings dealers. However, there are many residential furniture retail stores that actually serve as dealers. Dealerships often offer a trade discount to independent designers. In some geographic areas, some of the products sold at a dealership are available only through that dealer.

INTERNET SOURCING

Interior designers—and end users—have increasingly looked to the Internet for information and ordering of products. Thousands of sources are available online, and increasingly the vendors deal this way rather than providing printed catalogs. Regardless of their specialty or the size of their firm, interior designers must have electronic means of procuring goods for projects.

Computer technology opens the world to the designer. One can search catalogs and other information directly from manufacturers' Web sites. Internet catalog libraries have been created so that designers have access to the catalogs of numerous vendors and manufacturers. Many small business tradespeople and craftspeople sell specialty items via their own Web sites. Manufacturers and especially small vendors should recognize the benefit of a well-designed and informative Web site to draw designers to their product and service offerings.

The availability of pricing online varies greatly. Some companies that seek out the end user will have pricing available on their Web sites. Companies that deal more exclusively with the trade might require a designer to have a special code to access the price list. Otherwise, prices must be obtained from representatives, printed price lists, or dealers.

End users can view certain elements of a vendor's Web site, while others remain closed to end users but open to the trade. The designer will need to subscribe to an online library or obtain a special code to gain access to the trade-only information. This serves the same purpose as a closed showroom: it gives the interior designer access to product information and pricing that are not available to the general public. The information in these online libraries gives the small practitioner access to products from hundreds of manufacturers around the world. These resources add more suppliers to their libraries every day and have product listings for both commercial and residential needs. Some companies may also have chat rooms where designers can exchange information, and may provide online newsletters, planning tips and assistance, industry news, and other features.

TRADESPEOPLE AND CRAFTSPEOPLE

Tradespeople and *craftspeople* are another resource for goods and services to the design community. Many are also available to the end user. Cabinetmakers, painters, carpet and floor-covering installers, and wallpaper installers are a few examples of tradespeople and craftspeople that interior designers utilize to complete a project. The installation services these trade sources provide are especially important.

Some of these trade sources do not generally market directly to the end user. An example is a drapery workroom. There are also craftspeople who make custom products of various kinds, especially furniture items, and who work with interior designers and may market to end users.

It is important for designers to work with tradespeople and craftspeople who are dependable and trustworthy and consistently deliver quality. A designer needs to investigate new sources carefully. This investigation should include obtaining references from their clients and inspecting their work by visiting previous job-sites. Some tradespeople, such as painters and carpet installers, must be licensed contractors and hold bonds insuring their work. Those who are involved in structural work or installation of architectural finishes are generally required to be licensed by their state. Hiring unlicensed contractors in states that require licensing can leave the designer open to lawsuits.

When beginning to work with a new tradesperson, the designer should be sure that he or she understands how that tradesperson works, not just what he or she makes and the quality of the work. For example, will the cabinetmaker prepare working drawings of the custom furniture from just a plan and elevation, or is the designer expected to prepare all of the working drawings? If materials must be sent to the tradespeople, how will freight charges be handled? Will the installer accept delivery of goods (such as carpet) in the designer's name, or will the designer have to receive the goods and have the installer pick up the carpet from the designer? These are just a few of the many questions that the designer must ask of potential tradespeople.

CONSTRUCTION CONTRACTORS

Rachel's client has hired her to remodel the kitchen and family room. The client has indicated that he wants to replace the cabinets and appliances, and add a gas-burning fireplace in the family room. It is also likely that he will want an island with the range in the island and the client prefers that it be a gas range. Rachel realizes that she will need some guidance from consultants.

Perhaps it is easy to see that Rachel's project is just one example of design projects involving structural work that necessitates the use of one or more construction contractors. *General contractors* (often called GCs) are contractors that hold a license that allows them to contract for and supervise all phases of a construction project. Commercial designers regularly work with general contractors or construction management companies that oversee the entire project. A *construction manager* is an individual who oversees the construction project as an agent for either the general contractor or the project owner.

General contractors often hire *subcontractors* (*subs*) to do the specialized work. There are specialized subcontractors who do concrete work; plumbing; electrical work; framing; painting; carpet installation; and many other specialized trades and crafts. There can even be *secondary subcontractors* who are hired because a particular project requires special skills or equipment that the subcontractor does not have. For example, in construction, when a cinder-block stem wall is required, it is usually filled with a special cement mixture to strengthen the wall. The masonry subcontractor may hire a secondary subcontractor to take care of this job, because it requires a special piece of equipment.

In some states, designers must hold either a contractor's license or a specialty license to give instructions and supervisory information to subcontractors and installers—even carpet and wallpaper installers. An interior designer whose license is related to interior design practice (through a title or practice act) might not automatically be able to do the supervision granted by a contractor's license. The designer should know the law in his or her jurisdiction. Thus, designers must be careful about giving instructions to subs on the job. Designers should always request changes through the supervisor of the tradespeople involved or through the general contractor.

Select contractors and subs after thoroughly researching the company. They need to have the proper licenses and bonds to execute the required work. Ask to visit projects they have worked on. Also ask for references from designers and architects who have used the contractor. Do not hire contractors or subs that will not provide references or copies of their licenses!

It is common for a designer to obtain two or three quotes from different contractors. It is just good sense to let the contractor know you are getting other quotes. Naturally, the work should not proceed until a contract between the designer and the contractor, detailing what will be done and the price quoted for the job, is finalized. Remember that when you recommend contractors to the client, you could also be liable for problems even when the client pays the contractor directly for the work.

It is the responsibility of the interior designer to instruct the client, who may never have had a custom home constructed or experienced a remodeling or renovation project on a home or a commercial space, about the process that will take place. The designer should clarify the chain of command and how the various decisions and communications will take place, right from the beginning of the project to its completion.

It is important for the client to understand that he or she should not try to give directions or in any way supervise the subcontractors, unless, of course, the client is his or her own general contractor. If the client or the designer has a question or wants to make a change, the change should be discussed with the general contractor. When a decision is made, a change order should be issued by the designer to the general contractor, who will then direct the work to the subcontractor after a suitable change order has been prepared. Directions provided by the interior designer or the client that run counter to construction documents are often ignored, unless the subcontractor is clear that someone other than his or her foreman can provide that direction.

Making changes in a job after the contract is let (awarded) requires a change order. *Change orders* are documents that describe any modification in construction projects or interiors furnishing projects after the contract has been awarded. Change orders usually result in higher prices for the project, because something extra had to be done that was not called for in the original drawings and specifications. Change orders are also discussed in Chapter 12.

SELECTING TRADE SOURCES

Designers are constantly searching for high-quality tradespeople and subcontractors, as well as unusual products for their projects. Lead times can be quite long for many quality workers in the field, and the designer must explain time issues to clients at the inception of the project.

The first important part of selecting trade sources is determining what kinds of materials and catalogs will be necessary in the studio. An interior designer's library can easily become clogged with sample books, catalogs, flyers, and price lists. Manufacturers are now charging for their catalogs and samples, requiring designers to think carefully about what materials they place in their library. Of course, today many product catalogs are virtual catalogs—available on CDs or DVDs or viewable on the Internet. This helps, but the designer still requires information on the products and must know how to get the information that he or she needs about these items.

Establishing Vendor Accounts

Interior designers who sell merchandise to clients generally have to special-order the items, as only the biggest firms have a showroom with an inventory of sellable merchandise. Designers prefer to establish credit with the various vendors and suppliers they work with rather than paying up front when the order is placed. As with any consumer, the interior designer must establish a good credit relationship with a vendor in order to be able to pay on credit.

Most suppliers expect payment in full before the order is put into production. This payment in full might be in cash (checks, really) by the designer or when the designer has an open account with the vendor. Designers who must pay up front require clients to pay up front as well. Interior designers frequently require 100 percent payment by the client before the order is placed. Naturally, not all clients are willing to pay in full for something that may take several months to obtain. Thus, designers might need to have flexible prepayment terms.

To establish an account with a vendor or supplier (also called an *open account*), the designer or firm must first fill out a credit application. The information required on the credit application is similar to that which the designer may request of clients wishing to purchase on credit (and not using a credit card). Table 13-1 in Chapter 13 outlines the information that is normally required on a credit application. Be sure you understand what the credit limit will be so that you are not embarrassed by needing more credit than your limit allows. That definitely will mean late delivery of goods.

Open accounts are given only to designers who have a good credit history. In addition to having a good credit history, some are given an open account only when they order a specified dollar amount of goods from the supplier over some time period, which could be anywhere from one year to three years' duration. A good credit history is the key to obtaining an open account with a vendor. Designers and firms must be very vigilant in paying all bills on time. Late payments and nonpayments with one vendor will have a negative impact on the designer's ability to purchase from other vendors. Maintenance of a good credit history is why many interior design firms watch their finances so carefully on a monthly basis. It is also why many sole practitioners do not take much in the way of a salary from the business, so that they have plenty of funds in their accounts to take care of vendor orders where they have not been given an open account. Destroying a credit history with a vendor can lead to very serious consequences for the designer who wishes to sell merchandise to clients.

Members of ASID and IIDA have an added benefit of membership in that many companies are industry partners to the associations. These partnerships provide a wide range of information and product availability from hundreds of resources for members. Industry partners respect their membership with ASID and IIDA and are eager to assist practitioner members. Of course, other associations also have industry partners who can provide valuable assistance to designers in other professional organizations.

The firm's business plan gives management guidelines on what to keep as resources. If the firm is not doing residential design, there is little need for residential-grade carpet samples. Design firms that are lucky enough to work with high-end clients have little use for budget furniture catalogs. But then, these comments only state the obvious. How does a design firm really find and maintain the best sources? Some suggestions follow:

1. *Understand the focus and/or specialty of the practice*. Obviously, the focus of the practice is a primary determining factor as to what types of resources are needed in the studio or office.

2. *Review current resource materials on a regular basis*. Once a year, the design firm should review resource materials and eliminate items that are rarely used or available on the Internet.

3. *Discard old price lists* to avoid mispricing product specifications. Some manufacturer's representatives will provide this service.

4. *Obtain CD-ROM or DVD catalogs* for products that are used frequently.

5. *Carefully review new sources*. The design firm should keep only those new items that fit the design firm's product and jobs profile.

6. *Get to know the representatives* or the craftspeople from the resources the firm maintains. It is important to have clear answers to questions on pricing, delivery schedules, exclusivity, customs, warranties, quality, manufacturing, and terms of sale before ordering from a new source.

7. *Visit factories and workshops*. A great way to learn about a supplier's products is by arranging a tour of the factory or workshop. Special arrangements are generally required rather than just "dropping in" on a factory. If possible, arrange time to also talk to the order processing department.

8. *Try to work with sources on the firm's terms*. Small design firms need to find sources that will take lower prepayments with orders whenever possible. Establishing good credit with every source is the best way to improve terms.

9. *Work with sources that are geographically close* to the firm. Advantages of such sources include being able to have goods drop-shipped directly to the client, in addition to freight charges that are somewhat reduced.

10. *Establish policies for representatives' visits*. Unless designers enjoy constant interruptions, they should require reps to make appointments to show new items. Get to know the local or regional reps, as this relationship helps you receive the type of service you need. It is also a good idea to have a contact at factories and suppliers that the design firm uses frequently.

11. *Clarify payment and credit policies*. The smaller the design firm, the more likely it is that the supplier will require payment in full at the time of ordering. This is because most manufacturers and suppliers grant credit terms only to designers who order frequently or in large quantities.

12. *Do your job*. Designers sometimes try to pass the buck when they make a mistake or create a problem, blaming it on the trade source. A professional, responsible, and ethical interior designer who does his or her job does not to have to worry about passing the buck because of liability issues.

13. *Develop loyalty to sources*. Although it is not unusual for designers to use more than one company or trade source for certain products, establishing loyalty to sources will yield benefits to the design firm. One obvious benefit is granting of better credit terms. Another is that loyal sources will bend over backward to help out loyal designers.

14. *Do not demand or expect specification fees*. Reps and suppliers complain about designers who demand specification fees (an activity that is considered unethical by the professional associations). Specification fees must be revealed to clients even when freely granted by the supplier.

By now, readers should have some understanding of the vast amount of responsibility that an interior designer has in the execution of a design project. It is critical that the designer only take on projects for which he or she is qualified. Many things can go wrong, including providing incorrect information to vendors, making mistakes on drawings, and forgetting to tell tradespeople about site conditions or perhaps certain client peculiarities. The designer must do the necessary research to understand the proper specification of any product that goes into the project. The designer must carefully prepare the documents needed for the job. Above all, the interior designer should take care of any problems that arise, as quickly and professionally as possible.

WEB SITES RELEVANT TO THIS CHAPTER

www.www.highpointdesigncenter.com High Point Design Center

www.merchandisemart.com Merchandise Mart

www.pacificdesigncenter.com Pacific Design Center

An additional general resource for designers is www.interiordesignnet work.com

KEY TERMS

Change orders	Mart
Construction manager	Representatives
Factory reps	Reps
FF&E	Secondary subcontractors
General contractor (GC)	Showroom
Independent reps	Subcontractors (subs)
Jobbers	Trade sources
Manufacturer's dealer	Trunk show
Market	Turnkey design
Market center	Vendor

WHAT WOULD YOU DO?

1. Judy Smith has been working with a client, Mr. and Mrs. Stevenson, on their home for the past five years. The project has extended for this long because the client needs to do it in sections. Little by little, they have worked on the remodeling and finishing of their 4500-square-foot house in a small resort community. The house is a three-story Victorian on a quiet wooded lot in a residential area that has been rezoned for commercial use as well as residential.

   Six months ago, Mr. Stevenson informed Judy that they were going to convert the house into a bed and breakfast, now that he has retired from his job as a school principal. They hired Judy to continue to work with them on any additional remodeling that must be done in order to "cost-effectively" (as Mr. Stevenson remarked) get the property ready to accept its first guests as quickly as possible.

   Judy is a registered interior designer in her state but has never obtained a contractor's license. The Stevensons were told by the city that in order to convert the house to a bed and breakfast, they would have to bring the electrical and other mechanical systems up to code. Other mechanical and structural changes were needed in the kitchen and second-floor bedroom spaces that would be for guests. Judy has made some additional suggestions to change finish materials and space usage for the first floor to accommodate the greeting of guests and their use of the living room as a "lobby" living room. However, the Stevensons are reluctant to proceed with the changes, either those stipulated by the city or the suggestions from Judy.

2. Melinda and Phillip are partners in a design firm that focuses on residential projects. The firm is located on the West Coast and primarily designs projects in the upper part of California and the coastal regions of Oregon. Melinda and Phillip are committed to sustainable design and actually turn down work that cannot be designed using at least 50 percent green materials.

   A recent client was very pleased with their work on remodeling the client's home. The remodeling was done to mitigate the problems that two of their children were having with asthma. An important component of the remodeling was the removal of carpeting and installation of wood flooring. Melinda was very careful in discussing the flooring and installation processes with the vendor and the installer. She made it clear to the vendor and installer that they had to use green products and installation materials.

Melinda's client informs her that their children have had repeated asthmatic attacks since all the remodeling work was done. They want Melinda to have the flooring removed, as they believe that is the problem.

3. Margaret is an independent interior designer. Her client—a large family practice group—became interested in furniture items from a specific furniture manufacturer. They saw these items on display at a conference two of the doctors attended. They want Margaret to design the project with this product line. Margaret's contract stipulates that the doctors will buy all merchandise from her.

Margaret is not a dealer, nor does she have an agreement with this manufacturer to sell its products, but she has not told this to the doctors. She wants the product sale and the doctors want the specific product. Margaret is not sure how to solve her dilemma, because she does not want to tell the doctors that she really cannot order the goods directly from this manufacturer.

CHAPTER 11

The Project Management Process

After completing this chapter you should be able to:

- Discuss why project management is an important responsibility of an interior designer.
- List and discuss at least six key tasks of a project manager.
- Discuss typical tasks in the phases of a design project and how these tasks affect the responsibilities of a project manager.
- Explain how research, such as on evidence-based design, is valuable to a designer.
- Explain the role of the designer/specifier in a residential project and a commercial project.
- Explain the plan review process and its importance in the completion of a project.
- List and explain common deliverables in a residential project and a commercial project.
- Describe the differences between the project delivery methods discussed in the text.
- Be able to identify the stakeholders in a project program description.
- Describe the differences between a construction contract and a contract for design services.
- Explain how integrated design affects the work of the interior designer and the completion of a project.
- Explain the interaction responsibilities between a project manager and clients, and between a project manager and consultants for the project.
- What is integrated design and what effect does it have on the work of the interior designer?
- Describe the differences between a milestone chart, a bar chart, and a CPM chart for scheduling a design project.
- Discuss methods of project budgeting.
- Explain the importance of time management and time recording for interior designers.
- List and discuss the types of items that are important to retain in a project job file.
- Discuss how value engineering can help satisfy a client's need for budget control.
- Explain how BIM can make a project run more smoothly.

NCIDQ COMPONENT

Based on best information available, some material in this chapter might appear as part of the NCIDQ examination. The reader should not depend solely on this text for study material.

Regardless of the type of interior space, clients seek designers who have the key skills of managing the numerous details, making the necessary design decisions, and interacting with all the parties involved in a project. What these tasks (and others) collectively represent is *project management*.

Projects must be managed so that the required work is done quickly, correctly, and with as few problems as possible. Managing all these details is also critically important if the firm is to make a reasonable profit. This is not easy. Projects rarely progress without an assortment of challenges, worries, and delays.

Creating the design solutions and developing the documents are only part of the project management process. Many meetings occur between the designer and those involved in the project. In addition, students rarely see the detailed record-keeping that must be undertaken from the beginning to the end of the project.

Interior design projects continually become more complex, regardless of type of project. The designer's potential liability grows as clients expect more from design professionals. Having a complete understanding of the project management process is vital to students, as many may be thrust into some level of project responsibility soon after graduation when working for a smaller design firm.

This chapter offers a complete, though brief, overview of the project management process. Primary topics include the project management process and the role of the project manager. Other topics include understanding the role of the various parties to the project, scheduling and time management, and other issues critical to a general discussion of project management.

WHAT IS PROJECT MANAGEMENT?

Project management is the process of organizing and controlling all the tasks and resources for an interior design project from beginning to end to satisfactorily solve the client's problems, meet the client's desires, and provide a reasonable profit to the design firm. A project solution that does not solve the client's problems might be an aesthetic interior, but if it does not function or meet other needs, it will likely be considered an unsatisfactory solution. Projects must also yield a reasonable profit for the design firm, regardless of the method of compensation.

Effective project management begins with a detailed understanding of the client's goals and a comprehensive scope of services that defines what must be done. When defining the sequence of tasks, it is best to follow the generally accepted tasks of the design process: programming, schematic design, design development, contract documents preparation, and contract administration.

Another important part of effective project management concerns relationship management. The interior designer must exercise and maintain harmonious working relationships with the client, vendors, contractors, and everyone else involved. A design team can grow to dozens of individuals working for the same firm or joint ventures of design firms on mega-projects. Thus, being able to work with and direct a team is a vital skill.

It is rare for a design firm to work on only one project at a time. Even a sole proprietor has to have more than one project in process. Thus, scheduling becomes another critical task in project management. New projects should be accepted only after a determination of whether and how they will fit into the schedule of existing work. Office and project schedules must be refined and managed. The designer or team members responsible for the project are all likely working on phases of different projects. Thus, everyone must become skilled at multitasking and time management. Many interior designers could—and do—say, "It is getting difficult to project-manage today because there is so much to manage!"

To successfully manage a project, the *project manager* (also referred to as a PM), who most often is the interior designer in charge of the project, must use both the creative and analytical sides of the brain. The client is looking for a creative solution, yet in many cases the client is also looking for a solution that solves his or her problem, whether or not it is an award-winning creative solution. The client is also looking to the interior designer to manage all the details and installation of the project. Successful project management requires many things. Table 11-1 lists key tasks of the project manager.

In some firms, the project manager is not an interior designer involved in the actual design solution, but rather a specialized staff member. However, the PM's role is still to coordinate with the design team, the client, and other stakeholders for the completion of the project. The hundreds (if not thousands) of details that may be involved from the initial meeting to completion of the project must be controlled and coordinated by the project manager.

As for the project interior designer, he or she certainly wishes to provide a creative solution; that is why most designers go into the interior design profession in the first place. As a businessperson, the interior designer must also execute all of his or her responsibilities so that the firm can earn a reasonable profit. These goals are not in opposition to each other, for they require planning, communication, management, and business skills that all function together. Few designers can be successful without carefully managing their projects.

The skills used to perform project management tasks are acquired as the designer works alongside experienced interior designers. The designer learns about scheduling, for example, by first learning how long it takes for common tasks to be achieved and then by being responsible for scheduling. Learning the various management skills plays a critical part in the designer's success, so that he or she can control the project instead of letting the project control the designer.

TABLE 11-1.

Key tasks of a project manager

Prepare the proposal and contract.
Establish and oversee the project schedule.
Select a project team.
Serve as primary client contact.
Supervise the design team.
Establish and oversee the budget.
Coordinate with consultants.
Oversee the project files.
Supervise quality control.
Provide design input.
Utilize good communication skills.
Prepare and distribute project status reports.

Depending on the size of the firm and the role of the designers, a usual task of the project manager is to coordinate all the paperwork. Numerous items are used and filled out throughout the stages of a project. These are in addition to any actual floor plans, or other contract documents prepared to get the project built. Table 11-2 outlines these items for a residential project, but also includes items more commonly part of a commercial project. Please note,

TABLE 11-2.

The paperwork trail for a typical project

An effort has been made to include as many documents as are usually involved, but items may be included or excluded based on a firm's procedures. Drawings documents have been excluded from this list. Note that in one way or another, all these items can be correlated to a design contract for services. As a reference, the chapter in which the document is discussed or exhibited is included where applicable. The beginning section is for a typical residential project.

Interview forms and notes	Chapters 7, 11
Fee estimate forms	Chapter 6
Preliminary specification forms	Chapter 11
Design contract	Chapter 7
Project schedule	Chapter 11
Project budgeting	Chapters 6, 11
Credit application	Chapter 13
Product specifications/equipment lists	Chapter 12
Client approvals	Chapter 26
Sales confirmation forms	Chapter 13
Purchase orders for product sales	Chapter 13
Acknowledgments from vendors	Chapter 13
Transmittal letters as needed	Chapter 11
Delivery instructions from designer	Chapter 14
Installation floor plans	Chapter 12
Invoice from vendor upon shipment	Chapter 13
Shipping documents: packing list, freight bill, bill of lading	Chapter 14
Delivery acknowledged by client	Chapter 14
Invoice from designer to client for design fees and products	Chapter 13
Punch list after walk-through	Chapter 14
Repair tickets if necessary	Chapter 14
Client final payments (invoice)	Chapter 13
Thank-you note from designer to client	Chapter 14

These additional forms are possible parts of a commercial project and would be in addition to the items listed previously.

Staff interview forms	Chapters 7, 11
Feasibility study	Chapter 11
Construction agreement	Chapter 12
Specifications	Chapter 12
Bid documents (includes items listed in Table 12-5)	Chapter 12
Project progress reports	Chapter 12
Project schedules	Chapter 11
Punch list/deficiency reports	Chapter 14
Postoccupancy evaluations	Chapter 14
Certificate of occupancy	Chapter 14
Certificate of substantial completion	Chapter 14
Record drawings	Chapter 14
As-built drawings	Chapter 14
Certificate for payment	Chapter 14

however, that the actual items any design firm uses may vary from this list, and any particular firm or project may require items not included. If there is an example of the paperwork item within the text, the figure number is noted.

THE ROLE OF THE DESIGNER/SPECIFIER

Susan is one of the partners of an interior design firm specializing in hospitality projects. The contracts for these projects include specification of FF&E, but the merchandise is always purchased through the hotel's or restaurant's corporate offices. Susan's firm considers themselves to be designers/specifiers, since they do not sell merchandise but do prepare the plans and specifications.

Interior *designer/specifiers* can specialize in residential and/or commercial projects. They have made a determination that they do not wish to be involved in actually selling merchandise. Interior designers who work in architectural offices are another group of designers who infrequently involve themselves in direct sales of merchandise to clients. Designer/specifiers' responsibilities are otherwise the same for those who do design and sell products.

There are many responsibilities related to specifying a project, whether or not the designer will be directly selling the merchandise. Of these activities, three are of special concern to the designer who does not sell merchandise to clients: (1) estimating a project budget, (2) preparing the purchasing specifications, and (3) assisting the client in evaluating and selecting suppliers. Item 11-1 on the companion site is a sample worksheet for project estimating.

Estimating the project budget, as always, begins with the preliminary specifications of FF&E. The actual cost of the project cannot be known until either the client begins purchasing from suppliers or the bid process has been completed. Designer/specifiers who work with residential clients often budget or price a project based on the retail prices of the specified goods. As it is possible for the client to obtain some of the specified goods "on sale" or at a discount from a seller, the budgeted price will almost always be slightly higher than what the client actually pays for the completed project. Of course, if the client delays purchase of any of the items, the prices may be higher than the budgeted amounts.

When a designer/specifier works with a commercial client, the project will probably go out for competitive bidding. The final cost of the project to the client is not known until the bidding process is over. The designer cannot guarantee a firm price, but can budget based on methods such as: (1) a retail basis with estimates as to potential discounts, (2) a cost price plus percentage markup, or (3) a cost price plus a predetermined high–low negotiated markup. The first two are self-explanatory. The third budgeting option is less obvious and thus requires a bit of explanation.

Occasionally, a bid is set up so that the sellers who are providing prices must agree to only a specified markup on their cost. This condition is clearly indicated in the bid documents that the sellers obtain at the onset of the bid and on which they base their bids. Sellers must carefully consider if this negotiated or set markup is sufficient to justify bidding on the project. The budget is then closer to the actual purchase price, as the costs of the products are fairly well known by the designer.

Purchasing specifications can be as simple as what many designers call an equipment list or as complex as formal competitive bidding documents. A comprehensive equipment list provides quantities, descriptions, manufacturers' names, and a budgeted unit price (see Figure 11-1). The client then

Specification list for:
Ralph Smithson
Job Number 20547

Quantity	Manufacturer	Prod. No.	Description	Unit price	Extend price
2	B&B Italia	D277B	Diesis Sofa Fabric: COM Maharam 451801090 Mohair Color: 090 Magenta	$6500	$13,000
2	Cartwright	20/123	Club chair Fabric: Black Leather Finish: Ebony	3165	6330
2	Bernhardt	2BB 36/914	End table Finish: Frame—Black Top: Maple	2009	4018
1	Excel Custom		Custom Coffee Table 60 × 60 × 18 per drawings Finish: Marble	4500	4500
2	Atherton	L9968	Table Lamp Finish: Coffee	1295	2590
1	Amazing Custom Cabinets		Custom Entertainment Unit built to drawings (see attached) Finish: Maple and Ebony per drawings	27,300	27,300
			Total for Product		$57,738
			Freight and Delivery		4,619
			Sales Tax		3,975
			Total		**$66,332**

FIGURE 11-1.

A comprehensive equipment list used to prepare a project specification.

uses this equipment list when he or she shops for the necessary goods. Along with the equipment list, the designer might also provide the names and addresses of recommended sellers, installers, and craftspeople who can meet the demands of the designer and the client in completing the project.

When a formal bid is used to purchase goods and services, the designer is responsible for preparing the specifications for all of the FF&E. An explanation of the bid process and the documentation that must be included in a formal bid are discussed in Chapter 12.

Assisting the client with evaluation and selection of vendors who could supply the FF&E is another important task of the designer/specifier—of all designers, for that matter. By virtue of creating specifications, designers provide this evaluation process regardless of type of project. When a residential designer specifies products for the client, he or she has an expectation that the client is presold on the items, as they are discussed in detail throughout the project. Clients who purchase on their own might be tempted to find products other than what was specified. That is an important reason for including a disclaimer in the design contract about the designer's responsibility (see Chapter 7). This same or a similar clause should also be included in a contract for a commercial project that will be bid.

One might argue that the responsibility of assisting the client with evaluation and selection of sellers is more critical if formal bid documents are necessary. The bidding process allows any seller who feels that it is capable of supplying the specified merchandise to submit a bid to the client. But not all sellers are in fact able to fulfill the coordination and requirements of bids, especially for major projects. For example, although J. D. Furniture Store, which is a small retailer, may wish to bid on a project like a major hotel installation, the designer and client must determine whether J. D. Furniture Store really is capable of ordering, delivering, and installing the merchandise called for in the bid.

In some bids, the exact specification of merchandise is left a bit vague, so the client and the designer must evaluate alternative merchandise. Frequently, multiple sellers of office systems furniture get involved in bids. The designer must assist the client in determining if the products from several different manufacturers are sufficiently similar to the product named in the bid specification. Although the example is only for office systems, the designer may have to provide this same type of assistance for every single product specified.

BRINGING VALUE TO CLIENTS THROUGH DESIGN

In any given market, there are many—perhaps hundreds of—interior designers and others offering design services. Because there are so many people offering services, clients often do not see why one designer is worth one dollar figure while another charges less (or more). Some clients push designers to lower their fees, and/or provide a greater discount, and generally look for someone who will give them a bargain.

When buyers do not truly value what they are about to purchase, they try to negotiate anyone's fees and prices down—or walk away and hire someone who is willing to do it for a lower price. In a highly competitive market, such "price negotiating" is even more prevalent.

During initial meetings with clients, interior designers often find that they must educate the client on many topics, the most important of which is the value of design services. I have found, during my many years of presenting seminars on this topic, that many designers do not know how to discuss their value or the value of hiring a professional to perform design services.

Let's start at the beginning: the meaning of value. *Value* is "the importance or preciousness of something . . . the worth of something compared to the price paid or asked for it."[1] If the services to be provided are not important to the buyer, then he or she does not feel that they have much value. In other words, if buyers truly believe or perceive that one designer is no different from any other, they will not value the services of any.

From a business point of view, the buyer determines the value of a service or product, not the designer. Naturally, the interior designer feels that what he or she has to offer provides value and is "worth" the fees charged. However, if the client does not need, want, or value the services or products, then the perceived value to the client is not going to be very high.

Interior designers must be able to define the value they provide to clients in terms of benefits to the client. If the designer cannot translate his or her services into benefits that are important to a client, the client will not understand why the designer should be paid at all, whatever the quoted fees are.

Interior designers need to examine how they do business and realize that in a highly competitive market, satisfying the client is the critical issue, not creating what the designer perceives as great design. They need to think about how they provide value to clients so that they can readily provide answers to clients as to "what can you do for me?"

Here are some ways that interior designers provide value to clients:

- Utilize products that can enhance the safety and healthfulness of the interiors of homes and businesses. Your knowledge and expertise have value to clients.
- Design interiors that can create atmospheres that enhance the success of a business. This comes from a proven track record of work related to specialties.
- Build a reputation for excellent work and satisfied clients. Clients prefer to work with experts, and satisfied clients refer friends and colleagues.
- Plan interior spaces to be functionally efficient. Whether it is a residence, an office, or another type of space, making the spaces work for clients rather than against them adds value.
- Create living environments that enrich the home overall, especially for clients who have special needs, like families with aging parents or sick children.
- Make it clear to the client that the designer's role is to satisfy the client's needs and wants, not to stroke the designer's ego or impose the designer's personal tastes.
- Save the client time and money through judicious specification of products and design concepts. Make the process easy, but don't forget to include the client in the process.
- Enhance the financial value of the residence or business through excellent design.

These suggestions only scratch the surface of the ways in which interior design provides value to clients, whether their projects are residential or commercial. Value is an emotional experience, just as design is emotional. And the client's perception of value is just as important as the cost. When it comes to explaining the value of interior design, your focus must be on the clients and what they perceive as valuable. Only then will you be able to convince clients of your value to them.

PHASES OF AN INTERIOR DESIGN PROJECT

Project management is best understood when the parameters of a project are defined. Those parameters are defined using the scope of services, which should follow the phases of an interiors project. These phases mirror project phases in architecture and also follow the phases or performance domains as researched by the NCIDQ for the examination. The common five phases are: (1) programming, (2) schematic design, (3) design development, (4) preparation of contract documents, and (5) contract administration. An overview of typical tasks in each phase is discussed in this section; typical tasks were listed in Table 7-3 related to the development of the scope of services in a design contract.

Numerous tasks are performed in each phase: some distinctly different from those in other phases, and others that are similar from phase to phase. It should be pointed out that a client's needs might not require an interior designer to perform all the tasks of each phase for each project. That is why a checklist of required tasks is a helpful tool, both for developing the design contract and for project management.

The preprogramming and planning of a project that occur when the scope of services is developed for the design contract often result in a document called a work plan. The *work plan* "defines all the tasks or scope of work that is needed and includes clarification of deliverables, schedule, the needed resources and budget to take the project from inception to completion."[2] A work plan helps the designer clarify everything that has to be done and the correct order of tasks so that the project schedule can be determined.

Deliverables are documents and presentation materials that must be prepared to explain the design concepts and eventually allow the project to be built and installed. Examples are floor plans, sample boards, models, construction documents, and bid documents. They are called deliverables because they must be "delivered" (provided in some form) to the client.

Programming Phase

The *programming phase* is the information-gathering portion of an interior design project. The designer seeks as much information as possible on such things as client expectations, functional needs, aesthetics, and factors concerning the interior space itself. The programming phase is also an excellent time to deepen the relationship between the designer and the client.

Architects and some designers refer to programming as predesign. Because *predesign* essentially means information gathering and report generation prior to schematic design, a firm might use either term to describe those tasks undertaken to gather information and prepare to start sketches and preliminary selections. Nevertheless, this section uses the traditional and generally accepted term *programming* for this initial stage of the design project.

Typical tasks and information that must be gathered during programming include:

- Perform client interviews to determine the client's goals and objectives
- Visit the jobsite to gain information about the physical spaces
- Obtain floor plans, if available, or field-measure project spaces
- Inventory and analyze existing furnishings and equipment
- Interview users of the space, such as family members or employees, concerning likes/dislikes and needs
- Review applicable codes
- Determine the extent to which sustainable and environmental design issues might arise or be applicable

The interior designer must take careful notes in order to successfully design and prepare the documents required for completing the project. Designers are helped through this process by utilizing a variety of specialized forms, such as that shown in Figure 11-2. This form is also included on the companion Web site as item 11-2.

Client interview forms help firms define the client's needs relating to space requirements, and furnishings and equipment requirements. For large commercial office projects, designers might find that using employee questionnaires is more efficient. When the client wants to use existing equipment, the designer can use another form to analyze and inventory the furniture and equipment that the client already owns. These are just a few examples of the special forms designers create to help obtain the information they will need about the client's requirements and the interior space to be designed.

New Project Interview--Residential

Designer: _____ Date of Interview _____ Time: _____

Client: _____ **Project Location:**

Address: _____ Address: _____

_____ _____

_____ _____

Phone: _____ Site phone:_____

Cell phone: _____

Email: _____

☐ Existing client   ☐ New client

Heard about firm from: _____

Referred by: _____

Are you working with an architect?

Estimated budget: **Desired completion date:** _____

Construction: _____ Custom: _____

Furniture: _____ Accessories: _____

Project area/Scope of project:

Special considerations:

Occupants:

Children ages:

Health issues:

Pets:

Entertaining:

FIGURE 11-2.

The type of form that designers use to take notes at an initial meeting with a client. It can later assist in the development of a contract or in project specification research

Style preferences:

Color preferences:

What is the Budget?

Have you ever worked with an interior designer before?

Have you ever been involved in this type of project before?

Does anyone in the family to home improvements?

Bank reference:

Credit check

Reimbursable Expenses:

Notes:

FIGURE 11-2.

(*Continued*)

Research as a Project Benefit

The design process phases bear a direct relationship to research. The bulk of research occurs during the programming (predesign and) phase(s) as discussed previously. Research can, of course, be included in any phase of a project.

Chapter 14 discusses research that comes at the end of a project. Two of these research methodologies are the postoccupancy evaluation and the post-project evaluation. Postoccupancy evaluations help the designer and the project owner determine positives and negatives concerning the project solutions. A post-project evaluation can help a firm determine if the project was successful from a business point of view and assist it in doing future similar projects more effectively. Sample forms for both of these items are included on the companion Web site as items 14-2 and 14-3.

A much-discussed topic concerning project research is evidence-based design (EBD), which is done to expand the knowledge base of interior design. *Evidence-based design* is the "thoughtful use of the best available knowledge to improve design decisions." The concept of EBD is to use research to help determine how to go about designing an interior or a building. Evidence-based design helps to create better design outcomes.

Evidence-based design is most associated with healthcare design, but is also beginning to be used in the design of other types of facilities. EBD is being utilized to examine the successes and failures of other types of facilities, thus creating research and data that can be applied to future projects. An excellent resource concerning EBD in healthcare design is *Evidence-Based Healthcare Design* by Rosalyn Cama.

The point in bringing up research of this type in a business practices textbook is to encourage the practitioner—regardless of business size or type—that conducting project research can make the designer a better designer. One does not have to conduct formal EBD to obtain information from a completed project and apply it to future projects. By having statistics and other data available about a completed project, the designer can make better decisions about future similar projects.

This sort of research may not add substantially to the body of general interior design knowledge, but it certainly can be of benefit to the firm and the client. How does it benefit clients? As the interior designer gains insights into what works and what is not as successful, he or she makes better decisions for clients.

Research underlies so many project and business tasks undertaken by the professional interior designer. It is not something to be afraid of or forgotten upon graduation. Whether formal or informal, research during the design process or as part of business practices results in a more successful designer and practice.

*Hamilton and Watkins, 2009, p. 9.

Schematic Design Phase

The *schematic design phase* involves the execution of preliminary design decisions. These are accomplished through the development of written design concepts, bubble diagrams, adjacency matrices, block plans, preliminary floor plans, and any appropriate design sketches. In addition, the initial selection of furniture, materials, finishes, and equipment is made during this phase. Of course, the interior designer also includes applicable codes, accessibility guidelines, other regulations, and environmental standards required for the project in preliminary documents and selections. During this phase, the designer works with estimating forms for the architectural finishes, furniture specifications, construction estimates from contractors, and budgets. Estimating forms such as the one shown in Figure 11-3 help designers in the schematic design phase of the project.

Interior Design Source, LLC
PO BOX 164
Decatur, Alabama 35602
(Ph) 256-350-1123 FAX (256)350-2055
pdmasid@aol.com

Quote for Drapery/ Workroom Labor

Workroom:_____Phone:_____Date:_____

Client:_____ Room:_____

Please quote the following for me.

Yds. for fabric # 1_____
Yds. for fabric # 2_____
Yds. for fabric # 3_____
Yds. for fabric # 4_____
Yds. for fabric # 5_____
Yds. of trim_____
Yds. of lining:_____@$_____ = Total_____
　(you furnish- cotton sateen) flame retardant____ non flame retardant____

_____
Yds. of Inner lining ____ @ $_____ = Total_____

Labor for top treatment $_____x #. of treatments = total: $_____
Labor for drapery panels $ _____x #. of panels = total: $_____
Labor for roman shade: $ _____ea. = total $_____
Labor for balloon shade $_____ea. x # = total $_____
Labor for bedding with trim ____welting____ $_____
Labor for dust ruffle: $_____
Labor for pillow shams $_____ea. x #. ____ = total $_____
Labor for other pillows $_____ea. x #_____ = total $_____

Misc. items: (table cloths, specialty items) List:

Installation : $_____

Rods will be furnished_____ you furnish_____ Type_____
Fabric # 1_____ Fabric.# 2_____
Fabric.# 3_____ Fabric # 4_____
Fabric #5_____
Trim: #1_____ Trim # 2_____

FIGURE 11-3.

An estimating form to help the designer plan drapery treatments for a project. (Reproduced with permission of Phyllis Moore, FASID, Interior Design Source, LLC, Decatur, AL)

Client: _____Date:_____Pg. 2

Window size:

Outside width: _____Inside width_____ Install beyond frame_____inches

Finished length of panels:_____ of top treatment_____of shade_____
      Lowest point of swag_____longest jabot_____ shortest jabot_____
Finished mattress size: _____ Drop:_____Gusset_____
Tailored_____ throw_____coverlet_____pillow tuck_____
Dust ruffle: Drop:_____gathered:___tailored_____pleated_____lined_____
      With gussets:_____

Pillow sizes:

Sketches of window treatments and bedding:

Window # 1   Window # 2   Pillows:

FIGURE 11-3.

(*Continued*)

After review and client approval of preliminary graphic documents, the designer can move to the next phase of the project. Obtaining client sign-off is a best practice policy to help the designer to be properly paid for design work, especially if the client makes changes after approvals.

Design Development Phase

The *design development phase* involves final design decisions for plans, specifications, and any final presentation graphics. Depending on the designer's contract, he or she may also prepare construction specifications, at least at the preliminary level. It is critical that the interior designer conduct final consultations with any technical consultants to review any changes that were made after presentation of the schematic drawings to the client.

Along with these graphic documents, the designer prepares a more complete project budget. Figure 11-4 shows an example of a form that the designer might use to develop a budget estimate for a project that will not be put out for competitive bidding (as would be the case for most residential projects). Commercial projects often must be bid, so different documents are prepared for the project estimate. Once again, these documents are reviewed with the client, in a final presentation, before the contract documents are prepared. At the conclusion of the presentation, the designer should have obtained written client approvals of all drawings and specifications. These approvals are absolutely necessary before the project is moved to the contract documents stage.

The Design Collective Group, Inc. dba

DESIGN
pure + simple

301 N. PALM CANYON DRIVE SHOWROOM # 103
PALM SPRINGS, CA. 92262
VOICE: 760-841-1468 FAX: 561-745-0361

CLIENT PROPOSAL

Date _____ September 14, 2012 _____

Reference _____ #45-8976 _____

Please review and provide your approval of this work.

Name	Aaron and Evelyn Levy
Address	4682 Gene Autry Drive
City, St. Zip	Palm Springs CA 92262

SideMark	Levy Living Rm Area Rug
Deposit Required	50% Deposit At Time Of Order
Expected Ship Date	Approximately Jan 15, 2013

Ship To	Levy Residence
Address	4682 Gene Autry Drive
	Penthouse D
City, St, Zip	Palm Springs, CA 92262

Special Information   See Proposal for binding spec.

Quantity	Specification	Color / Finish	Each	Total
24 sq yds	Mayan Rivieria Sisal Carpet	784 / Mountain	22.99	551.76
	Width: 16-4"			
	Please Note: labor to fabricate will be billed directly from vendor			
	Deposit Required: $297.50			

Binding on rug
in paprika linen serge

Border made
from fabric from chair

Subtotal	551.76
Additional Charges	0.00
Sales Tax	44.14
TOTAL	595.90

Authorization To Proceed With This Proposal Subject To The Terms Of Agreement

BY: _____   Date: _____

FIGURE 11-4.

A proposal/estimate form showing items to be ordered for the client's project. (Reproduced with permission of Michael Thomas, FASID, CAPS, Design Collective Group Inc./Design Pure + Simple, Palm Springs, CA)

Contract Documents Phase

The *contract documents phase* of a design project involves final preparation of all the construction or working drawings (sometimes referred to as CDs), schedules, and specifications needed and required to build and install the design project. Contract documents are technical construction drawings, not furniture floor plans or other presentation drawings like perspectives. Care in the preparation of these drawings is very important, because serious liability issues arise if errors are made. Of course, interior designers can prepare the construction drawings only to the extent that the law in their jurisdiction allows. If the jurisdiction does not allow them to develop construction drawings, the designers will have to consult with architects, engineers, or other licensed individuals to be sure the drawings produced by licensed consultants meet client approvals. See Chapter 12 for a discussion of the bid process.

Competitive bidding requires the preparation of more detailed specifications than those used in most residential projects. When the project is to be bid, the designer is generally the party responsible for developing the complete bid package. Several other documents required in competitive bidding in addition to the specifications must be prepared.

Many residential projects and small commercial projects do not require a competitive bid. In these cases, project management at this stage includes preparing lists of recommended vendors or contractors in the name of the client or that are to be recommended to the client.

Contract Administration Phase

In the *contract administration phase* of the project, the competitive bid process is completed, orders are placed for all the furniture and equipment, and the actual construction and installation work are done. For a residential project, the project manager/designer's responsibility focuses on ordering or contracting for the furniture and other elements of the interior. However, depending on the contract, the residential designer might have other responsibilities as well, such as: coordination with the architect, contractor, and subcontractors; on-site supervision or review of installation of items in the specifications; on-site supervision of installation of furniture and accessories; and conduct of a walk-through with the client to inspect and note any omissions or damage.

For a project that was competitively bid, the interior designer's project management responsibility includes many more elements. The exact extent of this involvement varies by project and client, as many clients take on full responsibility for bidding or hire a consultant other than the interior designer to do this work.

At this point, please note a few key points of responsibility:

- Work supervision of the design team.
- Ordering of merchandise or letting of construction contracts.
- Coordination and cooperation with the architect, general contractor, and subcontractors.
- Review of shop drawings and submittals from vendors.
- On-site supervision of construction and installation of FF&E to the extent permitted by jurisdictional regulations.

To the designer, *on-site supervision* generally means making occasional trips to the jobsite as needed to be sure that all furniture and furnishings are being installed properly. Certain phases of the project require that the designer be on the jobsite for substantial periods of time. The client, however, often thinks that on-site supervision means the designer will be on the site all day, every day, seeing to every detail of the construction and installation. For most projects, this is, of course, impossible and impractical (and, depending on the designer's licensing, maybe even illegal). How much supervision and what kind of supervision—even who in the office or representing the office is to supervise—should be clearly spelled out in the scope of services and discussed with the client.

If the designer has the proper license, his or her responsibility may also include supervision of certain aspects of the construction of the space or installation of products. In most jurisdictions, someone who supervises construction or installation of architectural components (such as recessed lighting fixtures) must hold the proper license to legally perform installation supervision, or must be willing to relinquish this responsibility to a licensed contractor. You are strongly advised to learn what the law requires in your jurisdiction!

All postinstallation and postoccupancy activities are an acknowledged part of the contract administration phase. This includes a final site inspection called a *walk-through*, where the designer, with the client, determines if there are any omissions or damages. Notations are made on a form commonly called a *punch list*. Final payment to the designer is often withheld until all items on the punch list are taken care of. Larger design firms often prepare post-occupancy evaluations a short time after the client has moved in. A detailed discussion of contract administration tasks appears in Chapters 13 and 14.

One form that design firms use throughout the phases of the project is the *transmittal letter* (see Figure 11-5). This form letter can be used for many purposes. It can be sent to the client, consulting architects and/or engineers, subcontractors, leasing agents, manufacturers, or anyone else who is involved with or has an interest in the project. Another version of the transmittal letter is on the companion Web site as item 11-3.

The transmittal letter is designed to eliminate the need to write a separate letter or memo each time the designer transmits or asks for information. The fill-in-the-blank format makes it easy to use for a variety of purposes, though it is most commonly sent with materials or drawings of any kind. As can be seen by the example in Figure 11-5, it provides space to tell the receiver what is being sent and for what purpose, and it also gives instructions to the receiver for resubmittal or any action that the sender requires. It is an invaluable aid in speeding correspondence and stimulating action. Usually it is a two-part form: the original goes with the material being sent, and the copy is placed in the job file. Of course, a transmittal can also be sent via e-mail as an attachment.

PROJECT DELIVERY METHODS

Traditionally, projects have been created with more than one company involved in the process. For example, an architect or designer creates the design and plans for a client. A negotiated price or bids are obtained for the construction, and then the documents are handed off to a contractor, who hires subcontractors to complete the project. This type of delivery method is often referred to as *design-negotiate-build* or design-bid-build. For the most part, this is the main way residential projects are delivered. Many commercial projects are also delivered in this way.

Increasing numbers of commercial projects are delivered based on what is called design–build. In a *design–build* project, "a single contract is given to a single entity for both the design of the facility as well as the construction of the building."[3] In other words, one firm, such as a multidisciplinary architectural firm or a

JAIN MALKIN INC.
5070 Santa Fe Street
Suite C
San Diego CA 92109
858/ 454-3377
858/ 272-6199 Fax
www.jainmalkin.com

L E T T E R   O F   T R A N S M I T T A L

To:

Date:

Re:

Job No:

Sent Via: **Mail**

Purpose of Transmittal: ☐ For Review and Comment ☐ For Approval ☐ As Requested
☐ Correct and Resubmit ☐ For Your Use

Date	No. of Copies	Dwgs	Prints	Specs	Other	Description

Comments:

By:

Copies:

FIGURE 11-5.

A typical transmittal letter, which often accompanies other documents. (Reproduced with permission of Jain Malkin Inc., San Diego, CA)

large general contractor with architects on staff, prepares all the design concepts and documents and also is responsible for the actual construction of the project.

By going to a design–build delivery method, the project can more often be fast-tracked. *Fast-tracking* is just what it sounds like: a process to complete the project very quickly. In many cases, plans and construction documents are prepared "just in time" for the construction of those parts of the project. The project is fast-tracked in part because the negotiation for the design and construction is done at one time. The lengthy bidding process is nearly eliminated. Of course, for a design–build or fast-track project to function, the single source must have the appropriate design, construction contracting, and supervision personnel available, either as part of the firm or as a legal joint venture.

Clients can achieve effective cost control when using design–build. Everything is negotiated up front, as a fixed price can be determined for all phases of the project. If something goes wrong, the single-source firm cannot simply up-charge the client for changes. Another advantage to clients is that they have only one firm to deal with, rather than what can be dozens in a normal construction and FF&E project.

For the design–build firm, there is more liability and risk, as it takes on risks that are more often distributed to others. However, the potential revenue benefits have led many to bring these extra services into their design firms, so that they can offer more to potential clients. A very good reference on design–build is *Design-Build* by Jeffrey Beard, Michael Loulakis, and Edward Wundram.

STAKEHOLDERS

A project may seem to be an adventure that is embarked upon only by the client and the interior designer—but they are only the main players on the team. Anyone who is involved in the project and somehow has an interest in the project is commonly referred to as a *stakeholder*.

Any interior design project, particularly one that is large and complex, may have numerous stakeholders. Then again, the stakeholders might simply consist of the client, the interior designer, and the vendors who will eventually be hired to complete the installation; this is the case with many smaller projects.

The project manager (or project designer) is responsible for ensuring that all the members of this sometimes widely diverse group of stakeholders know what they are supposed to do and when and how they are supposed to do their tasks. The project manager also checks to be sure that they have accomplished their tasks. As any interior designer, from the sole practitioner to the senior project designer at the largest interior design firm, would agree, this is hardly ever an easy task. Managing the working relationships of the various stakeholders is always a challenge and a key task of the project designer/manager.

The most important stakeholder is the client. Clients expect the PM to keep them informed of the progress of the project. Some expect constant updates, while others are satisfied with weekly or even (on large projects) monthly updates. These might take the form of telephone calls, e-mails, memos, or other communications with the client. Information is important to most clients; many want to feel "in control" and believe that being informed is how they can maintain control. Others need to be kept informed of project progress because it affects their subsequent tasks and decisions.

Good client communication is an especially important key to ending a project with a satisfied client. Clients have, after all, decided to spend a great deal of money on your services and to accept your advice. That does not mean they will give you carte blanche with those funds or allow you to proceed without keeping them informed and involved.

Designers and project managers need to know which stakeholder can answer questions in a timely manner. The *single source of contact* is one particular individual who has the authority to make decisions regarding the project and to whom all communication is to be directed. The project manager or designer is that contact source for the design. Clients sometimes refer to their single source as the *owner's representative*. This individual might be an employee of the client or a consultant hired by the client. The owner's representative keeps the client informed using information passed on from the project manager. The terms *single source of contact* or *owner's representative* are more often used in relation to commercial projects than residential ones, as it is much more obvious who the contact is for a residence. However, residential clients sometimes use the services of an owner's representative, or a facilitator, to serve the same purpose.

Residential designers appreciate the concept of single-source decision making. This does not always happen with residential projects, as sometimes all family members wish to make (or at least be involved in) decisions. One way residential interior designers can protect themselves from problems of disagreement between the homeowners is for both to be asked to sign off on all paperwork and selections.

Here are a few more key issues in working with clients:

- Some want to clearly understand the project process. A clear scope of services set up in logical project order assists with this.
- Clients who have not worked with an interior designer before often require more education on the process.
- Clients enjoy visiting the jobsite—but sometimes these visits cause problems for the project manager, designer, and contractors. The project manager must make clear to the client what can and cannot be done while the client is visiting the jobsite.
- It is important that the client refrain from directly instructing workers on the jobsite. Be sure the clients understand that they should direct questions and changes to the proper foreman, to the project manager, or to the designer, not workers on the site.

In addition to the main client and the design firm, there are other potential stakeholders:

- Publicly funded projects include individuals who are interested in the completion of the project.
- Publicly funded projects often involve community leaders or city/town staff on the planning and building committee.
- Privately funded projects may involve a corporate board of directors or executive officers.
- Staff members who will work in the facility, or in some other way use the facility, may have input, just as family members have input regarding a residence.

Not all of these stakeholders will exist, and certainly not all of them will be at all the meetings, but the lead designer and project manager must keep them in mind when communicating to the source of contact and the group that will be making the decisions. Other possible project stakeholders include:

- Design staff, technical consultants, and vendors or trade sources.
- The lead designer, who may or may not also be the project manager.
- Design firm team members who may be assisting.
- Technical consultants. Architects, engineers, or specialty designers (such as a lighting designer) may be required. Even if these consultants are hired directly by the client, the interiors project manager must communicate with the consultants to ensure a well-designed project that proceeds smoothly.
- Vendors. They provide product information, pricing, samples, and other assistance that might be needed.
- General contractor and subcontractors. Instructions to the general contractor and the subcontractors must come from the project manager.

It certainly helps when all of these working relationships are well coordinated and run smoothly. Additional information about the people with whom the designer coordinates all of the tasks on an interior design project appears in Chapters 12 and 13.

SELECTING PROJECT TEAMS

Selecting a project team involves careful evaluation of each member's qualifications and skills, experience with like projects, and availability. A team must also be built upon delegated responsibility, trust, and strong relationships between team members.

Team selection starts with the project. The expected scope of services is naturally critical to team selection. The scope and skills needed are defined and identified, perhaps on a chart. Then the team leader can pencil in the names of potential team members next to the skill requirements. This will help the team leader more easily identify where highly skilled members will be needed versus involving less experienced designers.

Team member assignments must be made in relationship to other work that already exists. Although an experienced designer might be the person best suited to a particular project, that designer may already be fully committed to other projects. This means that less experienced staff members may be assigned parts of the project and have their work supervised by a senior member. This provides an opportunity for growth and challenge that the younger team members will welcome. Do not try to hide the fact that a less experienced person is working on the project from the client. The client has the right to know who is working on the project, and it is up to the team leader to ensure that members who have the right experience to do the work are assigned—and to reassure the client that this is so.

An important part of a well-functioning team is the delegation of work by the team leader. The leader cannot do it all himself or herself—that is why the team is needed. Too many leaders, however, can't really let go, and end up micromanaging the other members. Once work is delegated and responsibility is assigned to team members, the leader must allow those team members to do their jobs.

Lastly, the team must be selected so that the members respect one another. The team leader must be careful that one member does not let his or her ego get in the way of the group working together. Too many times I have seen one person in the group who is more highly skilled—and faster—at certain design tasks take over the work of those who are slower at producing work. Behavioral and communications programs can help with team building and team selection.

There are also several things that team members must remember. A long time ago, some unknown person said, "There is no 'I' in team." If you work for a sole practitioner or any small design firm, your willingness and ability to be a team player are crucial. Each individual in the company has a role on the team, though sometimes it is not very glamorous.

- Team members must put their egos on hold and work cooperatively with the other members.
- Negative thinking—especially about other team members—must be curtailed for the good of the team.
- Forcing other team members to go along with your ideas can be construed as unethical.
- Team members should feel that they are being heard.
- Remember that when the team wins, the individual wins.

PLAN REVIEW BOARDS

New construction, most major remodeling projects, and projects involving a change in occupancy require that a building permit be obtained from the local jurisdiction. The task of holding discussions with engineers and other jurisdictional staff involved in the review and approval process often falls to the project manager.

This review applies to residential as well as commercial use of the property. Exactly what is required and who can prepare the drawings will vary from jurisdiction to jurisdiction. For the most part, these decisions will be based on state licensing laws and local laws.

Before a building permit is issued, construction documents are evaluated by a local jurisdictional department. The *plan review board* (PRB) or design review board (DRB) evaluates the construction documents. These groups are responsible for ensuring that the plans meet codes and standard construction methodology required in the jurisdiction. This evaluation must be completed before building permits are issued.

The jurisdiction may require more than one set of drawings to be submitted. If the project is new construction or construction/remodeling, samples of building materials might also have to be submitted. Each jurisdiction has specific requirements as to what is to be submitted for review.

Depending on the contract responsibility, the type of project, and jurisdiction laws, the owner, architect, or interior designer submits copies of plans and specifications to the PRB. An interior designer can submit construction drawings under his or her name and seal for a building permit only if the interior designer is licensed or registered. Recall that in a few states interior designers are granted permitting rights. A permit application and fee are part of the process.

A member of the building department first reviews the plans (or performs a *plan check*) to ensure that the documents meet local codes. Large projects such as multiple dwellings and commercial projects will also be reviewed by the fire marshal. These individuals look for any omission or discrepancy in design as regulated by building, mechanical, fire, and accessibility codes and regulations. They will also look for compliance with all other local building and construction standards. Remember, the plans must meet the codes that apply in the jurisdiction of the actual project site, not that of the interior designer's office location.

Plans get *red-lined* (literally, are marked in red) to show where problems exist. Traditionally, drawings are marked up in red pencil or pen. Some jurisdictions may be able to do this process in a CAD format. If too many red marks are made, the plans are rejected and must be redrawn, and perhaps redesigned. If only a few red marks appear on the plans, the problems are usually worked out among the owner, architect, designer, contractor, and the building department prior to or during construction. The engineering department, planning and zoning department, state health department, or other groups that look specifically at compliance with regulations and codes within their jurisdictions also review many projects. For example, the state health department may review the drawings for a commercial kitchen or certain healthcare facilities.

Because meetings of the plan review board are subject to open meeting laws, anyone can sit in. Designers who have never been "under fire" at a PRB meeting should sit in on one sometime. If nothing else, it will make the designer more careful about the production of plans and specifications for all future projects!

With the exception of the installation of architectural finishes and the delivery of furniture, most construction or remodeling that is done on either residential or commercial sites requires a building permit. A *building permit* is an authorization from the city (or other jurisdiction) indicating that the plans and specifications submitted for construction meet local codes and regulations. It allows the construction work to proceed.

Laws do not universally allow an interior designer to submit plans to a jurisdiction's building department to obtain a building permit. When this authority is granted to a designer, it is said that the designer has *permitting privileges*. If the interior designer does not have permitting privileges, the construction documents submitted to obtain a building permit must be prepared and stamped by an architect.

Throughout the construction process, *building inspectors* will inspect the work. They will check to see that the project is built according to the plans, specifications, and appropriate methods. The interior designer (or general contractor) also will inspect the project. If an interior designer is not allowed to give direct supervisory instructions to subcontractors, he or she will send memos and change orders to either the client or the general contractor regarding discrepancies or changes that are needed.

Integrated Design

Integrated design—now often referred to as *integrative design*—is an emerging practice in which the numerous stakeholders in a project are included in the design from the beginning. Most interior design professionals would agree that being brought into a project at the beginning helps create the best solution and end result for the client. Unfortunately, too often that is not the case. With new construction, it is far more common for the interior designer to be hired (and thus become involved in the project) after the architect and others have completed the plans. Because of the problems that often arise, the process called integrative design has been gaining support.

This holistic approach seeks to build a better building or design project. "Integrated design recognizes that in the design-build industry the most successful projects bring all the stakeholders together from the beginning of design conceptualization through completion of the project."*

Naturally, a project is led by the owner of the property. This is because the owner is the stakeholder providing the purpose and use of the project—as well as paying the bills. The client may issue a request for proposals (RFP) to obtain the architect and the team of subconsultants, such as the engineers and, yes, the interior designer. Or the client may select the architect and the team in other ways that are within the parameters of the client's selection process.

"Every year more firms are adopting integrated practice, finding it can improve the quality and efficiency of the building process and result in both a better building and more satisfied client."** By utilizing integrated design and practice techniques, the project becomes a whole more easily rather than necessitating the integration of disparate parts—which takes more time and almost always results in higher costs to the client. In some respects, integrated design is similar to a design process called fast-tracking. (See the discussion earlier in this chapter.)

Team members must be willing to cooperate. One team member consistently trying to force his or her control upon the team can lead to disaster. Remember that the leader of the team is the client, even though the client is looking to the team to realize the concepts that the client is trying to achieve.

Team members must also be willing to work with an integrated and negotiated single contract rather than separate contracts with each of the individual design–build team members. This often means that the integrated design team will create a joint venture company, legally distinct from any individual company involved in the project. Joint ventures are discussed in Chapter 18.

It is important for interior designers, especially those involved in commercial design projects, to be familiar with integrated design, as more and more projects are being built using this process. Residential designers who become integral partners with architects or building contractors must also become familiar with integrated design to position themselves as part of the project team rather than an extension of the project leader, as has been done in the past.

New references on the topics of integrated design and design–build project processes are becoming available in book form. Information can also be obtained on the Internet, and a few of these sources are included in the references of this textbook.

*Piotrowski, 2011, p. 51.
**Elvin, 2007, p. 3.

PROJECT SCHEDULES

Scheduling of the design team's activities and the work that must be completed to construct and/or install the project is a very important project management responsibility. Project schedules are prepared during programming as part of the revised work plan, are refined during schematics, and are updated throughout the project. The project manager/designer carefully monitors the schedule, informing the client of any changes that might affect the due dates of upcoming activities and completion of the overall project. Project schedules help the designer maintain control of the project. Breaking down a large task into manageable units helps the designer get the task done on time.

Project schedules can take many forms, depending on who is using the information. Designers might use a schedule set up on a daily basis, or use week-by-week descriptions of what must be done to reach the target completion date. The project manager or design director needs a week-by-week or monthly schedule to aid in accepting, estimating, and assigning new work.

Computer software is available to assist with project scheduling. Sophisticated systems used by large design firms make scheduling for complex projects faster. Simpler programs for smaller firms are also available to help with scheduling. There are also scheduling software programs to help with selling appointments and subsequent billing.

Depending on the complexity of the software, the program can produce numerous reports once data about time lines, activities, and due dates have been entered. A design firm that will be involved in projects for large commercial corporations, public agencies, and the government will want to use a project management software program that is compatible with any used by the client. Simple project scheduling software for smaller design firms is available from several sources. Although the author does not endorse any particular software brands, a popular project scheduling software in the industry is Microsoft Project®. Due to cost, it is used primarily by larger design firms.

It is important that the scheduling system provide adequate visual displays of the work tasks and sequence of the tasks. The three methods most commonly used for visualizing the project schedule are the milestone, the bar chart, and the critical path method.

Milestone charts may be the easiest method of scheduling a project. In this method, the designer outlines the activities that are required for the project and then establishes the target dates for their completion (see Figure 11-6). Space can be included to indicate who is responsible for each activity. The actual date of completion should be noted, as this will aid in future estimating. The biggest advantage to the milestone chart is ease of use. It is a very good method for controlling the schedule of small projects that are not very complex. No specialized software is required, and it can be set up using common word-processing software; however, it may also be an option in specialized project management software.

A more graphic method of showing project scheduling is by use of a bar chart. Figure 11-7 provides an example. *Bar charts* (also called *Gantt charts*, named for Henry Gantt) consist of a description of tasks required on the left-hand side and horizontal bars on the right-hand side, showing the time required to complete the task in days, weeks, or months. Designers can use this chart as a management tool, to show their responsibility on a daily or weekly basis if they are working on more than one project. To assist with overall project management, the project manager can prepare a monthly chart for each designer to help the design manager determine whether someone is available for additional work.

A disadvantage of the bar chart is that it does not necessarily show how one activity affects another activity, or which is the most important activity

---

Project: Weldon Residence
Designer: Maryanne

Task Name	Days	Earliest Start	Earliest Finish	Latest Start	Latest Finish	Actual Finish
Interview Client	3	9/23/0X	9/26/0X	10/3/0X	10/8/0X	9/23/0X
Obtain Floor Plan	1	9/24/0X	9/25/0X	10/7/0X	10/8/0X	9/24/0X
Inventory Existing Furniture	1	9/25/0X	9/25/0X	10/7/0X	10/8/0X	10/5/0X
Sketch Preliminary Plan	7	9/26/0X	10/7/0X	10/8/0X	10/17/0X	10/6/0X
Make Preliminary Selections	5	9/26/0X	10/3/0X	10/10/0X	10/17/0X	10/7/0X
Prepare Preliminary Budget	2	10/6/0X	10/7/0X	10/15/0X	10/20/0X	10/8/0X
Meet with Client	1	10/7/0X	10/8/0X	10/17/0X	10/20/0X	10/8/0X
Revise Preliminary Plan	5	10/8/0X	10/15/0X	10/20/0X	10/27/0X	10/14/0X
Revise Selections	3	10/7/0X	10/20/0X	10/27/0X	10/30/0X	10/8/0X
Prepare Final Budget	1	10/20/0X	10/20/0X	10/29/0X	11/3/0X	10/23/0X
Make Final Presentation to Client	2	10/20/0X	10/22/0X	10/30/0X	11/3/0X	10/24/0X

FIGURE 11-6.

A sample milestone chart. The chart indicates the activities to be performed, the estimated days for completion, and the target dates for starting and stopping each activity.

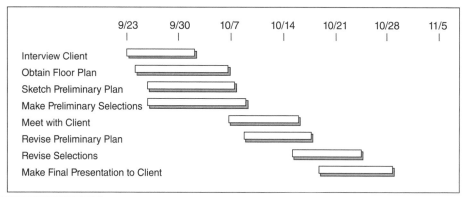

FIGURE 11-7.

A bar chart that graphically shows the time span required to complete designated project activities.

needed to complete the project on time. As readers know, many tasks in completing an interiors project overlap, with one task moving to completion while another begins. Analysis of the most important activities can be developed with more careful project analysis and a more complex color-coded bar chart. This tool works well for most small to somewhat complex projects, although it is not particularly appropriate for large or very complex projects. It can be done manually; some firms put bar charts up on a wall to show the project's or firm's progress on the work being done in-house. Computer software is also available for creating bar charts.

If the design project is very complex, so that the interrelationships of the required tasks are critical, the third method of scheduling may be called for: the *critical path method* (CPM). This scheduling method both displays and is dependent on the interrelationships of activities and the detailed tasks of each activity. Any one activity in a sequence cannot be completed unless the previous tasks and related activities have been completed. Generally, only the larger interior design firms find CPM appropriate for project scheduling, and only for large projects. Architects and the construction industry use CPM scheduling to maintain control of the interrelated tasks in the construction process. This method would be very difficult to manage manually, so some type of computer project management software is necessary.

Briefly, CPM scheduling starts by identifying the interrelationships among the tasks to be performed. This analysis shows the project manager which tasks must be done before the next or other tasks can be performed, thus establishing the critical path (see Figure 11-8). Here is a sample of a critical path for an interior design project: the designer obtains the client's needs, prepares floor plans, obtains the client's approval, orders products, and installs and/or delivers products. It is clear that it is impossible, as well as unwise, to try to do any one of these tasks before completing the one directly preceding it. As the interrelationships are entered into the computer, along with due dates and the duration of each task, the computer automatically makes the calculations and makes the adjustments for changes in the schedule. Then new charts are produced, which can be given in different formats to the interior design team members, the client, and other stakeholders.

PROJECT BUDGETING

Regardless of the type of project, establishing and sticking to the budget is a critical issue for both the client and the interior designer. Specifying a project that comes in significantly over the client's budget can lead to a potential lawsuit and ethics charges. These reasons alone make accurate project

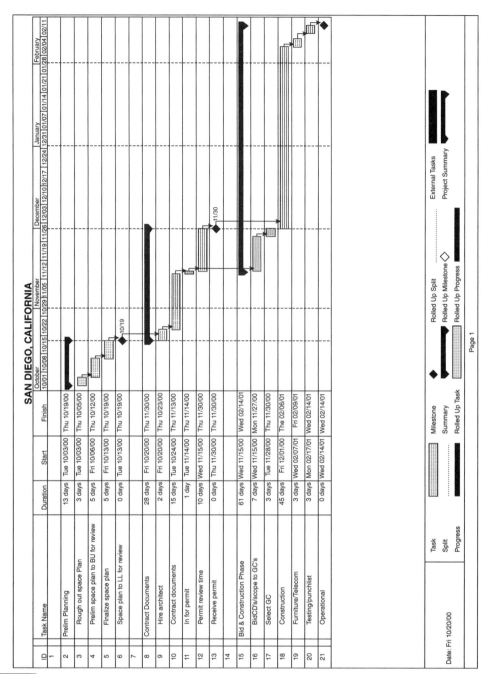

SAN DIEGO, CALIFORNIA

ID	Task Name	Duration	Start	Finish
1				
2	Prelim Planning	13 days	Tue 10/03/00	Thu 10/19/00
3	Rough out space Plan	3 days	Tue 10/03/00	Thu 10/05/00
4	Prelim space plan to BU for review	5 days	Fri 10/06/00	Thu 10/12/00
5	Finalize space plan	5 days	Fri 10/13/00	Thu 10/19/00
6	Space plan to LL for review	0 days	Tue 10/13/00	Thu 10/19/00
7				
8	Contract Documents	28 days	Fri 10/20/00	Thu 11/30/00
9	Hire architect	2 days	Fri 10/20/00	Thu 10/23/00
10	Contract documents	15 days	Tue 10/24/00	Thu 11/13/00
11	In for permit	1 day	Tue 11/14/00	Thu 11/14/00
12	Permit review time	10 days	Wed 11/15/00	Thu 11/30/00
13	Receive permit	0 days	Thu 11/30/00	Thu 11/30/00
14				
15	Bid & Construction Phase	61 days	Wed 11/15/00	Wed 02/14/01
16	BidCD's/scope to GC's	7 days	Wed 11/15/00	Mon 11/27/00
17	Select GC	3 days	Tue 11/28/00	Thu 11/30/00
18	Construction	45 days	Fri 12/01/00	The 02/06/01
19	Furniture/Telecom	3 days	Wed 02/07/01	Fri 02/09/01
20	Testing/punchlist	3 days	Mon 02/17/01	Wed 02/14/01
21	Operational	0 days	Wed 02/14/01	Wed 02/14/01

Date: Fri 10/20/00

Task / Split / Progress / Milestone / Summary / Rolled Up Task / Rolled Up Split / Rolled Up Milestone / Rolled Up Progress / External Tasks / Project Summary

Page 1

FIGURE 11-8.

Critical path method chart. (Reprinted with permission of Allyson (Grenier) Calvert, Phoenix, AZ)

budgeting a concern for designers. Clients rarely grant designers free rein with an unlimited budget. In fact, the budget that the client has in mind is almost always smaller than needed for reasonable accomplishment of the project. Many clients do not reveal the full nature or extent of the budget, fearing that the designer will always spend (at least) that much; by keeping it a secret, they think that perhaps the project will come in below what they wanted to spend.

Many interior designers are hired after other budget decisions for construction and structural elements of the project have already been made. This often heightens the challenge for the interior designer to implement creative ideas that will meet client needs and goals. It is never an easy task to convince the client to upgrade finishes, modify structural elements, or purchase higher-quality furnishings after these kinds of decisions have been made.

Project budgeting for the interiors primarily involves estimating the cost of furniture, architectural finishes, and accessories. Depending on the project, the designer might need to obtain estimates for non-load-bearing partitions, lighting, cabinets or other built-ins, and the like. For example, depending on its size, a new kitchen with all new cabinets, counters, wall and floor finishes, ceilings, and lighting can start at $25,000 for something modest, and can reach well over $100,000 for a large, complex kitchen—before appliances are included. The furniture alone for an office of around 175 square feet can start at about $35,000 (retail). How does the less experienced designer go about determining a budget?

One method that can be used concerns developing quality ranges. Design firms can develop three or four quality ranges from among the manufacturers with which they commonly do business. In a way, this is similar to the grade ranges of fabric for upholstered goods. The lowest grade or group of manufacturers includes those with budget lines. A second group consists of those that offer medium-quality goods—goods that would be serviceable and will provide several years of satisfactory use. A third group would include many of the high-end manufacturers, whose products are known for their high quality. The last group would be manufacturers that could supply custom goods or that are known to carry the very best quality items. Some design firms find it useful to develop a checklist that describes these ranges. These checklists are discussed with the client to clarify the differences among the product groups. The furniture representatives or the manufacturers' literature can be helpful sources of information when a firm develops these quality ranges.

A second budgeting technique is the use of "typicals." Commercial interior designers who have a significant amount of experience with certain kinds of spaces develop layouts of typical spaces, for example, offices or a doctor's exam room, or even a hotel guest room. At its simplest, this technique starts with an average or typical furniture arrangement. There can even be more than one typical arrangement for a similar space—something that is commonly done for hotel guest rooms. Adding a quality level to the typical space provides a budget idea that the designer can discuss with the client. Residential designers also find this method useful as a starting point when they are helping a client understand the potential overall cost of furnishing a portion of the home.

It is also possible to do product budgeting on a square-foot basis. In this case, the designer utilizes historical data that he or she has collected on a variety of project types and conditions. As preliminary discussions of project feasibility and budget are conducted, the designer can use these factors to clarify potential costs to the client. For example, a residential design firm can use this information to give a "ballpark" budget of all furniture and finishes for a high-end house based on the livable square footage of the house. A commercial designer may use historical square-foot factors to provide information to a client who is considering furnishing a law partner's office. The designer can even show the client that a contemporary-style office might cost X dollars per square foot, while a traditional style will cost some other factor per square foot.

Of course, the designer can also estimate each item by using standard materials, cost, and labor charges for individual items such as window treatments, carpeting, tile, and so on. Materials estimates can also be obtained from reference books. Designers often prefer this method, as the design of a residence and many types of commercial properties can be very customized and difficult to budget in a ballpark fashion.

There are, of course, a few built-in problems in using any of these techniques for budgeting. Clients may make decisions based on price rather than on the quality required. This may back designers into a corner, forcing them to use products or design concepts that do not result in the best finished project. Another problem is that the client may assume that the budget is the designer's final price and go elsewhere to find a less expensive solution. This is why most designers commonly quote budget ranges rather than single numbers. Ranges give the designer flexibility in the specification of products without always appearing to be over the budget when the actual prices are determined.

MANAGING AND RECORDING YOUR TIME

Many of the ways that an interior designer can be compensated for services are based on time—even when the designer does not charge by the hour. Everyone is restrained by time. There are only 24 hours in a day, and most do not want to work that many hours a day!

All of your design work must be accomplished during those hours you need to work or choose to work. Whether you charge based on time or some other method, managing and recording your time accurately does affect the bottom line. So does all the nonbillable time needed for other activities. An interior designer who is too busy to keep track of his or her time cannot bill accurately, cannot tell when additional staff must be hired to do nonbillable work, and cannot adequately schedule additional projects. Effective time management and faithful time recording are critical skills and tasks for the professional interior designer.

Time Management

As workloads continue to increase and clients continually demand that turn-around time on information be faster, time management can no longer be ignored. The Internet has brought us the opportunity (or problem) of working 24/7/365. Clients want answers *now*, not in a few days. We barely have time for our personal lives amid all our other responsibilities. There never seems to be enough time to get everything done. Getting into a habit of using good time management can help the designer do required tasks, on time and with a lowered level of stress. Table 11-3 lists 10 common time wasters.

To an interior designer, one of the absolute truths is that time equals money. Whether the designer is paid by the hour or receives compensation in some other way, the efficient, productive use of time has a direct bearing on the designer's yearly income. It is therefore very important for the interior designer to make the best use of his or her time while on the job.

TABLE 11-3.

Typical ways people waste time on the job

Inadequate planning
Telephone interruptions
Procrastination
Personal disorganization
Unrealistic time estimates
Attempting too much
Inability to say no
Crisis management
Socializing
Making mistakes

Time management and organization problems have existed for many years. The first book I found on the subject was *How to Get Control of Your Time and Your Life* by Alan Lakin, published in 1972. It remains a useful treatment of the subject, although you might find one of the other dozens of books on time management more effective for you. A few good references have been included for your further reading.

These theories were not developed to make you a slave to your job, but rather to help you organize your time to be as productive as possible. That does not mean that your time is planned so rigidly that there is no room for flexibility to meet emergencies. In interior design, it sometimes seems that every day is filled with emergencies. The purpose of time management is not to control time but to control the *use* of time. The basic premise involves creating to-do lists, prioritizing those lists, and keeping a calendar and a notebook handy; preferably all in the same notebook or electronic device. Figure 11-9 shows an example of a computer-based to-do list.

Time management is simple and is founded on the common, basic management responsibilities of planning, decision making, and control. You plan the day (or week or month) by making decisions about what (you hope)

Item	ABC	Daily Task List	Time Est.
		Check and respond to emails	:30
		Call Sally James: carpet pricing for Smith	:15
		Call Ned for lunch ?? Thursday	
		Verify RFP pickup for Hospice Center	:15
		Discuss Hospice Center proposal with Jim	:45
		Review Allegro plans with Tom	
		12:00 Lunch with Barbara W at Green Gables	1:30
		Finish Allegro plans review	1:00
		Check and respond to emails	:30
		4:00 Conference call with DKD	:45
		Time sheets	
		Specs for MicroAge 3rd Floor	

FIGURE 11-9.

A prioritized to-do list showing activities and time estimates for the completion of each task.

will be done and will not be done during any one time period. These plans and decisions then help you better control what you do with your time.

Time management experts discuss what is called the 80/20 rule. As it relates to time management, the *80/20 rule* maintains that when activities are arranged in order of importance, 80 percent of a person's time will be spent performing 20 percent of the activities. What this means is that in a list of 10 items, if a person accomplishes the 2 most important items, he or she has achieved 80 percent of the total value of time spent. Most companies can look at sales records and see that approximately 80 percent of the sales were generated by 20 percent of the sales staff. The main thrust of the 80/20 rule is that one should concentrate one's efforts on the few items on the list with the highest priority, to generate the greatest value or return. By the way, it does *not* mean that when you have accomplished those top two items, you can let the rest of the items on your list slide!

An effective tactic is to use a notebook organizer or an organizer on your smartphone that allows you to keep a calendar and to-do list easily accessible. It is also important to have phone numbers, e-mail addresses, and some sort of note-taking capability. Many designers still use a notebook that contains a monthly calendar, a day-to-day calendar divided by hours, pages for to-do lists, memo paper, and address pages. These elements are also generally available as apps for a smartphone or programs for a laptop. You might want to experiment with different systems to find what works best for you and the design firm you work for. Figure 11-10 is an example of a computer-based time management record.

The computer was supposed to help us eliminate paper. Instead, we still accumulate great piles and folders filled with paper. Being able to handle paper items only once is another great time management tactic. That is, read the paper, mail, memo, and so forth once, and then file it or discard it, rather than creating stacks of paper all over the office. You can easily accomplish this by setting aside a certain amount of time each day as part of your to-do lists for handling mail and filing. Forgetting to go through the mail consistently can lead to missing checks from clients and not paying bills in a timely fashion.

E-mail is another task that takes a large chunk of everyone's time each day. The first strategy is to allow a certain time each day to open e-mails and decide what must be done with each. Set up special in-boxes for current projects so that you do not lose important e-mails. Above all else, try to avoid checking your e-mail too often. It is a concentration breaker that does nothing but damage your productivity.

Time management also involves confident decision making, good organization, and learning how to deal with procrastination. It involves learning how to handle interruptions; how to delegate effectively; and even how to say no, which sometimes can be very difficult. Time management also requires that you (1) learn to reward yourself when you meet goals and (2) not beat yourself up when you are not making the progress that you would like.

Time management works, but it takes discipline to get into the habit of creating to-do lists and prioritizing them every day, and learning all the other techniques that will help you become a more effective employee or owner. Even though new habits are difficult to establish, it is necessary to keep at it if you intend to become a designer who rapidly earns promotions and responsibility.

Time Records

The habit of good time management makes recording the time worked on any project much easier. Recording time is an imperative when the designer charges by the hour. It also helps create a good history for how long it takes to design different kinds of projects. This is helpful when estimating fees for new projects.

Being "too busy to keep track of my time"—an excuse many designers offer when I ask them about time recording—does not justify refusing to use time management practices. Being too busy to keep track of his or her time

Thu Oct 26, 2000

Po To-Do's	
think about artafactual furniture	2-18-00
call barry for lunch	10-16-00
Proposals due on TSG Call C	10-26-00
verify FFE deliv sched on Credit union	10-26-00

7	
8	8:00a - 9:00a meet w K French re: PCC
9	
10	10:00a - 2:00p OSW Des Dev
11	
12	
1	
2	2:00p - 3:00p Az Biz conf call
3	
4	4:00p - 5:00p ASSCU weekly jobsite meeting
5	
6	
7	

Printed 8:43a 10/20/00

FIGURE 11-10.

A computer-based time record system sheet. (Reprinted with permission of Fred Messner, IIDA, Phoenix Design One, Inc., Tempe, AZ)

might mean that the designer is doing work that should be assigned to someone else. Delegating is an important business skill for owners and managers: They have to remember that they can't do everything themselves.

Keeping time records is not a difficult task. It does take discipline to accurately record time for the different activities being undertaken. A manual system requires one or two sheets of paper set up with space to describe the task performed and the amount of time spent on the task. (Naturally, this task can also be performed on the computer.) Be sure to separate billable from nonbillable time. A manual system such as this can utilize a simple form such as that shown in Figure 11-11. The form should have space for the client's name or the project's

		Time Record			
Designer:_____			Week of: _____		
			Page _____ of _____		
		Task	Billing		
Date	Project Code	Description/Notes	Time	Fee rate	Bill amount
		Totals			

FIGURE 11-11.

A sample form for keeping track of all billable hours worked by a design staff employee.

name as well as the designer's name. This form can record all the work done for the day or week and then be transferred to a form for individual projects. This form has been included on the companion Web site as item 11-4.

Many computer-based programs provide the same type of recordkeeping documents. Those are often designed to work in conjunction with a daily planner. The computer system allows a great deal of additional information to be included in the database. The computer system also can be interactive, so that each staff member can check on the appointments of other designers if necessary.

Time records are only as accurate as those charged with keeping them make them. How exact the records must be is a function of management control. It is impractical to try to record every single minute. Most companies record based on the quarter hour; that is, the designer reports work on any project or house time by 15-minute intervals. Designers record the activities of a normal workday plus any overtime.

Utilizing time management and time recording can lead to more effective use of time and prevent the loss of billable time. Clients will demand your undivided attention even though they know this is not practical. Time management helps you keep the promises you make. Accurate time recording helps ensure that you bill for all the time you have spent on a project, helping improve your profitability. Additional time management tips are included as item 11-5 on the companion Web site.

Reasons to Make Time Recordkeeping a Habit

Time equals money in interior design. Keeping track of time while working on projects helps you recognize whether a type of project is profitable for the time invested. Recording nonbillable time is also important, as it can help a practice owner realize what kind of assistance is needed with administrative tasks.

Here are several specific reasons to make time recordkeeping a habit:

1. Accurate time records are necessary for billing if the design firm is charging by the hour for professional services. Some clients wish to see time records before they pay the bill.

2. Time records help the designer or firm owner check on the progress of current jobs. This is necessary in order to determine if too much time is being used. If the project is running over the estimated time, the reasons must be analyzed. Does the client change his or her mind often? Is the designer nonproductive? Was there an error in the requirements or plans? Was enough time budgeted?

3. Keeping accurate time records helps a designer or the design firm determine what kinds of projects are actually profitable. When a firm is working with many clients who require a lot of hand-holding, or the firm spends a lot of time on activities like specification writing and drafting, certain fee methods provide more potential revenue (and profit margin) than others. This cannot be determined accurately if time records are not kept.

4. A record of time worked on previous projects helps the design firm determine budgets and fees for new projects. For example, if the firm knows that a 3000-square-foot model home can be completely designed in X hours, that information saves the firm time and errors in writing new contracts.

5. Historical time records can also help a firm decide if it even wants to take on certain kinds of projects, if they may be very time-consuming while returning a very small profit margin.

6. Time records can be of assistance to managers when they do employee performance reviews. Interior designers in many firms are looking for the majority of the designer's time to be billable. Time records help the firm determine if designers are productive for the firm. Depending on how important this is to the design firm, designers who are billing closest to their goals are more likely to receive salary increases or to be rewarded in other ways.

7. Time records and historical utilization records assist the firm's owner in making the overall budget and planning decisions necessary for the continued future health and growth of the design firm.

8. A wide variety of management control reports can be generated from time sheets.

PROJECT FILES OR JOB BOOKS

Janice received an e-mail from Mr. Smith, a client with whom Janice worked four years ago. Mr. Smith needed to replace chairs and the carpeting in his home office that had become damaged. Janice researched her job files and found the chair and carpet information. Mr. Smith wanted to match the carpet and upholstery, as he really liked it. Janice contacted the suppliers and was able to match the upholstery but not the carpet.

Keeping all the records and documents concerning a particular project so that the project designer—or anyone else in the office—can quickly track the answers to questions is a very important task for the project manager. Whether it is to answer a question on a project in process or to help a client out on a past project, a *project file* or project job book is the mechanism you need for this type of information control.

The project file usually consists of file folders or notebooks in which all the pertinent data and paperwork related to the work in progress is kept. It might be supplemented with boxes or other binders containing swatches and samples of materials. The project file serves as a complete record of all the designer's efforts to organize a project. It is also useful in creating the installation manual.

Keeping a project file up-to-date and organized requires discipline, just as time management does, but it is immensely useful. All the information the designer needs about the project is in one place. As questions arise or changes are made, the designer has a complete reference to use when talking to the client, vendors, or personnel in the design firm. The well-organized project file makes an impressive statement to the client about how the designer and the design firm keep control of projects.

If the designer in charge of the project is absent for any reason, the project file allows other members of the firm to seek out answers to clients' and vendors' questions. Even if the lead designer leaves the firm, another designer should be able to pick up the project file and complete the project.

As was the case for Janice and Mr. Smith, the project file is also invaluable as a future reference tool. If the client wants to replace items or is in need of repair of existing items, it is easy to check the project file for exact product information. If legal problems arise during or after the project, the project file will serve as a thorough reference tool for the firm. In addition, a project file is helpful as a sales tool in marketing efforts. Clients may wish to see how the firm expects to control their projects, so displaying a well-organized project file, with all its various parts, may be the answer.

Although projects are all different, many have similar qualities. Project files help the firm with projects that are similar in many ways. For example, project files can help determine the following:

1. Why the design time estimate was or was not accurate

2. Whether or not products performed as specified and if vendors were a problem

3. If taking additional work from the same client would be inadvisable, perhaps because the client made an inordinate number of changes

With so much project information being created and maintained on computers and other electronic devices, it is imperative for the designer to have backup systems and copies of the entire file of computer-generated documents. Firms usually make a good habit of backing up financial information, but do not always remember to do the same with correspondence, memos, e-mails, and drawings. Portable hard drives are very inexpensive for a small firm's backup storage. Some firms even use USB memory sticks as individual backup storage. Bigger firms routinely utilize offsite backup of company documents. If you use a portable hard drive or memory sticks, be sure you place them in a secure file unit, preferably one that is fire- and waterproof.

The project file should contain the following categories of information: meeting notes, correspondence, samples, and floor plans.

Meeting Notes

A piece of advice given to me by the first designer I worked for was to take a lot of notes at meetings. Not everyone has a memory for the many details that are discussed during meetings with clients, vendors, architects, and other stakeholders. Because interior designers often work on several projects at the same time, trying to keep all the information on each project straight without taking good notes is a recipe for disaster.

Most people do take notes, but some choose to trust their memories rather than put notes in writing. Perhaps they feel that by taking notes they are not giving their undivided attention to the client. However, memory is seldom perfect. Meeting notes can become important in court if any type of legal challenge or issue is raised.

Meeting notes should include the notes taken during the initial interview, which are used to develop the design contract, as well as all subsequent interview notes or forms obtained concerning client needs. Include the date and time of the meeting and the names of those in attendance. Notes need not be verbatim to be useful, but they should contain the salient details of the discussions. It is a good idea to retain the original notes taken during the various meetings that the designer has attended. Many designers send transcribed copies of meeting notes back to the client or other interested parties to be sure that there are no lingering misunderstandings. Telephone notes to any of these parties should also be kept in this section of the project file.

Do not trust your memory. Use a preprinted form, your laptop, or simply notebook paper. By the way, do not tape-record a meeting unless you have permission from all of those in attendance.

Correspondence

The meeting notes described in the preceding subsection are only one type of correspondence that should be retained in a project file. The primary document in the "correspondence" group is a copy of the signed design contract. Many firms find it best to retain the original, signed design contract in a separate file to protect it from loss or damage. Project designers use a copy that can be marked up.

File copies of all general correspondence sent to or received from the client in the project file. Insert any letters or memos and any e-mail messages. Print out a hard copy of your e-mail messages to a client and any responses from the client. Hard copies are important even if you have a separate in-box on your computer for each client and project. There is always the chance that the server will go down or the hard drive will crash when you most need to review e-mails in these computer-based files.

Keep file copies of correspondence to and from factories and representatives, including letters concerning pricing, special treatments or fabrics, custom work, availability for shipping, freight charges, and so on. Correspondence to and from architects, construction contractors, or subcontractors must also be retained. Again, all e-mails concerning the project should be printed out and placed in the project file.

Everything that goes into the file should be accurately dated. Do not throw away any of the preliminary work sheets, even when finalized sheets have replaced them. Sometimes a client signature for approvals is noted on a preliminary drawing and later disputed on the final drawings. Pricing information or brief notes might appear on preliminary sheets that may be needed to clarify or defend some action or decision. Leave cleaning out the files until after the project has been installed and all moneys have been collected.

A large number of original or, in some cases, photocopies of project documents should also be in the "correspondence" section of the project file. Table 11-4 lists some of these documents. In-depth discussions of many of these forms are contained in other chapters.

Samples

It is best practice to retain samples of textiles and other materials specified for a project. Samples should not be stuffed into a box or a folder with no identification. They must be accompanied by a full description, including the manufacturer, the product name and/or number, the color name or number, and a code for determining what furniture item (for upholstery) or room name/ number (for window treatments, wall treatments, and floor finishes) goes with which sample.

Samples may be organized piece by piece or room by room. Some firms use a small form printed on card stock. Others use a form such as the one shown in Figure 26-1 to help keep track of all the materials that have been specified for a project. The control sheet is ideal for setting up an installation manual so that the installation of furniture items will go more smoothly.

Storage systems for filing samples vary widely depending on the type of project. Residential designers find it convenient to maintain samples in boxes. Sturdy, solid-faced magazine storage boxes, clear plastic boxes (such as shoeboxes), or other appropriate-sized storage tubs can be used. Residential designers use storage boxes when fabric samples must be obtained in larger memo samples to appropriately show patterns to the client. Samples for smaller projects can often be contained within a large three-ring binder where other documents can also be organized. Commercial designers generally use a notebook or expandable, closed file folders to store samples. However, for some projects they would also use other storage boxes.

Floor Plans

The project file should have a printed copy of the final floor plan(s). If the project is very large, it might be convenient to have the large floor plans reduced on smaller sheets and include room-by-room plans. The copy of the signed, approved floor plans should also be included in the project file. Of course, backup copies of the CAD file should be maintained in a fireproof file or offsite location.

TABLE 11-4.

Documents typically included in a project file

Correspondence
Signed design contract
Memos and transmittals from vendors and suppliers
Meeting minutes and subsequent replies from client and vendors
Other correspondence related to the project

Project-Programming Documents
Client interview questionnaires
Job-site analysis
Space-programming questionnaires
Employee work area summaries
Existing furniture inventories

Project Specifications and Budgets
Furniture specification sheets
Estimates for architectural finishes and window treatments
Other budgeting forms
Samples and approved cuttings

Drawings
Preliminary plans drawn from site measures
Preliminary sketches, especially those approved by the client
Contract documents
Shop drawings
As-built documents

Bidding and Procurement
Bid specifications
Purchase orders
Acknowledgments
Invoices
Shipping documents
Change orders
Punch lists
Site inspection reports

Miscellaneous
Warranties
Maintenance documentation
Postoccupancy evaluations
Internal post-project documentation
Anything else pertinent to the project for future reference

Preliminary plans should be maintained until all moneys have been collected and the project has been fully installed and approved. Why worry about preliminary plans and sketches? Disputes during the progress of the project, as well as at the time of installation, often can be resolved by referring back to approved preliminary drawings and plans. In addition, maintaining these earlier plans and sketches gives the designer more leverage when charging clients for changes at the very end of the project.

The design firm should develop a system for coding the plans to the control sheets, as previously discussed, and to the written specifications. This makes it easy to identify specific items on the floor plan and is key in the development of installation manuals. An example of this is shown in Figure 12-1 concerning contract documents.

Other Items

For some projects, additional items should be placed in the project file. The smaller design firm will often maintain copies of many forms that normally would be in the bookkeeping area, in the warehouse, or in the hands of the managers. These items might include a copy of the formal bid specifications, equipment lists, invoices from manufacturers, time records, and freight information. If management produces them, follow-up notes concerning profitability, marketing information, problems, or successes may also be kept in the file.

BUILDING INFORMATION MODELING (BIM)

Building Information Modeling (BIM) "is the use of virtual building information models to develop building design solutions and design documentation, and to analyze construction processes."[4] Two-dimensional (2D) and three-dimensional (3D) drawings are combined with things such as specifications and cost data to help design architectural projects. BIM is not simply another type of CAD software, and it is not simply 3D image generation. This computer-based modeling system helps to define how a building is designed, through computer software techniques that improve visualization of the building and incorporation of other data such as costs into that design.

With this project delivery tool, changes are handled more efficiently and elegantly: when one thing is changed, the building components, specifications, and costs are also automatically changed. Errors are minimized through this type of automatic change management. Updates become simultaneous and instant, thus also reducing errors and omissions. For example, if it becomes necessary to eliminate a door opening, everyone's documentation is changed at the same time so that each team member is notified and no one is neglected.

Because of the nature of this software, the project team using BIM must be well organized and cooperative. It must also be well versed not only in computer drafting but in electronic communications methods. If the project team does not cooperate, the whole project can become chaotic and fragmented, and fail spectacularly. Some say that BIM works best within firms that already offer integrated practice, combining architecture, engineering, and design. Strong leadership from the client and key project design representative can make BIM work for other project joint ventures.

Here are some key advantages and disadvantages to BIM:

Advantages:
1. Leads to superior coordination of drawings and documents
2. Enables cost savings through somewhat reduced design labor costs
3. Expertise provides new markets for the design firm, including global work

Disadvantages:
1. Requires a learning curve for all firms involved in the project
2. May require changes in firm design and management philosophy
3. Is a fairly new technique that is not yet in common use

The BIM project management approach is not used by residential interior designers or even many interior designers in the commercial marketplace.

Commercial interior designers working for large firms or affiliated with an architectural practice might be involved with BIM. It is an emerging technique and provides opportunities for firms that are willing to dedicate themselves to learning how to apply BIM to selected projects. It also provides opportunities for individuals to become expert in an emerging part of the design–build industry.

VALUE ENGINEERING

Every client is looking for the very best value for the dollars spent on an interiors project. Few designers have had a client say, "Money is no object." A strategy borrowed from architecture and engineering practice that can help bring greater return on the dollars spent is the process of value engineering. *Value engineering* is a method of analyzing and specifying products and design solutions based on cost-effectiveness. The key concept in this strategy is to find acceptable substitutions for higher-cost design concepts in order to provide quality outcomes at lower cost. Although the term normally used is *value engineering*, it could also quite easily be called *value design practice*.

Value engineering is best applied at the early stages of a project, before many design decisions have been made and carried through to other phases of a design project. However, value engineering can be used at any phase of the design project. For the interior design of facilities, it can be very effectively applied to the specification of products or materials. When this method is utilized at the beginning of a project, it saves the designer time in analyzing various options against the known budget.

Some designers refer to value engineering as "making a silk purse out of a sow's ear." Of course, many designers feel that this is just not possible. A more positive approach to value engineering is to regard it as doing the very best design job possible at the lowest cost to the client. Sometimes this can be relatively simple, such as substituting a rayon blend fabric for silk on an upholstered item or using a textured vinyl wall covering rather than natural grass cloth.

Clients, however, may use the method as a pure cost-cutting mechanism, especially at the end of a project. This can create many difficulties for the interior designer. The best way to prevent this complication is to have frank and complete budget discussions with clients at the beginning of the project. Residential and commercial clients appreciate interior designers who show them up-front estimates for design projects. Residential clients, who may lose track of how expensive it is to design or remodel a home, appreciate budget estimates.

Value engineering can be another useful marketing tool for interior designers to show clients how they offer value and knowledge in design. In addition, applying value engineering in appropriate ways can be useful when the designer is trying to show how he or she differs from competitors.

Clients today are looking for greater value and lower prices. The recession may have forced this concept on clients who formerly did not have such an overwhelming concern for the "low bid" or low price. Like it or not, this concern is unlikely disappear for many years. Interior designers must recognize that clients at all economic levels and in all demographics are looking for value. And finding ways to make that silk purse from the sow's ear—value engineering—is part of the future of the profession.

WEB SITES RELEVANT TO THIS CHAPTER

www.aia.org American Institute of Architects

www.asid.org American Society of Interior Designers

www.interiordesigncanada.org Interior Designers of Canada

www.iida.org International Interior Design Association

www.pmi.org Project Management Institute

www.usgbc.org U.S. Green Building Council

KEY TERMS

80/20 rule

Bar chart

Building Information
   Modeling (BIM)

Building inspectors

Competitive bidding

Contract administration

Contract documents

Critical path method (CPM)

Deliverables

Design development

Design–build

Designer/specifier

Design-negotiate-build

Fast-tracking

Gantt chart

Integrated design

Milestone chart

Owner's representative

Plan check

Plan review boards (PRB)

Predesign

Programming

Project file

Project management

Project manager

Punch list

Red-lined

Schematic design

Single source of contact

Stakeholders

Transmittal letter

Typicals

Value engineering

Walk-through

Work plan

WHAT WOULD YOU DO?

1. KD Interiors has been hired to design and specify a 50,000-square-foot office complex for a county government agency. Because it is a government agency, the FF&E must go out for a competitive bid. At least 10 vendors have met the requirements for bidders and are expected to bid. Another 45 vendors have obtained the bid documents and are interested in bidding. The client has just informed the project manager at KD Interiors that the county wants the firm to help evaluate the bids, even though this was not contemplated or discussed when the design contract was negotiated.

2. Fred recently obtained a contract to remodel the kitchen and family room of a large house. He generally does his drawings using manual drafting; however, the contractor retained by the homeowner only works with CAD drawings. Fred did not feel he had time to learn CAD for the project, so he contacted Emily, an architect he met a few

months ago at a professional association event. Fred and Emily discussed whether she could do the drawings for Fred from his sketches.

At a meeting with the contractor, Fred did not disclose that Emily was not an employee—only that she would be doing the drawings. When the contractor contacts Emily about some issues with the drawings, she says that she is only creating the drawings for Fred and is not responsible for the accuracy or content of the design.

3. Susan is a designer in a small residential firm. A friend of hers, James, who owns his own design firm, has told her that he occasionally orders extra rolls of some wall coverings, billing the product to the clients whose project needed the wall covering. Rather than giving that extra material to the client who paid the bill, James donates it to charity, taking a tax deduction for the value of the material on his income taxes.

4. Alex Smith has been contracted by Ultimate Bed and Breakfast LLC to provide design services for a new B&B. Alex was interviewed by the owner of Ultimate but is working directly with the office manager, Sally. Sally has been approving all the specifications and plans and has given Alex approval to begin contracting for the interior renovation work. Alex arranges a construction agreement between Randolph Construction and Ultimate Bed and Breakfast, and Sally signs the agreement.

After the initial demolition has begun, Alex receives a frantic phone call from Sally telling him to stop the work. The owner is upset about some of the plans and costs for the renovation.

REFERENCES

1. *Oxford American Dictionary*, 2002, p. 1557.
2. Piotrowski and Rogers, 2007, supplemental materials.
3. Piotrowski and Rogers, 2007, p. 10.
4. Demkin, 2008, p. 986.

CHAPTER 12

Contract Documents and Specifications

After completing this chapter you should be able to:

- Compare the purpose and types of materials in a set of contract documents to a set of construction documents.
- Describe what kinds of schedules are included in a set of construction documents.
- Explain why it is better to use generic or trade names to identify products on construction drawings rather than actual product names.
- Discuss the differences between an open and closed specification and provide an example of each.
- Provide key characteristics and uses of proprietary, descriptive, performance, and reference specifications.
- Discuss the advantages and disadvantages of using proprietary specifications for a commercial project.
- Discuss why it is important for specifications to be written in a clear, concise manner and in accordance with the type of specification used.
- Explain the difference between a construction contract and a construction agreement.
- Explain the purpose of the competitive bid process.
- Explain why the competitive bid process is less often used for residential interiors projects.
- List and explain the documents needed for a competitive bid.
- Compare the purposes of the bid bond, performance bond, and labor and materials payment bond.
- Compare the purposes of addenda, change orders, and submittals.

NCIDQ COMPONENT

Based on best information available, some material in this chapter might appear as part of the NCIDQ examination. The reader should not depend solely on this text for study material.

Many projects require contract documents consisting of construction drawings, specifications, and schedules. Contract documents are used for the many residential and commercial projects when it is necessary for the client to obtain competitive bids, or prices, for the completion of an interiors project. Projects that have minimal or no construction work involved are often referred to as *FF&E projects*. That acronym stands for *furniture, fixtures, and equipment*.

Many industry standards affect the production of a complete set of contract documents. An understanding of what constitutes contract documents is necessary for any practitioner regardless of specialty. A residential designer might become involved in a project on which he or she prepares construction drawings and specifications for remodeling and additions to a home—assuming local laws allow those tasks to be performed by an interior design professional. Commercial interior designers frequently are involved in developing parts of the contract documents. The limitations on what they may actually produce are also established by state or local regulations.

This chapter discusses the documents associated with projects that must be competitively bid, with emphasis placed on formal bid specifications. It also includes a discussion of the bid process and the documents that are added to the construction drawings and specifications to complete the contract documents package.

Although much of this chapter may not apply to projects designed by the residential interior designer, it is necessary for all professionals to have an understanding of the documents and items discussed here. It is also important information that will likely be included in the NCIDQ examination multiple-choice section and indirectly in the practicum section.

CONTRACT DOCUMENTS

The fourth phase of a project is referred to as the contract documents phase. In this phase of a project, all the documents needed to build and bid (or purchase) the project are completed. A complete set of *contract documents*—often referred to as CDs—consists of all the construction drawings, specifications, and contracts or agreements between the designer and the project owner and others that might be involved in the construction of the project. CDs generally do not include furniture layout drawings.

Construction documents are thought of as the drawings and specifications portion of the contract documents. Be sure to note that there is a difference between contract documents and construction documents.

A set of contract documents is a legal document, constituting a contract, and thus ensures that the project will be executed according to the design concepts and wishes of the interior designer and the client. Technically, any variation from the construction documents without approval constitutes breach of contract.

Contract documents must be prepared carefully and accurately. Errors in the drawings or other documents will result in liability issues as well as potential lost revenue for the interior designer. Legal disputes can harm the designer's reputation and even result in penalties imposed by a court. Errors in contract documents can also lead to ethics complaints and, potentially, disciplinary measures by the designer's professional association. Table 12-1 lists the documents that are usually produced during the construction documents phase of a project.

Construction Drawings

Although the construction drawings are discussed separately from specifications, it is important to begin by saying that the two items are used collectively to complete a project: Together, they are the instructions on how to complete

TABLE 12-1.

Contract documents

> **Contract Documents**
>   Agreement between owner and contractor (also called *construction agreement*)
>   Conditions of the contract
>   Construction documents
>   Modifications: addenda and change orders
> **Construction Documents**
>   Drawings
>   Specifications
>   Schedules
> **Bid Documents**
>   Invitation to bid
>   Instructions to bidders
>   Bid form
>   Bid requirements
>   Construction drawings

the project. The drawings show visually what is to be done, while the specifications explain how the work is to be done and the quality of work required.

Many in the industry often call the construction drawings the *working drawings*. For an interiors project, a set of construction drawings would include dimensioned partition drawings; section drawings; mechanical drawings, including electrical and telephone location plans; reflected ceiling plans; plumbing plans; HVAC plans; other mechanical plans (such as for sprinklers in a commercial building); interior construction elevations; and construction details. Additional specialized drawings, such as plans from lighting designers, commercial kitchen and food-service designers, healthcare system designers, and others, might also be included. The person who designed the exterior structure would prepare any additional drawings.

Many interior and architectural firms also include equipment plans or furniture plans in the working drawings. Equipment plans show the location of, and identify by code, the movable equipment in the project. By *movable equipment*, we mean furniture and other equipment, such as refrigerators, that can be easily moved and are not part of the structure. Movable equipment is rarely bid with the construction of the walls. In most projects, furniture and equipment drawings are provided to the general contractor for information only. They are obviously necessary for the furniture bid.

Interior designers prepare furniture or equipment plans using a variety of techniques. Some are very detailed and in fact look a lot like a detailed rendered floor plan. Others are very simple, giving the bare essentials of shapes and sizes along with notes. The detail in these drawings is now controlled to some extent by the type of computer software that is utilized to create drawings. The equipment or furniture plan must also relate to the written specifications. Regardless of the technique used to produce the furniture/equipment plan, it must communicate to various stakeholders what goes where without the interior designer having to be on the jobsite.

For bidding purposes, the equipment plan must be very clear and understandable. When projects are to be bid, it is common for interior designers to prepare a separate equipment or furniture floor plan for information and use in installation. Some designers use codes that correspond to information in the written specifications to clarify each furniture item in the bid. Codes may be simple numbers or letters, accompanied by a furniture schedule describing these items of furniture (see Figure 12-1), or more complicated codes. Codes are

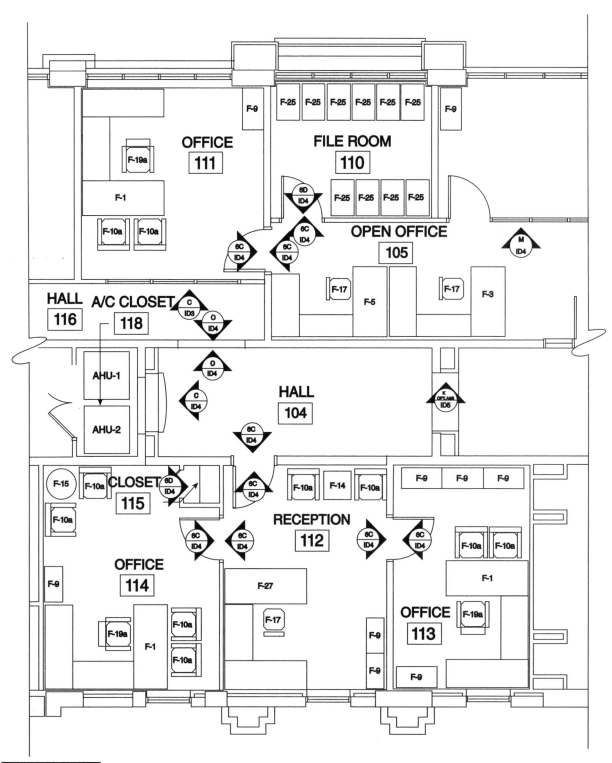

FIGURE 12-1.

Coded furniture schedule—partial floor plan. (Reproduced with permission of Sally Thompson, ASID, Personal Interiors by Sally Thompson, Inc., Gainesville, FL)

used to indicate generic types of furniture and furnishings, not specific product information, just as generic information is often used in notations on construction drawings. These codes are then further explained in the specifications.

The exact format for and coordination between plans and specifications must be clear enough for the vendors to know what they are bidding on. They must be easy enough for the design firm to produce and also to make any required changes to the plans. However, the design firm should individualize the formats, as plans and specs can also be used as a marketing tool.

Trade names and product numbers should not be used on the equipment plans, because it is too easy for errors to occur. Trade names and product numbers, if used, should be limited to the written specifications. All information in schedules or code keys should be generic descriptions. If the designer had to write product names and numbers many times, it would be all too easy to make errors such as number transpositions, resulting in an incorrect bid. If it became necessary to change something or substitute a different product, forgetting to make the changes in product numbers everywhere they appeared on the plans would cause incorrect bidding or the wrong product being ordered.

Although it is best to use generic names for furniture, furnishings, and room names, generic descriptions can lead to misinterpretations if the terms used are not clarified. For example, *chair* could mean guest chair, armchair, posture chair, club chair, dining chair, stool, occasional chair, or executive chair. *Table* could mean dining table, coffee table, end table, cocktail table, occasional table, conference table, table desk, or Parsons table. *Rest room* could mean the women's room, men's room, powder room, lavatory, bathroom, or lounge.

Many other examples of generic terminology for furniture, furnishings, and rooms exist. Although it is important for designers to use generic terms, it is equally important for terms to be consistent, clear, and defined within the specifications. To aid in defining generic terms, place a key either in the specifications or on one of the sheets of equipment plans.

Any number of books can further clarify how to prepare a set of construction drawings and equipment plans in detail. Several are mentioned in the references.

Schedules

Schedules are an important part of the instructions concerning how a project is to be completed. In this situation, a *schedule* is usually a tabular chart or graphic used to clarify project items that cannot easily and completely be distinguished from representations on floor plans and other construction drawings. A set of construction documents might include schedules for doors, windows, interior room finishes, ceiling heights and treatments, and lighting fixtures.

The format of these schedules varies greatly from office to office. Finish schedules are commonly prepared in tabular form, whereas door and window schedules are commonly prepared in graphic form. Tabular schedules are often computerized by using word-processing or spreadsheet programs or the CAD software used by the firm.

The information provided in the schedules that accompany the working drawings should be generic. Trade or manufacturer's names are supplied in the written specifications. For interiors projects that are not very large or complicated, some designers include a materials key with the finish schedule. The materials key is similar in format to the finish schedule, but it does name manufacturers. If it is used, it should be used only in the specifications. It would not be appropriate to use a materials key if a performance or descriptive specification were used.

SPECIFICATIONS

Even the most detailed construction drawings do not by themselves provide enough information for contractors to build or supply what is needed for an interiors or construction project. In fact, in court cases, the written word takes precedence over drawings.

The *specifications* portion of the contract documents (simply referred to as "specs" by many in the industry) contains the written instructions to the general contractors and vendors. The residential interior designer and many small interior design firms will likely use a simple, though detailed, specification list to clarify what is to be provided for the project.

Especially for commercial projects, larger design firms prepare specifications in a technical fashion and provide detailed information about the materials or products required, quality and workmanship expected, installation requirements, responsibilities of bidders, and the like. Specifications are needed for structural materials and designs as well as for the FF&E required for the interior. This section discusses the types of specifications used for the FF&E. If the reader needs information on the preparation of specifications for structural work, he or she should refer to the references section at the end of the book for suggestions.

When a designer decides to use a simpler form of specification, it is critical to clarify the quantities, description, and perhaps pricing. Figure 11-1 provided a sample of this type of specification. If a custom item or an attachment such as a mirror is part of the project, the interior designer may prepare notes concerning the quality and installation procedures required for those items, either as part of the equipment list or separately. Many of the documents discussed later in this chapter are more common in commercial design projects that must be put out for competitive bidding than in residential projects. It is important for all interior designers to understand these concepts, however.

When all or part of the construction and/or procurement of the goods must utilize the competitive bid process, a different type of specification is required. These detailed written specifications can be quite complex, and much care must be taken to avoid mistakes. Because it is easier for most people to interpret the written word than drawings, when there are discrepancies between the two, the courts often base their decisions on what appears in the written specifications. It is therefore essential for the designer to prepare the specifications clearly, without any ambiguity, errors, or omissions.

The specifications should complement the drawings, not duplicate them. Specifications should describe what is needed, along with quality standards. The drawings should show dimensional and location information. Drawings may also indicate quantities, sizes, generic identification of materials, and interrelationships of space, materials, and equipment. Some designers also provide quantities of the goods required in the written specifications. Although this is very helpful to the vendors who are bidding, vendors commonly are held responsible for the quantities.

When a specification is written for a product such that no other product can be substituted for it, it is commonly called a *closed specification*. Closed specifications require that only an exact match of the specification be provided by the vendor. In other words, whatever is specified for a Knoll Barcelona chair must be bid—no substitutions are permitted.

An *open specification* is one in which the owner is willing to consider substitutions for what was originally specified. This type of specification usually incorporates the words "or equal" into the specifications. *Or equal* means that products that are the same as, or very close to, what has been specified will be considered.

TABLE 12-2.

Sample of a very simple proprietary specification

Reception Area				
Item	**Quantity**	**Description**	**Unit**	**Total**
LC-5	4	Knoll 250LS Barcelona Chair Leather: Black		
T-3	1	Knoll 56T-MIN Mercer Coffee Table 44½″ × 44½″ Finish: Nero-Black Marble		

There are four customary kinds of formal specifications. These four types of specifications identify the goods and/or materials needed in different ways, so that the designer and the client can have better control over what is actually bid by vendors. The four types of specifications are (1) proprietary, (2) descriptive, (3) performance, and (4) reference.

Proprietary Specification

Anna's client is a private entity that requires competitive bids for furniture and equipment that will exceed $5000. The project budget for the accounting department has been estimated at $36,000. The client wants to use a particular manufacturer's products, as specified by Anna's firm. She plans to use a proprietary specification format for the bids, as there are at least five vendors that can provide a competitive bid on the furniture specification. If there were only one vendor, Anna would need to change the specifications in order to obtain the desired products for the client.

A *proprietary specification* names the products and materials by manufacturer's name, model number, or part number. With a proprietary specification, there is no doubt about what the designer and client wish to have bid (see Table 12-2). The basic proprietary specification is a closed specification that does not allow any substitutions. If more than one product is specified for each item, technically it is no longer a proprietary specification.

If the specifications permit no substitutions or do not have an "or equal" clause (which would allow substitutions), then the proprietary bid might be called a *base bid*. "The term *base bid* means that all people who wish to provide materials for the project must base their bid on the product named in the specification."[1] Note that the term *base bid* also has another meaning directly related to the actual bidding process, as discussed later in this chapter. A proprietary specification that permits substitutions is considered an open bid or open specification, because it allows other products to be substituted for the item specified. Again, if only a single source is named, it is considered a closed bid or closed specification.

The advantages of the proprietary specification are as follows:

1. It is the easiest specification to write. In many cases, the designer need only provide the basic descriptive information of manufacturer, product number, and finishes/fabrics to complete the specifications. When more detail is needed, manufacturers often provide information to the designer that can be reproduced in the specifications.

2. It is easier to use for preparing drawings. With known product sizes, drawings can be more accurate. The designer does not have to make allowances in the drawings for possible larger or smaller sizes of a product that might be bid.

3. The designer has maximum product control over the project. The carefully worked out design concept can be realized exactly as planned, as the products used to develop the design concept will be the ones purchased.

4. The time from invitation announcement to order entry is shorter, because the client need not evaluate alternate products.

5. Because everyone is bidding on exactly the same products, the competitive bid concept is more fully realized.

The disadvantages include the following:

1. Sometimes there are not sufficient numbers of bidders in a given market area that can provide the products.

2. This type of specification limits competition in some markets. When this is the case, it is often necessary to add an "or equal" clause in the specifications.

3. When the specifications must include an "or equal" clause, extra time is required for the designer and/or client to evaluate the bids and the substitutions.

4. Design control can be lost. What is "equal" is open to subjective judgment on the part of the client, the designer, and the bidders.

5. Design projects for government agencies generally require that more than one product be specified. A proprietary specification can be used in this case only if an "or equal" clause is inserted.

The specifications must include explanations of what procedures will be followed concerning the submission of alternates. This is done to protect all parties concerned when there is an "or equal" clause. A common practice recommended by the Construction Specifications Institute (CSI) is to submit requests related to substitutions prior to the close of the bid. These requests might include detailed descriptions of the substituted product. In some cases, clients ask that a sample product be submitted for evaluation prior to the close of the bid. Some firms require that vendors pay for the time the interior designer must spend in evaluation of substitutions, especially if the specs originally stated that substitutions were not allowed.

Descriptive Specification

A *descriptive specification* does not use a manufacturer's name or trade name for the goods being specified. Rather, it describes, often in elaborate detail, the materials, workmanship, fabrication methods, and installation of the required goods. The descriptive specification is considered an open-bid specification.

There are two advantages to the descriptive specification. First, it allows the designer to prescribe exactly what he or she wishes to specify for the project while not using a proprietary form of specification. When there are many similar products that have only subtle differences, such as with floor coverings, a descriptive specification helps to ensure that what is bid is actually equal to what is being specified, even if the goods come from different manufacturers. There are also situations in which the client wants a certain product for the project but would have a difficult time obtaining sufficient numbers of competitive bids if the client used a proprietary specification. A descriptive specification helps to narrow the "or equal" alternates so that the client can get what it wants.

TABLE 12-3.

Sample descriptive specification for open-office systems work surfaces

12.7 Work Surface		
A.		General
		1. Work surfaces shall suspend from architectural walls or freestanding panels. Components attached to the work surface shall be removable by hand or with the use of a minimum of tools.
		2. Vertical support elements (VSE 1–12) shall support hanging components on 1-inch intervals and shall easily allow for vertical height adjustment of the work surface.
B.		Component
		1. Work surfaces shall be made of warp-resistant materials and have squared corners and edges.
		2. Work surfaces shall be finished using high-pressure plastic laminates that are scratch and heat resistant (up to 250°) available in a variety of colors. Edges shall be finished with a matching vinyl material.
		3. All work surfaces must be provided with cantilever-type support brackets that allow for easy installation and removal from panels and wall-hanger strips with a minimum of tools.
		4. Work surface tops shall be capable of having various under-counter drawers, storage units, or other accessories suspended below, installed with a minimal use of tools.
		5. Cantilevered work surfaces shall be able to support up to 200 pounds when weight is located at the front edge of work surface. (Test data must be provided.)
		6. Work surfaces shall be available in the following nominal sizes:
WST-1:	24 inches deep by 30 inches wide	
WST-2:	24 inches deep by 36 inches wide	
WST-3:	24 inches deep by 42 inches wide	
WST-4:	24 inches deep by 48 inches wide	
WST-5:	24 inches deep by 54 inches wide	
WST-6:	24 inches deep by 60 inches wide	
WST-7:	24 inches deep by 66 inches wide	
WST-8:	24 inches deep by 72 inches wide	
WST-9:	30 inches deep by 30 inches wide	
WST-10:	30 inches deep by 36 inches wide	
WST-11:	30 inches deep by 42 inches wide	
WST-12:	30 inches deep by 48 inches wide	
WST-13:	30 inches deep by 60 inches wide	
WST-14:	30 inches deep by 66 inches wide	
WST-15:	30 inches deep by 72 inches wide	

Second, the descriptive specification can include critical performance criteria in situations for which a complete performance specification is not appropriate. With floor coverings again, many manufacturers have carpets that can meet the simple descriptive specification of such things as fiber, pitch, stitches per inch, and pile height. This may not be enough to ensure that the carpet or carpet quality required for the project is bid. Performance criteria related to such factors as static electricity, delamination, and crocking can be included in the specification for these kinds of goods. Other goods, such as furniture, which may not have such stringent requirements, can be written as descriptive specifications (see Table 12-3).

There are a number of disadvantages to using descriptive specifications:

1. It requires time to produce them, and they can be quite lengthy.

2. They require more precise and much more detailed descriptions of the products.

3. The volume of information needed to prepare descriptive specs can lead to errors, omissions, and loopholes that allow for products to be bid that were not intended.

4. The descriptive specification, unless it is written very carefully, can result in the designer losing control of the product and design concept. Omissions and errors in the specification could result in extra cost to the client and could also become the basis of a client lawsuit against the designer.

Performance Specification

Another type of open-bid specification is a *performance specification*, which is also written without trade names. The performance specification establishes the product requirements based on exact performance criteria. Any product that meets the performance criteria can be bid. The performance of the goods is based on the end product, and thus performance criteria are based on the accomplishment of that end. Performance specification criteria for carpeting are shown in Table 12-4. Performance results of a product are often the key to this type of specification.

Performance specifications are based on qualitative or measurable criteria and statements. It is common for specifications to require that certain tests be done and that certain methods of testing be used. Bidders must submit test data with their bids. This information is available from the manufacturers for the designer's use in writing the specifications. Manufacturers can provide testing information to the bidders.

When data from the manufacturer are not available or appear inconclusive, it may be necessary for the bidder to supply a sample of the product for testing, as is often the case with various textiles. For example, if the designer wished to use a carpet material on a wall, it would be necessary for the

---

TABLE 12-4.

Performance specification for carpeting

Specifications	
Pile Fiber Contents	100% Advanced Generation Nylon
Construction	Dense-Cut Pile Graphic
Gauge	1/10
Pile Height	.250
Pile Weight	30 oz.
Primary Back	Polypropylene
Secondary Back	ActionBac
Yarn Size	
Ply	2 Ply Heat Set
Dye Method	Beck Dyed
Total Weight	60 oz.
Stitches per Inch	8.3
Pattern Repeat	
Testing	
Radiant Density Panel (ASTM E-648)	Class 1
Smoke Density NBS (ASTM E-662)	Less than 450
FHA-HUD	
DOC FF-1–70	Passes
Static Propensity	Built-in Antistatic Control

Source: Reproduced with permission of Wade Carter, Interior Surfaces Guild, Scottsdale, AZ.
Notes: Specifications listed above are subject to normal manufacturing tolerances. Chair pads are necessary under office chairs, with roller casters to prevent premature or accelerated wear and to preserve appearance. Color may vary from dye lot to dye lot.

designer to specify some kind of performance criteria for that textile and for the manufacturer either to supply data regarding its use or to supply a sample that could be tested.

Some designers prefer this type of specification, because it allows for flexibility in what can be bid. Other designers feel that this same feature is a major problem with performance specifications. Ambiguities and confusion can sometimes occur, resulting in inappropriate products being bid. Advantages are the same as for the descriptive specification: full control when it is not appropriate to use proprietary specifications. Disadvantages are also the same: extra preparation and evaluation time, possible errors, possible loss of design concept, and loss of product control.

Reference Specification

A *reference specification* utilizes an established standard, such as the standards of the American Society for Testing and Materials (ASTM) and the American National Standards Institute (ANSI), rather than detailed written descriptions or performance criteria for required products. These established standards generally provide minimal acceptable standards of performance for various kinds of products. Because of this, the reference specification is considered an open bid.

The designer must check these standards to be sure that the minimums are satisfactory for the needs of the project. If the standard is too low, the reference specification cannot be used. It is also necessary for the designer to be fully familiar with the standards, because the standards sometimes provide options for materials or workmanship. The designer must be sure that he or she specifies the standard or level of standard required for the project. If this is not done, the bidder then has the option of using a lower standard than the one the designer may have intended to use. Reference specifications are more widely used in construction, but interior designers may use them for such things as wall and floor products and installation.

As readers might expect, there are advantages and disadvantages to the reference specification. One advantage is that a reference specification saves time, because only the standard must be stated; there is no need to write a long, detailed descriptive specification or performance specification. Another advantage is that a reference specification can be used to help explain a complex performance specification or descriptive specification for specialized products or installations. The disadvantage is that if the designer is not up-to-date on and fully aware of the standard, the designer may inadvertently permit products and workmanship that do not meet the desired requirements.

SPECIFICATIONS ORGANIZATION

When the FF&E for a project is put out for a competitive bid, it is standard practice to utilize a formalized organization for the specifications. The complexity of many projects can make true competitive analysis of bids very difficult, unless a standardized format is used to present information in an orderly fashion. As legal documents, specifications should be written in clear language and not omit necessary information. Even with the use of computer applications in the preparation of specifications, this document requires a great deal of time, thought, and care to ensure accuracy and completeness.

Following a standardized organization allows for greater speed and accuracy by the designer as well as by the vendors who will be providing bids. The furniture vendor is only interested in what furniture and furnishing items are required. The framer, electrician, plumber, and all the other trades are likewise only interested in what they are being asked to provide. Thus, standard organization helps each vendor find and bid on the products and processes most important to it.

The Construction Specifications Institute (CSI) developed the organizational format most frequently used in the design and construction professions. CSI is a nonprofit organization whose purpose is to improve professional documentation, especially specifications. With its membership spanning the full range of the construction professions, CSI has been able to develop a common language of construction and a standardized format for the preparation of specifications. Information on the CSI format materials can be obtained from www.csinet.org; materials may also be ordered using this Web site.

MasterFormat™, published by CSI, is the most widely accepted method of organizing specifications. Its detailed numbering system, organized by materials, trades, functions, and space relationships, reduces the chances of omitting important information. It also makes it much easier for the designer to make changes while the specs are being written.

The design firm can, of course, establish its own version of standardized specification language. All the popular word-processing software products provide sufficient flexibility for the designer to develop the template sections needed in a furniture and finishes specification. Software is available from CSI to assist firms in computerizing their specification tasks.

A design firm that frequently needs to use detailed specification formats may be interested in obtaining one of the standard text systems. Standard text systems (provided on discs) are available from trade associations, manufacturers, and some of the professional organizations. These standard text systems have a fill-in-the-blank format. However, these standard text systems require that users have a thorough understanding of the construction process, so that they know what to leave in and what to take out of the specification.

Another standardized specification program is the *MASTERSPEC Interior Design* (www.masterspec.com/masterspec) from ARCOM AIA. This program has short-form master specifications, which follow the CSI format. MASTERSPEC has specification information for interior construction, finish, and equipment items for several types of commercial facilities. It also has reference materials and provides background information on the various materials. This user-friendly system was the first set of specification standards for interior materials and products, and significantly simplifies the creation of intricate interior product specifications.

Specification Language

Whatever formats the firm chooses to use, specification language should be kept clear and direct. Clarity leaves little room for argument as to the designer's intent and what the client agreed to, and helps prevent potential legal and ethical complaints.

Language must be used carefully, as words can have double meanings or legal/technical meanings that are not carried into everyday use.[2] For example, *shall* and *will* are often used incorrectly. Though they are often thought of as similar or interchangeable, *shall* is used to indicate a command or mandate; *will* implies a choice. Another example is use of the word *all*, as in "The Contractor shall assume the responsibility for all unacceptable work." This sentence leaves no doubt about the contractor's responsibility.

In the field of interior design, sentence structure traditionally uses the indicative mood: for example, "The vendor shall remove all cartoning and packaging materials." (By the way, *cartoning* refers to the packaging, mostly cardboard, used to pack and ship furniture and other items.) Another alternative recommended by specification writing professionals is the use of the imperative mood. In this case, instructions do not use the phrases "the vendor shall" or the "contractor will." Words such as "shall" and "will" are omitted, creating an imperative sentence. If the preceding example were rewritten in the imperative mood, the sentence would read, "Remove all cartoning and packaging materials."

Writing technical specifications and preparing the remaining documents needed for a bid are time-consuming activities. In truth, most designers do not enjoy either activity. Small firms that infrequently produce formal contract documents and bid specifications may wish to hire specification-writing consultants. Independent practitioners provide consulting services to design professionals who do not feel qualified or who do not have the time to prepare construction and/or detailed interiors specification for bids. Larger firms may assign a staff member to be responsible for the preparation of all specifications issued by the firm. These specialists need to be experienced in interior design and/or architecture, and should have an eye for and interest in detail and a thorough knowledge of such things as materials, products, construction methods, and building codes. CSI has developed a certification process for qualified specifiers, who are entitled to refer to themselves as *certified construction specifiers (CCS)*. Information about this program is available from the CSI Web site.

SUSTAINABLE PRODUCT SPECIFICATIONS

Because sustainable or "green" design has continued to gain acceptance, it is important to include some brief information about preparing specifications that meet sustainable design goals. The first very important part of writing green specifications is to understand the language of sustainable and green design. The most accepted definition of *sustainable design* is design that "seeks to meet the needs of the present without compromising the ability of future generations to meet their needs."[3]

Many companies have jumped on the bandwagon of sustainable design as consumer interest in this topic widens. Although some truly embrace the concept of sustainable design, and the changes it necessitates in manufacturing, materials, and practices, some just practice what is called *greenwashing*. In greenwashing, a product or company does just enough to appear "green" to attract buyers. For example, a company may tout its sustainable practices because it recycles cardboard, even though it does nothing else related to truly green manufacturing or business practices.

If you are interested in designing and specifying sustainable products and processes, and supporting those companies that do so as well, you must become fully educated in sustainable design. Part of this education involves becoming LEED® (Leadership in Energy and Environmental Design) certified. LEED® certification—administered by the U.S. Green Building Council (USGBC) and the Canada Green Building Council (CaGBC)—is available for homes, commercial interiors, health care, retail, and other categories appropriate for other professionals. For detailed information, visit the Web sites www.usgbc.org and www.CaGBC.org.

Many jurisdictions, including the federal government, use the CSI system for green specification. This section provides a brief overview of how to incorporate sustainable products into specifications. This information comes from material written by Ross Spiegel that appears in *Sustainable Commercial Interiors* by Penny Bonda and Katie Sosnowchik.[4] Similar information is included in other texts on the topic and some of those have been included in the end-of-book references.

To begin specifying for sustainability:

- Compile a list of environmental attributes for the materials that might be specified for a project, such as recycled content or low VOC content.
- Evaluate the options available to see which meet the attributes criteria.
- Identify, research, and evaluate specific manufacturing processes, manufacturers, and materials (the most time- and effort-intensive step).
- Prepare the specifications. Be sure to incorporate specific criteria into the specifications in the appropriate sections.

CONSTRUCTION AGREEMENT

An important, if not critical, part of the contract documents package is the *construction agreement*. It is commonly called the *owner-contractor agreement*, because it is between the owner of the project and the contractor hired to execute the total contract documents package. It is also called a *prime contract* for this same reason. The construction contract includes the construction agreement along with the other parts of the contract documents, including drawings, general conditions, specifications, and other items discussed in this chapter such as addenda.

A construction agreement:

- Identifies the parties involved
- Defines the scope of work
- Includes clauses concerning the amount of payment and when it will be paid
- Gives a date of expected completion
- Contains other clauses concerning final completion and acceptance

The owner of the project can prepare the construction agreement or hire the architect or other legally appropriate professional to do so. It is not uncommon for this service to be part of the architect's contract. It is suggested that an attorney who is familiar with construction and architecture also advise on the form of the agreement. Preparation of drawings, making submissions for a building permit, and supervision of actual construction are regulated by the jurisdiction. Interior designers who do not have the legal authority to perform these tasks—but do so anyway—can experience serious legal and ethical consequences.

A format commonly used is one of the *AIA Standard Forms of Agreement Between Owner and Contractor*. The one most often used by interior designers is A-105–2007 AIA *Standard Form of Agreement for a Residential or Small Commercial Project*. Another is AIA-251–2007 *General Conditions of the Contract for Furniture, Furnishings and Equipment*. The agreement format and language actually used are defined by how the payment to the contractor will be made and whether the project delivery will be completed using a traditional approach of design-award-build, or another project delivery method. Readers can obtain copies of these and other AIA construction documents either from the AIA online (www.aia.org) or at a local chapter office of the AIA. The basic concepts discussed in Chapter 7 should be kept in mind during preparation of the agreement.

Payment is usually made by one of four methods: stipulated sum, cost plus fee, guaranteed maximum price, and unit price. A stipulated sum is just as it sounds: The owner agrees to pay a fixed amount to the contractor. The cost plus fee method is the cost of all labor and materials plus a fee for overhead and profit. In the guaranteed maximum price method, the compensation to the contractor is not to exceed a fixed amount. The unit-price compensation method is most often used in engineering projects, and seldom in architectural projects.

The interior design contract is often thought of more as an FF&E contract. This is because interior designers are not generally permitted to supervise construction work and the interiors agreement does not specify how the structural construction work is to be done. For example, if the interior designer is hired to design an addition to a house, it is likely (depending on the licensing laws in the jurisdiction) that a construction contract will be prepared for the structural work—especially for load-bearing areas—while the interior designer will prepare a design contract that covers the interior nonstructural work and FF&E.

Generally, the contractor chosen to handle the construction work also hires the subcontractors needed on the project. The owner of the project is, of course, permitted to hire these subs if he or she so chooses. If the owner hires subs, he or she must always use a construction agreement to be sure the work is done properly. The owner or the owner's representative needs to verify the subcontractor's capability to do the work. In large measure, this is why a general contractor is used: He or she has the experience to evaluate subcontractors quickly and effectively, whereas their work will probably be unfamiliar to an owner or interior designer.

COMPETITIVE BIDDING

Competitive bidding is a process whereby the client obtains comparative prices from a number of contractors and/or vendors for the construction or supply of the products needed for the project. The documents for the bid process are prepared by a design professional such as the interior designer. The actual bid process takes place after all the construction drawings, specifications, and schedules have been completed.

For commercial design projects, many clients require that prices for the FF&E be obtained from more than one source. Purchasing from only one supplier is rare with these clients, because the dollar amounts of the projects are so large. Millions of dollars could be spent on the furniture and equipment for a hotel, hospital, or large corporate office complex. The contract for the construction and/or procurement of furniture from a single supplier is done through negotiation rather than bidding.

In residential interior design, the purchasing process for FF&E is generally much simpler, with a single source—the project designer—providing the final pricing to the client. Purchasing goods directly from a vendor of the client's choosing is called *single-source purchasing*. The purchase is essentially negotiated. A residential project might use competitive bidding for the construction of the house, but rarely for the interior FF&E. Of course, the designer may have obtained pricing from more than one source, but the process does not require the complex competitive bidding described in this section.

Competitive bids almost always are required by law for projects involving federal, state, and local agencies, as well as for public businesses such as utilities. Most private businesses also require competitive bids on construction projects and large furniture or equipment orders. If the expected purchase is small, the client may not bother with competitive bids. What is "small" naturally varies from company to company.

There is another situation in which competitive bidding might not apply. Some clients can negotiate directly with a particular vendor because of some unique quality of the product, project, or circumstance. For example, if the client has a large inventory of a particular brand of office systems, the client may be able to negotiate directly for additional purchases, regardless of the size of each subsequent purchase.

The idea underlying the bid process is that it allows the client to purchase the products and services required for the project at a price that is as low as possible while maintaining the quality and intentions of the original design concept. This assumption is valid as long as the goods or services being bid on are either the same or can objectively be compared as equal. This, however, is not always possible. As you saw in the discussions on specifications, when substitutions are allowed, it becomes difficult for the interior designer and client to objectively evaluate the differences in the various products being bid on. Questions then arise about possible compromises that would still maintain the quality and/or design intentions of the specifications. When there are sufficient bidders of a like product, then competitive bids based on the original idea are possible. When a project is designed and/or specified in such a way that few bidders can supply the same product at a fair price, then the bid process might be suspect.

Client pressure to accept the lowest price can cause issues for the interior designer and client.

- The original design concept for the project may be lost when a product that does not have the same aesthetic appearance as the one originally specified might be purchased.
- When substitutions are allowed, the client may get a product that does not meet the performance criteria of the original design—which, of course, also becomes an issue for the designer.
- The competitive bidding process can be more expensive than other purchasing methods.
- A greater amount of preparation time is required, because of the complexity of contract documents and specifications for the goods and services, as well as all the other required bid documents.
- Time-consuming evaluations, either before the bid submittals or before the awarding of contracts, are required.
- There is a potential for claims and lawsuits related to the bid award if one or more bidders feel that the award was improper or the process was flawed.

Despite its problems, most major commercial and governmental owners continue to use competitive bidding for their projects. The interior designer must include the services for monitoring and coordinating the bid phase in his or her contract. This will help the designer keep control of the design concepts and aesthetic intent of the project. Architects have done this for years. Interior designers, regardless of the size of their practice, must do the same.

In addition to the contract documents, four bid documents must be produced in order to complete a bid: (1) the general conditions, (2) the invitation to bid, (3) instructions to bidders, and (4) the bid form. Bond forms—other forms associated with the bid process—are also briefly discussed. Table 12-5 lists the forms or other documents generally used during the competitive bidding process.

TABLE 12-5.

Sample list of the most common bidding documents

Contract documents
 Contract requirement forms
 Owner/contractor agreement
 Addenda and modifications that have become part of the contract
 Performance bond
 Payment bond
 Insurance certificates

Conditions of the contract
 General and supplemental conditions of the contract

Construction drawings
 Specifications
 Drawings
 Schedules

Bidding documents
 Invitation to bid
 Instructions to bidders
 Bid forms
 Bonds

Addenda and Modifications
 Additions to the bidding documents will also be part of the contract documents

General Conditions

Many conditions and much information are needed to establish the basic rules for the bids and the bid process. The document included in the bid documents that expresses these rules is a section of general conditions. These *general conditions* set forth the legal responsibilities, procedures, rights, and duties of each party to the contract. A standardized set of general conditions used by many designers and private business owners is the AIA form, AIA Document A201™-1997. It is commonly used because it has stood the test of time; however, the standardized form is quite long and cumbersome. Many designers and clients modify the conditions of the document to fit their particular situation.

Items covered in the general conditions include definitions, the names of the designer and owner, ownership of documents, the responsibilities of the designer and the owner, definitions and responsibilities of the contractors and subcontractors, clauses concerning payments, the time period of the project, claims, insurance, change orders, dispute resolution considerations, and other definitions or statements related to the contractual relationship of the parties.

For bids that concern only furniture, AIA Document A275™ID-2003, *General Conditions of the Contract for Furniture, Furnishings, and Equipment*, can be used. The general conditions in this document are similar in scope to the ones in document A201, but relate to interior furniture and furnishings rather than construction.

Because both of these forms are lengthy, generalized legal forms, it is necessary for the designer to prepare supplemental conditions for each project. The supplemental conditions spell out any conditions related to the specific project. For example, a supplemental condition that must be stated if the designer uses either of these AIA forms is that the words *designer* or *interior designer* should be substituted wherever the word *architect* is used.

Several kinds of documents may be available from interior design professional associations. Copyright law should be respected when using documents created and offered for use by the AIA, ASID, and IIDA. The designer must obtain permission from the association before making copies or modifying the documents in any way. Should the designer/specifier wish to prepare his or her own set of general conditions, they should be reviewed by the design firm's attorney before being submitted to the client. Copies of the forms from associations can be ordered from the organization's national office or Web site.

The Invitation to Bid

One task in the bid process is to determine who can submit a bid for the project. This process is tightly controlled by the client and might essentially be managed by the client or the client in conjunction with the design firm. The most common way to obtain bidders for a project is to prepare an invitation to bidders (also called an advertisement for bids).

The *invitation to bid* notifies potential bidders of the existence of a project. It might be a letter sent to a list of contractors and/or vendors, or an advertisement placed in the appropriate section of a newspaper. The invitation to bid will include instructions as to where the bid documents can be obtained. The information shown in Table 12-6 is commonly included in an invitation to bid. A sample of this form is shown as Item 12-1 on the companion Web site.

Government and public agencies most likely will advertise a bid in newspapers. This process is called *open competitive selection*. In this case, anyone interested in the project who meets the qualifications spelled out in the invitation to bid may submit a bid. Private businesses rarely advertise bids, though they may do so for a very large project. Some private organizations, through careful legal preparation, may have an acceptable *bid list* of potential designers and vendors who would receive the notifications. This selection process is called *closed competitive selection*, as it limits who will be allowed to bid on the project. In this situation, the client contacts several designers/vendors to make them aware of the project. Only those invited to bid in this manner are allowed to bid on the project.

The advantage of a bid list is that bidders are prequalified by the client; essentially, the client is saying that it will deal only with those designers and

TABLE 12-6.
Items commonly included in an invitation to bid

Identification of the client
Identification of the architect and interior designer
Project location
Description of the scope of work of the project
When and where bid documents can be obtained
Prequalification standards, if any
Description of any bonds or deposits that are required
Place, day, and time where bids are to be received
Statements concerning the client's right to reject any and all bids
Description of any laws or regulations affecting the bid
Identification of the company or organization responsible for issuing the bid

vendors that have experience with the particular kind of project for which the bid list has been prepared, and have proven personnel, capital to procure the goods, and so on. This also allows the client to receive a reasonable number of bids, rather than a very large number of bids that would require additional evaluation to eliminate unqualified bidders.

One disadvantage of closed competitive selection is that there might be too few bidders, possibly resulting in a higher price for the project. There is also the probability that less experienced, yet still qualified, designers and vendors will be prohibited from entering the bid process. Nevertheless, if it is possible to get a sufficient (by the client's estimation) number of qualified bidders through a prequalification bid list system, closed selection is a satisfactory and legal method of obtaining competitive bids.

The invitation to bid provides a summary of the project, the bid process, and other pertinent procedures for the project. It informs potential bidders of the project, its scope, and ways in which they can obtain further information. The invitation also states whether a security bond is required, how much it must be, and how long it will be held. The size or length of time for which the bond will be held may discourage some designers and vendors from bidding.

Instructions to Bidders

The *instructions to bidders* document informs bidders how to prepare their bid documents so that all submittals are in the same form. This makes it easier to compare bids from multiple vendors and makes the bid process fair to all who wish to participate. Some clients allow bidders not to bid on portions of the project. When this occurs, the items not bid on are called *exclusions*. Thus, one does not always start with absolutely comparable bids.

The instructions to bidders documents are not a contract offering, but information regarding the project bid. Many firms, with client approval, schedule a *pre-bid meeting* for all interested bidders and may give a tour of the site during the session. This pre-bid meeting gives all the bidders the chance to hear the same responses at the same time, rather than the design firm potentially having to constantly send out memoranda to all the bidders. Of course, other questions will arise after this meeting, so the design firm will issue addenda in response as needed.

Instructions to bidders commonly provide:

- Information on what form and format to use
- Information on how, where, and when bids are due
- Statements related to site visitation and familiarization responsibilities
- Statements related to resolution of discrepancies in document interpretation
- Information on how bids can be withdrawn
- The procedure for awarding the bid and conditions for rejecting bids
- Any other pertinent instructions that the client may require

Form A701™-1997 from the AIA is an example document that can be modified to meet the needs of an interiors project. Much of the information that is in the invitation to bid is repeated in the instructions to bidders.

Important parts of the instructions are the portions of the bid documents usually referred to as the "drawings and specifications." These consist of working drawings and/or equipment plans and the written specifications related to products, materials, and construction methods. The instructions to bidders should only mention where and how these documents can be obtained, how they are to be used by the bidder, and whether substitutions or exclusions are allowed (and if so how they are to be submitted). The actual drawings and specifications do not appear in this portion of the bid documents.

The Bid Form

To ensure fairness, the actual bid by all contractors or vendors must be submitted in the same way. The *bid form* (also sometimes called a *tender form*) is a document prepared by the designer or the client and provided to the bidders. The bid form is the document that the vendor uses to inform the client of its bid price. The format generally is set up as a form letter from the bidder to the client. The bid form has blank space in appropriate places to be filled in by the bidder. Figure 12-2 shows a sample bid form. This sample document has also been included on the companion Web site as Item 12-2. If no substitutions or exclusions are allowed in the instructions to bidders, a statement reinforcing disqualification of any bidder who submits a substitution or exclusion should be included here.

Although it is common for everything that has been specified in the construction documents and specifications to be included in the bid, it is also common for clients to ask for some things that will cost more than might fit into their budget. If a client anticipates that it may have a problem in meeting the budget with everything that has been designed, the client may provide a bid package that includes a specification for a base bid and alternate bids. The term *base bid* in this case means the amount of the project the vendor is prepared to supply that is the basic minimum specified, without consideration for alternatives. *Alternate bids* are amounts added to or subtracted from the base bid should the client add or subtract parts of the specified project. The base bid and alternate bids are ways for the client to keep the project within the project budget.

Bond Forms

The form submitting a bid for a project is only one part of the documents required of vendors and contractors. *Bond forms* are legal documents used to bind the designer or vendor to the contract as assurance that the designer or vendor will perform the requirements of the contract as agreed upon. They are required for the client's protection. Three bond forms are commonly used in the bidding process: (1) the bid bond, (2) the performance bond, and (3) the labor and materials payment bond.

The *bid bond* is required to ensure that the designer or vendor that is awarded the contract will sign the contract and execute the project. Proof of a bid bond is submitted with the bid. It is, in effect, a sort of insurance that those who are bidding are really going to provide what they have bid at the prices they have quoted. The vendor obtains the bid bond from a bonding or surety service for the construction, architecture, and interiors industry.

The bid bond may be a lump sum or a percentage amount of the bid. This security amount may be given by using a bond, cash, a certified check, or another method approved by the project owner. It is important to note that during construction, the "project owner" can be either the client who will occupy the space or the contractor who has responsibility to build out the project. In the latter case, the contractor relinquishes ownership to the client at an agreed-upon time. The bid bond of the successful bidder is usually held by the client for some time after the contract has been signed and other bid securities have been obtained. For unsuccessful bidders, the bid bond is returned promptly.

BID FORM FOR FURNISHINGS CONTRACT

CONTRACT NUMBER: _____

PROJECT: _____

BID OF: _____
                    (name of bidder)

- a Corporation organized under the laws of the State of _____
- a Partnership, with the following individuals as partners:

  _____

- a Limited Liability Company with the following member as General Manager:

  _____

- a Sole proprietor.

Present Bid To:

_____

    At: Hunter / Noble Inc.
             3114 N. 38th St.
             Phoenix, AZ

The Undersigned acknowledges receipt and review of the Project Documents, consisting of _____ pages of drawings and _____ pages of written specifications, and addenda No. _____ through _____, and hereby proposes to furnish all materials, labor, and miscellany necessary to provide and install the furniture and furnishings as specified in the aforementioned documents.

The Undersigned further agrees to hold his/her Bid open for thirty (30) days after the receipt of bids. Should the bidder be awarded the contract, he/she shall furnish a Performance Bond and a Labor and Materials Payment Bond in accordance with the General Conditions of the Bid, to the owner within ten (10) days after award of bid.

No substitutions or exclusions to what was specified shall be allowed. Any bidder not bidding on all items as specified shall be disqualified.

The undersigned agrees to supply and perform, in accordance with the specifications, all of the materials, labor, and miscellany as specified for:

_____Dollars   ($_____).

The Bid Bond and all other required documentation is attached by the undersigned bidder.

It is understood that the owner reserves the right to reject any or all bids, to withhold the award of bid for any reason, and reserves the right to hold all bids for thirty (30) days after the date of opening.

Date of Bid: _____

Name of Bidder: _____

Address of Bidder: _____

Authorized Officer: _____

FIGURE 12-2.

Sample bid form.

Why is this type of "insurance" necessary? If a firm has made an error in its bid, it may want to withdraw even after the bid has been awarded. Some firms submit bids only to find out how the competition is pricing services or products. Thus, a bid bond helps to prevent actually uninterested bidders from "shopping" the prices of competitors while ensuring that all bidders are serious in their intentions.

A *performance bond* is required from the winning bidder as a guarantee that the designer or vendor will complete the work as specified. A surety company agreeable to the client and the design firm provides the bond, thereby becoming liable to pay should the vendor or contractor fail to perform. It protects the client from any loss up to the amount of the bond incurred as a result of the designer's or vendor's failure to perform according to the contract. It is customary for the performance bond to be an amount equal to 100 percent of the value of the bid contract. The premium paid to a surety company for the bond insurance is a smaller percentage. The actual amount varies, based on the actual project conditions and the surety company. The performance bond is returned after satisfactory completion of the project.

A *labor and materials payment bond* is required of the winning bidder to guarantee that the designer or vendor will be responsible for paying for all the materials and labor that have been contracted for in the event that the designer or vendor defaults on the project. This is to prevent the client from being held responsible to subcontractors for goods not delivered by the winning bidder. This bond is also customarily an amount equal to 100 percent of the contract price. It too is returned after completion of the project.

A legal recourse related to the labor and materials payment bond is the *mechanic's lien*. A lien is an action filed by the contractor, subcontractor, or possibly the designer with the county clerk to prevent the owner of the property from giving or conveying title or a deed of trust to the named property until the mechanic who has filed the lien has been paid. In this situation, a *mechanic* is an employee, subcontractor, or vendor who has been hired to do work by the client or a general contractor.

More simply stated, contractors, subcontractors, their vendors, and, in some states, architects and interior designers may find it necessary to file a lien against the property to ensure that the owner of the property pays the designer or contractor any moneys due. A properly filed lien prevents the owner of the property from selling or conveying title of the property until the lien has been settled. Not all states have laws or regulations allowing mechanic's liens. The designer should check with the attorney general or registrar of contractors of his or her state to clarify how liens might affect the designer's business practices.

Bid Opening

The first submittal requirement is that the bid proposal or bid form be sent to the client or designer in a sealed envelope. The instructions to bidders will specify the exact labeling of the envelope, where it is to be delivered, to whom, and by what day and time. Failing to meet these requirements can lead to disqualification of the bid.

There are several reasons a bid can be disqualified if it is improperly submitted to the client or designer. If a bid is delivered after the day and time specified in the instructions, it will be left unopened and rejected. Any bid received that does not conform to the instructions can be rejected. It is also customary that bids cannot be withdrawn after the closing date and time for the receipt of bids, even if the bid opening has not yet taken place. However, the instructions may stipulate the conditions under which a bid can be withdrawn, especially if there are errors in it that would create a hardship for the bidder. In almost all situations, bidders should not be allowed to modify or alter a bid once it has been received and opened.

Once the bids are all received, there may be a public or private *bid opening* where the bids are actually opened. Bids for governmental agencies or public companies, such as utilities, are required to have the bid opening at an open public meeting. The place and time are noted in the invitation to bidders. At that meeting, the client or person charged with administering the bid announces each bidder and its bid price. The client usually does not award the bid at that time.

For private companies, the bid opening is not required by law to be open to the public. This means that a bidder might not have the opportunity to know what the competition has bid, if its own bid is low in comparison to all the others, or if the bidder made an error in reporting its prices. The designer and client must meet high ethical and professional standards when opening and awarding bids.

The invitation to bid should have informed bidders about the length of time the client will take to evaluate the bids and to make the decision as to who will be awarded the contract. Although most public agencies accept the lowest bid, they are not bound to do so if there are legitimate reasons for rejecting the lowest bid. Some negotiations may occur due to minor changes or product availability. The client must take care not to announce that firm X is the lowest bidder at the bid opening, as this announcement could later bind the client even if it wanted to reject the bid.

Even after the bids are opened, it remains possible that the bidding process will still involve negotiations. This might occur only with the winning bidder as small changes to the project are negotiated. If larger changes are needed that affect the price, it might be feasible to negotiate with the winning bidder, or it might be necessary to reject all bids and rebid the project. When a project involves government or public agencies, a negotiation may include a *best and final offer (BAFO)*. These types of clients often have more flexibility in the selection and negotiation of contracts with those who propose a bid amount. It might be that after the first submission of bids is reviewed, the client selects some of those bidders and asks them for their BAFO—in essence, another bid.

Depending on the provisions in the contract between the interior designer and the client, the designer will assist the client in evaluating the bids. This service can help a client determine the appropriateness of substitutions or any conditions that bidders may have included in their bid documents. After a reasonable length of time, the contractor or client will award the bid based on the bid values, negotiate further with the winning bidder (assuming that small changes must be made), or reject all bids and consider revising and rebidding the project.

Bid Award Notification

After the bids have been evaluated and a decision has been made as to who the successful bidder is, each bidder must be notified of the result. Should the owner wish to speed up the actual ordering and/or construction process, a *letter of intent* is sent to the winning bidder. This letter is a signal to the supplier or contractors to begin work on the project.

After the bid has been awarded, clients or the designer usually send a simple form letter to each of the unsuccessful bidders, thanking them for their participation. It is not legally necessary to inform them who the successful bidder was or the amount of the bid. It is often a good idea to state that the unsuccessful bids will be held for a certain length of time, as stated in the invitation to bid, in the event that the successful bidder withdraws. This means that the bids of unsuccessful bidders remain valid offers until the end of the holding period.

Other documents that concern the winning bidder and continuation of the project are discussed in Chapter 13.

MODIFICATIONS

No matter how hard designers try, nobody is perfect. Errors occur in preparation of the contract documents, and for many reasons, changes often have to be made in the plans or specifications once the work begins.

Modifications are changes in the construction documents. If the changes are made before the contract has been awarded, they are made by an addendum. Changes made after the contract has been awarded are made by issuing a change order.

Addenda

Addenda are additions or changes made to the contract documents once they are in the hands of contractors and vendors for determining their bid prices. Contracts for the construction work or FF&E purchasing have not yet been awarded or issued. This type of modification document is used only during the bidding stage, not after the contracts have been awarded. Any change in the project by use of an addendum becomes part of the contract documents.

A change in the project may be made because the client wants to alter some part of the project, even at this late date. Clarifications may also be needed because of a question from one or more of the bidders or because of errors or technical requirements regarding the documents that are discovered during the bid process. Addenda are used to clarify these changes in relationship to the previously prepared contract and/or construction documents.

Each addendum must be in writing and sent to all bidders who have obtained a set of the documents. Corrections or clarifications should not be made or accepted orally. All addenda should be prepared as quickly and as clearly as possible.

Addenda should come from the person who is responsible for creating the documents. If an allied professional or other design team member finds a questionable item, it should be called to the attention of the specification writer and/or preparer of the construction drawings, and that person should prepare and send the addendum. When addenda are mailed to bidders, there must be sufficient time for bidders to react to the addenda prior to the close of bid. Recall that notification begins upon receipt of the notification, not at the time of mailing. Addenda supersede and supplement the appropriate part or parts of the construction documents or bidding documents. A sample addendum letter is included as Item 12-3 on the companion Web site.

According to Harold J. Rosen, addenda are used to:[5]

1. Correct errors and omissions
2. Clarify ambiguities

3. Add to or reduce the scope of the work
4. Provide additional information that could affect the bid prices
5. Change the time and place for receipt of bids
6. Change the quality of the work
7. Issue additional names of qualified "or equal" products

Of course, other conditions or situations may arise that would require a change in the documents prior to awarding of the contract.

Note that an addendum can also be used to issue instructions after the contract has been awarded. However, when an addendum is used at this time, it really only constitutes a change order to the winning bidder or contractor.

Change Orders

Mrs. Brown visits a model home show and notices an interesting design of niches surrounding the fireplace in one model. She takes a photo of the wall and gives it to her designer, saying that she wants a similar design in her house, which is currently under construction. Fortunately, although that part of the house has been framed, the wallboard has not been installed. The designer issues a change order based on instructions from the client.

Change orders are written permissions or instructions concerning any aspect of the project that modify design concepts, construction designs, or product specifications. A change or modification made after the contract is awarded is documented with a change order. Change orders accepted and signed by the appropriate parties also become a part of the contract documents (see Figure 12-3).

Changes may be needed during the course of the project, and change orders are used to authorize and clarify these changes. Perhaps the client wants a window moved to a new location. Maybe the paint color for the doctor's suite must be different. A lighting fixture specified for the restaurant dining room might not be available by the time the project gets under way. Any of these occurrences, and many others, can arise during the actual construction, ordering, and installation of the project. The use of change orders is also discussed in Chapter 13. Item 12-4 on the companion Web site shows another version of a change order.

Interior designers should not allow any change to be made without a written change order being issued to all necessary parties. Of course, sometimes it is not within the interior designer's authority to issue a change order. Many designers and contractors allow changes to be made without giving written authorization or notification to the various parties. Clients have been known to tell the contractor to make a change and then forget to inform the interior designer. A seemingly simple change can, in fact, be quite a big deal. If the change is major, such as moving a window, it can affect other trades, schedules, space layouts, and product specifications, to name the most obvious. A good working relationship between the designer and the client and other stakeholders, as well as professional project management by the interior designer, can prevent changes being made without proper authorization and notification.

Additional charges may be appropriate for changes made after the contract has been awarded. Just as the interior designer wants to be compensated to replan a space once the client has given approval, a contractor or vendor will want to be compensated for making changes after the contract is in process. Changes made at this point usually cost the client much more than if the issue had been addressed and changes had been made before any contracts were issued.

Contemplated Change Notice <u>No. 2</u>

Date:
Project:

Project No.:

To: From:

Fax:
Total Pages: 3
_____

It is proposed to make the following changes - therefore, please promptly submit your total increased or decreased cost due to these changes for our approval. No work related to including this proposal shall be done until these costs have been approved an order issued.

Reason for Change

2△   .1 <u>Drawing 03</u>   Contractor to supply & install one duplex plus one voice/data outlet in Central Registry No. 516. See attached drawing 01.

          .2 <u>Drawing 03</u>   Contractor to supply & install one voice/data outlet in Area-8 No. 542. See attached drawing 01.

          .2 <u>Drawing S-1</u>   Contractor to revised beam size as per attached drawing S-1. See attached drawing S-1.

FIGURE 12-3.

A sample change order form. (Reproduced with permission of Charlene Conrad, B.F.A. in Fine Arts, IDNS, IDC, NCIDQ no. 09218; Conrad Interior Design, Halifax, Nova Scotia, Canada)

SUBMITTALS

Sometimes, at the beginning of contract administration or perhaps during the course of this phase, a vendor may have to provide materials, drawings, or documents for approval. As a group, these are referred to as *submittals*. For example, the vendor may have to submit items such as finish samples of wood for furniture, literature from manufacturers, or test results or certificates related to life safety code requirements. Vendor submittals of shop drawings and finish samples for custom pieces or special installations may also be required.

Vendors may also have to provide other types of submittals. One common submittal concerns updates to the designer and owner about construction or delivery schedules. In some cases, the bid documents and instructions to bidders may require that the vendor provide mock-ups. A *mock-up* is a full-scale representation of products or construction features. Examples include a full-scale wall with moldings; paint colors; setups of systems furniture so that the client can see the actual arrangement of the furniture; even the construction of a full-scale room, such as a patient room in a hospital, with all furniture, finishes, and equipment shown.

At some point, it finally becomes time for contracts or other agreements to be issued to begin the process of ordering the furniture, furnishings, and equipment. The process and documents associated with ordering products are discussed in Chapter 13. Of course, this process is very similar for projects that are not bid. Project finalization and postordering issues and forms are covered in Chapter 14.

WEB SITES RELEVANT TO THIS CHAPTER

www.aia.org American Institute of Architects

www.CaGBC Canadian Green Building Council

www.cmaanet.org Construction Management Association of America

www.csinet.org/masterformat Construction Specifications Institute

www.masterspec.com Published by ARCOM for the AIA

www.usgbc.org U.S. Green Building Council

KEY TERMS

Addenda	Competitive bidding
Alternate bid	Construction agreement
Base bid (actual bid)	Construction contract
Base bid (specification)	Construction documents
Best and final offer (BAFO)	Construction drawings
Bid bond	Contract documents (CDs)
Bid form (tender form)	Descriptive specification
Bid list	Exclusions
Bid opening	FF&E projects
Bond forms	General conditions
Change orders	Instructions to bidders
Closed competitive selection	Invitation to bid
Closed specification	Labor and materials payment bond

Letter of intent

Mechanic's lien

Modifications

Movable equipment

Open competitive selection

Open specification

Or equal

erformance bond

Performance specification

Prequalified

Prime contract

Proprietary specification

Reference specification

Schedules

Single-source purchasing

Specifications (specs)

Submittal

Working drawings

WHAT WOULD YOU DO?

1. Jennifer was working with Henry to review the dimensioned floor plans and elevations for the Cannon Group Accounting firm offices. Grace was completing the specifications for the furniture, while others in the design firm either had completed reviews or were working on other sheets in the drawings set. They were completing the contract documents so that bids could be obtained for the interior construction and furnishings. Jennifer found some errors in the drawings, but Henry said to ignore them, as the firm could send out an addendum once the drawings were issued. Later Jennifer discovered that Henry had not sent out any addendum.

2. Roger has been in the interior design industry for 20 years. He has designed both residential and commercial interiors and owns his own practice. Recently an attorney called Roger to ask if he would be an expert witness regarding a client's complaint against another interior designer. The project involved the design of a multimillion-dollar residence in an exclusive neighborhood.

   Roger knows this other designer by reputation but not personally. The dispute apparently concerns the quality of the installation of flooring, and the pricing of all the furniture specified. The client also claims that the designer exceeded the budget by a substantial amount.

3. John has been working with Mr. and Mrs. Smith for 10 years. He has done their primary residence, a second home, and now they wish him to help their daughter with her condominium. Through all that time and all those projects, the Smiths have never questioned John's fees or pricing.

   The Smiths' daughter, Jessica, told her parents that she thinks John is overcharging for an area rug, two lamps, and the dresser for her condo. Her suspicions were aroused, she said, after she looked up the products that John specified on the Internet. She found what she believes to be the exact same items at prices at least 30 percent less than John's bids.

4. Sam is the project manager and primary designer on a large medical office building for a major healthcare provider. His firm also has a subsidiary company that procures furniture for clients if the client wishes. This client didn't realize that Sam's design firm also had a sales division, as it is not located in the same office building. The existence of the sales division was revealed during the initial presentation for the design contract.

The client company made it very clear to Sam that the product specifications had to be put out to bid. They also told him that company policy required that at least 10 vendor bids be obtained. This project was budgeted at $176,000 at net.

There were two items in the specifications that the client was very interested in having in the specification package, as they had made these items standard at other locations. One was an ergonomically designed desk chair, and the other was a small side chair used in the exam rooms.

Sam prepared the specifications so that the minimum number of bidders could easily be achieved. While he was checking on fabric options for the ergonomic chair—he wanted to specify a COM fabric— Sam was offered an extra 10 percent discount on the ergonomic desk chairs below what other bidders would be able to purchase the chair for. He mentioned this to his boss, who promptly contacted the sales manager at the subsidiary company.

REFERENCES

1. Reznikoff, 1979, p. 231.
2. Ibid., p. 251.
3. World Commission on Environment and Development, 1987, p. 43.
4. Bonda and Sosnowchik, 2007, pp. 204–205.
5. Rosen, 1981, p. 177.

CHAPTER 13

Contract Administration: Construction and Order Processing

After completing this chapter you should be able to:

- Describe the essential business activities that occur during the construction phase of the project.
- Explain the procurement process and the role the interior design most often plays in that process.
- Discuss the role of the interior designer during contract administration should she or he *not* be involved in the procurement of goods for the project.
- Explain the importance of keeping the client informed as the procurement of merchandise is in progress.
- Explain the purpose of each of the project purchasing forms discussed.
- Explain why the client should be asked to sign the confirmation of purchase.
- Discuss each item that is needed on a purchase order and the importance of that information.
- Discuss why multiple copies of the purchase order are necessary.
- Complete mock purchase orders.
- Discuss why it is important to verify that the information on an acknowledgment matches what was on the purchase order.
- Explain the importance of invoices.
- Analyze the information on purchase orders, acknowledgments, and invoices.
- Explain what should be done when merchandise arrives damaged.
- Discuss the expediting task.

NCIDQ COMPONENT

Based on best information available, some material in this chapter might appear as part of the NCIDQ examination. The reader should not depend solely on this text for study material.

It is generally agreed that once the bids have been received and the contracts have been awarded for the primary work, the last phase of the project begins. This phase is referred to as *contract administration*, as outlined by the defined skills areas and project phases established by the National Council for Interior Design Qualification.

In contract administration, activity centers on the actual construction, placing of orders, and completion of the project. At this critical point in the project, all the other work that has been performed by the interior designer and others comes together to make design concepts become reality. All of the activities and responsibilities discussed in this chapter and the next require that the designer take utmost care in the execution of tasks, responsibilities, paperwork, and supervision, all of which are part of project management.

Most of the time, the interior designer is only indirectly involved in the construction of the building or interior. As the reader knows, the interior designer is very limited in what he or she can do concerning load-bearing construction. But this does not mean that the interior designer should be ignorant of the tasks and the paperwork that are necessary during this phase of the project.

This chapter begins with a brief discussion of the paperwork associated with contract administration related to construction that might be part of the designer's responsibilities. Because so many interior designers sell merchandise, the chapter provides a more detailed explanation of the paperwork involved in procuring merchandise for the client.

CONTRACT ADMINISTRATION: CONSTRUCTION

Exactly what role the interior designer plays in contract administration during the actual construction process depends on the laws and regulations within the jurisdiction of the project and the scope of services specified in the designer's contract. It can be very complex, involving activities such as obtaining permits, coordinating the procurement, and supervising the installation of the FF&E. It can involve supervising the installation or construction work of sub-contractors, conducting site inspections, and issuing documents related to the conclusion of the project work. Or it can focus on ordering merchandise and checking to be sure that it is delivered and placed properly.

Regardless of the designer's actual responsibility, the interior designer's role often involves reassuring the client about the process. Before orders are initiated and the construction process is started, the interior designer must spend time with the client explaining how the project will proceed. Clients become very nervous during a project. They see the changes taking place, but the changes always seem to happen too slowly. The designer should go over the schedule with the client at the very beginning of the project so that the client has a chance to ask questions and gain an understanding of how and when the construction and interior finishing, delivery, and installation will take place.

It is important for clients to understand the disruption that will occur during a remodeling or more extensive construction project. Remodeling a home cannot be done without some mess and inconvenience to the family. Major remodeling or additions might make it necessary for the family to move to other quarters for several months during the project. For commercial remodeling projects, few businesses can survive if they must totally shut down, even if the project is only to install new carpet.

If the client is moving into a new facility, the interior designer may include move management in his or her scope of services. *Move management* can include a wide range of services to help the client schedule packing and moving furniture and belongings into the new home or commercial site. For example, when a move is involved, scheduling must be planned so that employees can pack up their belongings that are in desks and file cabinets or inventory and mark items that are to be moved to the new location. Obviously, this is true of a family as well.

The construction and/or remodeling of many types of commercial facilities often must be scheduled outside normal business hours. This means that the interior designer must include any extra charges for after-hours or overtime work done by delivery and installation personnel in the estimates and final pricing of the project. Special permits for the construction and even delivery and/or installation of furniture may be required. Many times these types of moves are made over a single weekend: The move begins at the end of business on Friday, and the employees move back in on Monday morning. It can be a Herculean effort to schedule all that must be done, but this effort may be part of the interior designer's responsibilities.

Another important detail the client must understand is the scheduling of work. The designer should explain how each part of the construction and finishing of the project will be done and approximately when each phase will occur. Some clients appreciate a written schedule; others prefer that the designer keep them informed by e-mails or telephone calls.

It is important for clients to understand how the project will proceed, as there are reasons that on some days the project may have only one trade on the job and on others multiple tradespeople. The designer and tradespeople understand the problems that can occur when multiple tradespeople are on the jobsite at the same time. However, clients generally do not understand that problems can occur in this situation. For example, rough plumbing and rough wiring are both done when the building is in the same condition, but it is not a good idea for the designer to schedule both tradespeople to do their work on the same day. The plumbers may need to be where the electricians are, and vice versa. General contractors and job foremen have had to break up fights when electricians have unintentionally dropped wiring on the heads of plumbers. An entire project was shut down because nonunion furniture installers arrived on a jobsite where union workers were still working.

The designer needs to schedule regular meetings with the contractor and to make regular visits to the construction site. In this way, the designer will know what is going on and can easily keep the client informed of the progress of the project in relation to the interior designer's contract responsibilities. Designers issue *progress reports* to the client so that the client knows what is going on. This is especially helpful when the client wishes to be very involved in the project. For out-of-town projects, the designer must include the expenses of traveling to the project site in the contract and have these visits approved by the client prior to each visit. Design decisions regarding any necessary changes in the plans or the orders that are being placed for goods are made far more effectively with this kind of coordination.

Clients can become quite frustrated and stressed over the myriad decisions that they must make during the course of the project or during construction. The designer needs constantly to assure the client that everything is under control and to clarify where the project is on or off schedule. This, of course, means that the designer must be fully informed of the progress of the project so that the progress reports (whether given verbally or in writing) to the client are accurate. Holding weekly meetings with the client is not always necessary, but having periodic meetings with the client to discuss the schedule and what will be happening next are important to keeping the client comfortable with the progress of the project. Many large design firms have found that assigning an installation supervisor, in addition to a design project manager, is a very good investment for efficient project administration.

If problems occur that affect the timely completion of the project, it is critical that the designer so inform the client immediately. Thinking that "what the clients don't know won't hurt them" might sound appealing, but clients do need to know when things are going awry. As long as the designer or the firm is working on a solution to the problem, the client most likely will not become unduly upset when problems arise. If the designer has developed a solution to the problem before calling the client, the client will feel that the designer has already taken care of things.

Changes or corrections made because of errors and omissions that occur during construction must be brought to the attention of the interior designer. Changes can easily impact the aesthetic and functional goals of the project. Too often, the designer gets cut out of many of these decisions as the contractors and the client rush to complete the project. The interior designer must emphasize the importance of copying him or her on any change orders issued during construction by other stakeholders. Changes should be done only after a *change order* has been issued. (See Figure 12-3 in Chapter 12.)

The interior designer should also inform the client to be cautious about making arbitrary changes to the plans once the contracts have been let. Contractors often bid projects very low, and changes during the course of construction will be charged at far higher prices than the original bid. "It sure would be nice to have a window on that wall of the bedroom," says the client to the contractor. "Yes, I suppose it would. But that window will now cost you about $700, since the wall already has been framed. It would have cost only about $200 if you had thought of it sooner." (By the way, it is unlikely the contractor would tell the client that the window would have been $200 originally unless this was required by the contract.)

If the designer has only a minor role in the construction process, his or her energies will shift to administration of the ordering of goods. At an appropriate time, the FF&E for the project will be ordered. The ordering of architectural finishes is often included in the general construction contract rather than in the interiors contract, although this varies. Recall from Chapter 8 that anything that has to do with the actual building of the structure or that becomes physically attached to the structure is considered real property. In construction, this is often referred to as *capital construction* or *capital improvements*. The furniture, fixtures, and any equipment that is movable are generally not purchased as part of the capital construction. These various furniture items are considered *movable equipment* in construction terms.

When it is time for the designer to order movable equipment, the designer will either do so directly or will coordinate with vendors who will do so. For a commercial project, this does not happen until after the bids have been awarded to vendors. Now let us look at the paperwork and process involved in the ordering of goods for a client.

CONTRACT ADMINISTRATION: PROCUREMENT AND ORDER PROCESSING

Procuring furniture and other FF&E for clients requires processing a great deal of paperwork. Order processing is generally the responsibility of the designer in charge of the project. The ideal situation is to have an *expediter*—an individual who is familiar with the company's paperwork system and the requirements of the many manufacturers—be responsible for all order processing and the subsequent tracking function. Other roles of an expediter are discussed later in this chapter.

An office manager might also have this responsibility. In some cases, a vendor such as an office furnishings dealer will be responsible for the product procurement paperwork should that vendor win a competitive bid for the furnishings.

Order processing must be done very carefully, as many things can—and often do—go wrong. Product numbers can be transposed on a purchase order, resulting in the wrong merchandise being shipped. Sometimes the manufacturer puts the wrong item in the box so that the label on the box is correct but the wrong item is inside. Merchandise might be damaged in transit. Sometimes the ship date is weeks after the move-in date. These and many other problems frequently present themselves to designers who sell merchandise.

Clear policies and procedures must be established for ordering any merchandise and handling the paperwork. This is no time for sloppy handwriting, oral agreements, and procrastination in reviewing paperwork. Careful consideration of a client's creditworthiness is also a part of procuring products for clients. Profit margins on merchandise are too small and competition is too keen for any firm, large or small, to allow itself to be careless in conducting order processing.

Several paperwork items are commonly used in order processing. This section describes the documents generally used in the process, from the initial ordering of merchandise to jobsite delivery. Special attention is paid to the purchase order, acknowledgment, and invoice, as these are key items.

Credit Application

Unfortunately, some clients turn out to be bad credit risks. Firms that display items on a showroom floor or in inventory may find it impractical to require a credit check for small purchases, and many sales may be "cash and carry," paid for with a credit card. In contrast, before processing special orders or beginning extensive design services for clients unknown to the design firm, interior designers need to investigate these clients' creditworthiness. Policies regarding credit check should be set well before the situation arises. Management may decide, with the advice of the firm's accountant, that special-order purchases or design fees over some specific dollar amount will trigger a credit check be conducted by the design firm, or require that the prospective client complete a credit application.

The credit policy should include requirements concerning deposits, retainers, and payment terms. It has become routine for consumers to pay deposits or make payments to service providers before services are rendered. Readers are probably familiar with the insurance co-pays required before medical services are rendered, or advance payments (applied to the resulting fees) required by attorneys or accountants.

A credit application form should be easy for the client to fill out. After it has been completed, the form should be turned over to the design firm's financial institution or a credit agency for review and recommendation. The designer can check the credit of a residential client by requesting information from a credit reporting agency. Table 13-1 suggests several items that should be included on the credit application. The firm's accountant or banker may suggest other items for a credit review. When the designer is working with a commercial client, it is possible to obtain credit information on the business by contacting Dun & Bradstreet directly. A fee is charged by the bank, credit agency, or online credit reporting by D&B for these services.

Although the firm should take the opinion or recommendation of the financial institution or credit agency very seriously, the final decision as to whether to extend credit to the potential client remains that of the owner or the appropriate manager.

TABLE 13-1.

Items to include in a credit application

Note that this list includes information that should be obtained for a commercial client. Information on creditworthiness of residential clients can be obtained by means other than a credit application.
Purchaser's name
Purchaser's address, phone, fax, and e-mail
Contact person
Date business established
Bank references, including account numbers
Company name and DBA of commercial clients
Type of business (sole proprietorship, partnership, etc.) of business clients
Trade payment references of commercial clients
Federal tax ID or Social Security number
Amount of credit needed
Number of employees
General terms and conditions of extending credit are explained
Other items as recommended by the firm's accountant and/or attorney

A credit application never provides 100 percent assurance as to the creditworthiness or good intentions of a client. However, the procedure gives the design firm a better chance of working with clients who will honor their financial obligations. A sample credit application is included on the companion Web site as Item 13-1.

Confirmation of Purchase

Many firms proceed with merchandise orders on the basis of a verbal agreement from the client. This can be satisfactory for small "cash and carry" transactions with a relatively low value. Recall from Chapter 9 that an oral agreement to sell goods worth more than $5000 (with a base of $500 in some jurisdictions) is not legally binding. It is important for the designer to verify what value is considered binding in his or her jurisdiction.

Many firms require that a *confirmation of purchase*—also called a *sales agreement*, a *purchase agreement*, a *contract proposal* or simply *proposal*—be completed and signed by the client. This form legally requires the client to fulfill his or her financial responsibility to the designer concerning the purchase of merchandise. It also clarifies the designer's responsibilities as to what is to be ordered for the client. Company policy should be clear that no furniture or furnishings will be ordered or begun until signed purchase agreements have been obtained from the client.

The confirmation of purchase (we will use that term in this chapter) should be at least two pages (a duplicate form) so that the design firm and the client will each have a record of the sale (see Figure 13-1). Another example of a sales agreement is included on the companion Web site as Item 13-2. To be legally binding, the form must contain quantities, descriptions, and prices. The forms are numbered so that it is easier to track each form to the specific project. When signed by the client, the confirmation becomes a legal contract for selling the described merchandise.

Ordering merchandise without obtaining the client's signature is risky. A confirmation of purchase without the client's signature provides no concrete evidence that the client ever agreed to purchase the goods. The confirmation of purchase is also legally binding on designers, as they or the firm must sell the described merchandise at the prices quoted and their clients must pay for that

CATLIN INTERIORS, INC.
916 DANTE PLACE, SUITE 2
JACKSONVILLE, FL 32207
Phone: (904) 396-5522 Fax: (904) 396-4009

PROPOSAL
JONES / MR. & MRS. ROBERT
JONES
Proposal No.: 0001
September 27, 2012
Page 1 of 1

To: MR. & MRS. ROBERT JONES
     14144 MEADOWLARK WAY
     PLEASANTVILLE, FL 32265

Quantity	Description	Extended Price
	FOYER	
1 each	Custom Iron Console Table with Glass Top. Iron Legs have Texture Iron Finish: Oil Rubbed Bronze. Dimensions: 14" D x 68" W X 34" H. See attached photo. *Ref. #: 0004*	2,996.00
	FOYER	2,996.00
	LIVING ROOM	
2 each	Fully Upholstered Contemporary Club Chairs with Loose Pillow Back Cushion in Cream Basket Weave Fabric and Stained Legs. Comfort Down Seat with Blend Down Back. Fabric priced separately. Dimensions: 30" L x 25.5" D x 38"H. Arm height: 24" Seat height: 18" Wood Finish: Mink See attached photo. *Ref. #: 0003*	4,150.00
17 yards	Taupe Colored Basketweave Chenille Fabric for Loose Pillow Back Chairs. Fabric requires backing included in price. Fabric sample attached. *Ref. #: 0006*	3,419.00
	LIVING ROOM	7,569.00
	Item Total	10,565.00
	Freight	580.00
	Sales Tax	668.70
	Grand Total	11,813.70

Approved _____ Date _____

Requested Deposit   **$5,906.85**

Above pricing valid for 30 days. No returns on custom orders. Shipping charges of items are estimated and will be billed at their actual cost and are in addition to the above price quote. Installation Charges are not included in quote.

FIGURE 13-1.

A sales proposal (or sales agreement) used as the contract for the sale of merchandise. (Reproduced with permission of Juliana M. Catlin, FASID, Catlin Interiors, Inc., Jacksonville, FL)

same merchandise. It is impractical for a firm to use a series of these forms for a large volume of items. In such cases, a statement such as "The undersigned agrees to purchase the items described per the attached list" will suffice.

The *terms and conditions* are the seller's policies in regard to the sale of items or services to a buyer. The terms and conditions of the sale must be stated on the confirmation of purchase, and the client must be made aware of the terms (see Figure 13-2). Terms and conditions might relate to partial deliveries, changes in the jobsite, warehousing when the client is not ready to accept delivery, and warranties. The terms need not be as complex as those in the example; however, they should be complete enough to protect the interior design firm and inform the client of terms concerning the sale of goods. These terms and conditions should be prepared with the advice of the firm's attorney.

FACILITEC
INTERIORS FOR
BUSINESS

4501 EAST MCDOWELL RD.

PHOENIX, AZ 85008

PHONE 602/275-0101

FAX 602/275-0202

TERMS AND CONDITIONS

Applicant (hereafter referred to as **Customer**) agrees that the extension of credit by **Facilitec, Inc.** (hereafter referred to as **Facilitec**) shall be subject to and in consideration of the following Terms and Conditions:

1. Payment is due net 30 days from the invoice date. The **Customer** warrants and affirms that it is financially able to meet the commitments made to **Facilitec** and will pay promptly when due any invoice rendered by **Facilitec** on or before the due date set forth on each invoice. Any deposits required by the manufacturers will be billed to **Customer** and are due upon receipt.

2. The **Customer** should understand that **Facilitec** invoices for product as it is received at the **Facilitec** warehouse or at the job site. **Facilitec** cannot control the schedules of the manufacturers, therefore, multiple invoices can occur on a proposal. It is the **Customer's** responsibility to match the invoices to the corresponding **Facilitec** proposal. If the **Customer** requires a deviation from **Facilitec's** normal billing procedures, additional charges may be applicable.

3. **Customer** agrees to pay a finance charge of 1.5% per month (annual percentage rate of 18%) on all past due balances. Balances are past due after thirty (30) days from the invoice date.

4. At any time, any invoice is delinquent, the **Customer** understands that **Facilitec** may, at it's sole option, suspend credit terms to the **Customer**. If any legal action is required to collect monies due to **Facilitec**, the **Customer** promises to pay, in addition to finance charge, all costs of collection, including attorney's fees.

5. Partial shipments: **Facilitec** agrees to make every effort to deliver and install all products as quickly as possible. However, due to manufacturers shipping schedules and methods, **Facilitec** may only be able to deliver and install portions of the job at a time. **Customer** agrees to pay 90% of invoice amounts and may withhold 10% until completion of the job.

6. Storage: If **Customer** is unable or unwilling to accept installation or delivery of the products according to the specified schedule, the product may be stored at the **Customer's** request in the **Facilitec** warehouse, solely as a convenience to the **Customer**. **Customer** shall pay 90% of the invoice amount within thirty (30) days of the invoice date. In addition, **Customer** shall pay a warehouse charge of 1% per month of the invoice amount of such products so warehoused, payable monthly.

7. If **Customer** cancels an order with **Facilitec**, cancellation fees may be applicable.

_____
Company Name

_____
Company Address

_____
Date

_____
Authorized Signature

_____
Print Authorized Signature

_____
Phone Number

FIGURE 13-2.

Typical terms and conditions on the back side of a confirmation of purchase. (Reproduced with permission of Facilitec, Inc., Phoenix, AZ)

Many small design firms, especially sole practitioners, use the purchase order (discussed in the next section) as a confirmation of purchase. The contention is that some clients do not like to sign a lot of documents during the design process. This is a judgment call that is up to the owner. A purchase order may contain proprietary information, such as pricing, that the designer may wish to include on the purchase order but not necessarily reveal to the client unless the client is paying cost-plus for the merchandise. It is better business practice to separate the two tasks by using a sales confirmation that has been signed by the client before ordering goods.

It should be noted that a designer who is engaged in commercial design will also receive purchase orders from clients. In some ways, these can be considered a confirmation of purchase: although they come from the client, they are really purchase orders that signify the buying relationship. The designer must read these purchase orders carefully to ensure that the client is not asking for conditions that the designer is not willing to fulfill. Businesses are used to issuing a paper purchase order to proceed with a furniture order, but the order may also be faxed or e-mailed. As clients become more and more comfortable with purchasing goods over the Internet or by fax, even the smaller design firm must become familiar with these methods of confirming and ordering merchandise for interior design projects.

Purchase Orders

The *purchase order*, often referred to as a PO, is one of the most important forms of paperwork used in the contract administration phase. The purchase order is used to initiate orders for merchandise and services from manufacturers, tradespeople and craftspeople, and other vendors. Interior designers also use purchase orders to initiate orders for supplies or other items used by the design firm itself. Practically nothing should be purchased for clients without a *purchase order*.

The purchase order is another form of contract. It must be designed so that the vendor or supplier can easily find all the information needed to complete the order quickly and correctly. This information is central to establishing a contract for the sale of goods, as discussed in Chapter 9. The format must be standardized and must complement the recording methods of the remaining paperwork and the firm's accounting systems. The purposes of purchase orders are highlighted in Table 13-2.

All firms should have a policy prohibiting telephone orders to vendors. An order placed via telephone should not substitute for proper paperwork. Telephone orders are always problematic. In the first place, many manufacturers do not honor telephone orders until a follow-up written order is received

TABLE 13-2.

Purposes of a purchase order

1. Serves as the means of obtaining the needed goods and services in the client's interests.
2. Acts as a record of all outstanding orders. Needed for income tax calculations and loan applications.
3. Used to verify information on acknowledgments to be sure correct items were ordered.
4. Acts as a control mechanism for billing clients.
5. Can be used for checking the correct pricing of various suppliers.
6. Used to purchase items for the operations of the design firm.
7. Helps maintain accurate records when a hard copy is made of a digital purchase order.

(this negates any time advantage the designer may hope to gain by a phone-in order). Mistakes can be made when the vendor attempts to record or interpret verbal instructions. Dimensions can easily be transposed, resulting in incorrectly made items. It is even scarier to think of designers placing orders over their cell phones while they are in the car!

A useful procedure prior to finalizing an order for items involving fabric is to request a *cutting for approval (CFA)* from the supplier. This notation can go on the purchase order if time is of the essence, or a separate form can be faxed to the fabric supplier so that the sample will be received in a timely fashion. When the sample has been approved, a notice can go to the supplier to proceed with the order. Of course, this same CFA procedure can be applied to wall coverings, floorings, and specialty finishes of many kinds. What this procedure does is help to ensure that the color of current stock will work with all the other materials that will be used.

Electronic purchase orders via fax or e-mail are commonplace in this industry. Remember, from the discussion in Chapter 9, that electronic orders are valid contracts. When the designer faxes a purchase order, it is a good idea for the designer to set the fax machine so that a transmission report will be printed for each order and page (see Figure 13-3). This provides a record that the fax was actually sent to the correct party. Vendors often fax back an acknowledgment showing the receipt and confirming the order. Because e-mails can be misdirected, it is also advisable to request a confirmation that the vendor received an e-mail order.

Many suppliers are able to accommodate online order entry. The design firm needs the appropriate online capability with a supplier to order online. In most situations, the designer does not follow up an online order with a paper purchase order, to avoid the risk of duplicating the order. However, including a purchase order number on the online order or otherwise referencing a PO number to the online order is necessary for the designer's recordkeeping. It is also vital for the designer to keep paper copies of fax transmissions and e-mails related to orders for clients.

The exact content and format of the purchase order should be established according to the needs of the individual firm and its accounting practices. The following information should be a part of the purchase order, either as preprinted information or left as blank space:

1. *Preprinted sequenced numbers.* Using numerically sequenced purchase orders allows the firm to keep track of each purchase order, whether it is used or voided and thrown out.

2. *The firm's name and billing address, telephone number, fax number, and e-mail address of an appropriate party.* Preprinted forms look more professional, avoid mailing or shipping errors resulting from illegible handwriting, and save time.

3. *Space for the supplier's/vendor's name and address.*

4. *Space for the "ship to" location.* This is very important if the design firm does not want the merchandise shipped to the design firm's office location. On occasion, designers require that orders be delivered to some location other than the designer's office. This is referred to as *drop-ship.* It usually means that the shipment will be made to the client's address or the jobsite.

5. *Preprinted boxes or space for additional shipping instructions.* These instructions relate to expected ship date, the preferred freight company, and collected or prepaid charges.

Fax Call Report

PERCEPTIONS
480-951 6120
Jan-16-2007 10:04AM

Job	Date	Time	Type	Identification	Duration	Pages	Result
153	1/16/2007	10:03:05AM	Send		1:07	1	OK

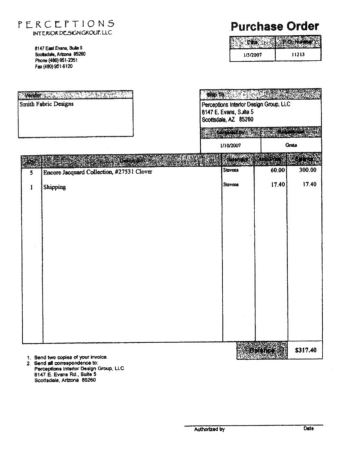

FIGURE 13-3.

Example of a fax transmission reply, showing that the fax was sent and what was sent. This type of report helps serve as a record of transmitted faxes. (Reproduced with permission of Greta Guelich, ASID, Perceptions Interior Design Group, LLC, Scottsdale, AZ)

6. *Space for the "tag for" information.* The *tag for information* (or "special info?" box as shown in Figure 13-4) can be placed at the bottom or the top of the purchase order. The client's name or a project number is usually written in this space as a further means of identifying the client who ordered the merchandise or service. Some design firms use project numbers rather than the client's name on all paperwork that

Purchase Order

The Design Collective Group, Inc. dba

DESIGN
pure + simple

301 N. PALM CANYON DRIVE SHOWROOM # 103
PALM SPRINGS, CA. 92262
VOICE : 760 · 841 · 1468 FAX : 561 · 745 · 0361

Importance Notice: Within 5 days of Receipt, Vendor must provide our firm with an Acknowledgement, confirm costs and provide a firm delivery schedule. We reserve all rights to cancel without penalty if these terms are not met.

Our Reference Number _____ - _____ - _____

Order Date _____ , 20 _____

Vendor	Fibreworks Carpeting Inc
Address	
City, St, Zip	

SideMark	Levy Living Rm Area Rug
Deposit Required	50% Deposit At Time Of Order
Ship By Date	Need by December 15, 2012

Ship To	Design Collective Group
Address	Attn: Michael Baker
	1540 Palm Colony
City, St, Zip	Palm Springs, CA 92264

Terms: _____

- This Order is subject to cancellation if Vendor is not able to ship by date specified or fails to notify of delay
- No changes or substitutions without prior approval.
- Acknowledgements, shipments + invoices must be clearly marked with our REFERENCE NUMBER.
- Any additional costs must be pre-approved in writing.
- Vendor agrees that acceptance of this order with the terms outlined supercede all other terms and conditions.

Quantity	Specification	Color / Finish	Each	Total
24 sq yds	Mayan Rivieria Sisal Carpeting	784 / Mountain	10.00	240.00
	Width: 16-4"			

Additional Information:

Subtotal	240.00
Additional Charges	0.00
Shipping Costs	70.00
TOTAL	310.00

Authorization To Proceed With This Proposal Subject To The Terms Outlined Above:

BY: _____   Date: _____

WWW.SHOPDESIGNPUREANDSIMPLE.COM   WHITE COPY: VENDOR / YELLOW COPY: OFFICE / PINK COPY: CLIENT BINDER

FIGURE 13-4.

A purchase order form. (Reproduced with permission of Michael Thomas, FASID, CAPS, Design Collective Group/Design Pure + Simple, Palm Springs, CA)

travels out of the office, in order to maintain client confidentiality. Firms also put other brief instructions on the purchase order that will help the receiving party clearly identify where the items are to be located at the jobsite. Note that some firms use "side mark" to mean "tag for" on purchase orders.

Typically, the body of the purchase order has space for the following information, though each design firm may organize its purchase orders in a fashion that is satisfactory to the firm.

1. *Quantity*. Must be included for the supplier, and is required by the UCC to create a sales contract.

2. *Catalog number*. Include the exact sequence of numbers and/or letters that the supplier uses to call out the products in the catalog. Mistyping or reversing even one number can lead to the wrong product being shipped.

3. *Description*. The method that the supplier uses in the catalog should be followed. This helps prevent having the wrong item shipped. However, remember that many suppliers process orders by the catalog number on the purchase order, not the description. The description acts as a check against the catalog number. There is no guarantee that the supplier's order input person will read the description.

4. *Net price*. Including the expected net price on the purchase order acts as an additional accuracy check, especially when the designer orders only occasionally from a supplier. Of course, best practice is to know what the net price or price to the designer will be before the purchase order is prepared! Net pricing on the purchase order can also help the firm utilize a cost accounting method for managerial control. Note that the net price should *not* be included on the purchase order if a copy of the form will be given to the client.

5. *Line item number*. Many firms use *line item numbers* as another method of controlling an order. Each item on the sale order is given a line item number. This number is cross-referenced in the appropriate column on the purchase order. Problems and questions about orders can more easily be tracked with this number. Goods can also be tagged with the line item number. Note that multiples of the same item for the same order are considered one line item.

The bottom of the form should provide space for the authorizing signature. This signature will be either that of the firm's owner or of an authorized manager. Additional information that the design firm wishes the supplier to be aware of can be added in appropriate places: for example, instructions asking the supplier to acknowledge receipt of the purchase order and to provide an expected shipping date.

Each supplier involved in a project receives a separate purchase order. Orders for multiple items to the same supplier for the same client can, of course, be sent on the same purchase order. If the designer is placing orders for multiple items to the same supplier but for two or more *different* clients, a different purchase order should be prepared for each client. Even though some firms place two or more customer orders to the same manufacturer on the same purchase order, better control is maintained by initiating separate purchase orders for each customer.

If two suppliers are involved in the completion of one finished product, such as a sofa that will receive fabric from another vendor, the designer must prepare two different purchase orders. *Customer's own material (COM)* indicates that the designer is not using a fabric available from the chair or sofa manufacturer. One purchase order is written to the sofa supplier, referencing the COM fabric according to the supplier's requirements printed in the supplier's catalog. A second purchase order is written to the fabric supplier, referencing the information required by the sofa supplier. This information is often included as an expanded "tag for" block of information in the body of the purchase order, rather than in the normal "tag for" space. Most furniture manufacturers require that the fabric be shipped prepaid to the factory. The designer must be sure that the fabric supplier does this, and the designer must remember to add the estimated shipping charge to the cost of the sofa. It is, after all, part of the cost of completing the sofa.

For a small design firm, two to three copies of the purchase order are required. To help the firm visually track the various copies, it is best if each sheet is a different color. The first sheet is always white. The other copies may be any color. They are used as follows:

- The white, or original, copy is mailed or faxed to the supplier.
- The second copy should go in the "open purchase order file." If the order is being faxed, the original copy can go in the "open purchase order file" after an acknowledgment has been received from the supplier.
- The third copy should go in the client's active file and be used for reference.

The outstanding orders are tracked through the open purchase order file, which consists of all numerically sequenced purchase orders for goods that have not yet been received. In a small design firm, the designer, or perhaps a design assistant or the bookkeeper, may keep track of this file. Large firms will assign this responsibility to a nondesigner staff member such as an expediter. When acknowledgments are received, they should be checked for accuracy against the information on the purchase order. Discrepancies should be dealt with immediately. When merchandise has been received and delivered, the bookkeeper can bill the client. Orders not yet received can be tracked by checking the expected ship date on the order against the current date. If an order appears to be late, the designer who was responsible for placing the order should contact the supplier to establish the reason for the delay.

It is common for an additional copy of the purchase order to be sent to a warehouse or warehouse service. This helps the warehouse effectively service the design firm, because the warehouse will know in advance the quantity and expected arrival dates of all the merchandise that the firm has ordered. If, on occasion, the merchandise is shipped to the client's location rather than to the warehouse, the warehouse often has the responsibility to unload and inspect the merchandise as it comes off the truck.

Some firms use a copy of the purchase order as a delivery ticket. In this case, pricing is blocked out of the copy that is given to the client. The client signs or initials this copy to verify the items that have been delivered. When multiple items are on one order, vendors often ship what is ready even if the order is incomplete. These delayed items are referred to as *back orders*. Any back orders or items in need of repair can also be noted on the delivery-ticket copy of the purchase order. Item 13-3 on the companion Web site offers another version of a purchase order.

Acknowledgments

When a manufacturer receives a purchase order, it sends paperwork to the interior designer called an acknowledgment. *Acknowledgments* or confirmations (sometimes called order updates) not only confirm receipt of the order, they mirror back the items ordered by the designer to demonstrate understanding of the order (see Figure 13-5). Depending on the supplier and whether the purchase order was mailed, faxed, or e-mailed, the designer receives an acknowledgment anywhere from a few hours to 10 days later.

Although acknowledgments vary in format to suit the needs of specific suppliers, it is likely that the following kinds of information will be provided on them:

1. An order number assigned by the supplier.
2. The design firm's purchase order number.
3. The date on which the acknowledgment was prepared.
4. A scheduled shipping date. The order will be shipped sometime during that week, not necessarily on that day.
5. What the expected shipping situation will be (e.g., "Collect—Roadway" means that the design firm will have to pay the shipping charges and that the merchandise will come from the Roadway shipping company).
6. Notations as to who ordered the merchandise, the billing address, and the shipping address.
7. The "tag for" instructions.
8. A restatement of quantity, catalog number, description, and pricing information. Many manufacturers put the net price on the acknowledgment. However, others still quote retail prices. If the retail price is quoted, the acknowledgment will often also quote the discount that the designer will receive for that order.
9. Other information related to billing and shipping.

The supplier may send the design firm an original copy, a fax, or possibly an e-mail version of the acknowledgment. Each acknowledgment must be checked against the purchase order. E-mailed acknowledgments should be downloaded into the designer's order system, or hard copies should be printed so that the designer has a record of the transaction. The acknowledgment should be attached to the corresponding purchase order in the open purchase order file. A copy may be added to the active project file for reference purposes.

The acknowledgment information must be compared against the purchase order upon receipt of the acknowledgment, so that any discrepancies between the two forms can be found and reconciled. There is generally very little time for the designer or the client to make changes in an order. Major suppliers often give only 10 days and certainly no more than 3 weeks "from receipt of order" to make any changes in the order.

Any discrepancies—especially those in quantity, catalog number, description, or price—should be discussed with the manufacturer immediately. Delays in calling attention to errors often result in the design firm's receiving the wrong merchandise. Discrepancies regarding the expected shipping date or other shipping information also should be checked to see how they may affect project completion.

Someone must be responsible for checking all outstanding orders. In smaller design firms, the person responsible for checking the acknowledgments is the designer, an assistant, or the bookkeeper. Checking acknowledgments is

ACKNOWLEDGEMENT

Purchase Order #   10007598

Page 1 of 1

BILL TO: **Business One**
100 Circle Drive
Phoenix, AZ 85018
602-555-0000

SHIP TO: **Furniture Install Corp.**
2222 Main Street
Phoenix, AZ 85253

HBF SALES REP: Jane Smith

HBF DUNS #: 255555

CUSTOMER CONTACT:
NAME: John Jones c/o Cool Restaurant 6
PHONE: 602-555-0001
EMAIL: jjones@aol.com

SHIPPING INFORMATION:
CALL BEFORE DELIVERY
John Jones 602-555-0001

ACCOUNT INFORMATION:
ACCOUNT #: 545454
ORDER DATE: 01/01/07
ORDER ENTERED: 01/02/07

TERMS: Net 30
ORDER TAGGING: Cool Restaurant 6
ORDER RECEIVED: 01/01/07

HBF CONTACT:
T: 888-555-5555
F: 888-555-0000
E: hbf@furniture.com

LINE	QTY	STYLE	DESCRIPTION	GRADE FABRIC	NET	EXT
Prod Line:						
1	16	5018-30	Westwood Lounge Chair Armless 27"OW x 36"OD x 30-1/2"OH Finish: 11-Amazon Dark On Maple	F-HBF Nubby #807-44	$980.16	$15,681.60
2	3	5020-30	Westwood Sofa Finish: 11-Amazon Dark On Maple 84"OW x 39"OD x 30-1/2"OH	Grade 1 HBF Leather Vivace/Nero #703-90	$1,838	$5,514

FREIGHT/HANDLING $2,010
SALES TAX $1059.78

ORDER TOTAL	**$24,265.38**

IMPORTANT NOTICE
No Cancellation will be taken on this order if covers have been cut. This acknowledges your order as it
will be shipped. If incorrect please notify us immediately, in as much as upholstering fabrics are not guaranteed
by the mill. HBF will not be held responsible for wear or fading of any covering materials.
THIS IS IMPORTANT AND SHOULD NOT BE NEGLECTED.

Hickory Business
Furniture, Inc.
900 12th Street Dr. NW
Hickory, NC 28601
TEL 828.328.2064
FAX 828.328.8816

FIGURE 13-5.

An acknowledgment from a supplier. (Reproduced with permission of HBF (Hickory Business Furniture) & HBF Textiles, Hickory, NC)

usually the responsibility of an expediter in larger design firms. Discrepancies must be brought to the attention of the project designer so that he or she can determine how to deal with the problem and discuss possible alternatives with the client.

Many design firms use a "tickler file" keyed to the days of the month. This file is checked daily (in very large firms) or weekly to make sure that goods have been received within the expected ship dates. Checking can be done immediately on orders that are about to be shipped or that have not yet been received although the ship date has passed. Computer programs are useful tools in such situations.

Invoices

An *invoice* is simply a bill. The interior design firm sends out invoices to clients for services performed and/or goods purchased in the client's name. Suppliers send invoices to the designer for the goods or services that the interior design firm has ordered.

Invoices from suppliers are commonly sent at the same time the merchandise is shipped. The invoice generally arrives at the office a few days before the merchandise. Carefully check incoming invoices and acknowledgments. Many suppliers use invoices that look very similar to their acknowledgments; the only difference may be the label. An invoice must be paid, whereas acknowledgments are for information only. The invoice must correspond to what was ordered and should be checked against the purchase order and acknowledgment. The invoice must also be checked against what is actually received in order to properly set up delivery and bill the client. Figure 13-6 shows an invoice from a supplier to a designer. In this case, the invoice is for the item shown on the acknowledgment in Figure 13-5.

The invoice may include special pricing such as an extra cash discount for prompt payment (see Chapter 8). These discounts can amount to substantial savings for a design firm that pays the invoice within the specified time period. Not all suppliers offer this special discount to all designers. Manufacturers expect prompt payment from the interior designer.

Too many busy design firms delay or even forget to send invoices to clients. Best practices should include invoicing clients as quickly as possible, so as to keep receivables very low and good cash flow moving in the design firm. Poor cash management through slow billing can be a serious problem for any interior design firm. Delays in billing can also lead to a few unscrupulous clients not paying for goods or services at all.

Goods should be billed within 10 days after the goods have been delivered and accepted by the client (see Figure 13-7). Services should be billed once services have been completed, for short-duration projects; on a monthly basis, for larger projects; or on whatever billing basis for services was agreed to in the contract.

Including language such as "billing upon delivery" or "payment due ten days after receipt of invoice" on the contract for services or the sales confirmation alerts the client to payment requirements. Similar terms should be included on the invoice.

Some firms try to use item-by-item billing on large projects. This, of course, means that if the project has 20 items that are to be delivered and only 2 arrive, the firm delivers the 2 items and bills only for those 2 items. The next time more items arrive, they are also delivered and billed. Although this may help the firm's cash flow, it can increase costs and cause many headaches for the firm. There is a cost attached each time the delivery truck delivers goods to

```
Send check to:
        HBF & HBF Textiles
          P.O. Box 60571
       Charlotte, NC  28260-0571
Freight Charges NET - Shipments FOB Hickory
No anticipation allowed
```

PROFORMA

Purchase Order # 10007598

Page 1 of 1

BILL TO: **Business One**
100 Circle Drive
Phoenix, AZ 85018
602-555-0000

SHIP TO: **Furniture Install Corp.**
2222 Main Street
Phoenix, AZ 85253

HBF SALES REP: **Jane Smith**   HBF DUNS #: 255555

CUSTOMER CONTACT:
NAME: John Jones c/o Cool Restaurant 6
PHONE: 602-555-0001
EMAIL: jjones@aol.com

SHIPPING INFORMATION:
CALL BEFORE DELIVERY
John Jones 602-555-0001

ACCOUNT INFORMATION:
ACCOUNT #: 545454
ORDER DATE: 01/01/07
ORDER ENTERED: 01/02/07

TERMS: Net 30
ORDER TAGGING: Cool Restaurant 6
ORDER RECEIVED: 01/01/07
SHIP DATE: 03/06/07

HBF CONTACT:

T: 888-555-5555
F: 888-555-5555
E: hbf@furniture.com

LINE	QTY	STYLE	DESCRIPTION	GRADE FABRIC	NET	EXT
1	16	5018-30	Westwood Lounge Chair Armless Finish: 11-Amazon Dark	F-HBF Nubby #807-44	$980.16	$15,681.60
2	3	5020-30	Westwood Sofa Finish: 11-Amazon Dark	COL Leather 1/black	$1,838	$5,514

FREIGHT/HANDLING $2,010
SALES TAX $1,059.78

ORDER TOTAL   **$24,265.38**

IMPORTANT NOTICE
Total amount due.
THIS IS IMPORTANT AND SHOULD NOT BE NEGLECTED.

1/24/07 11:45 am

Hickory Business
Furniture, Inc.
900 12th Street Dr. NW
Hickory, NC 28601
TEL 828.328.2064
FAX 828.328.8816

FIGURE 13-6.

This pro forma invoice corresponds to the acknowledgment shown in Figure 13-5. (Reproduced with permission of HBF, Hickory, NC)

PERCEPTIONS
INTERIOR DESIGN GROUP, LLC

8147 East Evans, Suite 5
Scottsdale, Arizona 85260
Phone (480) 951-2351
Fax (480) 951-6120

Invoice

Date	Invoice #
1/2/2007	99796

Bill To

Quantity	Description	Each	Price
1	Lorts Nightstand #9649; Finish: Rirenze; Standard Distress, No wax Match to finish sample enclosed	1,160.85	1,160.85T

The designer acts as the client's agent for all products and services described above. The designer makes no guarentees beyond those of the supplier, if any. Fabrics and leathers are not guarenteed for color match, wearing or fading.

Terms: 80 percent payment required at the time of signing this invoice. Balance is due when products are ready for delivery or when services are completed. All prices are subject to additional charges for storage and freight.

Subtotal	**$1,160.85**
Tax (7.95%)	**$92.28**
Total	**$1,253.13**
80% Deposit	**$1,002.50**
Balance Due	**$250.63**

_____
ACCEPTED

FIGURE 13-7.

A sample invoice prepared by a design firm and sent to a client. (Reproduced with permission of Greta Guelich, ASID, Perceptions Interior Design Group, LLC, Scottsdale, AZ)

the client. There is also a cost associated with the preparation and mailing of invoices. Many commercial clients will not pay for goods delivered one at a time, but only upon completion of the work.

It is suggested that, whenever possible, deliveries be done in lots or only when the order is complete. This will reduce delivery and bookkeeping costs for multiple deliveries. An example invoice form from a designer to a client is included on the companion Web site as Item 13-4.

SHIPPING AND FREIGHT

In most cases the interior designer must add charges for shipping the goods to the designer's warehouse or the jobsite. Even locally available items will incur additional charges for delivery. These topics are discussed in other sections related to specific applications. Chapter 8 contains a discussion of how freight and delivery charges affect the price of the goods, Chapter 9 reviews freight concepts as regulated by the UCC, and Chapter 14 discusses delivery charges. In this chapter, we investigate the forms that are specifically related to shipping and freight services. The forms discussed here are the bill of lading, the packing list, and the freight bill.

There are various freight matters that result in additional paperwork management for the designer. The first is the *bill of lading:* the form that the supplier provides to the truck driver to show what is being shipped and who has title to the goods. The driver carries this form with him or her in the truck; the contents of the truck must match what is on the form. The bill of lading does not mirror a purchase order and may actually cover several purchase orders to the same design firm or even multiple firms. The bill of lading is not a detailed list, but rather a total quantity of items. If the entire shipment is to one firm, the designer or the warehouse must check the number of items that are delivered against the number on the bill of lading. Discrepancies in quantity should be noted on the bill, as should any notations regarding damages to merchandise. This may sound somewhat daunting, but in fact most small interior design firms never see a bill of lading, as the size of their orders from a supplier is too small.

Another form that accompanies the delivery is a *packing list*, which is commonly in a plastic envelope attached to the outside of one of the items being delivered. The packing list details by quantity and description what is being shipped from a manufacturer or supplier to the warehouse at a specific time. The packing list must be checked against all items taken from the truck and against the number on the bill of lading. Again, discrepancies should be noted on the bill of lading if one is provided to the designer.

The actual *freight bill* is another invoice. It is usually sent a few days after the shipment leaves the manufacturer. The freight bill comes from the shipping company, not the manufacturer, because it is the bill for the shipping service.

It is important for the designer or a representative of the design firm (the warehousing service) to inspect all the items as they arrive at the designer's warehouse or jobsite. Many one-person design firms allow merchandise to be delivered to the client without the designer being available at the time of delivery to inspect the goods. This can be very costly if merchandise has been damaged. Inspection prior to delivery allows damages or errors to be caught, eliminating client dissatisfaction.

Damaged cartons should be immediately opened and inspected as they are removed from the shipper's truck. Whenever practical, all items should be unwrapped or uncartoned so that they may be inspected for *concealed damage*—damage that may exist even though the carton or wrapping appears intact. One type of concealed damage that frequently occurs with wood furniture shipped in a box is called *box burns*. When this happens, the carton has rubbed against the wood and that contact has marred the finish. Concealed damage must be reported to the carrier and supplier as soon as possible. As the time from acceptance of shipment or the discovery of damages lengthens, successful claims become less probable.

Any damage to cartons, packing, and merchandise should be shown to the driver. Notations about damaged merchandise must be made on the bill of lading or copy of the packing list in order for the design firm to make successful claims. It is important to take pictures of damaged merchandise—even a damaged box before it is opened. This can greatly help the firm in filing its claims.

Because the filing of freight claims and disposition of the claims are very time-consuming, many larger firms forgo filing claims on minor damage and handle repairs themselves without requesting that the shipper or vendor make them. These charges are then costed as overhead expenses. Merchandise that has sustained substantial damage in transit should be refused. However, a freight claim must still be filed, and records such as photographs, showing the extent of the damage, must be kept.

Certain documentation is generally required when the firm files a freight claim:

1. The bill of lading
2. The paid freight bill
3. The manufacturer's invoice for the item
4. The inspection report prepared by the freight carrier
5. Documentation of repair costs
6. Documentation of additional freight costs (if any) resulting from the damage
7. Other written or photographic documentation that attests to the damage occurring before delivery to the jobsite or to the designer's warehouse

The fact that a shipment has been damaged or is otherwise incorrect does not mean the designer can demand that the shipper automatically return it to the vendor. Most manufacturers will not accept merchandise for return once it has been delivered to the purchasing firm or the design firm has accepted it. Therefore, the firm must get written permission to return damaged (or incorrectly shipped) merchandise, rather than simply sending the merchandise back to the manufacturer. Each manufacturer has its own policy concerning returns, and these policies must be adhered to if the firm is to receive proper credit.

Whenever the design firm contacts the freight carrier concerning a shipping question, it should have at hand the bill of lading number, the supplier's name and location, the date of shipment, the description and number of items shipped, and the delivery location. If the information needed is not on the manufacturer's invoice, this information, along with other needed information, can be obtained from the manufacturer.

EXPEDITING

This chapter has mentioned many times that someone from the firm must check all the paperwork going out and coming in to be sure that items are ordered correctly, that the item ordered is what will be shipped, and that the items received are the items ordered. Sole practitioners must do all this work themselves. Larger firms are able to use someone who has these responsibilities as the key tasks in his or her job description. The term for the person who is primarily responsible for the ordering and managing of these product orders is *expediter*.

An expediter is an individual who is familiar with the design firm's paperwork system and the various ordering and shipping requirements of manufacturers. In firms that are large enough to have a person responsible for this specific job function, the expediter is a person who constantly monitors all orders *after* the purchase orders have been sent and the acknowledgments have been received. He or she is responsible for the speedy processing of orders. Expediters might also be responsible for preparing purchase orders, but that would be an operational decision of the owner. In the following discussion, the expediter does not have the responsibility for preparing purchase orders.

The first activity of the expediter is to check the acknowledgment from the manufacturer against the purchase order. This is a vital step to ensure that all the information matches on the two forms and confirms that the correct products and/or services are being supplied. Discrepancies must be taken care of immediately.

The expediter then looks closely at the expected ship date. It must be determined that the products are going to ship within the time specified on the purchase order and that they will arrive when they were promised to the client. If the ship date is not what is expected, the expediter should inform the designer so that the proper action can be taken. Delays in shipping are often caused or complicated by items that include dependent items. A common example is the fabric for seating. If the fabric is delayed, the seating items will also be delayed. Depending on the length of the delay, the designer may need to discuss with the client the necessity of reselecting the fabric. Sometimes the expediter will contact the client or vendor by e-mail or send a facsimile form.

Sometimes merchandise may come sooner than expected or is purposely ordered early. Merchandise shipped earlier requires warehousing until the jobsite is ready. If this is the case, the designer must negotiate with the client as to who will be responsible for the charges and where the merchandise should be shipped. At the time of order, it is relatively easy for the design firm to request that the merchandise not be shipped until a date beyond the normal shipping date. There may be an extra charge if the manufacturer must warehouse the finished goods when the designer requests that a shipment be delayed.

More often, the ship date shown is later than expected. The designer must contact the client to let him or her know about the delay. Short-term delays may be inconvenient but are seldom critical. Delays of three or more weeks may necessitate cancellation of the original order and finding alternate products.

The expediter is also responsible for tracking shipments once they have left the manufacturer. A very good practice is to set up a tickler file by date for the acknowledgments. The expediter can then check weekly on the disposition of any order. He or she can alert the delivery people to an impending shipment and confirm where it is to be delivered by the trucking company.

It is particularly important to know the disposition of merchandise that is to be drop-shipped to a jobsite. Someone representing the design firm (or the design firm's warehouse service company) must be at the site to unload, inspect, and deliver the goods to the client. Truck drivers generally are not responsible for unloading the merchandise from the truck, unpacking it, or delivering it to the client. In some firms, the expediter may also be responsible for filing both return permissions and freight claims. However, a warehouse service may be able to provide these latter two services for the design firm.

Once shipments leave the manufacturer, the expediter and designer track them by the bill of lading number, not the purchase order number. The firm receives information from the freight company as to what this number is. The bill of lading number, along with the name and address of the design firm, the name and address of the delivery site, the name of the shipping company, the name and address of the original shipping location, a description and the number of pieces in the order, and the weight of the order must be available for tracking delayed shipments.

WEB SITES RELEVANT TO THIS CHAPTER

www.asid.org American Society of Interior Designers

www.iida.org International Interior Design Association

Manufacturers will have information on their Web sites concerning ordering.

KEY TERMS

Acknowledgment	Freight bill
Back order	Invoice
Bill of lading	Line item number
Box burns	Movable equipment
Capital construction	Move management
Concealed damage	Packing list
Confirmation of purchase	Procurement
Credit application	Procurement form
Customer's own material (COM)	Progress report
Cutting for approval (CFA)	Purchase order (PO)
Drop-ship	"Tag for"
Expediter	Terms and conditions

WHAT WOULD YOU DO?

1. Alice had worked with the Brown family off and on for three years, designing two homes and a small office for Mrs. Brown. Mr. and Mrs. Brown hired Alice six months ago to design a summer home in a resort area. The Browns convinced Alice to begin work even though a contract had not been signed; they said things like, "Oh, we have known each other for so long, is it really necessary for us to sign every piece of paper before you order things?" Alice relented and ordered $75,000 of furniture and finish products without a single client signature. Today she just heard that Mr. Brown's business is in receivership and that it is likely that the Browns will have to declare bankruptcy.

2. James was very excited about obtaining a contract to redesign a restaurant for an up-and-coming entrepreneur who had been receiving

lots of press. Part of James's contract with the client was to provide the furniture, booths, and custom millwork for the bar. The client told James that the furniture for the existing space and the new location should be ordered as soon as possible, as he wanted the remodeling to be done very quickly and not interfere with business. James agreed to order the chairs—which the client picked out from an Internet page— before other design work got under way. The client did give James a check for 75 percent of the price of the seating. For the past two weeks, James has been trying to get in touch with the client to go over plans and to obtain further payment on the chairs, as the manufacturer has demanded a 100 percent prepayment for the order. The client has not returned James's calls.

3. Peter ordered several furniture items for his client's condominium. The client paid a 50 percent deposit. The supplier delivered the furniture items to Peter's warehouse service, where they are being held pending delivery to the client. Peter has informed the client that the merchandise is in and ready to be delivered, but that he must be paid the full amount due before he will schedule the delivery. The client wants to see the furniture before paying, but Peter is adamant about prepayment, saying "I gave you a break by only asking for a 50 percent deposit at the beginning."

4. Marge Johnson designed a portion of a dentist's office and was paid a fee of $15,000 for the design services. Dr. Green also had her order the chairs for the waiting area and a custom desk, credenza, and bookcases for his office. The manufacturer of the custom furniture quoted a 10-week delivery because of the special finish and custom details specified by Johnson. Dr. Green approved these changes, and he also approved the delivery time before the orders were sent to the supplier.

Two weeks after the scheduled delivery of the office furniture, the manufacturer finally returns repeated inquiries by Johnson, informing her that they need another four weeks to complete the pieces: They are having trouble getting the right quality of wood for the veneer in order for the special finish to work. The manufacturer also wants the remainder of the price of the furniture paid in full immediately. When Johnson tells the client about the problem, Dr. Green says that he can make do with his old desk and to cancel the entire order.

CHAPTER 14

Contract Administration: Delivery and Project Closeout

After completing this chapter you should be able to:

- Explain why it is important for the client to sign for items delivered to the jobsite.
- Compare and contrast the delivery process with the installation process.
- Explain how the delivery ticket can be useful to the designer—beyond showing what was delivered.
- Compare an as-built floor plan to an original construction drawing.
- Describe why a "white gloves" approach to the delivery and installation process is so important.
- Explain what occurs during project closeout and any documents that are utilized.
- Discuss retainage and who it most commonly affects.
- Explain the difference between the certificate of occupancy and the certificate of substantial completion.
- Compare a postoccupancy evaluation for clients to one done solely for the design firm.
- Discuss the importance of good post-project follow-up, both for the design office and as it relates to customer service.

NCIDQ COMPONENT

Based on best information available, some material in this chapter might appear as part of the NCIDQ examination. The reader should not depend solely on this text for study material.

You have ordered the merchandise and await delivery, placement, and acceptance by the client. You then enter the part of the contract administration phase dealing with the final stages of a project after the merchandise is shipped. This chapter discusses the tasks and activities in this stage, which include delivery and installation, project closeout, and postoccupancy reviews.

In small design firms, the designer customarily administers these activities, with assistance from others only at the delivery stage. In larger design firms, other employees whose specialized job responsibilities center on completing the project handle many of these activities. The responsibilities of an expediter—discussed in Chapter 13—might include resolving delivery and installation issues.

Whether these activities are done by the project designer personally or are delegated to others, the project designer always retains ultimate responsibility for completion of the project. It is an important part of being a professional interior designer.

DELIVERY AND INSTALLATION

At this stage, the largest part of the project still remaining is delivery and installation of all the FF&E that are part of the designer's contract. Any existing furnishings that are to be reused must be placed in the spaces as well. As it relates to the services of the interior designer, *delivery* includes the activities concerned with moving furniture, furnishings, and equipment from the manufacturer's warehouse or showroom to the jobsite and placing each piece in its correct location. Delivery does not include any special activities of assembly, construction, or physical attachment of the products to the building; those tasks fall under *installation*.

The delivery process itself can be both stressful and exciting for clients as they finally see the design concepts take shape. Thus, a week or two prior to the delivery and installation of the furnishings, the designer must schedule a detailed pre-move-in meeting with the client or client's representative concerning delivery and installation. A key concern is to review the furniture/equipment plans. This is done to be sure that the clients have not changed their minds about the placement of any of the items. If items are to be relocated, revised plans must be prepared so that the delivery and installation workers are not forced to place or install items more than once. The larger the project, the more important this becomes—and the larger the project, the more likely it is that clients will want to make changes in furniture and equipment locations.

An extra service that the designer may wish to include in the contract is move management. Move management is a service to help the client with organizing the packing and relocation of furniture and other items. It is especially important for commercial projects and residential projects when a client is moving from one location to another. This service was discussed in Chapter 13.

Even if the interior designer is not part of the pre-move preparation, it is a stressful time for the designer as well as the client. Many problems can crop up at the last minute, making delivery a challenge. For example, delivery trucks have been known to have accidents; there may suddenly not be room available to maneuver large trucks on streets and in parking lots. These types of problems can affect a delivery even when there has been excellent planning for the move-in. It is important that the interior designer plan delivery supervision time into the design fee, because the designer will either be expected or want to be present to handle problems that might occur. Let's look first at delivery issues and paperwork.

The designer should prepare a delivery plan showing locations for all the furniture and other items for the job to let the delivery people know exactly where each piece should be located. These delivery plans are essential for smooth completion of the project. They must be updated to include any changes in item locations discussed at the pre-move-in meeting (see Figure 12-1). A floor plan keyed to the purchase order number and line item number is one way to do this if the project is small and does not involve many items. For larger projects, and especially in commercial design, other methods are used. Furniture items on the floor plan are keyed to the purchase order to facilitate delivery.

Instructions are given on the purchase order regarding where to ship the goods. Goods are most often shipped to a warehouse used by the designer before they are ultimately delivered to the jobsite. Design firms often depend on independent delivery service companies for delivery to the client's home or office. Products such as wall coverings and flooring are shipped to the company that will do the installation of those products. Large design firms with a showroom might have their own warehouse and delivery staff with company-owned trucks.

Regardless of how the goods reach the jobsite, delivery crews must be trained in the "white gloves" procedures that lead to satisfied customers. Firms that depend on delivery service providers must select these companies carefully and monitor the performance of the delivery service to ensure that the company can supply the quality of service the designer wishes for his or her clients. Clean uniforms, clean hands, and polite and respectful behavior, as well as respectful treatment of the client's property, should be mandatory expectations for delivery service employees. These are just some factors that help a firm continue high-level customer service.

Although it does take time to prepare delivery and installation drawings, such drawings are the easiest and simplest way for the designer to guarantee that all the specified goods will be delivered and installed in their proper locations. Preparation of these documents assures the designer that he or she will not be needed on the jobsite at all times. Showing the client that these kinds of documents have helped on projects in the past will also indicate to the client that the firm can deliver and install the products without the designer being there every minute of every day.

A delivery for a large commercial project often requires that parking lots or even parts of streets be closed to allow delivery trucks easy access to the building. If it is necessary to close a street, the client, designer, or contractor must arrange with the municipality and/or city police to obtain the proper permits for the closure. In a multistory building, the client, designer, or contractor will also have to arrange for access to freight elevators or one of the regular service elevators. Even the installation of furniture at a new home can result in upset neighbors complaining about the number of delivery or tradespeople's trucks that are constantly in the neighborhood and taking up parking space.

Clients often expect the designer to be present at all times during delivery and installation of merchandise. This is generally an impractical use of the designer's time. The designer should, however, build into the contract a reasonable amount of time to be spent on the jobsite during delivery and installation. This time should be estimated at the beginning of the project and included in the fees for the project. It should also be carefully explained to the client so that the client does not have unfounded expectations about the designer's full-time presence. If the designer is at the jobsite during this crucial time, he or she can reassure an anxious client who may not be sure about finishes and products as they are being installed and/or delivered.

The designer who is present during delivery and installation of merchandise can speed up the inspection process and, when questions arise, help answer them. How much time the designer spends at the jobsite during this phase will depend on the client, the contract, the particular complexity of the job, and the designer's availability.

It is good business practice for the client to sign documentation indicating what he or she has received during the delivery (or installation) portion of the project. This signifies acceptance and transfer of title, and thereby requires that the client pay for what was delivered. If a copy of the purchase order was sent to the warehouse service or to the designer's warehouse, the client can sign off on this form. Some firms use a separate delivery ticket that accompanies the merchandise. This ticket, shown in Figure 14-1, is at least a three-part form. The parts are distributed as follows:

1. The top or original copy goes to the client.
2. A second copy is sent to the billing office.
3. The third copy is retained by the warehouse whenever a back order, which is a partial shipment, is made.

Any notations regarding damages or discrepancies between what was delivered and what was ordered should be noted on the delivery paperwork. This helps clarify which damages are the responsibility of the design firm and which damages are the responsibility of the client.

Delivery service should include dusting and vacuuming of the merchandise, carefully inspection of it for any scratches or other damage, and removal of all cartons and packaging materials. It may also be the delivery team's responsibility to show the client how to operate certain items, such as adjustable office chairs. However, this is often the responsibility of the designer.

Now let's review important issues concerning installation services. Installation and assembly is the part of the delivery process during which merchandise is assembled, constructed, or installed as physical attachments to the building. Installation includes applying architectural finishes such as wall coverings, attaching such items as wall-hung bookcases and mirrors, and assembling open-office furniture, to name just a few.

Specialized sets of drawings are often necessary for installation of furniture such as open office systems. With open-office systems, design firms prepare one or more sheets of drawings to aid in the assembly. Plans that show panel configurations and finishes, electrical and telephone service, and either plans or elevations for the location of hanging components are examples.

Routine architectural finish schedules, as part of the construction documents, provide the information specifying the locations of these finishes. Wall graphics or designs in flooring materials are examples of drawings that might be needed for architectural finishes and included in the construction drawings. Graphic schedules or interior elevations inform the contractor of the locations of such items as mirrors, complex wall treatments, and various wall-hung units.

It is also important for the installation crew to take care of dusting, vacuuming, and removal of trash. Some companies do not perform such tasks as a routine part of their service, so the design firm should be sure that these tasks are included in its contract with the installer. If they are not included, the designer or client will be charged for the extra work.

A final issue concerning delivery and installation concerns confidentiality. Throughout the project, the interior designer will have learned many private, proprietary issues about the client or client's business. Designers are often given keys to homes and free access to many business properties during the

Page 1
DELIVERY TICKET SO36959
Job
Proposal   PR0028850
Print Date   01/10/07

Customer PO
SalesPerson

Contract Office Group, Inc.
931 Cadillac Court
Milpitas, CA 95035
PHONE: 408-262-6400
FAX: 408-262-1193

Sold To: **Ship To:**   **Install At:**
  JOHN DOE   Contract Office Group   JOHN DOE
                            931 Cadillac Court
                            Milpitas, CA 95035

Line Seq. No.	Description	Quantity	
1 SZT-20-721MA1	ZODY TASK CHAIR,FABRIC SEAT/MESH BACK	1	_____
	(721MA1) 4D,PAL BK,PNU/BS,FM/ADJ,ST/HRD		
	.1X- CHR FAB - GAUGE GRADE A		
	005 DEPTH		
	,MA- ZODY MESH		
	001 SUPPORT		
	,TR- SURFACE 3		
	00F BLACK		
	,TR- SURFACE 4		
	00F BLACK		
2 5G90012RG	KEYBOARD TRAY, 19"W X 10 5/8"D	1	_____
	W/SWIVEL MOUSE - 10" SWIVEL RIGHT		
	STANDARD PLATFORM		
	19" GEL WITH SYNTHETIC LEATHER COVER		
3 MPGEL10	10" MOUSE PAD W.GEL PALM	1	_____
	***** PROCESS ORDER AS QUICK-SHIP ****		
4 SV-LABOR-A	COG TO DELIVER & INSTALL CHAIR & KEYBOARD TRAY.	1	_____

Client Signature_____   **Date**_____

Delivered By Signature_____   **Date** _____

FIGURE 14-1.

This type of form can be used to accompany merchandise for delivery and/or installation. (Reproduced with permission of Leonard Alvarado/Contract Office Group, Milpitas, CA)

TABLE 14-1.

Project closeout document records for FF&E projects*

Copies of contract documents	Installation floor plans
Project site drawings to show as-built situations	Back-up copies of all documents (on DVDs, CDs, or USB drives)
Copies of construction drawings	Maintenance and use instructions for appropriate FF&E items
Copies of specifications or equipment lists of FF&E	As-built floor plans and other as-built documents
Purchase orders	Invoices to client for goods and other FF&E delivered to project
Acknowledgments	Invoices to client for design fees
Invoices from suppliers	Certificate of Substantial Completion and all punch lists
Payment records for invoices from suppliers	Records of repairs or requests for reorder of damaged goods
Bill of lading	Designer's time sheets
Packing list from shipments	Project closeout report
Freight/shipping bills	Invoices for final payments to suppliers
Payment records of shipping bills	Invoices to client for final payment for goods and services
Delivery tickets or records	Archive copies of CAD drawings

*Note: Not all items will be a part of all projects.

project. This means the client exhibits significant trust in the designer. During delivery and installation, vendors and staff also are exposed to the client's private affairs in much the same way. An important responsibility of the designer is to carefully select these vendors and staff with consideration for trustworthiness and confidentiality.

PROJECT CLOSEOUT

As the last of the products are being delivered and/or installed, the project reaches what is referred to as *project closeout*. This term is borrowed from architecture and the construction industry. The documents used in this phase might be referred to as *project record documents*. Now is the time for final inspections, giving any necessary documents (such as warranties) to the client, and approval of payments to subcontractors and/or vendors. A list of documents that might be included in the final project closeout phase is shown in Table 14-1. The first task that the designer must perform to close out a project is to make a final inspection, referred to as a *walk-through*.

Walk-Through

A *walk-through* is a final inspection of the jobsite, once everything has been delivered and installed, to be sure that everything that has been ordered is present and correctly installed. The designer, client, and perhaps the contractor conduct the walk-through. Any omissions and damages are noted on an inspection list most commonly called a *punch list*, which details everything that must still be taken care of. Some firms call the punch list the *site inspection report*.

The punch list should be completed for each room or area. This will make it easier for the delivery and repair people to find and complete the omissions or repairs. After it is signed by the client and designer, a copy goes to the client. The design firm uses a copy of the punch list to prepare work orders, repair tickets, and memos for completion of the work. When a firm charges design fees on a phased basis, the billing of the final part of the fee cannot be made until after the walk-through is done. Many clients will not make final payments until all the items on the punch list are taken care of. It is to the designer's benefit to take care of these items as quickly as possible. A sample punch list form is provided on the companion Web site as Item 14-1.

The walk-through is also a good time for the designer to fine-tune the project. Designers may realize that it can result in some additional specification or sale of merchandise. When the installation is winding down, clients often see the need for accessories or pieces of furniture that were cut from the original budget.

Complaints and Repairs

Regrettably, this is the stage at which many designers lose interest in the project. It is always more difficult (and sometimes annoying) for the designer to take care of nagging problems with an ongoing project than to be designing a new project. However, it is critical for good client relations and possible future referrals that complaints, repairs, omissions, and replacement of damaged items be taken care of as soon as possible. Unresolved problems cause bad feelings and can result in poor reviews from clients. Small, unresolved problems can also mean serious problems with the firm's cash flow, as uncollected receivables can mount. The design firm should have available for any repair work highly qualified furniture repair people who are experienced with all kinds of wood and metal furniture.

As much as possible, the firm's aim should be to take care of potential complaints and repairs before the client is even aware of an issue. When custom items are being manufactured, the interior designer should, if at all practicable, visit the workroom or shop to inspect the products before they are finished and prior to delivery. This helps catch problems that may occur during custom manufacture. A competent warehouse service that inspects and repairs furniture can eliminate minor damages before furniture is delivered to the client. Delivery personnel who handle the merchandise as if it were their own also avoid potential problems. The firm should hire only competent, experienced installers. If at all possible, delivering all the goods at one time helps to avoid a lot of complaints. The delivery and installation people must also be required to clean up the jobsite.

Final Documentation

As the project nears completion, several additional documents or permits may be provided to the client. The size and type of project will determine the necessity for any of these documents as the client is preparing to move into the project space.

The first is a *certificate of occupancy*. For projects where construction work has been performed, the property owner must receive this certificate before any interior movable furniture can be delivered or installed. This certificate applies to the structure and is obtained from the local building department after an inspection. Issuance of the certificate means that the building or space has been inspected, meets codes, and is approved for occupancy.

Another document is issued after the interior products have been delivered and installed and a punch list has been created. The designer or architect issues the *certificate of substantial completion* to clarify that everything has been done and indicates if something is missing. It is most commonly associated with a construction project and commercial projects. As part of issuing this certificate or notice, the designer also should make sure that any extra materials, such as extra carpeting, ceramic tile, and wall coverings, are left at the jobsite and that suppliers have cleaned the areas for which they are responsible. If doing so has been made part of the designer's responsibility, the interior designer may also obtain a certificate of occupancy.

For a construction project, the contractor is required to maintain a set of drawings at the jobsite. If any changes are made, they must be added to these *record drawings* so that a complete record of the construction work exists. These drawings are often referred to as *as-built drawings*, because they reflect how the interior or building was actually built rather than what was shown in the original construction drawings. Sometimes a client will request that the firm prepare a "clean" set of as-built drawings, meaning that changes are incorporated into the original drawing rather than added to the set of prints. However, the record drawings created during construction must also be retained. Of course, a copy of the specifications and of all the addenda and change orders are also kept with the record drawings set. When the project is completed, the record drawings are turned over to the interior designer or the architect by the contractor. A print or copy of the as-built drawings, the specifications, and addenda are then given to the client.

Depending on the interior designer's responsibility, contractors will invoice either the interior designer or the architect for work that has been completed. If the designer feels that the work has been done satisfactorily, he or she will issue a *certificate for payment*. This form tells the client that the supplier or contractor has completed parts or most of the work and has sent an invoice for that work, and that the interior designer recommends that the client pay the supplier for that work. Certificates for payment may be issued during the course of the project, as some subcontractors will complete all their work, have it inspected, and get final approval significantly prior to the end of the project.

The term *retainage* (also referred to as a *holdback*) is associated with the certificate for payment. Depending on the contract, the client may retain a certain amount—commonly 5 to 10 percent—to ensure that all the work is done properly and that any omissions or problems are taken care of.

Warranties and maintenance information on all equipment and products delivered as part of the project comprise another set of documents provided to the client at the end of the project. The vendors who supplied and installed the merchandise provide these documents. In addition to the documents, instructions that may be required on how to operate equipment are also provided by these vendors. If the interior designer sold the goods to the client, then he or she should be prepared to transfer the warranties and instructions and provide appropriate training to the client.

Commercial clients frequently request that the designer prepare maintenance schedules. In general, maintenance schedules inform the physical plant workers how to clean, wax, vacuum, remove stains from, and otherwise maintain the furniture, fabrics, and architectural finishes. Such a schedule can be made up from the information provided by the manufacturers. The preparation of a formal maintenance schedule is often treated as a separate design service, though it is sometimes included and charged for in the design contract.

When everything has been completed or otherwise is in accordance with the interior designer's contract, the client should make final payment to the interior designer.

POSTOCCUPANCY AND FOLLOW-UP

Good customer service and an excellent reputation come from the activities the designer conducts after the client has moved in and (hopefully) paid all the bills. The mere fact that everything that was supposed to get done has been done should not signal to the designer that he or she can forget about the project. Poor follow-up services, whether by the designer or someone responsible for repair work, can ruin an otherwise satisfactory relationship with a client. Designers should never forget that repeat business or referrals only come from satisfied clients.

An excellent way for the designer and client to review the success of a project is to do a postoccupancy evaluation. A *postoccupancy evaluation* (POE) is a thorough review of the project that includes a site visit. It is conducted perhaps a month or more after the project is completed. The goal of the POE is to determine, from both the designer's and the client's points of view, the success of the project solution and project management process and whether or not the client is satisfied. The rationale is twofold: (1) to understand client satisfaction or, more importantly, dissatisfaction with the project solutions; and (2) to improve the project processes that the interior design firm uses so that the firm can achieve even better results on future projects.

Criticism is never easy to take. Frankly, many firms do not get involved in postoccupancy evaluations of a project because the designers are afraid of hearing criticism or because they have already moved on to the next project. Nevertheless, it is shortsighted for the design firm or the designer not to seek feedback on client satisfaction (or dissatisfaction). If problems exist, the designer needs to find out and take care of them before they fester and become crises. For example, an employee who expresses dissatisfaction with a new office may not truly be unhappy with the office design, aesthetics, or furniture—he may really only need someone to tell him how to adjust the new desk chair! If this kind of problem goes undiscovered, employee criticisms can give the client the impression that the project was unsuccessful.

Formal postoccupancy evaluations can be included in the design contract or sold to the client as a separate service. These services can involve questionnaires or on-site surveys, the results of which are reported to the client. Commercial designers most frequently use the formal POE, though many of them do not. An informal postoccupancy evaluation, in which the interior designer interviews the client to determine his or her satisfaction with the project, can be done by any firm for free, or can be included for a nominal fee in the design contract's scope of services.

A postoccupancy evaluation is usually best conducted by means of some sort of questionnaire. Figure 14-2 shows a sample questionnaire. A sample form is included on the companion Web site as Item 14-2. The design firm can make up its own questionnaire structured to gather information on user satisfaction. Questions might concern the installation, aesthetics, and functional planning, or any other information that the individual designer and client want to obtain.

An in-house evaluation of the project, called by many a *post-project evaluation*, should be done soon after the project is completed. This evaluation should cover such things as a time analysis, to see if the project was completed within the time estimate; identification of any problems; and an analysis of performance by suppliers during the delivery process. It could even include a discussion of any issues with the client. The design director may also do a profitability analysis to evaluate whether the project itself was profitable. This

Postoccupancy Evaluation—Office Project

Project Area/Department_____ Date _____

The purpose of this evaluation is to help your company and the design firm assess the planning and design of your work area and the spaces of the department in the recent design project. Your answers are anonymous so please answer with complete candor.

Rate the following items using this rating scale:				
Very Satisfied	**Satisfied**	**Dissatisfied**	**Very Dissatisfied**	**Not Applicable To Me**
4	3	2	1	0

Rating

1. Work space allowance for office/work station _____
2. Layout of space and furniture meets functional work needs _____
3. Guest seating is adequate _____
4. Desk top space for paper work is adequate _____
5. Desk top space for equipment needs is adequate _____
6. Location/adjustability of my computer area _____
7. Adequate file drawer space for the next 6 months _____
8. Adequate shelves for reference materials in my office _____
9. Adequate non-file drawers for supplies in my office _____
10. Provision for security of work area and documents _____
11. Adjustability of my desk chair provides comfort _____
12. The light levels in my work area are comfortable _____
13. Task lights are adequate _____
14. My computer screen is free of glare _____
15. Acoustical privacy is adequate _____
16. Overall noise levels _____
17. The printer I use is conveniently located _____
18. The copy machine I use is conveniently located _____
19. Team areas or conference rooms are nearby _____
20. Adequate space for team sessions _____
21. Overall satisfaction with new office/work station _____
22. My work space is aesthetically pleasing _____

In this space provide comments you would like to include. Use the back of this sheet if you need to.

Thank you for your time in completing this evaluation, your candid ratings and comments!

FIGURE 14-2.

A simple postoccupancy evaluation (POE) form that can be used to evaluate an office design project. A POE document can take many formats, being adapted to meet the needs of the design firm and client.

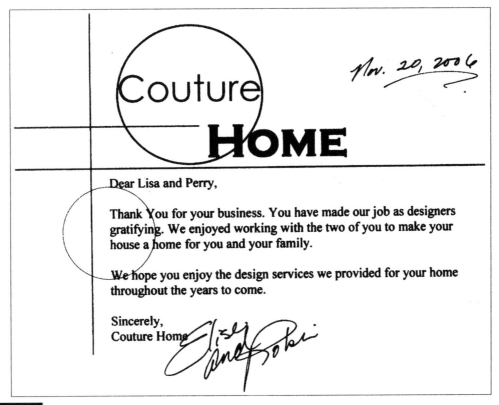

Nov. 20, 2006

Dear Lisa and Perry,

Thank You for your business. You have made our job as designers gratifying. We enjoyed working with the two of you to make your house a home for you and your family.

We hope you enjoy the design services we provided for your home throughout the years to come.

Sincerely,
Couture Home

FIGURE 14-3.

A sample note card thanking clients for their business. Good business practices mandate thank-you letters/ notes as an important follow-up. (Reproduced with permission of Robin Wagner, Wagner-Somerset Designs, Clifton, VA)

evaluation will help the design firm determine whether it should seek this kind of project in the future. Item 14-3 on the companion Web site is an example of this type of form.

Of course, the interior design firm or project manager should send a thank-you letter or postcard to the client at the conclusion of the project. Many designers drop off a small gift as part of the thank-you, such as a gift certificate for dinner or a floral arrangement.

A sincere thank-you note is most effective when it is handwritten, even if it is really a form letter. It shows an added measure of concern for the client and appreciation of his or her business (see Figure 14-3).

If a postoccupancy evaluation or meeting is not conducted, the design firm should solicit comments from the client on the handling of the project. Designers who are committed to providing their clients with excellent customer service carefully evaluate their clients' comments. They use the in-house evaluation and their clients' comments, obtained from follow-up mailings, to improve the service on any phase of the project that has been determined to be substandard. Poor customer service is, quite simply, unacceptable in a professional interior design practice.

WEB SITES RELEVANT TO THIS CHAPTER

You may wish to visit the sites for trucking firms concerning freight and shipping.

Manufacturer's Web sites will have information on shipping.

KEY TERMS

As-built drawings

Certificate of occupancy

Certificate of payment

Certificate of substantial completion

Delivery

Installation

Postoccupancy evaluation

Project closeout

Punch list

Record drawings

Retainage

Walk-through

WHAT WOULD YOU DO?

1. Dr. Milton and Dr. Sawyer hired George, Miller & Ross Design Group to plan and specify their new medical suite. They hired that firm primarily because of its reputation with green design. The doctors, whose practice specializes in allergies, want to have a LEED®-certified space to help attract new patients.

   As the design project proceeded, the clients began to have second thoughts about the costs of the green products. They asked the designers to use some "cost-effective" green products, but not to try for LEED® certification. The designers did the best they could and the doctors were pleased with the overall results.

   After the doctors moved in, they placed information on their Web site and within the practice reception area that the office had achieved LEED® certification.

2. David was embarrassed and upset when he found three notation errors in the construction drawings he had prepared for a retail store. The bid documents were released to prospective vendors yesterday. He decided to let the errors go and not tell his boss because he had made mistakes before and he was afraid he would lose his job.

3. An interior designer had been hired to specify the furniture for a cabin in a resort community. The designer was also hired to act as an owner's representative concerning the construction and interior finishing by the builder. The designer did have the proper licenses to do the work as an owner's representative.

   One of the many items the builder installed was the flooring material and all wall treatments as specified by the interior designer and approved by the client. The cost of these materials was part of the construction contract. There was an availability problem with the floor tile used throughout the first floor. After he told the interior designer about the problem, the builder replaced the original item with one that was more expensive but was in stock. The builder told the designer it was the only way to get the project done on time. He assumed that the designer had informed the client about the upcharge on the tile and went ahead and installed the more expensive tile, although he did not have a change order from the interior designer.

   On a visit to the jobsite (the client lived out of state), the husband noticed that the tile was different from the sample he thought he remembered. The designer said, "I sent you an e-mail about the tile. Your wife approved the change in material."

   "I don't remember receiving an e-mail or letter about the flooring," said the wife. "This whole project is way over budget. You claimed if we hired you as our agent, you could help keep costs down. You can pay for that mistake yourself!"

4. Kathleen specializes in work with seniors who are downsizing their homes or relocating to senior-living apartments. She was recently interviewed and hired to design a 50-unit assisted-living and nursing care facility.

   Kathleen specified tables and chairs for the dining room of the facility as well as the in-room guest chairs for the nursing care rooms. The catalog literature convinced Kathleen that the chairs would be appropriate for the ambulatory residents who sit in the assisted-living area of the facility, and that they should also work in the nursing care units. After all, the manufacturer was one of the many that specialize in furnishings for healthcare facilities.

   The purchasing agent for the facility points out that he had a bad experience with the exact same chair at another facility. Kathleen insists, "based on my experience," that the chairs will be just fine and orders them over the purchasing agent's objections.

CHAPTER 15

Creating and Managing an Interior Design Practice

After completing this chapter you should be able to:

- Describe the common characteristics of an entrepreneur.

- Evaluate your motivations regarding business ownership (using Table 15-1).

- Discuss at least three advantages and disadvantages of business ownership. Apply these to yourself as if you were about to start a business.

- Explain why it is important to obtain experience in the profession before starting a practice.

- Describe the functions of management, giving examples of how they work in an interior design firm.

- Explain the different styles of management and how each affects the work of an interior designer.

- Compare basic differences among at least three practice settings.

- Discuss some advantages and disadvantages of working alone.

- Explain the stages of a business and relate them to an interior design practice.

- Explain how planning decisions can affect the growth of a company.

- Describe how empowerment can benefit a firm.

- Discuss the kinds of research that must be undertaken when considering the purchase of an existing interior design business.

During both good times and bad, many consider starting a new interior design business. When the economy is good, designers feel it is time to spread their wings and work the way they want. When the economy is down, people who formerly worked for someone else take this as the opportunity to utilize their skills and gain experience as owner and designer.

Hundreds of thousands of new businesses are started every year, including an unknown number of interior design practices. The majority of these are small businesses with a sole practitioner or only a few employees. It is relatively easy to start a business, especially if the business is set up as a sole proprietorship (discussed in Chapter 18).

Even though it may be relatively simple to start, anyone who might consider this career track needs to do a lot of research, thinking, and planning. Wanting to be free to set one's own hours and "work the way you want to" are not the only things that need to be determined. Business skills as well as design skills are critical to having a successful interior design business. Motivation and determination must be evaluated and focused if you are to become a successful boss—even when the only person you are in charge of is you.

Planning helps the prospective business owner to clearly consider the business idea. Planning also helps determine if the idea is feasible. A plan for a new business is a tool for the owner to handle potential problems with thought rather than by pure gut reaction. Chapter 17 discusses how to go about creating a business plan for a new business.

Starting a new business also requires structure and an organization that will help it move toward profitability. The purpose of this organizational structure is to aid the owner and employees in understanding the various activities of the firm and to show who is responsible for those activities.

This chapter serves as an introduction to the idea of establishing an interior design practice. Practitioners who are ready to begin will find a wealth of information to help them make decisions as they plan and organize their practice. Students will learn that the decision to start a practice is not to be taken lightly, nor without experience in the field, no matter how tempting it might be to open a business right after graduation.

UNDERSTANDING MOTIVATIONS AND RISKS OF BUSINESS OWNERSHIP

The decision to start a new design practice must involve careful evaluation of your motivations for doing so, as well as a recognition of the risks inherent in undertaking business ownership. Unfortunately, too many people begin an interior design practice without carefully thinking through why they want their own business and the scope of the business concept. Running a professional interior design practice is a lot of hard work beyond the hard work necessary to design projects.

One of the first things to consider is personal motivation. Maybe your motivation comes from a desire to specialize in a way you could not work for an employer. You may be motivated by the idea of making more money or working for yourself. Or you may be motivated by a feeling that you can somehow "do it better" than other designers in the marketplace.

Whatever your motivations, the important point is to know and recognize what they are. Numerous questions that will help the potential business owner evaluate his or her motivations and attitudes concerning starting a new design practice are highlighted in Table 15-1. This exercise is very important and should not be taken lightly. A worksheet of this questionnaire is included on the companion Web site as Item 15-1.

Starting a business also involves risks—chief among them are legal and financial risks. There can be legal consequences to starting a business in your home. Many homeowners associations have very strict prohibitions on operating a business from a residence. Most jurisdictions also prohibit a business in the home if employees are hired.

Licensing or registration laws can affect the work of the interior designer beyond interior design title or licensing laws. Contracting for certain services in the client's name often requires licenses the designer must obtain. Clients may take legal action against you if you are negligent in performing the required

TABLE 15-1.

Personal motivations for and attitudes about starting a new design practice

These sample questions should be used to evaluate your motivations and attitudes toward starting your own business. If you are seriously thinking of starting your own business in the near future, use these questions only as a starting point to determine your interest and sincerity.

1. Why do you want to own your own business?
2. Are you dissatisfied with your present job? Why?
3. Are you prepared for the sacrifices of your personal time and energy that you will have to make?
4. How do your present skills and abilities prepare you for business ownership?
5. Do you have finances available to commit to the business venture, or must you obtain outside start-up financing?
6. Are you willing and able to survive financially without a regular salary or paycheck?
7. Do you have sufficient experience in the interior design industry to operate and maintain a design practice?
8. Do you have clients who will switch to your business if you leave your current employer?
9. Are you a self-starter, or do you need direction in your present work situation?
10. Are you willing to work the extra hours that are often required of a business owner?
11. Are you good at performing many tasks at the same time, or are you better when you only have to do one thing at a time?
12. What skills and abilities do you have that you can offer potential clients?
13. Why would a customer desire your services more than those of other interior designers?
14. Have you done any evaluation of potential competitors?
15. Are you prepared to handle the difficulties of operating your own business during the start-up year and beyond?
16. Can you work without others around, or do you need others to help keep you motivated?
17. What kinds of business skills or experiences do you have to operate a business?
18. Are you a good organizer?
19. Do you have a lot of self-confidence?
20. Is the financial risk involved in having your own business acceptable?
21. Is your present financial condition in a satisfactory state for you to start a business?
22. Are family members prepared to accept your long hours and lack of attention as you start and operate your own business?
23. If your business is to be located at home, do you have sufficient space and privacy to perform your work activities?
24. Can you define the kind of design firm you want in only three sentences?

services. Becoming involved in design work for which you are experienced and capable should help lessen the potential for negligent performance. It is critical to understand any limitations and requirements on the business concept before "hanging out your shingle."

Financial risk is affected by many factors. It can take tens of thousands of dollars to start up a design practice and survive during the first year alone. In addition, the entrepreneur must consider how he or she will pay personal expenses while waiting for revenues to be realized. Banks are reluctant to loan money to many small businesses for start-up funding. Besides, banks will not loan funds to a budding entrepreneur for living expenses, regardless of how great the business idea appears.

An evaluation of the personal financial risk entailed in starting a new design practice begins by determining the amount of funds you need each month to pay living expenses. Figure 15-1 is a simple form that will help you determine personal living expenses. Please note that this form is not all-inclusive; you may have personal living expenses that are not shown here. Be sure you include them in your calculations. A worksheet to calculate personal living expenses is included on the companion Web site as Item 15-2. It is generally suggested that the new business owner set aside at least one year's

Item	Monthly Amount	Annual	Notes
Housing			
Rent/mortgage			
Association fees			
Insurance			
Landscaping			
Property taxes			
Utilities			
Electric/gas			
Telephone and cell			
TV (cable)			
Internet			
Water/sewer			
Groceries			
Automobile			
Payment			
Gas/maintenance			
Insurance			
Plates/tags			
Autoclub			
Medical			
Health insurance			
Prescriptions			
Dental			
Miscellaneous			
Credit cards (total)			
Other loans			
Clothing & laundry			
Subscriptions*			
Child care			
Housekeeper			
Savings/investments			
Entertainment			
Gifts & charities			
Health club			
Other clubs**			
TOTAL			

*Magazines that are not business expenses

**Clubs that are non-business organizations

© Christine M. Piotrowski

FIGURE 15-1.

Personal expenses can be calculated on this form. It is helpful in budgeting for a new business venture.

living expenses before starting a small business. It can take a new business at least one year to generate enough revenue for the business to be able to pay the owner a salary.

The overall business concept has an impact on personal financial risk. The more ambitious the plans are for the business, the greater the risk. A practice that involves an employee or even a small showroom as part of the business concept will require a larger amount of start-up funds than many other arrangements. Any design practice with a high overhead will put more strain on the designer's ability to meet personal financial obligations as well as business obligations. Willingness to live on less while the business gets on its feet may be an important consideration. Careful evaluation, savings, and planning of personal financial responsibilities are very important parts of planning a new design practice.

Many practitioners and educators I have talked to have said to be sure and caution students against thinking of starting a design company too soon after graduation. It is quite common for students to be given an assignment in a business practices class to create a business for a fictitious company. However, receiving an "A" on that assignment does not guarantee success. Regardless of one's previous experience, age, or financial situation, starting a practice without experience in the field rarely leads to success for recent design program graduates.

What Is an Entrepreneur?

Most people regard anyone who starts a business as an entrepreneur. An *entrepreneur* is someone who is willing to take a risk by starting and managing his or her own business. Many entrepreneurs are also visionaries or innovators, doing things differently because they feel they have a better way to provide services or to manufacture and sell products.

It should not matter whether an interior design business is truly different and visionary. Given enough thought and planning, an interior designer can develop a design business idea that is cutting-edge for its area and contrasts with all the other design firms in the market. Providing services that clients want and meeting the needs of target clients is a good route to success in this profession.

Are there any specific characteristics of an entrepreneur that "guarantee" the individual and his or her business idea will be a success? Not really. An entrepreneur does need experience in the industry. Obtaining experience in the business world helps the individual understand that having a business means hard work and long hours. Entrepreneurs are also ambitious, are independent, have a lot of self-confidence, are passionate about their business, and are committed to making it work. They understand that it is common to put in long days, not thinking about punching in at 8:00 AM and out at 5:00 PM. A business owner understands long hours, working at home, and even not receiving much in the way of salary for perhaps many years. Much of what might otherwise be salary for the business owner must be retained in the business to help it become and remain financially stable.

Being the boss is fun. It is also risky and a ton of hard work. Knowing what it is that you are trying to accomplish with a design practice and how you are going to go about accomplishing that purpose are critical to business success.

ADVANTAGES AND DISADVANTAGES OF BUSINESS OWNERSHIP

Having independence to make your own decisions about clients and projects and expecting to earn greater income are probably the top reasons interior designers decide to start their own businesses. Certainly there are advantages to owning a business. Naturally, there are also disadvantages, and at times these will seem to outweigh the advantages. Part of the decision-making process in owning your own business is to look at both the advantages and the disadvantages—especially the disadvantages—of ownership to be sure that you are prepared to accept these constraints.

Advantages

- Independence. As the boss, the owner makes the decisions. For some, of course, this can turn into a disadvantage.
- Personal satisfaction in achieving success.
- Having the opportunity to perform the kind of design work the individual most enjoys.
- Job security. The job exists as long as the business succeeds and the owner wishes to remain in the business.
- Lifestyle. When you own the business, you can decide how many hours a week you work, where the business is located, when to spend more time with family, and other lifestyle matters.
- Making a potentially higher income drawn from the business's profits.
- Greater opportunity for personal recognition.
- Increased contact with clients, suppliers, and other industry members. The owner makes more client contacts, deals directly with suppliers, and has the opportunity to meet others in many areas of the design industry.
- Depending on the business form selected, there may be tax benefits.

Disadvantages

- Longer hours. Though you may start a business to work fewer hours, many entrepreneurs find they end up working 12-hour days, often 7 days a week, with little time off for vacations or for a personal or social life. This is especially true in the first few years of the life of the business.
- Greater stress. The stress of bringing in enough business to meet all the bills can weigh heavily.
- Financial risk. Personal assets are usually at risk, as new business owners typically finance a start-up with personal savings and personal credit.
- Legal liability. Owners are liable for their own actions, as well as those of their employees.
- Income may be minimal and even nonexistent during the first year or more. New business owners who have not thought out how to financially operate the business often find that the profits they expected are low.
- Greater tax burdens. For example, depending on the business form, the owner pays both the employer and employee portion of Social Security tax on income as self-employment tax.
- Need to satisfy customers. Even though a business owner is the boss, he or she is now controlled by the wishes of the client. There is no one else to negotiate with dissatisfied or demanding clients.

- Greater management responsibility. Business and employee management is the owner's responsibility. Many designers who start their own practice lack management skills.

- Less design input. As the business grows, the design owner often finds that he or she is spending less time on design and more time on managing the business.

- No employment benefits for the owner. Benefits such as workers' compensation and unemployment insurance do not exist for owners in most cases. Health insurance costs are also totally paid by the owner.

- Job security. The owner's job is secure only if the business remains active and solvent.

- Less flexibility. It is not easy to quit if the business owner finds that he or she does not enjoy ownership or otherwise no longer wishes to remain in business. A financial loss might result from closing down. It can also be difficult even to take a vacation.

It is an unfortunate reality that the disadvantages often outnumber and outweigh the advantages when it comes to business ownership. This reality should not discourage anyone from starting his or her own business—on the contrary! The intention in pointing out these issues is to be sure that the potential business owner realizes the risks involved and contemplates the business venture thoroughly before starting a new design practice. A good starting point to help the interior designer appraise the fundamental business idea is to answer the questions in Table 15-2. A worksheet of this table has been included on the companion site as Item 15-3.

FUNCTIONS OF MANAGEMENT

Starting an interior design business in which you are the sole employee and owner is risky in any economy. Ownership of an interior design practice comes with obligations that many have not recognized or faced. Most interior designers do not receive much formal management training. Whether the practice is a "me, myself, and I" arrangement or involves employees, owning a business requires management activities often beyond the experience and training of the would-be entrepreneur. Even if the designer has no desire to own a practice, understanding the manager's job will help him or her be a better employee.

So what does management encompass? At a general level, *management* consists of the effective direction of financial resources and staff members under the owner's or manager's control to positively affect the goals and objectives of the business. This concept applies to every business, from a small firm with a sole practitioner to a large, multidiscipline design firm with several layers of employees.

Management includes a multitude of tasks and responsibilities. In a small practice, the owner wears many hats: marketing for new clients, producing design project work, drafting contracts for new projects, billing and ordering goods, perhaps hiring and supervising an employee or two. And these examples are but a very few of the tasks involved in managing a practice. In a large firm, tasks may be delegated to different responsibility areas, each with a separate manager. For example, in a large firm it is unlikely that the manager supervising design employees will also be directly responsible for typing up invoices to clients.

TABLE 15-2.

A questionnaire to help the potential business owner define the business idea

These questions are intended to help you define your overall business idea, so answer them carefully. Be as specific as possible in your responses. The information from this questionnaire can be used to develop your business plan.

Have you clarified your design and business skills?
What experience do you have in interior design, architecture, and/or construction?
What experience do you have in sales and marketing?
What experience do you have in managing other individuals?
What business experience or knowledge do you have?

Define your business.
What services (exactly) will you offer initially?
Will you sell products?
Do you plan to have inventory?
How will you price your services (fee methods)?
How will you price the products you sell?
How will you receive and deliver goods to clients?
Have you considered what language will go into design contracts?

Do you know who your customers will be?
How many potential customers are in your business area?
How many of these customers do you think you can attract?
Will your customers perceive your prices as competitive?
Will your customers see a difference between your services and your competition's services?
What income group will your business appeal to?

What kind of finances will be required to start your business?
What business licenses will be required? Cost?
Are you going to start your business at home? Is this legally possible in your community?
If you are going to have your business in a commercial space, have you investigated rental costs?
What kind of equipment and furniture will be necessary to start your business? What is the estimated cost of purchase?
What are the possibilities for leasing these items?
What kind of income are you seeking for yourself for the first year? Use this (along with estimated expenses) to determine how much revenue you will need to generate monthly. Is this possible, considering your business idea, number of potential customers, and competition?

Have you researched the competition?
Who are your main competitors?
How many other firms like yours exist within two miles?
How many other firms like yours exist within your business area?
What can you do that your competition is not already doing?
Do you know how much your competition charges for its services/products?
Why would your customers buy from you rather than an existing competitor?

How will clients find out about your business?
Will you do mass mailings?
Will you use advertising? What kind and in what media?
Are you going to develop marketing tools, such as a brochure?
Have you considered the design of your letterhead and other business stationery?

Regardless of the size of the interior design practice, a manager performs four broad, generally accepted functions: planning, organizing, leading, and controlling. An important overall task related to these functions is decision making. Within these four broad functions are the important tasks that all successful managers undertake. Although the term *manager* is used extensively in this section, this discussion also applies to the owner of a small business or those working in a large design firm. Several tasks concerning these key functions are noted here.

The *planning function*

- Help chart the future direction of the firm.
- Use reasoning to proactively anticipate and solve problems.
- Focus on the big picture for long-term success.
- Provide direction for day-to-day decision making.
- Incorporate techniques and approaches for long-term strategic planning (discussed in detail in Chapter 20).

The *organizing function*

- Assist the manager in determining how best to use available resources.
- Determine roles for the different employees.
- Establish how projects will be done.

The *leadership function*

- Assemble individual talents and skills of the group into a cohesive whole.
- Delegate responsibility and authority.
- Mentor others to meet the goals of the design firm.
- Empower employees to make things happen themselves. *Empowerment* can be defined as "giving employees [who are] responsible for hands-on production or service activities the authority to make decisions or take action without prior approval."[1]

The *control function*

- Monitor the activities of employees to ensure that the plans, policies, and decisions of the manager and the firm are being carried out.
- Make adjustments or develop new evaluative mechanisms to help the firm achieve its goals and objectives.
- Monitor costs and expenses in relationship to the generation of revenue to enhance the possibility of profitability.

A primary, overarching function of the owner or manager, which applies to all four of the management functions, is decision making. *Decision making* is the act of making reasonable choices among the alternatives available. It is part of all the other management functions and seems to occur almost all the time in the manager's day. For example, the owner must decide which employees to assign to a new design project or who will be part of a team to complete a project.

These management functions are continually intermixed. Managers find themselves engaged in all these functions every day. This reality is part of the stress and excitement of the management role. There are many fine books on management in libraries and bookstores. Readers may wish to review one or more of these books (several are listed in the references at the end of the book) or even take a course in management to gain a more complete understanding of the management function.

When you own a firm, you are responsible for all aspects of the firm. An important topic when you have employees is leadership. This too is the subject of much investigation and research; almost any library will offer many books in this area. A brief article on leadership has been included on the companion Web site as Item 15-4.

MANAGEMENT STYLES

As an owner or manager, you will, of course, bring your own personality to management. Your management style likely will fit into one of the two categories of management style: autocratic (authoritative) or democratic (facilitative).

When a manager used an *autocratic* style of management, planning and decision making move from the top down, from the manager to the staff. Very little staff input is requested or even tolerated. This style of management is often apparent in small firms, where the owner performs all the management functions. For a sole proprietor, this is essentially the only choice for making decisions as to how things will be done. It is also practiced in many larger firms that have more structure and organizational levels.

An autocratic style does not mean that the manager is going to be a difficult person to work for. It does mean that the employees are expected to do the design work and project management in the way the owner/manager has dictated that it be done. An autocratic or authoritative manager allows little room for individual decision making and initiative.

In contrast, in a company that is managed in a *democratic* or facilitative style, staff input is desired and solicited; responsibility is often given to staff members to accomplish tasks without direct interaction from the manager. From an employee's point of view, this democratic style is usually most favored.

It is important to note that sometimes a democratic style of management can become a problem for the design firm. For example, if employees start making promises that the firm cannot keep, the reputation of the whole design firm is tarnished. The democratic manager must delegate but also set limits so that employee decisions do not work to the detriment of the firm.

A democratic type of manager can exist in any size firm, just as the autocratic type of manager can show up in any size firm. There is no way to predict which management style will predominate in a particular interior design firm. Design employees tend to prefer the democratic style of management, since most creative people like the freedom that this style of management provides. Knowing the style of management under which you work best can help you make a decision as to which employment offers you will accept. Knowing your own style of management will also help when you are hiring employees.

Types of Practice Organizations

The type of practice you start has a huge impact on many of the decisions you will make over the first several months, if not years, of the existence of your business. The exact nature of the business is as varied as owners' desires and business concepts. There are some common ways in which you might structure your design business. These are sometimes called *business models*.

An individually owned design business operating from a home office or commercial location.

A design business operating from a commercial location that is jointly owned by more than one individual. The business may focus on interior design or may be a combination of interiors and architecture.

A design studio that usually operates from a commercial location and includes some display of furniture or accessory items for sale.

A retail store featuring a combination of furniture items and accessories to meet your interests and goals. You will probably also provide interior design services.

This store may be focused on residential products, commercial products, or a combination.

A retail store specializing in an item such as accessories, lighting, or other interior products. Design services may also be provided.

A trade studio is an option when you have decided to represent interiors products for sale to other designers. Generally, this type of business does not offer products directly to the end user.

This by no means describes all the ways your design business may be structured or focused. It just provides a jumping-off point for you to consider as you plan your new venture. Many of the career options discussed in Chapter 5 can also be the basis of a business organization.

WORKING ALONE

Free to work when you want and how you want! Working alone has a lot of advantages, and is a big reason why many start an interior design practice. Working alone can also mean having the freedom to do interior design work in the way you really want to do it, without constraints being placed on you by a boss. It means that all the profits stay with the owner—you. However, "[f]ree isn't easy. It means risks. It means responsibility. It means hard work."[2]

Working alone also has disadvantages and pitfalls that can keep you from realizing the freedom that you imagined, as well as from realizing the profits from the business that you expected. Maintaining the discipline to keep to the task at hand is a big problem for many people working alone. Some find that they are procrastinators, putting off unpleasant or boring tasks like record-keeping. When you work alone, you are responsible for all of the business tasks as well as the design tasks. Then again, there is the possibility that the designer will become a workaholic, never taking time off to pursue personal interests.

Sometimes the realization of how alone "alone" can be is pretty hard to take. It is not easy for many who enjoy the social interaction that comes with working with other designers to make the transition to being the only one to answer the phone and do all the work. The silence of a home office can be unnerving and lonely. For many, it is a big test of willpower and discipline.

Too many designers start a business without understanding the risks. As a sole practitioner, it is up to you to develop business and find new clients. All businesses have expenses, and you will need to raise the funds through your project revenues to pay those expenses. If you make a mistake that causes physical or business harm, you are responsible for the consequences and perhaps even legal judgments. All of this and more come with starting a business and working alone.

Here are some guidelines that will help to make working alone a positive experience:

- Determine what you want to offer and whether those services are really needed by clients in your area.
- Understand that the probability of making a lot of money during the first year—even the first three years—is an illusion.
- Consider what success really means to you. Is it more money, freedom, or something else?
- Keep yourself charged up. Become involved in your professional association chapter, network with clients at their associations, or start a

network group of like-minded designers who could also use some camaraderie.

- Set goals that are challenging yet attainable. Do not undermine your confidence by setting goals that are impossible to meet.
- Give yourself a break. Take that mini-vacation. Attend a trade show or a conference. Have lunch with old friends. Look out the window and remember to smell the roses!

Owning one's own business and working alone are an exciting challenge as well as a scary proposition. It takes courage to start any new business. Carefully considering what you are trying to achieve and why, planning how to go about achieving those results, and then having the determination to do it will likely give you a great deal of pleasure and enjoyment!

THE STAGES OF A BUSINESS

One could suppose that a design firm exists on a continuum from start-up to its closing (for whatever reason). However, that is not really what happens. A design firm goes through several different stages as it survives and grows. These stages reflect the energy put into the business by the owner and employees, as well as the general viability of the business.

To understand these stages for an interior design business, it is helpful to look at the life cycles of products as described in marketing textbooks. When a new product first hits the market, sales will be low, as consumers have not really felt the need for the new product. Consider cell phones: for quite a while, only certain businesses and high-level executives had car phones, and only a few individuals even dreamed about mobile telephones. This first stage is called *market introduction*.

The next phase, called *market growth*, begins when sales of the product increase substantially, providing increased profits to the company. Depending on the product, this increase in sales and resulting profit can last a long time—as is the case with cell phones—or be fairly short-lived, as competitors start to sell similar products.

When a product becomes successful, competitors come into the market and sales of the original product decrease or the profit margin decreases. In this third phase, called *market maturity*, sales for the originating company fall off as competitors enter the market and siphon off sales. To some degree, this happened to the cell phone market as more and more companies jumped into the market. Reinvention has kept products like the iPhone on top of the cycle.

Unless something dramatic is done, the product enters the fourth and final phase—*market decline*—as sales of the product diminish for the original company as well as for most of the competition (see Figure 15-2). Obviously, in our example of cell phones, the market has not declined or even matured yet. It is still in a growth stage for all producers of this product. It continues to grow as the various products go through design and feature changes, creating a market for new sales.

The premise here is that similar stages exist for interior design businesses (Figure 15-3). In the earliest stage of any new practice, the emphasis is on introducing the company to the marketplace, obtaining clients, and earning revenues to sustain the firm. A client base must be established, and a good reputation for excellent design and customer service must be developed. The main concern is survival, and the focus is on producing work that will result in revenue. This is comparable to the market introduction stage of a product's life cycle.

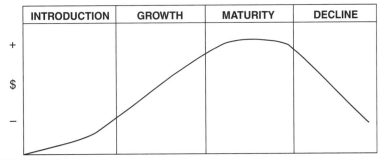

FIGURE 15-2.

The standard product life cycle.

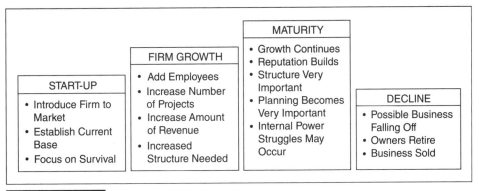

FIGURE 15-3.

The growth cycle of a typical interior design firm.

As the firm grows and employees are added, the focus of the business often changes. This stage is akin to the market growth stage in a product's life cycle. New organizational structure is needed to handle the added employees and the many challenges of increased business. The owner must consider whether he or she will spend time on design projects, marketing, or managing the firm. The small, personal, "family" business of the early days begins to disappear, because the owner has to be in too many places at the same time. Chaos can soon rule if the owner is uncomfortable with the added management responsibilities. This is often the time when the owner seeks out individuals with specialized management or other business skills so that the owner can continue to generate designs. Pressure heightens to increase revenues in order to pay for the added overhead. Organizational structure is very important at this stage.

Continued growth and expansion find the firm in a mature stage that it is hoped will never resemble the last stage of a product's life cycle, market decline. The design firm now has a confirmed reputation, perhaps even an award-winning staff. It probably also has become more specialized and can to some degree be choosy about clients and projects. It may have grown to the point that strong departmentalized units have been formed around specialties or services. A more formalized reporting structure, referred to as a *chain of command*, between one level of employee and another could be necessary in larger firms. Figure 27-1 shows an organizational chart that explains chain of command.

Of course, any interior design firm can enter the decline phase of the life cycle. A major contributing member of the firm might move on to start his or her own practice. Maybe the owner reaches a point at which doing design and managing the office are no longer of interest. Some owners reach retirement age and desire to retire. And, of course, some firms simply decline due to poor management, poor marketing, and mediocre financial management.

Regardless of the size of the firm, these stages or cycles are going to occur. Naturally, the larger the firm grows, the more critical and complex these issues become. Planning for growth, regardless of what form that growth takes, is important to the success of any company. A discussion of how to plan for continued growth appears in Chapter 20, along with the discussion of strategic planning.

BUYING AN EXISTING BUSINESS

One alternative for those who wish to have a practice without the challenges of starting from scratch is to buy an existing business. Many practitioners look forward to the day when they are in a position to sell their established business. They may reach this decision because they want to retire, or they may just have a feeling that withdrawal from the business is an appropriate idea.

There are many reasons why buying an existing business is a good idea. The new owner begins with an established client list, and many of these clients will potentially continue work with the new owner. Employees may stay on and help the new owner keep the business going. Organizational and process issues are lessened because an existing business is already structured. Initial start-up costs to run the business may be lower. (Of course, there will be costs involved in purchasing the business.) There is also less risk for the first year, as the existing client base and reputation of the company will help bring in new customers.

Naturally, there are some disadvantages as well. Buying a business is often more expensive than starting from scratch. It is important to investigate the reputation of the existing business to be sure it is in good standing. The prospective buyer must be sure that the existing target client suits his or her interests. You must be sure to do in-depth research regarding financial status, credit rating, and relationships with vendors; you do not want to buy a bunch of liabilities! Any inventory that is part of the purchase might be items that are difficult to sell to your future clients. Equipment—especially computers and other office machines—might be out-of-date and expensive to replace.

Before making an offer to purchase an existing business, the prospective owner should do at least these key tasks:

- Do plenty of research before you decide to buy someone else's business— no matter how great that other designer's reputation might be. Attorneys call this kind of research *due diligence*. A thorough research task involves finding out everything you can about all aspects of the business.

- Be sure you clearly understand why the business is for sale. Although it may be offered simply because the owner wishes to retire, it might also be put up for sale because of legal or financial problems.

- Develop a *letter of intent* that is a nonbinding offer to purchase the business. This letter of intent will help you obtain confidential information about the business, such as financial and client information. It can also serve as a draft of the information that your attorney feels should be included in the eventual purchase agreement.

- Talk to your accountant to see if the asking price is in line with that of other service businesses. Although your accountant might not have any local reference points, he or she may have contacts with accounting colleagues who can give comparison-pricing information in other cities or states.

- Carefully investigate the company's financial records for the past five years. A long financial history review will give you a better idea of how successful the firm and its name will be in the future. Of course, your accountant should be very involved in this review. Make sure you see profit and loss statements, balance sheets, and income tax forms for those five years.

- Beware of exaggerated profit claims or extensive client lists that do not seem logical or reasonable. Remember that due diligence is required concerning all aspects of the organization, including client lists and financial standing.

- Have your attorney determine if the company has ever been sued or has any judgments pending. You should also check other agencies, like the Registrar of Contractors, Better Business Bureau, and professional associations to which the owner belongs, to be sure there are no active or pending problems or complaints attaching to the company's name that could be harmful to you in the future.

- Remember that you are not only buying equipment, inventory, and library materials. You are buying the company name. Make sure that name is well regarded. Investigate the business by talking to vendors, past customers if possible, credit rating services, and other sources that can tell you something about a company.

This is only a brief overview of what is involved in deciding to buy a business. In-depth details on this decision process and valuation of a business the reader might wish to purchase are beyond the scope of this book. A few of the books listed in the references will provide additional guidance on these matters.

WEB SITES RELEVANT TO THIS CHAPTER

www.cra-arc.gc.ca Canada Revenue Agency

www.mbda.gov Minority Business Development Agency

www.score.org SCORE, a division of the U.S. Small Business Administration

www.sba.gov U.S. Small Business Administration

KEY TERMS

Autocratic management style	Letter of intent
Chain of command	Management
Control function	Market decline
Decision making	Market growth
Democratic management style	Market introduction
Due diligence	Market maturity
Empowerment	Planning function
Entrepreneur	

WHAT WOULD YOU DO?

1. George took his client to a furniture trade showroom to look at living room and bedroom items. Unbeknownst to George, the client had previously obtained a resale tax license, planning to use it to buy furniture directly from suppliers. The client returns to the showroom without George. The sales representative tells the client details about the discount and commission program that the furniture company has offered to George and is willing to offer to the client as well, since the client has a resale license.

2. Arne visits the purchasing manager for a long-standing client; he needs to drop off a revised floor plan for another section of the office complex. He didn't make an appointment, as he had already discussed the changes in the plan. Arne also brought some alternate fabric samples for conference room chairs.

   The purchasing manager is in his office, and as soon as Arne pokes his head in to say "hello," the client begins to berate Arne for his recommendation of vendors for the furniture being installed that week. "Those guys are idiots!" screams the client. "They have totally disrupted the office and now I understand they have damaged the carpet in the CEO's office! How could you recommend such incompetent fools?!" exclaims the purchasing manager.

3. Ralph and Michael have owned a residential design firm for four years. They have had several high-end clients and have also won awards for their design work. Recently, as the economy has become tight, they have been struggling to get new work that will cover their costs. A vendor with whom they have worked only a few times offers them a special discount for any merchandise they order from him during this year. The special discount also includes reimbursement for both of them to attend the High Point furniture show next year. The special discount and incentive trip are very appealing to Michael. Ralph, however, does not want to become involved with this vendor.

4. Joy Anderson specified window treatments, flooring, and furniture for two different clients living in two different high-rise condominiums located in the same city in the Southwest. The unit for the Joneses is on the 20th floor of a building in the central city. The living room is positioned in a corner and has windows on the south and west. The Brown's unit—located in a building eight miles away, is on the 9th floor of the building. Mrs. Brown's bedroom space has windows on the west, but the living room has windows facing north.

   Joy completed the design of the unit for Mrs. Brown last year. She got permission from Mrs. Brown to show photos of the residence in her portfolio, but is not allowed to indicate the location other than as being in a high-rise building.

   Mrs. Jones wants the drapery treatment that she saw in Joy's portfolio photo, which happens to be of the Brown residence, for her living room. Mrs. Jones insists on the drapery fabric shown in the photo of the Brown residence, along with a dark-colored carpet. Joy orders the merchandise, and both products are now ready for installation.

   In the meantime, Mrs. Brown and Mrs. Jones met at an art guild association's meeting a week ago. Mrs. Brown lamented about the sun fading of her drapery to Mrs. Jones. Mrs. Brown also told Mrs. Jones that she was having a hard time getting the interior designer (whom she did not name) to do anything about the fading. Now Mrs. Jones wants to cancel her order because she is afraid of sun fading as well.

REFERENCES

1. Ivancevich, Lorenzi, and Skinner, 1994, p. 261.
2. Fisher, 1995, p. 14.

CHAPTER 16

Advice and Counsel

After reading this chapter you should be able to:

- Explain the different roles an attorney plays in advising a practice owner.
- Understand the differences between an accountant, certified public accountant, and certified tax preparer.
- Be able to explain the basic accounting terms presented in Table 16-1.
- Discuss how a banker advises a practice owner.
- Compare debt capital and investment capital.
- Name and define the types of information a creditor will probably require for a business loan application.
- Discuss some ways in which a business can establish business credit with vendors.
- Identify the types of insurance that a sole practitioner operating out of his or her home should obtain.
- Identify the types of insurance that a partnership operating from a studio located in a shopping center will need.
- Explain malpractice and errors and omissions insurance.
- Discuss ways in which technical consultants might be used by a residential and commercial design practice.

NCIDQ COMPONENT

Based on best information available, some material in this chapter might appear as part of the NCIDQ examination. The reader should not depend solely on this text for study material. See the sections on working with attorneys, accountants, and other business specialists; insurance; financing a business; and business credit.

Whether you are a student assigned a project to create a business or a practitioner desiring to actually start a new business, understanding the roles of various business advisers is a natural and important step in starting an interior design firm. Very few people have expertise in all areas of business, so the prospective business owner should find the best advisers possible to help establish and maintain the interior design practice.

This chapter discusses the most important advisers one should consider engaging when starting—or operating—an interior design practice. They are:

- An attorney, who will render assistance in many legal areas
- An accountant, who provides information concerning financial and tax matters
- A banker, who may help obtain the financing needed to operate the interior design practice
- Insurance advisers, who help obtain proper insurance protection
- Technical consultants, who are the many allied professionals who help the interior designer with specialized design problems

This chapter also includes information on other key topics related to business advisers and advice. A discussion on sources of capital and establishing business credit follows the section on the importance of a banker as a business consultant. Additional information on many types of business insurance is also included. Note that this chapter's topics will also benefit the practitioner who has had a business for a few years and may be contemplating taking the business in a new direction.

ATTORNEY

The design firm owner must constantly be looking out for his or her best interests in a legal and ethical manner. Attorneys can assist the owner in understanding the numerous legal questions pertaining to starting a business, as well as issues that may arise during the life of the business. We hope the advice sought will not be necessitated by legal entanglements with clients; avoiding problems up front is much less expensive than retaining an attorney to handle a legal complication.

An interior design business may seek the advice of an attorney for several reasons. Here are some services that an attorney can provide on behalf of an interior design firm:

- Review design contract formats and clauses
- Advise on questions concerning liability
- Review leases, purchase agreements, purchase orders, and other business forms
- Advise the owner who is considering a change in the legal form of the business
- Provide counsel on how to avoid a potential lawsuit and represent the firm if it is sued
- Provide counsel concerning required licenses and permits
- Assist with intellectual property issues such as copyright
- Resolve employee rights, safety, and compensation questions
- Assist with questions concerning estate planning
- Assist with collection problems

Attorneys specialize in areas of legal practice. You should look for an attorney who has a strong background in business law. Obviously, an attorney familiar with the interior design, architecture, and building industry is more desirable than one who has never dealt with this industry before. The attorney for an interior designer or design business should be familiar with contract law, negotiation, and arbitration. Other business issues, such as copyright and labor law, may be more the area of specialists. Sometimes colleagues in a professional association will recommend their attorney; the local bar association may also be able to refer you to one or more prospective attorneys. There is additional information concerning hiring an attorney on the companion Web site as Item 16-1.

ACCOUNTANT

Financial recordkeeping is of the utmost importance for any interior design firm. The business needs accurate financial records to accurately report income to the state and federal government, to report sales taxes when merchandise is sold, and to help the owner understand the firm's financial position.

The firm owner or a bookkeeper performs day-to-day financial recordkeeping that may include daily posting, calculating, and verifying of financial records of the firm. A *bookkeeper* is an individual trained in financial recordkeeping who is hired to perform financial recordkeeping transactions. An *accountant* usually has more expertise than a bookkeeper in the preparation and analysis of financial reports, such as the balance sheet and profit and loss statement. Most new firms and sole practitioner practices will probably do their own recordkeeping or hire a bookkeeper. An accountant can help a new firm determine what accounts to set up, as well as suggesting a methodology for financial recordkeeping.

A *certified public accountant (CPA)* is an individual who has met educational and testing requirements established by the jurisdiction. A CPA holds a license to practice accounting that differs from the license of a bookkeeper or noncertified accountant. Another type of accountant is a *professional tax preparer,* who has the training and experience to interpret tax laws in relationship to the owner's actual business operations. A professional tax preparer is not necessarily a CPA, although this type of accountant will also be able to provide other accounting services. It is important to hire an accounting consultant who is familiar with the interior design business. Many general accountants, who are unfamiliar with the peculiarities of this industry, have problems in properly advising interior designers.

Accountants can do many things for a design firm besides prepare income tax returns and formal accounting reports. Some additional services include:

- Helping the small business owner organize financial and office management procedures and records.
- Preparing or advising on preparation of quarterly income tax statements and annual tax forms.
- Providing guidance as to what financial software program might be most appropriate for the business.
- Helping the owner to prepare records needed to obtain loans.
- Providing investment counseling.
- Advising on the firm's sales tax liabilities to various jurisdictions. City, county, and state or provincial jurisdictions have different regulations concerning sales taxes on goods and services sold to the consumer.

- Recommending operational changes that can help the firm reduce income taxes.
- Depending on the accountant's license, serving as the design practice's representative to the Internal Revenue Service concerning tax questions.
- Suggesting changes in business operations and procedures as the design practice grows.

An accountant who is familiar with interior design or architecture services is the ideal candidate for the interior design firm. It is important that the accountant be someone who will talk plainly and answer questions about the design firm's financial situation. Many small business owners become intimidated by their accountant and never understand the actual financial condition of the company. Item 16-2 on the companion Web site provides additional information you should consider when hiring an accountant.

Table 16-1 defines a few of the terms and reports concerning accounting that are discussed in this chapter. These items are discussed more thoroughly in Chapter 21, along with other basic accounting information.

BANKER

An ongoing relationship with a commercial banker is needed when a firm begins, as well as while it grows. A banker who is accustomed to with working with small businesses is especially useful. Getting to know your banker is important, as this relationship helps make it easier to obtain the loans needed for various business endeavors.

The prospective business owner should be sure that the loan officer and others with whom he or she is working will always be willing to explain how things work. Your banker should readily answer questions on, for example, how the loan process is structured or the charges for commercial checking accounts. (Commercial accounts are subject to charges and conditions that do not apply to personal accounts.)

The business will need a commercial checking account, a savings account, and perhaps a payroll account. A sole proprietorship—a common

---

TABLE 16-1.

Accounting terms and reports

Accounts. Financial entries with different names for clarification to show additions (increases) and subtractions (decreases) in the account.

Balance sheet. An accounting form that shows the firm's financial position at a particular moment in time, including a statement of its assets and liabilities; sometimes called a statement of financial position.

Expenses. The amount of a firm's outflows of resources as a consequence of the firm's efforts to earn revenue.

Income statement. An accounting report that formally displays all the revenues and expenses of a firm for a stated period of time. The result shows the net income (or loss) for the firm during the period; also called a profit and loss statement.

Net profit. The amount of funds left during an accounting period after all expenses are paid and any retained earnings are determined and funded.

Operating funds. The amount of funds that are required every month to operate and keep the business open for the month.

Revenue. The amount of inflows from the sale of goods or rendering of services during an accounting period.

Additional detailed accounting terms are defined and discussed in Chapter 21.

business form in interior design—should have a commercial checking account if the company name is a fictitious or trade name (see Chapter 19). Otherwise, a checking account (and other accounts) separate from the owner's personal checking account should be obtained to keep business funds separated from personal funds.

Small business owners often obtain business or "corporate" credit cards from the bank where they have their commercial account. These credit cards can be used for travel expenses, items that otherwise might be paid for with petty cash, or any number of other small expense items for the business. They should be used cautiously to purchase high-priced items for the business or otherwise pay business bills. Designers with good credit may use the business credit card to make purchases of goods that will be resold to clients.

Here are some additional services useful to an interior design firm available from a banker:

- Offer credit card services so clients can purchase on credit
- Make available payroll services when the firm has several employees
- Provide the designer with help in checking credit references of clients
- Offer assistance with cash management
- Provide information on investors who may wish to invest in, or loan money to, the firm
- Provide investment services such as money market accounts, individual retirement accounts (IRAs) and self-employed IRAs, and 401(k) retirement plans

SOURCES OF CAPITAL

Funding for the business can be obtained from a variety of sources. This section explains important financial terminology and sources of capital related to sources of business financing.

Let's begin by defining important financial terms:

- *Debt capital* represents funds that come from creditors as loans. Must be secured with some sort of collateral to help ensure repayment.
- *Collateral* is an asset pledged to repay a loan in the event the borrower cannot actually pay back (defaults) on the loan.
- A *secured loan* requires collateral as protection against nonpayment. Generally has a lower rate of interest than an unsecured loan.
- *Unsecured loans* do not require collateral. They are made on the basis of a business owner's ability to repay. A line of credit is an example of an unsecured loan.
- *Short-term loans* last for one year or less. These loans are generally for simple, daily operating expenses, like stationery.
- A *line of credit* is a type of short-term loan used to satisfy a temporary need for cash rather than long-term needs. It helps cover the purchase of inventory and credit purchases from suppliers. It usually cannot be used to buy equipment like a computer.
- *Long-term loans* are for more than one year and are usually granted to purchase capital items, like office equipment and delivery trucks, or the purchase—not rent—of an office location. These loans are obtained from private lenders, such as commercial banks and finance companies.

It is not unusual for a small interior design practice to be funded initially by personal funds. Once a budget is established, personal resources are accumulated to begin the firm. Some designers obtain additional start-up funds from family members.

Many entrepreneurs have used personal credit cards as a source of start-up capital. This convenient source, however, is very expensive with its high interest rates, and should be used cautiously. Relying on personal credit cards makes it far too easy for the new owner to go deeply into debt, causing problems concerning future personal credit needs. If a personal credit card is used for business purposes (the firm's accountant will advise as to the opportunity to do this), it should not be used for any personal expenses, so that personal and business expenses are not mixed.

At some point, every business needs outside financing beyond these personal sources. Banks are reluctant to finance a new business if the owner has little or no collateral. They generally shy away from making loans to small businesses until the business has shown that it is successful. The business owner will discuss with her accountant and banker opportunities for short- or long-term loans from a financial institution. It is critical for the prospective business owner to get his personal financial position in order before trying to obtain bank financing—or even obtaining a commercial credit card for the business.

When a bank business loan is not available, the business owner might consider alternative funding sources. Business loans are a major funding source for interior design practices, although they are not the only source of capital. A banker, along with the firm's accountant, can advise the entrepreneur on the pros and cons of various alternative funding sources based on the entrepreneur's personal situation.

Equity capital represents funds obtained from investors. They are gambling that they will receive a return on their investment, but they know that if the business fails, they may not even get their investment back. *Venture capital* is a common name associated with equity capital funds that come from investors. Venture capital for small interior design businesses is hard to obtain, however. Venture capitalists usually only invest large sums in businesses with very good potential for a high return on the investment.

Another type of investor term that has cropped up in the past several years is *angel investor*. Angel investors are more likely to invest in small entrepreneurial businesses like interior design practices, as they generally have less money to invest. Angel investors are often entrepreneurs themselves who want to see someone else succeed.

Someone who knows the interior designer but is not necessarily a relative is called an *affiliated angel investor*. For example, Sally's neighbor agrees to invest $25,000 in Sally's business. The agreement he works out with Sally is that he will obtain 10 percent of net profits. He will patiently wait for a return on his investment. Someone who is not connected with the designer and does not know him or her is called a *nonaffiliated angel investor*.

If the business is a corporation, investment funds will often be obtained through selling stock in the company. Even a small interior design practice can be organized as a corporation (see Chapter 18). Stock can be sold to anyone with a willingness to earn a small return on his or her stock purchase investment.

Loans for a small business can also be obtained by applying through the loan guarantee program with the U.S. Small Business Administration (SBA). The SBA itself does not give loans. Rather, it guarantees loans provided by an SBA agent-lending institution. Most new interior design firms do not need large sums, and many banks are unwilling to make small loans for this type of business. The loan guarantees from the SBA are more frequently for small amounts. Information on the SBA loan program can be obtained by checking the SBA Web site (listed in the "Web Sites" section at the end of this chapter and in the "Internet Resources" section of the reference list).

ESTABLISHING BUSINESS CREDIT

Naturally, establishing business credit is very important to any interior design firm, even more so for a firm that intends to sell merchandise. Anyone who has tried to buy a car or even to obtain a credit card has dealt with establishing credit. For most proprietorships and partnerships, business credit starts with a personal credit history of the individuals involved. If the business owners have good personal credit, the business will have an easier time obtaining credit. New corporations, which are legal entities themselves, must establish credit just like an individual.

Interior design firms that resell products need to establish credit with suppliers. This begins by having good practices established in obtaining up-front payments before ordering merchandise for a client. Funds received in advance of work completion or merchandise delivery will have to be returned if the project is terminated or (in many cases) if the order for the goods is canceled.

When a designer first begins to order from a supplier, it is necessary for the designer to pay the full price for the goods in advance of the shipment. This requirement is sometimes referred to as *pro forma credit*, which means the supplier must be paid in advance. Note that the term *pro forma* can mean in advance or hypothetical. This is why designers ask for a deposit or down payment from customers. Depending on the laws in the jurisdiction, the deposit or down payment can be used to make the required prepayment to suppliers.

As a designer establishes credit with a supplier, the designer will become eligible for *trade credit*. Trade credit is harder to obtain for new buyers and new design firms. When trade credit is available, the firm will be able to buy from a supplier without having to make an immediate prepayment. Suppliers may extend customers 30, 60, or even 90 days of credit without charging interest. Interest rates, payment terms, and penalties must be understood to prevent credit problems with suppliers.

The designer establishes credit with a supplier by filling out a credit application and meeting with an appropriate agent of the supplier. Credit and business information is verified, along with further checks on the designer's general credit rating through credit reporting organizations. The supplier then determines the credit limit and conditions for the designer so that he or she can order without making down payments.

A bad credit rating can cause serious problems for a business. Late payment of any bill from a supplier or other entity to which the business owes money affects the business's credit rating. This in turn can mean the design firm cannot purchase from a supplier without paying in full for any items desired. As the reader can imagine, that can be a substantial outlay of funds. Paying bills on time or even earlier than the due date supports a positive credit rating with more potential allowances from suppliers and others for credit.

For businesses, credit reporting agencies serve as clearinghouses on the soundness and creditworthiness of a business. Manufacturers and other suppliers the firm may use check these credit listings before extending credit to the firm. In turn, the design firm may check the credit rating of business clients before extending credit to them. This is discussed in Chapter 13. See the box on the credit agencies most related to the interior design industry.

The status of a credit rating, for an individual or for a business, is readily available. In some cases, these reports are free; other credit agencies charge a fee. Knowing the interior design firm's credit rating is very important to the owner of the firm, whether that owner operates a sole proprietorship or a large firm in a commercial office or studio. If there are errors, it is necessary for the owner/manager and/or the business to protest the errors and see that the credit history is corrected.

Credit Agencies for the Interior Design Industry

A national credit agency that gathers information on thousands of businesses, big and small, is Dun & Bradstreet (D&B). It obtains information on a business's operations, legal structure, financial condition, and payment history. It also reviews and makes available to a business owner who requests it information on a creditor's banking records, financial records such as income statement, the D&B credit rating, and whether legal proceedings against the business have occurred or are in process. The design firm should seek to have a good credit rating with D&B and can use the D&B reporting service to obtain information on the credit rating of potential business clients. Of course, the design firm will also check with Dun & Bradstreet to review the credit history of a commercial client (www.dnb.com).

The Allied Board of Trade (ABT) is a credit agency specific to the interior design industry. Designers register with ABT to show trade sources that they and/or the design firm are a member of the design community. An ABT membership will speed purchasing opportunities with many vendors in the home furnishings and commercial interior design industry. A listing with the ABT can be obtained only after the design firm completes an application process that reports a sales tax number and previous trade relations with suppliers, as well as meeting academic training and practical experience standards. The *Credit Green Book* references thousands of registered designers and is used both by interior designers to find trade sources and by suppliers to clarify credit information on designers (www.allied boardoftrade.com).

Another credit reporting agency important in the interior design industry is the Lyon Mercantile Group, Ltd., corporate group for the Lyon Furniture Mercantile Agency. Founded in 1876, Lyon began by providing credit information and collection services for the furniture industry.* Of importance to the interior design industry today is the Lyon Red Book, which is a credit rating reference book for the home furnishings industry. (This tool is also available on CD-ROM.) Information in the Red Book includes a firm's financial statements, credit activity, pay trends, and other information.

*www.lyoncredit.com/merc/history (March, 2012).

INSURANCE

Insurance is a necessity to minimize the many inherent risks that come with owning and operating a design business, regardless of size. Risk to the firm can come from the actions of the owners, employees, and even the suppliers hired by the designer. The firm with part-time or full-time employees may also be required by law to have certain kinds of insurance for employee protection. Design firms cannot afford to operate without appropriate business insurance.

We read every day of other events that can have an impact on business survival. Natural disasters, accidents, theft, and other unforeseen events create the need for insurance so that a business and its employees will be protected. A business that is hit by a tornado or flood may have a difficult time rebuilding and recovering from the destruction of the studio and contents. Insurance protection can help mitigate such losses.

Advice on appropriate insurance for your business should come from an insurance agent. An *independent insurance agent* commonly works for himself or herself and may represent more than one insurance company. An *exclusive agent* works for a particular company and only writes (sells) insurance policies from that one company. A *broker* also represents multiple companies. The difference between an independent agent and broker is that brokers most often only write commercial insurance, not personal. Regardless of what the agent is called, consult with an insurance agent who is familiar with commercial business insurance issues. Not all companies can provide the combination of business insurance an interior designer or firm might need. Professional associations, or sometimes an association chapter, sponsor certain types of insurance for members.

The self-employed business owner requires insurance similar to any other type of business. Professional liability and errors and omissions insurance are musts for any business owner. Insurance to protect the self-employed business owner from personal liability claims, interruptions in business, and the other situations and types of insurance discussed in the rest of this section are crucial for the self-employed interior designer.

The remainder of this section provides a brief overview of the typical types of insurance that are usually required or suggested for an interior design practice.

Professional Liability Insurance

Jim was designing a gift shop located in a strip shopping center. During the course of the project, he convinced the owner to use custom-made display cabinets and fixtures throughout the store rather than items from a display products vendor. He assured the owner that the cabinets would be ready on time. Three weeks before the store was scheduled to open, the cabinet fabricator's business closed for reasons unknown to Jim. The most important cabinets for the store had not been delivered to the store site, and the opening—planned around an important grand-opening party—could not occur as scheduled.

By commission or omission, there are many ways that an interior designer can have a situation occur that will require dependence upon professional liability insurance. Called *malpractice insurance* by many, *professional liability insurance* protects the design professional in the event an action causes acts, errors, or omissions in the course of work on the design project. One example is incorrect spatial layouts on design documents that delay the project or cause harm to the client's property. (Recall that "harm" in legal terms does not relate only to physical injury.) Another example is actual financial loss to the client because the project was not finished on time. Errors in the design plans that result in plans failing to comply with building codes is yet another example that can easily occur. This insurance also covers the interior designer should bodily injury or property damage occur as a result of the professional negligence of the designer. Has Jim's selection of the custom-cabinet shop resulted in professional negligence on Jim's part?

Interior designers can be held responsible for errors or omissions in work performed or advice given to a client. Often called *errors and omissions coverage (E&O),* this type of professional liability insurance provides protection should the interior designer or his or her employees make a mistake, which would be an error; or forget or not do something that was required, which is considered an omission. An example of an error is specifying a non-code-compliant material as a wall covering in the corridors of a hotel. Another example of an error is specifying the wrong wood veneer stain on cabinets for a kitchen remodeling. One example of an omission is forgetting to include smoke detectors in a remodeling of a residence. Another example of an omission is failing to make sure the type of recess-mounted lighting fixtures specified can be properly shielded from the ceiling insulation. In these examples, the designer technically has committed an act that could result in legal proceedings being filed by the client. E&O insurance provides coverage for claims should a court's decision go against the designer.

Property Damage, Liability, and Personal Injury Insurance

A group of insurance coverage referred to as *property damage, liability, and personal injury insurance* is also very important. Insurance policies that cover these areas of business are not all the same. The business owner can purchase combination policies or a policy for each type of coverage. When considering a combination policy, the owner needs to be very clear about what is and is not covered. For example, "property coverage" insurance might not include coverage for furniture and equipment used in the business unless it is specifically mentioned. If the interior design firm sells merchandise, property insurance should also cover display items and inventory.

A *business owner's policy* is a particularly important combination policy for any interior design firm that owns a studio, store, or warehouse. Many companies offer such package policies, which include various levels of property damage, liability, and personal injury insurance and often include business interruption insurance. Designers who rent space can obtain variations on this package to take care of their needs. Some insurance might be part of the lease, so be sure you understand what is covered. However, most insurance included in a lease is intended to protect the building owner's interests, not the tenants'. Additional insurance to cover your property within the leased space will be necessary. Table 16-2 provides an overview of the process for filing a claim.

TABLE 16-2.

Filing business insurance claims

When the business suffers a loss of any kind, it is necessary to file a claim with the firm's insurance agent immediately. These tips on filing insurance claims will help your insurer process any claims quickly and efficiently.
Keep records of all equipment and other resources you purchase to operate your business. Have copies of receipts for purchase that show the price paid for the item, whether it is a computer or even a reference book needed for the practice.
Contact the appropriate agent promptly after the event or loss. Waiting to contact the agent and file the claim could result in a loss for you.
Read your policies—have them handy on file—so that you know what your coverage and responsibilities are.
Contact the police in the case of theft or other events that might be deemed a crime.
If damage has occurred, take photographs as quickly as possible before anything is moved.
Unless directed otherwise by your insurance agent, get at least two bids on any repairs to be made to the property.
Protect the damaged property as best you can by making temporary repairs, such as having plywood installed over broken windows.*
Determine if there were any witnesses to the event, and get statements of what they saw.
If someone falls in your office, get a written statement and release from the injured party. This is especially important if the person leaves saying he or she is all right. Of course, if someone is injured, you may also need to call 9-1-1.

*Be careful about doing temporary repairs before your insurance adjuster has inspected the damage. If a temporary repair will prevent further damage, then photograph the existing condition first and then do the temporary repair.

Property damage insurance generally protects the building and its contents from loss due to fire, theft, windstorms, lightning strikes, and other types of loss detailed in the policy. Not all policies cover all potential types of loss, so the business owner may need an additional policy for some potential situations. Home-based businesses are likely to need supplemental coverage to protect damage to the home office and its equipment, because most homeowners policies do not provide this protection.

Supplemental coverage can be obtained for businesses located in areas that are prone to events like floods or earthquakes. Remember that the contents of the building—furniture, accessories, reference books, and office equipment—are considered personal property. The property damage insurance portion generally does not cover accounting records. *Liability insurance* protects the business should it be sued by a third party for injury or property damage due to negligence, product failure, or other claims of that kind. Note that the business can be sued for the acts of the owners, employees, agents, and suppliers. For example, one of your clients, Mrs. Smith, trips on a small area rug in the resource library of your studio; she falls and breaks her wrist. Liability insurance would cover the business in this case. In addition, if a carpet installer hired by the designer breaks a lamp at a client's home, the designer is potentially as liable as the installer.

Another type of liability insurance that is important for interior designers is *product liability insurance*. This insurance covers injuries caused by products that are designed, sold, or specified by the interior designer. For example, should one of the chairs sold for a doctor's medical suite break and cause injury to a patient, the interior designer could be sued. If you sell products from a vendor, the vendor will be more liable than you. If you design custom furniture, you will have more liability.[1] However, it is very common for the interior designer who has been involved in the design and specification of a project also to be named in the lawsuit, whether or not the designer custom-created a furniture item.

Personal injury insurance is part of liability coverage and provides insurance in case of slander, libel, defamation, false arrest, and other personal injury torts. These personal injury torts are discussed in Chapter 4.

Other Important Types of Insurance

There are several other important types of business insurance that might be needed. Some of these items are needed by firms with employees, and others might be recommended by the design firm's insurance agent. Generally, a small business with a limited number of employees will not be required to have some of these types of insurance. An insurance agent and the firm's accountant can provide guidance on this issue.

Commercial *automobile insurance* is necessary for the vehicles owned by a business. Auto insurance on a personal vehicle used by the business (say, a small van used for deliveries) might not provide coverage if the vehicle is used primarily for business purposes.

The interior design firm must also verify that employees have proper insurance for their vehicles that are used for business purposes. When an employee uses his or her car for business purposes, the business could be liable if he or she has an accident. The employee's vehicle is covered by the design firm only if the firm has purchased an employer's nonowned liability coverage policy. Personal insurance is generally the primary insurance on employee vehicles. Design firms that hire tradespeople should be sure that the tradesperson has auto insurance, so that the designer is not sued if the tradesperson has an accident while on a job for the designer.

Workers' compensation insurance is required by the jurisdiction when employees are added to the firm. Most jurisdictions require that the employer provide this insurance to protect the employee in case of work-related injury, whether the injury happens in the office or at a jobsite. Workers' compensation insurance is not available to sole proprietors, but it does cover their employees. Partners in and officers of other types of business forms may have the option, depending on state law.

Business income insurance (also called *business interruption insurance*) pays for the loss of net profit and for operating expenses in case a fire or other specifically covered event prevents the business from operating. The losses suffered by many companies after catastrophic earthquakes, hurricanes, terrorist attacks, and other events have been the end of many businesses. The business owner must be sure the policy covers events that might occur in the location of the business, as these are not "blanket" policies; the events covered must be specified in the policy and will be charged for accordingly.

Even with the use of computers, records of what clients owe to the firm can be easily lost due to fire or other events. *Accounts receivable insurance* covers the loss of accounts receivable records due to fire or other specific events. Of course, prevention is also important; the business owner must make sure to back up all files and store the backups in safe places.

Crime insurance protects the firm in case of theft of money or property. Depending on the policy, it may cover the company for theft by employees or by individuals other than employees. Not all policies cover both groups. Interior design businesses with showroom space must be concerned about shoplifting of small items. A break-in during which someone steals the office computer can have a devastating effect on the business if the data on that computer are not backed up on CDs or other media. Be aware that a personal laptop computer, not owned by the business but left at the business location and stolen, is not likely to be covered by business property insurance.

Owners and officers should make sure that they have some sort of personal *health and disability* insurance. It is also important that business partners agree to obtain health and disability insurance. A death, serious illness, or injury to one partner could devastate a business if that partner has no health or disability insurance. *Disability income insurance* provides continuing income if certain covered injuries or illnesses occur that prevent the business owner from working. The insurance provides benefits to help pay personal and business expenses. The employer may also wish to provide *health insurance* to employees as a benefit of working for the company.

Interior designers who work from home should purchase a separate rider for the equipment (such as computers) that they use at home but is primarily for business purposes. Most homeowners policies do not cover equipment used primarily for business purposes. There may also be other exclusions related to liability and injury on the residential property to clients or others doing business with the home-based design practitioner. This exclusion also can apply to the designer's personal automobile, if it is used for business.

There are many other specialized types of insurance that may be important for an interior design business based on the nature of the practice and business form. Consultation with the firm's attorney, accountant, and insurance advisor is indispensable to determine if other types of insurance are also necessary.

TECHNICAL CONSULTANTS

From time to time, Almost every interior design firm needs specialized technical consultants and allied professionals to assist with a project. An interior designer should not be afraid to admit the need for these professionals. Preparing documents and designs without the proper expertise and license is fraught with danger.

Technical consultants may be hired to obtain advice or to explain how part of a project will be accomplished. For example, a codes consultant may be retained to discuss code requirements for a particularly complex project. Some are engaged by the interior design firm to work on parts of the project that the interior designer is not legally allowed to design. An example is securing the input and design specifications from an architect or engineer for the design of a multistory residence to be located on sloped property.

Technical professionals are hired on a per-job basis by a small firm. Larger design firms often have one or more of these allied professionals on staff. The designer can include the fees for these consultants in the interior design contract or suggest that the client hire the consultant directly.

It is imperative that you understand the laws within your jurisdiction regarding what the interior design firm can do concerning technical construction and mechanical systems design. In some jurisdictions, the interior designer cannot even sell items that are affixed to the building or mechanical systems without a proper license. In addition, regulations do not allow a professional such as an architect to affix the architect's stamp to drawings that have been prepared by an interior designer unless the designer is an employee of the firm. In a similar vein, a registered interior designer cannot affix his or her stamp to drawings produced by a nonregistered interior designer.

A technical consultant might perform such duties as:

- Meeting with the client to determine needs related to his or her specialty
- Preparing drawings to be used to obtain needed permits
- Providing expertise not resident within the interior design firm
- Providing on-site supervision during the construction and/or installation of the project
- Working as a directly paid subconsultant or subcontractor to the design firm or the client

Table 16-3 lists a few of these specialists and how they can help the interior designer.

SOURCES OF INFORMATION AND ASSISTANCE

Many private organizations and government agencies provide consultation or reference materials to the business owner—far too many to list in this text. Information on many helpful organizations is provided in the "Web Sites" section of this chapter and the "Internet Resources" part of the reference list.

Private Organizations

The local chamber of commerce is a business lobbying and networking group for all sizes and types of local businesses; it works for the benefit of all

TABLE 16-3.

Common technical consultants

Depending on the project requirements and responsibilities of the designer, these consultants might be needed to complete the project scope.

Architects. Needed to prepare and review plans that require an architect's stamp. An architect's stamp is usually required on plans for residences of more than 3000 square feet and commercial spaces that will have more than 20 employees. Both these criteria vary according to local ordinances. Check with the building department of the project jurisdiction.

Electrical engineers. Provide advice and assistance on planning for/installation of electrical components for projects. Electrical engineers may also be needed to prepare and stamp electrical plans in order for the owner to obtain a building permit.

General contractors. Oversee all tradespersons needed for a project's build-out. Note that the term *build-out* is industry jargon for the construction process.

Specialty contractors or subcontractors. Provide advice on ways to build or specify interior design concepts. A cabinetmaker can advise the designer on how to detail drawings for a custom conference wall that might include storage, plumbing, and audiovisual equipment.

Lighting designers. Provide assistance with or the design and planning of specialized lighting concepts/components.

Commercial kitchen designers. Provide plans for commercial kitchens in restaurants, hotel food-service areas, healthcare food-service areas, and so forth.

Communications and technology. Specialize in helping to plan technical wiring for TV, Internet, computers, and other like items for today's high-tech homes and offices.

Acoustical engineers. Advise the interior designer on materials and finishes for architectural surfaces, and locations of acoustical treatments, to solve noise problems or build in desired acoustical qualities and properties.

Landscape architects, interior plantscapers, and florists. Advise the designer on the proper selection and positioning of plants in the interior; can also provide the designer with maintenance instructions.

Healthcare facility specialists. Consult on the design of offices of healthcare professions. Designers often hire nursing professionals as consultants.

Other consultants. The design business owner may wish to retain other specialty consultants from time to time. Examples include public relations, advertising and marketing agencies, employment agencies, management consultants, computer consultants, Web page designers, and communications consultants.

businesses in the community. It is a member organization welcoming all types of businesses to join the local chapter. The chamber of commerce does not necessarily offer direct assistance to businesses. Nonetheless, networking opportunities at local chapter meetings and programs sponsored by the local chapter can provide useful information about the business community. The chamber also provides information to consumers about businesses in the local area.

Universities and community colleges often have a small business development center or small business institutes. They are structured in conjunction with the U.S. Small Business Administration and the institution's business college. These groups provide seminars and one-on-one counseling to the small business owner.

Professional organizations in areas of business or the built environment profession can also help the business owner select a consultant. For example, the American Bar Association can provide assistance to business owners who are seeking an attorney. Local chapters of the interior design professional associations may have information on business advisors within the chapter area. However, it might be necessary to be a member of the association to obtain this type of contact information. Contact information on a specific trade association can be found in the *Encyclopedia of Associations*, available at libraries or by searching the Internet. An Internet search must be reasonably specific to narrow the search parameters.

Private outside consultants and business coaches are also an option. They provide the new entrepreneur or small business practitioner with advice or assistance specific to the business owner's needs. These consultants are most easily found through a search on the Internet or possibly through interior design professional associations.

Government Agencies

A great source where designers can obtain information on local regulations is from their state's department of commerce and department of revenue. Much information, including forms to apply for licenses and business formation documents specific to the jurisdiction, can be obtained via the Internet. Although the address may change by state, generally a Web site such as www.<state>.gov will direct you to the state department of commerce link. State income tax information for businesses is also available from the state department of revenue. State forms for applying for such things as business formation, business names, and resale licenses may also be available online through the state department of commerce or department of revenue.

Many cities have small business development centers or economic development offices. These offices can provide pamphlets, seminars, and one-on-one consulting services. You can locate them through the government section of the telephone white pages or the local government Web page. A small business resource center is frequently available at the local public library.

The Small Business Administration (SBA), a federal agency, provides many kinds of assistance to the small business owner. Assistance may come in the form of informational pamphlets and books, seminars, clinics, and one-on-one counseling. SCORE is the Service Corps of Retired Executives, an SBA group of volunteers that provides consulting to small business owners. SCORE volunteers can be contacted through the local SBA office. Numerous SBA publications are available online as PDF documents. In addition, the SBA may be able to provide financial assistance for qualified small businesses through its program of guaranteeing loans provided by member banks. The main address for the SBA is listed in the "Internet Resources" section of the reference list. Local offices may be found in the U.S. government section of the white pages in the local phone book.

The Internal Revenue Service has business tax kits for different business operations. Publication Number 334, "Tax Guide for Small Business," is especially useful to the owner of a sole proprietorship. Addresses for local IRS offices are in the U.S. government section of the white pages. Some additional tax forms are available online at the IRS Web site (www.irs.gov).

WEB SITES RELEVANT TO THIS CHAPTER

www.alliedboardoftrade.com Allied Board of Trade

www.cra-arc.gc.ca Canada Revenue Agency

www.dnb.com Dun and Bradstreet

www.irs.gov Internal Revenue Service

www.lyoncredit.com Lyon Credit Services, Inc.

www.score.org SCORE (Service Corp of Retired Executives)

www.sba.gov U.S. Small Business Administration

There are numerous associations for insurance agents, accountants, and attorneys. You may wish to search the Internet for sites of agencies or associations that will be local and specific to your needs.

KEY TERMS

Accountant

Accounts

Angel investor

Balance sheet

Banker

Bookkeeper

Certified public accountant (CPA)

Collateral

Debt capital

Equity capital

Errors and omissions (E&O)

Expenses

Income statement

Independent insurance agent

Liability insurance

Line of credit

Long-term loan

Malpractice insurance

Operating funds

Pro forma credit

Professional liability insurance

Profit

Profit and loss statement

Property damage insurance

Revenue

Secured loan

Short-term loan

Trade credit

Unsecured loan

Capital vs. Business

ORGANIZATIONS

Allied Board of Trade

Dun & Bradstreet (D&B)

Lyon Furniture Mercantile Agency

Service Corp of Retired Executives (SCORE)

U.S. Small Business Administration (SBA)

WHAT WOULD YOU DO?

1. Alex and Peter have been working in commercial interior design for a total of 14 years, with Alex having 2 more years of experience than Peter. They now feel it is time to combine their talents and start their own design firm specializing in hospitality spaces and offices. Alex and Peter can each contribute the same amount of money as start-up capital. They agree that they will share equally in the profits and management of the company. They are not sure if they should organize their firm as a partnership, an LLC, or a joint venture.

2. Shelly found an error in the specifications for a courthouse project. When she checked the equipment plans against the furniture specifications, the quantities of a certain chair did not match. She counted the item three times to be sure of her counts. Her boss told her to call the project interior designer at the issuing design firm for clarification. The project manager told her that the drawings were correct. Despite

Shelly's insistence, the project designer did not send out any clarification related to Shelly's question.

3. Carol charges a consultation fee that she feels covers approximately 75 percent of her time working on a project. Occasionally the consultation fee is based on an hourly fee, and sometimes it is a fixed fee. Carol also charges clients a cost plus percentage on any merchandise that they buy directly from Carol. Her residential clients have been satisfied with this arrangement until recently.

Two new clients complain that she is "double-dipping" by charging an hourly consultation fee as well as selling the merchandise at a markup. Carol tries to explain that her consultation fee does not in actuality "pay" her for the time she must put into creating drawings, shopping for products, and doing all the other work called out in her design contract. However, the clients tell her, "Choose one way of charging or we will hire someone else!"

REFERENCE

1. Steingold, 2005, p. 12/9.

CHAPTER 17

Preparing the Business Plan

After completing this chapter you should be able to:

- Discuss the purpose and use of a business plan for a new practice.
- Discuss the common parts of a business plan and the purpose of each part.
- Define a fictitious interior design business using the section "Define Your Business" in Table 17-1.
- Compare the advantages and disadvantages of operating a practice from a home office versus one located in a commercial site.
- Discuss the advantages and disadvantages of being a sole practitioner.
- Discuss the kinds of issues that small practitioners must be aware of as they obtain inventory items to sell.

NCIDQ COMPONENT

Based on best information available, some material in this chapter might appear as part of the NCIDQ examination. The reader should not depend solely on this text for study material. See the sections on setting up a business and leasing.

Far too many businesses fail—not because the economy is soft, but because the owner failed to plan. No one starts a business with the idea that it might fail, but success comes only after careful planning and preparation. According to the U.S. Small Business Administration, seven out of ten new firms last two years, and half survive at least five years.[1] Trying to find clients and funds to keep the business in operation are no small tasks.

Whether the business is entered into alone or with several partners or co-owners, many critical decisions must be made. A key aid in making those decisions is creating a written business plan before the doors are opened. Evaluating the business idea through a business plan helps the entrepreneur determine how feasible the idea might be. Interior design practice is much more than creating a library, finding sources, and obtaining a few initial clients. Planning helps the potential business owner see if the idea is feasible and what will be required to make it work.

A business plan does not guarantee success, but it helps the prospective business owner clearly consider the business idea. It provides an operational tool for handling potential problems with thought rather than pure gut reaction. It also helps establish such things as which design services will be offered, how many customers might potentially be interested in those services, and the amount of financial resources that will be necessary until revenue starts coming in.

THE BUSINESS PLAN

A business plan helps the new business owner think substantively and specifically as to what the business is all about and how it is going to operate. A *business plan* is a detailed definition of a business idea that explains how the business of this potential company will be executed.

A business plan:

- Creates the process and documentation that will help the prospective owner face the realities of starting a business
- Can help the prospective owner map a strategy for starting up the business
- Provides an opportunity to anticipate problems and develop ways to avoid them, if possible
- Helps the owner strategize how to cope with problems as they arise
- May help the firm obtain necessary funding from banks or other investors
- Gives the new firm a far greater chance of success than it would have without a plan.

As you start planning your new business, it is imperative to consider its purpose. "That's easy," you might say: "to provide interior design services to residential clients." Certainly that states a purpose, but most business consultants would say that a little more thought and specificity would be helpful. A clearly defined purpose helps to provide focus during initial planning as well as the first months of actual existence.

Any interior design practice can benefit from defining its purpose. Some call this purpose the mission of the business, as discussed in Chapter 20. Regardless of the type and size of the firm, a concept of a firm's mission helps it differentiate itself from other design firms. Defining its mission helps the owner clarify those differences, define the purpose of the business, and determine the services that will be offered. To help you define your business idea, complete the questionnaire in Table 15-2 about creating and managing a new practice.

Preparing a business plan takes time—it can take weeks or even months, depending on how much time can be devoted to researching and writing it. Although a plan will not eliminate problems, it helps the business owner understand what kind of assistance might be needed and how to better manage the whole of the business venture. If it is necessary to obtain outside financing from a bank or investors, more information will be needed, and this may add to the time needed for the research and writing. Advice from an attorney, accountant, banker, or consultant may be needed as well. Some of the decisions about how to structure the business can be made easier with advice from these types of professionals.

Table 17-1 lists some questions that you should answer about the proposed organizational structure of the new business. This will help with the overall research for the business idea and plan. Answering these questions before the doors are opened will go a long way toward allowing those doors—whether figurative or literal—to remain open for years to come.

When you develop your business plan, you are expressing your personal goals and ideas about what the firm is to be and do and how you hope it will

TABLE 17-1.

Key questions to ask about the organizational structure of a business start-up

---

Select a legal structure (see Chapter 18).
Sole proprietorship?
Partnership?
Corporation?
Limited liability company?

What licenses are required (see Chapter 19)?
Interior design registration?
Contractor's license?
Business licenses?
Transaction privilege tax license?

Select the name of the business (see Chapter 19).
Use your own name?
Use a fictitious name?

How will the business be financed for the first year (see Chapters 16 and 21)?
Personal investment by owner(s)?
Investments by friends or relatives?
Will loans be required?
Have an estimated cash flow and pro forma income statement been prepared for the first year?
Have personal living expenses for the first year been estimated?
Have start-up costs and expenses for the first year been estimated?

Where will the business be located (see Chapter 19)?
In a residence (will this violate zoning laws)?
In a commercial site?
Will customers be able to find the business location easily?
Can the business location (home or commercial site) easily be modified to meet your needs?
Will you rent or lease space?

Will the business have employees other than the owner(s) (see Chapters 19 and 27)?
Are any federal or state filings required?
What type of benefits will be provided to employees?
What kind of equipment will be provided for employees to do their jobs?
How will employees be recruited?

How will business financial records be maintained (see Chapter 21)?
What accounting bases will be used?
Who will do the daily bookkeeping?
Who will keep payroll and tax records?
Who will prepare any formal accounting records that are required?

Insurance requirements (see Chapter 16).
What kinds of insurance are needed initially?

How will the business be promoted and clients obtained (see Chapters 22 to 25)?
Do you have a marketing plan?
Do you know who your target clients are?
What marketing tools (such as a brochure or Web site) will be needed?
Will you market only to clients who are close to your business location?

(*Continued*)

TABLE 17-1.

(*Continued*)

Have you thought about how fees will be set (see Chapters 6 and 8)?
Will services only be provided, or will merchandise also be sold?
On what basis will fees be set?
How will fees be set?
Will compensation requirements be considered using more than one method?
Are you comfortable in quoting more than one fee method?
Do you know how to price any merchandise you purchase for clients?

Will design contracts or letters of agreement be used (see Chapter 7)?
What must be in a contract for it to be legally binding?
Have possible clauses been discussed with an attorney?
Will clients be billed for services covered in a design contract?
Will reimbursable expenses be billed?

Will the business require inventory (see Chapter 17)?
What will the initial inventory consist of and where will it be displayed and/or stored?
How will the purchase of initial inventory be financed?

TABLE 17-2.

Information to research for preparing a business plan

1. Analyze personal abilities and interests related to owning an interior design business.
2. Carefully consider the purpose and mission of the business, who prospective customers might be, and why the business is being started.
3. Develop a personal income plan that ensures payment of all personal expenses during the first year of the life of the business.
4. If you have hired employees or anticipate hiring additional employees, analyze operational needs and the required skills.
5. Analyze the potential market for the firm's services. Do not forget to research existing competition.
6. Draft a marketing plan that includes the specific aspect(s) of the market that the firm will address. Determine what services the firm will offer, target market, pricing policies, and considerations for advertising and/or promotional activities.
7. Determine which type of business formation will be used: a sole proprietorship, a partnership, a form of corporation, or possibly some other legal form.
8. Determine legal responsibilities and tax obligations. Consult with an attorney concerning contracts and liabilities, an accountant concerning recordkeeping, and an insurance representative regarding insurance obligations.
9. Estimate how much capital will be required to "open the doors." Estimate the first year's expenses. Determine sources of initial capital.
10. Develop a financial plan and income projections. Include projected balance sheets, income statements, and cash-flow forecasts.
11. Develop a concept of the firm's image: appearance of letterhead, business cards, exteriors of delivery trucks, title blocks for drawing paper, and so on.
12. Prepare an organizational plan that includes projected personnel needs, job descriptions, employee benefits, and purchasing procedures.
13. If the firm will engage in retail selling of inventoried goods, develop an inventory plan of what will be purchased, when it will be purchased, and where it will be stored.
14. Produce the business plan.

grow. Once completed, the business plan helps you determine if the idea is realistic and feasible. Having goals that can be measured by the firm's performance will help you determine what is going well and what must be adjusted to get back on track.

An important ingredient of all business plans is research. The items in Table 17-2 form a suggested sequence in which the research should be conducted to help prepare the sections shown in the outline. A typical outline is

TABLE 17-3.

Business plan outline

I. Business summary
A. Provide name(s) of owner(s) or board of directors members.
B. Give location of business.
C. Identify type of business formation (legal structure).
D. Describe business, including types of services to be performed.
E. Provide a summary of the owner's and/or manager's expertise in running the business.

II. Market research
A. Describe how the information concerning the business was obtained.
B. Describe the need for the firm's services in the community; include the number of potential clients.
C. Describe the known competition in as much detail as possible.
D. Detail existing sales for this kind of firm in the community (might be available from the local chamber of commerce).
E. Describe any industry or local trends that might affect the success of the projected business.

III. Marketing plan
A. Detail what portions of the market the business will address.
B. Describe what services the business will offer (may be detailed enough to explain how sample boards will be done).
C. Determine how services and/or products will be priced.
D. If a warehouse/delivery service is used, determine how these charges will be passed on to clients.
E. Outline what kinds of advertising and promotional activities will support the business.
F. Describe any problems concerning expected seasonal business, if applicable.

IV. Operational plan
A. Provide the organizational structure of the business.
B. Analyze hiring of personnel and job descriptions.
C. Describe how records will be kept and controlled.
D. Analyze employee benefits.
E. Project dealings with suppliers, delivery people, and subcontractors.
F. Frame customer relations.
G. Project personnel needs.

V. Financial information
A. Project initial capital and first-year estimates for keeping the business operating; detail how the money will be spent.
B. Estimate additional revenue (monthly) beyond break-even points.
C. Provide month-by-month, projected profit and loss statements.
D. Decide on accounting practices that will be used, especially those related to depreciation, leasing, and inventories.
E. Provide a beginning balance sheet.
F. Explain how projections were made.
G. Provide any additional information required of a corporation.

shown in Table 17-3, detailing the subject content of a well-thought-out business plan. As readers can see from these examples, the areas of skills and abilities; the marketplace; and operational considerations, such as pricing, expected capital required, and projected financial planning, must be thoroughly investigated, researched, and considered.

The actual writing of the business plan can begin after the research has been done or while the research process is ongoing. There is no single, surefire way to prepare a business plan, as the numerous books on the topic testify. Understand that a lender will be looking for certain kinds of information—primarily financial resources and estimates—if you are seeking a loan. Software programs exist to help with the business planning process. Many of the books in the reference list at the end of the book provide several outlines of business plans. A sample business plan has been included on the companion Web site as Item 17-1.

The business plan for a start-up is just that: the plan to start the business. When the doors open, new opportunities might arise that are outside the original plan. You need to look at any opportunities that come your way. You also need to look at challenges that could harm your business. The business plan helps you to determine if the opportunity is truly a good opportunity for the design practice. This ongoing use and review of the plan against what actually happens to the business is why you should never assume that once the plan is finished, that's it. Ongoing planning—called *strategic planning* and discussed in Chapter 20—is important to grow a business.

START-UP COSTS

Analyzing the financial needs and revenue expectations of the business is critical for the prospective business owner when developing a business plan. Financial planning for a new business should look at two factors: One is the amount of financial resources needed to pay for personal living expenses during a business start-up; the second is the business start-up costs.

The financial needs of a design practice will be similar regardless of the business location or type of practice. The exception is those businesses that decide to be more a retail studio or store, selling displayed and inventoried products. Though these types of businesses receive only minimal discussion in this section, they will need far greater financial resources.

Table 17-4 is a list of start-up expenses, composed of items that are both one-time and ongoing expenses. The one-time expenses required at start-up include those that must be paid before the business can open. Some start-up expenses become ongoing overhead expenses. Office supplies, telephone, and insurance are some of those items.

TABLE 17-4.

Common start-up expense items for a typical interior design firm

---

Initial, essential one-time expenses:
Office furniture (desks, file cabinets, shelves, etc.)
Office equipment (computer, printer, copy machine, telephones, other electronic equipment)
Remodeling of office/studio space
Initial inventory (if any)
Utility and lease deposits
Licenses and permits
Catalogs and samples
Miscellaneous office equipment (coffee maker, radio, camera, small refrigerator, etc.)

Ongoing expenses needed at start-up:
Stationery
Utilities
Phone, fax, cell phone
Internet provider
Web site/domain fees
Drawing supplies
General office supplies
Insurance premiums—related to the practice of interior design
Marketing materials, such as brochures, direct-mail items, and so forth

Professional expenses on an annual basis:
Possible consultant fees, such as accountant, attorney, insurance agent
Cleaning and janitorial fees
Transportation
Additional items or expenses that may be needed to initiate a design practice, as required

A third group of expenses that must be considered is those that are ongoing yet are not necessarily needed at the initial start-up of the business. Items such as owner's salary or draw, inventory (unless you open with inventory), payroll for assistants, and interest on loans and credit cards are examples. Budgeting worksheets that help you estimate start-up and ongoing business expenses will be quite useful in this regard. Worksheets for the information in Tables 17-4 and 17-5 are included on the companion Web site as Items 17-2 and 17-3.

If you are self-financing, as many sole proprietors do, developing an outline of business expenses will help you see what will be needed to start up and for the first year. Should outside financing be required, you will have to pay even more detailed attention to start-up financial planning.

Of course, anyone planning a new business would benefit from preparing detailed financial projections. Documents useful in this area are the pro forma income statement and other accounting reports. The business owner's accountant might help prepare any of these documents. In business terms, *pro forma* means a projection. It can also mean in advance. So, a pro forma income statement is one that has been created with projected numbers instead of actual numbers or in advance of actual numbers.

The basis of a pro forma income statement (also called a profit and loss statement, or P&L) is any known numbers, such as expected overhead expenses like rent and utilities. If you are unfamiliar with overhead expenses, it would be helpful for you to read that section of Chapter 21 before working on this section of the business plan.

Assumptions and "best guesses" as to what might happen in the future are factored in to produce the numbers on the pro forma income statement. Utilizing a pro forma statement requires homework on such things as the current and potential future economic situation, inflation, and changes in expenses. People more often overestimate than underestimate the projected revenue for a business.

By estimating the amount of start-up and ongoing business expenses for one year, you will gain an idea of the minimum amount of revenue needed for the year. When the amount of revenue collected in a year just matches the amount of expenses estimated for the year, the firm has only reached a *break-even point*. At this point, the firm is neither making nor losing money and thus has experienced no profits. Chapter 21 discusses the concept of break-even in more detail.

SETTING UP THE OFFICE

Many interior designers start their own business from a home office. That is a perfectly acceptable location for many, but not ideal for all. Business location is an important decision, but it is not the only one that will determine where you set up your office. This section looks at key issues you will need to consider in starting your own design firm.

Business Location

The location of the business can definitely have an impact on potential clients' opinion of the design professional. Clients want to know that they are dealing with a business professional, and a home office does not always project that image. "It is often hard to be taken seriously when your office is at home, because clients think it's just a hobby rather than a business," says one Arizona sole practitioner. The determination of which location is best—at home, in a

TABLE 17-5.

Home office location

> Locating the design practice at a home office has many economic advantages. It also presents challenges in terms of operating the business in a professional manner. It is important to check with your accountant to determine if a home office is a valid tax deduction for your business.
>
> **Location of home office:**
> - A studio with its own private entrance
> - Build an addition to the house—perhaps enclose or convert the garage
> - Dedicated room within the house
>
> **Operational issues:**
> - Privacy for telephone calls and faxes
> - Separate business telephone line
> - Minimal family background noise
> - Privacy for concentrated work
> - Where will meetings with clients take place?
>
> **Other considerations:**
> - Storage space for sample books and binders
> - Will CCRs prohibit small deliveries for items such as fabric?
> - Insurance for business activities conducted from home
> - What will happen when an assistant is needed?
> - Will you be able to create the appropriate business image from a home office?

Note: This is not an all-inclusive list. Other issues not listed here or discussed in this chapter may have an impact on the practice.

commercial office building, or in a retail center of some sort—depends on many factors, including the types of services that will be offered, the firm's expected client base, and funds available for start-up expenses.

Here are some key issues concerning the location of a home office. Other considerations are listed in Table 17-5.

Advantages

- Economical.
- Technology allows easy communication with clients and vendors.
- Convenient for those who have significant family responsibilities.
- Tax advantages exist for home offices, although special recordkeeping is needed.

Disadvantages

- Meetings with clients may be difficult, as the home design itself might not provide the image the designer wishes to project.
- Basic homeowners insurance likely will not cover business furniture and equipment.
- R-1 zoning for private residences does not allow employees to operate from the home business location.
- Neighbors may complain if delivery trucks often arrive at the home office.
- A homeowners association (HOA) may have conditions, covenants, and restrictions that restrict or prohibit a home-based business. *Conditions, covenants, and restrictions (CCRs)* are specific regulations for condominiums, townhouses, and even single-family dwellings in planned communities.

Zoning Terminology

- *Zoning restrictions*: Local government regulations that permit only certain types of land uses in given areas of the municipality.
  - *R-1* is the designation for single-family dwellings. It is expected that the primary use of the land will be for homes, not businesses.
  - *C-1* is the designation for most nonmanufacturing and nonindustrial businesses.
- *Zoning variance:* A request by a property owner to allow activities other than what is specifically defined for the zone. A home-based business may require a zoning variance.

A business office located in a commercially zoned part of town gives a different impression to many clients. Warranted or not, a commercial location may impress a client into feeling that the designer is more professional. In contrast, a client may perceive the designer in a commercial office location as more expensive than one working from a home office.

One factor that can affect a decision to locate in a commercial location is your target client market. For example, a design firm that seeks primarily the office corporate client often locates in the downtown business district. Residential design studios are often located near retail stores for furniture, carpet, lighting, and the like. This relationship could bring clients to the designer when they visit these other establishments.

Interior designers often locate in low-rise office complexes, where street entry and visibility are available. Some locate in mixed-use centers with other professionals, like accountants and operators of small retail stores of various kinds. Locating near peer groups and related professionals should be a primary consideration in selecting a commercial location. Some interior designers find this conducive to business, whereas others feel it is not a good idea to be located near potential competitors.

Naturally, an office in a commercial location has added expenses. The amount of rent, the terms of the lease, and how much of the utilities, insurance, and maintenance costs are covered by the landlord are important factors to consider. The amount of rent is directly related to the square-foot amount of space taken by the business; thus, careful planning of that space is needed before looking for rental space. If there is too little space, the office/studio will become quickly cluttered and will look unprofessional. Too big a space incurs unnecessary overhead expenses, draining revenues away from other uses and needs.

In a commercial space, the interior design practice owner will negotiate with the landlord concerning improvements to the space to suit the firm's needs. The amount of the landlord's allowance for interior partitions and improvements is important. Some locations do not cover much more than very basic painting, floor covering, and drop-in ceiling fixtures. If the allowances are minimal, the interior designer must decide to pay for *tenant improvements* (also called *leasehold improvements*) out of his or her own pocket. Everything that is done to the space by the landlord and tenant should be spelled out in a *tenant work letter* (also referred to as a *building standard work letter*). Tenant improvements are expenses that can in all likelihood be deducted as business expenses, but they are not recovered when moving out of the space. A few additional terms related to commercial space rental are provided in Table 17-6.

Another option for office space is to rent space in an executive office complex. In this case, the suites are already planned to meet specific size requirements. The tenants utilize a common conference room, group kitchen,

TABLE 17-6.

Selected leasing terminology

> *As is*. Space is rented without any changes to the interior.
>
> *Building standards*. Interior finishes provided by the landlord without charge to the tenant.
>
> *Build-out allowance*. Landlord provides a dollar amount per square foot to build partitions, provide basic architectural finishes, and install basic mechanical systems (such as lighting fixtures).
>
> *Demising wall*. A partition that divides one tenant space from another. Each tenant pays for one-half the thickness of the wall.
>
> *Rentable area*. The total amount of space required by the tenant on which the rent dollar amount (usually by the square foot) will be calculated.
>
> *Tenant improvements*. Upgrades to a leased space paid for by the tenant.
>
> *Tenant work letter*. A supplemental contract that details how the space will be finished by the landlord and what will be provided by the tenant.
>
> *Trade fixtures*. Items attached to the space rented by the tenant. Depending on the lease, they can be removed if no damage is done to the structure.

Note that this list is not all inclusive. Other terminology may also appear, affecting both how the lease will be prepared and the tenant's responsibilities.

and copy and mailroom, and pay for a receptionist who answers the phones and greets customers. This option provides a commercial solution for a sole practitioner who does not want to work out of a home office or get involved in a long lease at another type of office location. However, it is more expensive, and such space is limited. An executive office rarely provides the "growth" space needed when the design firm adds employees. As many a designer in an executive office location has said, it is also very expensive to pay for the extra office space needed to house the catalogs and samples of the business.

Equipping the Office/Studio

The equipment needed for an interior design office varies based on the business focus and the types of services to be performed. Readers who have worked in the interior design profession for several years will have some idea as to what kind of equipment they will need for their studio or office. It is always important to consider future needs, as many items will have to be replaced or upgraded as years go by.

A list of equipment items commonly needed for a new office is provided on the companion Web site as Item 17-4. The reader can review this list to determine personal needs. Naturally, this list is not all-inclusive. Some items on the list might not be needed right at start-up, and other items not on the initial list might come to mind later. Nevertheless, such a list provides a good starting point for estimating what is needed and how much should be budgeted for it. By the way, it is generally understood that the furniture and equipment used within the office by the staff are not items that can be sold to a client. This is really an accounting issue, but should be considered during planning as well.

Design firms must invest in software and computer hardware that are compatible with what is used in the industry. Being able to transmit any kind of document via e-mail or on a computer disc is important for both residential and commercial interior designers. There are far fewer problems with compatibility between one system and another—unless you are working with an older version of software or older hardware. Computer-aided drafting programs should be carefully selected for compatibility with potential project collaborators.

Business software that combines word processing, data management, and spreadsheets is the minimum standard. Contact management and presentation graphics capabilities are frequently included in business software suites. Project management software is important for firms involved in commercial design. An accounting program will provide the framework for financial recordkeeping. Readers should conduct prepurchase research according to their needs; I have made it a practice not to recommend specific software or software companies in this book.

The Design Library

The Internet has given designers the opportunity to reduce the size of their library. Product information can easily be obtained online. Photos that can be downloaded, as well as detailed information on the products, help reduce the design library. Pricing information might not be available online until the designer has established a trade relationship with a vendor.

Still, the design library has not disappeared. Maintaining actual samples of certain products and materials, as well as catalogs of information and photographs of furniture and equipment, remains an important part of the design office. Design firms located away from trade showrooms generally have larger libraries, because they cannot easily go to a mart or showroom for samples.

The design firm must carefully weigh the importance of taking or keeping a set of samples or catalogs with the likelihood that the products will be specified and perhaps sold to clients. Samples and catalogs in the firm's library should be maintained based on need, not just to have them around. Remember that samples and catalogs are not always free. Large fabric memo samples and cuttings often must be paid for if they are not returned.

Some manufacturer and vendor representatives will visit the small studio to update catalogs and price lists; however, this vendor service is more common for the larger office/studio. The business owner must take care of this chore on a regular basis so that he or she is less likely to inadvertently price goods using out-of-date lists or to specify discontinued goods.

Worktable space is ideal in the library so that items can be arranged to see how the color scheme will work. Stand-up-height worktables are useful for creating sample boards. Many designers display fabric books on pegboard, creating a backdrop that can be attractive if kept neat.

It is also possible to utilize reference libraries of product catalogs and samples that are maintained by an independent business serving interior designers, architects, and contractors. In this case, I am not referring to an online source. A membership fee is often required to gain access to the materials. Samples and catalogs can be checked out, but they must be returned or an invoice for the items will be sent to the designer. These reference libraries may also offer lunch seminars presented by vendors. The seminars, open to all in the industry, may charge a small fee if the designer is not a member of the reference library.

Inventory Issues

Every design firm accumulates some inventory. Any type of goods purchased and held by the business for potential resale to clients is considered *inventory*.

For accounting purposes, any goods being held at the design studio or a warehouse awaiting delivery to clients is technically also called inventory.

For many small interior design firms that do not have a showroom, inventory may consist of items that have been rejected by clients and cannot be returned to the vendor. Some inventory may also be accumulated as a designer who is searching for items for one client locates some unique item that might be used for some future client. These last two examples might be called unplanned inventory items.

For many firms, inventory builds not so much as a conscious choice by the owner to stock certain items as by accumulation of items rejected by clients that cannot be returned to the supplier. Rejections are going to occur, no matter how careful the design firm is in specification of products, client approval, and delivery method. It is especially important for the small firm to have good procedures and policies in place to prevent as many client returns and rejections as possible.

In some cases, a firm might purchase extra items for future clients. These inventory items represent dollars that the firm cannot use for anything else until the items are sold. Inventory held for possible sale also incurs storage costs and insurance liability, which constitute additional drains on financial resources.

Ideally, inventory items should be purchased based on the ability to sell them in a reasonable length of time—perhaps within a few months or weeks, certainly within the year. The designer should make sure that these items are not so special that none of the firm's other clients would be interested in buying them. For example, the designer should not stock up on Oriental-style vases if most of the firm's work is in 18th-century Georgian historical restoration.

Of course, it is usually good for business to maintain some items in inventory that turn over quickly and are common needs for your specific target clients. Having immediate access to some items represents an additional revenue source. Higher income margins might also be possible for some of these items.

An alternative to inventory purchasing is the use of quick ship programs from manufacturers. Many manufacturers have quick-ship programs through which a wide variety of goods can be obtained within a short period of time—often as quickly as two to five days—versus the regular shipping time of several weeks or even months. There are fewer options with quick-ship items, but when speed is the issue, it is an excellent alternative in many cases.

The design firm should keep good records as to how long items have been in inventory and even where they are located. These records will be needed for tax purposes. I have heard many designers comment that they have lost track of some items because those items had been in storage so long. If inventoried items become damaged or stolen, the records will help the firm recover insurance claims. Good records also help the design firm's owner know how to get rid of items—possibly at a designer's "ding-and-dent" sale through an association or even by making a donation to a charitable organization.

Green Office Management

You have to walk the talk! If you are interested in specializing in green design, or even if you simply want to have a more sustainable office environment, the suggestions in this section will help with this goal. If you are marketing a green design emphasis, it is really important to clients who have that interest that your business also operates "green." Of course, green office management is also a bonus for any size or type of practice.

Using green design and sustainable practices in your own business operations assures clients that you understand green design. Naturally, this goes beyond recycling. You must also be careful that you are not inadvertently participating in greenwashing, as this will turn off those clients with whom you most want to do business.

The following list provides several suggestions that you should incorporate into your business operations and design decisions.

It's about the Business

- Increasing staff productivity can reduce office energy costs. If more gets done during the normal workday, then less overtime is needed, and hence less extra utility costs.
- Using truly green products in the office can reduce employee absenteeism due to allergies and other health issues.
- Join the local chapter of USGBC or other groups that support green design.
- Make sure your marketing media ethically communicate your commitment to sustainable design practices.
- Only accept catalogs and paper items from suppliers that you use most often. Otherwise, you are renting space and buying bookcases and other storage units to hold items you never use.

Within the Office

- Install motion-sensor light switches in any room/space that gets only occasional use through the day.
- Use "standby" power electronic devices in the office to reduce energy use. Also, all those LED lights on those devices "steal" energy; turn them off if not needed.
- Set computer monitors to hibernate rather than display a screen saver when not in use.
- Use refillable pens rather than disposable ones.
- Use real cups, plates, glasses, and utensils rather than disposable ones.
- Cut down on office supplies in stock. Keep track of what is needed for about 60 days and only keep this much stock on hand.
- Don't add long, involved signatures—such as poetry, logos, and the like—at the end of your e-mails. Quite often, the recipient who prints out such a message ends up using an extra piece of paper that has only this signature on it. Use a brief signature instead.

WEB SITES RELEVANT TO THIS CHAPTER

www.amanet.org American Management Association

www.awed.org American Women's Economic Development Corporation

www.mbda.gov Minority Business Development Agency

www.score.org SCORE

www.usgbc.org U.S. Green Building Council

www.sba.gov U.S. Small Business Administration

KEY TERMS

"As is"

Building standards

Build-out allowance

Business plan

Conditions, covenants, and restrictions (CCRs)

Demising wall

Inventory

Pro forma

Rentable area

Tenant improvements

Tenant work letter

Trade fixtures

Zoning restrictions

Zoning variance

WHAT WOULD YOU DO?

1. Julie has been working as a designer at a residential furniture store for seven years. She has had many satisfied clients and also recently won a design award. Julie decides to start her own studio and spends a few months writing a business plan and budget before finally giving notice to her employer.

   Her business, located in a small executive office suite, has now been open for six months. Julie is fortunate in that a few of her previous clients have come over to her business because they liked Julie's work very much.

   One of those clients, Mr. Griffin, signed an agreement for redesign of the Griffins' living room. Mr. Griffin has become irritated with Julie because of the high prices for some of the items specified by Julie and signed for by Mrs. Griffin. Both Mr. and Mrs. Griffin reviewed the plans for the living room, but none of the sales agreements were signed until a few weeks later. Mrs. Griffin signed the sales agreements while Mr. Griffin was out of the country on business.

   He e-mails Julie to tell her he will not pay the invoice of $12,540 for an area rug and $23,978 for a sofa and two wing chairs, as he did not sign the sales proposal for these items.

2. Three years ago, Nancy started her residential design business, Nancy Smyth Interiors. She operated by herself for the first year and a half and then added a part-time assistant, Sue, who was a nearly-graduated intern from the local college. Six months later, Nancy hired Sue full-time. A few months later, Angie joined Nancy's company. Angie is an experienced designer with five years of practice. Angie and, to some degree, Sue have been able to bring in enough additional projects that Nancy is considering hiring an office manager. However, Nancy is concerned about Angie and the direction of the company, because Angie is increasingly designing projects in "Angie's style" rather than Nancy's. Nancy is not sure how to handle the situation that she believes is developing. To complicate Nancy's problems, Sue now feels she can ignore Nancy's directives just as Angie does.

3. Jesse, Steve, and Gwen attended the hospitality show in Las Vegas. Their expenses were reimbursed by their boss. At one of the vendor parties, Steve became drunk and unruly. Jesse and Gwen tried to calm him down, but he persisted in his rude behavior. At one point, Steve knocked over a display in a showroom, doing damage to the display and the wall. Fortunately, no one was hurt.

The following week, their boss receives a phone call from the vendor detailing what happened. The vendor tells the firm owner that he expects the design firm to pay for the damages and also says that all three of the firm's employees are banned from the vendor's showroom.

The owner calls the three into his office, wanting an explanation. "I guess I drank too much. Sorry," is all that Steve has to say. The others explain that it was a fairly wild party and lots of people were drinking too much—since the drinks were readily available from the vendor's bartender.

The owner is livid and fires Steve on the spot. He warns Jesse and Gwen that if anything even remotely like this happens again, it will result in their termination as well. Steve then says that he wants to take copies of project drawings he worked on in the past year, but the owner refuses. Steve then says that he will sue the owner for discrimination, since he did not fire Jesse and Gwen.

REFERENCE

1. U.S. SBA Web site, 2012, www.sba.gov/community/blogs.

CHAPTER 18

Business Formations

After completing this chapter you should be able to:

- Compare and contrast the different forms of business organization.
- Discuss at least three advantages and disadvantages of each different business organization.
- Compare the general partnership with the limited liability company (LLC).
- Discuss the differences in legal responsibility for the owner of a sole proprietorship, general partnership, LLC, and corporation.
- Discuss the difference between the limited liability partnership, a general partnership, and an LLC.
- Compare the LLC and regular corporation forms as they relate to interior design businesses.
- Discuss the benefits of the corporate form of business for an interior design firm, especially one with several employees.
- Explain the benefits of a joint venture when a project is too large for just one design firm.
- Explain the differences between the C corporation, the S corporation, and the LLC.
- Name the stakeholder owners of a sole proprietorship, general and limited partnership, LLC, and joint venture.

NCIDQ COMPONENT

Based on best information available, some material in this chapter might appear as part of the NCIDQ examination. The reader should not depend solely on this text for study material.

A very important decision for the person who is considering starting a design practice is the legal form the business should take. The legal business formation affects management structure, taxes, liability, financing, and investment potential. It is also important to understand all the available legal formations, as many businesses change their legal formations sometime during the life of the business. This is a perfectly acceptable business practice.

As discussed in Chapter 17, it is important for the interior designer to consult with an attorney and an accountant before he or she makes this choice. Although an attorney is not required to help set up all these forms of business, getting the advice of an attorney is always prudent. The prospective business owner should discuss the merits of the different business formations with his or her accountant as well, because the business formation chosen has direct income tax implications for the owners and the business.

It is appropriate for the student to study these business formations as a way of understanding the responsibilities of the owner. Many students look forward to having their own design firm sometime in the future.

Table 18-1 summarizes the key characteristics of each business formation discussed in this chapter. Many books are available concerning detailed specifics of each of the legal formations that a business could take, and many are listed in the reference list. This chapter and Chapter 19 also discuss the various licenses and filings that are required when starting and operating a business. This chapter focuses discussion on business formations in the United States.

SOLE PROPRIETORSHIP

The simplest and least expensive form of business ownership is the *sole proprietorship*. It is a business form that is started, owned, and operated by one individual. The owner and the business are considered one and the same, so the business has no existence without the owner. Because there is only one owner, that individual makes all the decisions as to how to organize and operate the business.

Note that a *sole practitioner* is technically not the same as a sole proprietor. The title of sole practitioner is usually used by a member of the legal profession. Nevertheless, many other professions, including interior design and architecture, use the term *sole practitioner* to refer to someone who works alone.

To initiate a business in this form, all the owner needs to do is establish a name and location for the company, obtain any required licenses, and begin operation. If the company name is anything other than the owner's personal name, it will be necessary to file documentation with a local authority in the county or state. For example, if the business uses a name such as Creative Retail Interiors, the owner will have to file a fictitious name form or trade name affidavit. This is discussed in Chapter 19.

Fees for business licenses, resale licenses, and registration of the business name are minimal. These fees may be under $500, depending on the jurisdictions. Some of these fees are annual, whereas others need to be paid only at the time the business is started.

It is advisable to open a bank account in the firm's name, obtain business stationery, and begin to establish credit with trade sources. A transaction sales tax (resale) license is required if the company plans to sell merchandise to clients. Table 18-2 highlights important advantages and disadvantages of this type of business formation.

A sole proprietorship flourishes because of the involvement and reputation of the owner. Likewise, income generation is stopped or slowed when a sole proprietor takes vacations or becomes ill. Sole proprietorships are harder to sell to others because of the tight connection with the owner. If it is sold, the value relates to the assets of the business and possible goodwill based on previous clients. However, clients may not stick with the business if it is sold to someone else.

TABLE 18-1.

Key characteristics of business formations

	Owners	Personal Liability of Owners	Who May Legally Obligate Business	Continuity	Organizational Paperwork	Business Profits Taxed
Sole Proprietorship	Sole proprietor	Unlimited personal liability	Sole proprietor	Ends when proprietor wishes; might be able to sell business	Minimal	Individual rates of proprietor
General Partnership	General partners	Unlimited personal liability	General partner	Ends with death of a partner; may be transferred with consent of all partners	Minimal; partnership agreement recommended	Supplement to Form 1040
Limited Partnership	General and limited partners	General partner has unlimited liability; limited partner has liability up to amount of investment	General partner only	Same as general partnership; limited partners can sell their share	Start-up filing required; partnership agreement recommended	Individual tax of general and limited partners
Corporation	Stockholders	Stockholders have no personal liability; officers and directors have liability	Board of directors and officers	Continues unless corporation ends by decision of board or reason of law; stock transferred without needed consent	Articles of incorporation; bylaws; annual meeting of stockholders	Corporation pays taxes on profits; stockholders pay personal taxes
S Corporation	Same as corporation	Same as corporation	Same as corporation	Same as corporation	Same as corporation	Taxed as partnership
Limited Liability Company	Members	Member's liability is limited to amount invested	Members or manager/ member	May have to dissolve, depending on state	Start-up filing; operations agreement recommended	Varies depending on number of members
Professional Corporation	"Partners"	Similar to corporation	"Partners"	Same as corporation	Same as corporation	Same as corporation

TABLE 18-2.

Advantages and disadvantages of the sole proprietorship

Advantages

It is simple to start.

There is great freedom in management.

All profits (and losses) go to the proprietor. Profits and losses are not shared with others.

There are minimal special fees and minimal formal actions necessary to create the proprietorship.

The federal government requires no filings to begin the business, until employees are hired.

Depending upon the location of the business, it is not required that the owner pay unemployment tax for any income.

Profits are taxed as income on the sole proprietor's regular income tax statement. Similarly, business expense deductions can reduce the individual income tax due.

Disadvantages

Owner has personal liability for all debts and taxes.

The owner could experience tax problems, since too often a sole proprietor mixes business and personal income. (This should not be done!)

It is more difficult to obtain business loans from banks.

Suppliers often require substantial down payments or payment in full prior to shipping, until credit is established.

A sole proprietorship that also operates in other states may have to obtain licenses or prepare other types of registrations to do business in those other states.

The sole proprietor cannot collect unemployment benefits if the business closes its doors.

In states with community property laws, if a couple divorces, the sole proprietor may be forced to sell or close the business in order to divide the proceeds of the business.

Sole proprietors must be careful not to mingle personal funds with business funds. Business funds should be deposited in a business account so that personal funds and business funds are not mixed. Commingling of funds can result in a very difficult problem if the individual is ever audited by tax authorities.

Sole proprietors must be especially careful in the operation of their business, because the owner has personal responsibility for all legal and financial liabilities of the business. If a client sues a sole proprietor, any damages the client wins can be collected from the firm's assets and, if necessary, from the owner's personal assets. The sole proprietor is also personally responsible for all the business's debts. Money owed to a vendor might have to come out of a personal savings account if the business's account balance is insufficient. The owner must pay self-employment taxes (Social Security and Medicare contributions) on business income even when a "salary" is not drawn. Income taxes for the business are filed as part of the owner's personal income tax reports. These types of financing, liability, and management issues are a constant challenge for sole proprietors. Having a good business coach or advisor is very important for these practitioners.

PARTNERSHIPS

Another relatively easy way to start a business is to form a partnership. Many interior design firms begin when two designers decide to join forces. Formal paperwork is not generally required, though it is strongly recommended to help clarify who is responsible for what business tasks. It is important to note that partners act on each other's behalf and have fiduciary responsibility to each other. For these reasons, it is important to consider carefully when deciding to join forces in a partnership.

Three types of partnerships can be created: the general partnership, the limited partnership, and the limited liability partnership.

General Partnership

A general partnership is a common business formation in the interior design profession. Essentially, a *general partnership* is formed when two or more people join for the purpose of creating a business and these people alone share in the profits and risks of the business.

Two or more interior designers often start a business as a general partnership (1) because it brings more design talent (perhaps some skill or experience that one partner lacks) to the company, (2) because of the assets and credit rating of the partners, and (3) because the responsibilities of the company can be shared.

It is relatively easy to legally form a general partnership. In many ways, it is very similar to establishing a sole proprietorship. States do not generally require a formal filing; however, it is widely recommended that a *partnership agreement* be prepared to avoid future problems. If a written partnership agreement does not exist, most states refer to the Uniform Partnership Act (UPA) to set the terms of the partnership.

The following are among the most common questions that must be answered by those developing a partnership agreement. The partners should discuss these same items even if a written agreement is not contemplated. An attorney may suggest additional items, depending on the nature of the business:

- What will be the name and address of the business location?
- Where will the partnership be located?
- What is the purpose of the partnership?
- What are the names and addresses of the partners?
- What are the responsibilities of each partner?
- How much capital will each partner contribute?
- How will business profits be distributed?
- How will business holdings be divided in the event of dissolution of the partnership?
- How will each partner's drawings (salary) be distributed?
- How will the partnership be dissolved in the event of a partner's disabling illness, death, retirement, or departure for some other reason?
- How can ownership be transferred to another partner?
- How will any other changes in the management or other agreements be made?
- Which partners have fiduciary responsibility?
- How will disputes be resolved?

Item 18-1 on the companion Web site is a worksheet for developing a partnership agreement. Some states may require registration of the general partnership with the secretary of state. A general partnership may also have to register the company name with an appropriate jurisdiction, especially if a fictitious name such as Creative Interior Designs is used. A firm name consisting of the partners' names, such as Brown and Williams Associates, may also have to be registered, depending on jurisdiction-specific law.

TABLE 18-3.

Advantages and disadvantages of a general partnership

Advantages
It is easy and inexpensive to start, similar to a sole proprietorship.
There is the benefit of having two or more people involved in the affairs of the business. Banks are likely to offer loans to a partnership based on the assets of both of the two people.
The tax responsibility on profits is paid on each partner's individual taxes. However, partnership profits must be reported on Schedule E of Form 1040. Other filings are required, however, for the partnership itself (see Chapter 10).
Partners do not have to pay unemployment taxes on partners' income.
Disadvantages
Disagreement between partners as to how to manage the partnership may create difficulties.
Profits are split as determined by the partnership agreement (or equally, if no written agreement has been prepared).
Dissolution of the partnership may occur due to one partner wishing to quit the business, or a partner's illness or death. Depending on many factors, the remaining partner may not be able to continue with the business.
Partnerships are required to file many more forms with the federal and state tax authorities than for a sole proprietorship (see Chapter 19).
A partnership doing business in other states may have to obtain licenses or file other registrations to do business in those other states.

General partners are equally responsible for the debts of the company (unless some other arrangement exists in the agreement). Thus, each general partner has unlimited financial liability for any losses or debts that the partnership incurs. Liability goes beyond the partners' initial investment. If assets of the partnership are insufficient to satisfy debts, personal assets (up to the limitations established in each state) of the partners are vulnerable.

It is very important to choose a general partner carefully. The bad acts of one partner impact the other. As with a sole proprietorship, partners are personally liable in lawsuits or for other legal claims. Because a partnership does not protect the personal assets of the partners from the penalties of litigation, a lawsuit could result in the plaintiff being awarded business assets as well as personal assets of both partners. The firm and each partner of the firm are responsible for the actions of all the other partners. Any wrongdoing by one partner or any promises made by one partner are also the responsibility and obligation of the other partners. Table 18-3 highlights other advantages and disadvantages of the partnership form of business.

Limited Partnership

A variation on the general partnership is the *limited partnership*. In a limited partnership, someone in addition to the working partners has decided to invest in the business. The investment is most often monetary resources, but it could consist of other resources having monetary value.

For example, Robert and Peter have decided to form a commercial interior design firm, but they do not have enough funding to get the company going. Robert asks his parents to invest in the company and they provide $15,000 for operating capital. An arrangement is made in which Robert's parents receive agreed payments but have no authority to operate or manage the business. In this situation, a limited partnership has been formed rather than a general partnership.

A limited partnership is formed, according to statutory requirements, when a limited partnership agreement is filed with the state in which the partnership was formed. Because of this requirement, it is more expensive to start up than a general partnership. If the limited partnership operates in other states, it may be necessary for the partners to file an agreement in those other states as well.

If a design practice decides to form as a limited partnership, it must have at least one general partner, with other partners who invest in the design practice designated as limited partners. The general partners have responsibility for the management of the firm, while the limited partner cannot. The role of a limited partner is restricted to that of investor, contributing assets toward the operation of the partnership. For this investment, the limited partners receive a portion of the profits. The limited partners have financial responsibility for the losses and debts of the partnership only up to the amount of each limited partner's investment in the firm.

The general partners in a limited partnership have the same legal responsibilities as members of a general partnership. A limited partner is liable only up to the amount of his or her investment. Should any one of the limited partners become involved in the management of the design firm, he or she is no longer a limited partner but is, rather, a general partner. When this happens, the former limited partner now shares in the liability of the firm, as do the other general partners. If any of the partners (limited or general) withdraws from the business, the business may have to cease operations.

The limited partnership is a less attractive alternative today because all states now permit a business form called a limited liability company (LLC).

Limited Liability Partnership (LLP)

A special type of limited partnership is the limited liability partnership. This type of partnership is generally limited to certain licensed professionals such as accountants, lawyers, architects, physicians, and engineers.

Not all states allow the creation of a limited liability partnership, so you must check with the secretary of state to determine if this is a feasible alternative for an interior design business. If it is allowed, this business formation must be registered with the state.

In this form of business, the owners have limited liability rather than blanket liability as in a general partnerships. Each partner can participate in managing the business, unlike the limited partner. Other advantages exist. To find out more about this type of business formation in your area, try an Internet search directed to your state's secretary of state or corporation commission.

LIMITED LIABILITY COMPANY

Interior design firms are finding the limited liability company to be an advantageous business formation in which to begin an interior design practice. The *limited liability company (LLC)* is a hybrid of the general partnership or sole proprietorship and the corporation. This business type is now available in all jurisdictions. Because the structure is defined by state statute, use of this organizational form must be carefully considered based on local laws.

Before forming an interior design business as a limited liability company, you should understand the laws that govern such a formation in your state. An LLC is organized under state law, and the requirements differ from state to state. Most often, specific legal forms for organizing an LLC must be filed with a state agency such as the state's secretary of state office. Filing fees are also charged. Table 18-4 mentions some additional points about the limited liability company.

Owners of LLCs are called *members*, not partners, and those who manage the business are called *managers*. Almost all states allow an LLC to be formed with only one person as the owner. Some members can be investors who have

TABLE 18-4.

Advantages and disadvantages of an LLC

Advantages

It is simpler to organize than a corporation. However, articles of organization and possibly an operating agreement will be required by the state.

Special meetings, such as corporate annual meetings of stockholders, are not required. Records must be kept to document decisions.

There is more flexibility in how profits and losses are allocated among the members than in a partnership.

It is managed like a general partnership (assuming there is more than one member).

There are few limitations on the number and nature of members.

LLC members are not employees, so the business does not have to pay unemployment taxes for the members.

Disadvantages

Licensed professionals, such as lawyers and accountants, are prohibited from registering their businesses as LLCs. This restriction might affect interior designers who work in states that have licensing for interior design.

Members who manage the firm must pay self-employment tax, because they are not employees. (Self-employment tax is discussed in Chapter 19.)

The loss of a member might result in dissolution of the LLC.

If the company does business in other states, it may have to register with those other states. This depends on state law. If the LLC was formed with only one member, it may have limited ability to conduct business in other states.

---

little or no management or actual work involvement in the firm. Like any business formation, the LLC can have employees who are not owner members.

The name of the company must contain the words "limited liability company" or use the initials "LLC" or "LC." For example, Robert is considering "IDS, LLC" rather than using his personal name. That name will have to be researched and approved by the state corporation commission or other appropriate agency before he can begin using the name.

One of the most attractive aspects of the limited liability company is that it affords the limited liability protection of a corporation. The liability is limited to a member's investment, thus protecting personal assets. A member has no personal liability even if the company is sued or faces large debt. The business itself faces these liability issues, not the members personally.

The LLC has certain tax advantages like a partnership or sole proprietorship, in that the member can treat his or her tax responsibility in one of those two ways rather than as a corporation. Thus, profits are taxed as they would be with either a partnership or a sole proprietorship; the choice was made by the members. For this reason, an accountant should be consulted before this form is elected.

It is possible for a design firm that starts out as a sole proprietorship or partnership to change its business formation to a limited liability company. To make this change, usually a form must be submitted to the state secretary of state's office, or articles of organization must be prepared and submitted to that same state agency. Changing from a partnership to an LLC may be more complicated, but it is not impossible. Item 18-2 on the companion Web site will help you organize the information needed to prepare documentation for a LLC. Information on forming an LLC can be obtained from the Internal Revenue Service (www.irs.gov/businesses/small).

CORPORATIONS

Setting up a corporation is the most time-consuming and expensive method of legally forming a business. However, there are advantages, as a firm grows and

TABLE 18-5.

Terms related to corporations

Corporation. An association of individuals created by statutory requirements and, as such, a legal entity; sometimes referred to as a *C corporation*.

Incorporate. To create a corporation.

Incorporation. The act or process of forming a corporation.

Private, or general, corporation. Formed for private, profit-making interests. It is the most common type of corporate structure.

Public corporation. Formed by some government agency for the benefit of the public, such as the U.S. Postal Service. The term *public corporation* can also refer to companies that sell stock on one of the formal stock exchanges, such as the New York Stock Exchange, the American Stock Exchange, or the NASDAQ.

Close corporation. Corporation in which all the shares of stock are owned by a few individuals and shares are not traded on any of the public markets; also called *family corporation* or *closely held corporation*.

The *S corporation* is identical to the common C corporation except for special tax status. See the section on S corporations later in this chapter.

Domestic corporation. A corporation formed in one state and doing business only in that state.

Foreign corporation. A corporation formed in one state but doing business in another state is referred to as a foreign corporation by the other state. A foreign corporation does not have an automatic right to operate in any state other than the one in which it was formed.

sees its existence continuing beyond that of a sole proprietorship or partnership, which can outweigh these costs. A *corporation* (sometimes referred to as a C corporation) is an association of individuals created according to statutory law; as such, it is a separate legal entity.

As a legal entity in and of itself, a corporation exists independent of its originators or any other person connected directly with the firm. The originators may sell their interest in the corporation to other stockholders or to outside parties at any time—and the corporation goes on. If the principals or any of the stockholders die or otherwise withdraw from the operation of the business, the corporation still remains legally intact. Table 18-5 defines important terms concerning the corporate form of business.

A corporation is legally and financially separate and distinct from any of its originating or ownership members (called *stockholders* or *shareholders*). Because it is a legal entity, the corporation can sue and be sued by others, it can enter into contracts, and it can commit crimes and be punished. If a suit is brought and the court finds against the design firm, only the corporate assets can be used to pay the business's debts and any damage awards. The corporation is legally and financially responsible, like any individual person. A stockholder's liability extends only to the value of his or her stock. Individual stockholders of a corporation cannot be sued as the corporation, cannot enter into contracts in the name of the corporation, and so on.

Each state establishes regulations concerning the chartering of a corporation and its general organizational and operational limitations. If a corporation engages in interstate commerce, the federal government will also regulate it. Although some states allow businesses to incorporate without hiring an attorney, it is a good idea to seek an attorney's advice for this legal formation. Firms generally incorporate in the state in which they do business. Firms doing business in other states may be required by those other states to incorporate in those other states as well.

Depending on the state of origination, a corporation may be formed by only one person, though generally more than one person is involved in the organization. The organizers of the corporation must prepare a document

TABLE 18-6.

A basic outline of items in the articles of incorporation

> An articles of incorporation document is required for a new corporation. Note that specific details will vary from state to state.
>
> 1. The name of the corporation
> 2. The purpose and nature of the business in which the corporation will engage
> 3. The initial capital structure
> 4. The number and classes of shares of stock
> 5. Shareholders' rights
> 6. The place where the corporation will do business
> 7. The names of the members of the initial board of directors
> 8. The names of the original incorporators and statutory agents
> 9. Other information as might be required by the state

called the *articles of incorporation*. Table 18-6 shows the general outline of articles of incorporation. A worksheet to develop the information needed within the corporate form articles of incorporation is provided in Item 18-3 on the companion Web site.

This document is most often prepared by an attorney and is submitted to the proper authority in the state. The name of the corporation must be approved by the state's secretary of state office or other appropriate state agency. When the articles of incorporation are completed, they are usually sent to the appropriate authority in the state, along with a filing fee. After approval, a certificate of incorporation is returned, along with the articles, by the state's secretary of state.

The first organizational meeting, the date of which is stated in the articles of incorporation, is then held. During this meeting, the board of directors is elected, the bylaws are prepared, discussions or actions concerning the sale of stock take place, and so on. When this agenda has been completed, the corporation may formally begin operation.

Corporate officers are required to inform the stockholders of the financial condition of the corporation and to conduct such other business as might be dictated by the board of directors or stockholders. An annual financial report must be prepared (usually by an independent accounting firm) and must be provided to the stockholders. Numerous reports must be filed on a monthly or quarterly basis with appropriate jurisdictions, making the corporate form of business a more intensive management challenge, especially if the corporation has employees.

Capital to start a corporation is generally obtained by selling stock in the corporation. People who wish to invest in the company will buy shares of stock. When the corporation is formed, the initial board of directors determines how many shares of stock will be issued and how much of this first issue will be sold. Later, the corporation may sell additional stock to raise more capital. Unlike limited partnerships, however, stock ownership does not automatically mean the stockholders share in the profits. Stock of a corporation that is some type of interior design firm is not openly traded on any stock market, so a large infusion of funds through the sale of stock is not easy to obtain.

A corporation can also raise capital by going to lending institutions and pledging future assets as collateral to secure the loans. Although this method is open to partnerships and sole proprietorships as well, it is much easier for a corporation to obtain loans than it is for these other forms of business. However, a purely service-oriented design corporation that carries no inventory and has little other collateral will still have difficulty obtaining a loan from a bank.

TABLE 18-7.

Advantages and disadvantages of the corporation form

Advantages

The corporation is a legal entity separate from its owners. No other business formation has this status.

Financial liability of the originators (or principals) and stockholders is limited to the amount of money each has invested in the corporation.

The personal assets of the principals and stockholders cannot be used to satisfy legal judgments against the corporation.

Corporations have continuity, even if the originators cease to be involved.

Capital for the business can be raised by selling stock.

A corporation can obtain debt financing (loans) more readily than other forms of business.

Shareholders elect the board of directors. This gives shareholders a say in the management of the corporation.

The nature of the corporation, even if it is only by legal appearance, may make it easier to attract employees.

Disadvantages

A corporation is the most complicated and expensive of the business formations.

Business continuity requires a great deal of paperwork.

Annual stockholders' meetings must be held.

The officers and directors of the corporation are liable for any criminal actions that they or their representatives perpetrate in the name of the corporation.

The names of officers and directors are considered public information available from the secretary of state. Shareholders' names are not generally public information.

Stockholders can only influence management by participating in the stockholders' meeting and election of the board of directors and officers.

Business activities are limited to those described in the articles of incorporation.

Corporations are more heavily regulated by state and federal agencies than the other business formations.

A corporation must qualify and register to do business in other states.

Tax issues for corporations are complex. The corporation must pay income tax on its profits. In addition, stockholders pay taxes on dividend income. The corporation's officers also pay employment taxes, Social Security and Medicare contributions, and unemployment taxes. The corporation must pay these same taxes for all employees of the corporation. If a designer forms an interior design business as a corporation, that designer/owner becomes an employee of the corporation. Technically, clients hire the corporation for design work, not the individual owner. The owner must sign contracts in the name of the corporation, not in his or her own name. As an employee, you are paid a salary—assuming you wish to be paid. Withholding and Social Security taxes must be paid to the federal government for salary paid to the owners just as they are for any other employee. And, of course, income tax will be paid on that salary.

Table 18-7 summarizes the advantages and disadvantages of the corporation business form.

S Corporation

The *S corporation* is a special form of corporation that affords many of the benefits of a corporation but does not pay taxes as a corporation. If a designer chooses to utilize the S corporation, he or she is essentially electing the manner in which he or she will be taxed. At one time, this form was formally called a subchapter S corporation. Because of the popularity of the LLC, the S corporation is not used as frequently today.

The S corporation is formed in a very similar manner to a corporation and is expected to meet all the same requirements as the corporation for articles of incorporation, stockholders' meetings, election of a board of directors, and so on. A business is formed as an S corporation because this entity provides liability protection and has a different tax structure that is often more favorable to owners. To understand the liability benefits, please review the corporation form of business in the previous section.

If a business elects to be an S corporation for tax reasons, it then pays taxes as a partnership or sole proprietorship.[1] Most states follow the federal government's lead on taxation. However, a few states tax the S corporation as a regular corporation. Check with your state treasury department or secretary of state office to be sure what rules are in effect in your state. The S corporation must file special tax reports with the government.

Designers also may wish to elect S corporation status in the early years of the business, when it is most likely to experience business losses. These losses are absorbed by the owner's and shareholders' personal income taxes rather than by the business, as the business itself does not pay income taxes. Owners and shareholders pay income tax on the profits of an S corporation in proportion to the share of stock they hold in the corporation. These payments are called *distributions*.

The owner of a design business who chooses to qualify it as an S corporation must apply to the Internal Revenue Service to do so. The eligibility requirements include the following:

- The firm must be a domestic corporation (incorporated within the United States).
- The shareholders can only be individuals, not other corporations or partnerships.
- There cannot be more than 100 shareholders.
- All shareholders must be American citizens.
- The corporation has only one class of stock.[2]

Any failure to meet these criteria will result in the termination of S status for the corporation. Because of these requirements, it is common for smaller, family, or closely held corporations to elect to be treated as S corporations. It is necessary to change to the regular corporate form when the firm no longer meets the eligibility requirements for S corporation status.

Because the advantages and disadvantages of an S corporation are very similar to those of a corporation, they will not be repeated here. Business owners who are considering an S corporation election should discuss this issue in detail with their accountants.

Professional Corporation

A *professional corporation* (referred to as a *professional association* or *professional service corporation* in some states) is a corporation formed by persons in professions such as law, medicine, dentistry, accounting, engineering, or architecture. If your state has interior design licensing, you may be able to use the professional corporation as the legal form of your business. In many states, only professional services that are licensed or have other legal authorization by the state may register as professional corporations.

The letters PC (professional corporation), PA (professional association), or PSC (professional service corporation) follow the name of the firm, identifying it as a professional corporation. All shareholders must be licensed to practice the service being provided, and the business is limited to a single profession. It should not be confused with a limited liability partnership, as the two are different business formations.

Merely because your state has licensing for interior design practice does not automatically mean that you may use the professional corporation for your legal business structure. Each state has guidelines governing which professions may use this business formation. Some have very limiting restrictions related to the professional corporation. Restrictive laws concerning professional corporations were passed in the latter part of the 20th century because many felt that professional service businesses gained too many tax advantages with this business formation.

The professional corporation is formed similarly to an ordinary corporation. Registration is done by filing documents with a state secretary of state or corporation commission office. Many professional corporations are considered professional service corporations, meaning that they provide services but sell no products. When this is the case, the tax liability is higher than for the regular corporation.[3]

All shareholders are liable to clients, even if only one member is negligent. Personal assets of shareholders are protected from business debts. However, any shareholder of a professional corporation who is found guilty of a negligent act is personally liable for the injury and damages.

JOINT VENTURE

Suppose that the design firm you work for has been approached by another design firm to respond to a request for proposal (RFP) for a boutique resort located in another country. Your firm has experience in working with international projects, and the other firm has extensive resort experience within the United States. The other firm wants your firm to join it in responding to the RFP and doing the project together. The other firm's owners propose that your two firms create a joint venture for this project.

When two or more persons or firms agree, on a temporary basis, to share in the responsibilities, losses, and profits of a particular project or business venture, they have elected to create a *joint venture*. The key to the joint venture is its temporary status. Neither firm loses its original identity, because the joint venture is almost always formed with a new name for the temporary partnership that exists only for the duration of the project. Both generally also go on with other projects that are separate from the joint venture project. When the project has been completed, the temporary partnership ends, and each firm goes back to working on a completely individual basis.

The joint venture is treated much like a partnership business formation, but it is for a limited time period or for a certain activity. Because two (or more) firms are creating a new firm—even for a temporary period—a formal agreement should be prepared. This agreement should explain the responsibilities of each party, the conditions of the arrangement, the manner in which the profits and losses will be divided, the method for paying employees, and so on. It is common to follow the outline of items in a general partnership agreement when drafting a joint venture agreement.

Not being a legal entity, the joint venture cannot be sued, but the individual members of the joint venture can be. Each firm independently, and the joint venture as a whole, are liable to the client. Depending on the state in which the joint venture is formed, the profits and losses of the venture are usually taxed as they would be for a partnership, or are passed along to the participating members of the joint venture.

This kind of business relationship most often is entered into for one of these reasons:

- The project is so large that no single firm—large or small—would have the time and support team within the existing firm to do it alone.
- The design project is in another state or foreign location. An out-of-state firm could benefit from the reputation and licensing of a local firm, or the experience of a firm that is familiar with working outside the country.
- To gain experience in the kind of project proposed, for which it currently has little or no experience. Perhaps one firm has experience in lighting and kitchen design for restaurants but needs additional staff for aesthetic design solutions. The joint venture creates a full-service design package for the project.
- The combination of firms makes a large staff available to complete the work even though each firm continues to do independent work. If one firm alone were to obtain the contract, it might be necessary to hire additional designers. It takes time to train new employees, and this can be quite costly. The temporary partnership brings the staffs of both firms together and might negate any need to hire additional employees on a short-term basis.
- A joint venture gives the two firms an opportunity to learn from each other in areas other than design. Although competing firms do not willingly give away their design and business secrets, some ideas and concepts can be shared while respecting the integrity and confidentiality of both firms.
- The joint venture provides a very strong design team. For the client, using the expertise of two firms can mean better design and follow-through. One firm may not have the support staff or expertise to complete the project in a timely fashion.

A joint venture is not the same as "partnering" with the various parties involved in a project in order to manage a project. Partnering is not a business formation: It is a way of managing a project. A joint venture *is* a specific form of business. Through the joint venture, both firms continue under their own individual identities and with projects other than the joint venture project. If the firms did not create a joint venture but wished to join together, one firm would have to merge with the other. This, of course, would mean that one firm would no longer exist.

There are disadvantages in participating in a joint venture. If the roles of each company are not clearly defined, one partner may be taken advantage of. Different management styles can interfere with smooth working relationships of those involved in the joint venture project. Any imbalance in expertise can cause problems when disagreements occur.

Care must be taken when deciding to enter into a joint venture. Thorough discussion of roles, responsibilities, and (of course) monetary investment is critical to the success or failure of the venture. Success naturally should be equally shared, and failure can harm both companies.

WEB SITES RELEVANT TO THIS CHAPTER

www.awed.org American Women's Economic Development Corporation

www.mbda.gov Minority Business Development Agency

www.nolo.com Nolo Publishing (for legal information)

www.score.org SCORE

www.irs.gov/business/small U.S. Internal Revenue Service

KEY TERMS

Close corporation	Limited liability partnership (LLP)
Corporation	Limited partner
Domestic corporation	Partnership
Foreign corporation	Partnership agreement
General partner	Private (or general) corporation
Incorporate	Professional corporation
Incorporation	Public corporation
Joint venture	S corporation
Limited liability company (LLC)	Sole proprietorship
Limited liability company members	Uniform Partnership Act (UPA)

WHAT WOULD YOU DO?

1. Jonathan and Henry have worked in interior design for several years, each working for a different commercial firm. Jonathan specialized in medical facilities and Henry was mostly involved in offices and some hospitality projects. They met when they were elected to the board of directors of their local professional association. Jonathan suggested at a postmeeting dinner that they team up and start their own design firm. They elected the partnership form of business and created a brief, loose agreement that focused on the dollars each would contribute to the firm.

   A year later, a client accuses Henry of overbilling and other activities that the client claims are fraudulent practices. Jonathan steps in to try to resolve the problems and understand what is going on, but the client refuses to speak to him. Three weeks later, the client sends a letter to the firm informing them that he is planning to speak to an attorney and is also filing ethics complaints against both of them.

2. Robert started his own firm after working for several years in residential interior design. He works by himself but has a part-time assistant to do ordering. Robert's design solutions often include custom casework as well as items purchased from vendors.

   He receives a phone call from the cabinetmaker whom he hired to manufacture custom cabinets for a kitchen project. The vendor complains that the instructions concerning the cabinets are very confusing. Robert tells his assistant to visit the cabinetmaker to straighten things out, as Robert has to go out of town to meet with another client.

The instructions the assistant gives turn out to be incorrect, leading to products that cannot be installed.

3. Ralph has worked for a design firm for a little more than a year. Clients on three projects of the eight for which he has been responsible have complained to the owner about his poor attitude, as well as his consistently poor record of responding to client communications about projects. Mr. Smith was particularly upset with Ralph's performance on his project.

   Three of the projects Ralph worked on during the year have won industry awards, including the project for Mr. Smith. The owner decides to fire Ralph after Mr. Smith calls and threatens to file a suit against the firm and an ethics complaint against Ralph. After talking to some colleagues at another firm, Ralph decides to look into suing the firm because of the termination.

4. Martha presented her design contract to Dr. Jones and Dr. Smith. All through her presentation and discussion of how she worked and how she saw this project progressing, she felt that obtaining the doctors' signatures on the contract would be easy. However, questions arose concerning the scope outlined and a few clauses in the contract, as well as the overall fee. Martha wants this project, as it will help her obtain other projects at a large medical office building that is only partially leased to tenants.

   Dr. Jones asks her to begin sketches of the floor plan right away, as they need to get those plans to the developer immediately. The doctor says he will not sign the contract until they see the floor plan.

REFERENCES

1. Nolo, "S Corporation Facts," 2005, www.nolo.com

2. S Corporations, www.irs.gov

3. Nolo, "Professional Corporations," 2012, www.nolo.com

CHAPTER 19

Business Legal Filings and Licenses

After completing this chapter you should be able to:

- Explain the importance and necessity of the employer identification number.
- Determine when a fictitious business name statement is required.
- Explain the differences between a business legal name and a trade name.
- Explain what types of interior design businesses are required to obtain a transaction privilege tax license.
- Describe the different filings necessary when a business has employees.
- Explain who must file self-employment tax and why.
- Compare the sales tax license to the use tax license.

NCIDQ COMPONENT

Based on best information available, some material in this chapter might appear as part of the NCIDQ examination. The reader should not depend solely on this text for study material. See the sections on business licenses and tax requirements.

One of the challenges of owning a design practice is the regular completion and filing of the various forms required by federal, state, and local jurisdictional laws. Serious adverse consequences await the business if the owner neglects to prepare and file required documents with the jurisdiction.

Some of the forms discussed in this chapter are needed to originate the business, whereas most are needed for the life of the business. Some states may not require all those listed, and other filings may be required by a specific state. Each city and county may also have forms for particular licenses, property taxes, or tax requirements that the business must obtain and file. Advice as to proper filings can be obtained from the firm's accountant and attorney.

Changes are made annually to many of the requirements for business filings, especially those relating to tax laws. The documents discussed in this chapter are broad guidelines as to what is required. The forms discussed relate to businesses formed in the United States.

BUSINESS LEGAL FILINGS

Legal filings for a new business will vary based on the type of business formation. A sole proprietorship need file only a very few forms to start the business, whereas a corporation must deal with quite a lot. This section discusses the most common forms required to start a business beyond those required for the legal formation. The forms and filings concerning employees are not one-time filings; they must be done throughout the life of the business.

Form SS-4: Application for Employer Identification Number

The form most commonly required of a business is *Form SS-4, Application for Employer Identification Number*, issued by the federal Internal Revenue Service. This *employer identification number (EIN)* identifies the business to the federal and state governments. It is used on income tax forms that must be submitted to the federal and state revenue services. Many states also require that the business obtain a *state employer identification number* using a different form. For reference, a copy of the Form SS-4 is included on the companion Web site as Item 19-1

All forms of business must obtain an EIN, with the possible exception of the sole proprietor. The owner of a sole proprietorship can use his or her Social Security number in place of an EIN. Most accountants recommend that the sole proprietor/sole practitioner obtain an EIN, as it will be required when the business hires employees. In addition, banks also require the business that wants to open a commercial account to have an EIN. States that issue state employer identification numbers usually require an EIN whether or not the business has employees.

When the interior design practice has been formed as a corporation, anyone working for the corporation is an employee. This means that even if only one individual actually generates income for the corporation and is a member of the board of directors/stockholders of the corporation, that individual would be considered an employee.

Sometimes a business must get a new EIN. If the business formation changes to a different type of formation, a new EIN will be needed for the new business—even if the name has not changed. For example, Mary Anne, the owner of Overview Interiors (a sole proprietorship), has taken on a partner, James. Because the business has changed from a sole proprietorship to a partnership, a new EIN must be obtained. The firm's accountant or attorney can provide guidance on specific issues.

The privilege of forming and operating a corporation rests with the states, so the state(s) in which the corporation intends to do business will require that all businesses formed as corporations be registered with the state before operations begin. In most cases, corporation identification numbers are obtained from the state department of revenue. This number may be different from a state employer identification number.

Fictitious Business Name Statement

Selecting a name for the new business is a very important task and a separate section appears later in this chapter to discuss issues related to that task. If the business name is something other than the legal names of the owners, it is necessary to file a *fictitious business name statement* with the appropriate state and possibly city offices. Many businesspeople refer to this as a *doing business as (DBA)* statement.

The main purpose in registering a fictitious business name is to identify to the state and to the general public the owner(s) responsible for any business formed within the state. In some states, it may also be necessary for the new business to publish a statement of ownership. This requirement varies depending on the legal form of the business. The federal government does not involve itself in business names other than through trademark registration.

Many sole practitioners use their legal name as their business name. Others choose a fictitious name. This filing is required of all sole proprietorships and partnerships and is usually filed with the county clerk or the state secretary of state.

Instead of a fictitious business name statement, corporations and LLCs must register the business name with the corporation commission and/or the state secretary of state (depending on the laws in the jurisdiction). It is relatively common for corporations to print a copy of the corporation papers in the business section of the local newspaper.

When the business uses a fictitious name, the owner must be sure that no other business in the state is already using that name. Research must be done to be sure that a fictitious business name is available. If the name is already being used, the state or county clerk will not allow another company to use the name. The reader should check with the jurisdiction in which the business will be located to know how to correctly and legally file the business name.

What's in a Name?

The name of a business affects the brand of the business and can mean positive promotional opportunities for the company. To some, a business name should clarify what the business offers—for example, "ABC Interior Design"—whereas others feel that is not necessary. For example, consider the business names Apple, Facebook, and Ford. They all invoke positive recognition, yet none of these names really clarify what the business sells. Some experts say that the more your company name communicates to potential customers, the greater the chance they will consider your firm.

Whether or not the name includes information about the business, the name of an interior design firm can raise positive recognition in the design firm's market area. The key in connection to the name is overall business branding and marketing. (Branding is discussed in Chapter 22.)

A business name can also give the firm a marketing boost. "New Visions" sounds like a larger company than "Thomas Jones Interior Consultant." If you plan to use a fictitious name, test it with friends and relatives to be sure it conveys the meaning you want. Also consider keeping the name short. A long name can be confusing.

In reality, a business can have two names: the legal name and a trade name. A *legal name* is the business's official name, which must always be used on legal documents such as contracts and tax returns. The *trade name*—dependent on the type of legal business formation used—is the one used in public, such as on stationery, business cards, and a Web site. A trade name can be any name not used by some other company. It can contain the name of the owner of the company, or it can be a made-up name.

Here's an example: "Mary Smith" is the legal name of a sole proprietorship interior design practice started by Mary Smith. If she adds terms like "interiors," "consulting," "design group," or "interior designer" to her name, it becomes a trade name: "Mary Smith Interior Design."

A name search should be performed to be sure some other business does not use the same business name—especially in your market area. Name searches can be done by using an Internet search engine such as Google (www.google.com), by checking local phone books in your area, and by reviewing trade name lists with the U.S. Patent and Trademark Office. You might also want to check Internet domain names if you want to use your company name as your domain name. Two large registration Web site addresses are www.register.com and www.networksolutions.com.

When you use a fictitious name, you may also wish to register the name as a trade name or a trademark. This is done through the U.S. federal government's U.S. Patent and Trademark Office (www.uspto.gov). You can also go to a private Web site (www.uspto.com) to search trade names. Registering the trade name or trademark gives you exclusive use of the item. This might be particularly important for a firm that plans to have offices in other jurisdictions than its home location. As long as your jurisdiction says that the name is usable, you do not have to register the name with the federal government.

The legal names and designations desired or required for limited liability companies and corporations require research and permission from a state agency. The state agency—often the office of the state secretary of state or corporation commission—will have a register of company names that are already in use. An LLC must register its name even if its business name is "Mary Smith, LLC." Partners that use their own names as the business name are handled similarly to a sole proprietorship. However, partnership names should also be checked, because a partnership such as "Smith and Randolph Partnership" might already be taken by another company.

For Firms with Employees

When a design firm hires employees—even part-timers—the owner becomes responsible for filing several other documents in addition to the EIN. Similar forms must be filed with the state. The employer will need to retain a copy of the Form W-4 completed by the employee. The employer also provides to the employee a copy of the Form W-2 for the employee's records. The manner in which these are collected, their amounts, and the reporting methods vary from state to state. Brief descriptions of these documents are provided. Many of the documents discussed in this section can be obtained online. The IRS Web site (www.irs.gov) is a primary site for finding these forms.

> *Form I-9, Employment Eligibility Verification.* The purpose of this form is to document that each new employee, whether a citizen or noncitizen of the United States, hired after November 6, 1986, is authorized to work in the United States. Because it is also unlawful for the company to discriminate in its hiring practices, companies are required to have all new applicants submit acceptable identification and work authorization information, primarily by using Form I-9. The individual or business that is doing the hiring must keep a record of the request and verification on file. You can obtain the most current versions of this form at www.uscis.gov/files from the U.S. Immigration Service.
>
> Federal *Form W-4, Employee's Withholding Allowance Certificate.* This form is filled out by an employee upon being hired. The employer is required to keep this form on file and must send a copy of the W-4 to the IRS. This form indicates the number of deductions to which the employee is entitled (or desires), which determines how much income tax is withheld from wages.
>
> Federal *Form W-2, Employer's Wage and Tax Statement.* This form is prepared by the employer and is sent to the employee no later than January 31 of the calendar year. Form W-2 shows all wages paid;

federal, state, and city taxes withheld; and Social Security taxes (shown as FICA) withheld for the employee.

Social Security and Medicare reporting. Businesses must pay contributions to the Social Security and Medicare programs for employees. The employee also will have a portion of wages withheld and sent to the program by the employer.

Federal *Form 1099.* This is called an informational form. It has many uses and is commonly used to report taxable income for individuals who are not employees of the firm. Examples are payments to installers or a nonemployee hired to do CAD work for the firm. At present, only amounts to nonemployees that total more than $600 must be reported on 1099s. There are other versions of and uses for this form. The business owner should consult with the firm's accountant to understand which forms are needed.

Unemployment taxes provide funds to eligible employees in the event that they are laid off from their jobs. This is a state requirement and funds are paid to the state. Almost all businesses with employees, even if there is only one employee, pay unemployment tax. The exceptions are sole proprietorships and partnerships that do not have to pay unemployment taxes on the compensation to the owners. Failing to pay these funds to the state can have serious consequences for the business.

Workers' compensation insurance is a state-mandated program providing funds to the employee to cover the expenses of work-related injuries. State laws generally require that most businesses, regardless of their size, provide workers' compensation insurance. Failing to pay these funds to the state can have serious consequences for the business.

LICENSES

The licenses that an interior design practitioner may need to obtain for a new business will vary based on local, state, and/or provincial laws. It is not possible to discuss fully all the specific licenses that might be required by the various jurisdictions. The owner of an interior design practice must check with the proper counsel to be sure he or she is fulfilling the requirements of each state and municipality in which the firm will be doing business.

An important point is to understand that a firm located in one state but doing business in another state may need to file specific forms or obtain licenses to operate in that other state. Note that "operating" can mean simply doing a project in that other jurisdiction. It does not mean that a branch of the business is located in the other state/jurisdiction.

The following is a brief discussion of the state licenses that are most commonly required of interior design practices. No federal licenses are required for interior design services or businesses. A possible exception is an industry-related business involved in the manufacturing of certain goods used in interiors.

Interior Design Licensure or Title Registration

Licensure and title registration laws in the United States and Canada vary by jurisdiction. Students and professionals must keep abreast of any new laws being considered in their jurisdiction and must be prepared to meet the specific requirements of all statutes, existing and new. In general, the state board of technical registration (or other similar agencies) sets the standards for licensing and title registration in conjunction with approval by state legislatures. The state boards are also responsible for enforcement and termination of license privileges.

Interior designers who are working in states where title registration or licensing requirements have been established must meet those regulations when they open a business. Depending on state laws, a designer working in a nonregulated state might be prohibited from even doing projects in regulated states. Regulated states generally allow a registered designer in another state to work in another regulated state. This is referred to as *reciprocity*. A designer who works for someone who is licensed might not have to be individually licensed as long as he or she is an employee. If the designer changes jobs or starts a business, the designer would need to obtain this important license or certification.

Additional discussion of licensing and title registration is presented in Chapter 2.

State and City Transaction Privilege (Sales) Tax License

It is imperative for businesses that intend to resell goods to the end user to obtain a state and city (if city sales tax is collected) *Transaction Privilege (Sales) Tax License*. This license is commonly referred to as a *resale license* or *seller's permit*. Sales tax must be collected on almost all goods (food being a notable exception) that are purchased by the end user/consumer in almost all states. Some jurisdictions require that sales tax be collected on design services as well.

The seller (interior designer) does not pay sales tax on goods that he or she buys and resells to a client. The sales tax license allows the interior designer to pass on the state sales tax to the client. If a designer does not charge the client the sales tax, the firm will have the obligation of paying that tax. If the business fails to do so, the taxing authority will hold the business responsible for the tax monies. The amount collected must be reported and paid on a monthly basis, whether or not sales for the period have occurred. These monthly reports must be filed as long as the business remains in existence.

In some states, the owner can obtain a city tax license form at the same time that he or she applies for the state license; the taxes are then collected by the state and are forwarded to the appropriate cities. If this joint license is not available from the state, the city license must be obtained separately. The city license serves the same function as the state license. If the design firm has offices/stores in more than one city or state, separate sales tax licenses will likely be required for each jurisdiction. Many states require, and accountants suggest, that a business obtain this license whether or not the business will be selling goods.

Legislators have increasingly started to require sales tax collection on some services, as a means to gain extra state income. The designer should carefully check whether sales tax must be charged on services. See Chapter 8 for additional information about sales taxes.

Use Tax Registration Certificate

Use tax is a companion to the sales tax. If the business will be purchasing goods from out of state for use or sale and these goods are taxable in the state in which the interior design firm is doing business, the business is required to obtain a *use tax certificate* and to pay sales tax on those items. This ensures that sales taxes or use taxes are collected either by the state that is selling the goods to the interior design firm or by the firm to the state if the goods are sold to end users.

Contractor's Licenses

In some states, an interior designer may be required to obtain a contractor's license. This is most often true when the interior designer's responsibilities include the hiring of trades to do construction work and supervision of that work, and when those charges are billed to the client through the interior designer. A license might also be needed even if only the purchase and supervision of the installation of architectural finishes is handled through the interior designer. This applies to both residential and commercial interior projects.

Exceptions are available only when the work is considered to be casual work for a small sum of money (specifics of this vary with the jurisdiction). Projects done by a professional interior designer rarely fall into the "casual work" category, however. Thus, such items as structural work, carpet laying, wall-covering installation, plumbing, and other items that are attachments to the building must be done only by a licensed contractor.

This is not to say that an interior designer must also be a contractor or have a general contractor's license. In fact, it is rare for interior designers to be required to obtain a general contractor's license or even one of the several specialized contractor's licenses for supervision of work. However, some states require these licenses or a specialty contractor's license to sell, contract for, or supervise the installation or construction of these types of products. If the interior designer does not have the contractor's license, he or she should instruct the client to hire contractors who hold these licenses to do the work.

Most states require that only licensed contractors perform work done for private residences and commercial facilities. If the designer hires unlicensed contractors to perform work that a licensed contractor must perform, the client may not have any legal obligation to pay the designer. It may also be a criminal offense for the interior designer to use the unlicensed contractor. The owner of the interior design firm should be familiar with the statutes of the state in which the firm is located, and of any state in which it may be doing business. Questions should be directed to the state registrar of contractors or other appropriate authority.

INCOME TAX BASICS

All businesses must pay federal income tax on business profits. The amount of tax that a business must pay on its income is based on many factors. The employer identification number discussed earlier is needed to file tax reports.

All forms of business have to pay *estimated taxes*, because federal and state income tax is on a "pay-as-you-go" basis. That means that the company must pay taxes quarterly on the amount of taxable income it expects to get.

Although estimated taxes are important for any size business to calculate and pay as required, it can be particularly important to the self-employed. With a self-employed individual, there is no employer to withhold a portion of wages with each paycheck. Usually, self-employed persons are required to pay estimated taxes based on the previous year's taxable amount. Penalties are imposed for underpayment of estimated taxes. Sole proprietors and other business owners should discuss the method of calculating and paying estimated taxes with the firm's accountant.

The exact taxable amount is affected by legal business deductions. These deductions generally relate to costs of operating and maintaining the business. Items such as marketing efforts, office supplies, and rent are just a few of the kinds of expenses that are deductible. It is beyond the scope of this book to discuss tax deductions. This issue should be covered in detail with the practitioner's accountant so that proper recordkeeping can be instituted at the very onset of the business. A brief discussion on income tax related to the different formations of businesses is presented in Chapter 18.

States also require that businesses pay state income tax on business profits. Because most states model their income tax reporting on the federal laws, the reporting methods are similar. Forms and actual reporting methods are, of course, different for each state.

A portion of the amount that is paid as estimated tax by the self-employed who own a sole proprietorship or partnership is a self-employment tax. The *self-employment tax* is paid on the income that a sole proprietor and any partners receive on their share of the owner's income of the business. It is the equivalent of the Social Security and Medicare tax paid by employees and employers on an employee's income. The form used in this case is Schedule SE (Form 1040), as shown in Figure 19-1. Another form important for the self-employed is Form 1040-Schedule C, on which the businessperson reports the profit and loss from a sole proprietorship. For informational purposes, a sample of Schedule SE (1040) and Form 1040-Schedule C are included on the companion Web site as Items 19-2 and 19-3, respectively.

Because the income of those who have ownership in certain business formations is considered self-employment income and is not subject to normal withholding taxes, the self-employed individual must report and pay this tax at the time at which normal income taxes are due. The government acts as an agent to collect this tax for the Social Security Administration.

In addition to income tax, many states tax the personal property of the business. In most cases, the personal property taxes cover furniture and equipment used in the business. Sellable inventory is not taxed. If a business owns any real estate, the business will also pay property tax. In most cases, these filings are sent to the county attorney or county assessor of the county in which the business is located rather than to the state revenue department. The county tax assessor automatically bills the owner of record annually for personal property taxes that are due.

Note that many tax guides are available from the IRS, some of which can be downloaded from www.irs.gov. Local and state agencies have numerous publications available that can help the new business owner clarify requirements within each jurisdiction.

WEB SITES RELEVANT TO THIS CHAPTER

www.cra-arc.gc.ca Canada Revenue Agency

www.uscis.gov U.S. Citizenship and Immigration Services

www.dol.gov U.S. Department of Labor

www.irs.gov U.S. Internal Revenue Service

www.uspto.gov U.S. Patent and Trademark Office

www.sba.gov U.S. Small Business Administration

Search sites within your jurisdiction to register a business name (usually with the state secretary of state or corporation commission).

SCHEDULE SE (Form 1040)	Self-Employment Tax	OMB No. 1545-0074
Department of the Treasury Internal Revenue Service (99)	▶ Attach to Form 1040 or Form 1040NR. ▶ See separate instructions.	2011 Attachment Sequence No. **17**

Name of person with **self-employment** income (as shown on Form 1040)	Social security number of person with **self-employment** income ▶

Before you begin: To determine if you must file Schedule SE, see the instructions.

May I Use Short Schedule SE or Must I Use Long Schedule SE?

Note. Use this flowchart **only if** you must file Schedule SE. If unsure, see *Who Must File Schedule SE* in the instructions.

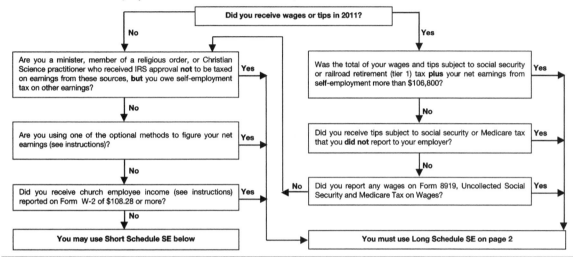

Section A—Short Schedule SE. **Caution.** Read above to see if you can use Short Schedule SE.

1a	Net farm profit or (loss) from Schedule F, line 34, and farm partnerships, Schedule K-1 (Form 1065), box 14, code A	**1a**
b	If you received social security retirement or disability benefits, enter the amount of Conservation Reserve Program payments included on Schedule F, line 4b, or listed on Schedule K-1 (Form 1065), box 20, code Y	**1b** ( )
2	Net profit or (loss) from Schedule C, line 31; Schedule C-EZ, line 3; Schedule K-1 (Form 1065), box 14, code A (other than farming); and Schedule K-1 (Form 1065-B), box 9, code J1. Ministers and members of religious orders, see instructions for types of income to report on this line. See instructions for other income to report	**2**
3	Combine lines 1a, 1b, and 2	**3**
4	Multiply line 3 by 92.35% (.9235). If less than $400, you do not owe self-employment tax; **do not** file this schedule unless you have an amount on line 1b . . . . ▶	**4**
	Note. If line 4 is less than $400 due to Conservation Reserve Program payments on line 1b, see instructions.	
5	**Self-employment tax.** If the amount on line 4 is:	
	• $106,800 or less, multiply line 4 by 13.3% (.133). Enter the result here and on **Form 1040, line 56, or Form 1040NR, line 54**	
	• More than $106,800, multiply line 4 by 2.9% (.029). Then, add $11,107.20 to the result. Enter the total here and on **Form 1040, line 56,** or **Form 1040NR, line 54**	**5**
6	**Deduction for employer-equivalent portion of self-employment tax.** If the amount on line 5 is:	
	• $14,204.40 or less, multiply line 5 by 57.51% (.5751)	
	• More than $14,204.40, multiply line 5 by 50% (.50) and add $1,067 to the result. Enter the result here and on **Form 1040, line 27,** or **Form 1040NR, line 27**	**6**

For Paperwork Reduction Act Notice, see your tax return instructions.	Cat. No. 11358Z	Schedule SE (Form 1040) 2011

FIGURE 19-1.

IRS Form Schedule SE (Form 1040), used to calculate the self-employment tax.

Schedule SE (Form 1040) 2011   Attachment Sequence No. **17**   Page **2**

Name of person with **self-employment** income (as shown on Form 1040)	Social security number of person with **self-employment** income ▶

Section B—Long Schedule SE

Part I   Self-Employment Tax

Note. If your only income subject to self-employment tax is **church employee income,** see instructions. Also see instructions for the definition of church employee income.

A   If you are a minister, member of a religious order, or Christian Science practitioner **and** you filed Form 4361, but you had $400 or more of **other** net earnings from self-employment, check here and continue with Part I . . . . ▶ ☐

1a	Net farm profit or (loss) from Schedule F, line 34, and farm partnerships, Schedule K-1 (Form 1065), box 14, code A. **Note.** Skip lines 1a and 1b if you use the farm optional method (see instructions)	**1a**		
b	If you received social security retirement or disability benefits, enter the amount of Conservation Reserve Program payments included on Schedule F, line 4b, or listed on Schedule K-1 (Form 1065), box 20, code Y	**1b**	(	)
2	Net profit or (loss) from Schedule C, line 31; Schedule C-EZ, line 3; Schedule K-1 (Form 1065), box 14, code A (other than farming); and Schedule K-1 (Form 1065-B), box 9, code J1. Ministers and members of religious orders, see instructions for types of income to report on this line. See instructions for other income to report. **Note.** Skip this line if you use the nonfarm optional method (see instructions)	**2**		
3	Combine lines 1a, 1b, and 2	**3**		
4a	If line 3 is more than zero, multiply line 3 by 92.35% (.9235). Otherwise, enter amount from line 3	**4a**		
	Note. If line 4a is less than $400 due to Conservation Reserve Program payments on line 1b, see instructions.			
b	If you elect one or both of the optional methods, enter the total of lines 15 and 17 here . .	**4b**		
c	Combine lines 4a and 4b. If less than $400, **stop**; you do not owe self-employment tax. **Exception.** If less than $400 and you had **church employee income,** enter -0- and continue ▶	**4c**		
5a	Enter your **church employee income** from Form W-2. See instructions for definition of church employee income . . . **5a**			
b	Multiply line 5a by 92.35% (.9235). If less than $100, enter -0-	**5b**		
6	Add lines 4c and 5b	**6**		
7	Maximum amount of combined wages and self-employment earnings subject to social security tax or the 4.2% portion of the 5.65% railroad retirement (tier 1) tax for 2011	**7**	106,800	00
8a	Total social security wages and tips (total of boxes 3 and 7 on Form(s) W-2) and railroad retirement (tier 1) compensation. If $106,800 or more, skip lines 8b through 10, and go to line 11 **8a**			
b	Unreported tips subject to social security tax (from Form 4137, line 10) **8b**			
c	Wages subject to social security tax (from Form 8919, line 10) **8c**			
d	Add lines 8a, 8b, and 8c	**8d**		
9	Subtract line 8d from line 7. If zero or less, enter -0- here and on line 10 and go to line 11 . ▶	**9**		
10	Multiply the **smaller** of line 6 or line 9 by 10.4% (.104)	**10**		
11	Multiply line 6 by 2.9% (.029)	**11**		
12	**Self-employment tax.** Add lines 10 and 11. Enter here and on **Form 1040, line 56,** or **Form 1040NR, line 54**	**12**		
13	**Deduction for employer-equivalent portion of self-employment tax.** Add the two following amounts. • 59.6% (.596) of line 10. • One-half of line 11. Enter the result here and on **Form 1040, line 27,** or **Form 1040NR, line 27** **13**			

Part II   Optional Methods To Figure Net Earnings   (see instructions)

Farm Optional Method. You may use this method **only** if **(a)** your gross farm income[1] was not more than $6,720, **or (b)** your net farm profits[2] were less than $4,851.

14	Maximum income for optional methods	**14**	4,480	00
15	Enter the **smaller** of: two-thirds (²/₃) of gross farm income[1] (not less than zero) or $4,480. Also include this amount on line 4b above	**15**		

Nonfarm Optional Method. You may use this method **only** if **(a)** your net nonfarm profits[3] were less than $4,851 and also less than 72.189% of your gross nonfarm income,[4] **and (b)** you had net earnings from self-employment of at least $400 in 2 of the prior 3 years. **Caution.** You may use this method no more than five times.

16	Subtract line 15 from line 14	**16**	
17	Enter the **smaller** of: two-thirds (²/₃) of gross nonfarm income[4] (not less than zero) **or** the amount on line 16. Also include this amount on line 4b above	**17**	

[1] From Sch. F, line 9, and Sch. K-1 (Form 1065), box 14, code B.

[2] From Sch. F, line 34, and Sch. K-1 (Form 1065), box 14, code A—minus the amount you would have entered on line 1b had you not used the optional method.

[3] From Sch. C, line 31; Sch. C-EZ, line 3; Sch. K-1 (Form 1065), box 14, code A; and Sch. K-1 (Form 1065-B), box 9, code J1.

[4] From Sch. C, line 7; Sch. C-EZ, line 1d; Sch. K-1 (Form 1065), box 14, code C; and Sch. K-1 (Form 1065-B), box 9, code J2.

Schedule SE (Form 1040) 2011

FIGURE 19-1.

(Continued)

KEY TERMS

Doing business as (DBA)

Legal name

Resale license

Self-employment tax

Seller's permit

Trade name

Unemployment taxes

Workers' compensation insurance

FILINGS

Employee's withholding allowance certificate—Form W-4

Employer identification number (EIN)

Employer's wage and tax statement—Form W-2

Fictitious business name statement

Form 1099 information forms

Social Security and Medicare reporting

Transaction privilege (sales) tax license

Use tax certificate

Work authorization verification—Form I-9

WHAT WOULD YOU DO?

1. Eric has owned a small residential interior design studio in a market area that has few competitors. His company has enough business that he has two student interns from a local design program, along with a full-time designer and an office manager. The full-time designer moved here from another state and is a professional-level member of one of the associations. She was also registered in that other state.

   Recently, Eric's advertising in the local paper has included the association logo. One of the interns talks to a professor, saying that she is pretty sure Eric is not a member of any association, since she has never seen any evidence to support that achievement. The student doesn't want to say anything to Eric and doesn't know what to do.

2. Barbara and Jane have had a design business for five years: a partnership called Excellence in Design. They have become specialized in an area of commercial interior design. It is important for both of them to protect the assets of the company and their personal assets.

   A recent problem with a client has them wondering about changing their business formation. In addition, Jane knows that Barbara wants to retire, or at least work only part time, in another two or three years. They have two full-time employees and one part-time employee.

3. Marsha charges a consultation fee that she feels covers the majority of her time working on a project. Occasionally the consultation fee is based on an hourly fee, and sometimes it is a fixed fee. Marsha added the consultation fee when she realized that clients were not recognizing the value she provided through her design solutions when she only charged a cost plus markup on the goods she sold. She also added

a consultation fee when it became clear that the markup percentage alone—which was very competitive in her market—was not providing a sufficient profit margin to cover expenses.

A client files a lawsuit against Marsha (and informs her that she also will file an ethics complaint). The client alleges that the design fee in addition to the markup on the products ordered by Marsha is an unfair duplication of fees.

CHAPTER 20

Strategic Planning: Designing the Future

After completing this chapter you should be able to:

- Explain the purpose of strategic planning and its benefits for a sole practitioner.
- Explain how and why planning is important for any interior design practice.
- Discuss how a company mission statement can be beneficial to a design firm.
- Identify through SWOT analysis at least three external factors that can have a positive impact on a firm.
- Discuss potential external threats to a design firm.
- Establish a business goal, along with strategies and tactics to make the goal achievable.
- Discuss why budgeting is such an important part of any planning process.
- Search out and investigate secondary sources of information to help gather better planning information for an interior design firm.
- Discuss how benchmarking can be valuable to a design firm.

Regardless of the size of an interior design practice, the business must be committed to planning. A firm does not become successful by opening its doors and expecting that a steady stream of clients will constantly be available. A firm must also be committed to long-range planning. Planning for the future helps to keep that stream of clients—and revenues—coming.

The type of planning that develops a future-oriented viewpoint and direction for a business is *strategic planning*. This long-term planning, along with annual business planning, helps the firm remain focused while at the same time looking for opportunities for desired growth.

Planning the business is an ongoing task for any owner who wants the company to grow. In fact, planning is necessary even for the owner who wants the firm to stay small and not become a huge management headache. Strategic planning is a specific process of planning that helps the business owner and employees determine where the firm wants to go in the future. This important planning process is a benefit to a firm of any size. The design firm does not have to be large to need to think about its future. The sole practitioner should be looking to his or her future goals as well.

This chapter focuses on the strategic plan as a management tool for the interior design practice to develop a positive future direction. It also discusses budgeting as part of the planning process and concludes with information about the importance of measuring performance of the planning process.

THE IMPORTANCE OF PLANNING

Many forces continually affect a business, especially the small business. The economy, the loss of an expected important client, the hiring of a key new employee, and even the health of the owner can all have an effect. A business strategy that can help firms survive the bad forces and increase the effect of good forces is planning—especially long-term planning.

Planning is second nature to an interior designer when it applies to projects for clients, yet many owners never seem to find time to plan the future of their business. This is unfortunate, as planning helps business owners find a clear direction and clarify the purpose of the business. It is also an important tool for the owner to use to keep control and be responsive to and competitive in the marketplace. A plan is a road map providing direction. It should never be thought of as something that, once written, cannot be modified.

According to Ivancevich, Lorenzi, and Skinner, "Planning enables a firm to respond quickly to changing business demands, market conditions, and customer expectations."[1] By utilizing planning, it is easier for the firm to set priorities. Understanding the importance of planning is essential, whether the reader is a business owner, employee, or student.

Planning will help a firm:

- Determine how to use its human and financial resources to the best advantage
- Determine priorities
- Formalize a mechanism for budgeting
- Measure and evaluate success, and find the right tools to measure with
- Integrate management and employee thinking so that they both have a common purpose

The primary reason for any business to use planning on a periodic basis is that businesses that fail to plan are more likely to fail. Businesses that do not plan often end up reacting instead of acting, thus allowing outside forces to control the business. Not knowing where the company is headed can lead to disjointed efforts and confused priorities.

Business planning helps the owner define and update his or her mission or vision of the firm by use of a mission statement. The *mission statement* (discussed further later in this chapter) is a philosophical statement that explains the direction and purpose of the design practice, its values, why it exists, and who it serves.

A written plan makes it much easier to evaluate what was planned, especially in terms of its mission statement versus what actually happened. Reviewing progress is an important part of planning. Six months or a year down the road, the owner and employees can look carefully at what was done and what was not accomplished as they prepare to plan for the next year. These variations or variances in planned versus actual can help the owner evaluate what happened so that negatives can be dealt with quickly before they become financial problems.

The business owner must realize that it is important for employees to be part of the planning process. It has been proven time and time again that businesses are more likely to be successful when the employees really feel that they are an integral part of the business. Employees may not have a direct financial stake in the business, but they have at least an emotional interest in the business succeeding—sometimes as much as the owner does. When employees are involved in planning, it is also much more likely that they will work to achieve the goals of the company.

Several types of plans are commonly used by businesses:

- The business plan, to organize a new business
- The marketing plan, to help define business development
- A financial plan, to help with budgeting and capital spending
- Various specific plans, such as human resources plans for hiring
- Strategic long-range planning, which is the focus of this chapter

Of course, it takes time to develop any of these plans. Many owners of small firms give this as the primary reason for neglecting this important management task. A compelling reason to plan is that, according to the Small Business Administration, failing to plan is one of the biggest reasons that small businesses fail. Even a sole practitioner can gain from strategic planning and the development of other plans when called for. The remainder of this chapter focuses on the strategic planning process that most facilitators and users of strategic planning employ.

STRATEGIC PLANNING BASICS

The very nature of the planning process requires the business owner and employees to look into the future. The type of long-range planning most often used and referred to in business is strategic planning. *Strategic planning* is a process for creating a specific written vision for the design firm and its future. It is comprehensive and future oriented, requiring the business owner and employees to predict what they would like to see for the business concerning the many operational and organizational areas of the design firm in the future.

As one might presume from the name, strategic planning comes from military planning. In the mid-20th century, big businesses looked for a way to better plan and become proactive in their markets. They turned to the concept of strategies as part of a detailed plan used by the military. Over time, the concept became a process of looking carefully at the internal resources a company had and the external forces that affect a business and utilizing this information to create a plan for the future of the company. With strategic planning, owners can act in the best interests of the company.

A strategic plan focuses primarily on the long term: three to five years into the future. However, many businesses create a "rolling strategic plan" that takes into consideration the current (or short-term) as well as the long-term goals of the company, making a separate annual plan unnecessary. A small firm might even use strategic planning to plan for only one year, although ideally such a plan looks further into the future than the coming year.

Strategic planning is not just a plan. It is a process that in a sense forces the owners and employees to look internally and externally in order to analyze where the firm is and where it wants to go. Many have said that the analysis process can be more valuable than the plan that results. Nevertheless, it should be obvious that a plan is very valuable.

TABLE 20-1.

A portion of a strategic plan for a small interior design practice

Goal 2: Increase marketing and promotional efforts to create potential client awareness of Johnson/Clark Designs.
Strategy 1 Review existing promotional materials.
Tactic 1: Collect copies of promotional materials used in the past three years.
Tactic 2: Categorize materials into types of promotional tools.
Strategy 2 Identify potential venues for speaking programs.
Tactic 1: Develop database of local target client professional associations.
Tactic 2: Develop database of target client professional associations in the three adjoining states.
Tactic 3: Develop database of any other possible clubs or groups that might host a program.
Strategy 3 Brainstorm with staff for at least six possible topics for programs.
Strategy 4 Identify potential venues for informational and educational articles to show our company's expertise.
Tactic 1: Obtain copies of all local magazines and other print media in our local market.
Tactic 2: Obtain copies of local magazines in major cities of the three adjoining states.

Generally, the steps in strategic planning look like this:

- Set forth (in writing) the mission or vision of the company.
- Analyze the business internally to determine strengths and weaknesses.
- Analyze outside forces that might affect the business to determine opportunities and threats.
- Develop goals and objectives for the next few years.

Table 20-1 shows a partial strategic plan. Strategic planning helps a business to act in a positive way regarding the forces that will inevitably affect it rather than constantly reacting and being in crisis mode. After reading this chapter, you might also find that you can adapt a similar process to do personal planning for your career.

MISSION STATEMENTS

A common component of the strategic plan is the *mission statement*, a concise philosophical statement that explains a firm's direction and purpose. It helps to clearly define the business and helps owners and employees recognize and identify what unique qualities the business brings to prospective clients. A mission statement helps the business owner with marketing decisions, operational choices, hiring, financing, and other management tasks.

A mission statement generally has an external focus, telling clients and other outsiders what the purpose of the firm is. Firms commonly display their mission statement on their Web site and perhaps other marketing materials.

This statement is a crucial part of strategic planning. Although it directs strategic planning from year to year, it is not unusual for it to change over time. Reviewing the existing mission statement at the early planning stages helps a prospective business owner think about the overall purpose of the business and determine if that purpose—and hence the mission statement—should be modified.

The creation of a mission statement starts by asking "Where does the firm want to go?" It is important that the mission be focused, not vague, though it is still a philosophical statement. Ideally, a mission statement contains a brief

Mission Statement:

Globus Design Associates applies interior design expertise to create life-enhancing spaces.

FIGURE 20-1.

A sample mission statement. (Reproduced with permission of Suzan Globus, FASID, LEED API+C, Globus Design Associates, Fair Haven, NJ)

description of the business, its customers, the services and products offered, and the geographic area served. It does not have to be long (many statements consist of only a few sentences), nor does it have to contain all these items. For example, "AB & C Interiors is a client-oriented residential interior design firm dedicated to providing creative design solutions that meet the client's needs first." Figure 20-1 is a sample mission statement from an interior design firm.

Many texts on how to go about making a strategic plan suggest writing or revising the mission statement before completing the rest of the work on the plan. Others recommend putting it off until the end. The in-depth analysis that a firm should do as part of the strategic planning process often leads design firms in slightly different directions than were initially expected. If the mission statement is reworked at the beginning of the process, it is recommended that it be revisited one more time after the rest of the strategic planning process is completed, to be sure it does not need any changes to conform to the strategic plan.

Some confuse a mission statement with a vision statement. A *vision statement* comes from the values and convictions of the owner of the firm and expresses what the firm hopes to become: the best, most creative hospitality design firm in the country. Vision statements are more internal, used to focus and direct the staff, and are less often communicated to clients and outsiders. Some of the references on strategic planning use "vision" instead of "mission" and vice versa. The point is to develop a simple expression of what the firm is trying to do so as to clarify its direction in achieving the goals and other activities and tasks of the company.

Figure 20-2 provides a sample vision and sample mission statement from an interior design firm. Note how they differ. Additional examples are included on the companion Web site as Item 20-1.

BUSINESS ANALYSIS

The next step is to analyze the business from the inside, as well as forces that might affect it from the outside. It would be unwise for an interior designer to start working on a project for a client without knowing the current situation of the space and the client's requirements. Likewise, it is unwise to try to create a plan for the future of the business without first analyzing the firm's current condition. By carefully looking at the forces that affect the design firm, the planning team can make better judgments for the future.

Vision:

Environments that bring positive and happy experiences.

Mission Statement:

To create enriching spaces that encourage productive environments and provide an atmosphere of pleasure and happiness. We believe in an inclusive process leading to creative solutions that support a long range vision of an environment that enriches the lives of our clients by providing for their needs and exciting their emotional expectations.

We believe in providing these services with integrity, research, and continued learning to promote the best solutions and lifelong relationships with our clients.

FIGURE 20-2.

Vision and mission statements. (Reproduced with permission of Phyllis D. Moore, FASID, Interior Design Source, LLC, Decatur, AL)

The most common way of doing this analysis is to use what is referred to as *SWOT analysis*. "SWOT" stands for **s**trengths, **w**eaknesses, **o**pportunities, and **t**hreats. Strengths and weaknesses are issues within the firm, whereas opportunities and threats come from outside.

Much useful planning information is obtained through SWOT analysis as a firm investigates what it does well. Equally important to a business (or individual) is investigating what cannot be done or what is being done in an inferior manner. As Peter Drucker points out, strength analysis "shows where there is need to improve or upgrade existing strengths and where new strengths have to be acquired."[2] Looking for a firm's weaknesses is also important so that actions can be taken to overcome and improve these areas.

Analyzing strengths and weaknesses requires investigating the internal resources and activities that the design firm can control. These include such things as the services the firm offers, financial resources, project management, and the way in which the firm is marketed. Understanding what the firm does very well is one consideration. Reviewing customer complaints is an example of a weakness that should be addressed.

External factors are the opportunities for, and threats to, the firm. Firms that are busy keeping up with their current day-to-day practice often miss seeing potential opportunities. For example, not reading the newspaper or subscribing to a local online news service makes it nearly impossible to know if a new corporate headquarters is moving into the area. Other external forces, such as government regulations, competition, technology, economic forecasts, and the firm's customers, can be opportunities or threats depending on exactly what is going on. Not keeping up to date with technology changes that can have an impact on marketing as well as productivity can be a threat.

Examples of SWOT items are shown in Table 20-2. Additional examples are included in Item 20-2 on the companion Web site. These examples should help guide you in conducting and writing your own SWOT analysis.

The easiest way to begin SWOT analysis is by reviewing the skills and interests of the owner and all the staff. Once the firm knows what skills and knowledge exist within it, analysis of how the firm operates and of company processes is important. Knowing "what we do" and "how we do it" can be an important part of a firm's strategic plan. These are important issues that can be resolved only through analysis and research.

TABLE 20-2.

Examples of items that might be included in a SWOT analysis

Strengths
Our firm is well known.
Our firm has a strong financial position.
Our firm has a focused client target market.

Weaknesses
Our firm receives too many customer service complaints.
Some support staff members have a bad attitude.
None of our designers are NCIDQ qualified.

Opportunities
Angel Carpeting is offering co-op advertising.
Our studio will be relocating to an uptown location to increase our potential for high-end clients.
A major competitor has overextended itself financially.

Threats
Three strong competitors have moved into our market area.
A former employee has taken away two former repeat clients in the last six months.
State licensing will be required for supervision of installations.

When the analysis shifts to external factors, it is often necessary to use primary and secondary sources of information. The easiest sources of information to access are secondary sources. *Secondary sources* are generally those sources of information that are already in existence or are produced by others. Any information that the firm gets from some source other than its own work is considered a secondary source. These include:

- Reports by local and federal governments
- Information from trade associations
- General business publications, such as the *Wall Street Journal*
- Local chamber of commerce publications
- Reporting services, such as the McGraw-Hill Construction Services Report (formerly referred to as the McGraw-Hill Dodge Reports)

Primary sources are sources of information that provide specifics from people who may have direct knowledge about the information being sought. Here are some examples:

- Casual conversations and networking
- Networking with contacts at agencies and professionals related to the firm's design specialties, such as real estate agents
- Contacts with vendors and subcontractors
- Observation—keeping one's eyes open for new construction
- Surveys and questionnaires developed by the design firm

These types of activities certainly take time and financial resources. Yet they can help a firm make better decisions as to what types of clients to pursue and how to use valuable resources, and envision the future of the firm.

BUSINESS GOALS, OBJECTIVES, STRATEGIES, AND TACTICS

When all the analysis and research have been completed, it is time for the design firm to begin developing the actual plan—often called the action plan. The keys to the action plan are the goals and objectives the firm wishes to accomplish.

An organization's *goals* are broad statements of what the firm wishes to achieve. These are usually established without regard to any time limit. In long-range strategic planning, it is often recommended that a goal be something to achieve in three to five years. An annual plan focuses on the coming year. Although the term *objectives* certainly has a different definition from *goals*, both terms are used in defining the broad statements. For simplicity, I use the term *goals*.

Goals are developed for as many operational areas of the company as are practical. In the best case, considerations are made for such areas as marketing, project management, operational management, finances, and personnel.

Establishing goals is an important aspect of financial and overall management control. For example, one of the goals for an interior design firm might be "to become an award-winning residential design firm within three years." Perhaps another goal for a firm may be to earn $1 million in revenue for the year.

Establishing goals creates end points, that is, something to achieve. It is easier to attain those goals when strategies and tactics are also developed. *Strategies* are specific statements that describe how the firm plans to achieve a goal. They are almost always combined with time limits. A sample strategy might be: "During the next year, we will refine our resource library to obtain materials on the highest-quality merchandise."

In many cases, tactics are helpful in implementing strategies to achieve goals. *Tactics* are highly specific actions that are needed to accomplish or carry out the strategies. A tactic for the strategy concerning the resource library might be to "clean out the library every six months."

All the goals, strategies, and tactics of the strategic plan must relate back to the firm's mission statement. Although it is common to revise the mission statement somewhat after the goals are established, the goals should always relate to the mission in the first place.

After the goals, strategies, and tactics have been defined and prioritized, the next step is to implement a review of the budget. Having a goal to become the premier in any kind of firm, with well-thought-out strategies and tactics to achieve that goal, is certainly a positive step. Not having the funds to carry out even the simplest of the tactics will discourage even the most enthusiastic owner and employee.

BUDGETING

Budgeting, in terms of the management planning function, involves creating annual managerial goals that can be expressed in specific, quantitative monetary terms. Strategic planning requires budgeting because many of the goals and tasks outlined in the plan necessitate the use of funds that the company might not have yet—but must plan to obtain.

We all work with a *budget*—a limited amount of money for a specific period of time to take care of bills and miscellaneous expenses. Businesses must budget as well. The difference between personal budgeting and business budgeting is that as an individual, you know what your income will be every two weeks represented by your expected salary. A business's funds fluctuate from month to month. Revenues constantly fluctuate while expenses stay more or less the same. This makes budgeting very important.

Budgeting

- Encourages the owner to plan for the financial needs of the company in a thoughtful and organized way
- Allows and encourages proactive management rather than reactive
- Permits the discovery of potential problem areas and provides the opportunity to determine a course of action before problems actually occur.
- Provides another opportunity for success
- Focuses the efforts of the whole organization toward the firm's annual goals by coordinating the efforts of all the various individuals and groups

Budgets can be drawn up as part of strategic planning, as plans are developed. However, it is more common for budgeting to be done when all the goals, strategies, and tactics have been determined and prioritized. This timing makes it easier for the owner and manager to estimate the financial and human resources necessary to accomplish important, agreed-upon goals and, if necessary, make adjustments to the goals. Prioritizing usually has the most effect on the budgeting part of the process. Something that at first seemed to be of highest priority might have to be downgraded when the cost of achieving that goal or doing that task is budgeted.

Strategies and tactics are the items that receive budget consideration, whereas goals are budgeted based on the total cost of the strategies and tactics needed to achieve the goals. Each strategy and tactic should be reviewed, and preliminary cost estimates for each item should be established. Revenue production strategies and tactics should also be budgeted. It is just as important for the firm to create revenue budgets as it is for the firm to determine what level of revenue is needed and is possible to accomplish for all the items that require cost outlays.

Forecasts of revenues and basic expenses for the coming year or future years begin with a review of figures for prior years (see Figure 20-3). With further analysis, budgeting for what the company will actually attempt to accomplish becomes more realistic.

The simplest and most common method of budgeting in many firms is to look at figures from the prior year and then, by applying various percentages of increase or decrease, come up with a new budget. This can work fairly well in normal circumstances, but could be disastrous in a slow economy or during a period in which the economy goes down or becomes volatile for some reason. The past is always a good starting point, but it should be used in conjunction with good research and future-oriented planning.

When new tactics are part of the plan, the firm will need to do some research. In some cases, this research might be done with the assistance of a consultant to establish a budget. For example, if the plan includes developing a Web site, it will be necessary to check with Web site designers to establish a budget for the design of the site, as well as the ongoing costs of a Web master and provider fees.

Some firms use the zero-based budgeting method as their starting point. This budgeting method received a lot of attention during the presidential administration of Jimmy Carter. *Zero-based budgeting* assumes that each year the managers of the firm start with a zero as their initial budget level and must

Design Department Proposed Budget 200x		
Revenue		
From Fees	420,000	500,000
Cost of Sales		
Direct Labor	271,875	290,000
Supplies	8,500	7,000
Reproduction Expense	9,350	7,500
Telephone (long distance)	3,700	4,800
Total Cost of Sales	293,425	309,300
Gross Margin	126,575	190,700
Total Cost of Sales	293,425	309,300
Gross Margin	126,575	190,700
Operating Expenses for Design Dept.		
Salaries	61,990	84,000
Payroll Taxes	16,000	24,000
Group Insurance	1,750	1,700
Promotion	2,750	2,000
Travel Reimbursements	6,800	7,000
Supplies and Postage	6,300	6,000
Professional Dues	3,000	2,500
Printing and Reproduction	8,400	10,000
Technical Consultants	12,900	5,000
Total Operating Expenses	119,890	142,200
Net Income	6,685	48,500
Profit to Sales	2%	10%

FIGURE 20-3.

A simple budget report helpful to owners in planning the upcoming business year.

justify all costs, as if the department or activity were starting new. This means that no costs are considered as ongoing from year to year. It also means that the firm must accurately forecast revenues to cover and, of course, exceed the expenses.

MEASURING PERFORMANCE

In any type of planning, it is important to establish a methodology for measuring performance. Some goals will take time to achieve, so a method of measuring performance can help the firm understand whether it is working its way toward the goal even though it is not there yet.

Establishing goals and objectives with no way of defining or determining success results in a meaningless expenditure of energy for the planning and writing process. Establishing some of the control mechanisms that will be used to evaluate financial and organizational success is also very important.

A formal measure of performance is *variance analysis*. Most commonly applied to financial or numeric data, variance analysis compares planned data to actual data. An example of variance analysis is a comparison of financial projections that have been prepared for the business plan to the firm's actual performance. Figure 21-10 show what this type of report would look like.

Performance can also be measured by doing post-project reviews at the conclusion of all significant projects. Such a review can be very formalized, using a form designed by the owner. Information such as the estimated project budgets versus the actual costs of the project can be compared. The numerical/financial data can also be supplemented with a short narrative review of the project. This post-project review is discussed further in Chapter 14. The firm's accountant, attorney, or the experience of the owner/manager might well suggest additional control reports.

It does not matter whether one is monitoring a strategic plan, a marketing plan, a personnel plan, or another type of plan. Stopping to review progress is essential to good business practice. A large firm might only have time for a formal annual review. A small design firm should look at the big picture painted by the plan a little more often—at least twice a year. Scheduling a half-day to review progress (or the lack thereof) is just as important as developing the plan in the first place.

The Triple Bottom Line

You may have heard the term *triple bottom line (TBL)*. It was coined in the 1990s by John Elkington and later expanded in his book *Cannibals with Forks: The Triple Bottom Line of 21st Century Business* (Oxford, UK: Capstone Press, 1997). It has become an influential business topic for firms involved in or supportive of sustainable design and social responsibility. It has received wide acknowledgment in the press over the intervening years.

The triple bottom line tries to establish value based on the parameters of people, planet, and profitability. It attempts to measure those parameters to help show how a firm looks to its client base and the general pubic beyond mere profit. The "people" parameter might include considerations for creating a healthy environment for employees. Considerations for "planet" often revolve around being highly green in practice within and outside the company. And, of course, "profit" relates to the firm's financial success.

The triple bottom line tactic is not normally used by an interior design firm unless the firm is quite large. Measuring the three Ps is not easy and generally is undertaken only by large firms. This brief insert of information is intended primarily to help define a term that some readers may have heard about and wish to explore; it is beyond the scope of this text to discuss this topic in depth. Readers who are highly motivated to have a green business are urged to investigate resources on the Internet and books such as Elkington's for more information.

BENCHMARKING

A technique that can help the owner both measure and understand how the business is doing is called benchmarking. *Benchmarking* is defined as "a strategic management approach that assesses capabilities by comparing the firm's activities or functions with those of other firms."[3] It is a way of determining which is the best company in the industry and then seeing if anything used by that company can be applied to your company.

The term *best practice* is associated with benchmarking. Here is a definition of best practice as applied to architecture: "a superior method or innovative practice that contributes to the improved performance of an organization, usually recognized as 'best' by peer organizations."[4] These best-practice processes can be adapted to almost all design firms, regardless of size.

A best practice is usually well defined and its results well documented. Just because some firm has a great deal of success with some process or methodology does not mean that the same process or methodology will work for everyone. However, those processes that have shown documented success can be beneficial to many firms. This section focuses on benchmarking, which can help small firms find and implement best practices.

Benchmarks for interior design practices are not easy to locate, because so much material concerning business performance is not openly or readily available outside a firm. Thus, it is perfectly reasonable to adopt benchmarking processes from other types of business in the industry, such as architecture, and even from outside the design–build industry.

There are ways to identify how one's firm is doing in some respects as compared to others. To begin, SWOT analysis will help point out the firm's weaknesses. Customer service complaints and follow-up surveys are also important ways to determine what is not working well. Of course, discussions with employees—though perhaps hard for the owner to hear—can also highlight and clarify weaknesses.

Naturally, you must also identify the competitors whom you believe are performing better than your firm. Internet and Web searches of design firms and reviews of literature such as trade magazines and local publications might help the owner find firms that are excelling in at least some areas. Doing this type of research helps the owner establish the benchmarks for improving processes.

Although it is likely that nearby competing firms will not be willing to share many trade secrets of how they do things, some firms are willing to share if they believe that disclosure will be a two-way street. Thus, you may have success through contacting owner colleagues from other cities whom you met through an association. Some small design firms have found luncheon "round tables" to be a good way for sole practitioners to share information. Perhaps these sessions could be led by a consultant who makes sure that everyone contributes.

You can also use the research techniques discussed earlier in this chapter. Surveys, informal conversations, and telephone discussions are all good ways to gain information. My book *Problem Solving and Critical Thinking for Designers* provides a chapter on research techniques.

Not every technique or bit of information obtained will be applicable to a specific firm. The owner must analyze what is discovered and determine which of these techniques are relevant and could be applied to his or her company.

It is also important to point out that, in some cases, benchmarks will be numerical data (e.g., revenue for the year, dollars of service revenue versus dollars of product sales revenue, number of hours billed, etc.). You can start this type of research with your own data and seek out any research that might be available on the Internet. By the way, most firms that bill services expect a minimum of 75 to 80 percent billable time worked by employees. In some firms this is 100 percent.

Logically, the next step is to implement appropriate benchmark practices in the firm. If an issue has been a low amount of billable time, it might well be easy to remedy the lack of time management and time recording. A firm's inability to attract high-quality clients compared to competitors is not an easy fix, but analysis of competitors' Web sites, advertising, and publication activities can begin to show a firm what it must do in comparison to others.

The professional associations may have literature available to members that help to establish benchmarks of best practice. Informational articles can also be unearthed on the Internet by careful research.

WEB SITES RELEVANT TO THIS CHAPTER

www.mbda.gov Minority Business Development Agency

www.score.org SCORE

www.sba.gov U.S. Small Business Administration

KEY TERMS

Benchmarking	Secondary sources
Best practices	Strategic planning
Budgeting	Strategies
Goals	SWOT analysis
Mission statement	Tactics
Primary sources	Variance analysis

WHAT WOULD YOU DO?

1. Sandy works in a state with interior design licensing legislation. She meets the requirements for registration, and has submitted her application to the board of technical registration. She is an employee of a design firm with six other designers, including the owners. The owners and two of the other designers are registered. When meeting with clients, the owners indicate that the company is registered and that their designers are also registered.

    After a particularly problematic project, a client reports Sandy to her professional association, claiming she was working without a license and breached the contract. In addition, the client claims that the faux finishing was not done properly and "ruined" the appearance of the house. The faux finisher has been to the house three times to try to resolve the client's concerns. In the meantime, the client refuses to pay the invoice for the faux finishing (billed by Sandy's company) and also refuses to pay the outstanding design fee. Those amounts total $23,000.

2. Mary Smith was hired by her client to prepare all the design work and documents necessary for the remodeling of the client's kitchen and for adding a family room space. Mary's contract included clauses stating that she would prepare working drawings and construction documents; supervise the work; and supply items including new appliances, architectural finishes, lighting (both architectural and movable), and furniture items. Mary's business is located in a jurisdiction that has interior design licensing regulations, but she has not gotten the license. The project, however, is located in a different state that does not have a licensing law for interior designers.

3. James has worked for a firm specializing in corporate offices for eight years and has enjoyed great success with that type of client. A change in ownership of the firm has prompted James to decide it is time to start his own company, which he will call James Jones Interiors. He will need an assistant, as he knows he will have some business from a

few clients who approached him just before he left his previous employer. What should James do to prepare himself to open his own business?

REFERENCES

1. Ivancevich, Lorenzi, and Skinner, 1994, p. 166.
2. Drucker, 1995, p. 43.
3. Gomez-Mejia, Balkin, and Cardy, 2005, p. 304.
4. Demkin, 2008, p. 766.

CHAPTER 21

Money Management

After completing this chapter you should be able to:

- Compare the differences between the cash accounting method and the accrual accounting method.
- Discuss the basic concept of the chart of accounts, debits, and credits.
- Explain the purpose of the income statement, balance sheet, and statement of cash flows.
- Understand and discuss the terminology of the income statement and balance sheet and relate that terminology to business examples.
- Explain the basic formula or financial outcome of a balance sheet.
- Correctly place dollar amounts into an income statement and balance sheet to show understanding of what these basic documents report.
- Discuss the difference between assets and liabilities.
- Identify items that are direct expenses and distinguish them from overhead expenses.
- Discuss ways to control overhead.
- Analyze a cash management forecast.
- Discuss some techniques that would be useful in ensuring good cash flow.
- Calculate the ratios shown in this chapter.
- Discuss the implications of the ratios and percentages introduced in this chapter.
- Discuss how financial management reports can be useful to the owner of an interior design practice.
- Explain "favorable" and "unfavorable" in variance analysis.
- Explain how break-even analysis can be important to the firm owner.

NCIDQ COMPONENT

Based on best information available, some material in this chapter might appear as part of the NCIDQ examination. The reader should not depend solely on this text for study material. See the sections on income statements, balance sheets, and basic financial practices.

Understanding basic financial accounting is not difficult. So let's start with a definition: *financial accounting* is the day-to-day and periodic measurement and reporting of a firm's monetary resources. It has been made easier by the number of accounting software packages available to help the small business owner. You use financial recordkeeping and reports to analyze and understand the financial position of your design firm. This measurement and reporting is also of interest to individuals outside the firm, such as bankers, government agencies, stockholders, and auditors.

Gaining knowledge in basic accounting is critical for any interior designer who sees business ownership as a professional goal. If you do not understand your business's financial situation, your business will not last very long. For that matter, it is important even if you don't see owning a business as a goal, because understanding the concepts of financial operations helps you be a better employee.

Basic financial recording begins with the accounts, journals, and ledgers set up to record the daily transactions of the design firm. These reports are prepared to help the owners maintain a firm hand on the finances. The information in these reports is used to create income statements, balance sheets, and statements of cash flow—the reports that are most commonly a part of financial accounting.

It is wise to engage an accountant to prepare reports, although accounting software programs can help the business owner develop them. Even though a business owner gets advice and counsel on financial issues from an accountant, it is still the owner's responsibility to understand what is happening with the finances of his or her company.

This chapter introduces readers to several essential components of financial accounting and financial management. Its purpose is not to teach you how to do accounting recordkeeping for your business. Rather, it discusses basic concepts to help you understand accounting recordkeeping.

The chapter begins with a discussion of the different accounting methods used to record information. In this edition, the discussion of the journal and ledgers has been moved toward the beginning to give readers a basic understanding of daily bookkeeping records. A review of the elements of the income statement, balance sheet, and the statement of cash flows (formally, the funds flow statement) follows. The chapter concludes with a discussion of cash management and computer software applications.

ACCOUNTING METHODS: ACCRUAL VERSUS CASH ACCOUNTING

An interior design practice must prepare specific standard financial reports at least once a year. Those reports are the income statement, balance sheet, and statement of cash flows. These reports help the business owner prepare income tax reporting forms and are usually needed when the business seeks business loans. These three reports start with the data recorded from daily financial transactions of sales and expenses. The type of accounting method used affects how this information is recorded.

The two most common accounting methods (or bases) are the accrual method and the cash accounting method. Central to the difference between the two methods is the time when revenue and expenses are recognized (recorded). *Revenue* is the amount of inflows from the sale of goods or the rendering of services during an accounting period. An *expense* is the amount of outflows of resources as a consequence of the efforts made by the firm to earn revenues. Rent, monthly utility bills, salaries, and advertising costs are examples of expenses.

With the *accrual accounting method*, revenue and expenses are recognized at the time they are earned (in the case of revenue) or incurred (in the case of expenses), whether or not the revenue has actually been collected or the expenses have actually been paid in the time frame (month and/or year) in which they were incurred. The accrual accounting method requires the use of double-entry accounting, making it somewhat more difficult to master. For example, furniture on order for a client would be considered revenue even though the payment for that order has not yet been received. A bill for the business telephone service is considered an expense even though the designer has not yet paid the bill.

In the *cash accounting method*, revenue and expenses are recognized in the period in which the firm actually receives the cash or actually pays the bills. Cash accounting is a single-entry system. It is a lot like a person's personal budgets and records. Revenue is recognized only when the design firm receives the check from a client in payment for an invoice. The expense amount of the telephone bill is recorded only when the owner actually sends a check to the telephone company.

A firm generally can use whichever accounting method it chooses, although accountants recommend the accrual method for firms that sell goods and maintain some inventory. Some firms use both accounting methods. Cash accounting is commonly used by small design practices for daily book-keeping purposes. It is simpler to use than the accrual accounting method and allows for use of single-entry accounting. The accrual method is used to determine tax liability. Because tax laws change annually and accounting standards also change on a regular basis, it is important for the business owner to discuss appropriate accounting methods with the company's accountant.

A design firm that has an inventory of goods or otherwise sells products will have to use the accrual method to determine its income tax responsibilities. It is also required for businesses with more than $5 million in annual sales or a firm whose business structure is a regular corporation (not an LLC). The accrual method is also recommended for any business that sells on credit, as the accrual method gives a more accurate picture of revenue and expenses.

To clarify the differences the accounting methods make in the gross income of a company, let's look at an example. During May, Maximum Interiors received a total of $11,400 in revenues. Of that, $5600 is from cash sales and $5800 is from invoices to clients on which payment has not yet been received. In the same month, expenses of $6500 were incurred for the period—$4500 has already been paid and $2000 is still due. Using the accrual method, there is a $4900 gross profit for the month. In this case, the profit is a "paper profit," as $5800 has not been collected yet (see Table 21-1).

Applying the cash method to the same example, only $5600 of revenue and $4500 of expenses are recognized for the month, because this is what was actually received or paid out. Using the cash accounting method, Maximum Interiors shows a $1100 profit for the month.

It is commonly recommended that all firms use the accrual method, because it provides a more comprehensive picture of profit and loss for the firm at any given period. Having a more accurate financial picture of the firm at all times helps the owner/manager make more intelligent management decisions. Moreover, with cash accounting, it is too easy for unpaid invoices to

TABLE 21-1.

Comparison of accrual and cash accounting methods

	Accrual Method	Cash Method
Revenue	$11,400	$ 5600
Expenses	−6500	−4500
Gross profit	$ 4900	$ 1100

accumulate, thus allowing debt to be overlooked, which would put the firm in a serious situation.

This chapter discusses accounting principles based on the accrual method.

ACCOUNTING RECORDS AND SYSTEMS

Every time the firm bills or collects funds from the client, or the firm orders or pays for goods for the client or the firm, those transactions must be recorded. *Transactions* are events that affect the financial activities of a firm, either as revenue generating or expense generating. Your daily financial recordkeeping is done to document monetary transactions. These accounting records are commonly referred to as the daily bookkeeping records. They are tools that you need to have to make decisions about operational issues.

Accurate financial recording is also critical for income tax purposes. It is essential that all these transactions be recorded accurately to meet legal and ethical standards of practice. The income statement, balance sheet, and statement of cash flows are summary reports generated from the information in the firm's accounting records.

Recording of financial transactions can be done with either single-entry or double-entry systems. A *single-entry system* is very simple. It is set up based on the income statement and includes business income and expense accounts. Because of its simplicity, it is used by many small businesses. However, many accountants feel that it is not an adequate or proper way of accounting for transactions.

Most accountants recommend using the *double-entry system* because of its built-in checks and balances. The double-entry bookkeeping system uses journals and ledgers (discussed later in this chapter) to aid in recordkeeping. The accounts are based on the entries found in both the income statement and the balance sheet. In the double-entry system, transactions are first entered in the journal and then summary information is transferred to the appropriate ledger. The next section provides additional information about the double-entry system.

Chart of Accounts

Financial organization is established in accounts. *Accounts* show additions (increases) to the account and subtractions (decreases) to the account that are represented in the income statement and balance sheet. Look at the income statement in Figure 21-6 and the balance sheet in Figure 21-7. Each of these terms is a summary term that is generated from dozens of separate subaccounts.

Even a small interior design business will have numerous accounts. A logical format must be created to manage all those accounts. The chart of accounts manages this logic. A *chart of accounts* is a list of all the accounts that a firm is using.

Figure 21-1 is a portion of a chart of accounts showing many of the major accounts typical of an interior design practice. An individual firm's chart of accounts may have other subheadings, but will likely have category headings very similar to those shown in the figure.

Typically, the major headings of the chart of accounts have account names that mirror the items shown on the balance sheet and income statement. The chart of accounts is a statement about how the firm categorizes the events that it seeks to control. These accounts can be further detailed to indicate such things as each customer's account or each vendor's account, to cite a few examples.

The chart of accounts is numbered in a logical order; the example in Figure 21-1 shows a typical order. Some of the account categories relate to the balance sheet: namely, Assets, Liabilities, and Owner's Equity. Others relate to income statement items: Revenues (or Income) and Expenses. The expenses

Sample Chart of Accounts

Account #	Description	Account #	Description
Assets		**Revenue**	
1000	Cash	6000	Sales of goods/products
1010	Cash: checking	6100	Freight in
1020	Cash: savings	6110	Delivery fees
1030	Petty cash	6200	Professional fees
1099	Total cash	6300	Reimbursable expenses
1100	Accounts receivable	6400	Cash discounts
1190	Allowance for bad debts		
1199	Total accounts receivable	**Expenses**	
1200	Inventory	7000	Cost of sales
1299	Total inventory	7100	Cost of goods sold
1300	Fixed assets	7125	Freight in
1310	Office furniture & fixtures	7200	Direct labor
1320	Office equipment	7300	Telephone
		7325	Supplies
		8150	Payroll tax
Liabilities		8200	Rent
2000	Accounts payable: cost of sales	8300	Telephone
2050	Accounts payable: general	8320	Utilities
2100	Accrued payroll	8400	Group insurance
2110	Federal withholding	8450	Insurance
2120	Unemployment compensation	8500	Professional consultants: attorney
2125	Social security	8550	Professional consultants: accountant
2200	Note payable		
2300	Interest payable	8600	Supplies
2400	Sales tax payable	8625	Catalogs/samples
3000	Long-term liabilities	8650	Postage
3010	Note payable long term	8675	Promotion
4000	Capital	8900	Depreciation expense
4100	Owner's capital	8925	Bank charges
4300	Owner's drawings	9000	Federal income tax
		9999	Net Income

FIGURE 21-1.

A partial chart of accounts for an interior design practice. (Excerpt from Christine M. Piotrowski, *Interior Design Management*, 1992, John Wiley & Sons.)

categories are commonly broken down into Direct Expenses, General Expenses, and Office Expenses. These accounts are numbered like this: 1000 assets; 2000 liabilities; 3000 equity accounts; 4000 retained earnings; 5000 income; 6000–8000 expense accounts. These code numbers are the ones used to cross-reference journal entries to posting entries. The chart of accounts should be set up so that it can increase in complexity as the firm grows, with appropriate accounts added as needed.

Because the amount of assets of a firm must always balance with the liabilities of the firm, the account record looks like the letter "T" in its simplest form. Accountants refer to these as *T-accounts* (see Figure 21-2). The left-hand side of the T-account is called the *debit* side, whereas the right-hand side is called the *credit* side. In these accounts, debit and credit have no meaning in accounting other than "left" and "right," respectively. They are not substitutes for the words "increase" or "decrease," since, for some accounts, the increase side of the T-account will be on the right and the decrease on the left. Figure 21-3 shows this accounting situation.

T-Accounts

Assets

(Increases on left, decreases on right)

Cash

DEBIT	CREDIT
300	900
1,700	450
1,000	

Accounts Receivable

DEBIT	CREDIT
8,700	9,100
7,500	
1,700	

Equities

(Decreases on left, increases on right)

Accounts Payable

DEBIT	CREDIT
900	
450	

Fees Revenue

DEBIT	CREDIT
	8,700
	7,500
	12,000

Note: These accounts are not represented to balance.

FIGURE 21-2.

A sample format of typical T-accounts.

Assets		=	Liabilities		+	Owner's Equity	
increase	decrease	=	increase	decrease	+	increase	decrease
(+) debit	(-) credit		(-) debit	(+) credit		(-) debit	(+) credit

FIGURE 21-3.

This example shows how some accounts show *increases* as a debit, whereas other accounts show *decreases* as a debit.

The Journal and Ledger

Following a business transaction, entries are made in a journal. A *journal* is a chronological record of all accounting transactions for the firm (see Figure 21-4). Journal entries show the date of occurrence, the name of the account to be debited or credited, the amount of the debit or credit, and a reference to the ledger account to which the entry has been posted. Entries are posted to different ledger accounts from the journal. *Posting*, therefore, is the transferring of a journal entry to the correct ledger account.

The *ledger*, often called a general ledger, is a group of accounts. If the bookkeeping is done manually, an actual general ledger book will be used to record all the entries. When computer software is utilized, the ledger will likely be the first place the data are entered; the software then updates accounts as appropriate. Various subsidiary ledgers often supplement the general ledger, providing detailed information to support the general ledger. For an interior design firm, an important subsidiary ledger is the accounts receivable ledger (see Figure 21-5). This ledger has separate accounts for each client who purchases on credit from the designer. A few other ledgers are as follows:

200X		Accounts	Ledger	Debit	Credit
Oct	6	Cash	1	1,250	
		Sales	26		1,250
	6	Accounts Receivable	2	3,400	
		Design Fees	3		3,400
	6	Inventory	5	17,700	
		Cash	1		7,000
		Accounts Payable	21		10,700

FIGURE 21-4.

An example of journal entries.

Sydney Orlando		Client #: R842
1526 E. Seaport Drive		

Date		Explanation	Debit		Credits		Balance	
May		Balance					150	00
	9	Sales Check # 6801	325	00			775	00
	14	Received on Account			500	00	225	00
	29	Sales Check # 7002	120	00			345	00
June	8	Received on Account			300	00	45	00

FIGURE 21-5.

A sample page for an accounts receivable ledger.

> *Cash receipts ledger*: Shows all the moneys received by the firm
>
> *Cash disbursements ledger*: Records moneys paid out to cover expenses
>
> *Accounts payable ledger*: Records amounts that the design firm owes to others
>
> *Purchase order ledger*: Shows outstanding orders for goods and/or services for clients or the firm
>
> *Payroll ledger*: Records payments to employees

Trial Balance

Assets must equal liabilities and debits must equal credits. This does not mean that debits and credits will be equal within each account, but rather that when all accounts are considered, they will be equal. A test to see if accounts are balanced and if all the accounts balance with the debit and credit sides totaled separately is called a *trial balance*.

There are two purposes of a trial balance. One is to check the accuracy of the posted entries to see if total debits equal total credits. The other is to establish summary balances in all accounts in order to prepare the balance sheet, income statement, and change in financial condition report. A trial balance can be done whenever the accounts are up-to-date.

BASIC FINANCIAL REPORTS: INCOME STATEMENT, BALANCE SHEET, AND STATEMENT OF CASH FLOWS

Regular review of a business's financial statements is a critical part of business ownership. The statements help you evaluate the financial performance of your business activities. The three most important and common business reports needed are the income statement, balance sheet, and statement of cash flows. Remember that the intent of these discussions is to help you understand the basic configuration of the reports—not how to prepare them.

Income Statement

The income statement helps the firm understand if it has actually made a profit for the period the statement covers. The *income statement*, commonly called a *profit and loss statement*, or *P&L*, formally reports all the revenues and expenses of the firm for a specific period of time. *Revenues* are the inflows of moneys to a company from the sale of goods and services. *Expenses* are the outflows of assets used to generate revenue and operate the business. The period of time a statement covers may be a month, a quarter, or a year. The result shows the net income (or loss) for the firm during the period.

Only the annual income statement report shows a profit or loss for the year. Monthly and quarterly income statements indicate whether, for those shorter time frames, the design firm was operating at a profit or a loss. Monthly and quarterly reports provide valuable information on which the owner can base decisions. Computer systems allow the owner to easily produce monthly profit and loss statements. How often to produce income statements is a decision that should be made in consultation with the firm's accountant.

The firm's accountant will help determine how much detail is needed in the income statement. The chart of accounts acts as the foundation for which items will be recorded in the revenue and expenses sections of the income statement. The sample in this chapter has been prepared to show more detail than many firms include. It has been done in this way to utilize cost accounting practices to measure and evaluate costs of doing business against the revenues that the firm has generated. In a cost accounting system, certain, if not all, costs directly related to the generation of revenue are "costed" or charged to the particular revenue-producing activity. This will help the owner get a clearer picture of his or her revenue-producing activities.

The easiest way to understand the parts of an income statement is to start at the top entry and work down through the various parts. Figure 21-6 should be referenced during discussion of the income statement.

 Item 21-1 on the companion Web site provides an example of an income statement for a small firm. Item 21-2 is a worksheet to develop an income statement.

For interior design firms, revenue results from design fees for services and the sale of merchandise that is ordered from vendors and billed to the client. Remember that when the client buys merchandise directly from the vendor (or hires a consultant such as an architect), those dollars do not represent revenue for the interior designer. Refer to the hypothetical income statement shown in Figure 21-6. Starting at the top:

The **DATE** indicates the time period that the income statement is reporting on. In our example, the heading indicates that the time period for this income statement is the whole year.

GROSS REVENUE is all the revenue generated by the firm for the time period. The term *gross* in accounting indicates that the figure represents funds prior to any deductions.

Income Statement
Grand Designs
For Year Ending December 31, 200X

Income

Gross Revenue		
From Fees:	185,350	
From Reimbursable Expenses	11,540	
From Sale of Goods		
Product	227,820	
Freight-in	24,680	
Delivery	14,100	
Installation	8,610	
Total Gross Revenue		$ 472,100
Other Revenue		
Interest	3,575	
Net Revenue		$ 475,675
Cost of Sales		
From Fees:		
Direct labor	35,800	
Supplies	2,350	
Reproduction expense	3,760	
Telephone / Fax (long distance)	1,290	
CAD—contract labor	6,750	
Reimbursable expenses	9,540	
From Products:		
Cost of Goods	177,699	
Freight-in	19,750	
Delivery	10,200	
Installation	7,650	
Total Cost of Sales		$ 274,789
Gross Margin		$ 200,886

Expense

Operating Expenses		
Salaries	30,940	
Payroll taxes	15,200	
Group insurance	6,000	
Rent	28,800	
Heat, power, and light	9,800	
Telephone	7,500	
Advertising and promotion	10,000	
Travel reimbursements	12,600	
Supplies	4,800	
Postage and express	1,300	
Depreciation expense (furniture and equip.)	5,600	
Depreciation expense (auto)	2,500	
Insurance	5,700	
Dues and subscriptions	2,750	
Professional development	1,800	
Professional consultants	3,000	
Printing and reproduction	2,200	
Interest expense	4,800	
Bank charges	1,750	
Web/Internet provider and serv.	2,400	
Misc. expenses	2,575	
Total Operating Expenses		$ 162,015
Net Income Before Taxes		$ 38,871

FIGURE 21-6.

An income statement showing the separation of direct expenses from overhead expenses.

Separate lines can be used to indicate which category of income results in a specific amount of revenue. This is shown in Figure 21-6: (1) fees for services; (2) product (sold to clients); (3) freight-in—the freight charges paid by the client; and (4) delivery—the delivery and/or installation charges billed to the client.

Thus, **Total Gross Revenue** is the total amount of revenue the firm generated by all means for the period of time noted.

Adjustments are made for returns, damages, or any extra discounts that the designer has offered. Adjustments are deducted from gross revenue to obtain net revenue, as shown on the example.

Firms may have revenue from sources beyond service fees and product sales, such as interest received on funds deposited in the company's bank accounts. These extra revenue sources should be shown separately.

Net Revenue is the term for the amount left over after adjustment amounts are subtracted from Total Gross Revenue. Some call this line item Net Sales.

On the income statement, the next items reported are those related to the cost of sales.

COST OF SALES refers to those costs incurred in the direct generation of revenues. This is also called *cost of goods sold* and relates to changes in inventory. Because these items are directly related to generation of revenue, they can be referred to as *direct expenses*. Identifying these expenses as fees for services and product sales, as shown in Figure 21-6, clarifies direct expenses to revenue categories.

Direct Labor is the time the designers spent directly involved in generation of the designs. Direct labor includes production of drawings, meetings with clients, and other time items determined by the firm. This amount is calculated from time sheets and salary amount paid to the designers.

Line items can also be identified for project expense items, such as supplies and long-distance telephone charges (as shown in the example) or other items deemed appropriate to be identified as a project expense rather than an overhead expense. These direct expenses are recorded to give a more accurate view of the profitability of the firm's activities.

Cost of sales from products corresponds to those shown in the revenues sections, and include:

- Cost of goods, which shows the change in inventory and any special orders delivered during the period
- Freight-in, which is the actual charges the firm has been billed for shipping
- Delivery and installation, the cost of delivery and/or installation charges from a warehouse service or salaries, cost of trucks, and equipment, if the design firm handles delivery services

Gross Margin is the amount left after expenses are subtracted from net revenue. Gross margin is sometimes called gross profit, although it does not truly represent profit. Gross margin also shows the amount of revenue that is available to cover overhead expenses.

OPERATING EXPENSES (also called *overhead expenses* or *selling and administrative expenses*) are those expenses that are incurred whether the firm produces any revenues or not. They are often thought of as the expenses incurred in keeping the doors open. Operating expenses are reported in as much detail as is needed by the firm. The expenses listed in Figure 21-6 represent common expense items for an interior design firm. Not all items are defined, as several are self-explanatory. Please note that your accountant or computer software may use or suggest slightly different terms for these items.

- Salaries: Amounts paid for non-revenue-generating labor activities of secretaries, accounting personnel, and owners. That portion of the design staff's salaries that cannot be considered direct labor should also be included in this line.

- Telephone: Normal local and long-distance telephone charges not considered a direct expense.

- Advertising and promotion: A variable expense for any type of promotional advertising. It can also represent the expense of a business lunch.

- Travel reimbursement: Costs of business travel not included in direct expenses.

- Depreciation expense: Capital equipment used for the operation of the business, such as a computer, has a declining value. This line item recognizes the reduced value.

- Professional development: Fees for seminars or classes.

- Professional consultants: Fees paid to the company attorney or accountant. Does not include consulting fees paid to an architect or other technical consultant on a project.

Total Operating Expenses. This is subtracted from gross margin.

A corporation-form business must show its estimated income taxes on the income statement. Business income profit for sole proprietorships or partnerships is personal income and is reported along with any other income made on individual or family tax statements. These forms do not necessarily show a provision for income tax.

Net Income before Taxes. Provision for income tax for corporation-form businesses. It is the estimated tax for the period.

NET INCOME (or loss) represents the amount of income (or loss) that results when all remaining expenses (deductions) are subtracted from gross margin, including any provisions for income tax. A positive result is what finally defines profit. A negative result is a loss.

Balance Sheet

The *balance sheet* shows the financial position of a firm at a particular moment in time by reporting assets and liabilities. The balance sheet is still sometimes called a *statement of financial position*. It helps the owner see the financial value of the firm, whereas the income statement shows the owner the profitability of the firm.

This report is composed of two parts that must equal each other—hence the term balance sheet. The two parts are called assets and liabilities. *Assets* are any kind of resource—tangible or intangible—that the firm owns or controls and that can be measured in monetary terms. *Liabilities* are claims by outsiders and/or owners against the assets of the firm as a result of past transactions or events.

There are two important formulas to keep in mind when reviewing a balance sheet:

Total assets = Liabilities + Owner's equity

Total assets − Liabilities = Owner's equity

The first reflects the final outcome of all balance sheets. The total amount of asset accounts must always equal the total amount of liability accounts. The second formula shows the breakdown of the two sections that make up the liabilities side of the balance sheet. *Owner's equity* represents moneys invested in the firm by the owners or stockholders. Liabilities accounts always

Balance Sheet
Bently and Jordan Interior Designs
As of January 31, 200x

Assets

Current Assets:

Cash	$ 8,625	
Accounts Receivable	31,750	
Inventory	11,900	
Supplies	1,250	
Prepaid Expenses	2,250	
Total Current Assets		$ 55,775

Fixed Assets:

Plant and Equipment:		
Office Furniture at Cost	$ 25,500	
Less: Accumulated depreciation	−2,400	
Office Equipment at Cost	11,500	
Less: Accumulated depreciation	−1,800	
Automobile at Cost	19,500	
Less: Accumulated depreciation	−5,600	
Net Plant and Equipment		46,700
Total Assets		$ 102,475

Liabilities

Current Liabilities:

Accounts Payable	$ 8,725	
Notes Payable	4,000	
Accrued Expenses	7,000	
Deferred Revenues	6,750	
Total Current Liabilities		$ 26,475

Other Liabilities:

Long-Term Debt		29,500
Total Liabilities		$ 55,975

Owner's Equity

Common Stock	$ 35,000	
Retained Earnings	11,500	
Total Owner's Equities		46,500
Total Equities		$ 102,475

FIGURE 21-7.

A typical balance sheet for an interior design firm that is a corporation.

have first claim on the assets of the firm and take priority over claims by the owners/investors.

Assets are typically shown on the left side or top of the page, and the liabilities are shown on the right side or bottom of the page. Figure 21-7 is a sample balance sheet for a small interior design practice; please refer to it in conjunction with this discussion.

Assets

There are three kinds of financial assets, and the categories are based on how quickly the asset can be converted to cash. *Current assets* are resources that can be converted to cash in less than one year. *Fixed assets*, also called *property, plant, and equipment*, are the long-lived items used by the firm. *Other assets* are such assets as patents, copyrights, and investment securities of another firm. These "other assets" are often considered intangible assets.

These are the most common *current assets* categories:

- *Cash* is funds in the firm's bank account, checking account, cash register, or petty cash box. By the way, *cash*, for accounting purposes, is money, checks, or items such as money orders that are accepted by banks.
- *Petty cash* is currency used to purchase small or minor items, such as office supplies, with cash on hand.
- *Accounts receivable* shows what clients or others owe to the firm as a result of sales or billings for services.
- *Inventory* shows items purchased for resale to the firm's customers.
- *Prepaid expense* is early payment of expenses, such as insurance policies or rent that may have to be paid in advance.
- *Supplies* on the balance sheet represents the value of normal office supplies.
- *Marketable securities* indicates that the sample firm has purchased stock in other companies and that the owners expect to sell that investment within the year.

Fixed assets or long-term assets include items that have long-term value to the design firm. Depending on the firm, it is common for three categories of assets to be reported: land and buildings, equipment, and other long-lived assets.

- *Land and buildings* will be shown if the firm owns its business location or any other firm-related building (such as a small warehouse). Note that in Figure 21-7, the company does not own its building, so it is not listed as an asset.
- *Equipment* represents furniture used by the office staff, computers, copying machines, delivery trucks, and so on.
- *Other assets* include investments in other firms and items of value to the firm, such as copyrights, trademarks, patents, licenses, and similar intangible assets that the firm might own. If the investments are to be held for more than one year, they are listed here. If they are expected to be sold within a year, they are listed under current assets.

Certain long-term assets, such as a computer, are understood in accounting to have limited usefulness and thus a reduced financial worth. *Depreciation* expresses the usage of a fixed asset in the firm's pursuit of revenue. Although many think of depreciation as a way to express the wearing out of an object, it more accurately relates to the usage of the object, not its physical wear and tear. Accountants predict what the useful life of the equipment will be and determine the depreciated value of the equipment for each year the firm owns the item. Depreciation is set for a fixed period of time and varies based on current tax laws.

Of special interest to the design firm is the value placed on copyrighted designs or patents on any furnishings the firm may have obtained. Patents and copyrights are *amortized*, which is a practice by which the value of the patent or copyright is reduced over time to record its usage in the firm's earning activities. Amortization is essentially the same as depreciation, except that it applies to intangible assets.

Liabilities

At any given time, a design firm will owe funds to others, such as the electric utility company, a custom cabinetmaker, or an employee. The firm also has an obligation to those who have invested in the firm, either as owners or purely for investment purposes. These types of obligations are considered *liabilities*. Liabilities always have first claim on the firm's assets, and all outstanding liabilities must be paid before owners or stockholders receive any funds should the business close for any reason.

The liabilities side of the balance sheet is made up of two sections: liabilities, which can be current and noncurrent (or long-term); and owner's equity. Owner's equity is discussed separately.

Current liabilities are obligations that are due within one year or less:

- *Accounts payable* are claims from suppliers or others for goods or services ordered by the firm (and possibly delivered) but not yet paid.
- *Notes payable* represent short-term loans, such as lines of credit obtained to pay for special orders for clients.
- *Accrued expenses* are the expenses owed for the period but not yet paid, such as salaries due, rent, and utility bills.
- *Deferred revenues* are revenues received for services or the future sale of goods that have not yet been delivered or performed. Retainers or deposits that the client has paid are common examples.
- *Current portion of long-term debt* shows how much of the long-term debt (e.g., debt resulting from the purchase of a delivery truck) is to be paid during the next one-year period.
- *Taxes payable* (sometimes called *estimated taxes*). This line represents the amount of income tax or other taxes owed to government agencies but not yet paid.
- *Noncurrent liabilities* are amounts that are owed but will not be paid during the coming one-year period. Most often, for an interior design firm this represents the balance of principal owed on a long-term loan for the purchase of a vehicle or the outstanding principal on the mortgage if the firm owns its office/studio building or space.

Owner's Equity

Owner's equity represents the amount of funds the owners have invested in the interior design firm. Some accountants use the term *net worth* in place of owner's equity. The majority of accountants do not like to use this term on the balance sheet because it gives a false idea that net worth actually represents the value of the company. This is not true, as this net worth/owner's equity amount is only "worth" actual assets after all liabilities are paid. In principle, it represents that the company has a worth on its own, but that is only the case if the total assets of the company actually exceed its total liabilities.

The owner's equity section on the balance sheet is actually part of the liabilities, but it is common to report it as a separate section, as shown in Figure 21-7. It is a liability account because the owners have claims on the assets of the business. However, it bears repeating that in the case of a business failure, the owners cannot recover any assets related to their owner's equity until after all other liabilities are paid.

How this section is shown on a balance sheet will vary, based on the business's legal formation. If the firm is a sole proprietorship, owner's equity would be shown as "Michael Smith, Capital" along with the amount Michael Smith invested to start the firm. If Smith invested additional funds at a later time, those additions would also be listed. It is not uncommon for the balance sheet for a sole proprietorship not to show an owner's equity section. These businesses retain earnings by maintaining all or most profits within the company assets. In this way, the company has additional funds for future company needs such as new computers.

For a partnership, it is customary to indicate the amount invested by each partner as a separate line, in much the same way as for a sole proprietorship. Tables 21-2 and 21-3 show the owner's equity section for these business formations. A partnership and a sole proprietorship also show a beginning and ending balance to reflect any withdrawals (or drawings) made by the owners against the assets, as shown in Table 21-2.

Drawings are amounts withdrawn by sole proprietors or partners as salaries. Drawings are not truly salaries, however, and are not treated as salaries in the bookkeeping process. A separate drawing account is set up for each partner.

A design firm that is a corporation would use the term *stockholders' equity* rather than owner's equity. For a corporation, terms related to this section of the balance sheet include:

- Capital stock and/or paid-in capital stock—The amount of money obtained to run the corporation.
  - *Par value*—The legal minimum claim on assets associated with the stock itself.
  - *Paid-in capital stock*—The excess of par value representing the claims on assets arising purely from the value of stock at the time of its issuance.
- Retained earnings—The claim on assets arising from the cumulative undistributed earnings of the corporation after dividends are paid to stockholders. Retained earnings do not refer to cash in and of itself. The earnings may be in some other form, such as a vehicle, equipment, or marketable securities.

TABLE 21-2.

Reporting format of owner's equity for a sole proprietorship on a balance sheet

Owner's Equity	
Michael Smith, capital as of January 1, 200x	$25,000
Deduct: 1999 drawings	−5,000
Michael Smith, capital as of December 31, 200x	$20,000

TABLE 21-3.

Reporting format of owner's equity for a partnership on a balance sheet

Owner's Equity	
Helen Sampson, capital	$15,000
Margaret Wallace, capital	10,000
Burt Anderson, capital	10,000
Total Partnership Equity	$35,000

There is no retained earnings section on the balance sheet of a sole proprietorship or a partnership.

Each general category is added to obtain total assets and total equities. Total assets must always equal total equities.

Statement of Cash Flows

The *statement of cash flows*—also known as a *funds flow statement*—reports all the inflows and outflows of cash due to the various activities of the company. Do not confuse the formal statement of cash flows with the cash management forecast. The former reports what has happened, whereas the latter reports what might happen. Cash management is discussed later in this chapter.

Owners make many kinds of decisions based on the information in a statement of cash flows. For example, perhaps the company is considering moving to a new office location. This report will help the owner determine if sufficient cash is regularly going to be available to pay higher rent. If the owner is considering the purchase of an office space, creditors will want to review this report before a decision to offer a loan is made.

A formal statement of cash flows will detail the changes in cash available from operations, any investing, and other financial activities over a given period of time. It also reports cash equivalents. *Cash equivalents* are very liquid, short-term investments, such as money market funds, that can be converted to cash quickly. *Operations activities* are the normal revenue-generating activities of the firm. Operations flows come primarily from the payments and receivables from clients, and the payments that the firm makes to others in the generation of revenues. Operations inflows can also come from other sources, such as interest earned.

Investment inflows and outflows result from lending money and receiving payments on those loans; purchasing or selling certain kinds of securities; and purchasing or selling assets such as property, buildings, or equipment that the firm owns.

Financing inflows and outflows come from the finances that the owners have invested in the company and subsequent payments to those owners for their investments, as well as payments received and returned to creditors, such as banks, for mortgages.

The most widely used format for this information is the direct method, shown in Figure 21-8.

The information used to prepare the statement of cash flows comes from the balance sheet, from the income statement, and, for corporations, from the retained earnings portion of the income statement. Although the report can be useful for those who need to review the financial condition of any type of business, it is primarily prepared for businesses in the corporation form. Many lending institutions require a cash-flow statement when a business seeks loans.

The methods for actually constructing these forms are quite complicated, and this task is generally done by the firm's accountant. They are not discussed here.

MANAGING YOUR FINANCES

Financial resources for all interior design businesses are limited. The smaller the design practice is, the greater the pressure on financial resources can become. Control and management of financial resources is a critical management function.

The income statement, balance sheet, and statement of cash flows are the primary pieces of information that an owner uses to manage the financial

Tanner Interior Design, LLC
Statement of Cash Flows
For the Year Ended December 31, 200x

Net Cash Flow from Operating Activities:	
Net Income	$ 120,400
Adjustments to Convert Net Income to Net Cash Flow from Operating Expenses:	
Depreciation Expense	10,600
Increase in Accounts Receivable	−25,650
Decrease in Inventory	22,300
Increase in Prepaid Expenses	−12,300
Decrease in Accounts Payable	−22,360
Increase in Accrued Expenses	−8,700
Net Cash Flow from Operating Activities	101,690
Cash Flows from Investing Activities:	
Purchasing of Equipment	−$ 22,500
Net Cash Used by Investing Activities	−22,500
Cash Flows from Financing Activities:	
Proceeds from Customer Retainers	18,900
Proceeds from Customer Deposits	33,000
Proceeds of Long-term Debt	27,000
Payments on Long-term Debt	−7,750
Cash Dividends Paid	−1,250
Net Cash Provided by Financing Activities	69,900
Net Increase in Cash	$ 149,090

FIGURE 21-8.

An example of a statement of cash flows using the direct method.

resources. For many firms, though, these reports do not provide enough information to assist the owner in making important financial decisions. Other financial management reports can be very useful.

Accountants call this type of information development for management *managerial accounting*. *Financial management*, or managerial accounting, is concerned with the analysis and reporting of all the financial aspects of the firm. This management task uses the information found in basic financial accounting reports and reconfigures the information for other specific uses. These additional reports help owners and managers analyze any financial or numerical information that is of interest to them.

A design firm owner can have the firm's accountant prepare the types of reports discussed in this section, but with today's computer software many of them can be produced by the manager. That way, only the reports of most interest to the owner or manager are prepared.

This section reviews several useful financial management tools that the owner can use to make financial decisions. It begins with a discussion of the all-important topic of cash management.

Cash Management

The constant inflow of cash that is needed to meet the cash demands of a firm as it pays bills is a crucial money management task. Although the statement of cash flows discussed earlier provides important information for the owner for long-range planning, it is less useful for day-to-day cash management. This section briefly discusses a simple report that can easily be prepared by a manager and can be used in cash management. This type of report should be done on a monthly basis. This is fairly easy with today's computer software.

First, do not confuse cash flow and cash management with profit. It is quite possible for a firm to have good cash flow and appear to be in a profitable position even while expenses are being delayed or deferred, affecting its actual profitability. At minimum, the firm must shoot for a break-even point of cash/revenue in and cash/expenses out. At break-even, the amount of revenue equals the amount of expenses due. Be advised that the lack of cash flow because of poor cash management is a primary reason for business failure.

Cash management is really cash forecasting. The firm estimates how much revenue will be realized each month (or quarter) and how much its expenses will be for that same time period. Because it is a forecast, the estimate for cash receipts (revenue) can never be 100 percent accurate. All kinds of things may happen to upset forecasts for obtaining revenue. A client might not pay bills on time or an expected project can be cancelled.

For this reason, it is also a good idea to project a small, though realistic, percentage above expected and needed cash receipts for the period. If this is done, then it is easier to meet actual needs if (and when) actual receipts are lower than the forecasts. Of course, it is also important to meet that cash inflow forecast if at all possible. It should also be remembered that not all income turns into cash immediately. Accounts receivables may take 30, 60, even 90 or more days to be received. So, although the cash could be recorded for several months, it should not be forecasted as in hand until the income has actually been received.

Cash forecasting of expenses is much easier. These outflows are usually known for any given period and are more easily controlled. Although the firm might forecast the purchase of a computer or inventory, these items can often be put off when cash receipts do not materialize as forecasted.

Figure 21-9 is an example of a simple cash management statement. Please use this example to follow along with the explanations of the parts of the statement. Notice how this report mimics the appearance of the income statement.

The cash management statement begins with the actual beginning cash balance for the most current month. The other months begin with estimated

Cash Management Statement: December to March 200x				
Description	Actual December	Projected January	Projected February	Projected March
Beginning Cash Balance	$ 8,000	$ 6,500	$ 19,100	$ 21,200
Projected Revenue	95,000	92,000	100,000	105,000
Other income		1,100	1,100	1,100
Projected Gross Revenue	103,000	99,600	120,200	127,300
Operating Expenses	77,000	78,000	79,000	81,000
Purchase computer	17,000			3,400
Purchase office furniture			17,500	
Line-of-credit debt	2,500	2,500	2,500	2,500
Ending Cash Balance	6,500	19,100	21,200	40,400

FIGURE 21-9.

A simple cash management statement. Notice how it repeats the format of an income statement.

cash balances. The next line shows the known and projected revenues for the months being projected. The projected revenues combine the known work-in-process amounts for each period with forecasts of additional work in each month. *Work in process* means work under way for any clients that have not yet been billed. Adding the beginning cash balance to the projected revenue provides the projected gross revenue.

Under the expenses, operating expenses are the projected combined expenses for each month. In the example, there is an allowance for a line of credit for a bank loan obtained in a previous month. This amount is the amount of principal and interest due each month. The expense section shows other known or projected expenses, such as the purchase of capital equipment. The last line shows the ending cash balance for each month.

The ending cash balance is carried up to the beginning cash balance line in the forecast months. The reader may wish to fill in April's figures to obtain the ending balance for the month (and to see how well the firm is doing). Item 21-3 is another sample cash flow statement, which can be found on the companion Web site.

A positive ending cash flow does not necessarily mean the firm is profitable. Even a company with good cash flow can be losing money. Sometimes the assets of a firm can be tied up in receivables or fixed assets. These assets help show a "profit" at the end of the income statement, but do not represent cash that is available to pay bills. Bills to vendors or others that are not paid or are deferred will still have to be paid one day.

Cash-flow reporting helps create a cash budget. This allows the owner to compare actual results of the business against forecasted goals to help prevent expenses from overtaking revenues and cash availability. Adjustments, made by holding down expenses or finding ways to increase revenues, are needed when forecasts are not met.

Many small design firms operate in markets in which they must survive on seasonal design business, such as the design of second homes in resort areas. Understanding on paper what the cash-flow situation will be in the slow months when these second-home owners are not procuring interior design work can help the design firm owner determine how to generate alternative revenue sources during those slow months.

New firms and those in the first year also have a built-in cash-flow problem. A new firm has many first-time expenses, such as stationery, office equipment, and marketing activities. Revenue is often delayed as the firm waits for full payment from clients. On top of this problem, many new businesses are required to pay in full and up front for merchandise that they purchase for clients. Obviously, the cash could easily be going out faster than it is coming in.

For design firms that do not sell merchandise, the cash-flow cycle is relatively short. Firms that sell merchandise often have a constant cash-flow problem because they have not received enough cash—from whatever source—to pay for the merchandise that is on order. Nevertheless, sufficient cash must become available to pay current bills.

It is important for you to realize that cash management and cash flow fall back on the cash accounting method rather than on the accrual accounting method. Good cash-flow records of cash receipts (deposits of cash) and outflows (when a check to a supplier or other liability account clears the bank) are necessary. To accurately record cash receipts, the owner must keep track of new orders or contracts for services, when deposits or retainers are to be received, when partial payments are expected, when deliveries of goods are expected, and so on.

Tips to Help Monitor Cash Flow

When the owner can see cash needs months in advance, this information encourages the owner to market beyond what is needed to pay today's bills. Small firms frequently develop the short-sighted habit of looking at the work they are doing right now, neglecting marketing until the current project is done. When this happens, a business may be without any revenue for weeks or even months as the owner finally gets around to seeking new business. Cash management actually forces the owner to recognize marketing efforts as an ongoing part of his or her ownership responsibilities.

Cash management also has a relationship to other business operations. Good, basic business practices aid in keeping cash flow operating efficiently. Here are a few examples:

- Constant monitoring of outstanding orders and receivables aids the firm in protecting narrow margins of profit.
- The firm must have good pricing policies for both fees and products.
- Credit reports on clients with whom the firm is unfamiliar should be obtained before the firm orders merchandise.
- Inventory, returns, and exchanges must be carefully monitored so that cash is not tied up in inventory. This cash cannot be used to pay other expenses.
- The firm must prepare design contracts to help protect it against possible stoppages or losses of revenue.
- The firm should require substantial retainers and deposits before work is begun or products are ordered.
- Careful timekeeping, scheduling, and project management are also helpful in cash-flow forecasting.
- A thorough monitoring of budgeted versus actual time estimates and fee estimates can eliminate project shortfalls.
- Constant monitoring of outstanding orders and receivables aids the firm in protecting narrow margins of profit.

Establishing policies that require substantial retainers and deposits, as well as tracking and collecting receivables, can help produce positive cash management. When the firm needs cash, the owners may be able to obtain short-term loans from the firm's banker. Keeping the banker informed of the financial situation of the design firm helps the firm in the loan approval process, as does a good history of prompt repayment of those loans. Going to the bank every time the firm needs cash to pay bills is not the best solution. Good management of the firm and the firm's cash flow is the answer.

Financial Ratios and Percentages

In addition to the reports and reporting methodologies discussed earlier in this chapter, design firm owners should become familiar with certain financial ratios and percentages. These provide many important clues to the success of, or possible problems in, the financial performance of an interior design firm. Ratios and percentages give an even clearer message regarding the business's overall financial success (or lack thereof). By using ratios and percentages, a designer can evaluate almost anything that can be measured in numerical terms.

Do not be afraid to learn about ratios and percentages. Ratios are quite common and are used every day by almost everyone in one way or another. In our everyday experiences, we might use ratios to determine the miles per gallon our car gets or to calculate a tip at a restaurant. The ability to calculate percentages is critical to determining the cost and selling prices of products.

As a reminder, a *ratio* is one number over another—the relationship between two or more things. With ratios, we are comparing two numbers. A ratio can become a percentage when we divide one number into another. To calculate a *percentage*, the large number (the denominator) must be divided into the small number (the numerator). For example, if we divide 75 by 100 (75/100), we will get a percentage of 75. When you are using ratios, remember that when you are comparing a part to the whole, the whole is always the denominator.

Accountants and financial analysts use many ratios to evaluate a business. Table 21-4 shows several financial ratios. Realize that analysis of financial ratios is not difficult to grasp. The information that these ratios provide can be critical to an owner's decisions about the current state and future of the firm.

Profit ratios help a design firm owner analyze how effectively the company is earning more income than it is spending in expenses. Obviously, a business can remain viable only if it sustains a profit. As a rule, profitability (or income) is affected by increases in volume and changes in price, or both. There are three primary ways a design firm can increase its profitability from fees. The first is to increase its fee base: for example, charging $100 per hour rather than $90 per hour or $3.25 a square foot rather than $2.75 per square foot. Another is to bill more hours at its design fee. This might simply involve being more productive and more accurate in billing time to a project. A third way is to find means of reducing expenses.

Efficiency ratios can be developed to review how well the business is operating. One very important efficiency ratio is the *average collection period ratio*. This ratio tells the business how many days, on average, it takes to collect accounts receivable. The faster clients pay their bills, the sooner the firm can pay its bills—a very positive situation for any size interior design firm. If this ratio is low, it means that the business is receiving payments from clients quickly. If it is high, it means that clients are taking a long time to pay, and this can seriously affect cash flow for the business.

Liquidity ratios show the design firm's ability to pay its debts. Of particular importance is the firm's ability to pay its current liabilities with available current assets. A second liquidity ratio is the working capital ratio. It measures the amount of cash that is available to operate the business on a daily basis. If a firm's working capital is less than its operating expenses, it may not be able to pay all of its current bills.

TABLE 21-4.

Financial ratios to determine the financial performance of the business

1. Profit margin on sales = Net income/Total sales
2. Return on total assets (ROA) = Net income/Total assets
3. Return on equity (ROE) = Net income/Owner's equity
4. Return on investment (ROI) = Net profits/Total assets
5. Current ratio = Current assets/Current liabilities
6. Quick ratio (or acid test) = Current assets − Inventory/Current liabilities
7. Debt ratio = Total debt/Total assets
8. Working capital = Current assets − Current liabilities
9. Net profit = Earnings before interest and taxes (EBIT)/Net sales
10. Return on investment = EBIT/Total assets − Total liabilities
11. Average collection period = Accounts receivables × 360/Total sales
12. Inventory turnover ratio = Cost of goods sold/Average inventory
13. Gross margin percentage = Gross margin dollars/Net revenue
14. Receivable turnover ratio = Annual sales/Total outstanding receivables

Debt ratios indicate how much of the firm's financing has come from debts—loans and lines of credit—rather than direct investment by the owners and/or stockholders. Potential new investors will be concerned about high debt ratios, because they indicate that the loans must be paid off before the firm yields any return on investments.

Ratios help determine the financial health of the firm and locate some of the potential financial or operational problems. Ratios are more important to the owner or manager than to employees. However, employees should understand that a lot of number crunching goes on behind the scenes in the operation of a design practice. Awareness brings about concern, and concern brings about the realization that every employee in the design firm affects the financial health of the company.

Reporting Performance

A management tool used by larger design firms is written reports. Management personnel and even project managers relay important information to the owners by creating these reports.

Two types of reports that are created and used by management to determine if the firm's plans are being accomplished are information reports and performance reports. *Information reports* are generally reports of financial or other numerical data. They are prepared in a narrative form and are used to provide information needed in the operation of the organization. A summary of an article related to general economic forecasts for the design firm's target market is an example.

The *performance report* consists primarily of financial or other numerical information. The data used to develop many performance reports can be found in the firm's usual financial reports, such as the P&L. Other performance reports can be generated from time records, accounts receivable records on design fees, and reimbursable expense records, to name a few.

Computer software programs create many kinds of reports with relative ease. However, not all reports that can be created are necessary. In fact, too many reports can confuse rather than help the owner. It is therefore necessary for the owner and the firm's accountant to determine which reports are desired, and to ensure that the ones produced are reliable and timely. What this means is that any report must be based on accurate data or information.

To be most useful, management reports must be accurate and timely. Accurate data is that which is truthful. For example, inaccurate time records are not truthful data reports. To be timely, reports should be based on weekly or perhaps monthly data. For example, weekly time sheets help the manager/owner decide which design staff member is available to begin work on a new project. Aged receivables reports are needed on a monthly basis to help project cash flow.

A data business tool used by many large firms is variance analysis. When utilizing *variance analysis*, the owner or manager looks at financial and numerical data in relation to the differences between planned (or budgeted) amounts and actual amounts. Basically, what happens in variance analysis is that data are reviewed to see differences in planned performance versus actual performance. Variance analysis is also discussed in Chapter 20.

In variance analysis, accountants use the terms favorable and unfavorable. An *unfavorable variance* generally means that the actual amount is more than the budgeted amount. A *favorable variance* generally means that the actual amount is less than the budgeted amount. For example, if the budgeted amount of direct labor for a project is 300 hours and the actual amount of hours worked is 365 hours, there is an unfavorable variance. Assuming there is the same number of budget hours, if the actual hours were 280, there would be a

Expense Report($) April 200X			
Expense	Actual	Budget	Variance over Budget
Salaries	$75,000	$78,500	$−3,500
Payroll taxes	4,575	5,000	−425
Group insurance	750	750	0
Rent	1,500	1,500	0
Heat, power, & light	650	500	150
Telephone	375	300	75
Promotion	450	525	−75
Travel reimbursements	790	600	190
Supplies and postage	450	500	−50
Depreciation expense	900	900	0
Insurance	750	750	0
Dues & subscriptions	250	150	100
Professional consultants	2,300	1,000	1,300
Printing and reproduction	570	450	120
Interest expense	875	875	0
Total Expenses	90,185	92,300	−2,115

FIGURE 21-10.

A sample performance report showing variance analysis for the overall expense report.

favorable variance. In Figure 21-10, you can see that there were unfavorable variances for several of the overhead expense items. If this trend continued, including the overall total expense variance, what effect would that have on the potential profitability of this particular firm? Item 21-4 on the companion Web site shows another detailed variance report.

A manager must not look only at the quantitative differences. For the data to be truly meaningful, he or she must also ask questions as to why the variances occur. Very often, there are logical reasons for a variance. For example, in Figure 21-10 the expense for heat, power, and light may have exceeded the budget because of a large amount of overtime required to complete a project. Can you think of some reasons why the salary expense was less than budgeted? The manager uses his or her judgment, after meetings with the individuals involved or a further review of billings, before making decisions on what to do about the variances.

Many kinds of reports can be generated from the data collected by the design firm, both in terms of financial information (such as revenue generated) and operational information (such as time records). Figure 21-11 is an example of a report concerning projected revenue—a very important report for any size or type of design firm.

Reports provide managers with much information on which to base decisions concerning all aspects of the office. To have the most utility, performance reports should be prepared on a monthly basis. Another example of a performance report is provided on the companion Web site as Item 21-5.

Other types of specific reports that can be useful, depending on the size and complexity of the interior design firm, are:

1. Revenues from sources—fees and sales of goods
2. Work in process and aged receivables
3. Aged accounts payables
4. Deferred income
5. Employee utilization and productivity
6. Comparisons of fees earned with budgeted estimates

7. Revenues by client type (or size of project)
8. Month-by-month profit and loss statements (with variances)
9. Budgets for capital equipment purchases
10. All overhead expenses or specific overhead expenses month to month

These examples are optional accounting and managerial information reports. Essentially, they should be prepared depending largely on the firm's ability to produce the required reports and on the owner's need to have the information. Computer applications allow fast turnaround of many reports. Ideally, most reports should be prepared within the first ten days of the month, on a monthly basis, when the previous month's data become available.

Even small design firms or sole proprietors can take advantage of performance reporting by using accounting and database management. Computer systems can link accounting and other numerical data to generate tabled reports relatively easily. Software that can also automatically prepare charts and graphs from the numerical data provides additional aid for the manager.

Creative Interior Design Projected Revenue by Client Type 200X, 200X (Est.), 200X (Est.)		
200X	200X	200X
Open Office Planning:		
Under 15,000 sq. ft. $ 23,500	$ 65,000	$ 75,000
15,000-30,000 sq. ft 12,000	36,000	40,000
Over 30,000 sq. ft. 20,800	27,000	35,000
Subtotal $ 56,300	$128,000	$ 150,000
Medical Facilities:		
Physician's suites 32,500	48,000	55,000
Hospitals 35,000	40,000	25,000
Subtotal $ 67,500	$ 88,000	$ 80,000
Banking Facilities:		
Branch offices 10,000	20,500	28,000
Corporate offices 15,500	20,000	30,000
Subtotal $ 25,500	$ 40,500	$ 58,000
Professional Offices:		
Attorneys 28,700	42,000	55,000
Accountants 13,600	25,000	30,000
Corporate 45,900	55,000	60,000
Real estate 5,000	7,500	10,000
Others 10,000	20,000	25,000
Subtotal $103,200	$149,500	$ 180,000
Hospitality:		
Restaurant 65,500	80,500	90,000
Lodging 38,500	49,000	72,000
Subtotal $104,000	$129,500	$ 162,000
Grand Total $356,500	$535,500	$630,000

FIGURE 21-11.

Performance report showing projected revenue by client type.

Break-Even Point

Few interior designers consider their businesses to be "nonprofits." Yet, many find themselves barely making a profit at the end of each tax year. This happens despite their best efforts at creating excellent interiors and being wonderful problem solvers for their clients.

Low profitability often occurs because many designers do not carefully control their operating expenses. These expenses must, at minimum, be in balance with the revenues that are generated. When this doesn't happen, a low profit or loss occurs.

One management tactic that can help with this situation is to plan for profit by establishing the firm's break-even point. The *break-even point* is when the dollars to operate the business are exactly equal to the dollars generated from revenues from all sales activity.

Too many designers forget to consider all the costs (or expenses) of operating the business as well as the costs of doing projects; thus, estimates for fees (and other sources of revenue) can easily fall short of revenue needs. When that happens, the firm is operating below the break-even point. When revenues exceed costs, then the firm is operating above the break-even point and making a profit.

Some costs will vary with the volume of work performed and revenue generated. Accountants call these costs *variable costs*. The biggest variable cost in an interior design firm is the direct labor—time actually spent on projects that create revenue—because it varies with the amount of projects that are done.

Fixed costs are those commonly thought of as overhead items, and stay essentially the same (or nearly so) every month. Generally, these expenses do not vary with the volume of work being done by a firm. Fixed costs increase somewhat as an expense such as rent or heat/power/light increases, but do not vary as much as the variable cost items.

Here are the steps in determining a firm's break-even point:

- Carefully determine fixed costs on a monthly basis.
- Determine salary and employee benefit costs such as Social Security contributions for all employees.
- Recognize the billing rate(s) of all employees.
- Recognize the amount of revenue generated from the sale of goods that pass through the design firm.
- Total all the costs and revenues—separating design fee costs from product costs.
- Subtract costs from revenues—separating design fees from product sales.
- The results of these last two items create break-even points.

By example, let's say that the total fixed costs (including salary expenses) for one month are $10,000. If we only consider funds from fees as the source of revenue, and the billing rate is $125 per hour for the owner, he or she must bill 80 hours in the month (assuming a 40-hour workweek or 160 hours per week) to break even. That might not seem like a lot of hours, but if the designer is a sole practitioner who must also take care of all the other tasks involved in the operation of a business, it means that the designer is only billing approximately 50 percent of his or her time per month. That really isn't a lot of productive use of the workweek!

Information about break-even analysis can also be found in many of the books listed in the references, including *Interior Design Management*, by this author.

CONTROLLING OVERHEAD

Losing control of overhead expenses not only means diminished profits, but can also result in a critical financial situation, leading in the worst-case scenario to the closing of the company. Keeping overhead expenses under control is an important task in producing a profit for any size design business.

Obviously, the larger the design firm, the more important controlling costs becomes. Yet, even the sole practitioner who works out of a home office needs to control overhead, or profit margins will be nonexistent. Although this section is directed to the interior design firm with employees, the sole practitioner will find key concepts to assist in cost control.

Remember that overhead items are those expenses necessary to keep the doors of the design firm open. For almost all businesses, overhead expenses exist even if no revenue is produced during a business day. Rent, utilities, and employee salaries are three examples.

Monthly reviews of these expenses are the starting point for controlling overhead. Reviews must be done so that the owners can clearly determine any areas of the business that have had increasing overhead costs. For example, the owner may see that the utility bills have risen and stayed high for a series of months. This could have occurred for several reasons, such as overtime or simply increases in the utility company's rates. Although it might not be possible to eliminate this increase—the workload is the workload—it can be taken into consideration when the owner is determining billing rates and fee methods for future projects.

Indirect labor—sometimes referred to as *house time*—is a frequent culprit in raising overhead expenses. *Indirect labor* is any work performed that cannot be directly charged to a particular revenue-producing account or project; that is, it cannot be charged to a client or at least to a project. A common example is when the design staff meets with manufacturers' representatives and vendors who drop by the office for a visit unrelated to any particular project.

There are many other kinds of overhead expenses. Here are several ways in which overhead expenses can sometimes be reduced to help improve profit margins:

- Purchase equipment rather than renting or leasing it.
- Negotiate for the best cell phone contracts possible—perhaps bundling or using multitasking services to include the office landlines and Internet.
- Make sure staff members are aware that business cell phones are not for personal use.
- Sublet office or studio space from another design firm (for the sole practitioner).
- When working with business professional advisers such as an attorney, have your questions prepared ahead of time so that the time with the professional is efficient.
- Arrange for in-house training seminars or utilize webinars for staff training rather than sending designers out of state.

The most important part of controlling costs is to know what the costs are. Many smaller interior design practices keep minimal records on direct or indirect expenses of operating the practice. For example, the author has heard from designers, "It takes too much time to record all my time." Yet not recording time can lead to loss of revenue and an undue increase in house time.

It is also easy for the detail-oriented interior designer to create obsessively meticulous methods and procedures to control overhead. Controlling overhead should not be an intrusion into the orderly completion of work in the firm. Determining which overhead activities will be controlled and studied should be carefully limited, to ensure positive assistance to the owner while not creating extra work for the staff. For example, I remember hearing about a firm that expected designers to keep track of the number of sheets of plot paper used in the development of a project. This type of micromanagement is generally a waste of time and rarely helps in lowering expenses.

Discussions with the firm's accountant to determine which areas of overhead need to be controlled, along with meetings to carefully explain to the staff the importance of these procedures, are vital when the owner is instituting methods to control overhead.

Another critical point related to overhead expense recording is that these items cannot be deducted from taxes without proper records. The IRS looks at expenses for entertainment, travel, and meal expenses very carefully. Good recordkeeping for those receipts from employees should be mandatory, along with records of major purchases made for operational equipment and use by the firm. Records and receipts are critical in case of an audit.

COMPUTER APPLICATIONS FOR ACCOUNTING

Computer applications for accounting and financial recordkeeping have become more useful and easier for interior designers over the years. Although some may still use a manual method of bookkeeping, accountants working with designers would prefer that the owners switch to a computerized system, for accuracy and speed. The choice of which system to use is affected by whether the firm will use a single-entry or double-entry system. It makes little difference to the IRS or state revenue departments whether an interior design firm utilizes a manual or computer system for financial recordkeeping.

Accounting software accommodates check writing to pay bills, preparation of payroll and payroll tax reports, and preparation of sales tax reports. Software programs also help the owner create useful managerial reports of many kinds. The firm's accountant can use the data generated by the accounting software to prepare income tax statements, as well as many other kinds of financial recordkeeping documents.

Software programs exist for both Windows® and Macintosh® computer systems that can be adopted by interior designers. I do not recommend any one particular accounting software program, but two still commonly used by interior design firms are QuickBooks Pro® and Sage Peachtree Accounting®. Other specialized programs that have been created specifically for interior designers are available; these combine accounting functions with other functions such as purchasing, project management, and order tracking.

Computer programs should not be expected to replace a qualified accountant. Selection of appropriate software should be made after the owner discusses all pertinent issues with the firm's accountant. The firm's accountant generally is familiar with different software programs for accounting needs and can help the design firm owner with this decision.

WEB SITES RELEVANT TO THIS CHAPTER

www.aahaq American Accounting Association

www.aicpa.org American Institute of CPAs

www.designmanager.com Design Manager
www.quickbooks.intuit.com QuickBooks accounting software
www.sage.com Sage Peachtree accounting software
www.sba.gov U.S. Small Business Administration

Other accounting software is available; the selection should made in consultation with the company's accountant.

KEY TERMS

Accounts	Fixed assets
Accounts payable	Fixed costs
Accounts receivable	Gross margin
Accrual accounting	Gross revenue
Accrued expenses	Income statement
Amortize	Journal
Assets	Ledger
Balance sheet	Liabilities
Break-even point	Net income
Cash	Overhead expenses
Cash accounting	Owner's equity
Chart of accounts	"Pass through"
Cost of sales	Performance reports
Credit	Posting
Current assets	Prepaid expense
Current liabilities	Profit and loss statement (P&L)
Debit	Retained earnings
Deferred revenues	Revenue
Depreciation	Single-entry system
Direct expenses	Statement of cash flow
Direct labor	T-account
Double-entry system	Transactions
Drawings	Trial balance
Expense	Unfavorable variance
Favorable variance	Variable costs
Financial accounting	Variance analysis
Financial management	Work in process

WHAT WOULD YOU DO?

1. Wallace Design Group experienced a 12 percent decrease in net income during 2011. Despite this, the owner added one interior designer and hired a full-time office assistant. The owner has been aggressively marketing for additional high-end residential projects, along with residential work for the smaller 1200- to 1500-square-foot house. In the firm's prime market area, new housing starts for homes over 3000 square feet have begun to show a small increase over the past six months.

The owner does not want to lay anyone off, especially the designer, because that designer has some great contacts. The space the owner uses for the office has room for one more designer, and the owner is thinking about offering to rent that space to a colleague, charging her rent and fees for the cooperative use of the office assistant.

2. George's firm has been working on the design and specification of a very large public utility office building in another state. The design contract calls for space-plan coordination with the architect, specification of all the furniture, and coordination with the architect on architectural finish specification. The project will be going out to bid for the purchase of the furniture.

   The person from the utility with whom George has been working has asked him to specify ergonomic desk seating for the offices. That amounts to 195 small executive chairs and another 57 large executive chairs. George wants the client to purchase a specific manufacturer's chairs, as they have the right "look" that George and the rest of the design team want for the project. The client likes the chair but is concerned about the price.

   George talks to a sales rep from another chair manufacturer who wants to bid on the project. That rep says, "I can get a good price if you can convince the client to let me make a presentation so that the utility negotiates a contract directly with the factory. I know I can get a deal from headquarters, especially if the company will also negotiate the desks."

3. An interior design firm has prepared drawings and plans for a residence. The couple who owns the house have agreed to purchase furniture and other items directly from the designer who did the design. Part of the project included the design of custom cabinets for the kitchen. The designer recommended the cabinetmaker, but the client paid the cabinetmaker directly.

   The fee for the project includes a percentage of the cost of all goods sold to the client through the design firm plus a design consultation fee. The designer bills the client for the furniture as well as the custom cabinets. The client refuses to pay the portion of the bill related to the cabinets.

4. Each month, Sally is responsible for developing two key reports on the activities of the interior design department. One of those reports shows the status of work in progress for the previous month and estimated work for the next month. A second report details design fees that are booked via new contracts, billings for the previous month, and expected billings for the next month. This report also compares this year's billings to last year's for the same months. Sally also generates a report on the direct expenses for last month and the expected direct expenses for the next month. Even without having a sample of each of these reports before you, how would these reports help Sally manage workload and operational decisions for the design department?

CHAPTER 22

Fundamentals of Marketing

After completing this chapter you should be able to:

- Evaluate a design firm's brand based on its Web site.
- Discuss why some firms' established brand helps them attract business without needing to do any marketing.
- Describe target marketing and the factors that are analyzed to determine a firm's target market.
- Explain how a niche can be of benefit as well as a problem for a small design firm.
- List and describe the four Ps of marketing.
- Explain what the product is in an interior design firm.
- Discuss how a client's perception of a design firm affects the firm's ability to attract clients.
- Explain why it is important to do a market analysis before developing a marketing plan.
- List the topics that should be explained in a firm's marketing plan.
- Discuss how a marketing plan can be useful to a small practice.

Many interior designers think that marketing consists of putting up a Web page or placing an advertisement in a magazine with the purpose of attracting clients. Others feel that they can leave their marketing to referrals. Marketing actually involves quite a bit more than that.

If you have ever taken a marketing class during your academic training, you have probably run into a definition of *marketing* that sounds something like this one from the American Marketing Association: "the process of planning and executing the conception, pricing, promotion, and distribution of ideas, goods, and services to create exchanges that satisfy individual and organizational goals."[1] Another definition of marketing includes the concept of moving goods and services from producers to consumers. Thus, marketing is much more than waiting for a customer to contact you because she saw your ad in a magazine or liked the contents of your Web site.

Design professionals must always be thinking past the current project and looking for ways to attract a constant flow of new projects. It is easy for an interior design firm to get lost in the crowd! The Internet allows firms in one part of the country—or world—to make contact with potential clients anywhere. Marketing must be planned and consistently nurtured for those new clients to be attracted to an interior design firm today.

When the economy is in turmoil, competition becomes extreme for the interior designer. When the economy is good, competition may be similarly robust, depending on the market, as many try to enter the industry. Understanding what is involved in effective marketing is essential to any size or type of interior design firm in both good and bad times. Interior design firms must always be vigilant as to what the general economy is doing, as it can have dramatic impacts on the interior design industry.

Marketing requires the owner to know what she wants from her business. It is an understanding of what clients value and are willing to pay for concerning her services. Marketing involves an understanding of the skills the designer has to offer to the clients with which she wants to work. It also requires an understanding of the different techniques that can be used to attract clients. Table 22-1 provides a context for the overall impact of marketing activities.

This chapter introduces readers to basic concepts underlying marketing, which provide the basis for decision making concerning the use of specific marketing techniques to execute a design firm's marketing plan. Chapters 23 and 24 discuss specific techniques and tools used for marketing an interior design business.

BRANDING

Much has been written about branding to help firms gain a competitive edge. A *brand* is "a type of product manufactured by a particular company under a particular name. Branding is the promotion of a particular product or company by means of advertising and distinctive design."[2] In other words, *branding* is the combination of images and encounters that the customer perceives, accepts, and experiences with a product. It is far more than just a logo on a business card.

As you can see by these definitions, branding is most commonly associated with products, but services can also be branded in a positive fashion. Think of FedEx, which provides shipping services, and Southwest Airlines, which provides low-cost travel. Even a person can become a brand in consumer's minds:

TABLE 22-1.

Marketing dynamics

Identify customer needs and wants.
Understand buyer behavior.
Analyze customer interest and demand.
Develop new products or services.
Manufacture or offer the new products or services.
Understand cost to offer the service or products.
Develop awareness of competitive pricing.
Price to ensure sales and reasonable profit margin.
Determine feasible selling price.
Develop a brand.
Determine which marketing tools to use.
Establish how the services and products will be made available to clients.
Utilize publicity and public relations.
Advertise to create awareness.
Determine where the services will be offered or products sold.
Use personal selling techniques.
Evaluate customer satisfaction.

consider Oprah Winfrey or Justin Bieber. Certainly, an interior design firm can work at developing a positive and lasting brand.

A brand becomes a valuable commodity when it automatically conjures up positive thoughts in clients and potential clients. There are sometimes simply too many choices, and often a client cannot see the difference between one design firm and another. At the least, brand identification helps to focus attention on a particular firm. Branding activity and a brand are not just what the firm tries to create. Success in branding is heavily dependent upon how the client perceives the firm and accepts the brand.

A successful brand starts with knowing what the firm is all about—its purpose and its values. The purpose and values of the firm are the framework, enhanced by excellent service, that results in client loyalty and trust. Loyalty and trust bring clients back when they need design services again and make them willing to refer their friends to the design firm. Thus, to create a brand, a firm needs to carefully consider and develop these elements:

Company name. A strong name helps develop the brand. Many designers use their own name, as many clients associate the work of an interior designer with the person. It is harder for a name such as ABC Designs to become a successful or useful brand, because it is harder for clients to relate the name to an individual or group of individuals. Chapter 19 discusses some of the issues surrounding the selection and registration of a company name.

Logos. A logo is usually a graphic that helps identify a business. A logo can bring instant recognition without even including the company name. Consider the apple logo for Apple computers.

Tag line or slogan. A few words that provide a strong concept of what the company does is called a *tag line*. Not very many interior design companies try to use a tag line or slogan. This is unfortunate, as a tag line can be very powerful. "Designing productive work spaces" is a tag line that might work for a commercial firm specializing in corporate offices or other types of commercial facilities.

Business color scheme. A color scheme that is carried through on all stationery and marketing materials adds to brand identification. Consider IBM blue as an example of how color helps identify a brand.

Exceptional customer service. Clients are looking for interior designers who will provide exceptional service. Being known for such things as returning phone calls and e-mails promptly, and keeping promises, adds to a firm's brand.

As the last element suggests, part of creating a brand is providing value. For a service business such as interior design, it is critical for the firm to emphasize its value to the client. It is equally—if not more—important to show the client how the firm can add value for the client.

How do designers add value? Materials suggestions and detailing in a residence add to the resale value of the house. An office designed to improve employee productivity, the restaurant interior designed to be so exciting that guests line up to get in to see the interior, or an assisted-living facility designed to help patients be very comfortable in the environment are other examples. Design solutions such as these are valuable to the client, and the designer's reputation for providing these types of services makes the designer valuable to the client. You might want to reread the section on how designers add value to clients in Chapter 11.

If the design firm or designer has been practicing for a few years or more, a brand of sorts has already been started. The firm or individual's brand begins with the reputation that the designer already has in the industry and market. Continually working to maintain an excellent reputation in the field is critical in this highly competitive business. Establishing a stronger brand identity builds on this reputation.

Remember that everything the firm or individual does somehow relates to the brand. Names, reputation, logos, corporate colors—all these are certainly important parts of the brand. But so are things such as how the phone is answered, the quality of customer service, and professional attitude. The image that a professional projects on a Web site or Facebook page, or via comments given on other social media outlets, all affect the brand and image of the designer and the firm. Keeping private life and professional life as separate as possible are important to a professional services provider regardless of experience level.

TARGET MARKETING

Not all potential clients looking for an interior designer are the right fit for a particular interior designer. Marketing to this broad spectrum of potential clients, especially for the small firm, is also wasteful of a very important resource—and that is, of course, money. Thus, a very important decision for an interior design practice is to determine the type of clients it seeks to attract to the business. At the most rudimentary level, this means deciding whether to serve clients who wish residential interior design services or those who want commercial interior design services. This decision can be considered the beginning of a business strategy called *target marketing*.

More precisely, *target marketing* is a marketing method that helps a firm identify one or more groups of potential customers who are most likely to utilize the firm's services. When a firm uses target marketing, it develops identifiable groups within the firm's total market, called market segments. A *market segment* is a group of customers that has some common characteristic. For example, everyone living within the city of New York City/Manhattan can be a market segment for a residential designer located in Manhattan. All doctors practicing in Dallas, Texas, can be a market segment for a commercial designer in Texas.

However, those examples are rather broad. Firms have greater success in target marketing when they are as specific as possible. It is difficult to attract every customer who may want some type of design services in these broad segments. By specifically defining smaller markets within a broad segment, firms will have greater success in attracting clients and thus will utilize marketing resources to the best advantage.

Of course, a firm can make a mistake and create too narrow a focus or target, thus limiting the number of potential clients. An example of this would be a firm located in a small city that targets a very specific type of commercial work, such as spas. Unless the designer is willing to travel for business, possibilities in that narrow a target market might be exhausted quickly within the local area.

Knowing what the design firm can do and wants to provide is only part of the challenge in reaching the right clients. The interior designer who is intent on expanding his or her market to high-quality clients must also find out what the client wants from an interior designer. As with any business, an interior designer cannot survive on providing what he or she thinks is needed rather than what clients actually need. That is like the traditional marketing example

TABLE 22-2.

Target characteristics used to help define a target segment and market

1. *Demographics*. These encompass characteristics such as age, gender, occupation, level of income, stage in family life cycle, religion, and race.

2. *Psychographics*. These concepts define a person's lifestyle interests and attitudes, such as hobbies, sports interests, personality traits, and abilities (or lack of abilities).

3. *Geographic*. These define a location of the targeted clients. For example, is the design firm willing to work only within the confines of the city in which the business is located, or is the firm willing to go out of state for work?

4. *Industry type*. This can be explained by differentiating the exact type of specialty within interior design. A commercial designer has many areas in which he or she can specialize, such as health care, retail, lodging, and so on. Residential designers can specialize as well; for instance, they may wish to limit their practices to designing apartments and condominiums rather than any type of residence.

5. *Benefits*. What is the client looking for? Benefits are related to why the customer buys. For example, the client may be looking for a more productive office staff and therefore may be seeking a design solution that will help meet that need.

6. *Product usage*. This defines how often the product or service is purchased or used. Although this factor relates more to product sales marketing than to design services marketing, it can be used to target services. Knowing how often a certain type of client will use design services will help the firm understand the type of marketing methods that it must use to attract repeat and new business.

of the companies that continued to make buggy whips when automobiles became popular. Target marketing provides a way to help designers solve both these problems.

Target marketing begins with an understanding of what services the firm can offer. A thorough analysis of what each employee can do and the kind of projects the firm has done in the past helps the firm determine what it can do in the future. This analysis may also help a firm determine if it can offer new services. Any new services may open up a new market segment and produce additional revenue for the firm.

Internal analysis of strengths, weaknesses, and previous general market interest should be followed by in-depth research so that the design firm can more clearly identify the market segments that most likely want and need the firm's services. Table 22-2 provides the characteristics that are most frequently used to differentiate market segments. There is information on buyer demographics in Chapter 25.

Information to develop target market segments comes from many sources. Information gathered from the library or other sources by someone other than the design firm is called *secondary research*. When research such as a questionnaire is undertaken to answer specific questions, it is called *primary research*. Primary research, obviously, is more expensive than secondary research. Here are principal examples of where target marketing information can be obtained:

- A firm's historic data on completed projects
- Reports and publications at the library
- The local chamber of commerce
- City building departments
- Small business development centers
- Questionnaires or interviews

Creating a clear understanding of the firm's target market is very important to the firm's overall marketing efforts. All firms have a limited amount of resources to put into marketing. Through target marketing, a firm can put its limited marketing resources to best use, locating and reaching potential clients who are most likely to be interested in the firm's services. It is one way of using scarce marketing dollars and time to fullest advantage. In addition, when a firm determines its target market, it is then easier to establish what marketing methods will work most effectively to attract target clients.

ESTABLISHING A NICHE

Some design firms have found that it is advantageous to establish a particular specialty in interior design. A few examples include Gensler in corporate design, and Wilson & Associates in hospitality. Specializing creates a targeted focus on some area of the industry that the owner finds particularly interesting and rewarding. It is easy to see how this would help a commercial designer.

Residential designers can also specialize. Consider a residential designer who only does condominiums in high-rise buildings or someone who only does contemporary-styled interiors of contemporary homes.

When the specialty has a very refined focus or is somehow unique, the firm has targeted a niche. According to Martin and Knoohuizen, a *niche* is "a design specialty that focuses its services to meet the needs of a specific group—or segment—of the total market."[3] Some marketing books do not even mention the term *niche;* they simply refer to this concept as *market segmentation*. The idea is to choose a specific segment or part of the total market in which the designer has an interest or expertise and to work only with clients in that segment.

Of course, some designers choose to specialize in two closely related segments. By becoming an expert in one or two segments, the designer can provide specialized services and focus the use of the firm's resources. Rather than market to all residential clients, consider the niche of condominiums in high-rise buildings. Another residential example is to specialize in helping clients downsize their homes by providing evaluation, restoration, and even disposal through resale of furnishings.

An advantage of developing a niche is that the designer will become very experienced in the niche area, researching and learning the peculiar functional problems of that niche. This allows the interior designer to be of special value to potential clients. When this happens, the client will not feel like the designer is learning on the job about the client's particular needs. Trying to be all things to all people is not usually the best strategy, whether the economy is strong or weak.

If a designer decides to specialize in a particular niche, he or she must be sure that sufficient work exists to support the goals of the design firm, meet business expenses, and generate a profit. Targeting too small or too unique a segment can mean that the designer does not have enough clients to keep working. This is why most niche designers market outside their immediate geographic area into different cities, states, and even countries.

The niche should also be something that the designer has a passion for. If the designer does not like doing residential design very much, taking up a niche in assisted-living facilities is not a good idea. Success is more likely to result for the interior designer when the niche is related to a special interest or passion. The specialty options listed in Tables 28-2 and 28-3 represent numerous potential niches; however, the possibilities are almost endless if one wishes (and can afford) to be very narrowly focused.

Good market research is needed to establish a business niche. Everything discussed in this chapter becomes vital. Coming up with an idea for a niche that has few potential clients or is past its prime is a disaster waiting to happen. The numbers of clients, the competition, and potential growth of the specialized area of design are all important factors. The experience level of the designer and the ease with which the designer can enter the niche also play a part in the designer's determination of whether a niche is a possibility and which niche might be right for the firm.

A brief discussion on one specialization—green design—is provided to help you see how the issues discussed here can affect a specialty. Similar thoughts are included in the "Global Design Work" section in Chapter 5.

Specializing in Green Design

Focusing a design practice on green or sustainable interior design requires a little more perseverance than other specialties. This is due to two issues that affect projects whether the client space is residential or commercial.

The first issue is that most clients have a strong belief that "green" equals higher costs for products. They may be interested in green design, but when it really comes down to it, they don't want to spend the extra money. Designers need to explain that although initial costs may be higher, over the lifetime of the products, the costs will diminish to where the cost differential is no longer a factor.

The second issue is that clients have heard so much greenwashing—misleading claims about a product's or service provider's ecological realities—that they have become skeptical. Even if you have LEED® certification, you will need to show clients through your marketing and words that you are committed to green design concepts and principles.

The following strategies will help in that endeavor:

- Learn all you can about sustainable design *before* you begin to market this specialty. Your expertise will help you be taken more seriously.
- Obtain the appropriate LEED® certification to help clients recognize your commitment.
- Use sustainable practices within your office as much as is financially possible.
- Know the differences in green product criteria to help recognize truly green suppliers. Also know why these products are more appropriate for your clients' needs.
- Develop marketing materials that explain your expertise and clarify your differences from designers who merely sell green products.
- Make funding available for continuing education opportunities, webinars, and conference attendance for staff growth.

As with any design specialty, start with careful planning of your green niche. Take the time to look at your strengths and weaknesses regarding embracing green design. Try to determine all you can about the client groups that are the most interested in green and sustainable design, to determine if there are sufficient numbers of clients in the market area where you wish to work. Make sure you have the knowledge and expertise in hand so that you don't make mistakes that hurt your business.

THE FOUR Ps OF MARKETING

Another part of developing a marketing plan and deciding how the firm will market involves clarification of the firm's marketing mix. The *marketing mix* consists of operational elements that the design firm can control in the process of marketing and selling goods and services. Traditionally, the marketing mix consists of the *four Ps of marketing*: four basic variables—**p**roduct, **p**lace, **p**romotion, and **p**rice—that create a firm's marketing mix. To some marketers, the four Ps have been expanded to the seven Ps, to include **p**eople, **p**rocess, and **p**hysical evidence. In fact, you may find that some marketers use even more terms for clarification of the marketing mix.

In terms of an interior design practice, the *product* is generally considered to be professional design services. The goods that some interior designers choose to sell are another part of the product variable. The firm must utilize its internal analysis and its preferred market area to determine which services and products potential clients need.

The second variable is *place*. Readers have no doubt heard the comment "location, location, location" associated with real estate, and the place variable does deal primarily with location. This begins with the location of the design firm in its market area. It also involves the realization that the firm must find methods to get to potential clients outside its immediate area. For example, someone located in a small city will have to market his services to clients in larger cities in order to grow the business.

The potential client finds out about the availability of a product through the third variable, *promotion*. Promotional activities inform potential clients of the existence of the design firm and the services that the firm offers, whether or not the designer is located in the same geographic area as the client. Promotional activities include public relations, the use of brochures, referrals, advertising, Web sites, and many other promotional techniques. These are discussed in detail in Chapters 23 and 24.

The last of the four traditional variables of marketing is *price*. Establishing the right price for the interior design firm's product is a difficult management activity. If the firm sets a price for services that is too high in relation to competition, the firm will not secure work with many clients. If the price for fees is set too low, clients will doubt the firm's ability to do the work and may not seriously consider using the design firm. Pricing for services is discussed in Chapter 6 and pricing for products is discussed in Chapter 8.

People, process, and physical evidence are factors that are often discussed concerning the marketing mix. These are especially relevant factors for service-oriented businesses. In the context of *people*, the firm's personnel and those hired or recommended by the design firm to assist with a project (such as carpet installers) are very important. Impressions do make a difference in a service-oriented business such as interior design, and are especially important to designers seeking work from high-end residential clients and many corporate business owners/leaders. Attitudes, behavior, and even how people are dressed will have an impact on clients.

Process refers to how the services are offered. There is, of course, a design process, but how each designer or design firm actually performs that process varies widely. Designers and the firm must determine the best way to provide services based on the target client. They may even find that it is necessary to offer slightly different ways of providing that design process based on target clients.

Physical evidence is a rather broad category of issues that affect the client's sensitivity to the design firm. A company Web site, its social media involvement, brochures, business cards, and office location of the firm are just some of the items concerning physical evidence. Cues such as the appearance of the office, or even the presentation of a clean business card, can provide indications to the client as to how business will be conducted and the quality of the work that will be produced.

These last three items also relate to perception. Although not generally included in the discussion of items that make up the marketing mix, perception is very important to the interior design professional. *Perception* is an intuitive process of gathering information about the people, places, events, and so forth, with which we come into contact. If a designer's image does not meet the client's perception of the image of a designer, the client is less likely to hire the designer. Perception also has an impact on the client's willingness to pay the price the designer is asking. If the client does not perceive the designer's services to be of high value, the client will not be willing to pay the price, even if the designer is a truly creative professional. Clients develop a negative opinion of interior designers who are not business professionals.

All these variables are important and must be investigated by the firm at its inception and throughout its existence. They all have an impact on the design firm's marketing plan; one is not really more important than another. Each is important by itself as well as in relation to the others. Ignoring one variable could upset the marketing mix and make it difficult, if not impossible, for the design firm to successfully market its services.

MARKETING ANALYSIS

Marketing analysis involves research regarding what is done to carry out the strategic plan discussed in Chapter 20. *Marketing analysis* involves gathering and analyzing data about such things as the abilities and interests of the staff, potential clients, the economy, and the competition. This research and analysis allows the firm to make better plans and decisions about the direction of the firm's business efforts. The goal of marketing analysis is to find out what the client wants and then to determine if and how the firm can provide it.

Due to the nature of this type of research, it is most commonly undertaken by a consulting firm rather than the design firm itself. Sometimes advertising agencies do marketing analyses. It is a time-consuming and detailed process better left to the experts. However, it is important for readers to understand what this research is about and what it results in.

Marketing analysis involves asking questions and seeking out information related to the firm's business goals. "What business are we in?" is an important question for any firm. The answer to this question must go beyond "We are in the business of providing interior design services." Almost every interior design firm and others in the built environment industry could say the same thing, so this nonspecific answer does not differentiate the firm at all from its competition. For the design firm to answer the question about what business it is in, it must first answer other questions. The key questions in Table 22-3 help the firm understand what business it is in (or wants to be in) and recognize the direction it wishes to take.

These questions relate to significant issues, especially for new or relatively new firms, or firms that are seeking to move into some sort of new market. Competition can be fierce, and a clear understanding of what business the firm is really in will help in attracting new clients.

A second step in marketing analysis is to conduct an in-depth review of the internal and external forces that can and do affect the firm. SWOT analysis, described in Chapter 20, is a common method of accomplishing this. (If you have not reviewed that chapter, please do so now.) The purpose of conducting a SWOT analysis for marketing plan development is to look at internal and external factors that can affect the firm's marketing goals.

Competition analysis is a critical part of conducting a marketing analysis once the issue of understanding what clients want has been resolved. Many

TABLE 22-3.

Questions to determine "What business are we in?"

> These questions will be helpful in developing a marketing plan, a mission statement, and a strategic plan.
>
> 1. What design services do we offer?
> 2. What design services could we offer that are needed in the marketplace?
> 3. What products do we intend to specify and sell?
> 4. Are there sufficient potential clients for the firm's services within a reasonable distance?
> 5. Who do we see as our primary and secondary customers?
> 6. How do we do what we do?
> 7. What quality of service do we endeavor to supply?
> 8. Is anyone else offering the services in the way our firm does?
> 9. Why should/would customers buy from our firm rather than from one of our competitors?
> 10. What are the trends in the profession, and how will these trends affect the firm's potential business?

small firms do not even recognize other designers within their local association chapter as potential competitors—yet they may well be. Understanding a competitor's design style and method of business, regardless of the size of the firm, will be an asset to a design firm that is interested in expanding its own market.

Marketing analysis should assist the design firm in determining marketing goals and budgets. It provides a body of knowledge about the firm's practice and staff, the kind and amount of clients available, general economic and legal trends or restrictions prevalent in the area, and the competition. The design firm can then use this knowledge to prepare a definite plan to achieve results that are specifically related to the firm's overall marketing or strategic plan.

Marketing analysis must not be a one-time endeavor. It should be considered a critical part of strategic planning and of the annual business plan.

MARKETING PLAN

A marketing plan should be developed in connection with a strategic or annual plan. It can be very formal, discussing the items listed in this section of the chapter, or it can be an action plan that addresses similar topics in a less formal manner. The development of a marketing plan is important, as it will help the firm determine what it should do to meet its marketing goals.

Marketing plans help create marketing goals and help establish how the firm intends to accomplish its goals through various strategies and tactics. A marketing plan looks at the future year's marketing activity, while the strategic plan develops overall long-term goals and activities. The firm should not ignore setting long-term marketing goals that are expected to take from three to five years (or more) to accomplish. The establishment of long-term goals is important so that the design firm can keep thinking ahead and anticipating the changing needs of its basic or desired market.

Marketing goals can take many forms and have many emphases. One might be to increase awareness of the firm in its present market. Perhaps it is to target a specific group of new clients. Conceivably the goal is to introduce the design firm to a totally new market location. Maybe the goal is to gain greater recognition as an expert in a certain area of design.

Whatever the goals eventually become, the process of creating a marketing plan and actually writing it down helps the owner and employees see the goals before them and create the means to best accomplish those goals. By developing a plan, the design firm considers which promotional tools are most appropriate to help achieve its goals. This decision then guides the firm in producing budgets to develop the appropriate tools and strategies.

Just as there is no perfect business plan, there is no one outline for a marketing plan for all interior design firms. Some firms will want to have a very formal plan with a table of contents, references, and budgeting information. If the plan is mostly to be used internally, so that the owners, managers, and staff know what is going on, a more informal format can be used. An informal action plan focused on marketing can outline goals with appropriate strategies and tactics for each goal in a logical sequence.

Many design firms find that hiring a marketing professional to consult with them for the preparation of a marketing plan saves time. Other firms decide to venture into this area on their own. It is well worth at least considering a professional marketing consultant to help with your marketing plan or any other aspect of your marketing needs. Item 22-1 on the companion Web site will help you make a decision about a marketing professional consultant.

A portion of a formal marketing plan is shown in Table 22-4. A sample informal action plan is shown in Table 22-5. The informal action plan is more common in the small firm. Larger interior design firms predominantly use formal plans that generally follow the outline overview set out here. Some of the items that the formal plan should cover include:

1. *An introduction*. Statements based on the information that was used to prepare the plan and statements about the use and purpose of the plan.

2. *Goals statement(s)*. A revised statement of general business goals based on the information gathered in the analysis.

3. *Capabilities*. A discussion of the firm's abilities, related to the kinds of clients who previously hired the firm.

4. *Services*. A listing of the services the firm can and is going to offer. Subsequent sections should discuss who will be responsible for these services and how they will be performed.

5. *Clientele*. Quantitative information as to potential numbers, market share, and possible growth in each client category. Both existing and new client objectives should be stated.

6. *Policy decisions*. A discussion of such things as how the firm will charge for services to clients, how the firm will charge for consultants, whether or not the firm will bill reimbursable expenses, whether or not the firm will sell merchandise, and what policies there will be related to purchasing of products for resale.

7. *Marketing organization*. A statement of who will be responsible for ongoing marketing analysis.

8. *Marketing effort*. Answers to such questions as, "In what ways will the firm accomplish its goals?" "How will it use advertising and public relations?" "How will results be monitored to see whether or not they are successful?" "How much financially will be committed to marketing?"

9. *Evaluation*. A discussion of how progress toward goals will be measured to judge the success of the marketing plan.

10. *Forecasts*. Amount of sales, profit, number of new clients, and additions to personnel; should be stated as both quantitative and qualitative measures.

TABLE 22-4.

A page from a sample marketing plan

II. Client Base
A. Current Year
    1. Our current client base is primarily from the Midland area. Current clients within the city limits represent 80 percent of total sales. The remaining 20 percent is made up of clients outside the city limits but within a 30-mile radius.
    2. The majority of current work is residential. Eighty-five percent of clients purchase merchandise and services for homes. Fifteen percent of clients purchase merchandise and services for offices or other commercial facilities.
    3. Services versus Merchandise

Of residential sales, 70 percent of all revenues are merchandise sales.
Twenty percent are from design fees, and 10 percent represent other services, such as repairs, which do not require the purchasing of additional merchandise.
Of commercial sales, 90 percent of all revenues are merchandise sales.
Design fees represent only 10 percent of revenues from commercial projects.

    4. Type of Purchaser

Sixty-five percent of residential customers purchase goods or services for their existing home.

    1. Sixty percent of purchases are for only a few replacement items in one or two rooms.
    2. Thirty percent of purchases are for new floor coverings, window coverings, and/or wall coverings.
    3. Ten percent of purchases are for many items in two or more rooms.

Twenty percent of residential customers purchase goods or services for a new house.

    1. Forty-five percent of purchases are for new floor coverings, window coverings, and/or wall coverings.
    2. Thirty-five percent of purchases are for only a few replacement items in one or two rooms.
    3. Twenty percent of purchases are for many items in two or more rooms.

Fifteen percent of residential customers purchase goods or services for a second (vacation or rental) house.

    1. Fifty-five percent of purchases are for only a few replacement items in one or two rooms.

TABLE 22-5.

Sample action plan for a small design firm

Goal: To increase client awareness of this design firm

Increase networking activities.
    Become a member of a good networking group.
    Take two Realtors to lunch each week.
    Discuss interrelationship with builders.

Advertise in low-cost magazine.
    Determine which local magazines are available in this market.
    Obtain their advertising rates.
    Work with a graphic designer to create a quarter-page ad.

Enter association awards competition.
    Make arrangements to photograph Jones residence.
    Obtain competition entry and follow through.
    Consider entering a national competition with Jones residence.

Goal: To change image/brand of this firm

Attend a seminar on branding.
    Read a book on branding.
    Contact three graphic design firms to discuss costs for redesign of logo, stationery, etc.
    Discuss image and brand with at least six past clients.

It is wise to involve the entire staff in the analysis and planning for the yearly marketing plan. Management will, of course, make the final decisions, but staff involvement and input help them buy into the plan and make it actually happen. If the staff does not believe in the plan, it will not be very successful.

As with any plan, it is important to institute a process of monitoring the progress and success of the plan. It does no good, and is, frankly, a waste of time and resources, for the firm to go through the process of developing and writing a marketing plan if it is not committed to executing that plan. Monitoring the plan's progress helps, though it cannot guarantee the success of the plan.

WEB SITES RELEVANT TO THIS CHAPTER

www.associationofmarketing.org Association of Marketing Professionals

www.marketingresearch.org The Marketing Research Association (MR)

www.sba.gov U.S. Small Business Administration

KEY TERMS

Branding	Niche
Demographics	Price
Four Ps of marketing	Promotion
Market analysis	Psychographics
Market segment	SWOT analysis
Marketing	Target marketing
Marketing mix	

WHAT WOULD YOU DO?

1. In the past three months, David's design firm has been experiencing some financial problems. He has not paid his installers on two jobs and is 45 days behind in those payments. He also owes a cabinetmaker $5000 for a custom cabinet. The installers are refusing to do any more work for David's company until they are paid in full for outstanding work. The cabinetmaker is angry because this has happened before, and he is threatening to put a lien on David's company if he is not paid in the next 10 days. All of David's current clients are up-to-date with their payments for any work or products needed for their projects. In other words, he has no outstanding receivables.

2. Margaret is finally in a financial position to venture out on her own and open a small studio. She told herself that she would wait until she had funds to have a studio in a commercial location, rather than work from home, to better attract the clients she wants. After a great deal of thinking and research, Margaret locates in a low-rise office building near a new residential development that is soon to be the general location of a new sports stadium and a lot of retail space. She wants to focus on residential clients in the new development as well as on small professional offices, as she has experience in both areas of

design. What key elements should be part of her business and marketing plans?

3. Lillian's and Robert's residential interior design firm (they are partners) has experienced a flurry of very recent project work. Counting on the inflow of expected revenue, Robert orders several thousand dollars' worth of accessories to have on hand in their small studio/showroom for future customers. The day before those accessory items are due to arrive, one of the customers cancels a contract for design services and an expected $100,000 of furnishings.

4. John and Kevin—who have specialized in food and beverage facilities—have also tried to get some projects with small hotels in outlying areas. Work has been a struggle for the past two years. Clients have put projects on hold, and most others they have contacted through mailings and phone calls have told the designers that there is no work for them.

   John and Kevin are wondering about starting to do seminars on designing food and beverage facilities. Rather than talk to designers, they think the market for their seminars should be independent restaurant and motel owners in outlying areas. They figure these people need the design help and that by presenting brief design seminars, they will also obtain some contracts.

REFERENCES

1. Bennett, 1995, p. 166.
2. *Oxford American College Dictionary*, 2002, p. 166.
3. Martin and Knoohuizen, 1995, p. 6.

CHAPTER 23

Promotional Basics

After completing this chapter you should be able to:

- Discuss the differences between promotion, public relations, and publicity activities.
- List several ways the press release can be used to promote a design firm.
- Prepare a simple press release.
- Describe the good and bad points of magazine advertising by interior designers.
- Discuss the types of social media included in this chapter and how each of them can be beneficial in business marketing.
- Discuss how social media outlets can help with business contacts.
- Explain why it is important to keep the social (personal) and business page separate on any social media outlet.
- Discuss several ways in which referrals can be used to improve the chances of promotional success for a design firm.
- Describe how networking helps to uncover new clients.

NCIDQ COMPONENT

Based on best information available, some material in this chapter might appear as part of the NCIDQ examination. The reader should not depend solely on this text for study material. See the sections on promotion, public relations, and publicity in particular.

During the good economic times the interior design industry experienced in the early 2000s, many new practices opened. Existing firms merged with other existing firms or designers broke away to start their own practices in the good economy. Unfortunately, during the following recession, many of these practices closed or have been greatly reduced in size.

Regardless of the state of the economy, design firms must cultivate new clients and new projects to keep employees actively involved in generating revenue. No firm can afford to let its message be lost among the competition.

How is this done? Through various promotional strategies and tools that are deemed appropriate to the design firm's mission, goals, and budget.

This chapter begins by clarifying the strategy of public relations and publicity activities. Other promotional tools discussed in this chapter include press releases, brochures, referrals, and networking. A section discussing Internet and social media marketing is also part of this chapter. These are all important, because they are the kinds of activities or tools that all design firms can use effectively to promote their practice. Additional promotional tools and strategies are discussed in Chapter 24.

PROMOTION

Opening an interior design practice is the "easy" part of business creation. Finding clients to support the business—in good times as well as bad—is the hard part. Many designers obtain their first clients by bringing along some of those with whom the designer worked at another firm. That is, if the former employer/owner does not object! For most, potential clients must be cultivated and enticed to talk to the designer through various activities that make the design firm known to potential clients.

Developing methods to get the word out about the design firm and seeking clients in the firm's target market is time consuming and comes with expenses for which the new firm must budget. Existing firms must also budget for continuing client development. It is a rare firm that has a continuous stream of new clients knocking on the door without client development.

Promotion is the method used to get the design firm's message—even the bare fact of its existence—before the client. In a practical sense, promotion "includes all the activities the company undertakes to communicate and promote its products [and services] to the target market."[1] Many people use the term *promotion* to mean public relations, but promotion is much more than public relations. Promotion also includes publicity, publishing, advertising, personal selling, and all the other strategies or techniques that help get a business's message to potential clients and its market in general. Promotional activities help a company grow regardless of its size or focus.

Competition plays an important part in what promotional activities a firm may decide to utilize to increase public awareness and attract new clients. A Web site is an essential tool in today's promotional tool bag for interior designers. Firms often find that entering competitions and seeking publication of projects in targeted magazines and newspapers is another good way to get the word out. And, of course, some firms believe that carefully designed and placed advertising is the way to make their existence known to potential clients.

Design firms are engaged in a continual search for new clients, new markets, and greater recognition. The promotional methods they use to find clients are critical to the ongoing life of the firm. In addition, individual designers may find that some of the methods discussed in this chapter and the next aid in promotion of the individual for various professional reasons.

Promotional tools are the devices the interior design firm uses to create awareness. They are generally created for relatively nonspecific general audiences. Table 23-1 lists the most common promotional tools used in the interior design profession. Note that this is not an all-inclusive list.

The design firm must select the promotional tools that will be most useful and (of course) cost-effective. One advertisement placed in a magazine or newspaper can cost thousands of dollars. The return on that one ad, however, is often negligible. Those same funds spent on quality photography, graphic

TABLE 23-1.

Typical methods of promoting the interior design practice

Public relations activities
Publicity
Using press releases
Internet marketing and social media marketing
Advertising
The company graphic image and logo
Business stationery
Letterhead, business cards
Photo portfolio
Referrals
Networking activities
Brochures
Design competitions
Direct-mail programs
Publication in magazines
Writing articles and books
Providing seminars and workshops
Premiums
Responding to requests for proposals (RFPs) from clients

design work for a Web site, or a printed marketing piece can bring numerous returns. Which promotional tools to use, when to use them, what goes into them, and how they are delivered to prospective clients all play a role in furthering the image desired by the firm.

PUBLIC RELATIONS

Getting out a positive impression of a designer or design firm is very important in this profession. A positive image helps bring in new clients. A firm with little in the way of a public image has a harder time obtaining new clients. Creating that public image falls within the concept of public relations. To be specific, *public relations (PR)* refers to all of a firm's efforts to create an image in order to affect the public's opinion of the firm.

Public relations and creating a public image concern the communication of information about the design firm through such devices as Web pages, brochures, news releases placed with the media, and even the design of the business card. Public relations can involve submitting articles on design-related topics to local publications or trade magazines; conducting an in-office product seminar for the public or other professionals; or even writing a book on a design topic. It can also consist of participating in special events in the community, making contributions to professional organization fund-raisers, or becoming involved in legislative efforts. Public relations refers to all of these and much more.

Crafting a positive image of the interior design firm can and does make a difference in the firm's ability to attract new business. If done internally, public relations work usually becomes the responsibility of the owner or a senior staff member in a bigger firm. There are many things the individual owner can do to strengthen the firm's public image. Preparing press releases—as discussed in this chapter—is one such activity.

Many firms, both small and large, hire a public relations or marketing professional to help them decide what activities and tools will best serve their marketing goals and resources. The public relations professional, being neutral, can make suggestions to help reach success faster. These specialists can also suggest outsourced specialists, such as a Web designer, to fully develop the PR tools.

Whatever the strategy is, the desired result is to gain positive recognition for the design firm in the public's mind. This recognition will eventually lead to future business and greater revenues.

PUBLICITY

Most public relations tactics—though not all—involve the expenditure of funds. Gaining public awareness of the design firm without necessarily spending anything to do so is ideal. This can be achieved through *publicity*. The aim of publicity is to attract attention or awareness without having to pay any media charges. "Publicity is what you use to get attention without paying for it. Publicity is the key to letting people know what you do."[2] When the firm has to pay for media attention, that promotional activity is called *advertising*, as discussed later in this chapter.

Designers who participate in events like a show-house or design competitions benefit from the publicity those types of events are able to provide. Positive publicity is highly sought after by design firms and traditionally has been the accepted form of promoting professional services. Publicity involves activities that the design firm may pay to develop, but the firm does not pay to place promotional information in any type of media.

Publicity takes many forms. It can be planned (good publicity) or accidental. Unfortunately, most accidental publicity is bad publicity. For example, several interior designers participated in their local chapter's show-house fundraiser. Their projects were published in a local magazine, achieving good publicity for each firm. Bad publicity, such as being named in the papers as the defendant in a personal injury suit, is not something that a design firm desires. Design firms seek to create planned publicity that will help potential clients view the firm in a good light and seek them out for design services.

Here are a few additional examples of good publicity:

- A press release sent to local media about the firm winning an award.
- Providing a free lecture about accessibility guidelines to a professional business group, such as accountants.
- Publication of project photos in the local newspaper's home section.
- Being named or even featured in a newspaper's "Home" section in an article on very special home designs. Sometimes such an article will include the name of the interior designer even if the article focuses on a builder or architect.
- Charitable and community service work, such as helping the community theater with props and set designs.
- Volunteering services on restoration projects.

These few examples are provided to get your outreach juices flowing. Many other activities that your firm and individuals within the firm become involved with can also result in positive publicity. Each publicity item adds to public image and awareness by potential new clients.

PRESS RELEASES

One relatively easy and very inexpensive way to obtain publicity for your firm is through a press release. A *press release* is a method of providing information about the design firm that might be of interest to the news media. The caveat about using press releases is that the information being provided has to be "newsworthy" or of significant value to the readers or viewers of the media to which the information was sent.

Here are a few quick examples:

- Publication of an article written by the designer
- Winning an award for design work
- Winning a contract to design a significant project such as a major hotel
- Offering a design seminar for the public
- Announcing the opening of a new design business or second location

Almost any kind of news or announcement can be prepared as a press release if it is truly a newsworthy event. Due to space constraints, in most cities, announcements about promotions and new hires are relegated to a minimal statement in a business briefs column of the newspaper, if they are published at all. If an industry-related publication exists in the area, many of the items previously listed will likely make it into those media, even if they are not included in general-readership media.

PR professionals have experience in preparing press releases; they also have many contacts with local and national print, radio, and television media. These contacts can be utilized to obtain the best coverage for press releases. If an in-house individual can use good journalistic techniques, however, then he or she can prepare a press release. Because preparing a press release is a relatively easy assignment, and is an inexpensive way to obtain some publicity for any size firm, it is covered here in some depth.

Preparing your own press releases is not difficult. There are several guidelines that can help get your press release read and potentially printed. Table 23-2 lists tips for preparing a press release. Figure 23-1 is a sample press release.

Being selective, especially at a local level, about who receives the press release may help get it noticed and published or even broadcasted. All areas of the media like to "scoop" their colleagues. Knowing that the design firm has attempted to provide that scoop just may help to get the press release noticed—particularly for very special news.

Review the policy of the publication before you send an e-mail. Many editors do not like to receive press releases from unknown sources via e-mail. Like everyone else, editors receive lots of e-mail every day, and some find it annoying to get a press release in this way. Do not e-mail graphics or other attachments with an unsolicited press release. The receiving party's computer may decide the e-mail is spam. Mention that graphics are available and briefly describe them. The editor will let you know if you should send the graphics.

Remember to follow up with a phone call to the editor when you send a press release. Public relations professionals do this to ensure that the message has been received, and you should do it as well. Even if the editor is not going to use your press release, it gives you the chance to talk to him or her briefly in order to better understand what the publication looks for, so that you will be prepared when future newsworthy items occur at your firm.

TABLE 23-2.

Tips on preparing a press release

Do not submit information that is primarily blatant promotion of the firm.
Use standard, concise journalistic style, using the classic five "Ws" and "H": who, what, when, where, why, and how.
Submit the information in a form that the publication can essentially use as is.
Do your homework before sending in a press release, as it might be necessary to modify the material for each publication.
Text should be typed double-spaced, with wide side margins for editorial comments.
The most significant information should be presented in the first paragraph; additional details can be presented in subsequent paragraphs.
Try to stick to a one-page release, as this will have the best chance of being published.
The contact information—name, address, telephone number, fax, and e-mail address of the contact person—should be placed at the top of the first page.
The words *Immediate Release* indicate that all the information in the text is timely and ready for publication. If this is the case, it should be indicated at the top. Otherwise, the date of preferred release should be clearly indicated.
Supplementary materials, such as line drawings or photographs, make an otherwise routine story more interesting.
Magazines prefer color transparencies or TIFF format digital photos. A TIFF version of a CAD drawing is also usable.
Black-and-white photographs should be glossy prints.
If people are in the photographs, provide their names and titles, along with signed publication releases.
Be sure that the client or organization has been informed about your press release and publication releases, and has provided written clearance for the information to be released.
If your photos were taken by a professional photographer, be sure you have a release to allow you to have the photo published by a third party and provide a credit line for the photographer.

Interior Associates, LLC

Contract Interior Designers

1776 E. Commerce Street

Atlanta, Georgia

For Immediate Release

For further information,

Contact: John Adams

404-555-3506

Interior Associates, LLC Awarded 20xx Golden Achievement Award

Atlanta, January 10 20xx—Interior Associates, LLC is the recipient of the twenty-sixth annual 20xx Golden Achievement Award presented at the _____ Community Service awards banquet on February 20, Patrick Smith, President, announced.

The award is granted to an interior design firm within the metropolitan Atlanta area that has achieved an outstanding record of community service during the year.

_____ notes the achievements of Interior Associates with the Northside Hospice, MacAlister Center for Battered Women, and the Home Start Youth Center as representative of the outstanding interior design work contributed by the firm. Jillian Connell, administrator for the MacAlister Center for Battered Women, said, "The sensitive design of our resident areas by Interior Associates has provided an atmosphere desperately needed in this facility."

Interior Associates, LLC, has been specializing in healthcare facilities as well as facilities for the aged for 25 years. The firm has completed projects throughout Georgia, as well as Florida, North Carolina, Tennessee, and Alabama.

FIGURE 23-1.

A sample press release. Please note that this is a fictitious release.

ADVERTISING

Advertising is defined as any kind of paid communication in media, such as newspapers, magazines, television, or radio. If a design firm pays the newspaper to run an announcement of some kind about the firm, it is considered advertising. If the newspaper runs an announcement or article about the firm and the firm does not pay for it, it is considered publicity.

Advertising as a means for professionals to promote their services was controversial until about the 1980s. Professional associations at that time relaxed their stand against members' advertising. Before that time, it was considered unprofessional to utilize paid advertising for the business development of design firms, as well as most professions.

There is no standard as to the use of paid advertising by interior design firms. For some firms, advertising plays an important part in the firm's overall promotional plan. Others never even consider using a paid advertisement for any reason. Most firms fall somewhere in between these two extremes, as competition in many markets has grown quite strong.

Advertisements may be aimed to create general awareness of the firm or to specifically attract customers to the firm. For example, many design firms place ads in local or specialty magazines to create awareness of the firm for potential clients in the targeted market. Often these advertisements include a photograph of a client installation to help potential clients understand the firm's design style.

Designers who produce revenue from selling products advertise more often. Their advertisements often announce a sale on inventory or special purchases. In general, the more the firm depends on product sales and showcases products in a retail store or a studio, the more the firm will use advertising (see Figure 23-2).

Due to the high cost of advertising, care must be taken in considering the why, when, how, and where of advertising. It is important for the design firm to understand what the goals are when placing and paying for an ad. One ad can eat up a small design firm's total marketing budget for the year. For example, a quarter-page black-and-white advertisement in many local magazines starts at $1500 for a one-time use. Color ads can run more than $3000 for a quarter-page insert. National magazines will charge far more.

FIGURE 23-2.

Magazine advertisement for an interior design firm. (Reproduced courtesy of Wagner-Somerset, Clifton, VA)

Newspaper advertisements are cheaper than those placed in magazines. They can reach a broader audience, but they also reach a generally untargeted audience. Ads in the newspaper announcing a sale on a particular product can bring in results quickly, but can also easily cost more than $500 for a small ad. Please note that the prices quoted for advertising vary greatly and may be different in the reader's market area.

Thus, part of the decision to advertise or not is affected by the firm's clients. If the design firm's clients are exclusively or primarily commercial, the advertising used will probably consist of print ads placed in trade magazines or newsletters targeted to commercial specialties. In business-to-business (B2B) advertising, the design firm needs to target where its clients are, and the local newspaper may or may not be a satisfactory location for a B2B ad.

Residential designers place print advertising in local home magazines, a regional publication such as *Mountain Living*, or national home magazines like *House Beautiful*. Today there is a wide assortment of business, trade, and residential consumer-oriented publications in which a design firm may choose to advertise.

Advertising for service businesses rarely brings an immediate response. A viable client might not contact the design firm until months after the advertisement has been published. This factor must be weighed against the cost of any form of advertising. Consequently, service-oriented interior design firms generally limit advertising and usually have limited success in using advertising to obtain new clients.

One common form of direct advertising that many designers do use is a Yellow Pages advertisement in the phone book. Many rely on ads that include the firm's name, address, and telephone number. Other firms, especially those that have showrooms and sell furniture, often take out larger Yellow Pages ads, to call more attention to their companies.

A type of advertising strategy that can be very useful is called *co-op advertising*. With this strategy, the manufacturer and designer generally share in the cost of the advertising, or the manufacturer provides an incentive to the designer to sell a particular product. Designers negotiate for the project designer's and the firm's name to be incorporated into the ad along with that of the manufacturer. These manufacturers' ads can appear in trade or shelter magazines, in the company's brochures and catalogs, on the firm's and manufacturer's Web pages—almost anywhere that the manufacturer chooses to advertise.

INTERNET AND SOCIAL MEDIA MARKETING

Interior design professionals have certainly embraced Internet marketing and recognized the importance of having a company Web site. All types of consumers are turning to the World Wide Web to find interior design service providers and even to pre-shop for products. Surfing the Web is not an activity only for the young; older consumers of every age group have become computer savvy.

Traditional marketing happens when a firm uses the various methods discussed in Chapters 22 through 24 to try to contact or make an impression on potential clients. Some marketers refer to this as *outbound marketing*. With the Internet, a concept called *inbound marketing* has emerged. Inbound marketing involves enticing the potential customer to contact or find the design firm. A Web site, blog, social media marketing, and referrals are some of many of the ways inbound marketing helps a firm be found.

At first, the Internet and the World Wide Web were just a great place for people to find information. Cyberspace opened up libraries around the world to researchers, educators, and students. In addition, it provided a place for writers to submit material on an almost limitless assortment of topics. The Internet quickly grew from being a vehicle for government agencies and the military to exchange information to being a wide-open highway of information, commerce, and marketing venues for anyone with electronic access.

Today the Internet has become a tremendous tool for interior design firms and others in the business world to market their services and products. Design company Web sites provide marketing information to a global potential market. Designers can search vendor sites for products of all kinds, and can purchase products from the wide array of vendors they find. Information on seemingly every topic imaginable is available by a simple search through a site such as Google or Yahoo!

E-commerce and e-tailing (electronic retailing) are quite common. However, a great deal of thought must go into this issue should a firm decide to sell via the Internet. It involves deciding what will be sold, pricing, purchasing arrangements, security for purchasing, display of product photos, and much more.

Let's get back to Web sites as a marketing tool. It would seem at first glance that any size interior design firm without a Web site is likely to be considered behind the times, but then again, simply having a domain address and site does not guarantee that clients will rush to the firm. A Web site does provide exposure—no question about that—but, like advertising, it rarely provides clients instantly.

As with any type of promotional tool, a firm should first decide why it might be necessary or desirable to have a Web site. The purpose of the site will help determine the design and contents of what will be displayed. It is common to include project photos, text describing the firm's design philosophy, and service offerings. A Web site can include a page for a client list, awards won, publications, and most anything else that can help a prospective client understand something about the firm. Interior designers naturally will include photos, but the site can also be designed to display brief videos, blogs, and any number of other options that the designer might wish to include.

Contact information is necessary so that a viewer can communicate with the firm. For the most part, this communication is initially undertaken via e-mail, though firms also include their addresses and phone numbers. Perhaps the firm wants the viewer to request information, make a personal phone call for an interview, or purchase something offered for sale on the Web site. Many Web sites provide a link to a frequently asked questions (FAQs) page, where the viewer will find a list of things that are often asked by other clients.

When the design firm chooses to market itself on the Internet, the relationship between client and design firm is harder to establish. Because of the lack of a physical connection, the relationship starts with the image projected on the Web site—and image definitely does come across on a Web site. The quality of the photos, the style of language in the text, and the colors used for backgrounds all play a part, just as they do in a printed brochure or hard-media promotional pieces.

Thought must also be given as to what to leave off the Web site. Including pricing for services or quoting discounts might seem like a good way to attract clients; however, it can also frighten them away, as the dollars or percentages quoted may be high in comparison to competitors. Exaggerated promises should also be avoided, as these exaggerations become expectations, and any lack of performance could lead to legal and ethical problems. The owner of the design firm must be absolutely certain that everything on the Web site and linked pages is truthful about the company.

TABLE 23-3.

Tips for using a Web site for marketing an interior design business

Why do you want a Web site?
Increase awareness
Sell products
Develop leads for design consulting
Provide information about the firm
Market worldwide
Develop a mailing list through the "hits"

What information could you include?
Job photos by project type
Owner and staff photos
Owner and staff resumés
Client list
Design philosophy
Services list
Client testimonials
News items about the firm
Places where projects have been published
Photos and descriptions of products to sell
Online place information distribution

Tips for creating a successful site
Make sure you know why you want a site
Keep it simple
Provide a reason for the viewer to come back to the Web site
Target the audience through design techniques
Respond quickly to inquiries
Keep it updated on a regular basis
Promote your Web site
Provide an easy way for potential clients to contact you
Keep your links to other sites at a minimum so that you don't lose the reader

This discussion is necessarily brief; a full discussion on how to design a Web site is beyond the space available in this book. There are many different opinions about what information should be placed on a Web site and how it should be presented. In addition, so much is changing relative to hardware, delivery, and software that it would be impossible to speak with sufficient depth in this text. You may wish to refer to some of the many references available to help when it comes time to design a Web site. Table 23-3 provides some additional tips and considerations on the use of Web sites for marketing.

Social Media Marketing

Utilizing some form of social media for marketing is a fact of life for professionals today. While the younger designer tends to be very comfortable in the cyber world, older designers are still finding their way. Comfort zones with the Web and e-mail do not automatically expand to create comfort with or acceptance of social media sites for business purposes. This section is not intended to explain in detail how to become social media savvy. There are numerous books that go into the depth of information needed to set up a useful site and the details of how to use social media for business networking. Several are included in the reference list.

"Social media is an opportunity, a new frontier, a space in cyberspace that gives you an individual place to play, builds awareness of you and for you, brands yourself, and from which you can potentially profit."[3] It is clear that clients use social media to find out something about a designer long before they shake hands. Employers also search for potential new employees' pages on social media sites to find out something about these persons even before they are offered an interview.

Social media is just that—social—and is used extensively to keep up with friends and family. It is also used extensively for business, as the flurry of new books on B2B social media use attest. It is absolutely critical to keep your online personal life and your business life separate—or at least compatible. A business professional has to be careful about what is revealed on the social side of a social media site.

Companies have interesting issues to deal with when company culture and rules conflict with employees' interests and activities on social media. Younger employees want to stay connected and often have no problem blending their personal and professional lives. Leaders of firms may become concerned that employees will give away confidential information about the firm and/or clients when this happens. Or the leaders of the firms may simply think that their employees spend too much time on social media or texting and not enough time on doing their jobs. Balancing control is thus a very important issue for many firms.

If you do a search for social media sites on Google or Yahoo!, you will discover perhaps hundreds of Web sites that can be considered social media sites. Of course, the most recognized are: Facebook, LinkedIn, Twitter, MySpace, and YouTube. You might also follow any number of the other sites that pop up on the "most popular sites" lists.

Let's focus on four of the most popular sites used by millions of people for business: Facebook, LinkedIn, Twitter, and YouTube. This section also includes some comments on how blogging can be beneficial to a design practitioner in a business context.

Facebook (www.facebook.com/business) is certainly the largest and fastest growing site for social networking. As you probably already know, a Facebook presence starts with your profile, but for business this is called a page. What I am going to briefly talk about here is how your Facebook page can be used for business purposes.

It's important to have a business-oriented page rather than a friends-and-relatives page; your clients are really not interested in seeing photos from your last vacation or your niece's babies. Many of your competitors may already have a business-oriented Facebook page and many of the companies you may wish to interview with likely have one as well.

To get your clients to "like" your Facebook page, you need to offer them something of value. This could be design ideas and tips or other information that you provide to help educate your client. The purpose is not just to educate them about you—that can be done on your Web site—but to validate your expertise.

Your best posts are those that you create. Research and write something that would be interesting to your potential clients, business friends, and friends of friends. This will help boost your reputation as an expert. You can, of course, alert friends to an article you read somewhere. But then you are boosting that author's reputation, not yours per se.

When you send messages and information that potential clients (or others in the industry) consider valuable, you hope that they will tell others about you. That gets someone else to "like" you and adds to your social media reputation.

Today, start gathering research information that you can use to create the items you will add to your business Facebook page. Draft three or four so that you have a supply—regular new information is something to shoot for. Then get your page designed, perhaps by an expert. Remember that you are trying to impress clients and entice business, not amuse your social friends.

Business people utilize *LinkedIn* (www.linkedin.com) for exposure, connections, and communication. Small business owners, employees of companies, and even major corporate officers can be found on LinkedIn. A LinkedIn presence helps you make contact with and be noticed by other professionals.

Your presence on LinkedIn begins by completing your profile. In your profile you can include a summary of your work experiences, skills, and accomplishments. This is the first thing a visitor to your profile will see, so it is important to provide strong information without getting too long-winded. You could also describe current and past jobs, education, publications in which you are represented or included, and awards. Other information can be included if you wish.

Your profile has space for recommendations that others have written about you. These recommendations come from people whom you have asked to write them, so you know that the recommendations will be positive. You will have the opportunity to ask the person to rework the recommendation; if they agree, you will have a nice, strong recommendation. Of course, you can also refuse to allow it to be posted if you think it in some way will be detrimental.

Special enhancements include adding a video, including a portfolio, and viewing information about who has looked at your profile page. You can also promote your Web site, blog, and Twitter connection if you wish to gain more exposure. The site is constantly making changes, so other link options might become available at any time.

A key component of LinkedIn is your "connections": the people who have asked to be "linked" to you or to whom you have asked to be linked. Once you are on the Web site, you can search for people you know or would like to know and ask to be connected to them. Some social media marketing books say quantity is king. The more people you are connected to, the greater the possibility that they will contact you for potential business. In my opinion, when you ask to be connected to someone, it is a good idea to use a short personal message to that person so he or she knows how you heard of them rather than the standard "I'd like to add you to my professional network on LinkedIn" option.

Another important part of LinkedIn is the "Groups" option. There are probably thousands of specialty groups on LinkedIn. There are likely hundreds related to interior design and the design industry. Joining groups that are compatible with your business interests allows you to converse with others around the world. You can join in on a conversation started by someone else or start your own topic within a group. You can even start your own group, to focus on your expertise or special interests. Groups you join will also be shown on your profile.

Because of the layout of the LinkedIn profile, you are essentially posting your resumé on line. Obviously, this is very helpful to someone who is actually looking for a job or desiring to change jobs. In this venue, though, you can provide more information than would normally be presented in a resumé.

All of these reasons—and others—make a presence on LinkedIn the first stop for a designer wishing to get involved in social media. Like all the rest of the options, however, to really gain from having a profile posted you must spend time to keep the profile up to date, and invest time in the options available to keep your name visible to those to whom you are connected.

Twitter (https://twitter.com) is probably quite familiar to a lot of the younger readers of this text. A *tweet* is a message with a maximum of 140 characters that Twitter users utilize to send comments about topics that they feel might interest potential clients, colleagues, and others. A Twitter post can provide simple bits of information to entice potential clients and others to reach out to your firm and vice versa. The tweet also allows an additional 20 characters for the user's name.

Obviously, you can make short comments through a tweet, but you can also provide links to other Internet sources. Maybe you want to tell others about an article you read in a magazine or online news service. You can provide that link in your tweet. You can also use tweets to promote your Web site, e-mail newsletter, LinkedIn page, or other appropriate links.

When someone shares a tweet with another person, it is called a *retweet*. This can be a fast way for information to be shared among many people. On many occasions, a particular topic will be of interest to a larger group. Hash-tags using the hash symbol (#) are combined with a few words or a phrase to connect the conversation.

Tweets can also be used for such things as:

- Liking Facebook pages
- Directing users to a landing page on your Web site
- Sharing a video
- Promoting a survey for information you want to gather
- Promoting a webinar or other seminar presentation

By the way, "landing pages are pages of a business Website that contain a form into which visitors can submit information in exchange for an offer."[4]

Tweeting can quickly become another of those time-consuming activities, so it is important for you to consider why you want to start tweeting and plan your regular involvement. Remember that tweeting is about providing information that will be of interest to those who connect with you. For example, you can give design tips that will attract residential clients, provide news about something like the ADA that might be of interest to commercial clients, or promote the fact that you will be in a certain town to give a seminar. It must, of course, be short—140 characters is the limit!

YouTube (www.youtube.com) is another very popular way of reaching out to potential clients, colleagues, and friends. YouTube is visually oriented and you can easily add video segments from many business activities. The videos last a maximum of 15 minutes for most users and are thus easy to create and produce.

Despite the common perception that it is only a social site, YouTube also allows you to set up a business site. You definitely should have separate social and business sites so that you can glory in your personal life on your social site and focus on potential clients on your business site.

One really great use of YouTube is for posting customer testimonials. Printing this information in brochures and other print marketing materials can be cumbersome. Additions and deletions on YouTube are quite easy to do. Because the nature of these testimonials is to be short and sweet, clients are more likely to give you the time to chat in a video that can be downloaded rather than asking them to write a letter.

Many businesses have found lots of uses for a YouTube presence. For example, you could do a video showing how your team prepares drawings, or the installation of furniture. YouTube videos can include guests who do a video in support of your business, such as an expert in kitchen design talking about sustainable products for the kitchen.

Once again, have a plan. Know what you are trying to do by using You-Tube for business. Because of the visual impact desired and the time it will take to create some of these videos, you must know what your purpose is for each segment. That also includes a plan for what will be shown and discussed in each segment.

Blogs If you have more to say that can be effectively communicated by tweeting, a blog may be an appropriate avenue to market your messages. You probably already have plenty of information and skills that will make blogging of benefit to your business. It doesn't take much to create a blog, as this is something that you can add to your Web site. Realize that the most benefits come from the communication back and forth with those who respond to your blog items. To successfully use a blog for marketing, you must commit to spending the time needed to keep up with the people who respond, as well as the time to create new blog topics.

Blogging helps you create a conversation with those who reach back to you. Not everyone out there will want to blog with you. Some think that bloggers are just show-offs trying to massage their egos and thus don't pay any attention to blogs. Others will give a blog enough of a chance to find that the information you are providing is there to help educate others, not just toot your own horn. So, targeting whom you are trying to reach is very important. Focusing the topics brought up on the blog is also necessary to reach as many in your target audience as possible.

Throwing out information is nice, as it can, if properly prepared, help demonstrate expertise. The content you send out in your blog posts has to be something that others will want to read and communicate back about. As with so much in marketing and business development, the first thing you need to do is figure out what you want to accomplish with your blog. Are you trying to establish expertise? Are you trying to attract new customers? What are your goals for having a blog?

You also need to determine how often you can actually post new items. It doesn't have to be every day, but once a month will not be very effective. Most marketers suggest at least a few times a week. Along with the posts, you must commit time to respond to those who respond to you. Eventually you will hit some topic posts that garner a lot of attention. You just have to spend some time responding to all those who have been interested enough in what you are saying to respond—positively or negatively.

Blogs don't have to be just words. You can post video content and audio content if you wish. If you are blogging about yourself and your design firm, the quality of your video content will be very important. Tempting though it might be to do your own video, you might want to work with a professional to shoot the video.

One other common strategy is to include guests on your blog. You might want to invite an expert in sustainable design to talk about flooring products, or a rug vendor to discuss the proper cleaning of rugs. This will help show those who find your blog that you are truly into this media marketing style to share your expertise and gain the confidence of potential clients.

The most popular social media sites can be accessed on smartphones, tablets, and of course computers. Your audience can get your posts from wherever they seek their information—a definite marketing advantage. However, you need to determine whom you are trying to reach before you jump on the social media bandwagon. So, it is back to those business and marketing planning efforts discussed in other chapters in this book.

You must also be willing to spend time on the sites and keep yours up to date. If you already have a Web site, the more action you get on these social sites, the higher up your Web site will be on Google. That is an important issue when you are trying to get clients to find you rather than the competition. It also gets you noticed on each of the sites you belong to. Finally, spending time on the sites helps you see what other professionals are doing and reveals potential contacts.

There are several resources in the reference list at the back of this book that will provide more detailed information about how social media sites can be used to market your firm. This list will keep growing, so don't forget to also check the Internet for additional articles and books that might be of assistance.

REFERRALS

Because so much of this profession is very personal, relationship building in interior design is critical. These good relationships are particularly important to residential interior designers. Word of mouth from past clients to their friends often results in new work. For some interior designers, especially sole practitioners, referrals may be the primary way in which they obtain new clients.

Word-of-mouth or referral marketing is an effective way to market interior design. A *referral* occurs when one client tells another person who may be looking for interior design services about a particular design firm. For years, many design firms have depended heavily on this method of promotion for finding new clients. It costs nothing, as no promotional materials are needed for a client to recommend the design firm to someone.

Referrals do not just happen, however. "Studies have shown that each time customers had a positive experience with you or your place of business, they will tell 4 other people. On the other hand, any time they have a negative experience, they'll tell 11 people."[5] Satisfied clients may not think about mentioning your firm to a friend or a business associate without prompting from the designer. However, they will tell everyone they know if the work was done incorrectly or poorly. It is human nature for clients to complain (even to total strangers) about poor service rather than to mention positive service. What this means is that the designer must "manage" referral marketing.

Here are some tips to improve success with referrals:

- Always provide a positive experience with existing clients. Do not let problems sour a relationship. Make sure that your reputation keeps improving.

- Do not make excuses when problems occur. Resolve the problem with professionalism and then move on with the client. Of course, it is best to avoid problems as much as possible through best-practice work.

- Make it a policy to always deliver more than you promise and never promise what you cannot deliver. When a client gets something positive that he or she did not expect, the client will generally be more interested in and enthusiastic about referring your company to others.

- Encourage referrals with information such as: "My business depends on referrals. Please consider mentioning my company to people whom you feel may benefit from my services."

- Join referral program groups. Some of these are affiliated with local professional associations, or may be part of a national database. There are also groups of various professionals that get together to discuss general business topics. These referral groups then try to help each other with referrals.

- Identify the clients who are most likely to provide referrals, and focus your efforts on them. Develop an in-depth mailing list and send them article reprints or other useful information items with a letter explaining how important referrals are to your business; this helps them help you.

- If your firm has employees, do not forget to instruct them in appropriate ways of obtaining referrals from people with whom they come in contact.

- Position yourself as an expert. Being very good at your niche in interior design means you will be thought of first when a client hears of someone who needs your expertise. If your firm provides excellent service and is expert in an area, clients will feel very comfortable recommending your firm to others.

Related to referrals are client testimonials. *Testimonials* are client statements made in a letter that the client sends or gives verbally to the designer concerning his or her satisfaction with the design firm's work. "Eric Smith provided our family with an outstanding solution to our need to add a small living space for my mother. His design solutions were supportive of our needs and he managed the project with great concern for detail" is an example of a testimonial.

A letter of reference—similar to a testimonial—states positive attributes about the design firm to either a specific client or in general. When design firms respond to requests for proposals from clients, letters of reference are often required to be submitted along with the other documents. Letters of reference are often longer than testimonials and often provide greater detail about the designer or the designer's work. It is also possible for an interior designer to ask the person who writes a letter of reference if the designer can also use a sentence or two as a testimonial.

Testimonials and letters of reference lend credibility, because someone else is making the positive comments or giving evidence to support claims made by the design firm. These testimonials and letters can also be used on Web sites, brochures, and other collateral marketing materials.

A word of caution about referral marketing and asking clients for referrals is in order. Never make it look like the firm is begging for work. The firm must focus on satisfaction and how it can help acquaintances of the client rather than on the design firm's need for business. If the designer somehow makes it sound like the firm is desperate or in real need of business, the client will wonder if something is suddenly wrong with the firm.

NETWORKING

Another word-of-mouth marketing technique that can be very successful is networking. According to the *American Heritage Dictionary*, a *network* is "an extended group of people with similar interests or concerns who interact and remain in informal contact for mutual assistance or support."[6] *Networking* is the cultivating of mutually beneficial relationships; it is getting to know people whom you can help and who can help you.

Networking for business relationships involves far more than getting together with colleagues at professional association meetings. Of course, many designers have had positive work-related networking experiences at professional association meetings. Nevertheless, networking has to go beyond the interior design chapter meeting, with attendance at events where you can meet potential new clients or others who can help provide referrals or tips on potential business needs.

The purpose of networking to develop business relationships is to use the networking opportunity to meet people outside the design industry who might help the designer with business opportunities. This kind of networking goes on at social and community clubs, seminars, church groups, schools, and the like. Because many of the reasons that a client will work with an interior designer are based on relationships, it is important to build contacts at groups where potential clients may participate.

Remember that networking is a two-way street; it should be mutually beneficial. Do not expect the other person to help you more than once if you are unwilling to help them. Becoming involved with your church's building committee just to meet potential clients and not contributing to the committee will leave a very sour taste in the mouths of the rest of the group.

When you use networking for business contacts, it is important to start with a plan.

- Determine what your purposes are for networking and who you want in your network.
- Learn to "work the room."
- Determine key individuals in your networking group.
- Go through your computer contact files or list the names of people who you think could help.
- Invite the networking individuals to lunch or coffee to talk about mutually beneficial topics. Remember that networking is a two-way street.
- Be willing to share information, and others will think of you as well.
- Make sure that you have business cards, and ask for cards from people who really interest you.
- Always have some small talk or conversation openers prepared.
- Remain current with the topics that interest your networking contacts.

When you attend a meeting such as a professional meeting, also have a plan. Ask the greeters if the people you are hoping to meet are expected. Perhaps they can even introduce you. When you attend a seminar or workshop, get to the class early so that you can introduce yourself to other participants and the speaker. Do not simply find people you know and stay with them all through the event.

Another important and successful networking tactic is to get to the meeting early and stay as late as you can. Getting there early allows you to scope out the meeting place and participate in the social part of the business or organization meeting. Staying to the end—even helping with the cleanup—can get you noticed. Some of the best contacts can be made at the end of the evening or meeting. The leaders of the organization almost always are among the last to leave a meeting or event.

Using networking to expand your group of acquaintances and to meet potential clients is a very effective and inexpensive marketing technique. Realize that a positive relationship with someone—even a business colleague—does not spring into existence overnight. Take the time to build your network with positive sharing, and before you know it, you will be called upon to share your knowledge in ways that you never expected. Pushing yourself on someone whom you have not met before can backfire, because they may find you aggressive or manipulative. Wanting to tell your story or ask your questions without giving something back is also impolite. Table 23-4 provides some additional tips on how to work a room in order to meet new people and expand your network.

TABLE 23-4.

Tips on how to work a room for networking effectiveness

Place your name tag on your right side. As you shake hands, the other person's eye will be directed to your name tag. Of course, some people believe that putting the name tag on a lower jacket pocket or belt is more interesting. If it suits your personality and the occasion, go for it!

Have a 10-second introduction prepared. When asked the common question, "What do you do?" have something to say besides, "Oh, I'm an interior designer." Perhaps you might say, "I help create unique home interiors" or "I assist companies in improving their bottom line."

If you want to give your business card to someone, ask the person for his or hers first. If the person does not offer you a card, then it is okay to ask for one.

Arrive early and stay until almost the end. It is the best time to meet the decision makers or VIPs.

Take care of eating at a meeting first, if possible; it is difficult to balance a drink and a plate of food while you get at your business cards. Freshen up and then progress to meeting people and exchanging cards.

Know why you are attending the meeting. If you want to meet people, plan to introduce yourself. Do not complain later that the meeting was a waste of time if you end up spending the evening with an old friend or sitting like a wallflower.

Do not drink too much alcohol. Sometimes it is a good idea not to drink at all during a meeting if you are trying to meet business contacts. At the very least, know your limit. Getting even a little tipsy is not a way to make a good impression.

Always have a sufficient number of business cards for the occasion. Nobody is impressed when you say, "I just gave out my last one." Use a card holder or put some in your jacket pocket.

Make others feel comfortable at meetings. If you have been to the meeting before and you see someone new, go up and talk to the person. Introduce the person to others. In a way, appoint yourself a hostess or host. At the very least, you will get to meet one or two new people and will gain experience at extending yourself.

Be sure to follow up in an appropriate manner. If you have promised to call or to send something to someone whom you have met, do so promptly. Be sure to get in touch with the chair, if you volunteered to help out at the next meeting. Do not forget a thank-you card/note, if one is appropriate.

WEB SITES RELEVANT TO THIS CHAPTER

www.marketingingpower.com American Marketing Association

www.facebook.com Facebook

www.linkedIn.com LinkedIn

www.prsa.org Public Relations Society of America

www.youtube.com YouTube

KEY TERMS

Advertising	Promotion
Blog	Promotional tools
Co-op advertising	Public relations (PR)
Inbound marketing	Publicity
Internet marketing	Referral
Landing page	Testimonial
Networking	TIFF format
Posts	Tweets
Press release	

WHAT WOULD YOU DO?

1. Alex was excited to receive word that a project his firm had completed in another state was to be awarded a special commendation by that state's environmental office for its excellence in sustainable design.

Alex has been working for several years to make a major impact in sustainable design, and this award, he thinks, will help bring his firm to a primary position in his state as well as assist with future promotion in other states. He wonders if a press release to the local media in his state would be a good first step in promoting this prestigious accomplishment. What should he include?

2. Kimberly is an interior designer working for a firm with a contract to do the interior design of a small resort. She goes to the jobsite prior to the installation of the furniture to make sure that the interior finish work is complete and the site is ready for the delivery of the merchandise. As she comes down a short flight of stairs in a two-story cabin, she trips and falls down the last three steps. Kimberly tries to break her fall, but instead she breaks her wrist and sustains a bad bruise on her left knee. She will have to miss about one week of work. Who is responsible to pay for Kimberly's medical care and loss of work: Kimberly, her boss, or the client?

3. "It takes days for Roger to return my phone messages. I even try to leave messages on his e-mail, and more times than not, he doesn't respond. Yesterday, the three e-mails I sent to him bounced back undeliverable, like he is blocking my e-mails!"

   These statements came from a disgruntled client who was complaining to Roger's boss at a residential furniture and design firm. The boss did what he could to calm the client down, but it didn't work very well. "I'll talk to Roger and make sure he returns your calls right away. I will also remind him that company policy forbids anyone from blocking e-mails," said the boss.

   When Roger comes to work the next day, the boss calls him into the office and tells him about the complaining client. "Oh, for goodness sakes! He's calling me all the time, asking stupid questions and wanting me on the jobsite every day. I'm working on five other projects and can't give him all my attention," claims Roger.

4. Robin and James joined a professional group consisting primarily of contractors. They joined the group in order to meet individuals working for or owning companies that might create referrals and collaborative work in interior design. Robin and James have a plan that they will both try to get to know at least three new people at each meeting. The only marketing tool they bring along for these visits is a good supply of business cards. The next day they meet to discuss their new contacts and how to take the next step in developing those relationships.

REFERENCES

1. Kotler, 2000, p. 87.
2. Fletcher and Rockler, 2000, p. 1.
3. Gitomer, 2011, p. 8.
4. Bodnar and Cohen, 2012, p. 14.
5. Burg, 1999, p. 114.
6. *American Heritage Dictionary*, 2000, p. 1181.

CHAPTER 24

Promotional Tools and Methods

After completing this chapter you should be able to:

- Explain the promotional benefits of well-designed logos and business stationery.
- Provide insights into the benefits of entering design competitions.
- Discuss the pros and cons of submitting projects to magazines as a promotional method.
- List several ways the company brochure can be used to promote a design firm.
- Discuss how direct mail can be both advantageous and disadvantageous to the firm for marketing purposes.
- Explain the benefits of writing articles as a way of exposing the design firm/designer to potential clients.
- Explain the benefits of a newsletter distributed through a Web site or direct mail.
- Compare the promotional benefits of speaking at an interior design professional meeting with those of speaking at a meeting of potential clients.
- Discuss how the RFP and RFQ system aids clients and interior designers.
- List the items that are traditionally required in an RFP.
- Explain how a hot-button issue can be the focus of promotional methods other than RFPs.
- Discuss effective ways for sole practitioners to promote themselves.
- Discuss effective ways for the design firm with a small design staff to promote the firm.

NCIDQ COMPONENT

Based on best information available, some material in this chapter might appear as part of the NCIDQ examination. The reader should not depend solely on this text for study material. Various sections may apply to the exam.

Competition, whether it is from other design firms or others in the built environment industry, makes it imperative for firms to look carefully at their marketing activities. Exactly which marketing and promotional methods a firm uses should be carefully considered in light of a strategic plan and budget constraints. Selecting appropriate methods helps effectively use marketing dollars.

Should the design firm be new or be trying to enter a new market, it will likely need a variety of promotional strategies to make itself known to potential clients. No firm can succeed without using some type of marketing beyond referrals.

This chapter looks at methods that are accepted as essential to the interior design firm: stationery appearance and photo portfolios appear at the top of that list. These are essential because they are the kinds of tools that all design firms can use effectively to promote any type of design practice.

Other promotional tools are also briefly discussed to provide ideas and guidance to the practice owner and student. Competitions are a good way to obtain publicity. Publication opportunities are sought after by any size and type of firm. Promotional tools such as direct marketing mailings, seminars, and premiums are included in this overview to give the practitioner some additional ideas on how to promote the practice.

The chapter concludes with a discussion of the request for proposal (RFP) as a marketing tool. Information about the presentation that follows the acceptance of a RFP is also included in this chapter.

This chapter and Chapter 23 should make it clear that there are many tools the interior design firm can utilize to promote itself to potential clients. Promotion and business development are crucial management tasks regardless of the size or type of firm.

THE GRAPHIC IMAGE AND STATIONERY

By *graphic image*, I am referring to the package of materials that the interior design firm uses to identify itself. This includes the company logo, business cards, letterhead and other stationery, business forms, and drawing paper identification. The firm's graphic image is usually incorporated into many marketing tools.

The logo is often considered the primary part of the graphic image. A *logo*, or mark, is a symbolic image of the company (see Figure 24-1). It can be a strong identification symbol for the firm, eventually helping to make the firm easily identifiable. It can be used on all of the firm's written communication, as

FIGURE 24-1.

A sample design firm's logo, used on the firm's stationery and related materials. (Reproduced with permission of James Tigges, Pinnacle Design, Inc., Phoenix, AZ)

well as on many other items related to the firm's business. The business card is a key tool incorporating the logo.

The design and color of the logo should be the same on all materials related to the firm. This will help clients connect the logo with the firm and help bring about client awareness and identification. Logos are displayed in many of the figures found throughout this chapter. The rest of the design of the business card, stationery, and so forth must be compatible with the logo.

Here are several points to consider when developing a logo:

- A logo can be a word, symbol, abstract form, letter-mark (like initials), or even a slogan.
- It should be designed so that it can easily be incorporated into all stationery and documents of the firm.
- It is created according to basic principles of design.
- Avoid trendy colors that will date the logo.
- Review color psychology so that the color or colors you choose convey the right emotion for your business.
- The design should be effective in black and white as well as color. It should also be easily readable on different backgrounds.
- The design of the logo should work in a variety of sizes so it can be used on various business stationery items (and other promotional or advertising items).
- A complex design—such as one using embossing, foils, and textures—will be expensive to print and may not translate well to uses other than on letterhead.
- A truly unique logo can be registered to protect it as a trademark so that no other company can use the same design.

There are many design options for stationery. Along with the company Web site, business stationery—especially the business card—makes an important first impression. The color of the paper stock and ink, the type size, the typeface, and the size of the finished format are just some of the factors that the design firm must consider when it is developing the firm's graphic image and stationery (see Figure 24-2).

Some typefaces are overly decorative: they may look great on some items but be difficult to read on others. It is a good idea to consider hiring a graphic designer to create any logo and stationery designs. Even though the interior designer may feel that he or she is perfectly capable of doing so, a graphic designer is more familiar with products and processes used to create the graphic image.

Business cards remain an important component of the array of promotional tools used by a design firm. The purpose of the business card is to help people remember the designer—especially potential clients or others who can help the designer in some way. All interior designer who are looking for new business should never be without a few business cards.

This small piece of stiffened paper, generally 3.5 inches by 2 inches, is sometimes thought of as a tiny billboard by which a company leaves an impression of sophistication, whimsy, or seriousness. Its simplest form is black type on white card stock. Many other, more sophisticated designs can be created, with color on one or both sides, foil, metallic inks, or just about anything else the design entails. A business card can be single-faced, double-sided, folded, square, embossed, and with or without cutouts.

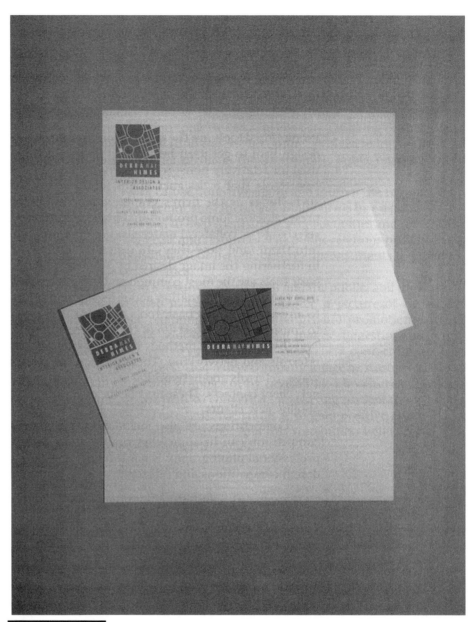

FIGURE 24-2.

Sample of a design firm's stationery and logo. (Reproduced with permission of Debra May Himes, ASID, Debra May Himes Interior Design & Associates, Mesa, AZ; photo by Dawson Henderson)

It is becoming increasingly difficult to include all the information that a design firm may want on its business card by using only one side. Positioning the firm's logo, name, address, telephone number, fax number, e-mail and Web addresses, cell or pager numbers, and, finally, the person's name, affiliation, and license number makes for really tiny print! Many design firms are resorting to using both sides or a folded card. This is entirely up to the firm owner.

We also obtain business cards from those who can help us with specifications, might lead us to other clients, or could provide other opportunities. This is not to say that one tries to give out one's cards indiscriminately. There actually is a bit of etiquette concerned with handing out business cards. Here are some tips:

- Do not offer your card as a way of starting a conversation. Offer a business card when the conversation is drawing to a close.
- If someone offers you his or her card, you generally provide him or her with yours as well, but it is okay not to exchange cards if you do not wish to.
- Always hand out clean, unbent cards. Carry them in a cardholder.
- Generally it is acceptable to write on the back of a card you receive, but do so out of sight of the person who gave you the card.
- If the other person says he or she is "out of cards," you could offer one of yours for him or her to write information on.
- Some people don't carry cards, but play a "power game" of collecting them from others.

PHOTO PORTFOLIO

Interior designers rely on a selection of project photos, displayed on a Web site, in a brochure, or in other ways, to help convince clients that the designer can do the kind of design they desire for their home or commercial space. A *photo portfolio* is a generic term for a library of project photos that can be used as part of many kinds of promotional tools. A book filled with photographs of installations can be shown to the client during the marketing stage of a design project. These photos help to show what the design firm can do.

Whether the designer or a professional photographer takes the photo, it is essential to get client permission before taking photos of their project. This is especially important if the photo might be used in any kind of publication. There should always be a clause in the design contract that gives the design firm permission to photograph and submit for publication all work, whether the firm expects to do this or not. This protects the designer from being sued for invasion of privacy. Anyone appearing in the photo should sign a photo release, especially if the photo is to be published.

It is important to know that when the designer hires a photographer to shoot an installation, the photographer retains the rights to the photos. Designers pay for use of those photos and must be clear with the photographer what uses are included in the fees. Merely because a designer has a photo of a project does not mean the designer has the right to have that photograph published.

If you wish to take your own photos, follow the guidance in the few tips provided here. These items should also be kept in mind when discussing photo shoots with a professional:

- The highest-quality reproductions of digital photos are achieved with TIFF format images.
- Magazine and book publishers prefer TIFF format.
- JPEG format images—which is more common for most nonprofessional shots—are compressed and are less desirable for publication.
- Those who self-photograph their projects usually underlight the space and thus end up with poor-quality photos.
- The designer who cannot afford a professional photographer should become familiar with the use of software like Photoshop® to improve image quality.

Numerous professional photographers still retain the use of film (rather than digital media) as an option. Photographs done in a transparency or negative format generally produce the sharp, high-quality images desired by magazine and book publishers. Enlargements made from negatives or transparencies are generally sharper than those from digital photos, unless the photo is from a high-quality digital camera. Photos on film also translate a bit better when they are used on copying machines to create color copies for proposals.

BROCHURES

A *brochure* can provide information to interest clients, grab their attention, and allow the design firm to showcase its design style and expertise. Brochures have certainly not disappeared despite the rise of Web sites. With the numerous publication software programs available, the designer can create many styles of brochures.

A brochure is sometimes referred to as *collateral material*, along with other kinds of marketing publications such as flyers, calendars, and inserts that can be sales materials. They can be prepared easily using many kinds of available software, making them a useful marketing tool. The brochure gives the firm the opportunity to show selections of its best work and to tell clients something about itself in a "leave-behind" that is relatively easy to produce. An example of a small "brochure" or leave-behind is the postcard (see Figure 24-3).

Here are some tips on preparing a brochure:

- The cover—if the piece is folded—should grab the eye; this is what gets the most attention.
- Use the highest-quality photography.
- A few quality photos will do more than many poor images.
- Use well-written and brief copy based on a client's needs.
- Provide a "taste" of what the firm is about rather than providing in-depth material. Otherwise, the client may not bother to call for more information.
- Include information about the firm and the services offered.
- Unless the brochure is printed in-house, avoid including material such as client lists or photos of people that can date the piece.

 Always remember that a brochure is not, by itself, going to win new clients. It is a promotional and sales tool to help in the long-term process of attracting new clients to the interior design firm. You may want to use a worksheet such as Item 24-1 on the companion Web site to help you focus on identifying your capabilities in interior design, and then use this information in the copy of a brochure or other types of promotional materials.

COMPETITIONS

Entering design competitions can garner publicity for the firm and provide additional materials for other marketing efforts. Because design peers judge competitions, peer recognition can be earned.

Design competitions on the local level are available primarily through association chapters. Local competitions provide a possible publicity outlet to

FIGURE 24-3.

A postcard mailer used as a "pass along" when a firm has an extensive Web site for promotion. (Reproduced with permission of Suzan Globus, FASID, Globus Design Associates, Fair Haven, NJ; photo by sjcarrphoto.com)

reach local clients. The award itself is always something that can be displayed in the office, and serves to announce to potential clients that the designer has a reputation for doing exceptional work. When the awards are announced in a local magazine, the designer can obtain reprints to give out to potential clients.

There are also national competitions, sponsored by associations as well as manufacturers and other groups. National competitions are announced at national conferences, and information about the awards is often published in trade magazines. You can find out about competitions through associations' announcements on their Web sites and announcements in trade magazines, and direct mailings to interior designers from various sources. Reprints can also be obtained for a firm's marketing efforts.

Design firms must target which competitions to enter. Entrance fees and project photography by a professional can be quite expensive. These costs must be weighed against the possible benefits. Time is also needed to prepare the materials in the required format. Care must be taken to prepare the materials exactly as required to prevent disqualification of the entry. Permissions from clients might also be required.

The photographs taken for a competition can be used in many ways: for the firm's photo portfolio, its Web site, and in brochures, newsletters, and direct-mail programs. A commercial firm might need them for proposal pamphlets. However, the designer must be sure that the contract with the photographer grants the designer rights to use the photos in other marketing tools.

The professional recognition that comes with winning or placing in a competition is very worthwhile. Entering and winning or placing in national competitions gains publicity for the designer beyond the local market. The fact that the designer has won an award often plays an important part in a client's decision to hire a designer, as it is another piece of evidence supporting the designer's expertise.

DIRECT MAIL

Direct mail can mean just about anything—from mailing letters to sending out brochures or newsletters. Because printing and postage are expenses, the key is to get the mailed items to the right people.

Everyone receives a lot of unsolicited junk mail. Many receivers will consider a promotional mailing from a design firm junk mail. Care must be taken in the content of the mailing as well as to whom the mailing is sent.

Here are some tips on utilizing direct mail as a marketing tool:

- Mailing lists should start with former clients.
- Additional addresses can come from a list service and other appropriate groups.
- Any marketing piece that is mailed should be flawlessly written, with good grammar and perfect spelling.
- Direct-mail items must be well designed and creatively thought out.
- The piece must have impact and should be designed to catch the eye of the receiver.
- Provide information that is interesting enough to entice the receiver to call or write for more information.
- Direct mailings to generate business from totally new clients often announce sales, holiday promotions, or seminars.
- Remember that nothing will happen automatically. For the greatest possible number of leads from direct mailings, the designer should follow up with a personal call.

Direct mail via e-mail must be handled carefully, as unsolicited commercial e-mails are spam. The law does not permit unsolicited e-mails (or faxes). It is important to check with your attorney to find out how to use e-mail and fax solicitations.

There are a great number of techniques and strategies in direct mail available for the designer to use as promotional tools to develop client leads.

The professional who wants to consider using direct mail is urged to check the references in the list at the end of this book. For direct-mail programs to businesses, the best book I have found remains Robert W. Bly's *Business to Business Direct Marketing*. A worksheet to help with the development of a direct mail piece is included on the companion Web site as Item 24-2.

PUBLICATION

There are many possible ways for the interior designer to utilize print media to gain publicity for the firm beyond the press release. Excellent-quality photographs are very important for many of these publication methods. In some cases, the publication will pay for the photography and even prepare the editorial material (the text), though this is not common. This section briefly discusses publication of projects, writing articles for publication, newsletters, case studies, and writing a book as a means of marketing.

Probably the most sought-after kind of publicity and promotion is *publication of projects* in trade and shelter magazines. A firm must carefully consider to which magazine or other print publication it should submit materials. Each publication has a slightly different target market and audience. Designers can contact a magazine's editorial offices to receive information about submission requirements.

Clients often view designers who have written *articles* as experts, or at least as having more expertise than others—and clients like to hire experts. "Publications provide one proof of who is real and who isn't . . . . Published work tells [a potential client] that the author must have substantial experience, and that she has reflected more deeply on her businesses than some."[1]

An editor who is looking for information that will be appropriate for the publication reviews all articles and other submissions. The writer must have some credentials, along with an ability to write, to be considered as a columnist or even a contributing writer to a publication.

Once an article has been published, the author can request reprints. These reprints can then be used as part of the design firm's total marketing plan and strategies. Reprints can be included in packets that are given to clients during marketing presentations or in packets that are mailed to prospective clients. Designers can also send along a reprint when they are writing to former clients.

Writing for Publication

Articles written by the designer and published in local or even national magazines are a great way to extend the designer's reputation and help with marketing. To get published, the designer must do some homework. Not everything that you think is a worthwhile article will be something an editor will want to publish.

Start by researching all the publications in the firm's area. Then investigate other publications that are of interest to the designer's target market. Determine what kinds of articles are commonly found in those publications.

Local publications are meant for both residents and tourists. This type of magazine occasionally has a few issues that contain articles on interesting interior design and architecture. Magazines such as *Phoenix Magazine, Los Angeles*, and *Chicago* are of this type. There may also be local business-oriented magazines that might seek articles from commercial interior designers.

Research back copies to see what style of writing and types of editorial material (the text is called editorial material) the magazine publishes. If what you want to submit does not fit the editorial content of the magazine, you will be wasting your time and that of the publication's editorial staff. Depending on the publication, you can find back copies at most libraries.

Come up with an idea that is interesting to the magazine's readers. Make sure it is something you know something about and can easily research for additional background, if necessary. Be prepared with photos or to discuss photos; interiors articles are naturally more interesting when they include good photographs.

It is best to send a query letter to the magazine editor before you spend much time developing an article. A *query letter* explains the concept of the article and even gives a little taste of it by including a first paragraph. If the editor is interested, he or she will send you information about the magazine's style guidelines, which contain information about margins, word count, requirements for camera-ready photographs or drawings, and basic grammatical style that is appropriate for the publication. Plan on keeping your article between 1000 and 1500 words. If the editor wants more, he or she will ask you for additional material.

Keep your expectations in check, as not all articles submitted to magazines will get published. Only a few magazines pay for articles. Payment is generally covered in the guidelines that will be sent to you upon request or if the editor is interested based on your query letter.

Although an article will not result in the phone ringing off the hook with new clients' inquiries, it does constitute one more promotional tool that the interior design firm can use. Published articles raise awareness; they get the design firm's name or designer's name in front of more clients than can be reached by the designer's efforts alone.

Newsletters have long been popular with architects and larger interior design firms. There are two basic kinds of newsletters. One is the simple in-house newsletter that tells everyone whose birthday is in that month and other tidbits of interest to employees. The other is the promotional newsletter that is used to inform clients about projects or otherwise provide valuable information for clients.

It takes commitment to begin publishing a newsletter, regardless of whether it is a printed collateral item or published on the Internet. Once the firm begins to publish a newsletter, it must follow through and be ready to produce this marketing piece on a consistent basis.

A promotional tool used by larger firms, especially in collaboration with manufacturers, is the *case study*. A case study of a particularly interesting or challenging project can be produced as a separate publication. A *case study* tells what the design program was and some unique features of the project, and may include before-and-after photographs. A case study can also discuss the solution and ideally will contain some quotes from the client regarding the quality of the project.

Writing a book is another way of demonstrating expertise and authority and can be a very effective promotional tool for the interior designer. Books take a substantial amount of time to write and require greater commitment than writing an article. However, it is a way of showing expertise and gaining credibility, especially if the topic is related to the designer's specialty. Publication of a book lends prestige to the interior designer and should be highlighted on his or her resumé and Web site.

You can get complete instructions on how to submit a manuscript proposal from many book publishers. In fact, you can go to the Web site for John Wiley & Sons and obtain information concerning submitting proposals to this publisher. There are also numerous reference books at bookstores on this topic.

Speaking at seminars or other gatherings can be a very rewarding process as well as an effective promotional tool. Designers can start their speaking efforts by volunteering to speak to civic and club groups on topics related to interior design. Even local business trade associations look for experts who can provide appropriate information for their monthly meetings. The designer who has speaking experience may wish to submit queries or proposals to national groups.

If the idea of giving a speech makes you cringe, you are not alone: Speaking in front of a group always ranks as one of the things people fear the most. Work up to giving a presentation by speaking to smaller groups. Volunteer to give a presentation or critique at interior design program classes. Chair an association committee so that you have to speak before groups. Take a public-speaking class (a good idea for students and also for professionals). The class can help you polish your presentation techniques and build confidence.

Prepare yourself and your speech. Consider topics on which you have expertise to be your mainstay. If you don't have time to prepare a good speech, then pass on the request or suggest a different topic. Not all programs have to be accompanied by visuals, but if you do, be sure they are of high quality. Bring plenty of business cards for after the program, but don't make this the focus of your program. Remember, you have been chosen to speak to the group to provide information of benefit to the attendees.

A marketing tool for some designers is the use of *premiums*. Have you been to a trade show or conference and received something like a ballpoint pen with a company name on it? A *premium* is an object that has a logo, slogan, or other words or graphics printed on it. A few examples are coffee mugs, memo pads, and pencils.

Premiums come in all types, colors, and price ranges. Even the small firm can offer a premium by having its logo and name printed on something small and useful, such as memo pads or pencils. This can also help with branding. Thus, if you want your firm to be known for quality, do not send out cheap pens that break after a few uses.

PROPOSALS AS A MARKETING TOOL

The proposal process has been around for many years. The term *proposal* has been used to mean a contract proposal or an overview of how the designer intends to proceed with a project. In the context of this section, however, *proposal* is a response to a *request for a proposal*—often abbreviated as RFP—issued by a client. It is not a contract or contract offer.

The proposal is a marketing tool very familiar to commercial interior design firms. It is used to "paint" a picture about the firm using information that might also be contained in the firm's Web site (or other marketing materials), but in a different format.

The client develops and issues the RFP. The client does this to determine interest in a project from many different design firms without having to hold separate meetings with each firm. Commercial clients almost always prepare an RFP for a large project and frequently use them for smaller projects as well.

The residential client is unlikely to use the formal RFP process. They do, however, use a similar concept: the interview. It is not unusual for a residential client to interview at least three interior designers before deciding on a firm for a project. These three interviewees are often arrived at in a simple way: The client does research on design firms and calls firms to discuss the project. This section focuses on the formal RFP as used by commercial firms as a marketing tool.

The RFP is used to narrow the field of potential design firms to a small group that the commercial client will actually interview. The client prepares the RFP document and makes it available to interested firms. A design firm prepares its response providing the information requested in the client's RFP. The firm is asked for such things as firm qualifications, resumés of the principals and designers who will do the project, a listing of past clients or references, and project budgeting.

Unlike what many residential designers consider to be a proposal (which includes pricing), the RFP does not necessarily contain specific pricing or cost information. That will be based on what the client requires and what the design firm wishes to include. The firm selected to do the project follows up the RFP at the selection stage with a formalized contract offer. It is a good idea to review the material in Chapter 7 on proposals versus contracts.

When a client decides to use the proposal process to obtain an interior design firm, the process might start with a *request for qualifications (RFQ)*. The request for qualifications—sometimes called a *letter of interest (LOI)*—is a way that clients can prescreen a number of firms by focusing on their experience and qualifications. Generally, the RFQ asks for staff resumés, brochures, references, and other experience documentation. After a client reviews the responses to the RFQ, it will use this prequalified group as the primary group to ask for RFP responses. The RFQ is most commonly used on very large projects, and might be something that only the largest interior design firms ever encounter. A sample RFP letter that a client would send to numerous design firms has been included on the companion Web site as Item 24-3.

The RFP is an efficient way for clients to obtain information from several firms and, to some extent, ideas on how to solve their project issues. A client issues an RFP to design firms whom it might like to consider for execution of a project. An RFP can also be issued to search the design market for a design firm that has the qualifications the client feels are important for the project (see Figure 24-4).

From the client's point of view, an RFP:

- Provides responses from firms that meet the specific requirements of the request; a firm that does not meet requirements will not reply
- Provides prequalification of only the most interested firms
- Makes it easier to eliminate firms that do not meet the qualifications without personally interviewing each company
- May stimulate responses from firms the client would not have thought of for the job
- Allows the client to review proposals at its convenience
- Keeps the client from having to invest a large amount of time interviewing design firms that may be unqualified

From the interior designer's point of view, the RFP:

- Helps the firm decide if it wishes to take on the project
- Provides an opportunity to be considered for some projects the firm might never have known about
- Puts a designer with the appropriate qualification in a better position to be granted an interview

The decision as to which firms the client will interview is determined primarily by the material provided in the proposal (response). This makes the

FIGURE 24-4.

Proposal materials in response to an RFP. (Reproduced with permission of Fred Messner, Phoenix Design One, Inc., Tempe, AZ; photo by Dawson Henderson)

proposal a very important document. Nevertheless, clients do not make a decision about a design firm purely on the basis of the proposals. After the proposals are reviewed, a list of design firms that the client most wants to interview emerges. This list is usually called a *short list*, because the number of firms is commonly limited to three to six (depending on the size and complexity of the project). Interviews are then set up with each firm on the short list. Table 24-1 outlines what is traditionally included in an RFP response.

It is very important to realize that the client controls the content and format of the proposal. The design firm must respond with the required

TABLE 24-1.

A typical outline of a proposal in response to an RFP

Note that the actual content of any proposal is governed by the information requested by the client.

Cover letter
Title page
Table of contents
Executive summary: Overview of contents
Problem analysis: Design firm's opportunity to explain its understanding of the client's needs
Scope of services: What will be done in response to what was required
Project experience: Information about projects similar in nature to the proposed project
Project approach: Information about how the firm will provide services and will manage the project
Staffing: Who will be responsible for the project
Staff resumés
Schedule
List of deliverables: Documents the firm expects to prepare for the project
Budget and fees
Financial information on the design firm
References
Miscellaneous optional information:
   Additional project case studies
   Article reprints
   Other information the firm wishes to provide

information in the proposal. Leaving out sections or making the proposal presentation different from what was requested can lead to disqualification. The client uses this control so that all proposals will be treated equally.

If a design firm decides to respond to an RFP, it will have to include information pertinent to each of these issues and perhaps others it may wish to include. The instructions in the RFP will inform the responding design firms how much latitude they have in what is to be stated and what additional information may be included. Each part is critical and must be written in response to the specific project, client, and instructions. Proposals for commercial projects can easily run about 25 pages for a small project and more than 50 pages for a complex project. So, this activity should not be taken lightly or done in haste.

Design firms that have been successful with the proposal process are exceptionally good at identifying hot-button issues within the RFP. A *hot-button issue* is one of critical concern to the client. For a school district, the hot-button issue might be quality design at an economical price. Clients do not always describe needs succinctly or obviously. In such a case, the design firm must then attempt to identify the issues. This, obviously, is more difficult and challenging for the design firm.

Table 24-2 provides several tips on preparing a RFP proposal. Many of the references can provide additional help with and ideas on preparing a proposal. The next section discusses the presentation phase of the proposal process.

Proposal Presentations

Preparing a response to an RFP takes a lot of commitment and time from any design firm. The hope is that it will be received in a more than satisfactory

TABLE 24-2.

Tips on preparing a proposal in response to an RFP

Good writing is a must.
Always be clear and factual, using language that clients will quickly and easily understand.
Ensure perfect spelling and grammar.
Make sure it completely speaks to the issues the client has stated.
Follow the outline the client has used rather than your own outline.
Be sure that content has addressed client hot-button issues. (A hot-button issue is one of critical importance to the client.)
Ensure that scope of services is not vague and that it contains sufficient descriptions to clarify what you will be doing.
Create an interesting-looking proposal with the use of photography and color photocopying.
Present material in two or three columns rather than one column.
Include testimonials from references using excerpts in quotes followed by the source name.
Integrate color in bullets or headlines.
Use looseleaf pages rather than permanent binding to make it easier to insert additional items and move things around.

manner so as to get the firm on the short list and be allowed to make a presentation. The client's *short list*, which is the list of firms it will allow to make a presentation, rarely includes more than three or four firms. Getting on the short list means the design firm can move to the next step of presenting to the client.

The presentation made after a proposal submission may be the first time the designer actually meets and talks with the client. It is important, therefore, to develop rapport with the client as well as to convey information the firm wishes the client to understand about the firm.

The presentation is likely to be given to a group referred to as the *selection committee*. The selection committee will probably include individuals that the design team has not met, so developing rapport is again vitally important. Having to make a presentation to a group should guide the designer in preparing the materials and selecting the type of materials that will be used.

These presentations are commonly given at the client's place of business. It is necessary to find out about the room, what audiovisual equipment can be supplied, what the presenter must bring, and the seating configuration of the space. Some designers prefer to use a conference table; others like a U-shaped table for a group. As the designer will be using the client's facility, he or she will need to ask what is available and whether arrangements can be made to accommodate the presentation style. It is likely that more than one firm will be presenting in a day, so changes in the arrangement of the conference room might not be possible.

Here are several additional key considerations in making this important presentation:

- A firm on the short list has already been judged competent to execute the project. Going over how great the firm is should not be a focus of the presentation at this point.

- It is essential that the presentation address the goals and needs of the client as stated in the RFP.

- It is essential that the firm address the key issues that are on the client's mind—whether or not they appear clearly in the RFP.
- The principal of the design firm generally makes the presentation or leads off the presentation. Others on the team who will do the project may also be part of the presentation team.
- Each person plays a part, explaining some important points about the project concepts and/or methods that will be employed to execute the project.
- It is very important for the firm to stick to the time limit established by the client.
- Appearances are important. Appropriate business apparel, clean and neat presentation materials and handouts, and working audiovisual equipment are a must.
- Listening to the comments and questions that the client makes, as well as watching body language, are critical to developing rapport and showing the client that the design firm will listen to the client's concerns and needs.
- Be sure that the team practices the presentation before giving it to the client. "Winging" a presentation is never a good idea. Practice also ensures that the team will stay within the designated time limit.
- Plan to arrive a little early so that you can set up your materials while the committee members take a break between presentations.

Knowing who is to be on the selection committee is not unethical. Asking about the committee members and then finding out something about each one is a good presentation strategy. This is not always easy to do, but phone calls to colleagues who have dealt with the client before can be helpful. Certainly it would be helpful to know their concerns about the project.

It is also important to involve the client in the presentation. Encourage questions and rehearse questions to ask members of the committee. Involving the client helps gauge client interest and confirmation of the ideas the firm is offering.

The order in which you present can make a difference. Some firms like to go first, feeling that they can make a good impression that way. Many other firms like to be last, believing that the last ideas and concepts the client hears for the day will be retained better. Presenting last also means that the client has been "educated" a little about the process and pros and cons of other firms. Questioning might be more intense because of what other firms have said.

During the presentation, be at ease with the committee members, and exhibit warmth, enthusiasm, and interest. Make sure that your presentation focuses on what the client needs to know about your firm and how you are going to solve the client's challenges. Do not bore them with anything that is not relevant to their primary concerns.

When it is over, say thank you, gather your materials, and leave without trying to hang around. It will probably take the committee a few days or weeks (depending on how many design firms are making presentations) to get back to you with the results. If you have answered a lot of questions or the group is particularly lively when you have finished, you can assume that the presentation was successful. If they are subdued . . . well, you tried!

Always go back to the office and critique the presentation: What seemed to go well? What went wrong? Learning from mistakes makes the firm better at presenting the next time. It is also appropriate to send the selection committee chairperson a thank-you letter within a few days. This is not only a polite bit of business etiquette, but also gives the firm one more chance to say a few words about how interested it is in executing the project.

WEB SITES RELEVANT TO THIS CHAPTER

www.aia.org American Institute of Architects

www.marketingingpower.com American Marketing Association

www.associationofmarketing.org Association of Marketing Professionals

www.thedma.org Direct Marketing Association

www.prsa.org Public Relations Society of America

www.sba.gov U.S. Small Business Administration

KEY TERMS

Brochure	Premium
Case study	Proposal
Collateral materials	Query letter
Direct mail	Request for proposal (RFP)
Graphic image	Request for qualifications (RFQ)
Hot-button issue	Selection committee
Letter of interest (LOI)	Short list
Logo (or mark)	
Photo portfolio	

WHAT WOULD YOU DO?

1. Marsha has a strongly held belief that abortions are wrong, but she has always kept this belief to herself. The design firm she works for recently obtained a contract for the remodeling and design of several offices for Planned Parenthood. Marsha is assigned the role as lead designer and project manager for this client.

2. Steve Johnson was hired by two doctors to design their new general practice space. Dr. Williams was given the responsibility of working with the designers, but both doctors met with the designer. They got along very well with Steve, and the project quickly moved into the design development phase.

   Steve brings Michael Hunter with him to the final review of the schematic plans. Michael had not previously met with the doctors. At the end of the presentation, Steve reintroduces Michael and tells the doctors that Michael will be taking over the remaining design and other responsibilities of the project. "I'm taking a year's leave of absence from the firm, leaving the firm next week. Michael will be taking over," says Steve.

   The clients suddenly become noticeably reserved but say nothing other than asking about Steve's absence. "I'm going to work on a master's degree with an emphasis in geriatrics," Steve says. "I want to specialize in assisted living and other senior facilities and feel I need the extra training."

Michael tries to contact the doctors three times in the next two weeks to go over the plans and specifications, but keeps getting excuses as to their availability. Three weeks later, the design firm receives a letter from the doctor's attorney giving notice of a breach of contract action. The doctors allege that because Steve would not be completing the project, the design firm is in breach.

3. The design process for a large second home progressed very satisfactorily, with client approvals at each stage of the process. Client approvals were obtained before any product was ordered, as stipulated in the design contract. The interior designer specified and provided all the movable furniture and custom cabinets except the cabinets in the kitchen and bathrooms.

    The interior designer convinced the client to purchase a custom entertainment center for the master suite and a custom entertainment center for the family room. The clients were excited about the design of both cabinets, especially when the designer explained the fine finish of both units and all the features that could be built into the cabinets.

    When the cabinetmaker began installing the custom unit in the family room, he realized it didn't fit into the designated alcove. He told the interior designer and client—who happened to be there at the time—that the cabinet had to go back to the shop for some adjustments for it to fit. The client asked the cabinetmaker who had made the mistake, and the cabinetmaker said that he had made the two pieces according to the drawings sent by the interior designer. "Didn't you check with the builder on the size of the alcove and verify that dimension before constructing the cabinet?" asked the interior designer. "I did check with him and nothing had changed from the drawings," retorted the cabinetmaker.

    Two weeks later, after the designer faxed a revised drawing and cost estimate for the family room cabinet, the client e-mails back and says he will not pay for something that the designer did not do correctly. He also cancels the entertainment center for the master suite, saying that he can no longer trust the designer.

REFERENCE

1. Harding, 1994, p. 24.

CHAPTER 25

Selling Strategies

After completing this chapter you should be able to:

■ Explain how selling is only one part of promotion and marketing.

■ Explain how selling differs from marketing.

■ Explain why it is important to understand that selling takes place in many different situations.

■ Discuss how the information on why it is harder to sell services than products can be used to improve the marketing of services.

■ Explain what it means for services to be "perishable."

■ Explain the buyer decision-making process and how it affects interior design services.

■ Explain the importance of building a professional relationship with clients.

■ Explain the selling technique of probing, and offer a suggested sequence of questions to help uncover a client's specific needs for interior design services.

■ Compare the use of features versus benefits in the offering of interior design services and a typical interior design product.

■ Explain what is meant by creating a win–win situation in a negotiation.

■ Describe why the environment in which a negotiation takes place can have an impact on the negotiation outcome.

■ List the steps in the selling process, and describe activities in each step.

■ Discuss several ideas on where to develop leads on potential customers.

NCIDQ COMPONENT

Based on best information available, some material in this chapter might appear as part of the NCIDQ examination. The reader should not depend solely on this text for study material. See the section on negotiation.

As a design professional, you will find that selling affects many of the interactions you have with a client. Personal selling—that is, one-on-one interaction—will take place when marketing to new clients, as will selling design concepts as the project progresses. Naturally, it will take personal selling to convince the client to sign the design contract in order to begin the project.

Only very rarely does an interior designer have the opportunity to become involved in a project without using some selling strategies. The best design idea will become a reality only if the designer and design firm can convince the client to buy it. Most of the time, a relationship between the client and the designer must be built, and the designer must work very hard to obtain final agreement from the client. Most of the time, the designer needs a lot of skill in selling to achieve an agreement.

Some designers find it extremely easy to sell concepts or products. Others feel frustrated by a lack of success in this area. We have all heard about the proverbial "born salesperson," but designers who can successfully sell ideas and products are not just "born." They have acquired a skill that improves with practice and experience. Learning techniques for selling more effectively also helps make the selling situation more successful.

This chapter discusses several selling concepts and techniques that many designers use. The focus of this chapter is on selling interior design services; however, much of what is discussed applies also to the selling of products. Chapter 26 focuses on design presentations and discusses the parts of the selling process that relate to making a successful presentation.

WHAT IS SELLING?

Interior designers generally do not like to think of themselves as salespeople or believe that what they do involves selling. Yet, their every interaction with clients actually does involve selling.

But what is selling? *Selling* consists of personal, often one-on-one, communication. According to the *World Book Encyclopedia*, selling "involves two-way communication between a salesperson and a customer. It enables the buyer to ask questions about a product [or service] and receive additional information about it immediately."[1] In selling, the designer must explain his or her services or perhaps his or her solution to the design project in a personal way, so as to instruct and bring the client to accept the company or design idea.

Interactions with clients create a constant stream of one-on-one and small-group communication exchanges that are, in essence, sales encounters. For example, it is critical for interior designers to be able to sell themselves just to obtain a meeting with a client. This gives the designer the opportunity to convince the client that he or she is the right person for the job. Then, the designer must sell concepts to the client throughout the design project. Selling continues even after the project is completed, if the designer wants additional work from the client.

In their interactions with clients, interior designers do their utmost to find out what their clients really want in the way of design services and products, and then try to provide those services and products. Satisfying clients and making a sale makes both parties winners. It is not necessary for the designer to try to sell clients what they do not want. In fact, it is bad for business.

Of course, it also takes marketing to find those clients to whom the designer can sell. As we saw from previous chapters, marketing takes many forms, and the designer might need to use several of those strategies to locate potential clients.

Some people do not like selling or salespeople, because they believe that selling involves manipulating people to get them to buy what they do not want. Unfortunately, many so-called salespeople practice this kind of selling. This is not the kind of selling we wish to talk about (or engage in).

Selling Exchanges

Selling exchanges occur in several ways. The most common method is *face-to-face* or personal selling. This is very personal selling, and many factors beyond what is said verbally can affect the success of the exchange. A buyer can be influenced by the way the seller is dressed, the seller's mannerisms, and a whole host of other subtle factors.

Selling can also occur via the *telephone*. Of course, I am not speaking of telemarketers, but of interior designers who have been contacted by a potential client who is seeking information about the designer's services. Interior designers do sometimes use what is called *cold-calling*, which is a telephone call to a person the designer does not know.

A third common selling exchange occurs in today's world by *e-mail*. It might be a "blast" e-mail sent to prospective clients or buyers, or a message in direct response to some initiative by the designer or client. Care must be taken in selling via e-mail, as there are federal regulations concerning the transmission of unsolicited e-mails.

An older technique that is still useful to many is *direct mail*. In this case the seller sends a letter or a brochure to a prospective client. The recipient might be someone that the designer has met, or the mailing may be sent unsolicited to a possible client—similar to a cold-call telephone sales effort. Direct mail can be useful for getting out the word on the design firm's existence, but because this type of unsolicited mail is considered "junk" it is often not received positively.

A final selling exchange occurs on the *Internet* through the company Web site. Clients often search out service providers on the Web. The site itself creates a selling situation, as the appearance and contents of the site "sell" the designer to some degree. The site should make it easy for the potential client to contact the designer for further information. It should also provide enough basic information for the client to be comfortable with the firm. Such informational items include a biography (bio), photos of project work, statements about the company, and how to get in touch with the firm.

SELLING SERVICES VERSUS PRODUCTS

Interior design, above all else, is about providing a service to the client. What makes selling interior design services so difficult is that the services to be performed are intangible. An *intangible* is something that is a concept and has no physical existence; it is a concept that the designer is selling the client. It is generally a lot easier to sell a product, because it is tangible: Clients can see it, feel it, and use it. They like it or they don't like it.

The intangible design service at first exists only in the mind of the designer. The designer must translate that concept into words and graphics that allow the client to understand it and "see" it as the designer sees it. How the living room will look or how the restaurant will look is difficult for many clients to understand. Often an interior becomes "real" for clients only when the project has been completed. However, the designer must convince the client to trust him or her in order for it to be completed.

It is very important for professionals and students to understand that what they are selling to clients is not the chair, sofa, desk, or other product.

Certainly, many interior designers also wish to sell those tangible items. But first and foremost, interior designers are selling intangibles:

- The ability to do what is required in a professional manner
- Concepts and ideas on how to meet the client's needs
- Knowledge as to which products are most appropriate
- Knowledge to meet codes and good planning precepts
- The ability to execute any other tasks needed to complete the project requirements

Selling a service means selling an action that is yet to be performed. For the client, it is difficult to know what he or she is going to get until it is done. In addition, the client does not keep the service; rather, the client keeps the result of the service—in this case, a beautiful, functional interior. Perhaps this is why so many clients have difficulty understanding what goes into doing an interiors project. The client often does not "see" all the work that is done to develop the concept of a project before he or she is presented with floor plans, boards, and specifications.

"Whereas most goods are produced first, then sold and consumed, most services are sold first and then produced and consumed simultaneously."[2] The designer must sell the client on his or her ability to solve the client's problem, execute the requirements of the project within a budget, and actually make it all happen. Clients must believe and trust that the designer knows what he or she is doing and will follow through on the tasks necessary to complete the project.

A service is also said to be *perishable*. Because a service only takes place *as* it is taking place, it cannot be inventoried or resold. Goods, of course, can be inventoried and sold or subsequently returned, and the product can then be resold to someone else.

In contrast, once a designer has committed to work for a client, he or she cannot spend that *same* time working for another client. Of course, designers often work on more than one project at a time, but not literally. You cannot draft a floor plan for one client and literally draft a different floor plan for another client at the same time, any more than a student can be studying for an exam and having fun at a party at the same time.

Successfully selling the design concept is the culmination of the design-selling responsibilities of the interior design professional. Understanding the differences between selling services and selling products reveals how important it is for the interior designer to understand the selling process and learn how to be successful in navigating that process. Neglecting to learn these differences will hamper the designer's ability to sell services and produce sufficient revenue to maintain the business.

THE BUYER DECISION-MAKING PROCESS

Buyers consciously or unconsciously go through a process when they desire to purchase something. It doesn't matter if the purchase is a product or service. It does matter, however, if the good or service has special value—such as the selection of a doctor or interior designer—or the cost of the good or service is rather high as perceived or defined by the buyer. The process is very similar for residential and commercial clients. It is often suggested that the commercial client may take longer to make a decision, as many decision-maker levels might be involved in the decision. Residential designers also say that many of their clients seemingly take forever to make a decision!

The recognized buyer decision-making process involves five steps:

Step 1. Recognition of a need for something. The stronger the need, the more quickly the buyer moves through this step and into the rest of the process.

Step 2. Looking for information about the purchase need. Information might be obtained from:

- Providers of the product or service
- Friends and relatives
- Advertising in traditional media or the Internet

Step 3. Evaluation of alternatives. This can be thought of as an extension of Step 2, because choices begin to narrow as information about the choices is obtained. Exactly what is important is very personal to the buyer. Price or cost is often part of the evaluation step.

Step 4. The purchase decision. A purchase decision can be impulsive or well thought out. Interior design services are rarely made impulsively. A big part of the purchase decision involves price or cost. In general, a reasonable price is relative based on how the client perceives price. Naturally, the more money the client has, the more reasonable a high price will seem—within limits. A reasonable price is also tied to the concept of value in the buyer's mind. The more the buyer values something, the greater the price he or she is willing to pay.

Step 5. Postpurchase evaluation. Sometimes the buyer has feelings of "remorse" after the purchase. Residential clients may suddenly feel that the sofa is too expensive or "isn't the right color." A commercial client may be concerned that the project doesn't quite meet goals and that the boss will be upset about the purchase.

On the other end of the spectrum is the buyer who is elated by the choices made and can't wait to proceed. Most are somewhere in the middle, happy to have made the decision or purchase and pleased to get the goods to the home or office or begin the actual design process.

There is much in the general business literature on this topic, as in general buyers have more disposable income right now than ever before. Several books in the reference list might be of interest to readers concerned with this topic.

BUYER DEMOGRAPHICS

Demographic information helps businesses clarify their potential clients based on specific information segments. Information can be collected concerning age, gender, affluence, interests, and almost any other segment a market researcher wishes to pursue. For this brief section on buyer demographics, I have chosen to highlight generational characteristics. This particular category has a significant impact on buyers in general.

Market researchers agree that there are four groups of buyers based on generational characteristics. The oldest group are the Matures, followed by the Baby Boomers, followed by Generation X, and then the millennium generation (also called Generation Y). It is important to keep in mind that the characteristics of a generation will vary from those at the older edge of the generation to those at the younger edge. For example, the older Baby Boomer may already be on a fixed income and more financially conservative than a younger Baby Boomer who is still working full time and has more discretionary income.

Here's a glimpse of consumer demographics based on generational characteristics.

The Matures, born between 1901 and 1945

- Financially conservative
- Retired and focused on health issues
- Cautious about whom they do business with
- Value trust and quality
- Characterized as a wealthy generation
- Seek fewer possessions and smaller homes
- Expect salespeople to respect them

The Baby Boomers, born between 1946 and 1964

- The richest generation, although they were hit hard by the 2008 recession
- Health and retention of "youthful ideals" are important; don't want to be reminded that they are getting older
- Worked or continue to work as business owners or business leaders
- Downsizing homes, but conspicuous consumption still important
- Quality is a high priority in services and possessions
- Love to bargain and haggle and are always looking for a reduction in price
- Prefer doing business face-to-face, though gradually utilizing technology such as social media

Generation X, born between 1965 and 1979

- Very tech savvy, especially for practical use
- Wide acceptance of online purchasing
- Entering peak earning years
- Tough customers; want proof, information
- Less trusting and may be less willing to work with Baby Boomers
- Highly educated; want to know a lot about products or services
- More environmentally savvy than older generations
- Ready to buy homes and big-ticket items

Generation Y, or Millennials, born after 1979

- Very tech savvy; lead in use of social media and online consumerism (this also influences referrals and decisions to buy)
- Very interested in environmental issues and social responsibility
- More diverse and highly educated
- A large constituency will make this generation a formidable consumer for many years
- Value individuality; most casual in dress; design conscious

- Influence Baby Boomer and Generation X purchasing
- Are impatient; look for "something for nothing"; seek approval from friends

Although not a generation of buyers, an important demographic to include in this discussion is called *cultural creatives*. Identified in the literature in the later part of the 20th century, cultural creatives influence many aspects of life today. They have also played a significant role in the growth of sustainable design.

"These creative, optimistic millions are at the leading edge of several kinds of cultural change, deeply affecting not only their own lives but over society as well."[3] They come from all income levels and all of the different generations, have jobs across the career spectrum, and are represented by a larger percentage of women than men. Some influence social issues, such as alternative health, whereas others are more concerned about environmentalism. This all means that they cannot be pinned down by standard demographics.

Their interest in environmental issues means they will be exceptionally motivated by the marketing messages and practices of interior designers and firms that focus on green design. They may already know quite a bit about the topic, so the designer who works with this client had better really know the ins and outs of sustainable design!

Designers—regardless of years of experience in the profession—need to understand what influences the different generations in their personal purchasing as well as their influences on the businesses they work in or own. Treating a Mature buyer like a Millennial buyer, and vice versa, will definitely mean "no sale," regardless of the designer's talent and experiences.

Detailed census data, including many demographic characteristics by state, are available on line from the U.S. Census Bureau (www.census.gov/). Additional statistical information can be obtained from the Bureau of Labor Statistics (www.bls.gov) and many other sources. There are also numerous books detailing buyers by generation, gender, and wealth. Several have been added to the reference list in this text. A classic starting point on buyer behavior is *Why We Buy* by Paco Underhill.

BUILDING CLIENT RELATIONSHIPS

Marketing and sales experts continually discuss the importance of building client relationships in this highly competitive world. We do it when we ask for the same waitress at a favorite restaurant: What is happening is that we are building a relationship with the waitress. Naturally, the designer seeks to build relationships with clients. In building client relationships, the focus is on helping the design firm and the client become partners, ideally in working toward long-term commitments.

Clients prefer to work with someone whom they already know, rather than finding a new interior designer. Relationships should be built so that clients think of the same designer and firm whenever they need interior design services. For the designer, working from time to time with former clients is also cost effective. The cost of prospecting for new clients is greater than that of maintaining existing client relationships.

It is not easy for designers to develop this type of partnership with many clients. Some clients only require design services once, maybe twice in a lifetime. These encounters may happen many years apart. Furthermore, for some clients, a lasting relationship is not desirable, because they had a bad experience. The converse is also true: Sometimes the designer does not want to continue the relationship with a very difficult client (and unfortunately, there are quite a few of them).

The interior design of a residence is an intensely personal experience for clients. It is their home. It is where they will raise the children, share family accomplishments and perhaps tragedies, and entertain friends and business associates. Bringing a stranger into the home can be difficult for the family. The designer must show concern, thoughtfulness, and empathy for the clients' interiors problems. Being totally businesslike certainly has its place, but so does having a sense of humor and knowing when it is all right to relax and be casual.

The interior design of a commercial space is less personal, but the relationship that must be built between the parties is no less important. The client must trust the designer to specify hundreds of thousands of dollars' worth of construction and products, using the client's financial resources. The client certainly must trust the designer to create an interior that solves the client's problems and meets whatever the client's goals and needs may be. This trust is a very important part of the relationship.

Developing sustainable relationships with clients is not an easy task. Despite the difficulties that may be encountered, doing so will very likely result in repeat business, referrals, and success for the design firm. The trust that must exist between the designer and the client takes time to build; it is easy to lose and difficult to gain but worth every effort to achieve.

SELLING TECHNIQUES

Design services do not sell themselves. The interior designer must use many kinds of selling and communication techniques to arrive at the point where the client is comfortable in making the decision to hire a designer or agreeing to allow the designer to continue with the design ideas offered. Using the selling techniques described throughout this chapter helps the designer reach those outcomes.

It is not possible to turn the reader into an expert salesperson with these few brief pages. It takes time and experience to become skillful at selling concepts and products to clients. Which techniques will help the designer sell his or her services and products is a very personal matter. What works well for one designer can lead to frustration and failure for another.

Two important characteristics are always present in the selling and presentation methods used by successful designers: *enthusiasm* for what they are doing and *interest* in the needs of the client. Successful professionals must have a genuine interest in their clients and the needs of those clients. When the designer realizes this, it is a lot easier to bring the encounter with the client to a successful conclusion. Showing a sincere interest in helping the client will yield positive results for the designer regardless of the techniques used to help sell the client.

Two techniques are briefly introduced in this section: probing, and features and benefits. These techniques come from tried-and-true methods of selling products, but readers will see how they can be applied to the discussion of and selling of interior design services.

Probing

"Mr. Jones, I understand that you need to remodel your office spaces due to the increase in the number of employees. I believe you said earlier that you are interested in using open-office systems as a possibility to increase the number of employees you can accommodate in your existing space," said Arthur Thompson, an interior designer.

This brief statement is an example of probing for information. *Probing* is a technique of asking different kinds of questions to uncover the client's needs. Some questions that the designer asks will elicit a closed response—yes or no—and thus are referred to as *closed probes*. Other questions are formulated to encourage the client to talk and give a lengthier response. This second kind of probing question is called an *open probe*. Which type of probe did Arthur use with Mr. Jones?

Closed-probe questions are geared toward eliciting specific information. They are also used when the client is not particularly responsive to other kinds of questions. For example, a designer might ask this short series of questions:

Designer: Do you have a preferred color scheme?

Client: Not really.

Designer: Do you prefer warmer colors, like oranges, rusts, and yellows?

Client: No.

Designer: Do you prefer cool colors, like blue and green?

Client: Yes.

Designer: Would a color scheme combining blues and greens be satisfactory to you?

Client: I think I would like that.

Open-probe questions, in contrast, attempt to get the client talking freely about some topic. They are also used to get the client to expand on previously mentioned information or to talk about broader concepts. For example, an interior designer is interviewing a doctor who plans to open a new family practice medical suite with other doctors. The designer might say, "Tell me about any ideas you have on how to accommodate small children and their parents in the waiting room." Hopefully, such a question will get the doctors to provide ideas on, or at least explain their perceptions of, this important topic.

What types of questions could Arthur ask to clarify the information he needs to expand on what was said in the opening example? What questions might Arthur ask to move on to other important programming information related to the opening example?

By means of a careful combination of open and closed probes, the designer can obtain the information required to discover the actual needs of the client. These kinds of questions can also be used successfully when the designer is handling objections that the client has raised during the actual work on a design project.

Features and Benefits

Another important selling technique that is useful in any kind of selling situation is that of describing features and benefits. *Features* are specific aspects or characteristics of a product or service; for example, a plastic laminate top is a feature of many desks. *Benefits* are features of a product or service that directly relate to a client's need for that product or service; for example, a benefit of the plastic laminate desktop might relate to the ease of maintenance (it is easily cleaned and will not mar as easily as a wooden desktop).

When the designer is discussing services, it is far more important to discuss the benefits of the service than any features, because it is more difficult to explain and understand the features of services. A feature of the design firm's

TABLE 25-1.

Tips for successful selling outcomes

Listen carefully to the client.
Ask questions that are thoughtful and that show you are listening.
Be sure to let the client talk; don't monopolize the conversation.
Have a positive attitude and be enthusiastic.
Never interrupt.
Never, ever argue!
Be polite and respectful toward the client.
Do not sound like you are begging for work.
Do not sound insincere.
Always work toward a win–win outcome.
Dress and sound like a professional.
Use third-party testimonials as evidence of the firm's expertise.
Remember that it takes time to build a relationship. Do not feel bad if you have to come back three or four times to close the sale.
Always say thank-you and follow up promptly on any promises.

services could be error-free working drawings. However, the client already expects drawings to be perfect. What, then, might be a benefit of the firm's service of preparing working drawings? One benefit is that the designer provides a one-stop, single source for project documents. When the designer is trying to think of benefits of services, he or she should think of outcomes that provide value to the client. What are some benefits of interior design services for a couple who is planning to build a custom home or for an organization that is planning to build a convention center?

Once the designer knows the client's needs, it is relatively easy for him or her to point out the various features and benefits of the designer's services or products as they relate to those needs. If the services and products meet the needs of the client, it will be much easier and quicker to obtain confirmation and close the sale.

Both probing and the features-and-benefits technique can assist the designer in the selling situation. Another technique related to the selling process is negotiation. Overcoming objections and methods of closing are discussed in Chapter 26. A few other ideas on how to have a successful selling outcome are offered in Table 25-1.

NEGOTIATING

You undoubtedly have already been involved in many negotiation situations, even if you have not yet worked in the interior design field. Perhaps you negotiated to get a few extra days from a professor to complete a project or a paper. Or it could have been to obtain a raise at a part-time job.

The professional interior designer is negotiating all the time—the subjects range from better pricing from a vendor or a more favorable installation date from the wallpaper hanger to the hourly fee charged by the designer's accountant. When you (or your client) want something that the other person may not want you to have, you are probably entering into a negotiating situation.

Let's be clear: *Negotiating* is an activity wherein two parties are trying to reach agreement about some point on which they currently disagree. In the ideal situation, the negotiation proceeds so that the two parties who start out on opposite sides of an issue come to a mutually agreeable conclusion. In other words, negotiating should create a *win–win* situation so that both parties are satisfied. If a negotiation creates an "I win, you lose" situation, then it is not a successful negotiation, because only one party is happy. The "I win, you lose" conclusion is not a negotiation, but rather manipulation—and manipulation has no place in the skill set of a successful interior designer.

Successful negotiation requires the use of strategies that are similar to those used in any other type of selling:

- Know your goals and objectives for entering into the negotiation.
- Try to anticipate what the other party might want and/or object to.
- Have the facts straight concerning your position.
- Know what your "bottom line" is.

As it might seem to suggest, negotiation involves discussion. Both you and the client (or whomever you are negotiating with) will state a position. You must carefully explain how you feel about the other person's position without being negative, but instead stressing the positive side of your position. The other party will counter with its position and reasons that its position is better, stronger, or more reasonable. Negotiations aimed at win–win solutions will always include some give-and-take, as (hopefully) each side sees some value in what the other party is saying.

For example, a client tells you that a $15,000 design fee is too high. She says someone else quoted only $10,000. You might counter by explaining the steps that will be needed to accomplish the scope of services, how you go through the design process, and the value that your services will provide. You could decide it is possible to delete a few of the steps in the scope, though the end result you understand the client wants may not be the same. Of course, many other approaches can be taken in this type of negotiation.

Eventually, after discussion and counterproposals, an agreement is reached—or not. One or the other party to the negotiation can sooner or later hit its bottom line, where it is no longer willing to budge. Someone gives in, or the parties agree to disagree and walk away.

Knowing when and where to negotiate is also important. Control of the environment is why designers prefer to make marketing presentations in their offices or studios rather than at the client's location. If the client greets you at the entry with a scowl and tells you about the terrible time she just had with the cable service, it is no time to negotiate or make a presentation with the expectation of obtaining a positive outcome. If possible, reschedule when the client is no longer frantic and angry. This type of thinking about when and where applies to other kinds of negotiations as well. If you can, conduct the negotiation for a raise somewhere other than your boss's office. Take your boss to lunch and discuss this topic in a neutral place.

Always giving in may garner work for designers, but eventually it will make them feel less valuable and make it harder each time to negotiate for what is really fair. On the other hand, being hardheaded and demanding his or her own way creates a very poor impression of the dilettante designer. Not many clients in today's competitive market will stand for that attitude anymore.

Skill in negotiation is not a gift that comes naturally to most professional designers, but it can be learned. Each successful negotiation affects how you conduct future negotiations. How you go about a negotiation session will also affect the future relationship between the individuals involved. Table 25-2 lists some tips that might help in negotiations.

TABLE 25-2.

Ideas for negotiation

Start with a plan. When you are about to negotiate an important design contract or a salary increase, do not fool yourself into thinking that you can pull it off without planning what you are going to say.

Only negotiate for what you are prepared to do or are able to do. Do not put anything on the table that you have no intention of doing or cannot accomplish.

Always be truthful. A successful negotiation depends on trust between the two parties. If the parties to a negotiation do not trust each other, they will never be able to negotiate anything successfully.

Have patience. The best negotiators know that it takes patience to work toward a win–win conclusion. Nobody likes being browbeaten or intimidated into making a decision. You gain an advantage when you take your time rather than rush.

Use your power. Power is based on perception. If you think you have it, you do. Using your power means having confidence in yourself and your point of view.

Understand that conflict is inevitable in many business situations. Not every client is really ready to work with a professional designer or can afford one; you may also not want to work with a particular client who contacts you.

TABLE 25-3.

Steps in the selling process

1. *Prospecting*. Locate viable prospective clients.
2. *Qualifying*. Clarify if these prospects can work with you.
3. *Preparation*. Do homework and prepare everything needed for the presentation.
4. *Presentation*. Make an appropriate presentation to the client.
5. *Overcoming objections*. Resolve client questions or concerns.
6. *Closing*. Ask for the sale or job.
7. *Follow-up*. Provide documentation or actions promised during the presentation.

THE SELLING PROCESS

If the selling process is to be successful for the interior designer, a flow of activities and communications has to take place. Table 25-3 outlines the seven generally accepted steps in the selling process. The steps concerning prospecting and qualifying are discussed in this chapter, as they focus on selling. Those concentrating on presentation and follow-up are discussed in Chapter 26.

Prospecting

It would be nice if clients purchased services from interior designers on a regular basis. Unfortunately, interior design services are not a commodity such as apparel that is purchased frequently, nor do designers generally have continuous-service jobs like professionals such as attorneys. Clients do sometimes come back to the same designer. That is a big reason why developing a good business and professional relationship with clients is so important. However, finding new clients is a continuing issue for most interior designers.

Finding new clients does, to some extent, include "digging around" for them. That is probably why the term *prospecting* has become associated with the sales process. *Prospecting* is the process of locating new clients and obtaining appointments with them in order to discuss how the design firm may assist the client. *Prospects* are potential clients in the firm's business area or target market who may require design services. They include clients who have worked with competitors, though not clients who already are under contract with competitors.

Potential clients are identified in many ways:

- Target-market research.
- Responses to the many promotional methods discussed in Chapters 23, 24, and 25.
- *Cold-calling*, which is contacting potential clients whom the designer has not met before. Telephone solicitations and direct mail are both cold-calling methodologies.
- *Warm calling* occurs when the designer has received an entrée to the client through a referral of some type. A designer does not know this potential client, however.

When a prospect begins to show interest in a firm, he or she might be referred to as a *lead*. A lead might be a client who calls the designer after seeing an article about the design firm in the newspaper or a trade magazine. By generating leads, the design firm identifies the best prospects for selling the interior design firm's services.

Many designers make the mistake of stopping the prospecting activity after obtaining one or a few new clients. This is a big mistake, as time must always be devoted to finding new work. Even having a project in hand does not automatically mean that the project will continue to its conclusion as described in the scope of services. And unfortunately, sometimes the client does not pay the bills for work that is done, leaving the designer with little income. Continuing to prospect and build strong relationships with clients is always necessary; any client might change designers for the next project. With a commercial client, the decision maker might leave the company.

An important issue is where to find prospects. The marketing methods discussed in Chapter 24 are to some extent passive on the designer's part, as many are built on waiting for a response from a potential client. Prospecting must also be active on the designer's part.

For residential interior designers, actively seeking clients most often involves getting referrals from former clients, vendors, and even social and civic activities. Thus, it should be easy to see that doing an outstanding job on every project for every client is important in getting referrals. Client referrals are critical, as many clients only want to work with service providers they know or whom friends of theirs know. You should go back to the section on referrals in Chapter 23 if you did not read it.

For commercial interior designers, actively seeking clients may involve:

- Attending trade conferences and possibly exhibiting at the conferences potential clients attend
- Reading trade publications of potential clients to help identify possible clients
- Reading local publications to determine new businesses opening in the market area

Do not be afraid to prospect for business. If you believe in your design skills and abilities, your confidence should be high when meeting with new clients. Boost your confidence by participating in networking groups where you will have to make presentations to groups or meet and mingle with people who are not directly affiliated with interior design. There are likely hundreds of groups in your area.

It is not uncommon for the designer to make a brief prospecting presentation before the client allows the designer to make a full presentation. Some designers refer to this encounter as the initial meeting. The initial meeting is discussed in Chapter 26.

Qualifying

Identifying potential prospects—or leads—is only the first step in the process. The designer must also qualify prospects. *Qualifying* means the designer determines whether there is sufficient reason to pursue a prospect. A *qualified prospect* is one who has been determined to be a reasonable client of the interior designer. Not all prospects will meet this criterion.

The designer's time is likely limited for prospecting and developing new business, as he or she must also continue work on existing projects. Consequently, it is important for the designer to devote time to those potential clients who have the greatest likelihood of retaining the designer—that is, those target clients identified in the marketing plan. Qualified prospects must have a need for interior design services, and not all potential clients in the firm's business area are really viable prospects. For the design firm that specializes in restaurant design, for example, facilities that have been open for only a year or so will not need design services for some time. Restaurants that have been open for several years, however, may be looking for some kind of assistance.

Qualified prospects must also be able to pay the fees expected by the interior designer. Can the potential client afford the fees the designer charges? There are certainly many potential clients that could utilize the services of an interior design professional, but not all will have the means to pay the fees and not all will be good credit risks. Credit ratings of commercial clients can be checked, and diplomatic discussions and questioning can be undertaken to find out whether a residential client has the income to afford hiring the designer. Of course, credit checks can also be conducted on residential clients.

Another qualifying criterion most associated with commercial design is whether the prospect has the authority to make a purchasing decision. The designer must get to the person who is in charge, or he or she could be wasting time. Sometimes it is not easy to get to a decision maker. Assistants to upper-level management personnel are very good at keeping unsolicited callers from getting to the executives.

A fully qualified lead usually results in an appointment for a face-to-face meeting. Now the designer is ready for the next step: the preparation of an initial consultation or other type of marketing presentation.

Preparation

Whatever the purpose of the presentation, preparation is needed. You have no doubt heard of or seen presentations made by a colleague where it is obvious that very little if any preparation was done. Students frequently make the mistake of presenting their projects without thinking through what they want to say. The lack of preparation can have huge negative implications.

I have heard of many designers who like to "wing" a presentation: They simply go to the meeting and discuss whatever comes up. This technique might work for a project presentation to clients with whom the designer has a good relationship. It is a very unwise choice for the designer when he or she is trying to win a contract with a new client or make a final presentation. "Winging it" rarely impresses a client.

Presentations or an initial meeting with a potential client where the designer is trying to win that client's business require preparation. The designer probably obtained valuable information about the direction and content of the presentation when the initial contact was made. The following are just a few of the questions that the designer must answer to prepare the best possible marketing presentation.

1. What are the prospective project requirements?
2. To whom will the presentation be made?
3. How many people will attend the presentation?
4. Where will the presentation take place?
5. Who from the design firm should be involved in the presentation?
6. What will the client want to know about the design firm?
7. What kind of graphics will be used as evidence of the design firm's design expertise?
8. What materials and documents will be given to the client to keep?

The answers to all of these questions, and perhaps others, will have an influence on the content and format of the presentation itself.

It is critical for the designer to ensure that the presentation addresses the prospective client's questions and concerns, as well as achieving the designer's objectives. Sufficient attention and time must be allowed to clarify those objectives and inform the clients about what they want to know. Obviously, the design firm's primary objective is to obtain the go-ahead to prepare a design contract. But there can be other goals as well. Making sure the prospective client learns about the design firm's design philosophy, methodology in project management, and expertise is very important.

An important step is to clarify the identity of the *decision makers*, the person or persons who have the authority to hire the designer. This is not always easy or obvious. In residential design, the designer rarely consults in this early stage with anyone but the owner of the home and the family, but who is the decision maker in the family—the husband or the wife? It is quite common for the designer to meet with only one of the household partners, but the person not frequently involved may be the actual decision maker. The interior designer must find this out as quickly and diplomatically as possible.

For a commercial project, it is not uncommon for the design firm to make the initial contact with a purchasing agent or even a secretary, rather than the owner or the principal of the company. In such cases, the designer may make an initial presentation to the purchasing agent and a more formal presentation to the owner at a later time. Presentations for many commercial projects often are made to a group of clients. For example, a medical office building may be owned by a group of doctors.

Understanding who the decision maker really is and having that individual be present at all meetings is ideal—but rarely the case for commercial projects. With a residential project, the designer may have to meet after 5:00 PM to get both partners to be present at meetings. Diplomatically observing that this will save time in the long run may help bring a reluctant residential decision maker to the meetings.

Here are some other important tips about preparation before the initial meeting with the client:

- Remember that when you present at the client's home or office, they control the presentation environment. When practicable, present at your office or a neutral location. This is not always feasible for residential projects, however.
- Plan your presentation to be sure it fits within the time limit the client has given you. An outline is always helpful in planning your time.
- Determine who from the design firm will be involved and each person's role in the meeting. For a commercial project, it might be important to have those actually involved in the design of the project at the meeting. However, anyone else who attends a meeting should also play an important part.
- Materials to be shown should relate to the project under consideration. Customize the media to the specific client project. A few items from other types of projects can be helpful to explain your design philosophy, but do not overwhelm the client with photos that do not pertain to the project.
- Make sure your equipment works for the presentation and can be comfortably viewed by everyone in the group. Bring your own projector to be sure you have what you need to show your graphics.
- Remember that preparation involves making an impression. There is an old saying that you only have one chance to make a first impression. Yes, professional dress and attitude make a difference for all clients.

In organizing the outline of the presentation, the designer should follow the basic form for outlining and organizing material for any report or presentation:

1. Tell them what you are going to tell them.
2. Tell them.
3. Tell them what you have just told them.
4. Ask for the sale.

The first step, "Tell them what you are going to tell them," quite simply involves creating an overview of the information that will be discussed at the meeting. Key items include reviewing the agenda, introducing other members of the design firm, and briefly describing what each person will discuss. The purpose of the first step is to stimulate the potential client's attention and interest. Even though the client has agreed to meet with the designer (which automatically suggests interest), the client still needs a reason to listen to the presentation. The designer must provide that reason during this first step.

The second step, "Tell them," consists of giving the body of the presentation itself. All of the material in this section on preparation indicates the kinds of information that the design firm likely needs to tell the client. What is important as to the "telling" is for all the presenters to be enthusiastic, alert to the client's body language, and responsive to the client's questions. Questions, by the way, are not bad. Questions mean the client is listening. In fact, the designer should involve clients by asking them questions. If the discussion digresses from the outline, the designer should go back to any item that he or she feels should still be covered.

Step 3, "Tell them what you have just told them," consists of giving a summary of the points that you made during the presentation. Always remind the client of the important points that he or she has heard. Remember to highlight the features and benefits of your services as they relate to the needs that the client has expressed.

The last step, "Ask for the sale," amounts to requesting that the client give the go-ahead for the design firm to prepare a design contract, sign an already prepared contract, or in some other way provide a positive conclusion to the presentation. In other words, this is the "close" of the marketing presentation. Chapter 26 discusses closing in more detail.

The biggest mistake the designer can make during the marketing presentation is to ignore the client's goals and questions. During this very early phase of a potential project, too many designers get carried away with telling their story and forget to tell the client what he or she wants to know. The designer who has been careful to answer the client's questions as well as covering what the design firm wishes to tell about itself will conclude the presentation on a positive note.

Chapter 26 discusses the remaining parts of the selling process, with emphasis on the presentation.

WEB SITES RELEVANT TO THIS CHAPTER

www.bls.gov Bureau of Labor Statistics

www.census.gov Census Bureau

www.nasp.com National Association of Sales Professionals

KEY TERMS

Benefits	Open probe
Closed probe	Probing
Cold-calling	Prospecting
Decision makers	Prospects
Features	Qualifying
Intangible	Selling
Lead	Warm calling
Negotiating	

WHAT WOULD YOU DO?

1. Rose Marie started her own design practice after having been fired from Miller/Jones Interior Architecture. Rose Marie was a competent designer, but about three months before her boss decided to fire her, she started making mistakes that cost the design firm in extra services and lost revenue. One example of her problems was a time when she had to leave town on family business: She did not leave any instructions for anyone else in the firm about her pending jobs. Rose Marie also failed to leave a forwarding phone number and didn't get in touch with the office for 10 days.

   During a presentation that Rose Marie is making to a new client, the client comments that he is also talking to the Miller/Jones firm.

Rose Marie makes very disparaging comments about Miller/Jones without mentioning that she was fired from that firm. The client hires Rose Marie instead.

2. Amanda and Tom were just finishing up their presentation to the building selection committee at the university for a redesign of the interior of the student union. They had made the short list and were very happy to have an opportunity to explain how their firm would approach the project should they be awarded the contract. Amanda has great one-on-one presence with clients, so she really worked hard on relating to and building rapport with the committee members. Tom focused on discussing the technical methodologies they would use.

   After the meeting, Amanda and Tom think that they have the project in the bag. A week later, though, the owner of the design firm receives a phone call from the chair of the building selection committee. He tells the firm owner that they are quite upset, because one of the committee members reported that he had experienced what he felt was improper behavior by one of the team members in an attempt to influence the committee's decision.

3. A client, Susan Brown, arrives for her appointment with Rita Jones of Master's Office Furniture carrying her laptop computer and some sample boards. After some pleasantries, Ms. Brown sets up her computer in order to show Rita some drawings.

   Ms. Brown explains, "We are planning to build six urgent-care centers in the immediate vicinity and two to four more in other parts of the state. They will all have the footprint shown in these drawings. We want your firm to provide a minimal amount of design time to specify upholstery fabric and wall accessories to fit into the environment of this state. Naturally, we will be buying all the furniture and finish materials from your firm except the floor coverings. Those will be provided by the contractor."

   Rita looks closely at the drawings on the laptop and notices a design title block from a design firm in another state. The sample boards look like a label that was glued to the board has been removed.

   "Why aren't you having the design firm that created the drawings do this work for you?" asks Rita.

   "Oh, we've paid them their fee and don't want to pay them for travel to this state," Ms. Brown replies.

REFERENCES

1. *World Book Encyclopedia*, 2000, p. 62.
2. Zeithaml and Bitner, 1996, p. 20.
3. Ray and Anderson, 2000, p. 4.

Design Presentations

After completing this chapter you should be able to:

- Discuss why it is important to know that presentations may be required in several different situations.
- Identify any differences between an initial presentation and a marketing presentation.
- Compare the focus of presentation points in a preliminary project presentation with those in a final project presentation.
- Discuss why it is important to prepare for any type of presentation.
- Explain why and how understanding body language can benefit the interior designer.
- Compare a general marketing presentation to a presentation given in response to an RFP.
- Discuss why it is important to know something about the people on a selection committee.
- Discuss strategies to overcome objections.
- Discuss why it is important for a designer to ask for the sale rather than waiting for the client to volunteer to buy.
- Discuss what kinds of things should be noted when following up on a marketing or initial meeting and the final presentation, beyond notes on the project scope itself.
- Summarize why it is important for a design professional to be aware of and use good business etiquette at all times.
- Discuss why making a good impression through one's business dress and behavior can make a difference in the success of an interior designer.

NCIDQ COMPONENT

Based on best information available, some material in this chapter might appear as part of the NCIDQ examination. The reader should not depend solely on this text for study material. See the sections on presentation techniques.

Winning clients is never easy. There is plenty of competition in all markets, so interior designers must take the matter of presenting themselves and the design firm very seriously. Even those with a strong reputation must sell themselves and their concepts and solutions.

In Chapter 25, we reviewed the first three stages of the selling process: prospecting, qualifying, and preparation. This chapter focuses on and emphasizes professional design presentations. The emphasis is appropriate because professional presentations are so critically important to the designer's overall activities.

The presentation made after the potential client has shown some initial interest in the design firm is arguably the most important of these activities. If the encounter does not go well and a relationship between the designer and the potential client is not begun, there will be no project to execute.

This chapter provides some basic guidelines for making design presentations. It also discusses the other stages of the sales process that bring the process to a conclusion: overcoming objections, closing, and follow-up.

The material under the heading "Good Impressions" is included here to bring to the forefront the importance of certain etiquette and issues related to presentations. Although the focus of this information is on the presentations made by practitioners, students can learn important tips about how to present their class projects.

PRESENTATIONS

Presentations are conducted for all sorts of reasons: to present information about the design firm; to land a new project; to go over plans and documents concerning the project. Even job interviews can be considered presentation interactions.

Presentation interactions can take many different forms, from casual to formal. They can be one-on-one meetings between the interior designer and the client or a group of clients. They can be held at the designer's studio, the client location, or even at a restaurant.

There are several common presentation situations with clients:

- Initial client interview
- Marketing presentation
- Presentation of the design contract
- Response to proposal presentation
- Presentation of design ideas during the course of a project
- Concept or final presentations to a client group

A presentation also serves the purpose of continuing to build the relationship with the client. The client hires an interior designer for design skill, experience, creativity, and other reasons. He or she also hires the interior designer because of a feeling of a relationship between the parties.

Both the client and the interior designer have goals for the outcome of the presentation. The designer is seeking agreement from the client to the design ideas presented. The client may have many goals, some of which may be completely hidden from the designer. Thus, as much as possible during each presentation, the designer should reinforce how he or she can and will solve the client's concerns and meet the client's goals.

Making any kind of presentation is very stressful for many professionals and students. Public speaking is one of the most feared activities. Although

TABLE 26-1.

Presentation tactics

Organize and plan the presentation ahead of time.
An agenda or outline for the presentation should be prepared, and the role of each participating member of the firm should be determined.
Stick to the time limit. Don't assume that you can go beyond the agreed time allowance.
Try to control the presentation by where it is held. Holding the meeting at the designer's office allows the designer to control the meeting and control potential interruptions.
If you must go to the client's location, try to make the presentation in a conference room (for a commercial project) or the dining room (for a residential project). Both are more neutral than an office or the living room. Prepare yourself for the possibility of interruptions.
Maintain good eye contact (an indication of honesty) about 50 percent of the time.
Do not be too informal until you have established a relationship with the client or the client has indicated that it is okay to be less formal.
Beware of using fillers like *er, well, okay, you see*, and *umm*. These words indicate powerlessness and nervousness. Use professional language without getting hung up in jargon or highly technical descriptions.
Do not distribute handouts, including the contract (unless the review of the contract is the actual purpose of the meeting) until the verbal portion of the presentation is nearly completed.
Focus on the client and his or her needs.

giving a design presentation is not exactly the same as public speaking, it still requires the designer to stand up (figuratively or literally) in front of one or more people and be in the spotlight. Presentation skills develop, and stress reduction occurs, according to the number of presentations given: the more the better.

The kind of preparation described in Chapter 25 can help alleviate butterflies in the stomach. There is no better way to get over being nervous than to make presentations, review what went wrong and right, and improve for the next opportunity.

A number of tactics can be used to improve presentation skills and effectiveness. Several are offered in Table 26-1. These tactics apply to almost all the different presentations that an interior designer might make. Please note that material about a marketing presentation has been placed on the Wiley companion Web site and marked Item 26-1.

Additional tips on making presentations are offered at the end of this chapter.

THE INITIAL CLIENT INTERVIEW

It would be nice if there were one surefire way to conduct the initial meeting with the client. The *initial interview*, of course, is the first time the designer presents any kind of information to the client. Unfortunately, there are as many ways to approach and conduct this important meeting as there are designers and clients. Still, there are several points to keep in mind, regardless of the type of client or specialty.

Having a plan for the initial meeting leads to greater success. A common suggestion is to develop an outline after reviewing the success (or lack thereof) of previous initial meetings. Some designers use forms such as the one shown in Figure 11-2 to help gather needed information.

The most important information for the designer to obtain during this initial meeting is an understanding of the scope of the project and the client's ideas on what has to be done. Not getting the scope right typically dooms even a promising project to failure. Another key piece of information is the budget. Clients are very likely to say that they don't know what the budget will be yet. You must do the best you can to determine budget constraints by careful and diplomatic questioning. That will save time and possible headaches and grief in the future. Naturally, many other key points must also be determined, and they should be listed on your outline or form.

Where is the best place to hold the presentation meeting? That will depend on the interior designer's personal preference and the type of project. Many interior designers like to visit the project site for the initial presentation, to help them get a feel for the project. Sometimes this is impractical if the project is under construction and a good space for the meeting is not available. Residential interior designers tend to like to make an initial presentation at the client's home or site. Commercial interior designers usually prefer to control the presentation environment, and thus conduct the meeting at their offices. Commercial designers often use PowerPoint presentations as part of an initial meeting and it is often easier to do that at the office.

"Take notes, take a lot of notes, always take notes" was advice given to me when I was just starting out in the profession. It is easy to forget small details as you run from one meeting to another appointment. You shouldn't tape-record the meeting unless the potential client gives you permission to do so. Don't forget to bring a tape measure in case you need to measure the space right away (although this is really a service you should do only after the contract is signed).

Avoid the temptation to give away design ideas at the first meeting. Clients of all types are often anxious to pick your brain for ideas—and then possibly hire someone else. Make it clear that the initial meeting is to obtain a clear picture of what the client needs and not to make design suggestions.

Of course, you must also be prepared to talk about yourself or your firm and how you proceed through the stages of a project. Bring along any brochures or other leave-behinds that you want to give clients to help them decide about you. They will also want to know how you charge. You certainly can discuss this issue in a broad sense by saying something like "I charge an hourly fee." Refrain from getting too specific. You can do that after you prepare a contract proposal.

Should you charge for the initial meeting? This is a recurring question with several possible answers. Many residential interior designers charge for an initial meeting; some of them credit that charge to the project once a contract is signed. Others feel that the initial meeting is a marketing expense and do not charge for it. Commercial designers—except those in the very highest echelons of the industry—do not charge for an initial meeting. If you do charge for the initial meeting, it is very important to make that clear to the client when you set up the meeting, not at the meeting itself.

PROJECT PRESENTATIONS

Interior design professionals must make numerous presentations during the course of any project. Each one is important in itself, whether it is a brief encounter or a lengthy meeting. Project presentations should also be considered important marketing opportunities, because any encounter with a client or potential clients is a chance to enhance or diminish the designer's reputation with the client. This section briefly discusses some key points concerning project presentations.

Preliminary Project Presentations

During the course of a project, the designer might make dozens of mini-presentations, referred to here as *preliminary project presentations*. The goal of the designer during a preliminary project presentation is to obtain client approval of whatever is being discussed. It is likely, however, that the client will have objections and discussions will be needed during some of these mini-presentations. A tactic some use is to make certain types of suggestions so as to guarantee that at least one of them will be vetoed, in order to direct the client toward the solution(s) the designer wishes to pursue.

Table 26-2 lists several characteristics of a preliminary presentation.

It is important for clients to sign off on approved products and floor plan proposals. A form such as the one in Figure 26-1 can be used to detail preliminary and final product specifications. This form has also been included on the companion Web site as Item 26-2.

Note that the form provides a space for the client to initial or sign. Signed approvals allow the designer to move on through the project with confidence. A client signature or even initials on the marked-up copy of the floor plan or specification indicates agreement to what is shown; thus, it also provides a mechanism for the designer to charge clients for work that has to be redone if the client changes his or her mind *after* the initial approval.

Final Project Presentations

It is customary to have a final presentation of the project documents at the end of the design development stage of the project. This final presentation is done to review the design decisions one last time. The goal of the final project presentation is to obtain the go-ahead to begin the remaining construction documents and specifications that will be needed. It is common that a few changes will still be necessary, however. All the client's last-minute concerns and hesitations must be resolved at this time so that the project can move forward. Keep the tips in Table 26-3 in mind when preparing for the final presentation.

Presentation of the final cost estimates or actual final cost of the project is also done at this time. The designer must be ready not only to defend design decisions, but also to answer any questions about costs of the project. It is advised that the designer once again obtain signed approvals on product selections and plans. The signed documents become part of the project files, just like those obtained during the preliminary presentation.

TABLE 26-2.

Characteristics of preliminary presentations

They are usually less formal than marketing and proposal presentations. Informality allows the necessary give-and-take that must occur in the early stages of the project.
Presentation style should create a comfortable atmosphere that involves the client.
Always give the client some choices during the presentation.
Changes in the plans can be sketched on the CAD sheets or on tracing paper.
Take plenty of notes to be sure all changes are incorporated into revised documents.
Obtain client sign-offs on all drawings and changes, as well as all product specifications.
The best place to make presentations will depend on the size and type of project.
Involve the client in the presentation by asking the client questions.
Questions that bring acceptance of the concepts under discussion usually lead to agreement for the whole concept.

Product Control Sheet

Job Name: _____   **Job #:** _____

Room/Areas: _____   **Control #:** _____

Item Specification			
Item Number:			
Manufacturer:			
Catalog Number:			
Case/Frame Finish:			
Hardware Finish:			
Size	W:	D:	Ht:
Other:			
Special Installation Instructions:			
Fabric:			
Grade:		Yards Required/Unit:	
Repeat:		Special Treatment:	
COM Supplier:			

Sketch/Photograph	Fabric Swatch

Delivery Time:	Shipping Location: _____
	_____
	_____

Unit Price (net):	Quantity:
Upholstery:	
Special handling:	Freight:
Total Item Net:	Delivery:

Client Signature: _____

© 2012, Christine M. Piotrowski

FIGURE 26-1.

A typical control sheet that can be used for client sign-off on each item on which agreement has been reached.

TABLE 26-3.

Five big mistakes when making presentations and selling

1. Talking too much and not listening
2. Using buzz words and terminology the client does not understand
3. Not paying attention to the client's needs and wants
4. Caring more about you than about the client
5. Failing to close/ask for the sale

As with the other types of presentations, it is a good idea for the designer to spend some time after the presentation has been made to review what went right and wrong during the presentation. A postpresentation review form can help formalize and organize the notes on what happened during the presentation. Obviously, this is more important if the client had lots of questions and problems with the final presentation documents. Generally, however, this presentation generates only minor changes to the plans, specifications, and other documents, so the designer can move ahead with preparation of the project bid documents or purchase orders. An example of a form that can be used to do a post-project review can be found on the companion Web site as Item 26-3.

Body Language

Nonverbal communication is said to be 75 to 90 percent of effective communication.* Experts such as Julius Fast believe that body language is a more accurate indication of a person's true feelings than the words he or she says. For the designer who understands how to interpret body language, it can be a very powerful tool in helping to sell.

The study of body language comes from scientific study of the meaning of body positions and gestures, called *kinesics*.** The clues we give through body positions and gestures often more accurately reflect what we are thinking than the words we use. Knowing how to read these signals helps designers to discern whether a client is really interested in what the designer is saying or even if the client is upset at what is being discussed—even though he or she hasn't said anything. We all give clues to what we are thinking through our body language.

One of the most important elements of body language is eye contact. Not making eye contact can be interpreted as meaning that you do not really think the other person is important. When you fail to make eye contact, you send a message that can be interpreted as arrogance: "I'm better than you." Both of these messages are bad to send to your client—or to anyone else, for that matter.

Another body language signal is what we do with our hands. We shake hands; we put our hands in our pants pockets, behind the back, or sometimes over our mouth slightly while talking, or we put our fingertips together to make a triangle. What do these gestures mean? We shake hands, of course, as a way to say "hello." Putting your hands in your pockets can be interpreted as meaning that you are secretive or unsure of yourself. Placing your hands behind your back can be a power stance; many police officers do this when they walk a beat. Someone who puts his or her fingers over his or her mouth while talking is commonly taken as not being very confident about what he or she is saying. It can also mean that the person is not being completely truthful. Let your hands fall naturally to your sides or perhaps fold them softly (so it does not look like you are madly gripping your hands) at your waist. If you are seated, fold your hands softly in your lap or rest them comfortably on the arm of the chair.

Placing your fingertips together to create a triangle with the hands is referred to as *steepling* (the shape resembles a church steeple). People who use this gesture usually feel they are in a position of power. They may be considered smug or egotistical.

Work at being relaxed and maintaining good posture when you stand to give a presentation. Face the client or group as much as you can rather than turning your back to them. Keep your hand movements slow and small; don't flail around with your hands or arms. Stand easy, without slouching. Walk with your head up, but not with your nose in the air!

When you are sitting, you can lean forward to show interest in what you are saying and what the client says in response to your statements. If the client leans or pushes away from the table, he or she may be losing interest in what is being said. Standing and leaning over the conference table or desk toward the other party is generally considered to be an aggressive posture. In response, most people will lean away from the person who is leaning toward them.

There are many other gestures and body positions that can help you better understand what your client, boss, coworkers, and others are actually saying when speaking. You may wish to read the books by Gerard Nierenberg and Henry Calero or Ken Delmar—listed in the references section—for more information. Here are a few more body language tips you might find useful.

A person shows impatience by:

Pushing away from table or desk

Tapping fingers or a pen or pencil on the table

Shifting from one foot to another while standing

Boredom is indicated when a person:

Turns body toward exit

Rests head in the hand

Doodles

Possible secretiveness and/or suspicion are indicated when a person:

Looks everywhere but at you

Smiles superficially or glances sideways

*Twitty-Villani, 1992, p. 2.
**Fast, 1970, p. 1.

CLOSING TECHNIQUES

Another important task for all designers is *closing*—that is, asking the client for the go-ahead to create a contract; asking the client to sign the contract; asking the client for approval of the plans and products specified. *Closing* is the art of knowing when to ask for the sale. If you are lucky and the client says, "I'll hire you," or "I'll take it," without your having to ask first, you probably do not even need to read this chapter at all.

Not asking for the sale is among the most common reasons that a client does not buy the designer's services and/or products. Why? Because some clients just want you to ask. Interior designers are very comfortable in designing elaborate, complex residences or commercial spaces. Some of these same designers, however, become very uncomfortable when the time comes to present and sell those concepts. Why are designers afraid to ask for the sale? Usually, plain and simple fear of the rejection that occurs when the client says no. However, a fact of life is that sometimes the client is going to say no or "I'm not sure."

I am not talking about hard-core, aggressive techniques to force someone to buy something or sign a contract. There are many other closing techniques that are very acceptable in this profession, as well as other service professions. The sooner the designer asks, the sooner the client may sign the agreement, and the sooner the designer can move on to another project.

In a very real sense, asking for the sale assumes that agreement has been reached on the issues being discussed. However, many people neglect to ask the questions that slowly confirm agreement. When this happens, and the designer tries to close before the client is close to saying yes, the designer is often met by one or more objections. Objections do not necessarily stop the presentation in its tracks; they are just obstacles to be overcome through additional questions and answers.

There are numerous how-to-sell books, each recommending various techniques. Some of those books are listed in the reference section. The following discusses some of the techniques that other professionals use with great success. They are easily applied to selling services and products in the interior design industry.

In Chapter 25, we discussed the use of features and benefits to help sell services and products. Try this closing method in combination with features and benefits. When you can meet at least two needs of the client based on your service features or benefits (or those of a product), use a trial close. A *trial close* is just that: you are trying to close by asking for the sale. Matching the client's needs with features and benefits shows the client that you are really trying to meet the client's needs and provide him or her with only what is needed, not what you want to sell. Remember, trying to close the sale means that you have reached an agreement on needs. Consider the following situation:

Designer: You said that you are looking for a comfortable sofa bed for the guest room, which will have a fabric that will be easy to maintain. Is that correct, Ms. Smith?

Smith: Yes, it is.

Designer: I have already shown you that an independent testing company has rated this sofa bed as having the most comfortable mattress on the market. This nylon basket-weave fabric that you like will be easy to maintain. Why don't I work up the final price with this fabric and see when we can deliver it to your home?

Assuming that the price is not an issue, if the client says this will be fine, you can finish with the selling portion of the meeting and only need to write up the paperwork. However, if the client says no, you must assume that something still remains to be resolved. You must ask more questions and discuss other features and benefits, and then try again to close.

Another frequently used technique is to close when the client agrees to a secondary issue concerning the sale. In the preceding example, when the designer obtained agreement about the fabric choice, he or she would then follow with questions related to the color of the fabric. When these two issues are resolved, then the designer will be ready to close.

Many designers use *third-party testimonials* (or references), which are statements or stories to help with the close. "A testimonial is a statement from a satisfied client praising you and your services."[1] Recalling how a previous client was satisfied by your firm's service or products often helps to alleviate fears during the decision-making process. "Grey Fox Restaurant felt our project management techniques were outstanding and was a major reason why their fast-track restaurant project opened on time" is an example.

Third-party testimonials or stories are very powerful. They do not represent the designer's opinions but those of a neutral third party. It is reasonable to ask clients who were particularly satisfied with your work for a testimonial. Do this by asking for comments and criticisms to improve your service in the future. You will likely gain a sentence or two that can then be used as part of your closing techniques or in other promotional situations. Remember always to ask for permission to quote the client!

Another closing technique—which must be used carefully—relates to a forthcoming event. For example, a client who appears hesitant to close the sale today might be encouraged if he or she knew that the price on the goods was going up in a few weeks. "I can only guarantee this price for the next 10 days, since we have already been informed of a price increase on January 1," the designer might say. This technique is perfectly legitimate *if it is true*. It should, however, only be used with complete honesty. It is unethical to tell a client that the price of the goods is going to go up when, in fact, it will not, or to tell the client that the plant will have to close for only two weeks when it will actually take longer.

These closing techniques and others are discussed in many sales books as methods that can help the designer obtain the client's signature on a design contract, perhaps achieve agreement on design concepts when reviewing plans, and sell products. Whether and how you use them is up to you.

OVERCOMING OBJECTIONS

To become successful at presenting concepts and selling services or products, one must understand how to overcome objections. *Objections* are disagreements with what was said or expressed by some other party. Objections can occur for many reasons. Table 26-4 identifies some of the most common.

In any selling or presentation situation, the client will have some objections to what is being discussed or proposed. Many of the top salespeople feel that unless the client makes some kind of objection, it is quite possible that the salesperson (designer) is not even making any headway. Others feel that an objection means the opposite: the clients are giving you a signal that they want to buy, but you have not convinced them yet.

TABLE 26-4.

Objections commonly raised by clients during presentations and selling encounters

Your price is too high.
Your service was not very good the last time we worked with your firm.
There is a question about the designer's experience with this type of project.
We don't like what has been proposed.
The competition is cheaper.
We cannot afford the service or product after all.
We do not believe your firm is big enough to handle the project.
A competitor is willing to do the design work on spec (for free).
The designer has not met our needs.
We must get approval from someone else.
We like the ideas but will purchase from a friend or relative in the business out of state.
Your low price, as compared to the competition, makes us suspicious.
We are not convinced that you can meet our schedule.
Our priorities have changed, and we need to spend the funds on something else.

One of the most common objections has to do with price. In fact, it is rare for price *not* to be an issue. "Your competition charges less per hour," "I can get free design services from another studio," or "The sofa is too expensive" are typical comments heard by interior designers. The literature on selling services and products strongly suggests that price is rarely the only factor in a price objection.

For the high-end residential client, price is generally not an actual concern, whereas quality certainly is. Perhaps the designer can overcome such objections by restating the quality characteristics of the product or by discussing how his or her services differ from those of the competition. A commercial client might object to price because the concepts presented do not represent or meet the needs of the client, or because something has gone wrong in the relationship and the value of the designer's services or experience has now become a question that translates into "the price is too high."

A second common objection is, "I need to talk this over with my spouse" (partner, boss, etc.). This objection often comes up for two reasons. First, the client is afraid of making a mistake and will not make a decision unless someone else agrees. Second, the designer has not been careful in setting up an appointment with the real decision maker(s)—the person or persons who will actually make the buying decision—in the first place.

When the client wants to discuss something with another person, there is not much the designer can do. Sometimes the designer can get an immediate decision by reviewing information about the service or product to help alleviate the client's concerns. But be careful about becoming a pushy salesperson, which could result in losing the sale altogether.

It is very important to try to involve the decision maker in presentations right from the beginning. This is not always going to happen in a presentation to a commercial client, as there are layers of responsibility to penetrate. In residential design, it is more likely that the decision makers will all be at the meetings—though, of course, this is not always the case. Whenever possible, the presentation should be arranged so that all the decision makers are present at the meeting. In this way, the designer need make only one presentation. Chapter 25 includes additional discussion about client decision makers.

An obvious part of overcoming an objection is actually listening to the objection. This sounds simplistic, but it is brought up because too many designers do not really listen to the client and miss the cues or even the words of the objections. It is imperative that the designer listen carefully to everything the client is saying—both verbally and nonverbally—so that the designer will not create this type of situation:

Sally Jones, a designer, is on a call with Bill Preoccupied, one of the project's designers. They are both at the office of Anthony Smith. Smith is responding to a question by Jones concerning color and style preferences for the remodeling of the office, and in the middle of that discourse, Smith says that he does not like a lot of browns and tans. Bill Preoccupied looks up from his notebook and says, "I really think that browns would be great in your new office." Both Jones and Smith stare at Preoccupied and then look at each other.

"Listening is a selfless act. You must suspend your own ego and interests and focus on the other person."[2] Listening also involves focusing your mind on what the person is saying rather than on what you are trying to say. Most people can tell when someone is truly listening or just pretending. Do not pretend. Listen, learn, succeed.

When objections occur, keep your sense of humor and perspective. The client is not going to like everything. Repeat the objection back and then ask questions to clarify what the problem might be. Then review the information you have already gathered about the client's needs and summarize your point of view in terms of the client's needs and objection. It is not necessary to assume that the client is right concerning the objection. However, be respectful and patient, as the client may not be familiar with industry concepts and terms. Never argue or tell the client that he or she is wrong—this will only put the client on the defensive.

Whatever the objection is, the designer must really listen to the objection and deal with it in a professional manner. Successful designers do not become successful by giving in to objections without trying to understand the nature of the objection and sway the client. However, never argue with the client. Getting the client angry not only means that the problem will remain unresolved, but also that the designer may lose the client.

FOLLOW-UP

A designer related this story: He was contacted by a client who, as he later found out, interviewed five designers for the remodeling of her kitchen. About 10 days after the interview, he received a call back saying that the client wanted to hire him. One of the reasons for this positive development was that he sent her a brief note thanking her for her time. He was the only one who did so, and the client liked this courtesy.

Many times we are too busy to follow up promptly with thank-you notes after a project is completed. Think how much of an impression it might make on clients to be thanked with a quick note after a marketing presentation! The designer should follow up on the marketing or proposal presentation with a letter and/or a phone call. The follow-up should include such things as thanking the client for his or her time, restating important points of the presentation, and emphasizing continued interest in working with the client. Any information or document that might have been promised during the presentation must be taken care of at this point as well. Delays in sending these additional documents could hurt the designer's chances of closing the sale. Figure 14-3 is an example of a simple thank you card.

Losing a sale can be a great lesson—if the designer takes the time to evaluate why he or she did not get the job. Whether the designer is experienced or new to the professional presentation process, his or her understanding of why he or she lost the job may be more important to future success than closing one sale. It is not pleasant to lose sales, but it is important for designers to try to find out why they did.

Records should also be kept on the results of marketing presentations and the completion of a project. This activity was discussed briefly in this chapter, at the end of the discussion on proposal presentations. Chapter 14 covers the post-project review discussion.

ADDITIONAL GUIDELINES FOR MAKING PRESENTATIONS

In this chapter, we have included many tips for making specific types of design presentations. Frequently, these tips overlap, as many are a useful part of any kind of presentation. In fact, many of the items discussed can be applied to job interviews, asking for a raise or promotion, and even dealing with personal relationships out of the office. Following are several additional presentation guidelines that students and designers alike might find useful in their professional practice:

- You only have one chance to make a first impression. Remember that the first 30 to 60 seconds create the strongest impression. Do your best to make this initial contact as professional and confidence-building as possible. Don't skip the next section on good impressions.

- Use professional language. Part of being a professional is sounding like a professional. Use proper language and speak distinctly.

- Anticipate the other person's responses and questions, but listen and don't interrupt. Trying to determine the other person's concerns will make you more thorough and professional.

- Tailor your presentation to the client, and be sure you are focusing on his or her needs.

- Be enthusiastic. Clients cannot get excited about a project if you are not.

- If you make a mistake, don't make a big deal out of it. Calling attention to the problem will only make you feel worse and may totally throw you off balance. Say something like, "Let me clarify that last point," and move on.

- Use gestures carefully. Gestures are helpful to emphasize important points. Hands that are constantly in motion are distracting.

- Talk to the client, not to the board or the screen. Too many presenters direct what they are saying to the board or screen rather than to the audience.

- Make sure your audiovisual equipment works and that sample boards will hold together for the presentation. This should be checked prior to the presentation (preferably during a rehearsal/practice presentation session). When you are going present at the client's location, expect to have to bring your own technology equipment.

- If the potential project is out of the country or with a foreign company, bone up on body language and customs of the other country. This kind of homework is absolutely necessary if your firm seeks to work with international clients (see Chapter 5).

- Prior to a presentation, do not consume milk products, salty foods, or alcohol. These items dehydrate most people. Be sure you have a glass of water handy in case your mouth gets dry.

- Practice, practice, practice! The more often you run through a presentation, especially with a colleague who can critique it, the better it will be; the more often you make presentations, the easier and more effective they will become.

GOOD IMPRESSIONS

We all play roles in our interactions with clients, vendors, peers, coworkers, friends, and associates. All of these roles are, to some degree, affected by the impression we make when we first meet. The language used in an e-mail can make a bad impression. Maybe a bad impression is created by misspelled words in written correspondence. It can arise from unnecessarily long voice messages, from being disorganized, and, yes, even in response to our appearance and apparel.

Good impressions are made by awareness of basic business etiquette and courtesy, regardless of the client or other with whom one interacts. Good impressions come from care, thoughtfulness, and awareness of the situation.

They also come from awareness of the position of the other person. Individuals who have power and influence expect those who provide services to them to understand their world—even if in reality it is unfamiliar territory for the designer. Good impressions help build respect.

It is important to point out that generational differences can have a large impact on a good impression. The older Baby Boomer client may be turned off by the behaviors and dress of younger-generational designers. Perhaps a younger-generational executive might think a Baby Boomer designer is stuffy. Because you are selling, you must be considerate of the other person in the encounter and accommodate his or her preferences and biases.

Transitioning from student to design professional includes understanding that casual dress and slang language have no place in the professional world. The material in this section is not presented to preach about etiquette, but to remind the entry-level design professional that there is a difference between the academic arena and the professional world. It was suggested more than once by many professionals who find entry-level designers lacking in these basic concepts.

According to Letitia Baldridge, former chief of staff for Jacqueline Kennedy, "An atmosphere in which people treat each other with consideration is obviously one in which a customer enjoys doing business. . . . A company with a well-mannered, high-class reputation attracts—and keeps—good people."[3] Respect for others, business etiquette, and plain old good manners are all part of being the consummate professional. These qualities help make a good impression on clients, colleagues, and others with whom the designer will interact on the job and in personal situations.

Image and Dress on the Job

Like it or not, first good impressions come from what we wear. Personal image and appropriate professional dress on the job do not always mesh. What we wear makes a difference in how people perceive us. Consider that much of what an individual communicates about himself or herself is conveyed by dress and body language. Remember the scene in the movie *Pretty Woman* when Julia Roberts goes shopping for clothing on Rodeo Drive in Beverly Hills?

Put on any well-tailored garment and you will probably find yourself standing up a little taller. In business, clothing does speak volumes to those with whom you interact. What is appropriate dress for one role is not necessarily appropriate for another. Casual Friday attire is fine within the office, but is unlikely to be appropriate for calling on clients. Wearing high heels is fine in the office and when calling on clients, but inappropriate for being on a construction jobsite.

There is a place for personal expression, and it's generally not going to be in the office environment. Modifying or improving your self-image in the working environment is a matter of learning ways to overcome the factors that hold you back from achieving greater success in your career.

Here are just a few common-sense tips for appropriate dress in the business office:

- Your firm will have a dress code, and the owner will set the tone.
- In general, men will be expected to wear suits and ties; women will likely be expected to wear skirted outfits, dresses, or nice pants suits.
- Designers working with residential clients have more flexibility in what they can wear, as design is a creative profession.

- People who wear suits are usually given more respect than those who do not. The jacket is as important for a woman as a suit is for a man, although a woman need not wear only suits.

- Designers in commercial firms will generally dress more conservatively. The well-tailored suit is always appropriate for meetings and giving presentations to clients, for both men and women.

- When calling on conservative clients, women who normally carry large handbags might want to consider switching to an attaché case instead.

- It is likely that your boss will expect your tattoos and piercings to be covered by apparel. Bosses do have the right to demand this.

- When you shop for business apparel, don't wear casual clothes or casual shoes. You will have a more accurate idea of what you will look like if you wear clothes similar to what you are considering buying.

- Fit is very important. Buy what fits, not what you think you will get into if you go on a diet. An expensive garment that fits poorly will look worse on you than a moderately priced garment that fits well.

Chapter 30 contains additional tips on dress for interviewing situations.

Communications

Interior designers spend a lot of time communicating with clients and industry colleagues. Good impressions in your communications come from care and courtesy.

A *telephone* greeting says a lot about the design firm, including the staff that answers after the initial pickup by a receptionist. An overly casual manner can skew a potential client's entire impression of the firm. This is true whether the phone is the office landline or a cell phone used for business. Keep in mind that the one who has something to gain from the conversation—generally the designer—should call back when a message has to be left for a client. Return messages from others promptly—no later than the next day, if this is at all possible. Clients expect responses right away even when that is not practical for the designer.

When considering *cell phone* usage, the best practice is to believe that the person you are with is the most important person—not the one on the other end of your cell phone connection. If you must use your cell phone around others, be conscious of how loudly you talk. Not everyone is interested in hearing your conversation. Make sure you separate business use of a cell phone from personal use. Only you are impressed by your own self-importance when you feel you must respond to a call on your cell phone when meeting with someone else.

Texting is certainly quieter than actual cell phone usage; however, the nose in the phone during reviewing or writing texts is also troublesome for many to observe. Keep in mind the previous admonition that the person you are with is more important than the text you just received. And regardless of the laws in your jurisdiction, do not text while driving!

E-mail is a ubiquitous communication tool today, but you must take care in what you send via this electronic mail system. Be assured that clients and others are maintaining a copy of any e-mails they receive. Likewise, the designer should maintain copies of e-mails received from clients and others involved in projects. If problems occur, these e-mails will create a paper trail that can be important in litigation and/or ethics complaints. Remember, once you click the Send button, there is no way to take back what you have sent. Ensure that the e-mail is going to the right address and person. And don't forget to check your spelling!

Written communications still take place. Letters, contracts, proposals, and all sorts of other correspondence must still be created via the old-fashioned methods of typing and printing hard copies. There is no excuse for misspelled words in written correspondence, especially given the quality of spell checkers today. Bad grammar can also be nearly eliminated by word-processing software. Remember, though, that not all spelling and grammar errors will be picked up electronically. Be sure you proofread what you are sending before placing it in an envelope.

Business Entertaining and Travel

A significant amount of business is conducted across a table in a restaurant. Interior designers often meet with clients at a restaurant after a presentation or to discuss a topic that does not require the review of plans and samples. Manufacturers' representatives often invite designers to lunch. An employee may go to lunch with a supervisor or the owner of the firm. The designer and colleagues at professional associations often meet elsewhere to chat and network.

Interior designers also travel on business to the client's jobsite, to showrooms, and conferences. Professional behavior is not something that can be left at the airline gate. It is not appropriate to dress in casual clothes for business travel, even when you are going alone to a meeting or jobsite location.

Here are some tips related to business entertainment and travel:

- Having the opportunity to travel on business does not mean that you should leave good manners at home. In fact, they may be even more important when you are traveling.
- Carry any essential documents—such as CDs, contracts, and handouts— in a briefcase as carry-on luggage, rather than in checked luggage.
- There is nothing funny about you or a colleague getting drunk at a conference and embarrassing the design firm.
- The main purpose of a business meal is to continue to develop rapport between the designer and the client, colleagues, or the boss. Business *is* discussed, but it is usually done after some small talk has occurred.
- If you are eating with a group of colleagues and you all need receipts, ask the server about separate checks or at least copies of the check.
- If you invite someone to a meal, the guest will assume that you will be paying for it.

A short article that provides additional information and tips on business etiquette can be found on the companion Web site as Item 26-4.

WEB SITES RELEVANT TO THIS CHAPTER

www.bls.gov Bureau of Labor Statistics

www.census.gov Census Bureau

www.nasp.com National Association of Sales Professionals

KEY TERMS

Body language	Objections
Closing	Relationship building
Feasibility studies	Third-party testimonials
Initial interview	Trial close

WHAT WOULD YOU DO?

1. The sales agreement for Turbo Designs clearly states that once the agreement is signed by the client, orders cannot be canceled after seven business days and that any cancellation request must be in writing. The designers have ordered furniture for the bedrooms, living room, and dining room. A few weeks after the agreements were signed, the client contacts the designer and tells her that the furniture order for the living room must be canceled. The husband objects to what he feels is the high cost of the furniture: "I've seen the same items on the Internet for a lot less!" he tells the designer.

   The designer reminds the client that the sales order has a no-cancellation policy. The husband e-mails the designer and says that unless the order for the living room furniture is canceled, he will cancel everything and, if necessary, sue the designer.

2. Barbara produced a set of working drawings showing the demolition and new layout and equipment specification on a remodeling of a kitchen and family room for her client. The fees for these drawings were included in the contract for the design services. When Barbara shows the client the drawings, the client suddenly says that he does not want to continue the project with Barbara. The client gives no reason for terminating the project contract. The client wants the drawings, but Barbara refuses unless he pays $2500 for the development of the drawings.

3. Sara is the owner of a commercial interior design firm that has been in business for eight years; it specializes in corporate and small business office facilities and some small hospitality projects. Sara receives a good lead on a project for an advertising agency. She calls the agency and is able to obtain an appointment to make a presentation of her firm for the project. Sara's firm has a staff of four interior designers, all of whom are NCIDQ certificate holders and are licensed in the state; the firm also holds a contractor's license. This would be an important project for Sara and the firm, because the advertising agency represents many important businesses of the type that Sara would like to have for clients. She is working carefully with her senior designer to determine what should be said and brought to the presentation.

REFERENCES

1. Bly, 1991, p. 30.
2. Excerpted with permission of Chandler House Press, from *Knockout Presentations* by Diane DiResta. p. 516. Copyright 1998 by Diane DiResta. www.chandlerhousepress.com
3. Baldridge, 1985, p. 3.

CHAPTER 27

Employee Management

After completing this chapter you should be able to:

- Discuss the agency relationship and how it affects the employee–employer relationship in an interior design office.
- Explain when a design staff member is considered an agent for an interior design office.
- Outline the legal duties the employer has to an employee, and the legal duties an employee has to the employer.
- Discuss the responsibilities of each of the job classifications of a design staff.
- Discuss the importance of job descriptions in general and how they help employers and employees.
- Discuss employment at will from the employer's point of view.
- Compare employment at will with a situation in which a designer has an employment contract with the employer.
- Explain how a noncompete clause in an employment contract might affect a designer (currently an employee) who is starting his or her own business; contrast with its effect on an employee who is going to work for another firm in the same geographic area.
- Outline the differences between an independent contractor and an employee.
- Explain why it is important for an employer to have a written contract with an independent contractor who provides CAD services.
- Identify and describe the different compensation methods found in interior design.
- Describe the different incentive compensation methods.
- Explain the importance to employees of performance evaluations.
- Discuss the pros and cons of an employee handbook for a small design firm.
- Explain why mentoring is important to entry-level designers, and outline how you might approach securing a mentor after graduation.
- Understand how to protect yourself from situations that might be considered sexual harassment.
- Briefly explain why the federal government has instituted employment laws.

NCIDQ COMPONENT

Based on best information available, some material in this chapter might appear as part of the NCIDQ examination. The reader should not depend solely on this text for study material. See the sections on basic employee management, agency, employment at will and contracts, and independent contractors.

Managing employees is almost always a challenging task for owners and design managers. Interior designers are generally self-motivated and do not need or like someone to stand over their shoulders to be sure they are working. Nevertheless, those in supervisory roles must be sure that employees are doing the work assigned in a manner deemed appropriate.

Hiring right is not an easy task. By "right" I mean hiring a person who fits the firm's culture in addition to having the skills to do the job. Processes that formalize personnel management can assist in the hiring, development, and retention of effective employees. Formalized processes also protect the employer should employees feel they have been treated unfairly. At the same time, formal personnel processes help employees understand what is expected of them and that the design firm intends to treat its employees fairly.

As an interior design firm grows, it becomes increasingly important for the owners and managers to define the firm's organizational structure and personnel management processes. Structure may not be something a designer likes, but it does help make the work flow more smoothly and should increase job satisfaction.

Individuals enter the interior design profession for many reasons. As would any professional, interior designers expect to be treated fairly, receive adequate compensation, and be given greater responsibility as their worth to a company and the industry grows. Employers expect employees to give loyalty and best efforts to the company that pays their salaries.

This chapter combines topics on employee management and employee legal issues. Both employers and employees should have an understanding of legal issues regarding employment. Although some statutes have an impact only on large design firms, many affect the small interior design firm as well. Meeting the spirit of employment laws is, at the very least, the ethical thing to do in any size or type of interior design firm.

Please note that the information on legal issues of employment constitutes only a brief overview; it should not be taken as a complete legal discussion of these topics nor considered legal advice. Employers or employees who have questions concerning potentially unfair treatment should discuss these matters with an attorney who is familiar with employment and human resources law.

THE AGENCY RELATIONSHIP

You are probably familiar with the fact that agents represent professional athletes during negotiations for contracts with sports teams. Agents also frequently represent a home buyer or seller. The employee–employer relationship within a design firm is also a form of agency relationship.

In common law, an *agency relationship* exists when one person or entity agrees to represent or do business for another person or entity. In the agency relationship, an *agent* is empowered to represent another person, called the *principal*. The agency relationship gives the principal the right to control the conduct of the agent in the matters entrusted to the agent. The agent for a sports figure cannot make a deal with a sports team if it is not agreed to by the principal (the sports figure). The individual working in the interests of the sports figure or a home buyer is an agent, not an employee.

However, employees do have a type of agency relationship with their employer. Let's first define an *employee:* "a person who works in the service of another person (the employer) under an express or implied contract of hire, under which the employer has the right to control the details of work performance."[1] In an interior design firm, the principal is the owner (or other controlling member), whereas the agents are all the employees, whether they are in management positions or staff positions.

In a pure agency relationship, the agent can negotiate and make contracts for the principal. Only certain individuals in the design firm other than the owner might be able to sign design contracts or other legal or financial documents such as purchase orders. An employee is a legal agent of the firm only if he or she has the authority to act in place of the owner.

In many other ways, employees are also agents, because they also represent the owner. For example, Roger and Kelley work for Marjorie. All three designers are expected to call on clients, obtain the information needed to prepare a design contract, and carry out the required design activities to complete the project. Only Marjorie, who is the owner, is allowed to sign the design contracts. If Roger or Kelley signed a design contract, the contract would not be binding on the firm.

Agreeing to go to work for an employer means that the employee understands that there are certain expectations and duties concerning the work relationship. Agency relationship is the legal concept that specifically spells out the extent of the relationship between the employer and the employee.

Unlike most contractual relationships, the conditions of the agency relationship do not have to be in writing. Accepting a position and knowing what the responsibilities of the position cover imply agreement. It is, of course, highly recommended that any employee who is an actual agent and who can sign contracts of any kind should also sign an employment contract upon hiring. The employment contract (discussed later in this chapter) spells out the actual agent responsibilities of the employee. Because all positions in the firm have different responsibilities and different levels of trust within the employer–employee relationship, it is important for employees to fully understand their responsibilities. Carefully prepared job descriptions (also discussed later in this chapter) explain these responsibilities.

Employees have duties to the employer and employers also have duties to employees. Each has a primary duty to the other to act in good faith toward the other. Each party in an agency relationship also has specific legal duties. Let us look first at the duties that the employer has to the employee.

Employer to Employee

Employees have an expectation to be paid a reasonable amount of compensation for the required work responsibilities. For most types of employees, the law does not define what this reasonable amount of compensation must be. In effect, the law states that compensation must conform to what is customary compensation for the services performed. Federal laws outline minimum wages for certain types of employees depending on the size of the company, but these laws rarely affect an interior designer.

The employer is also required to provide reimbursement to an employee for reasonable expenses incurred while the employee is working for and under the direction of the employer. For example, because Suzanne will be using her personal car to travel from the office to many jobsites, the firm owner will reimburse Suzanne for the use of her automobile when traveling on company business. The amount of that reimbursement is negotiable, but it is commonly set to the amount per mile allowed as a deduction on federal income taxes.

Another important duty of the employer is to assist and/or cooperate with the employee so that he or she is able to perform the agreed-upon services. For example, the firm owner will provide computer equipment and office furniture in the office for Suzanne to do her job. If the owner expects Suzanne to provide her own computer, Suzanne should expect some sort of reimbursement for upkeep on that computer. If the owner tells the employee that she must purchase all her own equipment in order to do her job, a judge may say that the owner is inhibiting Suzanne from performing her duties.

Federal and state regulations, as well as basic common law, require that the employer provide safe working conditions for employees. Should an employee feel that his or her working environment is unsafe, the employer cannot dismiss the employee for reporting unsafe conditions.

The preceding examples relate to general duties of the employer to the employee. Other employer duties may also exist, depending on the exact nature of the agreement between the employer and employee and changes in federal or state laws.

Employee to Employer

Accepting compensation from an employer automatically means that the employee has a duty to do the work assigned and follow the policies of the company. Whereas Melissa, as employer, has certain duties to Suzanne, Suzanne also has several basic duties to Melissa and the design firm for which she works. Additional duties may also be outlined by a formal agreement or written employment contract.

All employees have an obligation to perform their assigned duties with reasonable diligence and skill based on what would be considered common or reasonable for the job. For example, if Erica is hired on the basis of her skill in using architectural CAD software—purported by her to be at a high level—her employer has a right to expect that the work performed be representative of someone who fully understands the software. Rick, an entry-level designer, would not be expected to produce CAD drawings at the same level as Erica.

Many say that loyalty to employers (and vice versa) has diminished over the years. Nonetheless, a second important duty of the employee is to be loyal to the employer. An employee is expected to act in the interests of the employer, not for the benefit of any outside party or even of the employee himself or herself. This means that a designer who prepares the design work for a major client cannot be hired by that client to design an additional area for the client "on the side." If the designer engages in *moonlighting*—which occurs when an individual holds or engages in work outside his or her main job—the employer would have the right to terminate the employee for breach of the agency relationship because of this conflict of interest.

Here are some additional important duties of the employee to the employer:

- The employee must keep the employer informed of anything related to the relationship or work undertaken for the employer. "What the agent actually tells the principal is not relevant; what the agent *should have told* the principal is crucial."[2] Remember that agent is another term for employee.

- Employees must be loyal to their employers, and owe a duty to follow the employer's rules concerning business activities. An employee must follow all legal company rules, polices, and processes. Deviations without permission from the right supervisor technically violate this duty to the employer.

- Employees are hired because of the skills they possess, which relate to the tasks and responsibilities required by the employer. The employer expects employees to perform those tasks to the best of their ability.

- Some employees may have access to company funds, such as petty cash, to purchase supplies. The employee has a duty to keep a proper accounting of the inflows and outflows of funds or company property entrusted to him or her. A designer who has authorization to sign purchase orders for supplies would breach this duty if he or she used one of the purchase orders to obtain supplies for his or her own needs. In this case, the breach is also a criminal act, and the employer could press charges.

It is also important to note that when a client hires an interior designer, a form of agency relationship exists. It is not quite the same, however, as the employer–employee agency. Interior designers are not employees of the client in the same sense as has been described in this section. Comments about this form of agency relationship are included in Chapter 7 on design contracts. Employers are advised to discuss other specific issues with their attorney. Employees may also wish to consult with an attorney or read more about agency relationship in a business law book, several of which are mentioned in the reference list.

JOB CLASSIFICATIONS

The decision to hire an employee is made when the owner realizes that certain tasks can no longer be accomplished with the current staff. Adding design staff, or any staff for that matter, should not be taken lightly. The hiring process takes time—often time away from revenue generation. Regardless of a new employee's skills, a certain amount of time is needed to train that new employee. It also costs the firm a considerable amount of money to train even an experienced designer to become part of his or her new design "family."

In the long run, the most effective way of searching for and then hiring a new staff member is to begin by a careful analysis of that staff need. This holds true for a small firm as well as a large design firm. This often-avoided step can lead to hiring an inappropriate person regardless of the position.

Reviewing office procedures and defining project responsibility is an important part of that analysis. Job structuring can make the hiring effort less difficult and continuation of effective work among the existing staff less traumatic. Structuring of job responsibilities entails defining job classifications and job titles, and these are of benefit to everyone in the company.

As a firm grows, an organizational structure or chain of command emerges. This structure helps everyone in the organization understand the formal communication patterns. In a very large firm, an *organizational chart* graphically represents this structure. Figure 27-1 shows an organizational chart that includes the various job classifications common in an interior design office.

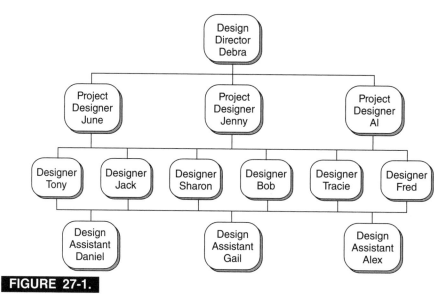

A sample organizational chart for an interior design firm.

Interior designers who work with corporate and many other commercial clients are very familiar with the idea of an organizational chart that shows the layers of responsibility. The issues of *chain of command* are more critical in larger firms. Although a formalized chain of command according to an organizational chart rarely exists in smaller design firms, issues regarding the chain of command do arise in the smaller firm as well. In many companies—even large corporations—the "real" chain of command does not always match or reflect the organizational chart.

A job title provides a sense of value for some individuals. Even the entry-level, recently graduated intern appreciates a job title when working full time. The job classifications discussed in this section use the titles that define responsibility level. In a large firm, job titles help show employees a way up the ladder of responsibility. Job titles also relate to the job descriptions that more specifically define responsibilities and required experience within a design firm. Job descriptions are discussed in detail after this section.

Principal

The owner of the interior design firm often uses the job title "principal" or "president." If there is more than one owner, the title *principal* is often used by all the different owners. In some firms, a partner can join the principal in upper-level management. A partner can be an owner or an upper-level employee who may or may not have some financial interest in the company. In large, multidisciplinary firms, the top officer of the design firm is often called chief executive officer (CEO) rather than principal or president.

The principal (for simplicity) provides the vision and direction of the company. He or she is the most direct link to clients and is responsible for the majority of initial client contacts and presentations to obtain new design work. A principal often finds that his or her time to spend on designing projects is reduced because of the greater administrative and marketing responsibility. Many find it important to remain involved in projects and hire others to take on many of the day-to-day management or administrative responsibilities.

Should a principal or partner be involved in a design project, his or her time would be billed at the highest rate quoted by the firm. The principal as a designer would be supervising project managers and other design staff in the execution of the design work.

Design Director

In some design firms, the individual responsible for managing the interior design professional staff has the title "design director." Firms might also use vice president of design, design manager, or perhaps some other title to indicate this person's leadership role. It is common for a design director's responsibilities to include administration, marketing, and design, although the principal rather than a design director can assume any of these responsibilities.

Here are key responsibilities and tasks of the design director:

- Administrative duties such as planning, hiring and firing, assigning work, and preparing contracts
- Preparing various management control reports, establishing policies, and attending management meetings
- Training and development of the design staff
- Making client contacts and subsequent presentations to prospective clients, either with the owner or individually
- Being involved in the development of marketing tools, such as brochures, Web site, and advertising
- Planning and participating in the development of marketing plans
- In conjunction with the owner, acting as the company's liaison with the public
- With guidance from the principal, setting the minimum standards for all design work that leaves the office

Design directors also have project design responsibility. It may be minimal in large, very active design firms, or it may be an important part of the manager's responsibility in a small firm.

In very large design firms, the leadership role concerning management of the design professional staff might be broken down into two or more areas. The design administration and marketing group might be responsible for all administrative functions, such as hiring, and all marketing activities of the interior design department. The design production group might be responsible for ensuring the quality of project execution. It would be common for these two groups to be headed by different individuals, who would report to a design department head such as a vice president.

Senior Designer

Senior designer or senior associate is the title often given to the very experienced interior design professional. Senior designers generally have five or more years of experience in interior design—similar to what would be expected of a project manager. A senior designer has extensive project responsibilities, is the lead designer, and may supervise other designers. Good communication skills are a must for this person if he or she is to manage a design team for a large project and work effectively with clients.

This position has critical client contact via assigned projects and perhaps during marketing presentations. As the lead designer, a senior designer meets with clients to determine their needs, prepares or directs others in the completion of design documents, and is responsible for order entry supervision and installation supervision. It is not unusual for the senior designer also to have specific administrative responsibilities assigned by the design director or principal.

Project Manager

The project manager often has different responsibilities than a senior designer and may be on a different level on the organizational chart or chain of command. Depending on the size of the firm, the project manager may have limited involvement in developing design concepts. Rather, many project managers find themselves primarily involved in administrative management of projects. This job requires good communication and organizational skills. In some firms, the project manager may be required to market the firm's design services and may even be required to negotiate design contracts. Specific tasks of a project manager were discussed in Chapter 11.

Designer

At the next level, professional employees are usually given such titles as designer or staff designer. Designers commonly are required to have two or more years of professional experience and well-developed technical design skills. On large projects, these individuals work under the supervision of a senior designer or project manager.

Designer-level employees may be involved in client interviewing and any information-gathering research needed for the project. They may be asked to prepare preliminary drawings and other documentation, preliminary product specifications, or other tasks assigned by the senior designer or project manager. On smaller projects, they may be responsible for all phases of the project. Administrative responsibility is limited.

Design Assistant

The entry-level position for most firms is commonly called design assistant or junior designer. Design assistants have little professional experience other than as interns, because they are usually recently graduated. They work under the direction of a more experienced designer for one or more years.

The kinds of work most commonly performed are drafting, preparation of sample boards, preparation of specifications lists for the FF&E, maintenance of the library, and other tasks assigned by the design director. After working for several months in a smaller firm, the design assistant usually is given responsibility for some small projects. As in the case of the designer, administrative responsibilities include only time and recordkeeping for his or her efforts.

Depending on the actual interior design practice and size of the firm, there may be some additional, specialized job classifications. Many firms have support personnel that provide administrative assistance. Larger design firms may have additional professional staff providing specialized assistance to the design staff. These other job classifications are noted in Table 27-1.

TABLE 27-1.

Other interior design job classifications

Space planner: Work responsibilities focus on space planning and use of space, not the specification of furniture and fixtures. Also called *TI (tenant improvement) specialist.*

CAD operator: Experienced in the use of computer-aided design equipment and software. Might be an interior designer or a computer operator. Although almost all interior designers are expected to have CAD experience, this specialty still exists.

Specification writer or estimator: Responsible for the preparation of finished specification documents and project budget estimates. May be trained in interior design.

Account executive: In firms whose focus is selling merchandise, the account executive is the lead in working with clients who require purchasing services and perhaps very little in the way of design services. Another common title for this job is *sales associate.*

Librarian: Responsible for maintaining resource materials; in some firms, will also be involved in writing purchase orders and the expediting functions. Might be an intern or entry-level designer or non-design-trained individual.

Graphic designer: Responsible for the design of graphics for such things as business cards and brochures, presentations, and presentation graphics for clients, as well as for similar graphics for the interior design firm.

Business development specialist: Exclusively works to identify and qualify potential clients, assists in developing presentations to obtain contracts, and is the liaison between the design firm and public relations and/or advertising specialists. Also called *marketing director.*

Administrative staff: Non-design staff providing secretarial, bookkeeping, and order-entry assistance to management and design staff. Also includes receptionists.

Human resources manager: A position in larger firms; professionally trained in dealing with hiring personnel and almost all other personnel issues not the responsibility of department heads.

JOB DESCRIPTIONS

Even in a small firm, it is important for the owner to develop job descriptions for staff members. The *job description* communicates the qualifications, skills, and responsibilities of each job classification within the firm. It is best prepared after job classifications and essential responsibilities of each position have been developed. Unfortunately, job descriptions are rare except in larger firms.

Job descriptions do have a place in almost any interior design firm:

- Job descriptions help growing firms organize and control the employee search task.
- They help to organize the work in the office and keep work on track.
- They help satisfy and reduce equal-opportunity complaints that might be raised by employees.
- Existing employees use them to see what qualifications and skills are required of higher-level positions.
- Job descriptions can also be provided to individuals who are being seriously considered for a position or upon being hired.

This employee management tool need not be elaborate. The small firm may find a simple structure, such as the one shown in Figure 27-2, satisfactory. Larger firms may find that detailed job descriptions are of greater value (see Figure 27-3). Prepared in outline form, they should contain statements that are specific enough to differentiate among individuals, yet broad enough to allow the manager some flexibility in hiring. The content of the job descriptions must be kept current and complete. They also must accurately reflect the desired

---

Interior Design Consultant
Creative Design Consultants, Inc.

This job classification requires that the employee assist the owner with projects. The employee is also expected to bring his or her own clients to the company.

Responsibilities:
Assist clients.
Evaluate and specify products to meet client needs.
Prepare layouts, plans, and other documents as required.
Prepare color boards or other finishes workups.
Obtain signed sales orders.
Prepare cost estimates for all work required on a project.
Complete all required purchase orders.
Coordinate installation and delivery.
Share in housekeeping chores in the office/studio/warehouse.

Qualifications:
Bachelor's degree in interior design. Associate's degree in interior design with work experience in interior design would substitute for a college degree.

Work Experience:
Minimum of two years' actual sales and interior design experience required.

Skills:
Portfolio should show training in color and product coordination, and the ability to space-plan.
CAD knowledge preferable—AutoCAD minimal.
Knowledge of standard computer software for business.
Knowledge of residential products and how to specify those products.
Proven sales record.

FIGURE 27-2.

A basic job description that can be used to define a design staff position in a small interior design firm.

skills required to perform the responsibilities of the positions. As much as possible, the descriptions should be stated in measurable terms to aid in performance evaluation. Item 27-1 on the companion Web site is a worksheet to help organize a job description.

Key parts of the job description are the statements related to responsibilities, qualifications, and skills required. The clearer these items are, the easier the hiring task will be. A detailed "Responsibilities" section helps the individual in the position knows what is expected of him or her.

The "Qualifications" section outlines the minimal educational requirements and the minimum amount of work experience (in years) that is required. Statements such as "graduation from at least a four-year college or university, with a major in interior design" set minimum criteria for an interior design position.

Statements concerning specific technical abilities, along with any skills or abilities of a general nature, can be outlined in the "Skills Required" section. It is often easier to finish writing this section after the "Responsibilities" section has been completed. It is important for the skills required to correlate with the responsibilities expected and the qualifications demanded. It is also important that these skills and general abilities be listed in the order of their significance. For example, for a firm that is involved in commercial interior design, CAD skill may be of primary importance for an entry-level design assistant; therefore, it should be listed first. For a firm that is involved in residential interior design, color coordination may be of primary importance for an entry-level design assistant.

A statement regarding to whom the person in the job described reports, either in a separate section or within the "Responsibilities" section, should be

---

Job Description

Job Title: Senior Designer
Reports To: Design Director
Pay Rate: Salary

Responsibilities:
The following describes the essential responsibilities of this job classification. Other duties may be assigned from time to time by the Design Director or Owner.

Determine scope of services required for projects.

Assist Design Director with development of design contracts and project scheduling.

Responsible for all phases and activities of design projects assigned, including but not limited to programming and data gathering, space-planning, furniture layouts, development of contract drawings, product specification, budgeting, presentations to the client, and jobsite supervision.

Maintain client confidence and good client relations.

Supervise design team members to complete projects. Team members will be assigned by Design Director.

Maintain client files for projects assigned, including all correspondence, drawings, and other materials, as described in our standard client file processes booklet.

Keep Design Director informed of project status on all projects and other duties assigned.

Attend all in-house meetings and programs.

Be available to meet with manufacturer's representatives as assigned by the Design Director. Maintain design proficiency by attending seminars and workshops.

Provide accurate time records to the Design Director each week.

Provide marketing assistance by participating in marketing presentations as requested and by informing Design Director of possible projects that might become known to the designer.

Supervisory Responsibilities
This job has no direct supervisory responsibilities; however, some direction of team members will be expected from time to time. This position does not participate in performance evaluations of team members.

Qualifications
Education: Bachelor's degree from a four-year college or university with a major in interior design; or an associate's degree and a minimum of four years of experience in lieu of a four-year degree.

Previous work experience: A minimum of four years full-time work experience.

Portfolio and resumé should show ability to perform the required tasks of a senior designer with full competence and skill.
    NCIDQ qualification required.
    Qualified to be licensed in this jurisdiction.
    Competence with AutoCAD, Revit, and SketchUp.
    Competence with other computer applications is also expected.

FIGURE 27-3.

A job description for a senior designer in a firm with numerous employees.

provided. This helps clarify the chain of command and also aids new employees in learning who their supervisor will be. Because people do leave their positions, reference is best made to a job title rather than an individual's name.

EMPLOYMENT AT WILL

Conducting an employee search take many hours of precious time away from revenue generation. Even with the use of the many electronic means available to employers today, hiring a new employee is not a task to be taken lightly. Employers are checking references more, investigating qualifications and personal attributes of the potential employee, and of course, conducting interviews looking for that "perfect" match.

When an employee is hired and not bound by a written contract, the hire is considered to be under the basic employment doctrine of employment at will. *Employment at will* means that an employee hired without a written contract, and who has no other written terms of his or her employment spelled out, can be fired by the employer at any time without any explanation. It also means that the employee can quit at any time without prior notice.

Traditionally, the courts have ruled that because the employee may quit at any time without giving a reason, the employer has the right to fire the employee at any time without giving a reason, as long as the firing does not violate any federal or state employment laws. Nevertheless, despite the persistence of the basic concept of employment at will, the employer must be careful when terminating any employee. The courts have also ruled that if promises were made during the interview, the employer might have implied an agreement, which then makes it harder to fire an employee.

Interior design has grown to be a very competitive business. Many design firms that never before thought of having professional staff sign employment agreements have begun to do so. Designers who work for a firm for a few years may later decide to start their own firm and often take some clients with them. If there is an employment-at-will situation with no contract, the designer perhaps has a legal right to do this, although he or she does not have an ethical right to take clients.

Both employers and employees should be aware of each other's rights with regard to employment and termination. Employers no longer can terminate an employee capriciously if the employee is fulfilling his or her duties in accordance with satisfactory levels of performance. Furthermore, employees have the right to retain their employment without fear of retaliation, sexual harassment, or discrimination. The box "Employee Termination Criteria" looks carefully at issues of termination and wrongful discharge.

Employee Termination Criteria

With the increased number of lawsuits and challenges over firings, the employer must be careful in terminating even an at-will employee. Employers should document employees' problematic activities. This is an important employer safeguard for defending against wrongful termination lawsuits. For the same reasons, the employee should have documentation of or copies of materials concerning any employment discussions concerning poor work performance.

There are some restrictions on the employer's right to terminate an employee under the employment-at-will doctrine. This list mentions the most common:

- An employee cannot be fired merely because of his or her sex, race, religion, age, or physical condition.
- An employer cannot fire an employee out of malice, in retaliation, or because of bad faith.
- The employee cannot be fired without due cause. An example of due cause might be because of a high number of absences from work without permission.
- Employees cannot be fired for performing "public obligations," such as jury duty or voting.
- Employees also cannot be fired for reporting company violations of health or safety laws (called *whistleblowing*).

Under employment at will, the employer can fire the employee without giving any reason. Yet employers should have reasons for terminating an employee—what attorneys often call "just cause." Of course, an employer can have many reasons or cause to terminate an employee that is perfectly legal. A few examples of these include insubordination, violating company rules, excessive lateness, low productivity, misappropriating company property, a downturn in business, being dishonest, and stealing from the company. Poor job performance is often the most difficult for the employer to justify unless a pattern of performance can be shown. This is a good reason for doing and documenting some type of formal performance evaluation.

Unfortunately, some employers take advantage of the employment-at-will doctrine and terminate employees unfairly. If an employee believes that he or she has been fired unfairly or not in accordance with his or her written or implied contract, the employee may have grounds for a wrongful discharge suit.

Wrongful discharge basically means that the employee has been fired without good cause. Litigation for wrongful discharge, also called unjust dismissal, is based on rulings by judges who feel that the employment laws passed by federal and state governments do not always go far enough to protect employees. Common-law wrongful discharge is based on legal precedent rather than on statutes.

Many courts have ruled that verbal agreements about working conditions constitute an implied contract between employer and employee. An *implied contract* is a contract formed by the actions of the parties rather than by an express written agreement. A written or oral assurance made to an employee by the employer can restrict the employer's right to fire the employee for anything other than cause. It is thus very important for employers not to make any long-term promises or statements about employment during interviews. Comments made during an interview, published in an employee handbook, and possibly other interactions at the time of hiring can inadvertently create implied contracts. Employers should make it clear that the hiring is at will and that no contract exists between the parties—unless, of course, a contract is desired, in which case it should be put in writing. The courts will look at many factors in determining whether an implied contract existed before deciding that a termination of employment was justified.

Both small and large firms should protect themselves from potential lawsuits by having and using appropriate management practices. Regular performance evaluations of all employees hired at will is one way to prove that a terminated employee was fired because of inadequate job performance. Documented meetings, during which the manager talks to and warns an employee that he or she is not meeting expectations, is another method the employer can use to protect its right to fire noncontract employees. Adding disclaimer statements to employee handbooks also affords the employer protection against lawsuits.

Employees who feel they have been wrongfully or illegally terminated have the burden of proof—and wrongful termination can sometimes be very difficult for the employee to prove. Employees can protect themselves by requesting written information regarding expectations and performance evaluations on a regular basis. It is also important for the employee to document any events that might relate to the firing. The employee should also maintain copies of performance evaluations that have been signed by the supervisor, as well as notes about any meetings concerning job performance.

Although it is currently harder for an employer to fire an employee for little or no reason, the courts still support the idea that the employer must retain the right to fire employees who are incompetent, unqualified, unwilling to work, and so on. As more and more court cases related to improper termination occur, it is important that both employers and employees take the hiring, evaluation, and termination processes seriously.

EMPLOYMENT CONTRACTS

Most employees in an interior design firm will be hired on the basis of employment at will. Firms with management, sales staff, or other specialized job functions may find this method of hiring unsatisfactory. When it is necessary to spell out the terms of employment, the firm will want to develop an employment contract.

An *employment contract* or agreement specifies the conditions of employment as well as benefits and special perquisites (perks). Written contracts are prepared to clarify more complex issues important to the employer or the employee. An interior designer who is responsible for the sale of goods or is otherwise eligible for a commission or a bonus may want a written contract to

---

Corporate Interiors Group, Inc.,
7000 N. Lincoln Avenue
Anywhere, Pennsylvania

August 200x

Mr. Tony Smith

8142 E. Dempster St.

Anywhere, Pennsylvania

Dear Tony:

Let me welcome you to the Corporate Interiors Group, Inc. family! We are very pleased you have decided to join our company.

The following constitutes the employment contract between Corporate Interiors Group, Inc., employer, and Tony Smith, employee.

Employment

You shall devote your full time and best efforts to interior design activities and perform these activities to the best of your ability. You are not allowed to work for clients or other design firms outside the employ of Corporate Interiors Group, Inc.

The starting job classification for your employment is **Project Manager.** The duties and responsibilities of a Project Manager include: marketing presentations, project design and specification, production of contract documents, working with designers and design assistants, job site supervision or coordination, and other duties and responsibilities as called out on the attached job description.

Compensation

Project Managers are compensated on a salary basis. Your starting salary will be _____ annually. This salary will be paid on the basis of 26 equal pay periods.

You are eligible for the bonus program after you have worked full-time for a period of three (3) consecutive months. Bonuses are determined based on a percentage of income. The details of the bonus calculations are outlined in the attachment, "Corporate Interiors Group, Inc. Bonus Policies." This attachment is considered part of this employment contract.

Project Managers are entitled to a _____ percent commission on all accessory specifications. Payment is made only after receipt of payment from the client.

Merit and cost-of-living increases are only awarded at the beginning of the calendar year. Merit raises are determined on the basis of performance reviews. Any salary increase thus earned will begin at the next regular pay period after the completion of performance reviews. Performance reviews are conducted for all employees during November and December. Cost-of-living increases are at the discretion of the owners, not the design department manager.

FIGURE 27-4.

An example of an employment contract for an interior design position.

Benefits

All benefits are described in detail in the company handbook. There is a company retirement plan. Eligibility and details are available from the Personnel Manager.

Termination

Your employment may be terminated by either party upon written notice. This notice must specify the date of termination and be hand-delivered or delivered by certified mail.

A. Within thirty (30) days of termination, you will be paid outstanding commission on sales of accessories made prior to your termination where all the merchandise has been delivered and accepted to the customer.

B. Commissions due on sales begun prior to your termination but not delivered prior to your termination will be paid within 30 days of receipt of payment by the customer.

C. Bonus payments will be prorated on the number of calendar days you worked between the last date of the previous bonus payment and the date of termination notice.

Noncompetition Provision

The employee may not go to work for a competitor of Corporate Interiors Group, Inc. for a period of 15 days from the date of termination of employment with Corporate Interiors Group, Inc.

The employee will not make available to a subsequent employer any confidential information concerning the operations and clients of Corporate Interiors Group.

Return of Company Property

Upon termination of employment, the employee will surrender all handbooks, files, equipment, price lists, catalogs, customer information, and other company records or property. The use of photographs for a personal portfolio of projects for which the employee was primarily responsible when an employee of Corporate Interiors Group can be used only if Corporate Interiors Group is cited as the employer.

Modifications to the Contract

No changes, modifications, additions, or deletions shall be made to this contract unless those changes, modifications, additions, or deletions are in writing, and are signed by both parties.

The above constitutes the total legal agreement between the parties named. Signatures below signify agreement to the terms of the employment contract. One copy shall be placed in your employment file. The second copy should be retained by the employee.

_____	_____
Tony Smith, Employee	**Date**
_____	_____
Jordan Jones, President	**Date**
Corporate Interiors Group, Inc.	

Attachments:

    Job description, Project Manager

    Corporate Interiors Group, Inc. Bonus Policies

FIGURE 27-4.

(_Continued_)

spell out what will be paid and how the commission or bonus will be paid. Firms may wish to protect company policies such as discount structures, client lists, and operating procedures that competitors would like to have if an employee goes to a competitor. Many employers also use written contracts that prohibit the employee from taking clients to competing firms if the employee quits. Figure 27-4 shows a sample employment contract.

In general, the written employment contract covers the following, although other items might also be included:

1. *Compensation*. Explain how the employee will be paid (hourly, weekly, biweekly, etc.). If by commission, the method of payment should be detailed.

2. *Employee benefits*. Specific employee benefits may have been negotiated that are different from those offered to other employees. This is especially true for management and senior designer staff.

3. *Employment responsibilities*. The employee's job responsibilities should be explained in detail so that expectations are clear. Many companies refer to and attach a copy of the appropriate job description.

4. *Grounds for termination*. It is critical for both the employer and the employee that statements about termination procedures and policies and the manner in which either party must give notice be included in the contract. For the protection of the employee, these statements should also outline how any outstanding commission (if commission is part of the compensation method) is to be paid.

5. *Termination for cause*. This clause protects the employee from being terminated for some capricious reason. Valid causes for termination include negligence, incompetence, dishonesty, disloyalty, and nonadherence to company policies.

6. *Territory rights*. Sales personnel may be limited to working with clients only in certain territories; if so, this fact should be stated in the contract. This territory might be certain cities or states, or even certain clients.

7. *Noncompete agreement*. The noncompete clause is also often called a *restrictive covenant* or noncompetition clause. This type of clause applies to the employee after he or she leaves the company, placing some limits on where and/or how the employee may work after separation regardless of the reason. Interior design firms most frequently use noncompete clauses to prevent an employee from taking clients with the employee. It may also be written to prevent employees from taking other privileged company information, such as discount structures, to another job.

   A restrictive covenant is enforceable by the court as long as it does not last for an unreasonable length of time or unfairly restrict the individual from making a living in a similar way in the same location as the former employer. What length of time and what area are considered reasonable is up to the court.

8. *Ownership of work*. A clause dealing with ownership of work product is not unusual in an interior design firm employee contract. The design work one undertakes as an employee belongs to the employer and this work is considered *work product*. Regardless of the existence of this clause, the interior designer must get permission of the employer (or former employer) to use any drawings or documents created for the employer's clients in the employee's portfolio. The use of work product

in a portfolio when one is looking for another job or starting one's own firm without permission can also be an ethics violation.

An employment contract need not be in writing. Technically, an oral employment contract is formed when the employer and employee have agreed about things with respect to responsibilities, compensation, and terms of employment. These types of agreements form the basis of an implied contract. Many experts on employee rights suggest that the employee prepare a letter summarizing the oral agreements discussed during the job interview and then send this letter to the employer. It is far more pleasant for both the employer and the employee to be in agreement concerning the terms of employment, compensation, and other conditions of the employment relationship rather than at odds about those conditions later on in court.

Employment contracts can protect both the employee and the employer. If the employer requests that a written contract be signed, the prospective employee should be certain that he or she understands all the terms of the contract.

INDEPENDENT CONTRACTORS

Small and medium-sized interior design firms sometimes seek out the assistance of individuals who can provide specific services to the firm while not becoming employees of the design firm. Individuals who work on the design portion of a project can be hired in an emergency or on an as-needed basis. Tradespeople who install merchandise such as carpeting, or a delivery crew that works for a delivery service, are also essentially independent contractors rather than employees of the designer. This section focuses on design professionals as independent contractors.

A design firm might hire a designer on a temporary basis to provide specific short-term services to complete work that in-house staff does not have the expertise or time to handle. According to the Internal Revenue Service (IRS), the general rule is that an individual is an *independent contractor* if the employing company has the right to control or direct only the result of the work and not the means and methods of accomplishing that result.[3]

The independent contractor usually has a specific, short-term working relationship with the firm, and the work is often defined by a written contract. The hiring firm is not required to pay benefits to an independent contractor, as that individual is not an employee.

The primary matters that define a worker as an independent contractor or employee focus on the degree of control that the employer has over the worker. The greater the control, the more likely it is that the worker is an employee. Along with this are the degree to which the worker controls his or her own work schedule; whether the worker works solely for one employer or works for more than one at a time; and where the contracted work is being performed. Again, all these points relate back to the amount of control held by the employer.

The IRS does not consider part-time workers to be independent contractors. It may be that the part-time employee receives little, if any, company benefits, such as health insurance; nevertheless, the employer is required to withhold Social Security, workers' compensation, and other mandated contributions for all part-time workers.

There are strict guidelines defining who is an independent contractor. Table 27-2 summarizes these guidelines. If you are considering hiring someone as an independent contractor or are working as an independent contractor, you are urged to read IRS Publication 15-A for clarification of this type of employment status.

TABLE 27-2.

Guidelines for defining an independent contractor

According to the IRS, the following factors will be considered when determining whether an individual is considered an independent contractor or an employee. Individual state departments of revenue and workers' compensation insurance providers may also be called to audit whether an individual is an employee or an independent contractor.
The person hiring the independent contractor has no control over how, when, or where the contractor does the work for which he or she has been hired. This is a crucial issue in determining the status of an independent contractor.
An independent contractor uses his or her own methods to do the work and receives no training from the person who buys the services.
An independent contractor works under his or her own business name.
An independent contractor maintains his or her own business financial accounts and other business records.
An independent contractor hires his or her own assistants when necessary to complete the assignment.
An independent contractor works when and for whom he or she chooses. He or she also sets the hours of work, though this may be negotiated by the requirements of the assignment.
The independent contractor provides his or her own equipment and supplies to perform the job duties required.
The independent contractor is usually hired for a short time, with no expectation of permanent employment. Often the independent contractor is hired "for the job," which means only for a specifically defined task.
Payment for services is commonly at the end of the job or by means of one or more partial payments (depending on the length of the job).
The expenses of working are borne by the independent contractor, though some expenses may be billed to the buyer, based on the assignment.
An independent contractor can work for more than one company or individual at a time.
The independent contractor must engage in professional work that is distinctly different from that of the person hiring the contractor. Interior designers hired by interior design firms to do interior design work might not be considered independent contractors, especially if the other conditions mentioned earlier are not met.
An employee can be fired or quit at any time. An independent contractor agrees to work until the assignment has been completed and cannot be fired as long as he or she produces a result that meets the specifications of the assignment.
If the employer withholds federal income taxes, Social Security taxes, and pays unemployment taxes regarding the individual, the individual is likely to be considered an employee.

From IRS Publication No. 15-A (U.S. Department of the Treasury, Internal Revenue Service).

You have no doubt heard the word "freelancer" used in reference to interior designers (or others) who work independently. *Freelance* is generally accepted as meaning a self-employed worker. Interior designers and others who work freelance are generally independent contractors. For example, Mary is an interior designer who was laid off during the early part of the recession. She is very experienced in CAD and Revit. She created a sole proprietorship business offering CAD services to other designers. Thomas hired Mary to prepare construction drawings for him. Mary satisfactorily completed the required work and was not asked to do any other work for Thomas.

The use of independent contractors offers several advantages for employers when staff needs become evident.

- Independent contractors are not employees of the design firm and have no rights to the benefits that employees receive.
- Employers save money by hiring an independent contractor even though they may pay a contractor more per hour.
- Employers are not required to withhold deductions for income taxes, or to pay or withhold Social Security contributions, Medicare contributions, or workers' compensation insurance from an independent contractor's fee.

- Employers are not liable for the negligent acts of independent contractors while they are performing their contractual work responsibilities.

An obvious advantage for someone who works as an independent contractor is the freedom to work on the types of projects he or she chooses. Another is to work the number of hours he or she may wish to work during the week, rather than a normal 40-hour-plus week like many design employees. The per-hour fee may also be greater than the salary paid to an employee. However, obtaining projects/clients can be as difficult as for any design firm. Not being compensated for 40 hours of work can result in a reduced income regardless of the hourly fee.

As far as independent contractors are concerned, they cannot file for unemployment insurance when the work has been completed. They are also most likely not entitled to workers' compensation insurance if they are injured while working for the contracting business. The independent contractor must pay self-employment tax on his or her income. If the worker does not report the income and pay self-employment taxes in accordance with IRS regulations, the worker can be subject to penalties by the IRS.

An advantage to the independent contractor that is a disadvantage to the employer is that the copyright to any designs created might belong to the independent contractor rather than to the employer. The contract between the two must clarify that ownership of the drawings and other documents prepared by the independent contractor belong to the employer.

Some design firms have taken advantage of the independent contractor designation when they hire individuals to prepare many kinds of design work. Whether it occurs by mistake or is intentional, this practice can have serious legal and tax consequences for both the employer and the workers.

A lot of problems that can arise concerning independent contractors can be reduced, if not entirely eliminated, if a written contract is developed between the parties before the work begins. Issues such as a specific description of services to be provided, duration of the agreement, how the contractor will be paid, and other issues that relate to the work required and the working arrangement should be spelled out.

Item 27-2 on the companion Web site is an article about outsourcing as it applies to interior design practice. Do not forget that the tradespeople, such as wallpaper hangers and carpet installers, hired by the interior designer to install a specific product are not considered employees and are considered to be independent contractors. Installers are independent contractors as long as the work they do and the equipment that they use to do the work are *not* controlled and provided by the designer who has hired them. Obviously, a designer has likely provided the materials or goods that they are installing, but the tools to install the goods are not. A designer who hires architects to review drawings that have been produced by the designer is hiring an independent contractor. Design firms that hire consultants are also hiring independent contractors.

COMPENSATION AND FRINGE BENEFITS

One of the largest, if not the largest, expense items for a firm is personnel expenses. Employees expect fair compensation for the skills and experience they bring and for the contribution they make to the design firm. Exactly how an employee is paid can be as important to the employee as the amount.

Because of the high expense, some employers try to hire staff for the lowest amount possible. Naturally, the concept of "you get what you pay for" does come into play in this situation: low pay may bring in an employee, but that individual may not have the experience or skills to make a very positive contribution to the firm's revenue. Consequently, determining fair and reasonable compensation is an important consideration for a design firm owner.

Although most readers think of their "pay for work" as salary, in reality there is more than one way for employees to be paid. Being paid a salary is only one of those ways. The method of paying an employee is better thought of as compensation. The term *compensation* is any kind of payment made to an employee for work performed. In addition to compensation, employees may receive other payments or other considerations. *Fringe benefits* are other kinds of payments that are optional. A few items that are considered fringe benefits are not optional and must be paid by the employer; these are discussed in the section on benefits. Fringe benefits, such as paid vacations and health insurance, also make a significant contribution to the total compensation package. We first consider typical methods of compensation and then discuss some common fringe benefits.

Compensation

This section starts with a few examples of how designers are commonly compensated. Harry works for a design firm that expects him to be in the office and prepare design documents, as well as perform other tasks common to either a residential or commercial designer. He is not expected to sell any merchandise, although he specifies FF&E. Harry is paid a salary. Joanne is an interior designer working for a furniture store, where her responsibilities include the sale of merchandise that the company stocks on its showroom floor or orders for clients. Joanne is paid a commission on the amount of goods she sells each month. Rob is a part-time employee who does CAD work for a design firm. He works anywhere from 15 to 20 hours a week while he also attends classes. Rob is paid by the hour. Rob is not an independent contractor because he does all his work at the design office under the supervision of senior designers. Harry and Joanne have received a bonus at the end of the calendar year during some of the years they worked.

These examples are the most common methods of compensating employees: straight salary, commission, and hourly wage. Bonus plans, technically called *incentive compensation*, are sometimes tied to any of these. The compensation program used by a particular firm is up to the owners and managers and is normally based on factors such as competition, company mission, type of practice, target client market, and, of course, requirements of state and federal laws. The preceding examples provide some specificity as to work situation. However, this is not meant to convey that any one compensation method is used only by the work situation described.

Let's look more closely at how Harry is compensated. The *straight salary* (or salary) method of compensation provides a fixed amount of salary to the employee no matter how many hours in the week he or she works. Of course, the firm still requires that Harry and other employees paid by the salary method work a normal workweek of 35 to 40 hours. The actual number of hours varies, as the workweek in offices ranges from 35 to 40 hours per week. By the way, that 40-hour workweek is merely a standard. Interior designers often find it necessary to work more than a 40-hour week. Harry's weekly salary is determined by dividing the yearly salary by 52 weeks. This is often paid every other week rather than once a week. This is the most common method of compensating interior design and other design professional staff, especially when product sales are not part of the compensation arrangement.

Some weeks it is necessary for Harry to work more than 40 hours in a week because of project schedules. Straight-salary employees are not eligible for any overtime pay when they work more than 40 hours in one week. They are also not expected to work "extra" for free, as that would not be fair compensation practice. In this case, the employee is usually expected to utilize compensatory time, at some convenient time. *Compensatory time* is time off during the normal workweek that makes up for the overtime hours an employee has worked. In all cases, the utilization of compensatory time must be approved by the manager so that the employee's absence will not be detrimental to the regular office work. In other words, when Harry has worked extra hours, he will ask permission of his boss to miss work on an agreed-upon day. Firms generally have an additional policy that compensatory time cannot be "saved up" for an extended period nor added at the beginning or end of a vacation period.

Joanne's work responsibilities are more involved with the selling of products than services, even though she also prepares floor plans for her clients' projects. Joanne is paid a commission on the amount of merchandise she sells to clients. *Commission* refers to some percentage of the gross sale, net sale, or gross margin of the merchandise sold. Being paid a commission is riskier for the employee because the amount paid is never guaranteed. The employee's compensation is based solely on what is sold. The flip side of that risk is that employees paid a commission might earn more over the course of the year than an employee paid a salary. Of course, they might also earn less if they have a bad year!

There are a few common methods of calculating commission; thus, some explanation is appropriate. Let's say that Joanne is paid a percentage of the *gross sale*. This means that the commission percentage is paid on the amount for which the client has actually been billed. For example, if the designer is paid 10 percent of the gross sale and the client has been billed $50,000, the commission owed to the employee is $5000.

Another way to compensate an employee who is on commission is basing the commission on the *net sale*. When commission is based on the *net sale*, the percentage is calculated after certain items have been deducted. Deductions could include discounts, freight charges, delivery charges, returns—even interior design services of in-house designers. For example, assume that same gross sale of $50,000 with a 10 percent commission on the net sale. From the $50,000, the company deducts $1000 for delivery and freight charges. The commission that should be paid to the designer would thus be $4900.

Many companies that deal in commercial furniture items pay commission on the goods and other products sold based on the gross margin of the sale. In the *gross margin method* of paying a commission, the commission percentage is not based on the selling price to the client. *Gross margin* (also called gross profit) is the difference between the selling price and the cost price of the goods or services being sold. In the preceding example of a $50,000 gross sale, with a 10 percent commission, assume that the cost price of the sale is $25,000. The amount of commission paid in this case would be $2500.

The preceding example makes it seem as if employees who are paid based on gross margin are not making much for their efforts compared to the other commission methods. In some respects, this is correct. To provide greater incentive, some firms utilizing the gross margin commission method might incorporate a sliding scale of commission. In this situation, different percentages are paid depending on the amount of the gross margin percentage. For instance, if the gross margin is 90 percent (nearly retail price), the commission percentage might be 45 percent. If the gross margin is only 5 percent (nearly cost price), the commission percentage might be only 2 percent. Designers are motivated to sell merchandise and services for the highest gross margin possible in order to receive the most commission possible. It should be noted, however, that depending on the type of work (residential or commercial) and competition, it might not be possible to sell merchandise at a very high gross margin.

Another common compensation method is the hourly wage. When an employee is paid an *hourly wage*, he or she is paid some rate for every hour worked. Although most firms talk about how they pay employees based on an hourly wage, interior design professional staff are rarely actually paid by the hour. Because of the nature of interior design work, the hourly wage is used less often as a method of compensation, except when it is relatively easy to monitor the employee's productivity and work responsibilities. The more common use of an hourly wage is to compensate entry-level employees and "production" employees, such as secretaries, bookkeepers, tech employees such as CAD specialists, and delivery people.

In the example at the beginning of this section, Rob was paid an hourly wage. Rob only works part time, so this compensation method is very appropriate. William is another employee whose job responsibility it is to prepare CAD drawings and other production documents for other designers. William is a full-time employee, and he is also paid an hourly wage. William's weekly "salary" is computed by figuring the average workday (e.g., 8 hours) and the average workweek (e.g., 40 hours). If an employee is paid $20 an hour, his or her weekly gross salary would be $800 per week for a 40-hour workweek. (This same concept holds true, of course, for Rob or any other part-time employee.) Because the federal wage and hour laws apply to design firms and employees who are not considered professional staff, the firm has to pay hourly-wage employees overtime for any hours worked beyond the normal workweek when they are full-time employees. This amounts to time-and-a-half for weekday overtime work and double time for work done on Sundays and holidays.

Another issue to discuss is the concept of an employee's gross salary, not what the employee takes home and is free to spend. *Gross salary*, as anyone who has held some kind of a job realizes, is the amount of employee compensation before any deductions. The employer must withhold (deduct) amounts for federal income tax, Social Security and Medicare contributions, possibly state income taxes, and possibly voluntary contributions for such things as health insurance. As you no doubt know by now, Social Security contributions show up on the paycheck stub as FICA; FICA stands for Federal Insurance Contributions Act. Social Security is the common term for FICA. The amount of compensation left after these deductions is called *net pay* or *take-home pay*. It is common for the basic withholdings and deductions for taxes and Social Security to amount to 20 to 35 percent of gross pay.

Often, larger design firms provide methods for employees to earn or achieve supplementary income in addition to their regular compensation. *Incentive compensation* is the term for any payment over and above regular compensation. Incentive compensation is primarily awarded to hourly and salaried employees. Two common types of incentive compensation are merit pay and bonus plans. *Merit pay* is an amount added to an individual's basic annual compensation amount, often as a reward for quality work done in the past. It is commonly referred to as a raise or salary increase. For example, Gail is a senior designer at a firm specializing in hospitality projects. During the last year as the senior designer on a major project, her work was recognized with a competition award for outstanding design using sustainable design concepts.

Due to the extra publicity this award gave the design firm, the owner gave Gail a merit pay increase. This increase in her salary remains in effect into future years with the company. Merit pay is an increase that can go to all employees, but usually is given to those individuals whose high level of performance during the past year warrants it. Merit increases are rarely paid to employees who work on commission.

A *bonus plan* is a method of paying extra compensation to employees based on their producing more than a specific personal quota. Bonuses are most commonly paid to design employees who sell merchandise. If they meet or exceed their sales quotas, the employees are paid some kind of bonus. Because designers who are responsible for creative design work cannot easily establish a quota of design work, bonuses are less often paid to these individuals. However, some interior design firms do have a bonus plan that rewards creative staff. Bonuses are usually based on the employee meeting or exceeding the amount of contracts budgeted or on exceeding a budgeted amount of specifications on a certain kind of furniture or furnishings. A bonus is not an ongoing compensation increase; it is awarded only for the year in which the work was done. Of course, individuals can earn bonuses every year. The bonus is the type of incentive compensation most commonly paid to those on commission and not eligible for a merit increase.

Another kind of compensation that may be added to the basic annual compensation is a cost-of-living adjustment. *A cost-of-living adjustment* (also referred to as COLA) is generally given across the board, meaning that all employees—except those paid salary or commission—may receive a cost-of-living adjustment to help offset increases in inflation.

Fringe Benefits

The amount of salary paid to an individual who takes a position with a design firm is only part of the employer's total compensation package. In some situations, the kind of fringe benefits offered might be a deciding factor in obtaining the services of a particular individual.

Fringe benefits can include a large variety of additional payments or benefits. A benefit can be payment of association dues or a trip to a major show like NeoCon. One of the most common fringe benefits is paid vacation and health insurance paid in part or wholly by the employer. In a very small firm, the fringe benefits will be quite minimal, such as two weeks of paid vacation time. Large firms may offer several types of fringe benefits. Most design firms are too small to become subject to federal or state rules concerning employee fringe benefits. Some benefits are also taxable to the employee, though the most common types are generally not taxable. The individual should, as always, check with an accountant to be sure that fringe benefits are handled properly.

The kind of fringe benefits and the amounts that can be paid to an employee and consequently deducted by the owner of the company vary based on the type of legal business formation. This is an important consideration for companies that begin as partnerships and corporations or experience rapid ongoing growth. Offering fringe benefits can entice highly qualified individuals to work for a particular firm. Thus, the amount of this extra compensation varies widely for interior design firms. The most typical fringe benefits are listed in Table 27-3.

Other benefits that would not be paid directly to the employee, but must be paid by the employer, include Social Security tax contributions, workers' compensation taxes, and unemployment insurance taxes. These are benefits that the employee may or may not draw on for some time. Social Security is not

TABLE 27-3.

The employee benefits most commonly provided by businesses

Actual required benefits will be different based on the size of the firm.
Voluntary benefits
Health insurance
Life insurance
Supplemental insurance such as dental, disability, and vision care
Retirement plan, such as profit sharing
Paid holidays, vacations, and sick leave
Employee purchase discounts
Payment of employee professional association dues
Payment of NCIDQ or other testing and licensing fees
Reimbursement for employee use of personal automobile
Payments for employee educational enhancements
Required "benefits"
Unemployment taxes
Social Security insurance
Workers' compensation insurance
Note that health insurance may become mandatory depending on actions of Congress.

payable until the employee retires (or is physically disabled and can no longer work). Workers' compensation covers on-the-job injuries, and unemployment insurance is only paid, under certain circumstances, if the employee has been laid off from the design firm.

When an individual is applying for a job, is considering a promotion, or is weighing the merits of staying with the present employer, he or she must look carefully at the complete benefits package. A position with one firm with a slightly lower salary but a good employer-paid health insurance program may be better than another position where the salary is a bit higher but no health insurance program is available to employees.

THE PERFORMANCE EVALUATION

Design practice owners must make decisions about who gets a raise, a promotion, extra training, or even who gets to travel to market at company expense. While small firm owners may make these decisions by the "seat of their pants" method, it is more equitable when an evaluation tool is used to help with these decisions.

A *performance evaluation* is a systematic evaluation of the positive and negative work efforts of an employee. It is especially important to use this type of tool when making decisions about raises, promotions, and even termination. The performance evaluation is a positive management activity that always gets a bad rap as an unpleasant task for both the employee and the owner/manager. Part of the reason this is so difficult for design managers is that few have any training in, or experience with, the performance evaluation process.

In many design practices, the performance evaluation consists of an informal mental review of each employee's work contribution. This informal review is almost always based on the manager's subjective opinions rather than on any objective evaluation of the employee's performance of his or her job responsibilities. Considering the increase in employee lawsuits with regard to discrimination, harassment, and unfair termination, it is important for owners and managers to use more formal performance evaluations.

TABLE 27-4.

Guidelines for performance evaluations

A performance evaluation should be designed to:
Encourage employee development, based on understood employee responsibilities.
Enhance the employer-employee relationship.
Provide for supervision and training of design staff, as needed, by a staff member.
Provide an objective aid in determining compensation increases and promotions.
Define guidelines for how a performance evaluation affects dismissals.
Help motivate employees to achieve agreed-upon goals related to responsibilities and job performance.
Provide guidelines for performance levels with new goals and responsibilities.
Aid in determining the need for new hires.
Protect the employer from false claims by employees.
Make available written records of performance and reprimands if a former employee claims wrongful discharge.

Conducting performance evaluations as a positive process does take time. The firm owner must try to allow for time to consider each employee's performance and discuss these impressions with the employee. Performance evaluations do not have to be done constantly, but should be done at regular intervals that make sense to the busy owner. The firm owner should not make these discussions a time for negative criticism; rather, they should be seen as an opportunity to help direct an employee's progress and development. This helps make the evaluation discussion less anxiety producing for employees.

Objective evaluations can help employees be more effective, productive, and loyal to employers. Table 27-4 provides some guidelines for use of the performance evaluation.

From a legal standpoint, written evaluations also help protect the employer if an employee files a formal grievance. Written notes and evaluations placed in each employee's personnel file provide the design firm owner with a credible document to use if any employee claims that some type of discriminatory practice exists or unfair termination has occurred.

An article detailing the performance evaluation process can be found on the companion Web site as Item 27-3. A sample performance evaluation also has been added to the companion Web site as Item 27-4.

The employer should follow up the performance evaluation with monitoring of the employee's progress. Some areas and employees may need special monitoring, and the employer must be ready to spend the time either training or working with the employee. Remember that performance evaluations fail when the employer treats evaluation and development as the important issues in a formal performance evaluation process.

THE EMPLOYEE HANDBOOK

Adding one or two employees to a firm with five or fewer employees does not generally cause confusion in terms of everyone learning and adhering to the company rules and policies. However, when there are multiple employees, it is important for the firm to develop an employee handbook.

The purpose of an *employee handbook* is to provide owners, managers, and employees with a concise reference regarding the company's policies. It usually includes general operating policies, such as those related to special-ordering merchandise for clients, as well as personnel policies. Some design firms have one handbook that describes personnel issues and one or more additional handbooks that explain operational policies.

Personnel policies are the primary reason that employee handbooks are developed. Having written policy statements helps ensure that policies are applied fairly and consistently. To be sure all policies are current, the owner should review the handbook once a year. The state Department of Labor can advise the owner on current labor policies. Of course, the firm's attorney can also advise on specific legal issues that might arise regarding the contents of the handbook. It is also advisable that all employees sign a form acknowledging that they have received, reviewed, and understand the contents of the handbook.

Employers must recognize that a carelessly written employee handbook can create serious legal and personnel issues. Language in an employee handbook can create employment obligations that the employer did not intend. Many courts have determined that promises or statements in a handbook concerning continuing employment create an implied contract. An *implied contract* is one in which "a contract [is] implied by the direct or indirect acts of the parties."[4] Such legal interpretations and complications may make the small business owner shy away from preparing an employee handbook—but it is a useful management tool for any size interior design business.

The company owner can enlist the assistance of staff in the development of a new or revised handbook. Many policies may already exist in writing, or employees may already know what they are, even if they are not written down. Some information, such as paid holidays and vacation or sick time allowances, may have to be obtained from company records. The firm's attorney should review the employee handbook before it is issued to employees.

The organization and contents of the handbook should be logical and concise. Clear and precise wording is important, as is the use of terminology that everyone understands. For example, the firm may wish to use a format that mirrors the logical sequence of events of an organization. In this case, issues related to hiring would be placed first; hours of work, absenteeism, and employee benefits would be placed in the middle; and policies relating to when an employee leaves the company, including termination, would be placed at the end.

Information concerning termination is of particular importance. In the case of termination without cause, if the handbook describes a procedure for dismissal, an employee cannot be terminated unless the firm follows that procedure.

It is important for the owner and/or managers to meet with employees to explain why the handbook was prepared, to define the purpose of the handbook, and to go over its contents with employees. Even if employees have not been a part of the process of creating the handbook, at least they will feel less threatened by a new set of rules if the rules are explained to them before the rules are put into effect. Revisions should also be reviewed with employees before they take effect.

The handbook establishes the policies needed to aid owners and managers in control and decision making. However, the business owner must always remember that strictly enforced rules may lead to a disgruntled group of self-motivated, self-directed individuals—the type of person who often seeks a career in interior design. Table 27-5 summarizes the common parts of employee handbooks.

Written policies related to operational and personnel issues aid the owners and managers of the firm in running the practice in a professional

TABLE 27-5.

Common parts of an employee handbook

A. Overview.

B. Introduction. Provides an overview of the company.

C. Organization. Provides a description of the company's responsibility areas and organizational structure.

D. Employment and hiring policies. Details hiring procedures, whether and when performance evaluations are performed, and promotion policies.

E. Compensation. Details compensation policies for all levels of employees. This section commonly defines pay periods, bonuses, and fringe benefits (if any).

F. Time off. Details company paid holidays (if any), vacation policies, sick leave, and other paid or nonpaid days off.

G. Training. Provides information about any company training or reimbursement for training for educational purposes.

H. General rules and policies. Details workweek, overtime, tardiness, and such things as use of company phone and mail for personal business, dress code, and other general work conditions.

I. Leaving the company. Includes information on termination policies, expected notice, severance pay (if any), and policies on references.

manner. Written policies also help clarify how things are done and where employees stand in their relationship to the firm. Employees will adhere to policies that are clear and can be easily followed. Employers need to keep in mind that an employee handbook is never really finished. It must be reviewed periodically and modified if necessary to meet the changes in company policies. Item 27-5 on the companion Web site provides a sample section of an employee handbook.

MENTORING

Training and mentoring new employees, regardless of their level of experience in the profession, is vitally important and cannot be taken lightly. *Mentoring* is training, guiding, or advising someone to help that individual attain a higher level of success. Although mentoring can be a kind of training, it involves much more than training an employee in how to follow the operational procedures of a firm. Someone who acts as a mentor to another designer often provides career advice that goes beyond what might be appropriate to the immediate situation.

Mentors come from many different places. A mentor can be someone in the firm. Large design firms often have a formal mentoring program in which a senior designer works with entry-level and junior designers to help them learn the ropes and improve their skills. Owners of small design firms must make themselves available to mentor their employees. A mentor within the firm helps the individual increase his or her understanding of and worth to that company.

Sometimes designers must find mentors outside the design firm in which they work. Perhaps it is someone the designer meets at an association meeting or an alumnus from the designer's college. Having a mentor from some other firm or part of the industry gives the individual someone to talk to about issues that he or she might not want to discuss with a colleague.

When someone comes to you seeking a mentor—whether or not you own the company—remember to:

- Keep the discussions confidential.
- Accept a mentorship relationship only if you can be sincerely helpful to the other person.

- Give constructive criticism when the person asks you to critique his or her work.
- Not talk too much! Ask the mentoree questions and let him or her think out loud. Sometimes all a mentor has to do to be helpful is act as a sounding board.

SEXUAL HARASSMENT

Sexual harassment is a type of discrimination forbidden by federal statute Title VII of the Civil Rights Act of 1964, and is monitored by the U.S. Equal Employment Opportunity Commission (EEOC). Readers should note that a few additional statutes have also been enacted that are not detailed in this brief overview; you can find information on these other statutes by going to www. eeoc.gov/laws/index.

"Sexual harassment is generally defined as sexual advances, requests for sexual favors, and other verbal or physical conduct of a sexual nature when submission to such conduct is made either explicitly or implicitly a term or condition of employment or some related activity."[5] Sexual harassment can affect women or men, gay or straight. It can happen in the interior design office, whether large or small, and in other firms involved in the built environment industry. Unfortunately, many in the industry have been subject to sexual harassment at one time or another. Remember that both men and women can be harassed or become harassers.

We most often think of sexual harassment between an employer and employee occurring when a business owner or supervisor of an employee makes unwelcome sexual advances toward an employee or subordinate. For example, Rachel is told she will receive a promotion if she gives sexual favors to a superior. This example is an illustration of the type of sexual harassment called *quid pro quo*, which is Latin for "something for something." It is the most commonly understood type of sexual harassment.

Another common type of sexual harassment is the situation when actions by others create what is called a *hostile work environment*. This second type is more subjective, as it is harder to prove and is generally not specifically linked to a promotion, raise, or the like. Examples are the posting of explicit cartoons in the work environment; the telling of offensive jokes or the use of offensive gestures or language can also create a hostile work environment.

Sexual harassment behavior can also occur between office peers. It can be considered sexual harassment depending on the work relationship of the office peers. However, peer harassment is not illegal under EEOC laws in the same way as employee–employer harassment. For example, Bonnie is a relatively new interior design employee at a design firm with several men and one other female designer. The group goes out frequently on Friday late afternoons for drinks at a restaurant after work. Bonnie, trying to fit in, joined the group on some of these Friday afternoons. A few of the men told off-color jokes that Bonnie did not appreciate, and she was actually offended by some of these jokes. She wasn't sure what to do. She may feel that their behavior is harassment, but if none of these people are her employer or supervisor there is generally no legal recourse for Bonnie. By the way, if her fellow employees constantly tell such jokes and make such comments at the workplace during work time, Bonnie may be able to prove a case of hostile work environment.

Sexual harassment is not easy to prove. In many cases, it is one person's word against the other's. The first thing that should be done is to tell the person exhibiting the unwanted behavior to stop. This can be very difficult for the person being harassed, but experts say that it is actually very effective. Telling the offending person to stop lets the person know that the words or behavior are unwelcome and offensive to the recipient. Experts suggest that a brief letter demanding cessation of the behavior can be effective if a face-to-face discussion is uncomfortable. Of course, keeping a copy of the letter is *always* imperative.

Documentation of any situation is also imperative. When harassment occurs, the employee should check with other employees to determine if the harassment is widespread. Documentation of harassment by supervisors is very important because employees are often fired when these situations occur and the employer often cites work deficiencies as the reason for termination. The documentation will help show that discrimination, not work deficiency, was the basis of the termination.

The individual should file a written complaint with the proper supervisor or person in authority if the behavior is coming from a coworker, client, or others outside the firm. If a designer feels that he or she is being harassed by a supervisor, he or she should, as soon as possible, document any details about the episode. If the individual is working in a small firm and the harassment is coming from the owner, the designer should still submit the letter to the owner. In larger firms, the individual might need to file the complaint with the human resources manager—who might not be the same person as the interior design supervisor.

If nothing positive results from the written complaint, the designer should speak to someone at the EEOC or state fair-employment office before going to an attorney and filing a lawsuit. In fact, it is necessary for an individual to have filed a complaint with the EEOC before filing a federal lawsuit. If the EEOC feels a complaint has merit, it will issue a letter that allows the complainant to take the case to court. Delays in contacting the proper authority might be interpreted as acceptance of the behavior and could jeopardize a claim, if one is filed later.

Sexual harassment is unwanted sexual advances or sexual connotations. If the individual accepts the behavior, he or she cannot later claim that the actions constitute harassment. Do not tolerate this kind of behavior from coworkers, bosses—even clients. Learn more about sexual harassment by reading one of the books in the reference list or any of the other numerous books and articles on this subject.

There are also situations concerning harassment in the workplace that may or may not involve sexual harassment. Discrimination issues are discussed in the next section as well as in Chapters 29 and 30.

FEDERAL LAWS REGULATING EMPLOYMENT

An employer must use diligent care in hiring, working with, and terminating employees. Because of a lack of training in employment issues, the owners of interior design practices—especially small firms—can easily fall victim to inappropriate behavior in the supervisory relationship with employees. Numerous laws at the federal and state levels were enacted during the 20th century to protect employees. Many of the laws intended to protect employees have more of an impact on firms that are unionized. As it is almost unheard of for an interior design firm to be unionized, there will be no attempt in this text to discuss those laws. The U.S. Equal Employment Opportunity Commission enforces federal employment laws.

Several situations do involve federal laws and affect employment in the nonunion professional interior design office. This section discusses two of those in some detail and very briefly mentions several others.

Workers' Compensation

Unfortunately, an employee can be injured on the job, either within the interior design office, on a jobsite, or possibly at other locations connected with the ordinary work of the employee. *Workers' compensation* is actually state law mandating that the employer pay for medical treatment of an employee should the employee be injured on the job—regardless of who was at fault. In essence, by accepting workers' compensation coverage, the employee gives up the right to sue the employer for matters related to the injury. The employer must have insurance, pay into a state fund, or be in essence self-insured to cover the medical expenses if an employee is injured or dies on the job.

The compensation limits are defined by state statute, and the level of responsibilities will thus vary. The key is that regardless of the state the design firm is located in, if the firm has employees, it will have to have workers' compensation insurance. It is thus a very good idea to always check with the state where you are working or where you own your company to know what is expected in that state. The department names differ from state to state, but information can be obtained by going to the Web site of your state government or the U.S. Department of Labor's Web site (www.dol.gov).

Employment Discrimination

Congress and state legislatures want to be sure that individuals are able to fairly obtain and hold jobs. Although these laws generally apply to firms with 15 or more employees—either full-time or part-time—all interior design firms should abide by their intent. Even a small design firm with only one or two employees must avoid discriminatory hiring and working relationships with employees.

Title VII of the Civil Rights Act of 1964, along with the Equal Employment Opportunity Act of 1972 and the Civil Rights Act of 1991, prohibit an employer from discriminating on the basis of sex, race, color, religion, or national origin. An employer cannot discriminate against an employee in terms of hiring, promotions, pay raises, benefits, firing, or many other work-related issues. For example, Jane has repeatedly asked for flexibility in her work hours to accommodate her taking a class at the community college. Each time, her requests are refused and no reason is given for the refusal. Harvey was granted the same request the first time he asked. On the face of it, it appears that Jane has grounds for filing a discrimination complaint.

During the job interviewing and hiring process, employers are also expected to abide by federal laws barring discrimination. It is illegal for employers to ask, either verbally or on a job application, for such things as the employee's (1) age, (2) date of birth, (3) maiden name, (4) marital status, or (5) gender, or for any other information related to age, gender, religion, national origin, race, or marital status. It is possible for the employer to obtain information in less direct ways, if the information would have a significant impact on the interviewee's ability to perform the job responsibilities. More information on this issue is presented in Chapter 30.

A law that is familiar to most readers is the American with Disabilities Act (ADA). This act primarily concerns accommodation in public buildings, but it also affects the workplace. Title I of the ADA affects the hiring and promoting of employees. This portion of the ADA restrains employers from discriminating against any handicapped person who is otherwise qualified for a job and mandates that the employer make "reasonable accommodation" in the structuring of the job and/or modification of the work as necessary for the employee to do the job. Employers with 15 or more employees are required to comply with these legal requirements.

The first line of defense for an employee in any kind of discrimination matter is discussed in the section on sexual harassment. Documentation by the employee of what transpired in a conversation or other actions will be necessary. The EEOC and/or state labor relations departments most commonly review complaints before any lawsuits may be filed. Should the EEOC determine that there is sufficient cause, it will file a civil lawsuit against the employer in the name of the employee. If the employee wishes to talk to an attorney, it is important that the discussion occur with an attorney who specializes in labor law. Not all attorneys will understand the intricacies of discrimination in the workplace well enough to be able to best advise a client.

Other Employment Laws

Here are brief descriptions of other employment laws or regulations that may affect an interior design business:

- The Equal Pay Act of 1963—an amendment to the Fair Labor Standards Act—requires that employers pay all employees who have the same basic work responsibilities and work experience the same amount of salary or wages.

- The Age Discrimination in Employment Act of 1967, which was amended in 1990, prohibits employer discrimination based on the age of the employee. It specifically prohibits discrimination concerning employees 40 years old or older.

- Firms that wish to seek design work with the federal government must comply with Executive Order 11246, which requires firms that do more than $10,000 of business with the federal government to have nondiscrimination clauses in their contracts.

- The Fair Labor Standards Act, commonly called the wage-hour law. It primarily governs wages for employees who are working in companies that are involved in interstate commerce and hourly wage employees. This particular law may not pertain to interior designers who are paid a salary rather than an hourly wage.

- The Occupational Safety and Health Act (OSHA) of 1970 regulates workplace safety. OSHA inspectors, although primarily concerned with production facilities, do make inspections in the office environment, and may inspect an interior design office for such things as properly located fire extinguishers.

There are additional laws that generally only affect firms with numerous employees. In some cases, "numerous" means 15 or more employees; in others, it is 20 or more employees. The employer must be sure that it meets all obligations toward employees that are established by state or federal laws. Readers should check with an attorney and may also wish to review one or more of the books listed in the reference list. There is also much online information on the topics of employee rights and/or employer responsibilities.

WEB SITES RELEVANT TO THIS CHAPTER

www.dol.gov Department of Labor

www.eeoc.gov Equal Employment Opportunity Commission

www.irs.gov Internal Revenue Service

www.mbda.gov Minority Business Development Agency

www.nolo.com Nolo—publications on employment issues

www.osha.gov Occupational Safety and Health Administration

www.sba.gov Small Business Administration

www.ssa.gov Social Security Administration

KEY TERMS

Agency relationship

Agent

Bonus plan

Chain of command

Commission

Compensation

Compensatory time

Cost-of-living adjustment (COLA)

Employee handbook

Employment at will

Employment contract

Fringe benefits

Gross margin

Gross salary

Hourly wage

Implied contract

Incentive compensation

Independent contractor

Job description

Mentoring

Merit pay

Noncompete agreement

Performance evaluation

Principal

Quid pro quo

Restrictive covenant

Sexual harassment

Straight salary

Work product

Workers' compensation

Wrongful discharge

FEDERAL EMPLOYMENT LAWS AND COMMISSIONS

Age Discrimination in Employment Act of 1967/1990

Americans with Disabilities Act Title I

Civil Rights Act of 1991

Equal Employment Opportunity Act of 1972

Equal Employment Opportunity Commission (EEOC)

Equal Pay Act of 1963

Executive Order 11246

Fair Labor Standards Act (wage/hour law)

Occupational Safety and Health Act (OSHA) of 1970

Title VII of the Civil Rights Act of 1964

WHAT WOULD YOU DO?

1. Monica has had an unfortunate bout of illness recently. In addition, her young son has also been sick. This has forced her to miss several days, and once a few weeks, of work each month for the past six months. Although she is entitled to some sick leave each month, the time she has missed exceeds that amount. Her work as a project designer at the firm has repeatedly had to be done by others. However, the work she has accomplished herself has been at a high level and complimented by clients.

   Her boss calls her into his office and informs her that if she misses any more work, he will have to let her go. "All this personal time off is interfering with your ability to get projects completed on time. Other designers have to pick up your slack," her boss says to her at that meeting.

2. The active housing market has led to fast growth for Paul's residential design firm. In the last year, he and his business partners, Ron and Judy, have had to add an office manager and two designers. One is a senior-level designer and one is an entry-level designer who was hired after serving an internship.

   Paul is the managing partner and has been completely stressed out by the overwhelming personnel management issues that keep occurring. Judy thinks they need to add two more employees, but Paul feels that the office is in a certain amount of chaos as it is. Adding people might not be the right choice even though everyone is working 10- to 12-hour days six days a week to keep up. What would you do if you were Paul?

3. Mary worked for a large commercial interior design firm where the number of male employees outnumbered the women. For the most part this was not a problem, as several of the men were willing to provide mentoring and help and good camaraderie to Mary. However, two of the men constantly told off-color jokes and, at lunch meetings at some restaurants, not only ignored Mary in their discussions but also made comments about waitstaff that seemed out of line. After one exceptionally difficult in-house staff meeting, Mary complained to her boss about their rude behavior. He said he would look into it, but after a few weeks, nothing has changed.

REFERENCES

1. Reprinted from p. 543 in *Black's Law Dictionary*, 7th ed., by Bryan A. Garner, ed., 1999, with permission of the West Group.

2. Jentz et al., 1987, p. 479.

3. IRS, 2006, Publication 15-A.

4. Brown and Sukys, 1997, p. 98.

5. Jones and Philcox, 2000, p. 92.

CHAPTER 28

Goals and Career Options

After completing this chapter you should be able to:

- Explain why it is important to set goals.
- Discuss factors that make goal setting difficult for some people.
- Define and explain what a personal mission statement is and why it is a helpful tool for students and professionals.
- Complete the personal goals exercise and the professional goals exercise.
- Discuss the factors that should be considered when making a decision concerning an initial career path.
- Discuss the pros and cons of a career path as a generalist versus a specialist in an area of design.

The interior design profession offers students and professionals numerous options and directions for career opportunities. For many, the direction in the profession seems very logical and direct. "I intend to design residential interiors." "My goal is to be involved in the design of restaurants and hotels," say others. Clearly, this latter sentiment could mean any number of commercial specialties.

Part of one's effort to determine a path in the profession involves personal and professional goal setting. Goals provide direction in our lives. Professional goals help make choices and decisions that arise during our careers easier to navigate. Personal goals help to balance professional activity for a fuller life. Setting goals is risky and takes commitment, but if the goals we set are goals that interest us, they likely will be fulfilled. It takes time to reach goals. Just as Rome was not built in a day, obtaining the credentials to create designs that are purchased by custom furniture manufacturers, or presented awards by magazines and associations, or perhaps work for a major manufacturer does not come overnight.

We also discuss career options and specialties in this chapter. These brief descriptions will assist readers in understanding that the interior design field encompasses substantially more than designing homes. Commercial interior design has taken on increasing importance over the past 60 years with the planning and design of hotels, restaurants, medical facilities, and offices of every kind.

Regardless of where you start in the profession, 5, 10, or 15 years later, you might find yourself doing something totally different in the field. To many designers, this is just one more exciting aspect of this profession.

A PERSONAL MISSION STATEMENT

Many readers have heard of Steven Covey and his very popular book *The Seven Habits of Highly Effective People*. To Covey, a personal mission statement helps a person set a direction for what that person wants to do in his or her personal and professional life. Much like a business mission statement, "it focuses on what you want to be (character) and to do (contributions and achievements) and on the values or principles upon which being and doing are based."[1]

A personal mission statement will help you define your focus, which, in turn, will help you determine on what you most wish to spend your emotional, psychological, and financial resources. According to Covey, a personal mission statement will help you more effectively handle the changes that will constantly affect your life.

Creating a personal mission statement starts with allowing your innermost self to make you aware of what you most want in life—not just today, but in the future. It starts by determining the end you most desire, such as to own a successful design practice, to be the principal project designer at one of the top five design firms in the country, to have both a satisfying family and professional life, or anything else you can imagine.

Here is a brief example of a personal mission statement:

> *To believe in myself and allow myself to try, to experiment, to experience, thus to learn.*
>
> *To strive each day to be willing to pay the price to achieve greater happiness, confidence, and spiritual growth.*
>
> *To do some work that benefits others and that is enjoyable to me.*
>
> *To treat others based on the principles that I hold as important.*

It is a good idea to draft a personal mission statement before you continue reading this chapter. Think of what you want to be known for at the end of your career, or even your life. Consider the roles that you now play within your family, in your career (or potential career), with friends, and in the community at large. Determine your values—what makes you the person that you are. Make notes about the things, words, places, and activities that inspire or excite you. Then take some time away from the hustle and bustle of your daily life to write down a personal mission statement. It doesn't have to be structured like the example. Any format or length will do. You can use Item 28-1 on the companion Web site to develop a personal mission statement.

After reading this chapter, you might want to revise your statement, or you may find that it's fine as it is. Then again, nothing says that you can't rewrite your personal mission statement in a year or more. In fact, it is perfectly natural that it might change as the years go by. This is because new opportunities you can't envision today will possibly present themselves.

PERSONAL AND PROFESSIONAL GOALS

Our world certainly has grown more complex, challenging, and stressful. It can be filled with opportunities for anyone who is willing to seek and achieve success in the interior design profession. Of course, the general economic condition can have an impact on the number of opportunities that exist in any particular geographic area.

Despite economic lows, the interior design profession offers students and professionals numerous options and directions for career opportunities. An effective way of helping to determine career options is through determining and setting personal goals.

Many students and professionals have a goal of going out on their own, having their own studio. Work experience is gained in order to eventually reach that goal. Goals become refined and maybe even changed completely from one type of design to another. Yet for many, sometimes these goals are never reached because many individuals do not actually set their own goals for the future.

Goal success does not just suddenly materialize. It is achieved through hard work, determination, and planning. Sometimes family, friends, children—all of these and others—may enter the picture and delay or prevent an individual from reaching personal and professional goals. But in most cases, the inability to achieve a goal or a dream is not due to other individuals or job responsibilities; rather, it is usually due to a lack of planning and failure to set goals—or maybe setting the wrong goals.

What Are Goals?

Every year, new books—and Web sites—appear about setting goals. In these "how to" publications, authors constantly discuss how individuals with the greatest success have set goals all through their careers.

Without some kind of direction, your personal and professional life can be very frustrating and unfulfilling. Many people live their lives flying by the seat of their pants, purely on going with the flow. For a few lucky people, this method works fine. Unfortunately, for the majority of us, living life purely on the fly leaves us somewhere other than where we want to be.

There is nothing wrong with just experiencing life—letting it happen. However, according to Brian Tracy, "Success is goals, and all else is commentary. All successful people are intensely goal oriented."[2] Whatever your concept of success is, it will be far easier to achieve it if you have a "destination" with goals to help you reach the success you desire. Always consider that goals are concrete ideas requiring effort and commitment to achieve.

Most people have dreams, but many have no goals. There is a difference. Dreams are hopes and imagined fantasies, whereas goals are concrete ideas that represent something a person wants to achieve. Philosophically, goals are brief stops along the way of life that mark achievement in an individual's personal and professional life. Owning your own studio someday is not an end in itself, even though it may have been the goal. Once you achieve that milestone, you must be ready to create new goals related to the success and growth of the studio. "A goal is the ongoing pursuit of a worthy objective until accomplished."[3]

Whether an individual is a student who is still negotiating his or her way through design classes or a professional who has been actively practicing in interior design for several years, personal and professional goal setting is important. When tighter job markets limit choices, students must have a clearer idea of the types of jobs they are interested in pursuing, while remaining open to any reasonable opportunity. The professional who feels unfulfilled needs to take stock of what he or she has accomplished and the skills that he or she possesses.

Even though you may have some general idea about what you want out of your personal and professional life, without some kind of concrete plan, you will find yourself reacting to what happens to you rather than having some control over events in your life. Take control. Develop goals that are meaningful for your professional and personal life and watch those goals help you achieve the vision of what you want for your life!

Risks in Goal Setting

Setting a goal requires commitment of time, energy, and mental processes. Some people do not wish to really make a commitment of any kind beyond their immediate physiological needs. In setting goals, a person runs the risk of failure, that is, of not achieving the goal. But not achieving the goal does not automatically mean failure. The goal may be unattainable at the present time for one reason or another.

Not accomplishing a goal should never be thought of as failure because there can be many reasons that the goal was not accomplished. Chief among these is that the goal may have been set so high that it was unattainable in any reasonable length of time. Maybe the goal was set too high based on the experience level of the individual. Designing high-end residences is a great goal, but not attainable for someone straight out of college.

Another reason people do not set goals is because of the risk of feeling the pain of failure. It is emotionally difficult to admit that you have not achieved some goal that you would like to have accomplished. Of course, it is painful to "fail," but not trying is also emotionally painful. Everyone fails occasionally, and learning from the failure and resolving to fix the issue, or try harder, or do whatever is needed to succeed the next time is very important for successful people.

Here are a few worthwhile thoughts to keep in mind when setting goals:

- Set goals that satisfy you—not parents, a boyfriend or girlfriend, a spouse, or peers. Goals that are set to please others or because they expect it of you will rarely satisfy you.
- Clarify your purpose in setting a particular goal. You have to know what you want and why it is important in order to work at achieving the goal.
- Some goals are unattainable without the proper experience, so certain goals take time to achieve. Be prepared to "pay your dues" in the process of achieving some of your goals.
- Be sure you are honest with yourself in setting goals. Sometimes our temperament, habits, or behavior interfere with achievement of goals.
- Do not be afraid to change goals or change direction. Life is not perfect, and reality usually does not match fantasy. Be flexible in goal setting.
- Unexpected circumstances and a lack of understanding of career requirements are just a few things that can affect your ability to reach your goals.

There is one indisputable fact about life: Life will change. For most, change means growth. So don't be afraid to grow. Being open to a change of plans may offer you an opportunity for personal and professional growth that you had not even considered.

Setting Personal Goals

Whether or not you write a personal mission statement, the best way to set goals is to try to look at yourself in terms of the future. Steven Covey calls it "beginning with the end in mind."[4] In many ways, a similar approach is to write your own obituary today—a rather jarring thought at the age of 21 or at any age. This exercise in goal setting was required by an instructor whom I had in college. The idea was to focus on long-range goal setting. Occasionally, we all need to look at what we want to be remembered for—what we hope we will be

TABLE 28-1.

Personal goals exercise

The purpose of this exercise is to analyze your skills, interests, and abilities in relation to the kind of job opportunities you will be seeking in interior design. Completing this exercise will make you more aware of what you have to offer your present or future employers. It will also help you discover goals that you need to work on in the next year or so.

1. What is your primary interest in interior design?
2. What or who influenced your interest in this profession (family, teacher, mentor, the media, work experience, etc.)?
3. What kind of skills in interior design do you have right now?
4. What special skill(s) do you have to offer your present employer or another employer?
5. If you were going to a job interview tomorrow, what specific career goal would you share with the interviewer?
6. What could you do right now to improve your chances of getting the job you most want?
7. List three of your biggest successes.
8. List five goals you wish to accomplish during the next calendar year.
9. List three goals you hope to accomplish by the time you are 30 years old.
10. List three goals you hope to accomplish by the time you are 50 years old.
11. Assuming it were possible for you to achieve any goal in interior design, what would it be?
12. List 10 mini-goals needed to support the goal stated in number 11.

able to accomplish by the time we pass away. Writing that obituary, or at least beginning with the end in mind, has helped many to more clearly see a focus for future actions.

Understandably, writing your own obituary is an unsettling thing to do. It may be easier to start thinking about what you want to accomplish by the time you are 30, 40, 50, and at retirement age. And, if you find *that* too difficult to do, just try to figure out where you want to be in your professional and personal life during the next five years. Be sure that you include considerations for your personal life as well as professional life. Let me be one of the first to tell you that your professional life should not *be* your life.

If you are unsure of what you want to accomplish, it might help if you use Tables 28-1 and 28-2 to get started. Find a quiet place where you can think undisturbed. Be brutally honest with yourself as you answer the questions in these two tables. Worksheets for Table 28-1 and 28-2 have been included on the companion Web site as Items 28-2 and 28-3.

Once you have some idea of where you want to be, you can start looking at goals in terms of the concrete things that you need to accomplish in order to achieve them. Those specific actions are thought of as strategies.

Strategies are specific actions that are needed to achieve goals. For example, Beth has a goal of owning her own studio by the time she is 35. Assuming that Beth is a 23-year-old student who is about to graduate, what strategies might she need to plan out to achieve that goal?

Here are a few sample strategies:

Work with a residential firm for five years to gain experience in residential practice. Perhaps also work for a commercial firm to gain experience in that area of design.

If necessary, take additional business classes at a community college or enter an MBA program to gain the business knowledge to own and operate a studio.

What are some additional strategies that might be feasible and useful for Beth?

TABLE 28-2.

Professional goals questionnaire

In these questions, you are asked to look at a variety of issues concerning your professional and personal life. Combined with the questions in Table 28-1, these questions give you an opportunity to look at some additional issues that can help clarify your professional and personal goals.

1. List at least three things that drew you into a career in interior design. Write several comments about each of these items.
2. List any three people you most admire. Write down a few words or sentences that explain why you admire them.
3. List three or four companies (or types of firms) that provide the kinds of design work you wish to do.
4. Which of the following is most important to you in your career: money, recognition, self-satisfaction, or creative expression?
5. If you had the means to do so, what would you most like to do—personally and professionally? Remember, no restrictions.
6. What do you think you need to change to make yourself happier in your professional and personal life?
7. What frustrates you most about your professional and personal life?
8. What do you like most about work in interior design? What do you like least?
9. When are you at your best and most secure (professionally and personally)?
10. Do you prefer to work independently or with a group?
11. Write a paragraph that sums up what you most want to be remembered for in your professional (and/or personal) life.
12. On a sheet of paper, make two columns. On the top of one column, write the word *Problem;* on the other, the word *Solution.* Then, in the "Problem" column, write those things that you feel are holding you back or are problems in your professional and/or personal life. In the "Solution" column, write down potential solutions to each problem. In some cases, you may find that you are really writing down thoughts rather than true solutions, but those thoughts will help you find solutions to the problems.

The process is the same for any goal, and in some ways is never ending. New opportunities arise all the time—the trick is to recognize and act upon them. Unexpected problems and challenges might derail you momentarily or even forever. Although staying on track to accomplish goals in the shorter term is always a good idea, keeping oneself open to opportunities that might have long-term implications is important. But isn't that part of the fun?

CAREER DECISIONS

Your first real job in the interior design profession is a significant milestone. For everyone, it is the first step on a journey that can lead to a rewarding and successful future in a career full of challenges and excitement. That first position can also chart a direction toward a goal for the future; more often, it becomes a stepping stone to other opportunities.

Interests in specific kinds of design work obviously influence career options. Outside interests or experiences from a previous career can move you toward a particular specialty. Understanding who you are and what your interests are will help you make the decision as to which area to go into in interior design. Completing the sections on goals earlier in the chapter can be quite helpful.

Few designers remain with the same company for decades. It is likely that you will be with three or more firms before you retire. Some sources say graduates may change jobs as many as 10 times before they retire. And that's okay: It is important to keep yourself open to new opportunities, especially after you have gained some on-the-job experience.

At the beginning of your career, be advised that employers will expect you to "pay your dues"—and this does not mean to a professional association.

Despite the new employee's training and talent, the interior design firm will want to train and observe the employee for some period of time before giving him or her substantial project responsibility. In many cases this means doing what graduates refer to as "menial work," such as maintaining the library, calling for pricing, gathering materials for presentations, and organizing sample boards. There is nothing wrong, however, with maintaining the library. All of these tasks are part of the design process and are undertaken by the most experienced professional as well as the beginner.

It simply takes time to transition from entry-level recent graduate (or new employee) to having the responsibility of dealing directly with clients. The IDEP program (briefly described in Chapter 2) can help speed this transition, as it encourages employers to involve entry-level designers broadly in the whole of the design process. Internships also play a vital role in speeding transition.

Here are several factors that may influence your career decisions:

- In a small firm, the new employee might be able to work on a variety of projects sooner than those who begin work at a larger design firm.
- Expectations for productive work—alongside experienced designers— will be high in a small firm.
- Entry-level designers generally progress more slowly in larger firms.
- Larger firms give an entry-level designer the opportunity to see how a variety of bigger projects are handled by playing a role on a team.
- Compensation and benefits should be weighed carefully; sometimes working for a firm at a lower salary is the better choice because of the experiences that the new designer can have with that firm.
- Promotions come slowly in design; it most likely will take an entry-level designer two years or so to move up to the next job level in a design firm.

One of the fascinating aspects of the interior design profession is the variety of ways in which an individual can work in the field. Although some areas do require training or experience beyond the undergraduate level or the normal interior design degree, many offer positions that the trained interior designer can achieve with work experience in the field.

This *is* a challenging, exciting—sometimes frustrating—profession. But it is also a great way to make a living! A certain amount of patience is necessary in this profession.

DESIGN CAREER SPECIALTIES

There are two recognized branches of the interior design profession. The one with which most readers are familiar is residential interior design, which of course is the design of houses and private living spaces. The other is commercial interior design, which is the design of many kinds of public businesses and private or government facilities.

However, there are many other career options beyond "residential" and "commercial" interior design within the profession and built environment industry. These specialty career areas might focus on a narrower or even an additional range of knowledge and skills suitable for the specialty, such as lighting design, barrier-free design consulting, and interior design management.

This section explains many of these career options so that readers can get an idea of the work of the specialty. It is not all-inclusive, because one could argue that a focus on any one type of space or service also creates a specialty.

Preparing for Career Specialization

There have been lots of arguments in the past few years as to whether interior designers should be generalists or specialists. It is believed that when the economy is slow or flat, a generalist can find projects of some kind while a specialist might find himself twiddling his thumbs. Both arguments have merit.

The generalist feels that she is able to design any kind of space, whether it is a residence or a commercial facility of some kind. However, clients have increasingly indicated that they like to hire experts. A client who hires someone to design a private residence wants that designer to understand the needs of residential design. A client who hires someone to design a store or medical office wants to know that the interior designer is familiar with that client's business and design needs. This brief section discusses decisions the designer must make if he or she wishes to specialize rather than be a generalist.

Many specialty areas require extensive job experience and even additional education. For example, a designer does not become successful at the design of healthcare spaces without experience and knowledge about healthcare practice. But how can one find out what experience or education is required for any specific career option in interior design?

Researching the specialty is one way of understanding that specialty. Reading textbooks, design books, and trade publications on the specialty is one easy way to learn about it. Interior design and architecture trade magazines provide impressions of what it is like to design all types of interiors.

Another way to prepare for career specialization is to interview designers who already work in that segment of the design field. Interior designers are like most people: They love to talk about what they do and are flattered to find out that others are interested in their work. It is suggested that the individual ask for no more than 30 minutes of the designer's time; this shows respect for his or her professional responsibilities.

Personal experience can be another way to learn about a specialty. Some students become interested in healthcare design because of a family member's health problems. Those who work their way through college with jobs in retail stores often become interested in visual merchandising or retail design. Family members and family friends certainly influence a career direction and may also influence a specialty focus. For example, perhaps an uncle is a veterinarian who talks about the importance of the interior for keeping animals calm during office visits.

It is advisable to seek additional coursework that will indirectly provide general background information about a design specialization. For example, someone who wishes to specialize in hospitality design should take some introductory classes in the hospitality industry. Those who wish to work in retail design would be wise to take merchandising and visual merchandising classes.

Students should also recognize that many specialized interior design firms might not hire an entry-level designer. I have heard from numerous specialized firm principals over the years that they simply do not hire entry-level designers. In general, the reason is that the lack of actual work experience prevents an entry-level designer from working at the pace and intensity needed in such firms. "We need designers who can hit the ground running," commented one such principal. "Entry-level designers, regardless of the quality of their talent, cannot do this," the principal continued. Their advice is for students to get good-quality actual work experience and learn what it is really like to work in design before they apply for a job in a highly specialized design firm. Of course, there is no reason a newly graduated student could not apply

TABLE 28-3.

Partial list of residential interior design specialties

Single-family homes	Model homes and apartments
Townhouses	Dormitories
Condominiums	Sustainable design
Patio homes	Senior housing
Apartments	Apartments in assisted-living facilities
Manufactured housing units	Color consultation
Vacation homes	Historical restoration/renovation
Residential restoration	Custom closets/storage
Kitchen and/or bathroom design	Residential children's spaces
Home offices	Renovation for the physically challenged
Home theater design	Private yachts and houseboats
Music rooms/game rooms	Home staging

anyway. Being in the right place at the right time has gotten many designers their first job.

Residential Interior Design

Residential interior design deals with private living spaces, most frequently the freestanding, single-family home, as well as many other types of private residences. Designers might also specialize in functional areas within the umbrella of a residence, such as kitchen and bath design. Other specialty areas are listed in Table 28-3.

An important characteristic of residential interior design is the personal relationship that usually develops between the client and the designer. The ability to get along with people and develop sensitivity in questioning clients, to uncover their needs and wants, is very important. Residential clients are quite particular about what they buy and how their home reflects their image. Tact and diplomacy are a must, when showing the client the realities of good and bad design ideas and translating expressed desires into a design concept with which the client can live.

Commercial Interior Design

Commercial interior design—sometimes called contract interior design—involves the design and specification of public spaces, such as offices, hotels, hospitals, restaurants, and so on. There are many kinds of public spaces, and it is normal for a commercial designer to focus his or her practice on only one area or perhaps on a few types of related public spaces. Depending on the size of the design firm, a firm might offer expertise in multiple specialties. Table 28-4 is a partial list of the specialties that exist within commercial interior design.

An important skill for today's commercial interior designer is to have knowledge and appreciation of the client's business. This knowledge helps the designer ask better questions about the needs and goals of the client during programming. The designer also realizes that clients are different even when they are in similar business categories. Therefore, the designer needs to understand the business of the business in order to make appropriate design decisions.

It is also important to realize that the client who has contracted with the designer is often only one of the users/stakeholders that must be satisfied. The

TABLE 28-4.

Partial list of commercial interior design specialties

Almost any kind of commercial or business facility can become a specialty in interior design. Choosing too narrow a specialty, however, can limit the amount of business the interior designer will be able to obtain.

General offices

Facility planning

Corporate executive offices

LEED® specialist

Professional offices

Law
Advertising/public relations
Accounting
Stockbrokers and investment brokers
Real estate and real estate development
Financial institutions: banks, credit unions, and trading centers
Architecture, engineering, and interior design
Consultants of various kinds

Health care
Hospitals and health maintenance group facilities
Medical specialty office suites
Nursing homes and assisted-living facilities
Medical and dental office suites
Outpatient laboratories and radiological treatment facilities
Psychiatric facilities
Rehabilitation facilities
Medical laboratories
Veterinary clinics

Hospitality and recreation
Hotel, motels, and resorts
Restaurants, coffee shops, etc.
Commercial kitchens
Recreational facilities
Health clubs and spas
Country clubs
National and state park facilities
Amusement park facilities
Sports complexes
Auditoriums and theaters
Museums
Convention centers
Casinos
Set design: movies and television

Retail facilities/merchandising
Malls and shopping centers
Department stores
Specialized retail stores
Gift shops in hotels, airports, and other facilities
Store visual merchandising
Displays for trade shows
Showrooms
Galleries
Boutiques

TABLE 28-4.

(*Continued*)

Educational and institutional facilities
Colleges, universities, and community colleges
Secondary and elementary schools
Day-care centers and nursery schools
Private schools
Churches and other religious facilities

Government offices (federal, state, and local)
Courthouses and courtrooms
Prisons

Industrial facilities
Corporate offices
Manufacturing facilities
Training facilities
Employee service areas, such as lunchrooms and fitness centers

Transportation
Airports, bus terminals, train depots, etc.
Tour ship design
Custom and commercial airplane interiors
Boats and ships
Recreational vehicles

Adaptive use

Restoration of historic commercial sites

Commercial products design

satisfaction of employees and the public or the clientele of the business directly affects the success of the design and future business. Not understanding and designing in relationship to this issue can result in a nice-looking interior for an unhappy client.

Facility Planners

Many corporations and institutional organizations realize the economic benefit of having their own planning and design team. *Facility planners* are part of the facility management department, which is responsible for the physical plant (the building and its systems). The facility management department ensures that everything involved in the business—building, equipment, and people—is organized and arranged to best function together to meet the management's goals.

Designers might work as facility planners or be hired by the corporation to work with in-house facility planners. Specialized degrees in facility planning are available, but many facility planners are interior designers or architects.

The job of facility manager, sometimes in the same department as a facility planner, is a more specialized career and requires additional training in psychology, physical plant management, and engineering.

Lighting Designers

Although all designers learn something about lighting concepts and lighting design as part of their curriculum, lighting interiors to create special environments involves skills and experience that the average interior designer does not have. Designers can specialize in lighting design, continually learning about new products but also about all the intricacies of lighting science and design application. There are firms that specialize in providing consulting to other designers, as well as to clients, in the lighting design of all types of spaces, both residential and commercial in context.

Sales Representatives

Sales representatives, also called *sales reps*, may work in retail furniture and furnishings stores and dealerships, in manufacturers' showrooms, and as outside sales reps for manufacturers. Sales reps in retail stores might be referred to as *sales associates*. A sales associate is not always an interior designer, but rather someone who is skilled in sales techniques. Many retail stores and office furnishings dealers hire interior designers to be sales associates. Additional information on sales representatives and dealers is provided in Chapter 10.

Barrier-Free or Universal Design

Although compliance with accessibility standards is required for new construction, many owners of public buildings that were built prior to adoption of accessibility standards are unsure of what must be done to comply with the standards. A career option for some designers experienced with barrier-free design concepts is consulting to businesses to help them comply with standards—either before or after a lawsuit is filed. For example, the prime designer might not be knowledgeable about current barrier-free requirements; in this instance, that firm may engage a consulting designer to review plans for new or remodeled facilities to be sure that the plans will meet the legal requirements prior to submittal for building permits.

Sustainable Design

Designers who focus on sustainable design assist the owners and developers of commercial facilities and home owners who are increasingly interested in sustainable design. Their practice focuses on the use of products and methodologies to lessen impact on the natural environment and improve the interior environment.

Helping to provide standards in this area is the LEED® (Leadership in Energy and Environmental Design) program from the U.S. Green Building Council (USGBC). This program has established both standards for sustainable designed buildings and a professional accreditation program. LEED®-accredited designers might work for any type or size of interior design or architectural firm.

CAD Specialist

CAD specialists, sometimes called CAD technicians, rarely are responsible for design decisions. Because the majority of designers today are CAD qualified, this career is less often an option. Some designers may still choose to remain technicians and assist designers and architects by producing the drawings that are required to finish a job. This type of work is often outsourced, so the enterprising CAD specialist can create an independent business. The Internet allows CAD work to be done almost anywhere in the world.

Other Computer Specialists

Large design firms and independent consultants might choose to pursue work as "tech" specialists. Although it is often thought of only in relation to information technology (IT), this job specialty actually includes individuals who choose to work exclusively using one or more types of programs or specialty tasks. Specification writing and preparation of bid documents are examples.

Professional Renderers

Many in design feel that rendering is becoming a lost art. However, clients and other designers continue to utilize renderings to express design concepts to clients and for clients to use to market properties. The professional renderer is very skilled in perspective and various rendering media, including the use of 2D and 3D CAD programs. He or she may be employed by a large interior design or architectural firm, or may be self-employed as a freelance renderer.

Model Builders

Similar to the professional renderers are model builders. These individuals may also be professional renderers, or they may only produce architectural and interior models. Multidisciplinary firms might have model builders on staff, although there are many model building companies and freelance model builders. Model building requires that the individual have an excellent sense of scale, knowledge of the kinds of material that can be used to produce a scale model, a concern for detail, and patience to do the work required in model building.

Product Designers

Interior designers who have gained a strong reputation in the field and experience in the custom design of products may supplement or modify their practice to focus on product design. Designers can start their own company to produce their designs or license their designs to a manufacturer. Product designers working directly for a manufacturer may need to have an industrial design background.

Interior Design Management

A position in interior design management requires extensive experience in the field or experience in general management. Most design directors are former designers. It is important for the design director to have knowledge of interior design and good general business knowledge or experience related to the management of personnel, marketing, and general business principles.

Marketing Specialists

Large interior design firms frequently utilize a marketing specialist to prospect and market for new clients. This person may be an interior designer who has a special ability to market, or a business major with an emphasis in marketing. The marketing specialist is expected to locate new clients and to respond to inquiries from potential clients.

Teaching

A very satisfying way to "give back" to the profession is to join the faculty of an interior design program. The minimal educational requirement for a full-time faculty position is a master's degree, in addition to some professional experience. Most programs, regardless of size and type of institution, expect that faculty members will continue their education beyond a master's degree, engage in academic research and publishing, and/or remain active in the design profession. Interior design programs also hire practitioners as adjunct or visiting instructors to teach part-time.

Museum Work

Interior designers with experience or additional training in museum, restoration, or curatorial areas can work for one of the many historic site museums that exist. This can be very rewarding work for those individuals who have a keen interest in history and restoration. Most of these job opportunities require advanced degree work in such areas as art history, history, and archaeology.

Journalism

A journalism career is possible for interior designers who are very good writers or who have had training in journalism. The position might be with a large city newspaper or a trade or shelter magazine. Some designers who find their way into full-time journalism positions might also serve as design critics.

Merchandising and Exhibit Design

Many of the skills that an interior designer learns can be applied to visual merchandising, display, and exhibit presentation. Department stores, retail specialty shops, mall management corporations, galleries, and trade show coordinators require merchandise displays. Department stores have in-house visual merchandising departments to oversee their constantly changing merchandise displays. Others work for exhibit companies that specialize in the coordination and setup of trade show and convention displays.

Architectural Photographers

An architectural photographer today is usually someone who has trained to be a professional photographer. These individuals specialize in the photography of exteriors and interiors, and are hired by the interior designer, the architect, or the owner of the building.

As a final note, this section has provided just a glimpse at the wide variety of opportunities in the interior design industry. Many of these career options are possible with a degree major in interior design, whereas others require at least several years of experience in the field. Some also require additional education, training, or advanced degrees for eligibility. Several other specialties that might be of interest to readers are listed in Table 28-5.

TABLE 28-5.

Additional career options related to the interior design profession

Acoustic design	Real estate
Lighting design	Tenant improvement planning
Art consulting	Installation supervisor
Client representative/facilitator	Contract administrator
Feng shui consultant	Construction supervision
Color consultant	Wayfinding design
Expert witness	Feasibility studies
Codes consultant	Behavioral factors design
Universal design specialist	Security design
CAD specialist	Specification writer
Graphic design	

WEB SITES RELEVANT TO THIS CHAPTER

www.asid.org/careers American Society of Interior Designers

www.careersininteriordesign.com Careers in Interior Design

www.interiordesigncanada.org Interior Designers of Canada

www.iida.org International Interior Design Association

www.bls.gov U.S. Bureau of Labor Statistics

KEY TERMS

Commercial interior design	Personal goals
Contract interior design	Professional goals
Facility planner	Residential interior design
Goals	

WHAT WOULD YOU DO?

1. A good friend of yours works for another interior design firm in the area. You know that she applied for membership in one of the professional associations because you both applied at the same time. Your application is still pending, and you know hers is as well. At a meeting, you noticed that her card had the appellation "ASID" after her name. This puzzles you because you know that she has not yet passed the NCIDQ examination. In fact, she is not even eligible, since you both graduated only six months ago.

2. Marilyn has been working very hard for the past nine weeks with a very difficult client, Mr. Norton, owner and developer of a facility for Alzheimer patients. He constantly challenges her suggestions and has already demanded four major changes in the specifications of products and three changes in the equipment plans for the common areas for the facility her firm is designing for his company. His primary argument is that she is overspecifying materials, using "expensive" products when cheaper ones would do—at least as far as he is concerned.

"You have not even come close to staying within the budget we discussed at the beginning of this project. I insist that you find something besides that expensive cubicle curtain and drapery fabric and find me a cheaper chair for the dining room," Mr. Norton exclaims. "It's not that the cubicle curtain and drapery fabric is expensive, but it must meet a certain level of code compliance, which this one does. Less expensive chairs will not hold up to the special needs of the residents who need an armchair," responds Marilyn. "I don't care about that!" explodes Mr. Norton.

3. Sandra was hired by Hayden Residential Designs four years ago. She started as an intern and was promoted to designer a year later. Because of her exceptional sales results, she was promoted again just six months ago to senior designer. A month ago, Ms. Mill, the design director, discussed with Sandra some problems that clients had been expressing about Sandra's performance over the past several months. Sandra was told at that time that she needed to correct the attitude that clients complained about. Yesterday another client called the owner, Jim Hayden, and was very angry about some things that Sandra said at a meeting.

4. Mark made a point of setting and reviewing his goals every three months. He even took a day during a weekend to go through the effort. Yet Mark felt like he was not getting anywhere. He finally took a long look at what he was doing and his goals and discovered that he started many things to get moving toward his goals, but never seemed to finish up what was needed to fully accomplish them.

REFERENCES

1. Covey, 1989, p. 106.
2. Tracy, 2003, p. 7.
3. Canfield et al., 2000, p. 61.
4. Covey, 1989, p. 97.

CHAPTER 29

The Job Search

After completing this chapter you should be able to:

- Explain the importance of an organized job search.
- Explain how an informational interview can be helpful to your overall job search.
- Discuss the purpose of the resumé.
- Explain the characteristics of the different types of resumés and when each can be used.
- Draft your resumé with emphasis on a career objective or career summary.
- Explain why an entry-level designer should place educational achievements before work achievements on a resumé.
- Discuss why it is important to be careful about what kind of personal information is included in the resumé.
- Explain the purpose of a cover letter and list what it should contain.
- Outline the types of items that are most often included in a portfolio.
- Explain why a portfolio is never finished.
- Discuss how you can tailor your portfolio to a job interview at a residential versus a commercial firm.
- Compare and contrast an electronic resumé to a paper resumé.
- Discuss benefits and disadvantages of creating an electronic version of your portfolio.

The job search can be a time-consuming and stress-producing period. The ease with which you may find the first—or next—job fluctuates wildly in direct relationship to the economy. In good times, plenty of jobs are available at all levels. When the economy becomes tight, even seasoned professionals have a hard time finding new employment opportunities. The process of finding an interior design position can seem like a roller-coaster ride at any time.

Because the interior design profession does ebb and flow with the economy, students and design professionals must be thorough in their approach to their career efforts. When they are ready to make a move or to start the job search process, they must do so with careful thought and planning. This job search process starts with the material that was covered in Chapter 28.

Critical to the job search are strategies related to the development of the resumé, cover letter, and portfolio. This chapter provides in-depth guidance on how employers review resumés, the job interview, and follow-up. This chapter also consolidates the previous edition's information on the digital job search. These topics are separated so that readers can be introduced to and study the basic job search topics before moving on to how these items are affected by digital media.

Books you might find at a bookstore are going to be much more general in nature, though many may also be helpful. The few books available that specifically relate to the design profession job search are generally related to the development of the portfolio and are, of course, very valuable to the candidate. The Internet now contains a vast variety of information as well, some of which is directed toward the interior design profession.

THE SEARCH IS ON

The job search may be a quick process, or it can seem to take forever. In good times graduates have their choice of jobs. Professionals can sometimes write their own ticket in a booming market location. In a tough market, job seekers must be willing to take less than an ideal situation and even be more creative in search strategies.

Whether the market for interior design jobs is good or poor, for the student, the job search begins long before graduation. The student must evaluate what part of the profession holds the most interest for him or her. Does the student dislike making presentations and therefore not want to be a salesperson? Does the student find making technical working drawings boring but working with colors exciting? Is there a geographic preference? These kinds of questions, along with many others, must be asked to help with the job search. Sometimes using a book such as Richard Nelson Bolles's *What Color Is Your Parachute?* is a help in determining career goals more precisely. Table 29-1 provides some tips on the job search process.

Information about the specialties of the interior design field, responsibilities within different work environments, and potential employers is available from many sources. College advisers and career counselors can be helpful sources of information regarding different design companies. Students can join student chapters of professional associations, attend the professional chapter

TABLE 29-1.

Tips on the job search process

1. Have a strategy and plan. Know what you are looking for and what your "bottom line" might be. By bottom line I mean the level of job (junior designer rather than project designer)—especially important in a down economy.
2. Be realistic. Salary and benefits are not going to be as high as you might expect, regardless of the level of your skills. But you also shouldn't sell your skills at a bargain-basement price. Be prepared to negotiate salary, benefits, hours of work, and other considerations of employment.
3. Evaluate your skills carefully. If you are deficient in some skill that is important to the type of job you seek, get training at a community college or possibly an online program (for a codes class, for example).
4. Be prepared. Make sure your portfolio is always in excellent shape and your resumé is ready to go. Don't forget that when you attend a professional meeting, you are also interacting with people who may be looking for an employee. Always dress and act the part of the consummate professional in professional situations.
5. Use social media—carefully. Certainly social media is an avenue to potential job openings. However, job seekers need to be careful about what is posted on any social media site they participate in. Employers will look you up on Facebook and all the other sites. A fun-loving photo on your personal page might be great for friends, but can give the wrong impression to a potential employer.

meetings at the local level, and perhaps participate on committees. Students can also talk to relatives and friends who might have worked with designers or who know someone in the industry. The book *Becoming an Interior Designer* by this author provides insights and input from interior designers in numerous specialties from all over the country. If you are looking to move to a new city, perhaps your professors can make suggestions. Obviously, the Internet can also be a great help in this situation.

One of the best ways to understand what the interior design field is all about is to schedule an *informational interview* with an interior designer who works in the type of situation in which you have an interest. In this case, you are doing the interviewing rather than the designer. Here are some important strategies if you go this route:

- Plan several questions that you want to ask the designer.
- Be precise about what you want to know.
- Assume that you will have from 15 to 30 minutes for this interview.
- Call at least a week ahead of time to ask for the meeting.
- Be prompt, be pleasant, and do not try to turn it into a job interview.
- Dress professionally and be respectful.
- Don't overstay your time unless the designer seems to be willing to let the clock continue to run.
- Don't forget to send a thank-you card!

You might also find job announcements through university career placement offices. Positions with corporations might be available through this source. Department stores, print media, and the federal government may also interview for design staff through the career placement office.

Reliable standbys for gathering information on design firms include Web searches, Yellow Pages ads, local publications, and classified ads. This type of research does not reveal current job openings, but it provides material about companies that might have them. Yellow Pages ads do not always provide the name of the owner or manager of a design firm, but they can give some information related to the company. Firms that sell a lot of merchandise often list in their ads the product lines that the firm carries. These product lines will help the student determine if the firm is primarily a residential or a commercial interior design firm. Don't just look under "interior design": Many companies will have larger ads listed under "furniture" and "office furniture."

Social media sites like LinkedIn can also help the job seeker find openings. Groups in LinkedIn generally allow group members to post job openings or allow a group member to "advertise" for a job. Whether the seeker is a student who is ready to graduate or a professional who needs or wants to make a job change, the Internet has become a primary way to locate jobs. Unfortunately, because so many people use this search strategy, it is easy to get lost in the crowd.

Professionals who are looking for new positions usually hear about job openings by word of mouth. Others discreetly put out the word to allied associates, such as sales reps, that they are looking for a new position. Quite a lot of job searching and interviewing occurs during trade shows, like NeoCon in Chicago. This is especially true for designers and others who are interested in sales positions. However, design firms may also advertise that they will be interviewing during one of the NeoCon shows.

Employed professionals who are looking for another position must be discreet. The search has to go on while they are still completing current responsibilities. Disregarding your current work responsibilities to go out on interviews is a very bad idea. Understandably, employers do not like their employees looking for another job while they are still working. Yet, of course, not everyone can afford to quit a current job in order to look for a new one. Almost all books on searching for a job advise readers not to quit the current job before they have obtained a new job.

Here are a few hints for the professional who is seeking a new job while presently employed:

- Do not use company time, telephones, or supplies for the job search.
- Do not fake client appointments in order to go on interviews.
- It is acceptable to schedule appointments during the lunch hour.
- Use vacation time to interview for out-of-town jobs; do not call in sick.
- Under the employment-at-will doctrine, you should give some notice when you are ready to leave, though it is not mandatory. Someone has to be prepared to take over any projects that you are leaving behind.

Searching for a position that suits the graduate or experienced professional requires thought and planning—just like any interior design project. You must manage this process right from the beginning. It helps to keep a record of all correspondence, keeping copies of each letter and resumé that you send out, and recording phone calls and other contacts. Taking notes during phone calls and preparing follow-up notes after interviews are also useful techniques. Look at each negative response as an opportunity to learn how to make future inquiries positive. Most importantly, don't give up!

The strategies listed in this section, and in the later discussion on digital job search, are all ways to locate potential jobs.

Executive Search Firms

Professional employment agencies or executive search firms can help you locate a design job. Don't let the title "executive" lead you to think that such a firm is only for the very experienced. Some will not take on a recent graduate or someone with only a few years of experience; that can be determined with a quick phone call. If you wish to use this method of locating a job, you need to do some homework about the search companies before you sign on with one.

These professional employment agencies are sometimes called *headhunters*. That name used to refer to companies that search out and essentially "steal" an executive or an employee from one firm in order to place that employee in another firm. Today the term is commonly used to refer to any executive search firm.

An executive search firm works on a commission that generally is paid by the hiring employer. Because of this, the search firm is interested in helping the employer, not necessarily you. The search firm's task is to fill contracts with employers. These firms are usually looking for the senior-level designer or manager-level positions in the design firm. A contingency firm looks for a wider range of types and salary levels of positions. This type of agency might be a better opportunity for the less experienced designer.

If you decide to use an executive search firm, investigate it thoroughly to be sure that it deals with the interior design and architecture industries. If you are going to use an executive search firm, know what you are looking for before you approach one. You also need to understand all the restrictions and fees involved. You could waste a lot of time waiting for the firm to find you something if you don't fit its profile. Names of executive search firms that specialize in interior design and architecture positions can sometimes be found in the classified sections of trade magazines. If you are interested in working with an agency, you may want to check *The Directory of Executive Recruiters* at a local library to find recruiters in your area and field.

Some executive recruiting companies may want you to sign an exclusive agreement with them. Employment experts suggest that you do not do so: It is not appropriate for them to ask this, and it also limits your possibilities.

RESUMÉS

Whether you are a student embarking on your first position in the profession or an experienced professional wanting to move on to new challenges, one of the most important tools you will use to obtain a position is a resumé. A *resumé* is a summary of a person's qualifications. It must instantly communicate fundamental information related to your work experience, education, special skills related to the desired position, and career objectives.

Resumés can be from one page in length to multiple pages. Graduating students rarely require more than one page for a resumé, due to their limited work experience. It is a rare student who needs more than two pages unless the graduate is a second-career individual.

Professionals generally require at least two pages, and may need a longer resumé if they have extensive experience. Remember that those who review resumés do not have time to read exceedingly long documents. Pertinent information should be communicated distinctly and briefly.

Certain kinds of information are expected in all resumés. How this information is presented varies somewhat with the format used by the applicant, as discussed later in this chapter. Understand that your resumé plays a significant part in whether you will obtain an interview. In some companies, a resumé is also important in reviews for promotions.

As you read the remaining parts of this section, remember that fudging in your resumé is never, ever acceptable. There are many ways an employer can verify information, so always be truthful.

A resumé is always accompanied by a cover letter if it is mailed or faxed. If the resumé is e-mailed, it is more courteous to send a short note along with the resumé. A worksheet to help you develop your resumé has been included on the companion Web site as Item 29-1. A list of active verbs that can be used in resumés and cover letters is provided in Table 29-2. You may want to refer to Figure 29-1 as you read through these next sections.

Contact Information

Contact information generally heads up a resumé. This is simply your full name, mailing address, telephone number, cell phone number, e-mail address, and perhaps a fax number. Do not forget to include any professional association affiliations (used correctly) in the contact information. Never put your Social Security number on the resumé!

Be sure you include your daytime phone number, as that is the number a prospective employer is most likely to call. Students should consider including both a permanent address and an address at school. Do not use a fax or e-mail address at work as part of your contact information. Do not allow job search mailings to come to your current job location.

TABLE 29-2.

Some active verbs that can be used in resumés and cover letters

Accomplished	Demonstrated	Negotiated
Achieved	Designed	Organized
Arranged	Developed	Performed
Assisted	Directed	Prepared
Collected	Established	Presented
Communicated	Executed	Reviewed
Composed	Formalized	Scheduled
Conceptualized	Gathered	Selected
Conducted	Improved	Supervised
Contributed	Initiated	Trained
Coordinated	Introduced	Wrote
Created	Managed	

Be very careful about receiving phone calls concerning job searches at your current place of employment. Your boss will not be pleased to discover that you are using company time to look for another job.

Although these items are common and the employer needs some way to get in touch with you, privacy issues have become more prevalent in recent years. You may wish to set up a separate e-mail account for the job search and only use a cell phone number (rather than a home number) in your contact information.

A *heading* can be part of the contact information or a separate item. A heading is particularly important with an electronic version of the resumé, but can also be of benefit on a standard one. A separate heading line is no longer than a short sentence. Something as simple as: "Resumé of James Jones" or "Proven sales winner!" can work. The intention is for this headline or subject line of an electronic version to catch the employer's attention and cause them to open your mailing.

Career Summary and Career Objective

The *career summary*, in a few brief sentences, provides a significant statement concerning your ability to handle the job for which you are applying. It usually contains brief snapshot information about your skills and accomplishments. You will provide specifics in the "Work Experiences" section of the resumé. A career summary in combination with a career objective statement is also effective for a professional who is making a major job shift. For the student who is beginning a career, a *career objective* is often more appropriate.

A *career objective* talks about what you want to do rather than what you have already accomplished. For example, "Energetic recent graduate seeking employment with a creative residential design firm that also includes opportunities to design assisted-living facilities."

A career summary for an experienced interior designer might read, "Senior project manager with 11 years' experience in hospitality design with

Sandra A. Mathews, ASID
200 Mocking Bird Lane
Richmond, Virginia 23375
Phone (314) 555-2000
E-mail sandram@xxx.net

Key Word Summary

Ten years' experience in health care, hospitality, and corporate office design. Project Manager, Senior Designer. AutoCAD 2000, PowerPoint, Microsoft Project. Marketing responsibility, team management, NCIDQ certified, ASID chapter leadership, BS Interior Design.

Design Experience

Carson Jefferies, Inc. Richmond, VA.

1994 to present. Project Designer
1991–1994 Senior Designer

- Direct design teams of 3–8 professionals in design of hospitality and healthcare projects.
- Space-plan and design corporate offices. Familiar with Haworth and Herman Miller systems.
- Responsible for obtaining contracts of over $230,000 in fees in past two years.
- Hired and scheduled subcontractors and supervised installations.
- Developed two presentations using PowerPoint, which have become templates for company.

Associated Interior Architects. Del Mar, CA.

1989–1991 Designer

- Space-plan and design executive offices, law offices, and banking facilities.
- Assisted senior designers with drafting, product research, and specification writing.
- Assisted in space-planning two open-office systems projects of over 25,000 square feet each.

Education

U.C. San Diego

Part-time, 19XX–19XX. Classes in Marketing.

Arizona State University

19XX Bachelor of Design Science. Major: Contract Interior Design

Professional Affiliations

International Interior Design Association, Professional member
Chapter Publicity Committee
American Society of Interior Designers, Professional member
American Institute of Architects, Affiliate member
NCIDQ Certificate # 55555

FIGURE 29-1.

Chronological resumé prepared by a professional, shown in a format acceptable for electronic transmission or scanning.

one of the top design firms in the country. Experienced in all aspects of the design process, certified in AutoCAD, Revit, and SketchUp. Recipient of numerous awards for creative work." Here is an example for a professional who is seeking a position as a representative with a manufacturer: "Ten years' sales experience for office furnishings dealers, specializing in Herman Miller and Steelcase open-office systems. Exceeded sales goals 11 out of 15 years."

When you are using a career objective, it is important that it not be so narrow as to limit other possibilities—assuming you are open to other possibilities—or so broad that it seems that you have no direction or objective. Consider this objective: "A position as an interior designer." It is too vague and indicates to the employer that you have not given much thought to your future.

Whether sent electronically or on paper, be sure you are also using key words that will attract attention at the particular organization or job. It is also important to include quick mention of licenses or certifications if your heading did not show this.

Education

For the recent graduate, a most important block of information on a resumé summarizes his or her education. This section follows the career objective for students, because it is the primary "experience" a student has had up to this point. A professional commonly places educational information after work experience information.

It is best to begin this section with academic training first. Supplemental courses and seminar attendance should be listed after academic degrees. Begin first with the highest degree you have earned. Include the name of the institution and its location; the kind of degree earned and the year granted; major and minor; and any academic or career-related activities. Students should list a grade-point average only if it was exceptionally high. About a year after graduation, drop the grade-point average from the resumé. Students do not need to list high school education, unless it was a prestigious school or a foreign educational institution.

For professionals already in practice, employers are not particularly interested in grade-point average or academic activities. Professionals should, however, include professional continuing education units (CEUs) and any other formal educational training in this section. However, if the professional has taken a large number of CEU classes, he or she should list only the most recent and any others that show updating related to the job being sought. You can always provide a supplemental sheet.

Professional Accomplishments

Professional accomplishments should include information on certifications, licensing, and awards. A subheading can be used under "Education," or you can include a separate section such as "Certifications and Awards" or "Professional Accomplishments." Involvement in professional associations should be listed with the proper acronym. If you have been involved in a large number of committees, consider listing only the ones for which you have served as an officer or chair. If your list of awards and involvement is long, you can always prepare a supplement that details this information and provide it if requested by the employer.

Work Experience

Depending on which format you choose for your resumé, the work experience portion will be written differently. It is important to focus on what you accomplished in each job. Even students can provide some brief comments concerning accomplishments during an internship in the work experience section. Truth is vital, as embellishments that either don't sound real or are discovered to be false will inevitably be discovered and your reputation and credibility harmed.

Traditionally, this section lists the name and location of the company, the years worked for each, and the titles of the positions held. One or more brief narrative statements about skills developed, responsibilities, and/or accomplishments in each position follow this. Students will want to place the internship first in the work experience section, followed by summaries of part-time jobs.

Professionals need to list projects for which they have been responsible. The organization of this information varies with the job objective. It is not necessary to list every single project on which you have worked. If you have extensive experience, highlight the key projects that might be of interest to the prospective employer. For example, it would make more of an impression to note that you were the project designer for a restaurant in the Bellagio Hotel than to include an unrelated list of small projects on which you worked three years ago. Be selective about your project list so that your resumé does not become too long. Also, ethics are involved here, so you must be careful about how you take credit for work on which you might have been a team member but not the project designer.

Personal Information

The most important personal information on a resumé will be contact information. Anything else is up to the individual.

Including marital status, names of children, service records, height, weight, and health conditions provides information that an employer cannot legally ask about except within the bounds discussed in Chapter 30. Volunteering this information could prejudice a decision, and the applicant would not have any grounds for challenging the prejudiced decision.

That is also true of certain community activities in which you may have participated. Unfortunately, these can also unwittingly cause a prospective employer to discriminate against you. There would be nothing you could do, since you volunteered the information.

Depending on the position, it might be beneficial to include information about travel experiences, especially foreign travel. A firm that does global work will be interested in someone who has had the opportunity to travel—especially on a study tour.

Skills and Key Words

Technology has increased the importance of being sure that you include reference terms identifying skills in interior design. Skills terms and key words are especially important in an electronic version of your resumé. In that context, an employer can scan resumés for an assortment of key words. Any resumé that contains those words will go into the "save" pile, whereas those that do not include those terms will likely be ignored.

An interior design firm is going to look for terms and words such as AutoCAD, Revit, and other software titles; project management; LEED® specialist; building codes; and other terms that key into skill sets, knowledge areas, and design tasks that are critical for the firm's staff. A firm may also look for other terms or key words, like sales experience, space-planning, and product coordination. Obviously, these are only a small sampling of the kinds of key words and skills employers will be searching for.

Fluency in any foreign language will be an important skill for large firms doing global business. Fluency, by the way, means that you can speak, write, and read the language as well as a native. Conversational skill means you can speak it but might not be able to read and write it very well. Language skills are also important to many small firms in many markets.

Another approach for experienced professionals is to include a section highlighting core competencies or areas of expertise. This emphasizes that you know how to apply knowledge in the field, and it indicates skill attainment at an advanced level. A few examples are bid specification coordination, accessibility evaluation, and sustainability problem solving.

References

It is not necessary to list references on a resumé or even to provide them without a request from the prospective employer. Most references are not checked until after the interview and before an offer has been made. When creating your list of references, you should ask the persons beforehand if you can list them.

Most employers assume that the work and education history are the starting point for your references. These are the people whom they will likely want to contact first. Unless the employer asks for a copy of a list of references, or references are required in any employment application that must be filled out, most of the discussion of references will occur during the interview.

A professional who is seeking a job while he or she is still working may not want the current employer to know that he or she is looking for a job elsewhere. If this knowledge gets back to the current employer, the professional could be instantly terminated. You can clarify why you do not want the prospective employer to contact a current employer during the job interview. You might be asked why, so be sure you have an answer prepared.

If you are concerned that a previous employer may give a bad reference, ask that the employer not be contacted. You will have to provide a brief explanation of the circumstances surrounding this request to the prospective employer, however.

Many employers no longer give a reference—good or bad—for a former employee. This extends, in some cases, to student interns as well. Employers are concerned about the possibility of being sued by former employees if it can be shown that the bad reference is the reason the employee did not get the job. Thus, the applications from some employers contain language that releases former employers from liability for what is said in a reference.

Students can also use the services of college career placement offices to maintain references. This is a convenience for those who are asked to provide personal references, as they only have to write the reference once; thereafter it is kept on file at the placement office. Prospective employers then request a copy of the reference from the placement office.

Physical Appearance of a Resumé

"The resumé and letter came in handwritten, on lined notebook paper. It wasn't even on letter-size paper! It sure got my attention—that is, I promptly put it in the do not call file!" claimed a design director. There are thousands of stories like this told by design directors. They are constantly amazed at how many resumés they receive that were created apparently without any thought to appearance.

The appearance of the resumé can, by itself, make a good or bad impression. Trying to create something to get attention can work, but for most firm owners and managers, creativity in the presentation of resumés and cover letters is mostly an inconvenience. They are interested in the content, not fancy typefaces, designs, or origami folding. Today, print resumés might automatically be scanned, and one with fancy typefaces or other creative elements that do not scan might thus be discarded.

Here are several basic tips for the printed version of a resumé. Some of these tips may not apply to a digital version, so check that section as well. Note that these basic tips essentially apply to the cover letter, too:

- Use white, buff, or a light gray paper; light pastels are also acceptable. Use quality bond paper. Use a business-size envelope (referred to as number 10) or a large flat envelope that is 9 inches by 12 inches.
- The text should reproduce as a dark black image.
- Make sure to have perfect spelling and good grammar.
- Using a different font in the contact information is acceptable, as long as it is legible. Serif fonts, such as Times Roman and New Century Schoolbook, are easier to read than sans serif fonts.
- Use bold headings in the body of the resumé so that they stand out and attract attention.
- Double-spacing between major sections, with single spacing within each section, is best.
- Letter-quality laser printers produce the best printouts; do not send photocopies.

Don't forget to proofread your resumé two or three times over a period of time or have someone else do so. Spell checkers do not always catch all misspelled words. Proofreading will also help you edit down long sentences into tighter content that gets to the essence of what you are trying to convey.

RESUMÉ FORMAT

The three most common resumé formats remain the chronological, the functional, and the combination. No one format works best in all cases. Which of the basic formats you should use depends on the intended audience and the purpose of the resumé. The experienced designer who is attempting to make a career change from "on-the-boards designer" to salesperson will need a different format from the technician who is trying to obtain a position of total project responsibility. A student's resumé will be formatted differently from that of an individual who has been out of work for some reason for a number of years.

By far the most commonly used format is the *chronological resumé*, which lists all experience in reverse chronological order. *Functional resumés* do not give specific employment history and are sometimes used by individuals who have been out of work for some time. The *combination format* generally combines the chronological and functional resumé to help eliminate the negative perceptions that sometimes attach to a functional resumé. Information about how to structure an electronic resumé is also included later in this chapter.

Chronological Resumé

The style of resumé that remains the most common is the one that provides information in reverse chronological order. It is called a chronological resumé and states work experiences (and educational history) exactly when they occurred, starting with the most recent first. This type of resumé is easy to

Mary Anderson

1234 Granite Avenue Circle City, Arizona 602-555-9782 E-Mail: mary@xxx.com

OBJECTIVE: Entry-level design position.

EDUCATION: Arizona Southern University, Wilcox, AZ.

B.S., Major: Interior Design

Minor: Marketing

EXPERIENCE:

Intern.

Design One, Phoenix, AZ Summer, 20XX
Responsible for some drafting and space-planning of an office and small house
Participation in client meetings, interaction, and project presentations
Library upkeep

Draftsperson

Desert Construction Co, Circle City, AZ. Summer, 200X
Assisted in the preparation of working drawings for custom home builder.

COMPUTER SKILLS

AutoCAD

Microsoft Office

Microsoft PowerPoint for presentations

ACTIVITIES

American Society of Interior Designers, Student Chapter

Phi Kappa Phi Honor Society

FIGURE 29-2.

Example of a poorly written student resumé.

follow and clearly shows the individual's work history. Many employers prefer this traditional format for resumés.

The chronological format is not recommended, however, if the job seeker has a spotty work record or has been out of the workforce for some time. It also might not be appropriate for someone who is seeking to make a significant change in his or her career.

Experienced professionals should provide work history followed by educational experience. If the experienced (and older) designer places education first, it can draw attention to age, which, unfortunately, can lead to discrimination. Work history is more important than educational experience for the experienced professional anyway. Students should place educational experience first, as that is the most recent activity.

When you are listing your educational experience, you would commonly list the school and the degree information. It is not necessary to list the year you obtained your degree, as this can become an age identifier. Include academic honors if you have them. Figure 29-1, presented earlier, is an example of a resumé for an experienced designer. Figures 29-2 and 29-3 use the chronological format for a student who is ready for the job market. Figure 29-2 is an example of a poorly written resumé that will not get much attention from an employer. Figure 29-3 shows this same student resumé better prepared. It clearly shows how too little information can mean the resumé is ignored.

Mary Anderson

1234 Granite Avenue, Circle City, Arizona 602-555-9782 E-Mail: mary@xxx.com

Objective

Entry-level design position with a commercial interior design firm specializing in health care and hospitality. Particularly interested in a challenging position that will increase my experience and involvement in interior design.

Education

Arizona Southern University, Wilcox, AZ

    B.S., Major: Interior Design.

    Minor: Marketing.

    GPA 3.8/4.0.

Experience

Summer, 20XX

Design One, Phoenix, AZ.

    Intern.

        Commercial and residential firm specializing in hospitality.

        Space-planning and design documents for a bed and breakfast and two other projects.

        Client meetings, interaction, and project presentations.

        Meetings with manufacturer's representatives.

Summer, 200X

Desert Construction Co, Circle City, AZ

    Draftsperson

        Assisted in the preparation of working drawings for custom home builder.

Computer Skill

AutoCAD 13 and 14

Microsoft Office Word and Excel for documents and spreadsheets

Microsoft PowerPoint for presentations

Honors/Activities

American Society of Interior Designers

Student Chapter, 200X–20XX

Chapter Treasurer, 20XX

Volunteer for the Showhouse (Phoenix chapter)

Phi Kappa Phi Honor Society, Arizona Southern Chapter

FIGURE 29-3.

Chronological resumé prepared by a student who is seeking a first job (a corrected version of the example in Figure 29-2).

Functional Resumé

The *functional resumé* emphasizes qualifications and skills, rather than the order in which they were obtained. Emphasizing overall qualifications is intended to quickly interest the employer in your qualifications and possibly overlook a spotty work record.

Many employers do not like the functional resumé, because they are concerned with a prospective employee's work history, so this tactic often does not work. However, it is still an option for many job applicants. When an applicant presents a functional resumé, it is not uncommon for the prospective employer to ask for a chronological work history as well.

For an experienced professional who perhaps is looking for freelance contract work, a functional resumé can help focus on the experiences in design that are probably going to be needed for that type of work situation. For example, someone wishing to do freelance CAD work will want to focus on job experience and skills with CAD (see Figure 29-4).

WILLIAM C. BLAKE

| 9700 N. 19th Street | Tallahassee, FL 32000 | (P) 850.555.9876 | blake@xxx.com |

Summary

Highly motivated individual seeking an entry-level position in interior design. Previous work experience provides superior work ethic and demonstrated ability to successfully work with others. Negotiated contracts in public relations areas.

Major Work Experiences

Interior Design

Part-time design assistant for a residential design firm. Select finishes and products, develop sample boards, prepare furniture floor plans under direction of design firm owner.

Technical Writer

Three years' experience in large architectural firm. Responsible for developing proposals and other marketing materials. Collaborated with the firm's PR consultant on many projects.

Event Planner

Two years working as an assistant to a major event planner in Nashville, TN. Obtained pricing information, developed schedules, supervised small party set-ups.

Public Relations

Ten years' public relations experience in private sector. Excellent print media placement record. Good writer and researcher. Skilled in organizing special events. Worked with several interior design and architecture firms. Involved in contract negotiations for events.

Education

Florida State University 200x. Bachelor of Arts: Interior Design
O'More College of Design. Intermittent. Took design classes part-time.
University of Michigan 1984 Bachelor of Science Major: Journalism/Public Relations

Affiliations

American Society of Interior Designers, Student Member
Publishers Publicity Association
Public Relations Society of America

FIGURE 29-4.

Functional resumé prepared by an individual who has made a career change.

Combination Resumé

A *combination resumé* utilizes characteristics of both the chronological and the functional resumé and combines them into one. Usually, this results in a resumé in which functional skills are described, as in the normal functional resumé, followed by a brief chronological listing of educational and work experiences. A combination resumé highlights skills that are related to the job being sought and deemphasizes either a limited or a spotty work history. This kind of format can work very well for students whose skills learned in school and internships will be of greater interest to a prospective employer than work history that consists of a series of part-time jobs. Figure 29-5 is an example of a resumé using the combination format.

THE COVER LETTER

This section discusses the cover letter in terms of traditional job searches. The cover letter or memo that accompanies an electronic job search is discussed later in the chapter.

Never send out a resumé without a *cover letter*. This letter is an opportunity for you to personally introduce yourself in such a way that the employer (you hope) will have no alternative but to read your resumé and call you for an interview immediately. Those items, in a nutshell, are the purposes for always including a cover letter.

Cover letters will likely be created for different purposes. Some are in response to an advertisement that you saw in a newspaper. Another can be the result of a personal contact with the employer, perhaps someone you met at an association meeting. Others are sent based on a recommendation by a professor or an interior designer. Tailoring the cover letter to each company accomplishes a positive objective. Each letter must sound as if it were written only for that company, even if it contains primarily "stock" paragraphs used in practically every letter you send.

With the purpose of the cover letter in mind, as always, start by doing some homework. Begin with the company's Web site. Naturally, it provides a lot of information about the company to tell you if this might be a good fit. Students can also begin a file of advertising they see in local and trade magazines on firms in which they have an interest. This can provide good information and allow you to show that you know something about the company.

Once you have determined which companies you wish to apply to, try to discover the name of the person who will do the interviewing. For most companies today, that will come from the company Web site's "About Us" and "Contact Us" sections. A letter addressed to a specific person creates a better impression that one addressed to "Personnel Director" or "To whom it may concern." With a broadcast letter—which is one that is sent to numerous firms—do as much research on each firm as you can to try to make sure you will be a good match.

Content and Appearance

Because the cover letter is never a long document, careful thought must be given to the sequence of information provided. It is important for the letter to get the reader's attention quickly and to make him or her want to read your resumé and then call you for an interview. Positive attention is gained by using good business-writing techniques, professional language, and perfect spelling.

Jennifer Alvarado

1875 Wacker Drive,
Chicago, Illinois,
312-555-3000

Summary

- Four years' commercial sales experience for an office furnishings dealer
- Experienced in marketing interior design services
- Design project team manager
- Seven years commercial interior design: government and corporate
- Three years residential interior design
- Computer skills: Microsoft Office, Project, and Act!

Sales and Marketing Skills

Maintained numerous commercial accounts with last employer. Developed many new accounts with government agencies and corporate. Generated over seven million dollars in sales last year (second-highest total for ten sales people). Equaled or exceeded sales goals each year.

Developed successful marketing strategies for two interior design firms and two contractors.

Supervision Skills

Hired, trained, and supervised two sales assistants to help manage my accounts. First sales assistant recently began working as sales representative. Also supervised design assistants when working as a project team manager. Overall project manager for several large government agency projects.

Design Skills

Experienced in commercial space planning and interior design. Familiar with open-office systems products, and various qualities of commercial and residential furniture and furnishings products. Some experience in residential design/sales.

Work History

1998 to present	Account Representative	Quality Office Furnishings, Inc.	Chicago, IL.
1996–1998	Interior Designer	Smyth Design Consultants	Evanston, IL.
1991–1996	Interior Designer	Best Interiors, Inc.	Chicago, IL.
1988–1991	Design Associate	Regal Home Furnishings	OAK Park, IL.

Education

Southern Illinois University. 1988. Bachelor of Science. Major: Interior Design.

Professional Membership

American Society of Interior Designers, Professional member since 1994.
NCIDQ certified. Certificate # 55555

FIGURE 29-5.

A combination-style resumé for a professional seeking new responsibilities in her career as a sales representative.

Applicant's name

Address

Area code and phone number

Date

Name and title of employer

Name of company

Address

City, State, Zip Code

Dear Mr. (Mrs. or Ms.) Smith:

The first paragraph should state the reason for the letter. Give the employer information about the specific position for which you are applying. If you are responding to an advertisement or have gotten the contact through someone the employer will know, state that information.

The second and third paragraphs are where you can provide some specific information about yourself and why you are interested in working for the firm. Include statements that explain how previous academic training or work experience qualifies you for the position. Relate your skills and experience to the company's needs or the job requirements.

For professionals with several years of experience, the third paragraph will probably be necessary to complete the basic information you wish to tell the employer. Whether you are a student or professional, do not simply repeat what the employer can read in the resumé—expand or clarify upon what you have stated in your resumé.

A final paragraph thanks the reader for his or her time and indicates your desire for a personal interview. Be concise. If you are going to be in the city at a particular time, mention that you will be calling to set up an interview at that time. If you intend to get back to the employer rather than wait for him or her to call you, indicate that. Or say something like, "I look forward to hearing from you soon." Remember to say thank you "for your consideration" or use other appropriate wording.

Add a closing greeting such as "Sincerely,"

(leave four lines for your signature)

Type your full name

Enclosure (or Enc.). This is used to indicate you are sending something with the letter, in this case, your resumé.

FIGURE 29-6.

A sample cover letter showing what should go into each section of the letter.

Business writing consultants and employment counselors generally recommend that the cover letter contain about four paragraphs, each with a particular purpose (see Figure 29-6). The first paragraph should attract attention by concisely stating the purpose of your letter. Write with enthusiasm and interest. Let the prospective employer know that you know something about the company and why you want to work there. The first paragraph should also briefly explain where you heard of the company, such as a job announcement on LinkedIn. If it is a letter of inquiry, this should be clearly stated (see Figure 29-7).

The second and third paragraphs should contain specific information about the applicant's skills and interests in the position. Explain how your skills relate to the job that was advertised or otherwise meet the employer's needs.

Julie Adams
8090 S. Willamette Street
Philadelphia, Pennsylvania
215-555-1448
E-mail jadams@xxx.com

October 26, 200x

Mr. Timothy O'Niel
AAD, Inc.
1237 N. 17th Street, N.W.
Washington, D.C.
202-555-1400

Dear Mr. O'Niel:

Over an eight-year period, I have worked as a Designer and most recently a Senior Designer at a highly respected commercial design firm in Philadelphia. At this point in my career, I seek an opportunity to apply my design and supervisory skills in a management position.

During the last few years I have been personally responsible for obtaining and designing many of the largest projects ever undertaken at my company. As a Senior Designer I am responsible for supervising design teams in the execution of projects.

It is not difficult to hear flattering comments about the quality design work produced at AAD, Inc. I believe the negotiation and design skills that I have refined at Design Three will further add to the success of your firm. In addition, I grew up in Baltimore and have a strong association with the Washington, DC, and Baltimore markets.

As you will see from the enclosed resumé, I have broad commercial experience in health care, hospitality, corporate offices, and university facilities.

Over the past four years, I have been preparing myself for management by enrolling in courses in pursuit of a master's degree in business.

I have considerable talent, enthusiasm, and interest to offer as a design manager to AAD, Inc. and would appreciate the opportunity to meet with you personally to discuss such a position. I will call you next week to confirm a convenient time for a personal interview.

Sincerely yours,

Julie Adams

Enc.

FIGURE 29-7.

A cover letter in which an individual is inquiring about a possible position at a firm. Note how the applicant starts the letter.

Focus your attention on the employer's known or probable needs. This translates to showing the employer that you have done some homework about the company. Including statements related to those specific needs helps make the kind of impression that can get you an interview. Statements about your personal goals and interests as they relate to the particular position and company can also be placed in these paragraphs.

Present the information in these paragraphs in terms of its importance to the position as you understand it. Mention a few skills or accomplishments, but

TABLE 29-3.

Tips for preparing a cover letter

- Address the letter by the employer's name—never "To Whom It May Concern."
- When you can drop names, do so: "I was referred to your company by John Jones, the owner of Jones Thompson Flooring."
- Discuss accomplishments and results. This goes for the resumé as well.
- Be brief and concise. Use good grammar and correct spelling.
- It is okay to use industry jargon and buzzwords. However, you had better know what any jargon you put in your letter means.
- Do not include negative information (such as "I left ABC Interiors because of a disagreement with the owner"). This might come up in the interview, but you will have a better chance of explaining it then.
- Do not make your letter sound like you are begging for a job.
- Always say thank you at the end.

don't summarize your resumé. For example, if you have CAD skills, state what version. Accomplishments, such as sales records and management experience (see Figure 29-7), are important items for experienced designers to include. Students should point out the skills in which they are particularly proficient related to coursework or internship experiences.

The last paragraph should tell the prospective employer that you want an interview. You want the employer to call you, but do not wait for the employer to respond. The last paragraph should include a reference to the enclosed resumé as well as the availability of your portfolio for review.

It is often recommended that you state you will be calling the employer concerning an appointment for an interview. This naturally is very important if you have decided to travel to a location for your job search. It is not a good idea to expect the employer to meet with you when you are ready. They have meetings and work to accomplish, so you must be flexible with meeting times. Do not bother to call the employer on Mondays or Fridays, as many are in meetings on those days. And do not expect to be asked for even an informational interview if your letter arrives only a few days before you do!

Use a simple ending, such as in Figure 29-7. Thank the employer for taking the time to review the letter and resumé. Leave four spaces for your signature, with your name spelled out below. Because you are including a resumé, place the word *Enclosure* or the abbreviation *Enc.* below your signature. Table 29-3 provides some additional tips on preparing cover letters.

The *physical appearance* of the cover letter should meet standard business letter criteria and be a good companion to the resumé. Keep the cover letter to one page; you want the employer to read your resumé and not spend a lot of time with the letter itself. The previous examples show how to set up the contact information and salutation.

The appearance of the cover letter can quite easily attract attention—positive or negative. Using fancy type styles, funny folds, logo-style designs, and pastel colors may fuel your creative side, but, as with a resumé, they detract more than help. You may include a logo, design element, or graphic, but use discretion. Unless you are applying for a job as a graphic designer, your graphic should not be more interesting than your text.

Perfect spelling and good grammar are mandatory. Have someone else read the letter, perhaps a professor if you are a student. A professional who still does not feel comfortable writing may want to hire a freelance writer or resumé writer to help with preparing the cover letter. Go back to the section on the physical appearance of the resumé for additional formatting information.

PORTFOLIOS

Portfolios are of critical importance to an interior designer at any level of practice. This visual field requires visual "proofs" of one's ability to design interiors. Simply stated, a *portfolio* is a visual presentation of what you can do as an interior designer. The term *portfolio* is also used to refer to the binder in which the visual items are placed.

Your portfolio must show your best work. Although you may have many items to potentially include, not all of them will be used when you interview for jobs. When this is the case, the portfolio should contain design work that relates to the design position you are seeking and the needs of the prospective employer. Something that Maureen Mitton, author of *Portfolios for Interior Designers*, suggests is to create an inventory of the items you have available for a portfolio. This will help you create one that is individualized for each job interview.

Before we get deeper into the discussion of what should go into a portfolio, it is important to emphasize that there is an ethics issue concerning portfolios. Recall that the work product of an employee belongs to the design firm, not the employee. When you decide to look for another job, association codes of conduct specifically state that you cannot take drawings or other documents without permission.

Your portfolio is never really "finished," as it must be constantly updated and refined to meet current or expected needs in the job search process. At first it will be filled with projects from classes and then replaced by drawings and project photos of professional work. For the student, it must present the breadth of the student's abilities. For the experienced professional, the portfolio must show a range of work, with emphasis on the present. This is another reason to have a list of the potential portfolio items.

Students often make the mistake of including something from each of the studio classes they take. The employer is not really interested in the work you did your first year, nor are many interested in seeing that work to appreciate the progression of your talents. They assume that you are constantly improving your skills over time and want to know what you can do for them right now. A professional's portfolio will be more extensive than a student's and will only show drawings or photographs of completed projects.

Here are some quick tips on the overall concept of a portfolio:

- Items should show that you have the skills for the job for which you are applying.
- Portfolio items should be self-explanatory even though you will most likely be presenting them to the prospective employer. Written explanations should not simply state what can be seen in the graphics.
- Organization of the items is key to helping make your portfolio self-explanatory. Remember that a portfolio tells a visual story about you. Each piece that you include demonstrates how you can help the prospective employer.
- A sloppy portfolio tells a huge negative story about you. Be neat, and make sure everything is attached (as necessary) before you leave your house!

What to Include

After you have inventoried—or certainly collected items in an organized fashion—the items you feel could go into a portfolio, it is time to decide how to organize everything. Because you may only have 30 to 60 minutes for the entire interview, you need to limit the number of items in your portfolio. Twenty-five to thirty items or pages should be sufficient, especially if they directly demonstrate the skills needed for the position. You probably will not want to have more than about 45 items in the portfolio, as it will either bore the reviewer or decrease the time available for the interviewer to ask you questions.

It is helpful to have each section of the portfolio labeled. Pieces that are not self-explanatory should have brief, written descriptions of the design project or the piece. This is particularly important when you are not there to explain the items in the portfolio. They also help you remember key concepts that you want to cover; if you are nervous, you might inadvertently skip them. Hand lettering is considered an important skill by many design firms, so written materials could be hand lettered. However, word-processed documents are certainly acceptable.

Select items that show employers you have an understanding of the issues involved in designing interiors. This is especially important for students. You must include items that showcase your technical, creative, and problem-solving skills. A variety of items will thus be needed, from a complete project to parts of a project, a series of concept sketches, and other items such as photos of models.

The items selected should be your best work and provide examples of all the skills you possess. Table 29-4 suggests many of the items that should be included if at all possible. Professors can help guide you on this choice.

As you begin to organize your portfolio, you will select items for both types of specialties and then focus the items before you go for an interview. Obviously, a student's portfolio will not necessarily have an extensive selection of either residential or commercial projects, so a student must show a variety of items that

TABLE 29-4.

Items commonly included in a portfolio

Examples of these items should be included and organized to show your skills in relationship to the job for which you are applying. Be sure you only show work YOU did. If projects were done by teams, bring the parts you were responsible for, not what someone else did.

Students
- At least one complete project with all required documents
- Sketches that show the decision-making process
- Freehand sketches and thumbnails
- Programming sketches or documents (i.e., bubble diagrams and adjacency diagrams)
- Furniture floor plans
- Working drawings
    Dimensioned plans
    Mechanical plans
    Elevations, sections, and details
    Millwork designs
- CAD drawings
- Manual drafting
- Color boards
- Exhibits of hand lettering skills
- Perspectives and/or isometric drawings
- Technical renderings in any media in which you are competent

Professionals
- Project photos or slides
- Publication reprints
- Articles you wrote
- Specifications

will help demonstrate his or her skills in the techniques and processes of interior design. Begin with a high-quality piece or a project that showcases a whole project. It should end with another quality piece to serve as a "last impression" of what you can do. Do not include poor-quality work or work you feel you have to apologize for—if it is not very good, either rework it or leave it out.

The professional may find it easier to emphasize certain types of work, but may also have to show the breadth of his or her experience in designing projects when making a job change. As much as possible, do not include a large number of items showing residential projects if you are interviewing with a commercial firm, and vice versa. Professionals will want to lead with a recent award-winning project and may even include a copy of the award certificate.

A question that many students ask is whether it is acceptable to rework project solutions once they have been graded. There is no easy answer to this, but it certainly can be considered. However, any "reworked" projects should still reflect what you are capable of doing. Sometimes this depends on creating an overall appearance; an example is changing to the same color boards when you initially used different colors of boards for each project.

Depending on what kinds of projects you have done in school, you might need to develop new documents. Because of the job, you might want to develop such items as cabinet drawings, construction drawings in CAD, and rendered perspectives that were not originally done for a project. You can explain what you recently added in order to more completely show your current skills.

Today the vast majority of portfolio work is transferred to digital media. This fact must be considered when you are selecting items and deciding whether to rework a project presentation. Photograph sample and project boards as soon as possible after having completed them, before they can become damaged. Some employers may want to see original drawings (not CAD) so that they can evaluate basic drawing skills, or samples of material boards so that they can determine your skill in this task.

Store projects, drawings, models, and so on carefully so that they do not become damaged. A former student of mine lost all her original work when her apartment roof leaked. She had no photos of any of her work. Be sure you make backups of photos as extra "insurance."

Because professionals generally are not allowed to take drawings and documents made while employed at a design firm, you may have to spend the time and money to photograph finished projects. However, be sure you obtain the client's permission to photograph the interiors and that you have permission to duplicate work done at your place of employment. The rights clause in a design contract that relates to photographs does not cover a designer's personal use of photos.

Even though the portfolio is a visual tool, it should also contain certain written documents. Include one or two clean copies of your resumé and references list even if you have already mailed these to the employer. If you sent your portfolio to an employer—which sometimes happens when you are interested in a firm at a distance from your residence—enclose a cover letter. This cover letter will be similar to the one that accompanies your mailed resumé, but can also be modified to focus attention on your portfolio.

Each of these written items should be placed in plastic sleeves within the portfolio, with the cover letter first and the resumé second. A table of contents is a nice touch. To have a complete visual package, consider coordinating the paper color of your enclosed cover letter and resumé to the overall theme you have used in the portfolio. Keep in mind, however, that strong colors for the cover letter and resume are generally not recommended.

Format of the Portfolio Binder

A key decision that you will make as you create the portfolio relates to the format. You will be carrying your portfolio in taxicabs, automobiles, trains, buses, and airplanes. Items will be laid out on conference tables and desks, and may possibly even be mailed across the country. Although you may have created a digital portfolio, some employers will want to see "real" items—and this requires the use of a binder. Therefore, you might want to have both large- and small-format items available. When you are finalizing the schedule for an interview, you can inquire about any preferences the prospective employer may have.

The common format size for boards and drawings in academia is 20 inches by 30 inches; however, portfolios are actually often smaller. The 8-by-10-inch, 11-by-14-inch, and 14-by-17-inch formats are easier to present and transport. Photography allows for reducing the 20-by-30-inch traditional size to smaller formats.

Whatever format you decide to use, it is important as much as possible to present all the examples consistently in either a vertical or a horizontal manner. This will aid you during the interview because you will not have to keep flipping the portfolio around. This will also cause less visual confusion in a digital format. An option is to group horizontal-format items separately from vertical-format items.

There are different methods of binding pages, so choose one that will give you flexibility. The most common are plastic pages (available in different sizes) that are held in place with nylon or metal screws. Depending on the brand, you can add and subtract pages easily. Many items, such as sketches, renderings, and plans, can be mounted on paper that matches mat board or black photographic paper and can be inserted into plastic notebook sleeves. Remember that each side of the plastic sleeve is a "page." Use this to your advantage as you organize drawings and written statements.

For written items, try to stick to one type font. Multiple type fonts can inadvertently make the portfolio look messy. You have to be careful about reducing a large original. CAD drawings are generally not a problem, but hand-drafted items may be difficult to read, and details may be difficult to discern. Larger sheets can be neatly folded.

The physical binder itself should be of good quality and look very professional. Drawings rolled up in a tube may be convenient to carry, but they do not communicate the right level of professionalism, nor do the cardboard portfolios that many students use during college. It is not, however, necessary to spend a lot of money on leather-bound books. When you ship the portfolio, also arrange to pay for the return shipping costs when the prospective employer sends it back to you so that the employer will not have to pay these charges.

Two excellent resources for the development of portfolios are the books by Maureen Mitton and by Harold Linton. See the general reference list at the end of this book.

DIGITAL JOB SEARCH STRATEGIES

Resumés are *not* out of date in the digital age for the job search. A resumé can be your most important marketing tool, whether sent digitally or via "snail mail." Marketing tool? Yes, to market you! This section briefly discusses using the Internet for job searches, structuring a resumé for transmittal via the Internet, and constructing a portfolio on a CD or in DVD format.

In the digital job search—for that matter, any job search—a targeted approach works best. Do you know what specific type of job you want? In this case, what *targeting* means is that the resumé and cover letter are customized to the firm you are approaching, whenever possible. It does not mean that you are so finely focused and narrowly defined that you are not considered for anything else. Homework—knowing what a firm might be looking for—is the basis for this type of targeting.

The all-purpose resumé you perhaps drafted earlier in this chapter must now be fine-tuned. Because it is so easy to customize your resumé and cover letter with word-processing software, the generic version that you might have used for each job location is out.

Even the generic resumé posted on multiple locations will not get you the attention you want and need today. Here are some realities of the job search in the digital world:

- Use specific key words related to the interior design profession and your skills to attract attention.
- Connect to a specific company's needs—made easier by researching its Web site before you push "Send."
- Edit your resumé information into short sentences (not using bullets if in plain text) that make sense and stand out against others' blocks of text.
- Be sure you have used perfect grammar and spelling—there's no excuse for misspelled words.
- Be careful about everything you post on e-mail, social media, and other ways an employer can find out about you on the Web. A wild personal life broadcasted on social media could cost you a job.

Keep in mind, when posting your resumé and portfolio on a Web site, not to include too much. If your site or materials take too long to download, the employer may give up and never see your great work. Sometimes people think that information about themselves on their personal Web site is a good idea. However, placing information such as marital status, photos of the family, and even personal interests provides information that can lead to discrimination against you, just as it can when included on a resumé.

When you post your resumé to a site—whether it is your own site or one of the job Web sites like Monster—you want to be cyber safe. Be sure you understand the privacy policies of the posting site. The same cautions mentioned for the resumé and cover letter apply here.

The Digital Job Search

The Internet has become popular for job searches because it is cheap. You can use the Internet for a job search in many ways. One way applicants use it is to post information about themselves—usually their resumés—online. Another is by taking advantage of the job banks available on association Web sites. You need to be a member to use this service, but even students may be able to avail themselves of this service. Don't forget to check out allied groups such as the National Association of Home Builders (www.nahb.org), the Hospitality Industry Network (www.newh.org), and others mentioned in other chapters and the resources sections of this book.

Another online way of finding employment is to search the Web sites of interior design firms. Many have links on their Web sites where candidates can obtain information about possible openings and how to apply for those positions. If the firm does not have a link for application, the site will still provide information about the firm that can help a candidate determine if that is the type of firm he or she might want to work for. One can always contact the firm via e-mail links or in another manner.

Social Web sites, especially LinkedIn, are other places to look for job openings. Once you open a LinkedIn page, you should join groups related to interior design. Within these group discussions, job announcements and job-seeking postings appear. Although some may be for experienced designers, others are worded to allow students to apply. Note that many are also international positions. An important part of using a social site is that your page be professional in content—including a professional photo—to give the best impression.

We all use e-mail, and e-mail has become a common way for individuals to inquire about or apply for jobs. Creative and individualized e-mail addresses that are provocative may be fun among friends, but they have no place in the job search. You don't need to eliminate your favorite e-mail address if you don't want to, but during the job search and on the job, realize that suggestive, provocative, and downright rude e-mail addresses will not be acceptable.

Other search locations can be used as well. One of the best known is www.monster.com. A site specific to interior design is www.interiordesignjobs.com. Others can be found by searching "interior design jobs" on a search engine. At these sites you can post your resumé, look for posted jobs, get job-hunting tips, and much more. You can search by specific city as well. I do not recommend or endorse any one site as best or better than another.

Commercial sites aid both the applicant and the employer. Fees are generally required by either party to use the online services, although some sites do not charge. You must sign up with one of these sites; thereafter, you can post a resumé or a job opening.

Sites for local and regional publications might also have postings for jobs in or related to interior design. Web sites for trade magazines might be yet another a source of postings. These are just a few of the most common ways to use the Internet for your job search.

A caution for those who think that searching via digital methods is the only way to go in the 21st century. As related by a professor and design professional, the interior design industry is small, even though it seems very big. Personal contacts through involvement in professional association chapter activities, attending trade fairs, meeting designers through informational interviews, and other opportunities to meet professional designers cannot be overlooked.

Digital Resumés and Cover Letters

Design firms receive resumés by fax and e-mail as often as (if not more often than) by regular mail. Preparing a resumé for fax transmission requires no special manipulation. Posting a resumé by e-mail, anticipating that it might be scanned by the employer via computer, or otherwise posting on an Internet job site requires the candidate to use some special techniques (see Figure 29-8).

For the most part, your electronic resumé or cover letter will be very similar to the printed versions. Your cover letter will use the same content suggestions made previously. The resumé must include the same categories of information, also discussed previously. The differences lie primarily in how you present the information.

If you mail a cover letter and resumé to an employer—especially a corporation or large architecture or interior design firm—it is likely that they will be electronically scanned. Larger employers use scanners and specialized

<u>**Michael Smith**</u>

From: "Michael Smith" <msmith33@xxx.net>
To: "Albert Jones" <ajones@jonesarchitecture.xxx>
Sent: Monday July 17, 200x 9:27 AM
Subject: employment request

Dear Mr. Jones
jones architecture and design

I am very interested in talking to you about the job opening your firm advertised in the Sunday newspaper. I believe I would be a perfect fit for your firm. Allow me to tell you why.

* I have a bachelor's degree in interior design from a FIDER accredited school with a 3.9 GPA.
* The internship I completed last summer was at a design firm very similar to yours. I received high praise from the intern supervisor.
* I have worked part time through school and understand what "work" means.
* My language skills include fluency in Spanish and some German.
* I have taken extra AutoCAD classes to improve my skills.
* My family lives in your city now.

You will see by my resume that I am the person you are looking for to join your firm. I can send you a partial electronic portfolio when we discuss an appointment to meet you in person.

I appreciate your time very much. I know you are very busy.
Michael Smith

Mike Smith
Ravenswood Street
Anywhere, USA
Phone (111) 555-4567
E-mail msmith33@xxx.net

OBJECTIVE: Entry-level design position with a commercial interior design firm associated with an architect. Want a challenging position which will help me grow as a professional in commercial design and contribute to a high-quality design firm.

EDUCATION: University of Florida
          Bachelor of Design, Major Interior Design
          GPA 3.9/4.0.

EXPERIENCE
          Summer 200x and Fall 200x
          Gainesville Design Services
          Intern: Commercial firm specializing in offices and retail.

FIGURE 29-8.

An example of a resumé sent via e-mail preceded by a cover letter.

Produced drawings for senior designers, prepared specification selections.
Attended client meetings and office meetings with representatives.

Summer, 200x.
Alliance Construction Co. Atlanta, GA.
Draftsperson.
Assisted in the preparation of working drawings for custom home builder.

COMPUTER SKILLS
AutoCAD 200x
Microsoft Office Word
Microsoft PowerPoint

LANGUAGE SKILLS
Spanish. Can speak and write fluently.
German. Can speak some.

HONORS/ACTIVITIES
American Society of Interior Designers
Student Chapter President 200x
Student Chapter Treasurer 200x

FIGURE 29-8.

(*Continued*)

software to speed up the process of eliminating those that do not meet their specific needs. Software scans for key words so that the employer can quickly narrow the number of resumés even further.

Key words are especially important when using digital methods for the job search. Employers can program their scanner software to look for key words such as AutoCad, Revit, space-planner, ASID, IIDA, licensed, and so on. The employer uses similar tactics when going to a resumé posting site on the Web. Table 29-5 provides several other tips concerning scanned resumés and cover letters.

Sending a document via e-mail is another method frequently used in electronic job hunting. A downside is that when an e-mail is sent to a specific person, that person might not see the e-mail for a few days. If it is sent to the firm's general "contact us" link, it might not get to the right person for even longer. It is best not to include your resumé in the body of the e-mail. The formatting will not always convert properly.

For appearance sake, it is best to e-mail the resumé as an attachment. Ideally, convert the resumé and cover letter to PDF format so that the recipient cannot make changes. Make a comment about the attached cover letter and resumé in the e-mail. This "introduction" should be brief, however. If you have met the employer before, be sure you remind the prospective employer about your earlier conversation.

Although you will have records of the e-mails you have sent out on your server or hard drive, it is a good idea to print out copies for your file. This will

TABLE 29-5.

Tips for scanned resumés and cover letters

- The version of your resumé you think might be scanned should follow some very specific guidelines. Scanners are sensitive and will eliminate those that it cannot read properly.
- Print only on white paper with little texture.
- Do not use bullets, underlining, boldface type, boxes, other graphics, or italics.
- Use quotation marks (" ") to call attention to special words.
- Do not use fanciful fonts. Use simple fonts such as Times Roman, Courier, Helvetica, or Ariel.
- Use a type size of 12 or 14 points.
- Some acronyms will be recognized depending on the key words that are entered by the employer. If you are not sure, spell them out.
- Print using a laser printer for the best-quality image.
- Send the letter and resumé in a large, flat envelope. Folds and stapled paper can confuse the scanner.
- Do not bracket your phone number. Use periods for divisions (e.g., 123.456.7890).
- Do not put information in boxes, as the scanner software may not read this information.
- Make absolutely sure there are no misspelled words or typos.

help you keep track of your job search efforts, just like with other record-keeping suggested in the chapter. It's a good idea to test out your items by sending them to a friend or even yourself. That way you can determine if any changes in typeface, spacing, and so on are needed.

Another alternative is to post your resumé on the Web. We have already discussed this in the preceding job search section, but a few more specific comments related to resumés are in order. Posting your resumé on the Internet can give you more flexibility with content and design than sending either an e-mail or a regular printed version. You are able to use boldface, italics, colors, different font sizes, and even graphics to call attention to your information: "This on-line presence . . . demonstrates to employers your awareness of technology and may be a little extra that puts you ahead of the competition."[1] Here are a few other hints for using a Web resumé:

- Avoid photographs of yourself that are casual or suggestive. Use only professional-looking photos.
- Understand that including a photo can reveal information that can be used to discriminate against you.
- Do not use too many links; you may lose the potential employer.
- Do not include salary information from current or past jobs.
- Watch the contrast of font colors against the background color(s); text has to be easily readable.
- Use simple graphics that will not take too long to download.

You may want to check the reference list for books that can help further if you wish to prepare an electronic resumé.

Digital Portfolios

A digital portfolio is a reasonably economical way of developing a portfolio. You can take digital photographs of boards and drawings; then make prints of these items or post them on the Web. Digital photos and scanned items can be manipulated to suit your format and even, in some cases, to repair small errors.

Even when you digitize, don't discard your original work. Employers often want to see actual work, especially from students. Digital photos can hide mistakes that viewing original work will reveal. Digital photos of drawings also change the scale of technical drawings, thus potentially hiding errors—another issue employers have, especially with the work of students.

Project photos are best taken by professional photographers. They will have better-quality digital cameras than most do-it-yourself photographers. For a professional, these project photos are the bulk of your portfolio, and you need to show your work in the best way possible. Don't forget to negotiate the rights (permissions) to use the photos taken by professional photographers in your work portfolio, on your Web site, and in other marketing media.

Digital portfolios can be prepared in a variety of ways. Items are easily saved on DVDs due to their large storage capacity. USB flash drives are also great because they can store a lot of material and are easy to carry. Portfolio pages of drawings and PDFs are copied to these drives, and then Adobe Acrobat Reader allows just about anyone to view the images. This is an easy way to produce a digital portfolio.

Applicants can use these same media to create an individualized portfolio that can be sent to and even kept by the employer. For security, however, it is best to use a DVD-R read-only disc so that the receiver cannot alter it.

With DVD media, you can create a preprogrammed presentation where the viewer experiences your portfolio as you want him or her to, without interruption. Special software is needed to facilitate this type of presentation. This way you get the viewer's undivided attention during the presentation. You can integrate animation, voice-overs, and music to make it even more personalized. In addition, you control the timing, sequence, and pace of the information in your presentation.

A DVD can also be created so that the viewer has options for moving from one section to another of the material. When the viewer controls the presentation, he or she can focus on areas of interest and skip others. For example, if the company is looking for someone for its hospitality department, the design director can skip work related to other types of facilities and concentrate on the quality of solutions and technical work in hospitality.

These presentations can also be programmed into a personal Web site or posted to a Web site hosting interior design portfolios. Two sites that host interior design portfolios are www.slideshare.net and www.carbonmade.com, among others. Note that these are mentioned for reference and the author does not specifically endorse either. Other sites also allow portfolio postings.

You may be able to link your Web site with one of the job search sites. A caution for Web site portfolios is that you must be careful about image file size and the number of images you include. Employers may become impatient waiting for a complex portfolio to download. If the portfolio is sent as a large e-mail or e-mail attachment, the recipient's system may interpret it as spam.

Help is available to those who cannot prepare a Web site themselves. Students may be able to receive assistance in setting up a digital portfolio from departmental or university computer centers. Professionals and students can also get help in this area from software like iWeb and Microsoft Front-Page. Commercial copy centers might offer helpful services, or you can hire a graphic designer or a Web site designer to do your site. Several books are out now on how to use the computer to create a digital portfolio. Maureen Mitton's book, *Portfolios for Interior Designers*, is an excellent resource for preparing a digital portfolio. Some of these titles appear in the reference list at the end of this text.

WEB SITES RELEVANT TO THIS CHAPTER

www.asid.org American Society of Interior Designers

www.careeronestop.org Career One Stop (a division of the U.S. Department of Labor)

www.newh.org Hospitality Industry Network

www.interiordesigncanada.org Interior Designers of Canada

www.interiordesignjobs.com Interior Design Jobs

www.iida.org International Interior Design Association

www.monster.com Monster

www.nahb.org National Association of Home Builders

www.carbonmade.com site to post portfolios

www.slideshare.net site to post portfolios

You may also want to search the Web sites of other professional associations for career and job-hunting information. Numerous additional sites can be found by searching topics such as resumés, cover letters, and job interviews.

KEY TERMS

Career objective	Functional resumé
Career summary	Headhunter
Chronological resumé	Informational interview
Combination resumé	Portfolio
Cover letter	Resumé
Digital portfolio	
Enclosure	

WHAT WOULD YOU DO?

1. Mary was very excited about the opportunity to work with a local television celebrity. Four months ago, Mary had planned and specified furniture for the very large living room and dining spaces of his house. The items specified for the living room included two custom-made end tables and a matching coffee table, all of which were oversized. The materials and finishes of these items matched custom cabinets designed for the dining room. The custom tables and cabinets were nearly ready for delivery. Most of the other furniture had already been delivered.

   Yesterday Mary received a call from the celebrity's assistant. The message was that the order for the rest of the furniture not already delivered was canceled. "He won't need any of those other items, as he has just accepted a position with a station in San Francisco and will not need those items anymore. Since he will not be taking them, he also wants the deposit back on those items."

2. Reston Carpet, Inc., is a supplier of carpet for use in homes and offices. Over the telephone, a sales representative for Reston offers to sell Diane Smith of Smith Anderson Interiors 325 yards of Magnum

plush carpet at a price of $21 per square yard. The Reston sales representative also verbally agrees to keep the offer open for 21 days and hold the stock for that time. Smith tells him that the offer appears to be fine and that Smith will let Reston know of Smith's acceptance within the next week after she confirms the price with her client. Five days later, the Reston rep sends Smith an e-mail that Reston has withdrawn the offer. Smith immediately telephones the Reston rep and accepts the $21-per-square-yard price for the 325 yards of carpet she needs for her project. The Reston factory claims that a sales contract was never formed between Reston and Smith and refuses to sell the carpet to Smith at that price.

3. Sara, working at an office furnishings dealer as a designer, mentions to her boss that a client appears to be ready to order 50 traditional desks and credenzas from a certain manufacturer. The boss, thinking that this will be a good opportunity to get some of this popular desk into inventory, orders an additional 10 units. After the order has been placed, Sara learns, but neglects to tell her boss—for more than a week—that the client has changed his mind and will not order the desks for at least six months. The boss is now responsible for paying for all the desks and credenzas because it is too late to cancel the order with the manufacturer. What might the boss do; what should Sara have done?

4. A good friend of yours who works at another design firm in town tells you about a situation that happened to her two weeks ago. She went on a trip with her boss to an out-of-town jobsite, where their client meetings lasted two days. Your friend tells you that her boss made a pass at her. "It wasn't the first time," she says. "He has made comments at work that I just don't think are appropriate," she continues.

She says that she is quite concerned because she likes working there and in every other respect the firm is a great place to work. "I don't know what to do. I already told this jerk designer that I am not interested," she confides.

REFERENCE

1. Nemich and Jandt, 1999, p. 75.

CHAPTER 30

On the Job

After completing this chapter you should be able to:

- Appreciate some of the factors that employers use to evaluate a resumé, and use this information to develop a better resumé and handle an interview successfully.

- Discuss the necessity of preparing for a job interview, including the importance of doing "homework" about the interviewing firm.

- Discuss why and how your apparel and other personal appearance issues can affect a job interview.

- Explain the importance of projecting the right image for the job interview through good business etiquette.

- Discuss how to handle an interview session when you are no longer interested in the position.

- Explain diplomatic responses to illegal or improper questions posed during the job interview.

- Draft a generic thank-you letter to be used following a job interview.

- Discuss why it is important for a new hire to make a good impression the first few weeks on the job.

- Discuss why the section on job strategies is important to the entry-level designer as well as the established professional.

Each of us grows in our own way as we seek fulfillment in our careers. For the student, the first job is an important first step in establishing a successful and satisfying career in the interior design profession. As the professional gains experience in the field, he or she seeks greater levels of responsibility and challenges in the workplace. Often it is necessary to seek new responsibility in another firm, even in another city.

Interviewing for a job is not to be taken lightly. You need to prepare yourself for each one of these important presentations and negotiation sessions. You are presenting yourself to a potential employer who needs to be impressed by both your skills and your personality and professionalism. As you discover more about the company, you will "negotiate" to become a part of the company.

Becoming a part of an interior design firm for the first time is an exciting feeling, as you will finally get to do the work that you have trained to do. The work you get assigned in the beginning might seem trivial at first, but that is because they need to see you up close and personal to see what you really can do. It gets better; always remember that—assuming, of course, that you give it your all every day.

This chapter provides information about how employers review resumés and cover letters, which may help you in your preparation of these important tools. It continues with an extensive discussion on interviewing, providing tips on negotiating for and during that stress-producing event.

The chapter includes a section for the professional who has been working for some time and considering making a move. It provides some insights for consideration in this regard. Making a career change is never an easy decision, but sometimes it is necessary to improve one's responsibility challenges and income opportunities. The chapter also includes a new section concerning on-the-job strategies. For many, it is more advantageous to stay with a current firm than to move on. The new section briefly discusses this topic.

HOW EMPLOYERS REVIEW RESUMÉS AND COVER LETTERS

Employers receive dozens of resumés every week—if not every day—whether or not they have an opening. Knowing how to catch their attention might move your resumé to the top of the pile and possibly get you an interview.

Naturally, when employers do not have any openings, they do not have the time to read each application in depth. Another important part of your job search is to provide something in the cover letter and resumé that gives them a reason to look at yours now. Understanding what they look for is crucial to a successful job search.

Certain features will almost always automatically eliminate a letter from consideration: such things as poor spelling, sloppy appearance, a "To Whom It May Concern" salutation, too many pages, or an obvious lack of skills top this long list.

Generally, the first thing an employer will do is scan application letters and other mailings for relevance to the firm. They may manually or possibly electronically scan for key words. Those that do not match will be put in a separate pile and may or may not ever be read again. If the company currently has no openings, an employer may give the cover letter a glance, note that the resumé mentions certain skills that the company generally needs, and determine if they are worth retaining for future reference.

There are several other items that an employer either looks for or uses to evaluate a resumé:

1. *Reference to how the applicant heard of the job opening or the firm.* "I was excited about your advertisement in the Sunday *Gazette* for a design assistant." "I enjoyed our chance to discuss a possible position with your firm when we met at the chapter IIDA meeting." These types of comments show the prospective employer that you can make a connection with the employer and that you know something about the firm.

2. *Use of key words or phrases to catch the reviewer's attention.* Employers are looking for certain skills, accomplishments, educational background, and other items specifically related to their design specialty. When those key words or phrases are used (e.g., "AutoCAD 20XX," "increased sales," "award-winning project"), they will catch the reviewer's eye, and he or she will likely slow down and pay more attention to the letter and resumé.

3. *Relevance to the design firm.* Employers are impressed when an applicant has done some research about the firm. For example, craft career objective and career summary statements that relate to the work done by the firm to which you are applying. The applicant's skills should also be relevant to the design firm's skills needs.

4. *Clarity of employment history.* Employers want to know what the applicant did and where he or she worked prior to applying for the current position. The employment history section naturally tells the prospective employer what you have done in the past and have to offer. Whenever possible, include comments that quantify your experience, as these will stand out.

5. *Achievement.* Employers want to hire an individual with a proven level of accomplishment. They are looking for indications of successful project management, profit making, or anything else indicating that the applicant knows how to achieve goals. This is another reason to think about outcomes, quantifying accomplishments, and skill sets as you write your resumé.

6. *Good communication skills.* Designers do not just communicate through their drawings. Writing and verbal skills are at least equal in importance to technical skills for some positions, and may be more important for others. Accurate proofreading of written materials is very important.

7. *"Creative writing."* Employers become suspicious of resumés filled with more active verbs or claims of accomplishment than seem reasonable for the individual's apparent level of experience. Out-and-out lying is easily discovered; just don't ever do it. Always be truthful in what you include in the resume and cover letter.

8. *Broad interests.* Most employers want to hire individuals who are loyal and dedicated to the interior design profession, but they do not want one-dimensional employees. Indicate involvement in professional associations, community groups, and other outside activities. Be careful not to go overboard, however. You may sound too busy with hobbies and outside interests to have time to work. You might also unintentionally provide information that can cause the employer to discriminate against you.

9. *Compensation and salary history.* Some applicants include salary history or compensation requests in the documentation. An employer is going to look at whether this information is in or out of line with the company. Many suggest not including this information unless it is specifically requested by the prospective company.

10. *Neatness.* This is obvious, but it is worth repeating.

THE JOB INTERVIEW

A job interview is a stressful situation regardless of whether you are a student or an experienced professional. All your preparation and hard work have gotten you to this point. You are ready to present yourself and your skills through a personal interview. This is your chance to make a good impression, to convince the employer that you are the one person in the world who can handle the job.

In just about every reference book, you will read that the interview is where little things more often than not torpedo a candidate. The hints and comments in this section, we hope, will help you to achieve success as you move through the interview process.

The planning and preparation for your interview are no less important than any other kind of planning and preparation discussed in this text. Here are some strategies and reminders about that preparation:

- *Organize your portfolio.* Go through your portfolio and be sure that every item is where you want it for the interview. Familiarize yourself with what you are going to show the interviewer, and confirm in your mind the order in which you wish to show it. Make sure you have a copy of your resumé, references, and a pen in the portfolio. If your portfolio is on a computer, be sure you have any cables you might need.

- *Ensure neat appearance and good grooming.* Check the outfit you wish to wear to be sure it is clean and pressed and shoes are shined. As necessary, trim your hair and take care of other personal grooming needs.

- *Verify details.* Twenty-four to forty-eight hours before the interview, call to double-check on details such as time, the person who will be interviewing you, and how to pronounce his or her name. Clarify if more than one person will be interviewing you. If so, request an agenda, so that you will know how much time you will be spending with each person.

- *Know where you are going.* If you are traveling to another city, find out where to park or how to get to the office. You can, of course, use the Internet to help with this.

- *Prepare yourself.* Your mental preparation includes anticipating and thinking about the kinds of questions the interviewer may ask you and that you may want to ask the interviewer about the company. Some common questions are included at the end of this section. Also, if you are bringing a laptop to show your portfolio, make sure it works properly.

- *Know the time frame.* Initial interviews can be as short as 30 minutes or can last 2 hours, though an hour is the average. In either case, plan to spend about 20 minutes showing your portfolio and the rest of the time answering questions.

Lateness and no-shows are nearly inexcusable. If for any reason you cannot keep the interview appointment, call and personally talk to the interviewer to tell him or her. Don't be late unless it is due to something totally beyond your control—but if you must be late, be sure you call. To avoid being late, make a point of arriving at the office or studio at least 10 to 15 minutes early. These few extra minutes will give you a cushion in case you experience a traffic jam or difficulty in finding the office. It also gives you a chance to relax and collect yourself before going into the interview. If at all possible before you check in with the receptionist, go to the restroom to check your overall appearance.

When you check in with the receptionist, be sure to smile and tell the receptionist who you are, with whom you have an appointment, and what time the appointment is for. Remember to be friendly and cordial but professional with everyone you meet. Most likely, you will be told to have a seat. You can mentally prepare yourself by reviewing points you would like to make. For the most part, though, it is better to have done that before you arrive, and instead use any wait time to try to relax and think positively about the way you will conduct yourself and the outcome of the interview. Try to use this time to compose yourself by reading a magazine. Try to relax; don't fiddle with your portfolio, briefcase, or handbag. And turn off your cell phone!

You may be asked to fill out a company job application form before the interview. Many companies use standardized forms to obtain specific information they feel is key to their review process. Job application forms ask for such information as contact information, job history, education, and credentials and references. Note that the job application cannot ask for information that is considered illegal, such as marital status and age. More on that is included later in this chapter.

If by chance you are interviewing out of state, there is a possibility that someone from the office will meet you at the airport. Of course, you will know this ahead of time, and your preparation for this is to travel in professional casual dress. If you know you are going right into the interview from the airport, then you should travel in business apparel. It also helps to know what the person looks like or to arrange a meeting place so you can easily contact this person. Additional tips and strategies are included in the article labeled Item 30-1 on the companion Web site.

What to Wear to an Interview

What you wear to the job interview is a part of the overall impression that you will leave with the interviewer. It will not get you the job, but it might lose it for you. Many interior design professionals find it acceptable to be trendy or even casual in their everyday business apparel. However, most interviewers expect more conservative apparel for the interviewee. If you have researched the company as well as you can, you will have some idea of what normal business attire is like at that design firm. Nonetheless, it is smart to dress more conservatively even if you know the firm is very casual about normal work attire.

Here are some quick tips:

- Wear apparel that is comfortable and professionally appropriate.
- Business suits for men and women are standard, with ties for men.
- For women, sundresses, sleeveless dresses, or low-cut dresses do not project the kind of impression that businesspeople like to see.
- Refrain from wearing anything that attracts more attention to your outfit than to yourself.
- Hide tattoos as best you can and carefully consider whether you want to retain any body piercings.
- What you wear to the interview and the image you project can have an impact on the salary offered. Someone who comes to a job interview sloppily dressed will be taken less seriously even if he or she is highly talented.

Refer back to Chapter 26 for additional discussion of general business clothing.

The Interview—First Impressions

As an old advertisement once put it, "You only have one chance to make a first impression." Now is that chance, and it can be absolutely critical to the outcome of your interview. However, you are not concerned: you have done your homework, know what you want to say, and have even practiced that first encounter. When your interviewer arrives and greets you, be prepared to shake hands. Prepare for this by having your portfolio, handbag, or attaché case positioned so that you can pick them up with your left hand, leaving the right hand free to shake hands. Smile! Say hello, introduce yourself. You want this job, don't you?

When you arrive at the conference room or office where the interview will be held, wait for some indication from the interviewer as to where to sit. If he or she does not make any indication as to where to sit, choose a chair that is either directly across from the interviewer or at a 90-degree angle. These two positions make it easier to show your portfolio and maintain eye contact.

Remember that the purpose of the interview is for the employer to get to know you personally, ask you questions, and try to evaluate whether you would be a good addition to the firm. The interviewer will be looking for information and personal conduct that shows you will be able to do the job and will fit in with the existing team. If the applicant is an experienced professional, the interviewer is also looking for clues that he or she is even willing to work for the firm.

The interview is a time for you to evaluate whether this particular firm is really the kind of firm for which you wish to work. Just because a firm has a good reputation does not mean that you will want to work for it. Create your own internal list of what you want to know about the company through the questions you will ask during the interview.

As you are being interviewed, keep several things in mind:

- Refrain from distracting mannerisms such as fussing with your hair or accessories, or playing with a paper clip or pen.
- Pay attention to your own body language; don't slouch or otherwise allow your body language to communicate disinterest.
- Listen carefully at all times. Don't fall into the trap of thinking about what you want to say while the other person is talking.
- Ask for clarification if the interviewer says something you don't understand.
- Think before you speak, and do not interrupt the interviewer.
- Use eye contact; smile, and show interest.

Interview Styles

Remember that the first "interview" encounter is when you greet the receptionist upon your arrival. When a firm is large enough to have someone at the front desk, he or she knows you are coming and has been told to evaluate the encounter with you. That is why arriving early enough to gather your thoughts and yourself before you enter the office or studio is so important.

There are many different styles of interviewing. In some cases, the employer will purposely ask you questions that will put you under even more stress than you are already experiencing. The idea, as far as the employer is concerned, is to find out how you might react under the worst conditions. This probably does not happen in interviews with interior design firms very often, but stress-inducing questions could come up. Stay calm, recognize what the interviewer is doing (it's not a personal attack), and do not become sarcastic or defensive. If the interview is conducted in a particularly stressful or abrasive manner, you might not want to work at that company anyway!

Another style of interviewing is the situational interview. In this case, the interviewer will ask a lot of questions like, "What would you do if the client vetoed every single design idea you presented at the final presentation?" The interviewer is trying to see how you think on your feet. These kinds of questions are most likely to be asked if you are applying for a management position, or perhaps a project manager position, rather than a position as a designer. In any case, think about your answers and take these questions seriously.

Some firms use team interviews. This means that more than one person will question you during the interview or you will be passed from staff member to staff member during the interview period. This happens frequently in larger design firms, where an ability to fit into the team and the existing company culture are important. Understand that everyone probably has a preplanned part to play in the interview. One interviewer may be casual, another may be formal, and another may appear not to be interviewing you at all but observing your behavior. Be respectful of everyone, and be prepared for a long interview process.

Most interviews in interior design are not designed to induce stress. In fact, many owners and managers of design firms with whom I have talked insist that they try to make the candidate as comfortable and at ease as possible—but you will feel stressed.

Focus on your qualifications in terms of what you can do for the company. Graduating students need to indicate a willingness to learn. Be enthusiastic in your answers, and stress your positive characteristics, but do not exaggerate your experience or your abilities. It will not take much time for the employer to find out that you are not an expert with CAD if you said you were but are not. Absolutely do not try to pass off someone else's work as your own in your portfolio. That, too, will be found out very quickly and will always result in dismissal.

The Interview Discussion

The interview discussion itself will include several themes. First, the employer will ask you questions to see if you fit with the needs of the company. He or she will be looking for various clues in your answers and demeanor to help with the hire/no hire decision. Second, you will have the opportunity to present your portfolio. Naturally, this is your chance to convince the employer that you have the skills to work at the company and do the job that is available. Third, you will have the opportunity to ask questions of the employer to help you determine if this is the firm you want to work for, clarify responsibilities, and acquire other information that is important to you.

The kinds of questions asked during the interview are discussed in the next sections. It is important to develop some good strategies for handling the interview discussion in a positive way.

During your interview, never bring up personal problems, argue, blame others, or beg for the job. Even if you left your previous job under difficult circumstances, do not blame anyone at the other company for your problems. This tags you as a difficult person and will probably influence the interviewer to pass you over. If you are asked if you were ever fired, be honest. It is not necessary to go into a long, detailed discussion of what happened. Make some brief comments about what happened and hope the interviewer moves on.

Be well prepared in presenting your portfolio. You *are* well prepared, because you have organized your materials and practiced this all-important task. Don't rush through this presentation, but also don't spend an inordinate amount of time on each item. Don't make excuses or apologize for work that is less than perfectly executed. If the work is of poor quality, you should not have included it. Explain what is good about the piece, not what is bad. Don't forget to clarify what part of a group project you did when presenting work that is not totally your own. And be enthusiastic without being boastful or obnoxious about your skills.

During the interview, you may realize that you are not interested in working for that company. It is important that you complete the interview but promptly inform the firm that you are not interested in pursuing the position further. Those of you who are students should not accept an interview if you really have no interest in working for the company. Some students like to go on interviews to "practice" for the job they want. This is poor business etiquette that can come back to haunt you later. An informational interview (discussed in Chapter 29) is quite different from arranging for an actual interview to use as "practice."

One very good clue that the employer is interested in you is if the interviewer suggests showing you around the studio or office. This is usually done only if the candidate interests the employer and he or she wants to introduce you to staff members. However, if you have not actually been offered the position, don't assume anything. Every once in a while, an employer just tries to be nice and shows off the studio but doesn't offer you a job.

For the most part, if you are offered a position, be prepared either to accept or reject it at that time. If you are offered a position that is different from the one you expected or you are being offered a lower salary than you were expecting, it is acceptable to ask for time to consider the offer. If you really want the position, say so. Do not leave without knowing what the salary range is if you have been given an offer.

It is very common for a firm to interview several people for even an entry-level position. If you are not made an offer but there is no indication that you have been rejected, ask the interviewer when he or she will be ready with a decision. This will help you decide about making other interview appointments or making a decision about another offer.

Watch for clues that the interview is drawing to a close. A few common ones are the interviewer begins to stack the job application, your resumé, and his or her notes together; or the interviewer pushes his or her chair back in preparation for getting up. This is the time to summarize your interest in the position and why you are the best candidate. State this in a few sentences so that you do not overstay your welcome at the end. When the interview is over, get up and leave promptly.

If an offer is made and you accept it, be sure that you understand what day you are to start, the time, and anything else that you need to take care of, either prior to your first day or during your first day on the job. If you don't get an offer, you will probably be disappointed, but you still need to be gracious and professional. Say something that indicates you are interested in the job if you really are. It is important to keep a good attitude at this point because needs change in interior design all the time. The firm that doesn't need you today may have work come in that requires hiring additional staff next week.

Don't forget to thank the interviewer for his or her time, regardless of the outcome. As soon as reasonable after the interview, prepare some notes on how the interview went. This is naturally very important if you do not get an offer so you can correct any issues in your presentation. But it is also important when you get an offer. Your notes concerning salary and responsibilities are very important, as most interior design jobs do not include a written offer or contract.

TYPICAL INTERVIEW QUESTIONS

There are many kinds of questions that are commonly asked in interviews. Interviewers will ask questions to find out about your personality and demeanor. They want to determine whether you will fit into the existing group. They will ask questions to determine your overall interest in interior design and the specialty area that you are interested in pursuing. If you are a recent graduate, the interviewer probably will ask you about your educational background and the classes you took.

Typically, an employer will ask you to discuss your strengths and weaknesses. Whenever possible, discuss your strengths related to specific examples. Perhaps CAD is a particular strength, so consider mentioning grades in those classes or extra workshops you have taken. Weaknesses are harder to discuss. Deal with any of these in a straightforward manner, focusing on how you are trying to overcome the weakness.

Questions are likely to come up to find out about your ambitions in the field and, to some degree, your future plans with regard to your career. Interviewers may even ask questions to find out if you have any "skeletons in the closet," to discover whether you left a prior job under bad circumstances. It is important that you prepare yourself for these questions in advance. The questions shown in Table 30-1 are typical of ones asked in an interior design interview. This table has been included as a work sheet on the companion Web site as Item 30-2 so that you can draft your responses. You may want to think of some others as well.

Your Interview Questions

You too will have questions when you interview. Some of the ones you initially planned to ask may have been answered during the interview discussion. Some of them are going to involve salary and benefits. Others concerning responsibilities are also common. You might not have much time to ask your questions, so use the time to help you better understand the company and show the employer that you are the right person for the job. Questions you might ask include:

- Can you describe your expectations of me during the first year?
- What are the job responsibilities of this position?
- Will I be working with only one designer or several (for an entry-level position)?
- How many people work in the company?
- What are the company's plans for growth or expansion?
- Are many other people being interviewed?
- How will I be evaluated for raises and promotion possibilities?
- When will you be making a decision?

Salary discussions might occur during the course of the interview or near the end. Compensation will most likely not be brought up until late in the discussion. Employers are going to want to know what kind of salary you are looking for. Be prepared to give a salary range, but if possible wait to do so until the employer has indicated what the salary will be. If you are already employed in the profession, they will ask what you are currently being paid. If you ask for too much, you probably won't be given an offer. If you ask for too little, they may believe you don't have any confidence in your skills and thus drop you from consideration.

Employers, of course, want to hire you at as low a salary as is reasonable for the position. But do not sell yourself short. If the salary offer is way below

TABLE 30-1.

Common interview questions

General Questions for Any Candidate
Why did you decide to become an interior designer?
What do you know about our company?
How did you hear about our company?
Why do you wish to work for us?
Have you applied to any other companies?
Tell me about the qualifications you have for this position.
Are you willing to do the traveling out of town that is necessary for this position?
Tell me about yourself.
How long have you lived in this city?
How much compensation are you expecting?
What will you add to our company?
Describe what you consider to be your weaknesses.
How do you plan to overcome those weaknesses?
Could you name a coworker we could contact who could tell us something about you?
Do you have any objections to taking our item1 psychological tests?

Questions Common for Entry-Level Positions
Why did you select the college or school you attended?
Why did you select a major in interior design?
Did you have any leadership experience in college?
How do you think your colleagues in your major would describe you?
How do you view this job in relationship to your long-term goals?
Describe your reactions when your work was criticized.
What are your ambitions for the future?
How long would you expect to stay with our company?
Did you find it comfortable to work in the classroom studio?
How long do you think it will take you to make a meaningful contribution to our firm?

Common Questions for Candidates with Prior Professional Experience
Tell me about your previous experience and how those positions relate to this position.
How do you think you can best contribute to this firm?
Why are you looking for another position?
Are you a leader?
What are your ambitions for the future?
You appear to be overqualified for this job. Why are you applying for this position?
If you are offered a position with this company, tell me what you would do during the first month on the job.
How much are you worth?
How would you describe your supervisory (management) style?
How have you increased sales or profits at your present employer?
How do you think your present boss would describe you?
May we contact your present employer?
Please tell me how many days of work you missed last year.

what you need to live on or is way below what you understand the competition is paying, say so. Remember that benefits such as health insurance, reimbursement of professional association dues, and employee discounts are important parts of the compensation package.

It is important to consider these benefits along with long-term professional factors. A job with a firm that has a national reputation can yield long-term benefits even if you leave after a few years. You might be able to negotiate certain benefits like NCIDQ fees and professional dues payments in place of some basic compensation.

Compensation levels are often based on several factors. Most commonly, compensation is based on years of experience in the profession, along with other beneficial and relevant experience. Education and technical skills also affect compensation. Possibly your reputation, based on such things as awards, authorship and publication, and/or skills as a speaker, can also have an impact on compensation levels. You should reread the section in Chapter 27 on compensation and benefits.

If you are interviewing in a city with which you are unfamiliar, research the cost of living there before you go for an interview. Investigate costs of housing, food, gas, and other items of daily life. You might be able to get this information from a local bank or the chamber of commerce.

Compensation in Interior Design

Compensation in interior design is difficult to determine with any precision. This is because so many businesses are sole proprietorships and privately held businesses. Thus, the data on compensation are limited, sometimes consisting only of word-of-mouth reports in an individual's market area.

Nonetheless, a good source for general information on salary and other compensation is the U.S. Department of Labor's Bureau of Labor Statistics (BLS). The BLS regularly researches wages for hundreds of occupations, including interior design. The information in the BLS statistical report is drawn from data on larger firms, and this may vary considerably from the actual compensation you may hear about in your area.

As of 2011—the latest report—the hourly mean wage for those offering specialized design services was $25.39 per hour with an annual mean wage of $52,810. Even with the poor economy, these are increases from the information available at the time the fourth edition of this book was prepared.

This report also indicated that the top paying areas or states were California, New York, Texas, Florida, and Illinois, with the highest mean annual wage for these states being New York with $65,540. You can find information specific to your state and some of the larger metropolitan areas by going to the Bureau's Web site (www.bls.gov.oes.current). Search for occupational category 27-1025.

Median wage information on many cities can be accessed from other sites. The U.S. Department of Labor sites (www.careeronestop.org) and (www.salaries.com) can provide salary ranges for your area. *Interior Design* magazine also reports some salary and industry data that can help you understand potential compensation levels. They report information from the overall design "Giants," hospitality Giants, and Green providers. Remember that these figures are for the largest firms in the country.

Salary information might be available from the professional associations. However, note that these organizations often quote the Bureau of Labor Statistics for their information. The ASID report, *The Interior Design Profession: Facts and Figures*, provides much useful data on the profession in the United States and Canada. You can purchase a copy of this report from ASID.

You must recognize that salary rates will vary by geographic location, size of the design firm, specialty of the firm, and even the number of employees. Salaries in some geographic locations will appear high because the cost of living in that city/area is higher than in many other locations.

A large firm with substantial revenues will be able to pay employees more than a small firm with a limited number of employees. A design specialty such as residential might include commission on the sale of merchandise as part of a compensation package, whereas a firm specializing in retail design, for example, that does not sell merchandise cannot offer a commission as extra compensation. All of these factors should be kept in mind when discussing salary and compensation.

ILLEGAL QUESTIONS

U.S. law states that some types of questions are inappropriate to ask during an interview; the laws prohibit interviewers from using them, and they cannot appear on a job application. These questions relate, but are not limited, to age, sex, religion, marital status, parental status, sexual preference, and ethnic origin. For example, the employer cannot directly ask you how old you are, your date of birth, your religion, or your native tongue.

There are ways in which certain normally illegal questions can be asked so as to make them permissible. This is especially true if the question has a direct bearing on an individual's ability to perform the job. It is legal for an employer to ask something like, "Are you between the ages of 23 and 50?" or "Are you a citizen of this country?" The key, of course, is whether the questions and the way in which they are asked are being used to discriminate against potential employees. You may wish to review appropriate sections from the books of Lewin G. Joel III, Fred S. Steingold, and Steven Mitchell Sack (see the reference list) for specific ways in which questions can and cannot be asked during interviews or on job applications.

Questions directed at women, such as asking whether she is single or married, what her husband does for a living, or whether she plans to have children, are all considered illegal. Sometimes these questions come up in very casual ways, such as, "Are you going to be able to work evenings and weekends when needed?" This question could be innocent or actually a ploy to find out if you have children and child care responsibilities. These discriminatory kinds of questions must not influence the employer's decision as to whether to offer a job to an individual.

When you are asked a question that you believe to be illegal or that you feel uncomfortable answering, you must be prepared to say something. Many of the job-hunting books suggest that you answer the question; others suggest not offering personal information. Another way of handling this situation is to say something like, "I do not understand what that has to do with the requirements of the job or my qualifications to do the job." When the interviewer responds, comment on how that will not be a problem for you, without necessarily detailing or revealing personal information.

If the interviewer asks too many of these kinds of questions or ignores your hesitancy in answering them, you always have the right to terminate the interview and obtain a job somewhere else. It is sad to say, but discrimination in hiring decisions does occur. However, if you feel you have been denied a job based on discrimination, you have recourse should you choose to pursue it. "You may have a cause of action if you can prove that you were discriminated against in the job application process . . . . If you feel you have a legitimate gripe, the first step is to file a complaint with your state human rights commission or the EEOC."[1] Of course, you can hire a private attorney and file a civil suit if you wish. Only you can decide whether you want to work for a firm that appears to discriminate.

FOLLOW-UP

Even if you have been offered and you have accepted a position, the interview process is not complete. Should you accept the position, there may be some follow-up tasks to be performed at the office, such as completing additional paperwork. Most likely this will be done on your first day on the job. You will also likely have some additional questions concerning that first day.

Perhaps you have been offered a position but have asked for time to consider the offer. It is best if you call the interviewer promptly and follow up with a refusal or acceptance letter. In most situations, the employer is hoping for an immediate response. Depending on the situation, you can ask for 24 to 48 hours. Waiting longer can be a problem and can indicate to the prospective employer that you are not interested. When you respond within a reasonable time frame, the company knows whether you are interested in the position and, in the case of your refusal, has a letter for the company's records.

You have to be careful to ask for time to decide if you have other interviews scheduled. If you have another interview that day, do not keep one employer dangling to see if someone else might have a better offer. Be sure to consider the offer in front of you carefully, comparing it to your goals, to help you decide whether to accept. A highly qualified designer is likely to get more than one offer or be speaking to more than one firm, and the employers know this. If you are interested, let the person in front of you know that fact, as well as that you are also interviewing with other firms. In all honesty, this is a delicate situation in which there is, unfortunately, no perfect answer.

More likely, you will not receive an offer immediately because the company is also interviewing other people. An important task shortly after the interview is to prepare notes detailing what was talked about, as part of your job search recordkeeping. If an offer was not made or you were rejected, these notes will help you determine and understand what might have gone wrong so that you can correct the errors during future interviews.

If an offer is made and you accept it, a written summary from your perspective is also important. Notes related to salary, benefits, and expected performance levels will be essential in the future to remind you of the agreed-upon responsibilities on which you will later be evaluated. Many designers now request that offers be put in writing. This writing does not have to be a formal employment contract, as described in Chapter 27, but it should include key points concerning salary, benefits, and work responsibilities.

Good business etiquette also calls for you to send a thank-you note or letter to the interviewer immediately after the interview. If you have not yet received an offer, this courtesy will indicate to the prospective employer that you are a professional. Even if the firm does not have an opening for you, you will be remembered later. Thank the interviewer for giving you his or her time; restate your interest in the position, if you are still interested; and follow through with providing any information that you agreed to supply. Figure 30-1 shows a sample letter with suggested content.

Some job-hunting experts suggest sending an e-mail thank-you instead of one by snail mail. Considering the number of e-mails a business owner receives each day, many employers will appreciate a handwritten thank-you note. A follow-up phone call is also appropriate in place of a note, especially if the interviewer has so indicated. It might be a good way to set up a second interview or provide some information that for some reason you did not have at the time of the initial interview.

If you are interested in a position with the firm but you know that the firm is still interviewing others, it is necessary to keep the design firm interested in you. Be sure to add something in your note or letter summarizing your qualifications and stating how you can contribute to the company.

YOUR FIRST JOB

The transition from student to professional is not easy for most individuals. The last semester of school can be a nerve-wracking time. Projects are generally complex, the quality of work must be very high, and grades become even more

Marilyn Norton
2571 N. Paradise Lane
Sacramento, California
(916) 555-2410

February 18, 200x

Mr. Sandford Hopkins
Hopkins, Dodge, and Russell, Inc.
1849 Grass Valley Avenue
Reno, Nevada

Dear Mr. Hopkins:

Thank you for giving me the opportunity to meet with you yesterday and discussing my joining your firm as a Project Designer.

While you interview the other individuals you are considering, I hope you will take the time to examine my resumé and will decide in my favor. I feel confident in my ability to be a productive contributor to the on-going success of Hopkins, Dodge, and Russell.

I would like to review three important facts that show I am the most qualified candidate for the position of Project Designer. First, I have seven years' experience with a full-service commercial design firm, where my responsibilities involved all areas of a design project from programming through contract administration. Second, my experience and knowledge of AutoCAD 14, 2000, and PowerPoint allow me to contribute immediately to your firm. Third, since I am already NCIDQ certified, you will be hiring a designer who will easily be licensed in Nevada.

Should you need any further information, I will be happy to provide it. I look forward to your positive response to my application at the end of the week, when you conclude your remaining interviews. Thank you again for your time and consideration.

Sincerely,

Marilyn Norton

FIGURE 30-1.

A sample follow-up thank-you letter that would be sent after a job interview.

important. Added to that stress is the development of portfolios, job searching, and internships. A great way to make the transition from student to practitioner is an internship. Internships help students see how all the coursework they have taken relates to the work done in the "real world."

Despite these stresses, many designers talk about how excited they were to finally use the skills they spent so many years honing in classes. Becoming a professional colleague to other interior designers feels so much better than being a student!

Your first job becomes the groundwork for your career. This is not to say that your first job represents what you will always do in interior design. If you ask any professional who has been working for 15 years or more about his or her career path, you will find that a career in interior design is never a straight path. It zigs and zags and even may throw you a few curves. I once had a student who always finished her commercial projects very quickly in comparison to everyone else in the class. I asked her about it one day, and she said, "I hate doing commercial projects so much, I just want to get it over with." Naturally, her first job was with a residential design firm. About a year later, she was visiting the school, and we got to talking. "Say, do you know of any commercial design firms that are hiring?" she asked. "I hate residential design!"

Naturally, how work works is different in different companies. Some firms are relatively relaxed and informal, whereas others might have a formal structure that makes it feel like working in the corporate world. How work works in a particular firm will in all likelihood be a key component of training during the first few days on the job.

Your first job is where you will learn to work in interior design:

- You will learn methods of doing a project not covered in school. This is because each professional has a personal way of working.
- You will begin to make business and industry contacts as you socialize with professionals in your area.
- You will become very familiar with certain product lines and crafts-people that you can confidently recommend to clients.
- Attending and participating in professional meetings will help you gain confidence in dealing with people you do not know.
- You will learn how to dress, how to "talk," and how to act like an interior design professional.

Because it is your first job, do not be cavalier about the experience. Most of you will learn very quickly that you must park your egos at the door, because you will be directed, reprimanded, and pushed to learn by bosses, other designers, and even clients. This is not school, and this first job in interior design is probably not like any other job you have ever had.

Just because you graduated from a wonderful, accredited school (or anywhere else, for that matter) does not mean that you know more than your boss. I have often told students, much to their chagrin, that now that they are graduating they will begin to learn about work and how to do interior design. Table 30-2 provides several truths about that first job.

TABLE 30-2.

On-the-job policies and truths

- They really mean you are to be there at 8:00 AM every day.
- One hour for lunch means one hour.
- Talking to friends on the phone is not allowed. Keep your personal life outside the office.
- Many project decisions are made within minutes, not days or weeks.
- Observe how others work, ask thoughtful questions, and listen a lot so that your decision-making skills keep improving.
- Reading magazines because you have "nothing to do" is not a positive task.
- If you make a mistake, don't fret over it and lie. Own up to a mistake and learn so you don't repeat the same mistake.
- You can't take every Friday off to meet up with friends for a long weekend.
- The boss is always right even when he or she is wrong.
- The boss is not likely to pat employees on the back every time they do something right. "Grades" don't happen on a weekly basis.
- December 24th is not a holiday. Nor are a lot of other days you may have normally had off.
- You will get criticized in front of others, and it will not feel pleasant.
- The boss will probably not give you positive feedback all the time—get over it.

Though truthful, the preceding comments may seem a little harsh—or possibly condescending—as well. The work environment is not school, and your time is not your own but the company's. Maybe you will be lucky and have a boss who mentors and congratulates more than criticizes. Those really hard instructors are that way for a reason, because interior design is a demanding, sometimes high-stress, and always time-sensitive profession, whether you are just starting or own the company.

Design professionals expect entry-level employees to come ready to work—even if that means cleaning up the library from time to time. They expect the entry-level professional to be a team player, be disciplined, and be well organized.

They don't expect you to know everything; they also expect you to ask questions. When you aren't sure, the only dumb question is the one you don't ask. Doing it correctly means a lot to the senior staff and clients. Aspire to learn all you can about the business, and there will likely be no end to your success.

Many recent graduates feel they are entitled to take on large responsibilities and do very important work right off the bat. Get over it. Few new employees who have little previous work experience are going to be allowed to take on projects by themselves, meeting with clients and doing plans and specifications without supervision. You have to "pay your dues" and learn how the company that hires you does things and expects you to do the work. Their way may be quite different from what you learned in school. It doesn't mean you were taught wrong. It just means there are many ways to do essentially the same tasks. Learn how your company wants work done, and you will have a successful probationary period and possibly a long association with the company.

Table 30-3 offers a few suggestions about how you can prepare yourself for the transition from student to professional. I am sure your professors will have others. If you missed it, you should also go back to Chapter 5 and read the section on expectations.

TABLE 30-3.

Suggestions to assist students in the transition to professional

Talk to professionals who are doing the work you want to do. People love to talk about what they do and their work. Make appointments and come prepared with about 15 good questions to ask that will help you find out what it is like to work at a particular kind of company or in a particular type of design specialty.

Examine your motives and establish goals. Set goals that interest you. Think about what you want to do two, five, or ten years from now.

Get involved with a professional association. Visit chapter meetings of the different organizations in your area. Students are always welcome. When you are sure about which one(s) you want to join, get involved. Volunteer for committees. It is a great way to get to know people in the business.

Begin to be a professional. One or two days a week—maybe for studio classes—dress professionally, as if you were going to the office. Get used to being dressed up. You will also likely feel more confident on those days.

Begin to work like a professional. Use a time management system of some kind. Treat the school day as a workday; that is, start the day at 8:00 AM and work until 5:00 PM.

During your internship:

—Don't play the critic. You are there to learn, not to criticize the company.
—Don't be lazy or blasé. If you want a good recommendation from this company, cheerfully complete all assigned tasks.
—Look for things to do or to help out as well.
—Ask questions. They expect you to ask questions.
—If you want to work for this company, show that you want to be there by doing all that is asked and then some.
—When you have nothing to do, look for or ask for something to do. Straighten catalogs or review samples and catalogs.
—You can learn a lot about current products by cleaning up the library from time to time.

ON-THE-JOB STRATEGIES

Leaving a current job voluntarily is certainly a solution when dissatisfaction occurs. Many designers have suffered through involuntary separation from a job due to the economy or for cause. Certainly, many wish to advance their careers doing what they are doing and/or stay with a particular company.

When you accept a position with a company, do so with the expectation you are going to be there for a while. When you accepted the position, you should have had some idea of what the expectations of you would be. You should also have been made aware of responsibilities and even how long it might be before you would be given added responsibilities.

As an entry-level employee, don't look down your nose at tasks that you feel are beneath you. As far as the company is concerned, you have the knowledge to be hired, but you may not yet understand how they do things. As was pointed out, keeping the library up may not sound like what you want to do in interior design, but you can also look at it as a way to learn sources. So keep your expectations in check.

Professionals need to continually examine how they are doing their jobs. Becoming more productive (yes, more productive) and staying interested in enhancing the company's reputation are two important keys to advancing your career. For the professional who has worked for a few years, simple things like coming in on time, volunteering to complete tasks others don't want to do, not complaining, and giving a positive impression of your company through your behavior are all important.

Long-term professionals must also look to enhance their careers through newer challenges that don't always involve bringing in new clients. Volunteering to work on committees of professional associations can help you meet influential people at the national level. Agreeing to critique student work or lecture to students adds to your apparent expertise. Being visible in the community by speaking to community groups about design topics of interest to the general public is also a great thing.

Career advancement goes back to discussions earlier in this book, particularly in Chapter 28. You have to have an idea of what it is you want to accomplish in the interior design profession so that you can plan how to achieve your goals. Career advancement does not happen by treading water and just taking what comes as it comes. Although good things have happened to many professionals that way, the truly successful have had a vision and a plan.

These brief thoughts and the items in Table 30-4 are only a small smattering of things that you can do to advance your career.

MAKING A CAREER CHANGE

At some point, many interior design professionals start thinking about making a career change. I have encountered numerous senior designers who have left full-time practice in order to teach at a university or community college. Other designers seek the possibilities of additional income by obtaining positions as sales reps with manufacturers and vendors. And, frankly, some leave the profession to do something out of the profession.

There are many reasons why someone makes a career change after years in the profession. Some common reasons are:

- Lack of respect by boss
- Contributions to the firm are not valued
- Lack of challenge

TABLE 30-4.

Career advancement strategies

- Develop goals and a plan.
- Improve your professional skills, especially the technical ones related to execution of interior design projects.
- Obtain appropriate additional education, such as in codes, management, accounting, and marketing.
- Obtain credentials that enhance your expertise: NCIDQ certification, licenses, LEED® accreditation, CAP certification, and others.
- Become involved in a professional association for professional growth and professional networking.
- Seek out and join (or at least go to meetings of) professional associations or groups where your potential clients attend.
- Become comfortable speaking in public and/or speaking to strangers. Join groups like Toastmasters to help with this skill.
- Be positive and don't complain.
- Be dependable. Go above and beyond your expected responsibilities when practicable.
- Be a team player, not a prima donna.
- Leave your personal problems at home.
- If you are set on leaving, plan with money in the bank for expenses, an up-to-date resumé, and—once again—a plan.

- Office environment has become difficult and overly stressful
- Work responsibilities have negatively affected personal life responsibilities
- Compensation has become stagnant
- No longer find the work interesting

Not everyone develops these negative feelings. Most interior designers find the profession challenging and satisfying. Some stay with a single firm for many years, perhaps working their way up to management or partnership. Nevertheless, any job is stressful at times, and even when the economy is booming this profession can be very competitive.

One day you may find that your current job does not suit your needs anymore. "You can come up with a million (untrue) reasons why you can't leave a situation you dislike. But when you deny reality (or the depth of your unhappiness), it has a way of catching up with you."[2]

Before you cut the cord and quit your job or close your studio, you had best think about what it is you still want to do and why you think you are dissatisfied. Lots of jobs require long hours. Lots of jobs are stressful. And in lots of jobs you have to work with (in some way or another) difficult people. It is critical that you assess your current situation at work, your skills, and your interests in new directions.

Look at the job you have, and perhaps talk with someone you trust who can help you see if the current situation isn't really awful but just has to be fine-tuned. If you work for someone else, discuss changes in your responsibilities within the company. Think about whether options like a marketing emphasis rather than strictly design planning can work in the current job, and then talk to the boss about how you could do this. When it's your own business, make contact with a business coach who can help you find new options for your business efforts.

If you are unhappy and think you want a totally new direction, you may need to go all the way back to books that can help clarify interests. You can start by answering the questions in Table 30-5. You might also find Robert Bolles's *What Color Is Your Parachute?* a useful tool to help you redefine your

TABLE 30-5.

Questions to help evaluate a possible job or career change

- What is scariest about changing careers?
- List three to five reasons why you want to leave your present job.
- List three to five reasons why you should stay in your present job.
- What was the reason—the last straw—that helped you decide to leave?
- Did you regret leaving a previous job?
- Do you wish that you had left that other job (or this one) sooner?
- Is there a particular circumstance that would convince you to stay?
- If you leave, how will you support yourself during a transition should you be fired during the job search?
- If you leave, are you really acting in your own best interests?
- Why do you think it is time to make a total career change?
- What will you be looking for in a new career that the current one does not provide?
- Are you prepared for a major difference in income if you embark on a totally new career?
- Do you have a plan for your future related to making a career change?

interests. They don't make you investigate the whole of the situation, but they can get you headed in a promising direction.

An important part of the evaluation and decision process is talking to someone who knows you well and will keep your confidences as you contemplate making a career change. If it is going to be something dramatic, such as moving from a design/planning position to one in sales, talk to people who already are working in that position, especially those who have been designers before. They can help you understand what it is like to make a transition and warn you about problems with making a career change.

When you are certain about your new career path, make sure that you can afford to make the change. As discussed in Chapters 15–20, starting your own practice is neither inexpensive nor easy. And teaching salaries—if that is what you are contemplating—are not on a par with the compensation that senior designers are accustomed to.

Finding a new job, especially in a different field, takes time. Figuring out for sure what it is you want to do and where you want to do it is just the start. You need to consider any impact on your family. When you are going to be able to interview without the boss finding out is another consideration.

You might also need to obtain different credentials to seek out a new career option. Full-time faculty at most institutions are generally required to have a master's degree. Becoming involved in sustainable design can involve obtaining LEED® certification or accreditation. Moving to a state that has licensing laws may also require that you get more education or meet other standards.

An important issue is to not burn your bridges. Walking in and quitting one day without giving notice and with projects unfinished will cause a lot of problems for both the company and you. The company may not be very willing to give you a recommendation, assuming you need it. You might not be able to take current clients with you to your new position or even use past projects as part of a portfolio.

Once you know what you are going to do, give ample notice, say thank you for the experience of working there, and say good-bye gracefully. And remember, for most of you, Thomas Wolfe was right—you can't go home again. It is unlikely that you will want to return to your old position, and it is also unlikely that they will want you back. So think very carefully before making a change.

WEB SITES RELEVANT TO THIS CHAPTER

www.asid.org American Society of Interior Designers

www.careeronestop.org careeronestop (a division of the U.S. Department of Labor

www.newh.org Hospitality Industry Network

www.interiordesigncanada.org Interior Designers of Canada

www.interiordesignjobs.com Interior Design Jobs

www.iida.org International Interior Design Association

www.monster.com Monster (a job search site)

www.bls.gov U.S. Bureau of Labor Statistics

You may also want to search the Web sites of other professional associations for career and job-hunting information. Numerous additional sites can be found by searching topics such as resumés, cover letters, and job interviews.

KEY TERMS

Career strategies

First impressions

Illegal questions

Interview styles

WHAT WOULD YOU DO?

1. Mary was very excited about getting an interview with a particular design firm. Even though she was new to the city, the firm had a great reputation for cutting-edge design and was highly recommended as a place to really learn and move up in the field.

   When she arrived for her interview, she had to wait 45 minutes in the lobby. Chad, the design director, finally came out and led her to the conference room. He introduced Mary to Karen and Don, two designers in the firm. After a few minutes of pleasantries, Don asked Mary why she wanted to work at this company. While she was responding, Karen left the room. Then Chad asked her to show them her portfolio. As she was explaining the projects in her book, Karen returned to the conference room along with the owner of the company, Eric.

   After she was done with her portfolio, Eric asked her why they should hire her. As Mary began to respond, Eric's cell phone went off and he took the call. Don told her to go ahead and answer anyway, which she did. Eric asked her to repeat what she said, and before she could answer, he asked her if she was married, if she had any kids, and if she planned on having any more kids.

2. Alice has worked for a 25-person commercial design firm for only about 3 months. She was hired right out of school, and her hiring was based in part on a terrific portfolio. Her portfolio and her comments at the interview indicated that she had very good CAD and Revit skills. By the time of her 90-day performance evaluation, it had become obvious that Alice was struggling with the drawing assignments given to her by the design director. During her 90-day performance review,

she was asked about problems and then was asked to bring in her portfolio for a second meeting. At that second meeting, Alice admits that some of her portfolio work was done by a friend.

3. Kelly is asked during a job interview if she has any small children. "You see, this job requires that the designers be free to travel around the state as well as other states to meet with clients," says the employer. Kelly hesitates, as she has a four-year-old child.

   She is very interested in working at this firm, which has a fantastic reputation. She knows they work with clients who own large private residences in three states. The pay is slightly less than what Kelly was hoping for, but she feels that she could get by since her husband works from home.

4. Alan has worked in the interior design profession for nine years. He worked in a residential design firm for three years and commercial design firm for six years. He has been increasingly frustrated with his current employer due to a lack of salary increases and responsibility.

   He talks to a sales representative who is a friend about jobs working for manufacturers or suppliers. His friend says that many firms, but not the one he works for, would positively consider Alan's experience. "If you are unhappy, maybe you should check around. Of course, the salary for a rep is very up and down, meaning it can be great one month and bad the next," comments his friend.

   Alan decides to first talk to his boss because he thinks he might be in line for a promotion. A week later, his boss informs him that Alan is going to be laid off in 30 days. Alan then hears that his boss hired a woman with only five years' experience for essentially the job that Alan had.

REFERENCES

1. Lewin, 1996, p. 46.
2. Hirsch, 1996, p. 149.

NCIDQ Definition of Interior Design

National Council for Interior Design Qualification approved by the Board of Directors in 2004.

Interior design is a multifaceted profession in which creative and technical solutions are applied within a structure to achieve a built interior environment. These solutions are functional, enhance the quality of life and culture of the occupants, and are aesthetically attractive. Designs are created in response to and coordinated with the building shell, and acknowledge the physical location and social context of the project. Designs must adhere to code and regulatory requirements, and encourage the principles of environmental sustainability. The interior design process follows a systematic and coordinated methodology, including research, analysis, and integration of knowledge into the creative process, whereby the needs and resources of the client are satisfied to produce an interior space that fulfills the project goals.

Interior design includes a scope of services performed by a professional design practitioner, qualified by means of education, experience, and examination, to protect and enhance the life, health, safety, and welfare of the public. These services may include any or all of the following tasks:

- Research and analysis of the client's goals and requirements; and development of documents, drawings, and diagrams that outline those needs;
- Formulation of preliminary space plans and two- and three-dimensional design concept studies and sketches that integrate the client's program needs and are based on knowledge of the principles of interior design and theories of human behavior;
- Confirmation that preliminary space plans and design concepts are safe, functional, aesthetically appropriate, and meet all public health, safety, and welfare requirements, including code, accessibility, environmental, and sustainability guidelines;
- Selection of colors, materials, and finishes to appropriately convey the design concept, and to meet socio-psychological, functional, maintenance, life-cycle performance, environmental, and safety requirements;
- Selection and specification of furniture, fixtures, equipment, and millwork, including layout drawings and detailed product description; and provision of contract documentation to facilitate pricing, procurement, and installation of furniture;

- Provision of project management services, including preparation of project budgets and schedules;

- Preparation of construction documents, consisting of plans, elevations, details, and specifications, to illustrate non-structural and/or non-seismic partition layouts, power and communications locations, reflected ceiling plans and lighting designs, materials and finishes, and furniture layouts;

- Preparation of construction documents to adhere to regional building and fire codes, municipal codes, and any other jurisdictional statutes, regulations, and guidelines applicable to the interior space;

- Coordination and collaboration with other allied design professionals who may be retained to provide consulting services, including but not limited to architects, structural, mechanical and electrical engineers, and various specialty consultants;

- Confirmation that construction documents for non-structural and/or non-seismic construction are signed and sealed by the responsible interior designer, as applicable to jurisdictional requirements for filing with code enforcement officials;

- Administration of contract documents, bids, and negotiations as the client's agent;

- Observation and reporting on the implementation of projects while in progress and upon completion, as a representative of and on behalf of the client; and conducting post-occupancy evaluation reports.

Reprinted with permission from the National Council for Interior Design Qualification. This definition can be downloaded from www.ncidq.org.

80/20 rule. A business rule applicable to many situations, stating that from a list of 10 items arranged in the order of importance, if one accomplishes only the 2 most important items, one achieves 80 percent of the total value of time spent.

Acceptance. In contract law, what occurs when one person agrees to exactly the conditions in the contract proposed by the other party.

Accountant. Person who provides information concerning financial and tax matters. This individual has more expertise and training than a bookkeeper.

Accounts. Financial entries with different names for clarity to show additions (increases) and subtractions (decreases) to the account.

Accounts payable. Claims from suppliers for goods or services ordered (and possibly delivered) but not yet paid for.

Accounts receivable. What others owe to the firm as a result of the sale of, or billing for, goods and services.

Accrual accounting. An accounting method in which revenues and expenses are recognized at the time they are earned (in the case of revenues) or incurred (in the case of expenses), regardless of whether the revenue has actually been collected or the expenses have actually been paid.

Accrued expenses. Expenses owed to others for a given time period but not yet paid; salary owed during an accounting period but not yet paid is an example.

Acknowledgment. The paperwork form that a supplier sends to a designer to indicate what the supplier interprets the designer's order to be; sometimes called a confirmation.

Actual freight. The cost of transportation of the goods from the supplier to the designer's warehouse or the jobsite.

Addenda (order updates). Corrections or changes made to contract documents and written by the person or firm responsible for the original set of contract documents. (*Addendum* is the singular form.)

Administrative law. Law created by rules and decisions of agencies of federal, state, and local governments.

Advertising. Any kind of paid communication in media, such as newspapers, magazines, television, radio, or Internet sites.

Advertising allowance. A special discount or other incentive given when a designer uses a manufacturer's product in promotions and advertising.

Agency relationship. The common-law relationship that exists when one person or entity agrees to represent or do business for another person or entity. Today's employer–employee relationship is a reflection of the agency relationship.

Agent. A person who is authorized or empowered to represent another person.

Alternate bid. In competitive bidding, amounts added to or subtracted from the base bid should the client add or subtract parts of the specified project.

Amortize. Concept that the value of intangible assets, such as copyrights, patents, and trademarks, is reduced; similar to *depreciate*.

Angel investor. Entrepreneur who wants to see someone else succeed and may invest in a business such as interior design.

Arbitration. A means of settling a dispute in which a disinterested third party evaluates the arguments of two parties to a contract.

As-built drawings. Working drawings prepared after a project has been completed, indicating exactly what was built rather than what may have been shown in the construction drawings.

As is. Condition of space rented without any changes to the interior. Applies to many other situations in which a good is sold in the condition it currently exists and is not represented as new.

Assets. Any kind of resource—tangible or intangible—that a firm owns or controls and that can be measured in monetary terms.

Assignment. Transfer of rights in a contract to a party that was not originally a party to the contract.

Assumption of risk. Legal doctrine holding that a plaintiff who knowingly and willingly enters into a risky situation cannot recover damages if harm or injury occurs.

Atelier. Term for shopkeepers. See *Ensembliers*.

Autocratic management style. Business conduct in which the owner performs all the management functions. Usually very little input is solicited from staff members on how to operate the business.

Back orders. Items that a vendor cannot ship with other merchandise or are otherwise not available for some period of time.

Balance sheet. An accounting form that shows the financial position of a firm at a particular moment in time, including a statement of its assets and liabilities; sometimes called a statement of financial position.

Bar chart. A scheduling method consisting of a description of tasks required on the left-hand side and horizontal bars on the right-hand side showing the time (in days, weeks, or months) that is required to complete each task.

Barrier-free regulations. Codes created and enforced to make public buildings more accessible to the handicapped and disabled.

Base bid. A proprietary specification that contains an "or equal" substitution allowance; all bidders must base their bids on the goods specified by product name.

Basis of the bargain. Information provided by a salesperson that is the primary influence on the buyer's decision to buy a product.

Benchmarking. The practice of assessing a firm's data in comparison to data from other companies in the industry to determine capabilities.

Benefits. Features of a product or a service that relate to the needs of the client.

Best and final offer (BAFO). A negotiation requirement in some projects involving government or public agencies.

Best practices. Superior performance and practice.

Bid. An offer for the amount a person will pay to provide the required specified goods and/or services.

Bid bond. Bond required of all bidders to ensure that the designer or vendor who has been awarded a contract will sign the contract.

Bid form. Document prepared by the designer or the client and provided to the bidders. The bidders submit their prices for the goods or services on this form. Sometimes also called a tender form.

Bid list. A list of acceptable potential designers and/or vendors who may receive bid notifications. They are selected by the project owner through prequalification.

Bid opening. The time when the owner of a project reveals who has bid on the project. In most situations, the bid opening is private, and only the owner and the designer who is responsible for creating the contract documents are present. Government agencies and many public utilities are required to hold bid openings that are open to the public. In this case, anyone may attend the bid opening and find out what others have bid for the project.

Billable hours. The number of hours that a designer works on projects under a contract for design fees. The fees can be charged by any method, if the client is actually being charged for the hours that the designer works.

Billing rate. A dollar amount, combining salary, benefits, overhead, and profit, that is used as the basis for charging clients for services; usually expressed as an hourly rate.

Bill of lading. The form that the supplier provides to the truck driver to show what is being shipped and who has title to the goods.

BIM (Building Information Modeling). Acronym for a design system that combines graphic and project data to define how a building is designed through computer software.

Blog. A Web site where users can read and exchange information.

Body language. Nonverbal communication.

Bond forms. Legal documents used to oblige the designer or vendor to the contract as assurance that the designer or vendor will perform the requirements of the contract as agreed upon. Three common bond forms are the bid bond, the performance bond, and the labor and materials payment bond.

Bonus plan. Method of paying extra compensation based on the employee's producing more than a specified personal quota.

Bookkeeper. An individual trained in financial recordkeeping who is hired to perform financial recordkeeping transactions and duties.

Box burns. Furniture damage caused when a shipping carton rubs against fabric or frame materials.

Brand. The combination of images and encounters that the customer perceives, accepts, and experiences with a company. It is not just a logo mark.

Branding. The combination of images and encounters the customer perceives, accepts, and experiences with a product or a firm.

Breach of contract. Breach simply means "to break." A breach occurs when one of the parties to a contract does not perform its duties as spelled out in the terms of the contract.

Break-even point. The point at which revenues equal expenses. At this point, the firm is neither making nor losing money.

Brochure. Printed marketing piece that provides information to interest clients, grab their attention, and allow the design firm to showcase its design style and expertise.

Budgeting. Process that involves annual managerial goals expressed in specific quantitative, usually monetary, terms. Encourages the manager to plan for the various events that may affect the firm rather than to react to them.

Building codes. Regulations that primarily concern structural and mechanical features of buildings.

Building inspector. Person (usually a municipal employee) who checks to see that the project is built according to the plans, specifications, and appropriate methods.

Building permit. A permit granted by local governmental agencies that allows the construction of a new building or major interior remodeling.

Building standards. Interior finishes provided by the landlord without charge to the tenant.

Building standard work letter. A document that outlines what quantity and quality of work will be undertaken by the developer in the construction of a tenant's office or other commercial space.

Build-out. An industry term for the construction process.

Build-out allowance. Dollar amount that a landlord provides per square foot to build partitions and to install basic mechanical systems such as lighting fixtures and architectural finishes.

Business plan. A detailed definition of a business idea and explanation of how the business of this potential company will be executed.

Buyer. A person who contracts to purchase or who does purchase some goods.

Buying a job. A practice in which a firm prices goods or services at an unusually low rate in order to make the sale or get the contract.

Capital construction. The cost for actually building the structural components; also referred to as capital improvements.

Career objective. A statement that explains what kind of work the job applicant seeks; generally used in the resumé and/or cover letter.

Career summary. In a resumé, a significant statement of experience and skills concerning the applicant's ability to handle the job for which he or she is applying.

Cartoning. Boxes or other packing materials.

Case law. See Common law.

Case study. A marketing tool that tells what the design program was for a particular client and discusses some unique features of the project.

Cash. The cash on hand in the firm's bank accounts, checking accounts, cash registers, or petty cash boxes; considered a current asset.

Cash accounting. Accounting method whereby revenue and expense items are recognized in the time period in which the firm actually receives the cash or actually pays the bills.

Cash discount. An accounting term referring to an extra discount given when a designer or design firm pays an invoice promptly. A notation that commonly looks like "2/10 net 30" appears on the invoice to notify the designer or design firm of the cash discount.

Catalog price. Supplier's list in which prices can be designated "suggested retail," "list," "retail," "net," or "wholesale." These different terms have different meanings regarding the price the designer must pay for the goods.

Certificate for payment. A form telling the client that the supplier has completed parts of, or most of, the work and that the supplier has sent an invoice for that work. This certificate recommends that the client pay the supplier's invoice.

Certificate of occupancy (CO). A document provided by the local building department after the construction of a building has been completed, indicating that the owner may now legally occupy the building.

Certificate of substantial completion. A form that reports what has been done and indicates if something is missing concerning construction of the structural elements.

Certification. A term most frequently associated with legislation that defines who may use a certain title. Also might be called registration.

Certified public accountant (CPA). An individual who has met educational and testing requirements established by the jurisdiction for the accounting profession.

Chain of command. The formal reporting links that exist between one level of employee and another; helps everyone in the organization understand what the formal communication patterns are.

Change order. Written permission or instructions concerning any aspect of a project that modify design concepts, construction designs, or product specifications.

Chart of accounts. A list of all the accounts that a firm is using.

Chronological resumé. States educational and work experiences exactly when they occurred, in reverse chronological order.

Click-on agreement. Contract formed when purchasing on the Internet by way of clicking on a box that says something like "I agree" or "Accept."

Close corporation. A corporation whose shares of stock are commonly held by only a few individuals. The stock is not traded on any of the public stock markets; also called family corporation or closely held corporation.

Closed competitive selection. Occurs when those on an acceptable list of potential bidders receive notifications of impending bids and are allowed to bid on a project.

Closed probe. A sales technique in which the designer asks the client a question that generally results in a closed (yes/no) response from the client.

Closed specification. A bid specification that is written for one particular product, such that another product cannot be substituted for what has been specified.

Closing. The art of knowing when to ask for the sale.

Codes. Systematic bodies of law created by federal, state, and local jurisdictions to ensure the safety of the public.

Codes of conduct. A set of ethical principles.

Cold-calling. Contacting potential clients whom the designer has never met before.

Collateral. Money or property that is pledged as security in case a loan is not paid. The loan giver takes the collateral if the person who takes out the loan defaults.

Collateral materials. Marketing publications, such as brochures, flyers, calendars, and inserts, that can be used as sales materials.

Combination fee. Use of more than one method of charging a client.

Combination resumé. Utilizes qualities of both the chronological and the functional resumé forms and combines them in one resumé.

Commercial interior design. The branch of interior design concerned with the planning and specifying of interior products used in public spaces, such as offices, hotels, airports, hospitals, and so on; sometimes called contract interior design or contract design because it involves a contract for services.

Commission. A method by which an agent acting on behalf of the employer is paid; usually a percentage amount paid to the agent (interior designer), calculated on the agent's sale of goods and/or services.

Common law. Law created by court decisions and governing areas not regulated by statute or administrative law.

Compensation. The method of paying an employee for work performed.

Compensatory damages. A sum of money equal to the financial loss that the harmed party suffered due to a breach of contract.

Compensatory time. Time off given to salaried employees during the normal workweek to make up for overtime hours they have worked.

Competitive bidding. A process whereby the client has an opportunity to obtain comparative prices from a number of contractors and/or vendors for the construction or supply of the project.

Complete performance. Occurs when the terms expressed in the contract are fully accomplished in the manner in which they are specified in the contract.

Concealed damage. Damage to goods that is not obvious because the original packaging is not damaged. Most often occurs when items are shipped in cartons.

Conditions, covenants, and restrictions (CCRs). Specific regulations for condominiums, townhouses, and some other types of residences in planned communities. If a community has CCRs, it might not allow a business to operate out of a residence located in the community.

Confirmation of purchase. The business form that spells out what goods the designer has agreed to order or sell to the client; also called a sales agreement, purchase agreement, or contract proposal.

Conflict of interest. Occurs when a person puts his or her self-interest before his or her public or fiduciary responsibilities.

Conforming goods. The delivered goods as described in the sales agreement.

Consideration. Something of value that is exchanged as it relates to the contract; the legal term for the "price" that the offeree "pays."

Constitutional law. The highest level of law in the United States, expressed in the federal and state constitutions.

Construction agreement. An agreement between the owner of the project and the contractor hired to execute the total contract documents package. Also called a prime contract.

Construction documents. All of the working drawings, schedules, and specifications that describe what is required for the completion of a project.

Construction drawings. The typical plans, elevations, and details required for building a structure or an interior.

Construction manager. An individual who oversees the construction project as an agent for either the general contractor or the owner.

Consultation fee. Means of charging a client who wants ideas from a designer but does not need complete design services.

Continuing education unit (CEU). Short-term coursework in a wide variety of topical interests of a professional nature.

Contract. A promise or agreement made between two or more parties for performing or not performing some act. The performance or lack of performance of this act can be enforced by the courts.

Contract administration phase. The fifth phase of a design project, in which the competitive bid process is completed, the project is actually constructed, orders for goods are issued, and the goods ordered are placed or installed.

Contract design. See Commercial interior design.

Contract documents. All the drawings and specifications that together describe what is required for a project, along with contracts or agreements between the project owner and the designer and other stakeholders.

Contract documents phase. The fourth stage of the design project; involves the final preparation of all construction or working drawings (sometimes referred to as CDs), schedules, and specifications that are required to build and install the design project.

Contractual capacity. The legal capacity to enter into a contract.

Contributory negligence. A defense to negligence, in which the defendant must show that both sides were negligent and that injury resulted.

Control function. A management function in which a manager monitors the activities of the firm and takes any steps necessary to ensure that the plans, policies, and decisions of the manager and the firm are being carried out.

Conversion. A legal tort in which the rightful property of one person is taken by another; can also be a (statutory) crime of theft.

Co-op advertising. System in which a manufacturer and designer generally share in the cost of the advertising, or the manufacturer provides an incentive to the designer to sell the particular product being advertised.

Copyright. Time-limited legal protection granted to the creators of written materials and graphic designs.

Copyright notification (notice). To begin the legal protection of written materials and graphic designs, the following must appear in a conspicuous place on the work: (1) "Copyright," "COPR" (for copyright), or the copyright symbol ©, (2) year of publication, and (3) the name of the copyright claimant.

Corporation. An association of individuals, created by meeting statutory requirements, which is a legal entity. The corporation has existence independent of its originators or any other member or stockholder. It can sue and be sued by others, enter into contracts, commit crimes, and be punished. A corporation has powers and duties distinct from those of any of its members and survives even after the death of any or all of its stockholders.

Cost-of-living adjustment (COLA). An across-the-board compensation increase, meant to offset inflation.

Cost of sales. Expenses incurred or paid in the direct generation of revenues. Called cost of goods sold in retail sales businesses; in this case, it refers to changes in inventory.

Cost plus percentage markup. A design fee method that allows the design firm to add a specific percentage to the net cost of the merchandise being purchased by a client.

Cost price. The price that the designer must pay for the goods.

Counteroffer. An agreement to the offer in which the terms of the offer have been changed.

Cover letter. A letter that accompanies a resumé or other business documentation.

Credit. In accounting, the right-hand side of an account.

Credit application. A form filled out by a potential client to assure the designer that the client is creditworthy and has the ability to pay for the project costs.

Crime. A wrong against society that is defined and regulated by statute.

Critical path method (CPM). A scheduling method that begins by identifying the inter-relationships of the tasks to be performed. This analysis shows the designer which tasks must be done before the next or other tasks can be performed, thus establishing the critical path.

Current assets. Resources that the firm would normally convert to cash in less than one year.

Current liabilities. Obligations that are due within one year or less.

Customer's own material (COM). Designation when a designer uses a fabric on a specially ordered, upholstered furniture item that is different from one of the fabrics available from the furniture manufacturer.

Cutting for approval (CFA). A request for a sample of a current dye lot of textiles, wall covering, or other finish so that the designer can approve it before an order is finalized.

Cyber law. Laws dealing with utilization of the Internet and computers.

Daily rate. A fee amount charged for a full day's work, usually based on an hourly rate. Generally not used for creative time.

Damages. Money awarded to the party that has been harmed as a result of breach of contract or commission of a tort.

Debit. In accounting, the left-hand side of an account.

Debt capital. Business loans that come from creditors such as commercial banks.

Decision makers. The people who are authorized to make decisions for the client.

Decision making. The act of making reasonable choices between available alternatives; an important part of the management function.

Deep discounting. An extremely large discount from the suggested retail price that is given to a designer or a design firm that places very large orders.

Defamation. The wrongful harming of a person's good reputation. If the defamation is in writing, it is called libel; if it is oral, it is called slander.

Deferred revenues. Revenues received for services that have not yet been rendered or the sale of goods that have not yet been delivered.

Delegation. Transfer of responsibilities from one person to another.

Deliverables. Documents and presentation materials that are given to the client to explain design concepts.

Delivery. The activities concerned with moving tangible items from the showroom or warehouse to the jobsite and placing them in their correct locations.

Demising wall. A partition that divides one tenant space from another. Each tenant pays for one-half the thickness of the wall.

Democratic management style. Staff input is desired and responsibility is often given to staff members to accomplish tasks without direct interaction from the manager.

Demographics. Characteristics such as age, gender, and occupation that marketers can use to help identify customer groups.

Deposit. Money that is part of the purchase price, prepaid by the buyer as security in contracts for the sale of goods or real estate.

Depreciation. Concept that capital equipment has a limited, useful life; intended to express the usage of a fixed asset in the firm's pursuit of revenue.

Descriptive specification. Describes, often in elaborate detail, the materials, workmanship, fabrication methods, and installation of the required goods.

Design–build. Process in which a single contract is awarded to handle both the design and the construction of a project.

Design development phase. Project stage in which final design decisions are made regarding plans, specifications, and preparation of final presentation documents.

Designer/specifier. Interior designer who only infrequently becomes involved in direct sales of merchandise to clients. Designer/specifiers' responsibilities are otherwise the same as for those who do design and sell products.

Design-negotiate-build. Project in which each part is handled under a separate contract, such as a contract to design, to build, and to purchase furniture.

Destination contract. Shipping/freight method in which a manufacturer retains title to the goods until they are delivered to the buyer's delivery address; also referred to as FOB destination.

Direct expenses. Items that can be directly attributed to the generation of revenue.

Direct labor. The time employees spend directly involved in the generation of revenues for the firm.

Direct mail. Printed marketing material—from letters to brochures or newsletters—that is sent to prospective clients by regular postal mailing.

Direct personnel expense (DPE). A number that includes not only the salary of employees but also any cost of benefits, such as unemployment taxes, medical insurance, and paid holidays.

Disbursements. See Reimbursable expenses.

Disciplinary procedures. Means of handling ethics complaints against members received by a professional association; may vary according to jurisdiction.

Discount. A reduction, usually stated as a percentage, from the suggested retail price. A full or normal discount from suggested retail is 50 percent.

Doing business as (DBA). A filing required when the name of the business is other than the names of the owners.

Domestic corporation. A corporation formed in one state and doing business only in that state. Domestic corporations are also corporations formed within the United States.

Door-to-door. Method of charging by which the client is charged from the time the designer or the delivery truck leaves the designer's studio or warehouse loading dock to the time it leaves the client's location.

Double-dipping. A slang term sometimes used by clients directed toward designers who earn revenue from the design and specification of products and also from selling the merchandise specified.

Double-entry system. An accounting system that uses information in the accounting journals and ledgers and in which the accounts are based on the entries found in both the income statement and the balance sheet.

Down payment. A portion of the total selling price paid at the time goods are ordered.

Drawings. In accounting, withdrawals from the profits of a business by owners in sole proprietorships and partnerships.

Drop-ship. Shipping/freight method in which the designer requests that a manufacturer ship goods to an address other than the designer's business location or warehouse.

Due diligence. A process of doing thorough research to find out all that one can about any type of topic.

Duty of care. Common-law doctrine holding that in one's interactions with others, one must use the care a reasonable person in the same or similar situation would.

Electronic signature. A signature affixed by electronic means on an e-mail, faxed letter of agreement, or other electronic message.

Electronic Signatures in Global and National Commerce Act (ESIGN). Model law adopted by most of the states that helps to enforce contracts transmitted electronically; allows the use and recognizes the validity of electronic signatures in many situations.

Employee handbook. A concise reference of company policies for all employees.

Employer identification number (EIN). A government-assigned number that identifies the business to various federal and state government agencies.

Employment at will. The doctrine that an employee who is not bound by a written contract and who has no other writing spelling out the terms of his or her employment has the right to quit his or her job without notice but can also be fired by the employer at any time, with no explanation.

Employment contract. Contract specifying conditions of employment as well as special perks and benefits between designer and employer.

Empowerment. Giving employees the opportunity and authority to carry out the activities of the company without prior approval of a supervisor or manager.

Enclosure. A term placed at the end of a cover letter to indicate that something has been attached to or accompanies the cover letter.

End user. The ultimate consumer of goods or services; can also mean consumer.

Ensembliers. Shopkeepers and shops dealing with interior products; also called *ateliers*.

Entrepreneur. Someone who starts and manages his or her own business.

Equities. Claims on a balance sheet by outsiders and/or owners against the total assets of the firm.

Equity capital. Business funding that comes from investors such as stockholders.

Errors and omissions coverage (E&O). Insurance that covers an interior designer in the event he or she is responsible for errors or omissions in work performed or advice given to a client.

ESIGN Act. See Electronic Signatures in Global and National Commerce Act.

Ethical standards. What is right and wrong in relation to the professional behavior of the members and even the practice of a profession.

Ethics. Principles that impact a person's or group's behavior.

Exclusions. Portions of a competitive bid on which a vendor does not bid.

Expediter. An individual who is familiar with the design firm's paperwork system and the various ordering and shipping requirements of manufacturers; responsible for the speedy processing of orders.

Expenses. The amount of outflows of a firm's resources as a consequence of the efforts made by the firm to earn revenues.

Express warranties. Promises, claims, descriptions, or affirmations made about a product's performance, quality, or condition that form the "basis of the bargain."

Factory reps. Manufacturer's representatives who work only for one particular manufacturer as employees of the company.

False imprisonment. The intentional confinement of a person for an appreciable duration of time without justification.

Fast-track. Design and construction using a process to complete the project very quickly. In many cases, certain plans and construction documents are prepared "just in time" for the construction of those parts of the project.

Favorable variance. In accounting and budgeting, when the actual amount is less than the budgeted amount.

Feasibility studies. In-depth estimates of the planning and specifications that will be needed for a project.

Features. Specific aspects or characteristics of a service or a product; used during selling.

FF&E (furniture, furnishings, and equipment). Acronym for projects that have minimal or no construction work involved.

Fictitious business name statement. A filing required when a business is operating under a name other than that of the owner(s).

Fiduciary duties. Mandatory practices and behavior for an individual who acts in a position of trust or confidence for someone else.

Financial accounting. The day-to-day and periodic measurement and reporting of accounting information for use by individuals outside or inside the firm.

Financial management. Act of planning and analyzing all the financial aspects of a firm in order to help owners manage and control the performance of the firm; often called managerial accounting.

Fire safety (life safety) codes. Statutes and/or regulations that mandate a reasonable measure of safety in a building from fire, explosions, or other comparable emergencies.

Firm offer. An offer for the sale of goods in writing, made by a merchant, whether or not any consideration has been given by a buyer.

Fixed assets. Resources (also called property, plant, and equipment) that are the long-lived items used by the firm.

Fixed costs. Expenses or costs that are commonly thought of as overhead items and stay essentially the same or nearly so every month.

Fixed-fee method. Some dollar value determined by a designer for the performance of all the services required on a project. The client is then charged that amount, whether the project takes a shorter or longer time than the estimate; also called the flat-fee method or lump-sum method.

Fixture. In tax terms, a product that could be considered personal property that has become affixed to a building.

Flat fee. See Fixed-fee method.

FOB, Destination. Shipping/delivery option in which the manufacturer retains ownership of the goods, pays all shipping expense, and assumes all risks until the goods reach the destination.

FOB, Factory. Shipping/delivery option in which the buyer assumes ownership or title of the goods when they are loaded on the truck at the factory. The buyer assumes the transportation expenses and all risks.

FOB, factory—freight prepaid. Shipping/delivery option in which the interior designer has ownership and responsibility for damages during transit, but the manufacturer pays the transportation charges to the destination.

Foreign corporation. A corporation formed in one state but doing business in another state is a foreign corporation to that other state.

Four Ps of marketing. The four basic variables (product, place, promotion, and price) that create a firm's marketing mix.

Fraud. When someone intentionally misrepresents facts to deceive another party for personal gain.

Free on board (FOB). Shipping/delivery option in which the shipper must assume the expense of loading the goods onto the truck as well as the expense and risk for shipping the goods to the FOB destination; also referred to as freight on board.

Freight. The cost and process involved in the delivery of goods from the manufacturer to a destination. Also called shipping.

Freight bill. The invoice (bill) from the shipping company for moving goods from the supplier to the designer or the receiving location.

Freight factor. An expense or cost that the designer adds to the selling price or the cost price of any goods ordered for the client that are shipped to the designer's warehouse.

Fringe benefits. Direct or indirect additional payments made to the employee for work performed; may include paid vacations, profit-sharing plans, and group health insurance.

Full discount price. The discount given by most manufacturers, 50 percent off the suggested retail. This is also called net price.

Functional resumé. Presents information in order to emphasize qualifications and skills of the applicant, rather than the order in which they were obtained.

Gantt chart. A bar chart.

General conditions. Documents that set forth the legal responsibilities, procedures, rights, and duties of each party to a construction project; part of the bid documents.

General contractor. Individual or company that holds a license to contract and supervise all phases of a construction project; often called the GC.

General partnership. When two or more people join together for a business purpose; they alone share in the profits and risks of the business.

Goals. Broad statements, without regard to any time limit, about what a firm wishes to achieve.

Goods. Tangible items that have physical existence and can be moved.

Graphic image. The package of materials that the interior design firm uses to identify itself; includes the company logo, business cards, letterhead and other stationery, business forms, and drawing-paper identification.

Gross margin. The difference between revenues and cost of sales. Represents the amount of revenue available to cover overhead (selling and administrative) expenses.

Gross profit. Another term for gross margin. Does not represent profit.

Gross revenue. All the revenue, prior to any deductions, generated by the firm for a given accounting period.

Gross salary. The amount of employee compensation before any deductions are taken.

Headhunter. A slang term for a professional executive search and employment agency that will search out an employee from one firm in order to place the employee with another firm.

Hot-button issue. An issue that has critical importance to the client.

Hourly fee. The most common method of charging for services. It is based on the firm's direct personnel expense. For each hour or portion of an hour that a designer works on a project, the client is charged some dollar amount.

Hourly wage. A compensation method in which an employee is paid some dollar amount per hour for every hour worked.

HTML. Hypertext Markup Language; the computer language source code used to develop World Wide Web sites.

Implied contract. A contract formed by the actions of the parties rather than by an expressed written agreement.

Inbound marketing. Enticing the potential customer to contact or find a design firm through marketing on the Web, social media sites, or other means.

Incentive compensation. Compensation over and above regular compensation.

Income statement. An accounting document that formally reports all the revenues and expenses of a firm for a stated period of time. The result shows the net income (or loss) of the firm during the period; also called a profit and loss statement.

Incorporate. To create a corporation.

Incorporation. The act or process of forming a corporation.

Independent contractor. Someone who works for himself or herself and is not subject to the control of an employer.

Independent design firm. A firm that has no affiliation with a particular product and may not have any products displayed for sale in its office or studio.

Independent insurance agent. Person who commonly works for himself or herself and may represent more than one insurance company.

Independent reps. Manufacturer's representatives who work for themselves or a sales-representing group; usually handle several manufacturers' products.

Indirect job costs. Charges that add to project costs but are not associated with normal service expenses.

Inferior performance. Work that varies quite considerably from what is required or promised in a contract.

Informational interview. An informal interview that allows a student to find out something about the work in a particular profession.

Infringement. Any unauthorized use of copyrighted, patented, or trademarked materials.

Initial interview. The first time the designer presents to the potential client.

In lots. Products for one order are transported from the manufacturer to the designer in partial shipments.

Installation. The specialized part of the delivery process that involves assembly, construction, or physical attachment of products to the building.

Instructions to bidders. A document that informs bidders how to prepare bids for submittal so that all submittals will be in the same form.

Intangibles. An item or concept that does not have physical existence.

Integrated design. Process in which stakeholders in a project are included in the design from the beginning. It is a holistic approach to design and construction; also referred to as integrative design.

Intellectual property. Creative achievements such as writings, drawings, or various other media.

Intentional torts. Acts committed by a plaintiff on purpose and with knowledge that they were wrongful.

Internship. A supervised work experience within an interior design firm or other appropriate company within the industry; generally a part of the required curriculum.

Invasion of privacy. A legal harm against a person's right to freedom from others' prying eyes.

Inventory. Goods purchased and held by the business for resale to clients.

Invitation to bid. Summary of the project, the bid process, and other pertinent procedures for the project. It informs potential bidders of the project, its scope, and where to obtain further information; also called an advertisement for bids.

Invoice. A bill sent from the manufacturer or supplier to the designer indicating how much the designer must pay. The designer also uses an invoice to bill the client for goods and/or services provided.

Jobbers. Wholesalers who purchase smaller quantities of goods from manufacturers—usually a specific category of goods—and resell them to the trade.

Job description. Communicates the qualifications, skills, and responsibilities of each job classification within a design firm.

Job posting. A company notice, description, or post, on its Web site or other locations, regarding an employment opening or opportunity in the firm.

Joint venture. A temporary contractual association of two or more persons or firms in which they agree to share in the responsibilities, losses, and profits of a particular project or business venture.

Journal. In accounting, a chronological record of all accounting transactions for a firm.

JPEG format. In digital photography, a method of compressing an image that creates a usable—but not suitable for publication—version of a photograph. (JPEG stands for Joint Photographic Experts Group.)

Keystone. A discounting term that means a 50 percent discount from a suggested retail price.

Kickback. Money, or possibly some other incentive, offered in return for a favor between two parties.

Kinesics. The scientific study of the meaning of body positions and gestures.

Labor and materials payment bond. Bond required from the winning bidder to guarantee that, should the designer or vendor default on the project, the designer or vendor would be responsible for paying for all of the materials and labor that have been contracted for.

Landing page. A page on a Web site where visitors enter information so that they can get additional information or some other item.

Lead. A prospect that has begun to show interest in a firm or designer.

Ledger. In accounting, a group of accounts; often called a general ledger.

Legal injury or harm. Some legally recognizable loss, harm, wrong, or invasion; may be physical, economic, or (in some situations) psychological/emotional.

Legality. In contract law, doctrine that a valid contract exists only when it concerns the performance of some legal act.

Legal name. The business's official name, which must always be used on legal documents such as contracts and tax returns.

Letter of agreement. A simplified form of contract.

Letter of intent. (1) A letter sent to the winning bidder allowing that firm to begin work on a project. (2) A letter offering to buy a design business.

Letter of interest (LOI). Response to a client that has requested information on the qualifications of prospective design firms before publishing a request for proposal. Also called a request for qualifications (RFQ).

Liabilities. In accounting, amounts that the firm owes to others due to past transactions or events. Liabilities always have first claim on the firm's assets.

Liability insurance. Protects the business should it be sued by a third party for injury or property damage due to negligence, product failure, or other claims of that kind.

Libel. A wrongful harming of a person's good name through a written communication.

Licensing. A term most frequently associated with a state or province whose legislation defines who may practice interior design.

Lien. A legal claim or notice that someone other than the person who has ownership or possession of goods has a security interest in the goods.

Limited liability company (LLC). A type of business formation that is a hybrid of the general partnership and the corporation and that grants limited liability to its members.

Limited liability partnership (LLP). A partnership formation limited to licensed professionals; may not be available in all states.

Limited partner. Investor that contributes assets toward the operation of a partnership but may not participate in management of the partnership.

Limited partnership. A business formation created according to statutory requirements, with at least one general partner and one or more partners who are designated as limited partners.

Line item number. Numerical identification of an item on a sales order. This number helps the firm cross-reference merchandise to purchase orders and other documents.

Line of credit. Short-term business loan that lasts for one year or less.

List price. Generally accepted as being the same as suggested retail price—a price to the consumer.

Logo. A symbolic image of a company or an organization; also called a mark.

Long-term loan. Loans that are for a term of more than one year; usually granted to purchase capital items or an office location.

Lump sum. A fee that covers all the work and expenses required in the scope of services; must be carefully calculated because the designer knows that the fee cannot be increased beyond the fixed amount.

Malpractice insurance. See Professional liability insurance.

Management. The effective direction of staff members and financial resources under a manager's control toward goals and objectives that the owners of the firm have established.

Manufacturer's dealer. Retailer that features selected products from a particular manufacturer in a showroom that is open to the public.

Manufacturer's suggested retail price (MSRP). A price established by the manufacturer. It is also simply called retail price.

Markdown. A term used in retail to represent discounts taken from the normal selling price.

Market. In reference to designer resources, a term that many interior designers use to mean one of the annual shows held at the marts.

Market analysis. Investigation and planning activity that involves gathering and analyzing data concerning such things as the abilities and interests of the staff, potential clients, the economy, and the competition, so that the owner and managers can make better plans and decisions about the direction of the firm's business efforts.

Market centers. Concentrations of trade sources in one area of a city.

Market decline. The part of the business life cycle in which product sales are decreasing and the product value to buyers is diminishing.

Market growth. The second stage of a business or product life cycle, in which sales of the product or business increase substantially, providing increased profits to the company.

Marketing. All the activities of moving goods and services from producers to consumers.

Marketing mix. Operational elements that the design firm can control in the process of marketing and selling goods and services.

Market introduction. The first phase of the life cycle of a product.

Market maturity. The third phase of the business or product life cycle, in which sales for the originating company fall off as competitors enter the market and siphon off sales.

Market segment. A group of customers that has a common characteristic.

Markup. A term used in retail to represent percentage amounts (converted to dollars) added to the net or cost price to the designer.

Mart. A building in which many firms have separate showrooms or share showroom space.

Mechanic's lien. A legal recourse related to the labor and materials payment bond, that prevents the owner of the property from giving or selling the property to anyone until the lien has been satisfied.

Mentoring. Training or advising an individual to help him or her attain a higher level of success.

Merchant. Anyone who is involved with the buying and/or selling of the kinds of goods in which he or she is dealing; a person acting in a mercantile capacity.

Merit pay. An amount added to an individual's basic annual compensation amount, often as a reward for quality work done in the past.

Milestone chart. An easy scheduling method whereby a designer outlines the activities required to do the project and establishes a target date for the completion of each task.

Mirror image rule. Unequivocal acceptance of the offer in a contractual situation.

Misrepresentation. The altering of facts to deceive or the use of fraud for personal gain.

Mission statement. A philosophical statement of what the firm sees as its role in a profession; contains broad statements of what the firm wishes to achieve during an unspecified time period.

Mock-up. A full-scale, usually nonfunctional, portion of a design project, such as a hotel guest room.

Modifications. Additions or changes made to the contract documents (see also Addenda and Change order).

Moonlighting. Holding or engaging in work outside one's main job.

Movable equipment. Items such as furniture, accessories, and equipment that are not fixed to a building structure.

Move management. A process to help a client get ready to move and effect the actual move from one location to another.

Multiple. A billing rate based on a calculation of salary rate, expenses, and a profit margin. Also called a multiplier.

Multiple discounts. A series of discounts from the suggested retail price, given by manufacturers to designers for placing very large orders.

Mutual assent. Legal doctrine holding that the giving of a contractual offer and acceptance of the offer must be done willingly.

Mutual understanding. Contract clause stating that the contract, as written, is the full and complete terms and conditions of the agreement and that both parties accept this as being so.

Negligence. A failure by one party to use due care, resulting in injury sustained by another person or a person's property.

Negotiating. Activity that occurs when two parties are trying to reach agreement about some point.

Net income (or loss). The amount of income or loss that results when all expenses are subtracted from revenues. If the result is positive, net income represents the dollar amount of profit the firm has made for the given time period. If the result is negative, net loss indicates that expenses have exceeded revenues for the given time period.

Net price. A price representing a 50 percent discount from suggested retail.

Networking. Cultivating mutually beneficial relationships for the purpose of marketing oneself or one's design firm.

Niche. A very specific or unique focus concerning services or products provided by a firm.

Noncompete agreement. An employment contract clause that places some limits on where and/or how the employee may work after leaving, regardless of the reason. Also called a restrictive covenant.

Nonconforming goods. Any goods that are not as described in a sales order or a purchase order.

Not to exceed limit. A fee "ceiling" in a design contract or predetermined limit to complete the project requirements.

Objections. Disagreements with what was said or expressed by some other party.

Offer. In contract law, one party makes an offer to provide something or do something for another party.

Offeree. The person to whom an offer has been made in a contract negotiation.

Offeror. The person who makes the offer in a contract negotiation.

On the boards. Refers to manual drafting and other traditional tasks of the designer.

Open competitive selection. Process in which clients, such as government agencies, advertise impending bids so that anyone who is interested in the project and meets the qualifications that are spelled out in the invitation to bid may submit a bid.

Open probe. A sales technique in which the designer asks the client a question that generally results in an open-ended response; encourages the client to talk.

Open specification. A bid specification written in such a way that many products can be substituted for the item being specified.

Open terms. Situation arising when items are left off a purchase order; in this case, the purchasing agreement may not be valid.

Operating funds. Funds needed to keep the doors to the firm open and in business.

Oral agreement. An agreement made without any written contract or other writing explaining its terms.

Ordinances. Laws created by local governments, such as those regulating zoning, building codes, and traffic issues.

Or equal. Term in a specification that allows bidders to substitute what they believe to be products of quality equal to that which was specified.

Other assets. Financial assets such as patents, copyrights, and investment securities in another firm.

Overhead expenses. Those expenses incurred whether the firm produces any revenues or not; also called selling and administrative expenses.

Owner's equity. The section on the balance sheet showing the amount the owners have invested in the firm.

Owner's representative. Someone hired by the client to act on his or her behalf with the designer and others involved in a project.

Packing list. A detailed list, by quantity and description, of what is being shipped to the designer from a manufacturer or a supplier. It is commonly placed in a plastic envelope attached to the outside of one of the items being shipped.

Partnership. When two or more individuals agree to form a business.

Partnership agreement. A written description of the responsibilities of each person in a business partnership.

Pass through. In accounting, the transaction in which goods or services are billed by the interior designer to the client or end user.

Patent. An exclusive right to make, sell, and use a product for a specific period of time.

Percentage off retail method. A fee method in which a percentage is determined and the dollar amount is subtracted from the retail price of the merchandise.

Percentage of merchandise and product services method. A fee method that allows the designer to negotiate a percentage of profit on the cost of the goods and installation that will be involved in a project.

Per diem. A dollar amount charged to the client to cover hotel, meals, and transportation costs when it is necessary for the designer to travel out of town in the interests of the project; can also refer to a day rate for services.

Performance. In contract law, when each party does or provides what was agreed upon in the contract, performance has occurred. There are three types of performance: (1) complete, (2) substantial, and (3) inferior.

Performance bond. Bond required of the winning bidder as a guarantee that the designer or vendor will complete the work as specified and will protect the client from any loss, up to the amount of the bond, incurred as a result of the designer's or vendor's failure to perform according to the contract.

Performance evaluation. Systematic evaluation of the positive and negative work efforts of an employee. Used to review past performance in relation to agreed-upon responsibilities, and forms the basis for salary increases, promotions, and/or retention.

Performance reports. Reports consisting primarily of financial or other numerical information of interest to the owners and managers of the design firm.

Performance specification. A specification establishing product requirements based on exact performance criteria. These criteria must be based on qualitative or measurable statements.

Permitting privileges. Permission by a governmental entity for a designer to submit plans to the building department of a jurisdiction to obtain a building permit.

Permitting statute. Legislation or ordinance that allows interior designers to submit plans for building permits.

Personal goals. Goals for the nonemployment aspects of life.

Photo portfolio. A collection of photographs, slides, or other photographic media that represents projects for which the designer was responsible; used as a promotional tool.

Piggyback. A freight term for when a truck's trailer is loaded on a train flatcar and is shipped by train to the general destination.

Plaintiff. An injured person who brings a lawsuit against the party who allegedly harmed him or her.

Plan check. A municipal building department's review of construction documents done before the department issues a building permit.

Planning function. Managerial task that involves research into capabilities and resources so as to provide direction for the firm.

Plan review board. A local government agency whose responsibility it is to review construction drawings prior to issuance of building permits.

Portfolio. A visual presentation of what an individual can do as an interior designer.

Posting. In accounting, the transfer of a journal entry to the correct ledger account.

Postoccupancy evaluation (POE). Site visit and project review that are conducted to discover the existence of any problems in the design and installation of a project.

Posts. Information added to various social media Web sites.

Practice acts. Guidelines established by legislation concerning what a person can or cannot do in the practice of a profession in a particular state. Individuals whose profession is guided by practice acts must register with a state board and meet exacting requirements.

Predesign Information gathering and report generation done before a schematic design is started. Is an alternative term to Programming.

Premium. A giveaway product that has a logo, slogan, or other words or graphics printed on it, such as a T-shirt or a coffee mug.

Prepaid expense. The early payment of expenses in a period paid prior to when they are due, such as rent.

Prequalified. Refers to vendors or others who have been determined to be suitable to provide services and products to the company or to submit bids.

Press release. Information provided by the design firm or its representatives that might be of interest to the news media.

Prestige pricing. Unusually high cost of certain special products due to status or special aspects, like exceptional quality or materials, associated with the product.

Price. Any kind of payment from a buyer to a seller, including money, goods, services, or real property.

Price-fixing. An illegal practice where two or more businesses agree to sell merchandise or services at the same price.

Primary sources. Firsthand data sources, such as a questionnaire or survey.

Prime contract. See Construction agreement.

Principal. In an employment or agency relationship, the person for whom the agent acts. The owner of a business is a principal.

Private (general) corporation. The most common type of corporation formed for private, profit-making interests.

Probing. A selling technique of asking questions to uncover the needs of a client.

Pro bono. Providing something at no charge.

Procurement. Process of obtaining the goods and/or services needed for a design project.

Procurement form. *See* Purchase order.

Products liability. Tort law related to negligence and strict liability and contract law related to warranty.

Professional corporation. A special form of corporation created by individuals in professions such as law, architecture, and accounting.

Professional goals. Statements of desires and intentions that help to determine career options and make choices and decisions that arise during a career.

Professional liability insurance. Protects the design professional in the event an action causes acts, errors, or omissions in the course of work on the design project; often called malpractice insurance.

Professional negligence. Tort committed when the designer fails to use due care in carrying out his or her design responsibilities as normally expected by a professional.

Professions. Occupations with a recognized and accepted knowledge base, skills, and training.

Profit. What results when all expenses, including estimated taxes, have been deducted from all revenues for a particular period.

Profit and loss (P&L) statement. Another name for the income statement.

Pro forma. Projected financial information, such as the pro forma income statement.

Pro forma credit. Credit allowed or applied "in advance."

Programming phase. The information-gathering portion of an interior design project.

Progress report. Correspondence or verbal report made to the client so that the client is kept informed of the progress of the project and any problems.

Project closeout. The point at which a project has reached the time for final inspection and necessary documents are provided to the client to bring the project to completion.

Project file. File folders or notebooks in which the designer keeps all the pertinent data and paperwork related to a project in progress.

Project management. A process of organizing and controlling an interior design project from beginning to end so as to satisfactorily solve a client's problems and provide a reasonable profit to the design firm.

Project manager. Individual who is responsible for making site visits and telephone calls to keep a project on track; also the job title for a designer who has overall responsibility for all phases of a design project.

Promotion. Providing information about services or products from the seller to the buyer; includes publicity, publishing, advertising, and direct selling.

Promotional tools. A variety of methods and items to promote a business; includes press releases, brochures, and company logos, among others.

Proposal. An overview or other response to a request for a proposal (RFP) from a client. It is not necessarily a contract, although some designers use the term to mean a contract.

Proprietary information. Information, graphics, or other property that belongs to a particular person or firm.

Proprietary specification. Specification that lists products by the manufacturer's name, model number, and/or part number.

Prospecting. The process of locating new clients and obtaining appointments with them.

Prospects. Potential clients in a firm's business area.

Proximate cause. A legal term that connects unreasonable conduct of one party to any harm caused by that conduct.

Psychographics. Concepts defining a person's lifestyle interests and attitudes, such as hobbies, sports, and other interests.

Publication. When the creator of a copyrightable work has distributed the work to another without restricting the use of the work.

Public corporation. Business formed by some government agency for the benefit of the public. The U.S. Postal Service is an example.

Publicity. A direct form of promotion that is not paid for.

Public relations (PR). All the efforts of a firm that go into creating an image that positively affects the public's opinion of the firm.

Puffing. A salesperson's statements of opinion, not facts, about a product.

Punch list. A list that records in detail everything that must be taken care of in order for a project or installation to be completed; also called the site inspection report.

Punitive damages. Compensation in a tort or breach of contract case; given to punish the guilty party for its infliction of grievous harm.

Purchase order (PO). The business form that a designer uses to order goods and/or services for the client or to order supplies needed by the design firm.

Qualifying. Determining whether a potential client is really worth pursuing as a prospective client.

Quantity discount. A discount greater than the normal 50 percent discount, given because a large quantity of merchandise has been purchased at one time.

Query letter. Communication explaining the concept of an article to a magazine or other media editor; usually gives a little taste of the article by including the first paragraph.

Quid pro quo. Latin for "something for something." It is associated with the most commonly understood type of sexual harassment.

Ratio. One number over (divided by) another—the relationship between two or more things.

Record drawings. The set of drawings kept at the jobsite on which any changes made to the building are recorded. These will later be used to create the as-built drawings.

Red-lining. Notes or corrections made in red pencil or other medium that call attention to problems or errors on drawings that a jurisdiction checks before issuing a building permit.

Reference price. The amount customers internally acknowledge as the price they believe is reasonable.

Reference specification. Specification that uses an established standard, such as the standards of the American Society for Testing and Materials (ASTM) or the American National Standards Institute (ANSI), rather than written, detailed descriptions or performance criteria for required products.

Referral. Occurs when a client (or other party) tells another person who may be looking for interior design services about a particular design firm.

Registration. Legislation that defines who may use a certain title such as "registered interior designer." See also certification.

Reimbursable expenses. Costs that are not part of the design contract but are incurred in the interest of completing the project. Sometimes referred to as disbursements.

Relationship building. Activity that involves getting to know clients sufficiently well to have a good business connection with them.

Rentable area. The total amount of space required by the tenant on which the rent dollar amount (usually by the square foot) will be calculated.

Representatives (reps). The men and women who act as the informational source to the interior designer about various manufacturers' products. Independent reps work for themselves and are usually responsible for many different manufacturers' products. Factory reps work, as employees, for only one manufacturer.

Request for proposal (RFP). A document used by clients to obtain specific information about a large number of design firms that might be interested in providing design services for a project.

Request for qualifications (RFQ). A document used by clients to obtain information on the staff and general qualifications of a design firm before the client issues a request for proposal mailing; also called a letter of interest (LOI).

Resale license. A license required by most state and local jurisdictions when a business sells merchandise to a consumer. Also called a seller's permit.

Residential interior design. The plans and/or specifications of interior materials and products that are used in private residences.

Restocking charge. A fee charged by the designer for taking back merchandise that the client has ordered but does not want.

Restraint of trade. Contracts or arrangements intentionally made to be detrimental to the public good and generally have a negative effect on the potential for fair competition in a given market.

Restrictive covenant. An employment contract provision that does not allow an employee to work for a competitor; also called a noncompete agreement.

Resumé. A summary of a designer's qualifications.

Retail method. A fee method in which the design fee is derived by charging the retail or suggested retail price for goods sold to clients.

Retail price. Generally means the same thing as suggested retail price; the price quoted to the consumer.

Retainage. Money held back by the client to ensure that all the work, omissions, and problems associated with the project are taken care of.

Retained earnings. The claim on the assets arising from the cumulative, undistributed earnings of the corporation for use in the business after dividends are paid to stockholders.

Retainer. Payments to a professional to cover future service or advice by that professional. In interior design, the retainer is customarily paid at the signing of the contractual agreement.

Revenue. The amount of inflows from the sale of goods or rendering of services during an accounting period.

Right of refusal. A buyer's legal right to change his or her mind after a contract has been signed. Generally, a buyer has 72 hours to refuse the purchase of goods or services; in many jurisdictions, though, the right of refusal applies only to contracts signed in a residence.

Sale. Occurs when the seller transfers title or ownership of the goods to a buyer and the buyer provides some consideration to the seller.

Sale on approval. When the buyer takes the product without paying up front, but is obligated to pay if he or she keeps the product after some agreed-upon time.

Sales tax. Tax collected on goods considered to be tangible personal property when those goods are sold to clients.

Schedule. A tabular chart or graphic used to clarify sizes, location, finishes, and other information related to certain nonconstruction parts of an interior or structure; commonly prepared for doors, windows, and interior room finishes.

Schematic design phase. The phase of the design project in which preliminary design decisions are made and documents are prepared.

Scope creep. Situation in which project requirements become larger than originally intended due to client requests.

Scope of services. A detailed list of the tasks that must be accomplished to complete a design project. It is used to estimate the time involved and the design fees, regardless of fee method utilized.

S corporation. A special form of corporation that affords many of the benefits of a corporation but that pays taxes as a partnership; formally called a subchapter S corporation.

Seasonal discount. A special discount given to retailers to purchase certain goods earlier than normal. The goods are generally associated with a season or a holiday.

Secondary sources. Information that generally comes from existing materials, such as magazine or newspaper articles.

Secondary subcontractor. A subcontractor hired by another subcontractor to do or provide a portion of the work required of the first subcontractor.

Secured loan. A loan for which collateral is required as protection against possible nonpayment.

Selection committee. A group representing the client that will hear presentations from designers. The committee assists the project owner in determining which firm to hire to do the project.

Self-employment tax. A tax that self-employed individuals must pay on income earned.

Seller. Any person who sells or contracts to sell goods to others.

Seller's permit. See Resale license.

Selling. Finding out what a client wants and needs through the use of personal communication and then providing that good or service.

Selling price. The actual price that is quoted to the client.

Sexual harassment. Unwelcome sexual advances or requests for sexual favors from a supervisor directed at an employee in order for the employee to be hired or promoted, or to otherwise influence the work performance of the employee.

Shipment contract. Shipping/freight method in which the title to the goods passes to the buyer when the manufacturer (seller) places the merchandise into the hands of the shipper. Also called shipping contract.

Shop right. Legal doctrine stating that the employer holds a nonexclusive license to any creation or invention of tangible products an employee designs that are created as part of the employee's normal working duties.

Short list. A small number of interior designers or design firms that a client selects from a larger group to make presentations in order to negotiate a contract for design services.

Showroom. Leased or owned space that a manufacturer uses at a market center or other location to display merchandise to the trade; also used in reference to a retail store.

Signature. Name written (or electronically affixed) on a contract by a party who is legally authorized to do so. According to contract law, the person being charged—the client—must sign the contract for it to be enforceable.

Single-entry system. A simple bookkeeping system that is based on the income statement and includes business income and expense accounts.

Single source of contact. One particular individual who has the authority to make decisions regarding a project for the design firm as well as the client.

Single-source purchasing. System in which the client purchases goods from only one vendor. This term is most often used in commercial interior design.

Slander. The wrongful harming of a person's good reputation through oral communication.

Small claims court. A court that hears civil actions in which the damages sought are for a small amount.

Social responsibility. Use of the designer's expertise and time, usually on a volunteer or pro bono basis, to enhance and enrich the interiors of nonprofits and public places or otherwise perform community service.

Sole practitioner. Term for a business professional who is working on his or her own.

Sole proprietorship. The simplest and least expensive form of business, in which the company and the individual owner are one and the same.

Spam. Unsolicited mail or e-mail.

Specifications. The written instructions to contractors and vendors concerning the materials and methods of construction or the interior products that are to be bid on a project.

Specific performance. A type of remedy related to breach of contract, in which a court orders the breaching party to carry out the specific, breached terms of the contract.

Square-foot method. A method of calculating fees whereby the designer determines a rate per square foot and multiplies it by the amount of square footage of the project.

Stakeholders. All the parties to a project who have a vested interest in the completion of the project, such as the client, interior designer, architect, and vendors.

Statement of cash flows. An accounting statement reporting, for a specific period, the changes in cash flows from operating, investing, and financing activities.

Statute of Frauds. Statutory requirements mandating written contracts in certain circumstances. For the interior designer, these include a contract for the sale of goods that have a value of more than $500 to $5000 (depending on the jurisdiction), any contract that will take more than one year to complete, and any sale of real estate.

Statutory law. Laws created by governmental entities such as the U.S. Congress and state legislatures; also referred to as statutes.

Stocking dealer. A vendor that stocks a certain inventory level of goods at all times. These sellers and designers often receive larger discounts because of the volume of products they carry.

Straight salary. A fixed amount of salary paid to an employee no matter how many hours in the week he or she works.

Strategic planning. A process for creating a specific written vision for a firm and the future of that firm.

Strategies. Specific actions that are part of a business or marketing plan for which definite time limits within the year have been set for completion.

Strict liability. Tort doctrine under which a seller is held liable for injury to others resulting from a defective product, regardless of fault.

Subcontractor. An individual or company that is licensed to contract and perform specialized work on an interiors or construction project; also called a sub.

Submittals. Materials, drawings, or documents that the vendor may have to provide to the designer or contractor for approval.

Substantial completion. Contract performance that cannot vary greatly from what has been specified in the contract.

Suggested retail price. A term related to the price to be used by the seller and suggested by the manufacturer.

SWOT analysis. A planning technique used by firms to develop many kinds of plans. SWOT stands for strengths, weaknesses, opportunities, and threats.

Tactics. Highly specific actions needed to accomplish goals and strategies; they are even more specific than strategies and are usually short-term.

Tag for. Information that a designer requests a manufacturer to affix to the goods and note on the invoice to help the designer deliver the goods to the correct client.

Tangible personal property. Any property that is movable, can be touched, or has physical existence.

Target marketing. Marketing method that helps a design firm identify one or more groups of potential customers who are most likely to utilize the firm's services.

Tenant improvements. Improvements to a commercial space paid for by the tenant; also called leasehold improvements.

Tenant work letter. A contract that spells out everything that is done to a leased space by the landlord and tenant. Also referred to as a building standard work letter.

Termination for cause. Employment status that protects the employee from being fired for some capricious reason. Reasons for termination for cause include negligence, incompetence, dishonesty, disloyalty, and failure to follow company policies.

Terms and conditions. The seller's policies in regard to the selling of items or services to a buyer.

Testimonial. Statement that the client makes in a letter that he or she sends, or that the client gives verbally to the designer concerning the client's satisfaction with the design firm's work.

Third party. An individual or company that is somehow involved in the project or relationship but is not a party to or signatory of the original contract between the designer and the client.

Third-party testimonials. A statement from a former client used as a reference to help sell the designer's services and/or merchandise to a new client.

Three Es. Short name for education, experience, and examination. Relates to the background that professionals and educators feel is necessary to become an interior design professional.

TIFF. Stands for Tagged Image File Format. A method of reproducing digital photos that produces a high-quality image suitable for publication.

Title. In sales law, refers to the legal ownership of goods. The person who holds title to the goods owns the goods.

Title acts. Legislative measures concerned with limiting the use of certain professional titles by individuals who meet agreed-upon qualifications and who have registered with a state board.

Tort. A civil wrong committed against another party that causes injury to the harmed party. Torts are not created or legislated by statute.

Trade credit. A supplier's extension of credit to allow a designer to purchase without paying up front.

Trade discount. Discount given as a courtesy by some vendors to designers and others in the trade. The discount is usually a small percentage off retail.

Trade fixtures. Items attached to the rented space by a tenant. Depending on the lease, they can be removed if no damage is made to the structure.

Trademark. Legal protection for distinctive names, logos, or symbols.

Trade name. The business name used in public, such as on stationery.

Trade sources. Groups of manufacturers, suppliers, and tradespeople that provide the various goods and services a designer uses to complete an interiors project.

Transaction privilege (sales) tax license. Form issued by state and municipal taxing authorities that allows the interior designer to pass on the state sales tax to the consumer. Also called a seller's permit.

Transmittal letter. A form letter that a designer can use to send information to anyone involved with the project or to anyone from whom information has been requested.

Trial balance. A test to see if accounts are balanced and if all the accounts balance when the debit and credit sides are totaled separately.

Trial close. Asking for the sale. This can occur before the buyer has given a substantial indication that he or she is interested in buying.

Trunk show. An event when a manufacturer's rep invites one or more interior designers to view a small selection of new merchandise.

Turnkey project. In architecture, a project that commonly includes financing assistance, property acquisition, and all the design and specification services associated with architecture or interior design. Also referred to as turnkey design.

Tweets. Information provided through the Twitter Web site.

Unemployment taxes. Funds provided by the employer to eligible employees in the event that they are laid off from their jobs; paid to the employee through the state.

Unfavorable variance. In accounting and budgeting, when the actual amount is more than the budgeted amount.

Uniform Commercial Code (UCC). The body of law governing the relationships between the various levels of buyers and sellers in business transactions.

Uniform Electronic Transaction Act (UETA). Model law adopted by most of the states that helps to enforce contracts transmitted electronically.

Uniform laws. Laws developed and suggested for adoption by all states, to bring consistency to the numerous versions of similar laws passed by individual states.

Unsecured loan. A loan that does not require collateral as a guarantee.

Use tax. A tax on goods that a business purchases from a supplier in another state for use within the state in which the purchasing business is located.

Utilization rate. A factor identifying the amount of time that a designer spends on billable hours versus nonbillable work.

Value engineering. A method of analyzing and specifying products and design solutions based on cost-effectiveness.

Value-oriented fee method. A fee method by which a design firm prices its services based on the value or quality of the services rather than on the cost of doing those services; also called value-based method.

Variable costs. Costs that change according to the volume of work performed and revenue generated.

Variance analysis. A managerial technique in which one looks at financial and numerical data in relation to the differences between planned or budgeted amounts and actual amounts.

Vendor. Someone who sells products or services either to the end user or to another merchant, like the designer.

Vignette. A display of furniture and furnishings in a store or a showroom that simulates an actual room.

Walk-through. A final inspection of a jobsite to be sure that everything ordered is present and that any omissions or damaged goods are noted.

Warm calling. Contacting a potential client for a possible interview when the designer has received an entrée to the client through a referral of some type.

Warranty. A statement or representation made by a seller concerning goods. Warranties are related to quality, fitness of purpose, or title.

Warranty of title. Representation that the seller has title or legal ownership to the goods and can legally sell them to others.

Whistleblowing. Reporting a company's health or safety violations. Employees cannot be fired or otherwise retaliated against for whistleblowing.

Wholesale price. A special price given to a merchant, from a merchant at a value lower than what the goods would cost the consumer.

Workers' compensation insurance. An insurance program paid for by the employer that provides funds to the employee to cover the expenses of work-related injuries.

Work for hire. Concept that an employee who creates something within the scope of normal work responsibilities relinquishes copyright ownership of the design to the employer.

Working drawings. Another term for construction drawings.

Work in process. Work that is under way for a client that has not yet been billed.

Work plan. Comprehensive listing of all the tasks that are required to complete an interior design project.

Work product. Drawings, documents, and other products prepared by an employee that are actually owned by the employer.

Wrongful discharge. Firing an employee without good cause.

Zone pricing. System in which a manufacturer determines two or more shipping zones based on geographic distances from the factory. Each zone has a different price for the product.

Zoning restrictions. Local government's legal constraints of land use in given areas of the city.

Zoning variance. A request by a property owner to the local jurisdiction to allow activities other than what is specifically defined for the zone.

GENERAL REFERENCES

ARTICLES AND COLLATERAL MATERIALS

The listed articles, brochures, material from Web sites, and other collateral materials represent only a small number of items on the topics in this book.

Abercrombie, Stanley. 1999. "Design Revolution: 100 Years That Changed Our World." *Interior Design*. December. pp. 141–98.

———. 1987. "News: Leaders Meet." *Interior Design*. October.

American Academy of Healthcare Interior Designers. 2012. "Certification." Available at www.aahid.org

American Institute of Architects, California Council. 2007. "Integrated Project Delivery."

American Society of Interior Designers. 2012. *Environmental Scanning Report*.

———. *How to Get Your Work Published*. 2009. Available at www.asid.org

———. 2012. *The Interior Design Profession: Facts and Figures*.

———. 2011. *ASID Code of Ethics and Professional Conduct*. Available at www.asid.org

———. 2011. *Interior Design in the New Economy*.

———. 2006. Web site information.

———. 2005. *Consumer Use of Design Services*.

———. 2005. *The History of ASID*.

———. 2005. *Inside Small and Medium Design Firms*.

———. 2005. *Know Your Client*.

———. 2000. "Primary Basis of Complaints Being Filed." Information from ASID Ethics Office. August.

———. 2000. "Procedures for Filing an Ethics Complaint." ASID Web site. June.

———. 1999. "The Road Map to Growth." *ASID ICON*. November.

———. 1998. *ASID Code of Ethics and Professional Conduct*. Washington, DC: ASID.

———. 1998. "Design Fees and Profits." *ASID Professional Designer*. September/October.

———. 1998. "Design Specialties." *ASID Professional Designer*. July/August.

———. 1998. *Strategic Mapping Research. Phase III*. June.

———. 1998. "Strategic Planning for the Small Design Practice." *ASID Professional Designer*. March/April.

———. 1997. "Clients Are Impressed by Project Management." *ASID Professional Designer*. March/April. p. 17.

Bacskai, Andrew. 2001. "Inside the Big Guys." *ASID ICON*. November. pp. 20–24.

———. 2002. "Body of Evidence." *ASID ICON*. March. pp. 27–30.

Bast, Jan. 2008. "Stretching Your Ethical Muscle." *Interiors & Sources*. March. p. 62.

Bauer, Natalie. 2004. "Fringe Benefits." *Perspective*. Spring. pp. 24–28.

Berens, Michael. 2008. "Using Research in Design Practice." *ASID ICON*. September/October. pp. 30–31.

Bernardo, Stephanie. 1985. "Fire Me . . . and I'll Sue!" *Success!* July/August.

Brake, Alan G. 2011. "Power Tools." *Perspective*. Fall/Winter. pp. 16–20.

Brandt, Roslyn. 1995. "Can You Manage?" *Contract*. April. pp. 76–77.

Brown, Tim. 2008. "Design Thinking." *Harvard Business Review*. June. pp. 84–92.

Burke, Kimberly. 2002. "The 24–7 Work Week: The New Norm." *ASID ICON*. August. pp. 24–28.

Busch, Jennifer Thiele. 2000. "Wanted: Architects and Designers for Hire." *Contract*. September. p. 96.

———. "Socially Responsible Design: Making a Difference." *Contract*. February. p. 42.

"Buyers Guide." 2006. *Interior Design*. April.

"Buyers Guide." 2000. *Interior Design*. January

Caan, Shashi. 2003. "The Future of Design: Finding the Soul of Our Art." *Perspective*. Winter. pp. 41–43.

Career One Stop. 2011. "Occupational Profile: Interior Designers." Available at www.careerinfonet.org

Castlelman, Betty. 1987. "How Will Licensing Affect Me?" *Designers West*. June.

Collins, James C., and Jerry I. Porras. 1996. "Building Your Company's Vision." *Harvard Business Review*. September/October. pp. 65–77.

Congdon, Chris. 2010. "Generation Y Gets to Work." *ASID ICON*. March/April. pp. 10–15.

Conlon, Ginger. 2000. "Cashing In." *Sales and Marketing Management*. June. pp. 95–102.

Corlin, Len. 1986. "Marts Accelerate Development." *Contract*. December.

Cornell University Law School. 2012. "UCC Article 2—Sales." Available at www.law.cornell.edu/ucc

Costello, Katriel. 2005. "All Business?" *Perspective*. Fall. pp. 10–14.

Dahle, Cheryl. 1998. "Fast Start: Your First 60 Days." *Fast Company*. June/July.

Dale, P. Adrianne. 1995. "The Ethics Process: Inside Perspective." *ASID Report*. September.

Danko, Shelia. 2010. "On Designing Change." *Journal of Interior Design*. vol. 36, no. 1.

Dennis, Lisa D. 2003. "Value Propositions: It's About the Customer, Not You!" Knowledge Associates. Available at www.knowledgence.com

"Design Revolution: 100 Years That Changed Our World." 1999. *Interior Design*. December.

Deutsch, Randy. 2012. "Leading in the Age of BIM." *Design Intelligence*. Available at www.di.net

Ebstein, Barbara. 1985. "Licensing: The Design Concern for the Eighties." *ASID Report*. January–March.

Farley, Susan E. "Guarding against Knock Offs." *ASID ICON*. Spring 2005. pp. 42–48.

Federal Trade Commission. 2012. *A Businessperson's Guide to Federal Warranty Law*. Available at www.business.ftc.gov

Finter, Andrea. 1985. "Senior Designers' Average Pay: $37,300." *Contract*. June.

———. 1984. "Designer Salary Poll Links Job Tenure and Compensation." *Contract*. July.

Foti, Ross. 2004. "In Search of Excellence." *Perspective*. Winter. pp. 25–26.

Foundation for Interior Design Education Research. 2006. Web site information.

———. 1993. *FIDER Fact Kit*. February.

Gaulden, Joan. 2000. "The Business Value of the Internet." Seminar handout.

Gerasimo, Pilar. 2001. "Another Satisfied Customer?" *ASID ICON*. March. pp. 11–14.

———. 2000. "25 Ways Your Business Will Change." *ASID ICON*. November. pp. 30–33.

Gibson, Woody. 1980. "Design Wages Depend on Function." *Contract*. October.

Goldsborough, Reid. 1999. "Changing the Future of Doing Business." *Interiors & Sources*. June. pp. 40–41.

Goldsborough, Reid, and Angela Frucci. 2001. "Working the Web." *ASID ICON*. June. pp. 12–19.

Gueft, Olga. 1980. "The Past as Prologue: The First 50 Years. 1931–1981: An Overview." *American Society of Interior Designers Annual Report*.

Guest, Rita Carson. 2007. "ASID Update: What Is Good Interior Design Worth to the Bottom Line?" *Interiors and Sources*. October.

Gura, Judith B. Fall. 1999. "Modernism at the Millennium." *Echoes*.

Hammonds, Keith H. 1999. "How We Sell." *Fast Company*. November. pp. 294–306.

Harragan, Betty Lehan. 1986. "Career Advice." *Working Woman*. September.

Hemmings, Sonya Goodwin. 2005. "Going Abroad Smart." Bizaz.com. September/October. pp. 70–72.

Henderson, James P. 2003. *Practice Analysis Study for the Profession of Interior Design*. National Council for Interior Design Qualification.

Herman Miller, Inc. 1994. *A Brief History of Herman Miller*.

Holst, Beth. 2008. "Placing Value on a Credential." *Interiors & Sources*. April. p. 54.

Hughes, Nina. June 1987. "Interiors Platform." *Interiors*.

Imperato, Gina. 1998. "How to Give Good Feedback." *Fast Company*. September.

Institute of Business Designers. 1993. *CEUs and You. A Guide to Developing a Self-Directed Learning Path for the Professional Member* [brochure]. February.

———. 1993. *Membership Information* [brochure].

———. 1992. *History of IBD*. Unpublished manuscript.

———. 1989. *Code of Professional Conduct* [brochure].

———. 1980. *Code of Ethics* [pamphlet]. p. 105.

Interior Design Educators Council. 2006. Web site information.

———. 1999. Membership brochure. June.

———. 1994. "Members of Interior Design Organizations Vote on Unification." Press release. May.

———. 1992. Membership brochure.

Interior Designers of Canada. 2006. Web site information.

"Interiors & Sources 2006 Directory & Source Guide." 2006. *Interiors & Sources*.

"Interiors & Sources 2000 Directory and Source Guide." 2000. *Interiors & Sources*. January.

Internal Revenue Service. 2011. "Independent Contractor (Self-Employed) or Employee?" Available at www.irs.gov

———. 2006. *Publication No. 15-A. Employer's Supplemental Tax Guide*. January. Washington, DC: U.S. Department of the Treasury.

———. 1999. *Starting a Business and Keeping Records*. Publication No. 583. Washington, DC: U.S. Department of the Treasury.

———. 1999. *Tax Guide for Small Business*. Publication No. 334. Washington, DC: U.S. Department of the Treasury.

International Codes Council. 2000. As reported by ASID Grassroots [brochure]. April.

International Federation of Interior Architects/Designers. 2012. Information from Web site. Available at www.ifiworld.org

International Interior Design Association. 2006. Web site information.

———. 1997. *IIDA Code of Ethics*.

International Society of Interior Designers. 1992. *Membership information* [brochure].

———. 1984. *Perspective*. Fall.

"The Internet: What Does It Look Like?" 2000. *Fast Company*. March.

Jensen, Charlotte S. 2001. "Design versus Decoration." *Interiors & Sources*. September. p. 91.

Joiner, Colene. 1998. "Your Code of Ethics: How Can It Help You?" *ASID Professional Designer*. May/June.

Jones, Carol. 1999. "Defining a Profession: Some Things Never Change." *Interiors & Sources*. September.

Kaplinger, Eunice, and Susan Ray-Degges. 1998. "Can Ethics Be Taught or Is It Too Late?" *Journal of Interior Design*. vol. 24, no. 1.

Kapusta, Tom. 2009. "The Success Value of a Triple Bottom Line." *Facility Management Journal*. November/December.

Kettler, Kerwin. 1985. "Is There More to Licensing than a License?" *Designer Specifier*. May.

Kroelinger, Michael D. 1993. *Mission and Benefits of Unification*. Unpublished material.

———. 1992. "Unified Voice Update." *Perspective*. Institute of Business Designers. Spring.

Kubany, Elizabeth Harrison, and Charles D. Linn. 1999. "How to Increase Your Fees in a Tough Market." *Architectural Record*. November.

———. 1999. "Why Architects Don't Charge Enough." *Architectural Record*. October.

Lande, Kim. 2005. "Entrepreneurial Eyes." *Perspective*. Winter. pp. 44–48.

Leonard, Woody. 2000. "The New Internet Security Threats." *SmartBusiness*. July.

Ligos, Melinda. 2000. "Clicks and Misses." *Sales and Marketing Management*. June. pp. 69–76.

Loebelson, Andrew. 1996. "Interior Design Giants." *Interior Design*. January.

———. 1985. "Mart Fever Is Epidemic." *Contract*. December.

Long, Deborah H. 2000. *Ethics and the Design Profession*. Continuing Education Monograph Series. National Council for Interior Design Qualification.

———. 1998. "Why We Need Ethical Decision-Making Skills." *ASID Professional Designer*. May/June.

Marans, Ron. 2012. "Back to Business: 100 Giants." *Interior Design*. January. pp. 84–98.

Marberry, Sara. 2003. "Giving Back to the Design Profession." *Perspective*. Spring. pp. 27–32.

Martin, Caren, and Denise Guerin. *Body of Knowledge: 2010 Edition*. Published jointly by American Society of Interior Designers, Council for Interior Design Accreditation (formerly FIDER), Interior Designers of Canada, International Interior Design Association, and National Council for Interior Design Qualification.

———. 2006. *The Interior Design Profession's Body of Knowledge: 2005 Edition*. Published jointly by American Society of Interior Designers, Council for Interior Design Accreditation (formerly FIDER), Interior Designers of Canada, International Interior Design Association, and National Council for Interior Design Qualification. Available from www.idbok.org.

Martin, Jane D., and Nancy Knoohuizen. 1997. "Create a 'Bang' with Easy-to-Use Marketing Techniques." *ASID Professional Designer*. July/August. pp. 14–15.

McCarroll, Thomas. 1992. "Entrepreneurs: Starting Over." *Time*. January 6.

McCracken, Laurin, and Ann Carper. 1992. "Designers on Stage." *Contract*. November. pp. 66–67.

McDonough, William, and Michael Braungart. 2002. "Beyond the Triple Bottom Line." Available at www.mcdonough.com/writings

McLain-Kark, Joan H., and Ruey-Er, Tang. 1986. "Computer Usage and Attitudes toward Computers in the Interior Design Field." *Journal of Interior Design Education and Research*. Fall. vol. 12. pp. 25–32.

Merchandise Mart Properties. 2000. *The Merchandise Mart Buyers Guide*. June.

Merle, Jan S. 1995. "The Internet: Hype or Harbinger of Business, 90s Style?" *ASID Report*. November/December. pp. 16–18.

Milshtein, Amy. 1994. "First Timers." *Contract*. November. p. 84.

Morton, Jennie. 2011. "BIM—The Intelligent Choice for O&M." *Buildings*. August.

Muoio, Anna. 2000. "Should I Go .com?" *Fast Company*. July. pp. 164–172.

National Conference of Commissioners on Uniform State Laws (NCCUSL). 2003. "Amendments UCC Article 2." Available at www.nccusl.org

National Council for Interior Design Qualification. 2006. Web site information.

———. 1998. *Analysis of the Interior Design Profession*. NCIDQ.

National Institute of Building Sciences (WBDG). 2012. "Engage the Integrated Design Process." Available at www.wbdg.org

———. 2010. "Engage the Integrated Design Process". Available at www.wbdg.org

National Institute of Business Management. 1998. *Fire at Will: Terminating Your Employees Legally*. Special Bulletin No. 239A. National Institute of Business Management.

Nolo. 2011. "Working as an Independent Contractor FAQ." Available at www.nolo.com

Nolo Web site. 2005. "Corporation Basics." October. Available at www.nolo.com

———. 2005. "Professional Corporations." October. Available at www.nolo.com

———. 2005. "S Corporation Facts." October. Available at www.nolo.com

"Nondiscrimination on the Basis of Disability by Public Accommodations and in Commercial Facilities; Final Rule." 1991. *Federal Register*. vol. 56, no. 144. Washington, DC: Department of Justice.

Olivieri, Georgy. 2011. "Q&A: The Future of Design." *Metropolis*. Available at www.metropolismag.com

"Open vs. Closed: The Results Are In." 1992. *Interior Design*. June.

Peterson, John. 2011. "The Virtuous Circle: Pro Bono Service and the Interior Design Practice." *Perspective*. Spring/Summer. pp. 8–14.

Piotrowski, Christine M. 1998. "Strategic Planning for the Small Design Practice." *ASID Professional Designer*. March/April. pp. 18–21.

Polites, Nicholas. "Arkansas Enacts Tiered Licensing System: Interior Designers Weigh Consequences." *Interior Design*. July 1993.

Portillo, Margaret, and Tiiu Poldma. 2010. "Janus Perspective: Looking Forward, Looking Back." *Journal of Interior Design*. pp. v–viii.

Ranallo, Anne Brooks. 2005. "Life-Long Learning." *Perspective*. Fall. pp. 36–42.

Rayle, Martha G. 1992. "Unified Voice Task Force (UVTF) Update." Newsletter published by American Society of Interior Designers. April.

Rebholz, Jenny S. 2009. "Putting the 'i' in Team." *Perspective*. March/April. pp. 18–21.

———. 2006. "Power in Numbers: Marketing to Boomers." *ASID ICON*. Spring. pp. 52–56.

———. 2005. "Practice Innovators." *ASID ICON*. Winter. pp. 62–64.

Reh, F. John. 2012. "How to Use Benchmarking in Business." *About .com Management*. Available at www.management.about.com

Rosenfeld, Jill. 2000. "Information as If Understanding Mattered." *Fast Company*. March. pp. 203–19.

Ross, Jim. 2002. "The Art of Self Promotion." *ASID ICON*. May. pp. 10–13.

Ross, Ken L. 2001. "Dare to Compare: Improving Your Practice through Benchmarking." *Design Intelligence*. Available at www.di.net

Ross, Ken L., Jr., and Gail Burns. 2003. "The Role of Mentoring in the Design Profession." *Perspective*. Winter. pp. 17–20.

Row, Heath. 1998. "These Cards Mean Business." *Fast Company*. August. p. 62.

Russell, Beverly. 1992. "Into the Ninth Decade: A Historic View of 'Interior Design' through the Contribution of Women." *IBD Perspective*. Fall.

———. 1985. "Interiors Business: New Moves toward Interior Design Licensing." *Interiors*. March.

Ryan, Rene. 2011. "Redesigning the Future." *IIDA Perspective*. Available at www.iida.org

Sandham, Lisa. 2008. "The Need to LEED." *Interiors & Sources*. September. pp. 60–61.

Sawasy, Mitchell E. 2008. "International Design: Holding the Key to a Changing Economy." *Interiors & Sources*. September. pp. 56–57.

Schlereth, Laura. 2010. "Prioritizing Project Management." *Perspective*. Spring. pp. 32–36.

Schonfeld, Erick. 2000. "Corporations of the World, Unite! You Have Nothing to Lose but Your Supply Chains!" *Fast Company*. June. pp. 123–32.

Schrank, Jenny. 2012. "Taking Business Abroad." *ASID ICON*. Fall.

Senn, Jan. 2000. "Motivating Your Staff." *ASID ICON*. November. pp. 8–10.

Siegel, Alan M. 1995. "ASID Code of Ethics and Professional Conduct: A Primer." *ASID Report*. September.

Simpson, Scott. 2010. "Design Goes Global." *Design Intelligence*. Available at www.di.net

Slavin, Maeve. 1983. "Jobs Are Not What They Used to Be." *Interiors*. September.

"The Source Guide 2006." 2006. *Contract*. January.

"The Source Guide 1999–2000." 2000. *Contract*. January.

Staffelbach, Andre. 1992. "Does the Public Consider You a Professional?" *IBD Perspective*. Summer.

Stern, Linda. 1995. "The Perfect Proposal." *Home Office Computing*. February. pp. 81–86.

Stern, Natalie. 1982. "Top Contract Furniture Sales People Can Boost Earnings 33% with Timed Move." *Contract*. November.

Strogoff, Michael. 2003. "Coping with Success: Growing Pains of Successful Design Firms." *ASID ICON*. November. pp. 20–26.

Sykes, Claire. 2005. "Managing Your Organization with Morals in Mind." *Office Solutions*. May/June. pp. 34–35.

Talarico, Wendy. 1999. "Listening to Computer Experts." *Architectural Record*. August. pp. 74–78.

Taraska, Julie. 2011. "The Social Network: It's a Design Conversation You Shouldn't Be Missing." *Perspective*. Fall/Winter. pp. 31–33.

Taute, Michelle. 2005. "Compass vs. Computer." *Perspective*. Winter. pp. 22–25.

Tingas, Pauline. "Taking Orders." 2006. *Perspective*. Spring. pp. 44–50.

Tobias, Sheila, and Alma Lantz. 1985. "Performance Appraisal." *Working Woman*. November.

"Triple Bottom Line." 2009. *The Economist*. Available at www.economist.com

Unified Voice Task Force. 1994. Newsletter sent to IBD members. April.

———. 1993. "Interior Design Organizations Target July 1994 for Unification." Press release. September.

U.S. Small Business Administration. *Developing a Strategic Business Plan*. no. MP21.

———. 2011. *Independent Contractors vs. Employees*. Available at www.sba.gov

———. 1998. *State of Small Business: A Report of the President*.

———. 1991. *State of Small Business: A Report of the President*.

U.S. Bureau of Labor Statistics. 2012. "Occupational Employment Statistics: 27-1025 Interior Designers" (as of August 2012). Available at www.bls.gov/oes

———. 2010. *Occupational Outlook Handbook*. Available at www.bls.gov/ooh

U.S. Green Building Council. 2012. "LEED Certification." Available at www.usgbc.org

Vollmer, John L. 2000. "Sole Practitioner: Self-Employed or Contingent Worker? Investigating Worker Misclassification and Its Implications to Commercial Interior Design." *Journal of Interior Design*. vol. 26, no. 1. pp. 56–61.

Voss, Judy. 1996. "White Paper on the Recent History of the Open Office." Holland, MI: Haworth.

Wagner, Michael. 1985. "Interiors Business. Salaries and Bonuses Are Up for Designers." *Interiors*. September.

Warshaw, Michael. 1998. "Get a Life." *Fast Company*. June/July.

Webber, Alan M. 1998. "Are You a Star at Work?" *Fast Company*. June/July.

Weigand, John. 2006. "Defining Ourselves." *Perspective*. Winter. pp. 26–34.

White, Allison Carll. 2009. "What's in a Name? Interior Design and/or Interior Architecture: The Discussion Continues." *Journal of Interior Design*. vol. 35, no. 1.

Whitemyer, David. 2006. "Practice (and Title) Makes Perfect." *Perspective*. Winter. pp. 16–20.

Wilson, Trisha. 2011. "Corporate Philanthropy." *Contract*. January/February.

Zeiger, Lisa. 1999. "House Fraus." *Interiors*. September.

BOOKS

Aaker, David A. 1995. *Developing Business Strategies*, 4th ed. Hoboken, NJ: John Wiley & Sons.

Aaker, David A., V. Kumar, and George S. Day. 1998. *Marketing Research*, 6th ed. Hoboken, NJ: John Wiley & Sons.

Abercrombie, Nicholas, Stephen Hill, and Bryan S. Turner. 2000. *The Penguin Dictionary of Sociology*, 4th ed. New York: Penguin Books.

———. 1994. *The Penguin Dictionary of Sociology*. New York: Allen Lane Publications (Penguin Books).

Abramowitz, Ava J. 2002. *Architect's Essentials of Contract Negotiation*. Hoboken, NJ: John Wiley & Sons.

Alderman, Robert L. 1982. *How to Make More Money at Interior Design*. New York: Whitney Communications Corp.

———. 1997. *How to Prosper as an Interior Designer*. Hoboken, NJ: John Wiley & Sons.

Alexander, Roy, and Charles B. Roth. 2004. *Secrets of Closing Sales*, 7th ed. Paramus, NJ: Penguin/Portfolio.

Allen, David. 2003. *Ready for Anything*. New York: Viking/Penguin.

Allen, Jeffrey G. 1997. *The Complete Q & A Job Interview Book*, 2nd ed. Hoboken, NJ: John Wiley & Sons.

Allwork, Ronald. 1961. *AID Interior Design and Decoration Manual of Professional Practice*, 2nd ed. New York: American Institute of Interior Designers.

American Heritage Dictionary of the English Language. 2000. 4th ed. Boston: Houghton-Mifflin.

Anthoy, Robert N., and James S. Reece. 1983. *Accounting Text and Cases*, 7th ed. Homewood, IL: Richard D. Irwin.

Applegate, Jane. 1995. *Strategies for Small Business Success*. New York: Plume.

Atkins, James B., and Grant A. Simpson. 2008. *Managing Project Risk*. Hoboken, NJ: John Wiley & Sons.

Augustin, Sally, and Cindy Coleman. 2012. *The Designer's Guide to Doing Research: Applying Knowledge to Inform Design*. Hoboken, NJ: John Wiley & Sons.

Axtell, Roger E. 1997. *Do's and Taboos around the World for Women in Business*. Hoboken, NJ: John Wiley & Sons.

———. 1991. *Gestures*. Hoboken, NJ: John Wiley & Sons.

Baker, Ronald J. 2006. *Pricing on Purpose*. Hoboken, NJ: John Wiley & Sons.

Baldrige, Letitia. 1993. *Letitia Baldrige's New Complete Guide to Executive Manners*. New York: Rawson Associates.

———. 1985. *Letitia Baldrige's Complete Guide to Executive Manners*. New York: Rawson Associates.

Ball, Victoria. 1982. *Opportunities in Interior Design*. Skokie, IL: VGM Career Horizons.

Ballast, David K. 2010. *Interior Design Reference Manual: Everything You Need to Know to Pass the NCIDQ Exam*, 4th ed. Belmont, CA: Professional Publications.

———. 2006. *Interior Design Reference Manual*, 3rd ed. Belmont, CA.: Professional Publications.

———. 2002. *Interior Construction & Detailing*. Belmont, CA: Professional Publications.

Bangs, David H., Jr. 2005. *Business Plans Made Easy*, 3rd ed. Irvine, CA: Entrepreneur Media.

———. 1998. *The Market Planning Guide*, 5th ed. Chicago, IL: Upstart Publishing.

———. 1995. *The Business Planning Guide*, 7th ed. Chicago, IL: Upstart Publishing.

Barnhart, Tod. 1995. *The Five Rituals of Wealth*. New York: HarperCollins.

Barr, Vilma. 1995. *Promotion Strategies for Design and Construction Firms*. New York: Van Nostrand Reinhold.

Beam, Burton T., Jr., and John J. McFadden. 1998. *Employee Benefits*, 5th ed. Homewood, IL: Dearborn Financial Publishing.

Beard, Jeffrey L., Michael C. Loulakis, and Edward C. Wundram. 2001. *Design-Build*. New York: McGraw-Hill.

Beatty, Richard H. 2000. *The Resume Kit*, 4th ed. Hoboken, NJ: John Wiley & Sons.

Becher, Tony. 1999. *Professional Practices*. New Brunswick, NJ: Transaction.

Beckwith, Harry. 2007. *You, Inc.* New York: Time Warner Books.

———. 2000. *The Invisible Touch*. New York. Time Warner Books.

Belker, Lorin B., and Gary S. Topchik. 2005. *The First-Time Manager*, 5th ed. New York: American Management Association.

Bender, Peer Urs. 1995. *Secrets of Power Presentations*. Willodale, Ontario: Firefly Books.

Bennett, Peter D., ed. 1995. *Dictionary of Marketing Terms*, 2nd ed. Chicago, IL: American Marketing Association.

Bennis, Warren. 1994. *On Becoming a Leader*. Reading, MA: Perseus.

Berger, C. Jaye. 1994. *Interior Design Law and Business Practices*. Hoboken, NJ: John Wiley & Sons.

Berger, Warren. 2009. *Glimmer: How Design Can Transform Your Life, and Maybe Even the World*. New York: Penguin Press.

Berkowitz, Eric N., Roger A. Kerin, Steven W. Hartley, and William Rudelius. 1997. *Selling the Invisible*. New York: Time Warner Books.

———. 1994. *Marketing*, 4th ed. Burr Ridge, IL: Richard D. Irwin.

Berman, Karen, and Joe Knight (with John Case). 2006. *Financial Intelligence*. Cambridge, MA: Harvard Business School Press.

Besson, Taunee S. 1999. *Cover Letters*, 3rd ed. (National Employment Weekly Career Guides). Hoboken, NJ: John Wiley & Sons.

Bird, Polly. 2010. *Improve Your Time Management*. New York: McGraw-Hill.

Birnberg, Howard. 1999. *Project Management for Building Designers and Owners*. Boca Raton, FL: CRC Press.

————. 1992. *New Directions in Architectural and Engineering Practice*. New York: McGraw-Hill.

Bixler, Susan. 2005. *Professional Presence*, 2nd ed. New York: Perigee.

Bixler, Susan, and Nancy Nix-Rice. 1997. *The New Professional Image*. Holbrook, MA: Adams Media.

Black, Henry Campbell (with Joseph R. Nolan and Jacqueline M. Nolan-Haley). 1990. *Black's Law Dictionary*, 6th ed. St. Paul, MN: West Publishing.

Black's Law Dictionary. 2004. 8th ed. (Bryan A. Garner, ed.). St. Paul, MN: West Group.

Black's Law Dictionary. 1999. 7th ed. (Bryan A. Garner, ed.). St. Paul, MN: West Group.

Blades, William H. 1994. *Selling: The Mother of All Enterprise*. Phoenix, AZ: Marketing Methods Press.

Blanchard, Ken (with John P. Carlos and Alan Randolph). 1996. *Empowerment Takes More Than a Minute*. New York: MJF Books.

Blanchard, Ken, Donald Carew, and Eunice Parisi-Carew. 2000. *The One-Minute Manager Builds High-Performing Teams*. New York: William Morrow.

Bliss, Edwin. 1983. *Doing It Now*. New York: Bantam Books.

Blum, Laurie. 1996. *Free Money from the Federal Government for Small Businesses and Entrepreneurs*. Hoboken, NJ: John Wiley & Sons.

Bly, Robert W. 2008. *Persuasive Presentations for Business*. Irvine, CA: Entrepreneur Press.

————. 1998. *The Lead Generation Handbook*. New York: American Management Association.

————. 1998. *The Six Figure Consultant*. Chicago: Upstart Publishing.

————. 1994. *Business to Business Direct Marketing*. Lincolnwood, IL: NTC Business Books.

————. 1991. *Selling Your Services*. New York: Henry Holt.

Bodnar, Kipp, and Jeffrey L. Cohen. 2012. *The B2B Social Media Book*. Hoboken, NJ: John Wiley & Sons.

Bolles, Richard Nelson. 2007. *What Color Is Your Parachute?* Berkeley, CA: Ten Speed Press.

Bond, William J. 1997. *Going Solo*. New York: McGraw-Hill.

Bonda, Penny, and Katie Sosnowchik. 2007. *Sustainable Commercial Interiors*. Hoboken, NJ: John Wiley & Sons.

Bossidy, Larry, and Ram Charan. 2004. *Confronting Reality*. New York: Crown Press.

Bowie, Norman E., and Meg Schneider. 2011. *Business Ethics for Dummies*. Hoboken, NJ: John Wiley & Sons.

Breighner, Bart. 1995. *Face to Face Selling*. Indianapolis, IN: Park Avenue.

Brett, J. M. *Negotiating Globally*, 2nd ed. Hoboken, NJ: John Wiley & Sons.

Brown, Gordon W., and Paul A. Sukys. 1997. *Business Law*, 9th ed. New York: Glencoe/McGraw-Hill.

Browne, M. Neil, and Stuart M. Keeley. 2010. *Asking the Right Questions*, 9th ed. Upper Saddle River, NJ: Pearson/Prentice Hall.

Buhler, Patricia. 2002. *Human Resource Management*. Avon, MA: Adams Media.

Burg, Bob. 2006. *Endless Referrals*, 3rd ed. New York: McGraw-Hill.

————. 1999. *Endless Referrals*. New York: McGraw-Hill.

Burley-Allen, Madelyn. 1995. *Listening: The Forgotten Skill*. Hoboken, NJ: John Wiley & Sons.

Burstein, David, and Frank Stasiowski. 1982. *Project Management for the Design Professional*. New York: Watson-Guptill.

Caan, Shashi. 2011. *Rethinking Design and Interiors*. London: Laurence King Publishing.

Cabrera, Angel, and Gregory Unruh. 2012. *Being Global*. Boston, MA: Harvard Business Review Press.

Cama, Rosalyn. 2009. *Evidence-Based Healthcare Design*. Hoboken, NJ: John Wiley & Sons.

Campbell, Nina, and Caroline Seebohm. 1992. *Elsie de Wolfe: A Decorative Life*. New York: Clarkson N. Potter.

Canfield, Jack, Mark Victor Hansen, and Les Hewitt. 2000. *The Power of Focus*. Deerfield Beach, FL: Health Communications, Inc.

Caplan, Suzanne. 2000. *Finance and Accounting*. Holbrook, MA: Adams Media.

Carmichael, D. R., Steven B. Lilien, and Martin Mellman. 1999. *Accountant's Handbook*, 9th ed. New York: John Wiley & Sons.

Carron, Christian G. 1998. *Grand Rapids Furniture*. Grand Rapids, MI: Public Museum of Grand Rapids.

Casperson, Dana May. 1999. *Power Etiquette*. New York: American Management Association.

Chase, Landy, and Kevin Knebl. 2011. *The Social Media Sales Revolution*. New York: McGraw-Hill.

Chasteen, Lanny G., Richard E. Flaherty, and Melvin C. O'Connor. 1995. *Intermediate Accounting*, 9th ed. New York: McGraw-Hill.

Clark, Tim (in collaboration with Alexander Osterwalder and Yves Pigneur). 2012. *Business Model You*. Hoboken, NJ: John Wiley & Sons.

Clarkson, Kenneth W., Roger LeRoy Miller, and Gaylord A. Jentz. 1983. *West's Business Law, Text and Cases*, 2nd ed. St. Paul, MN: West Publishing.

Claxton, Lena, and Alison Woo. 2008. *How to Say It: Marketing with New Media*. New York: Prentice Hall.

Cochran, Chuck, and Donna Peerce. 1999. *Heart and Soul Internet Job Search*. Palo Alto, CA: Davies-Block Publishing.

Cohen, Jonathan. 2000. *Communication and Design with the Internet*. New York: W. W. Norton.

Collier's Encyclopedia. 1984. "Interior Design and Decoration." vol. 13. New York: Macmillan.

———. 1975. "Marketing." vol. 15. New York: Macmillan Educational Corp.

Collin, Simon. 1997. *Doing Business on the Internet*. London: Kogan, Page.

Collins, Dennis. 2012. *Business Ethics: How to Design and Manage Ethical Organizations*. Hoboken, NJ: John Wiley & Sons.

Concise Oxford American Dictionary. 2006. Oxford, NY: Oxford University Press.

Conry, Edward J., Gerald R. Ferrera, and Karla H. Fox. 1993. *The Legal Environment of Business*, 3rd ed. Boston: Allyn and Bacon.

Construction Specifications Institute. 2011. *The CSI Construction Contract Administration Practice Guide*. Hoboken, NJ: John Wiley & Sons.

Cook, Kenneth J. 1995. *AMA Complete Guide to Small Business Marketing*. Lincolnwood, IL: NTC Business Books.

———. 1994. *AMA Complete Guide to Strategic Planning for Small Business*. Chicago: American Marketing Association.

Cook, Marshall. 1999. *Time Management*. Holbrook, MA: Adams Media.

Cooke, Robert A. 1999. *Small Business Formation Handbook*. Hoboken, NJ: John Wiley & Sons.

Cottrell, Michelle. 2012. *Guide to the LEED-AP Interior Design and Construction (ID+C) Exam*. Hoboken, NJ: John Wiley & Sons.

Council for Interior Design Accreditation. 2006. *Accreditation Manual*. Available at www.accredit-id.org/resources.

Covey, Stephen R. 1989. *The Seven Habits of Highly Effective People*. New York: Fireside Books.

Covey, Stephen R., A. Roger Merrill, and Rebecca R. Merrill. 1994. *First Things First*. New York: Simon and Schuster.

Cowley, Michael, and Ellen Domb. 1997. *Beyond Strategic Vision*. Boston: Butterworth-Heinemann.

Cramer, James P. 1994. *Design Plus Enterprise*. Washington, DC: AIA Press.

Cramer, James P., and Scott Simpson. 2002. *How Firms Succeed*. Atlanta: Greenway Communications.

Crandall, Rick. 2003. *Marketing Your Services for People Who Hate to Sell*. Revised ed. New York: McGraw-Hill.

———. 1998. *1001 Ways to Market Your Services*. Lincolnwood, IL: Contemporary Books.

Crawford, Tad, and Eva Doman Bruck. 2001. *Business and Legal Forms for Interior Designers*. New York: Alworth Press.

Crompton, Diane, and Ellen Sautter. 2010. *Find a Job through Social Networking*. Indianapolis, IN: JISY Works Publishing.

Cushman, Robert F., and James C. Dobbs. 1991. *Design Professional's Handbook of Business and Law*. Hoboken, NJ: John Wiley & Sons.

Czinkota, Michael, Iikka A. Ronkanien, and Michael H. Moffett. 2011. *International Business*, 8th ed. Hoboken, NJ: John Wiley & Sons.

Czinkota, Michael R., Masaaki Kotabe, and David Mercer. 1997. *Marketing Management Text and Cases*. Cambridge, MA: Blackwell Publishing.

Daily, Frederick W. 2005. *Tax Savvy for Small Business*, 9th ed. Bethany Laurence Berkeley, CA: Nolo Press.

Dale, Paulette. 1999. "Did You Say Something, Susan?" *How Any Woman Can Gain Confidence with Assertive Communication*. Secaucus, NJ: Birch Lane Press.

Davidson, Jeff. 1994. *Marketing on a Shoestring*, 2nd ed. Hoboken, NJ: John Wiley & Sons.

Dawson, Roger. 1999. *Power Negotiating*, 2nd ed. Englewood Cliffs, NJ: Prentice Hall.

———. 1994. *The 13 Secrets of Power Performance*. Englewood Cliffs, NJ: Prentice Hall.

———. 1992. *Secrets of Power Persuasion*. Englewood Cliffs, NJ: Prentice Hall.

Delmar, Ken. 1984. *Winning Moves—The Body Language of Selling*. New York: Time Warner Books.

Demkin, Joseph A., executive ed. 2008. *The Architect's Handbook of Professional Practice*, 14th ed. Hoboken, NJ: John Wiley & Sons.

Deutsch, Randy. 2011. *BIM and Integrated Design: Strategies for Architectural Practice*. Hoboken, NJ: John Wiley & Sons.

de Wolfe, Elsie. 1913/1975. *The House in Good Taste*. Reprint ed. New York: Arno.

Dible, Donald M. 1974. *Up Your Own Organization*, 2nd ed. Reston, VA: Reston Publishing.

Dienhart, John W., and Jordan Curnutt. 1998. *Business Ethics*. Santa Barbara, CA: ABC-Clio.

DiFalco, Marcelle, and Jocelyn Greenkey Heiz. 2005. *The Big Sister's Guide to the World of Work*. New York: Fireside Books.

DiResta, Diane. 1998. *Knockout Presentations*. Worcester, MA: Chandler House Press.

Dohr, Joy H., and Margaret Portillo. 2011. *Design Thinking for Interiors*. Hoboken, NJ: John Wiley & Sons.

Drucker, Peter F. 1995. *Managing in a Time of Great Change*. New York: Truman Talley/Dutton.

———. 1973. *Management: Tasks, Responsibilities, Practices*. New York: Harper & Row.

Dun & Bradstreet. 1999. *D&B Business Rankings*. Bethlehem, PA: Dun & Bradstreet.

Dunung, Sanjyot P. 2006. *Starting and Growing Your Business*. New York: McGraw-Hill.

Edwards, Paul, and Sarah Edwards. 1999. *Working from Home*, 5th ed. New York: Tarcher/Putnam.

———. 1996. *Secrets of Self-Employment*. Revised ed. New York: Tarcher/Putnam.

Edwards, Paul, and Sarah Edwards (with Linda Rohrbough). 1998. *Getting Business to Come to You*, 2nd ed. New York: Tarcher/Putnam.

———. 1998. *Making Money in Cyberspace*. New York: Tarcher/Putnam.

Elias, Stephen. 1999. *Patent, Copyright and Trademark*, 3rd ed. Berkeley, CA: Nolo Press.

Elias, Stephen, and Patricia Gima. 2000. *Domain Names: How to Choose and Protect a Great Name for Your Website*. Berkeley, CA: Nolo Press.

Elkington, John. 1997. *Cannibals with Forks: The Triple Bottom Line of 21st Century Business*. Oxford, UK: Capstone Press.

Elvin, George. 2007. *Integrated Practice in Architecture*. Hoboken, NJ: John Wiley & Sons.

Emerson, Robert W. 2004. *Business Law*, 4th ed. Hauppauge, NY: Barron's.

Emery, Vince. 1996. *How to Grow Your Business on the Internet*. Scottsdale, AZ: Coriolis Group.

Entrepreneur Magazine. 1999. *Starting a Home-Based Business*, 2nd ed. Hoboken, NJ: John Wiley & Sons.

Entrepreneur Media, Inc. 1999. *The Entrepreneur Magazine Small Business Advisor*, 2nd ed. Hoboken, NJ: John Wiley & Sons.

Epstein, Lee. 1977. *Legal Forms for the Designer*. New York: N & E Hellman.

Eskenazi, Martin, and David Gallen. 1992. *Sexual Harassment. Know Your Rights!* New York: Carroll & Graf.

Esty, Daniel C., and P. J. Simmos. 2011. *The Green to Gold Business Playbook: How to Implement Sustainability Practices for Bottom-Line Results in Every Business Function*. Hoboken, NJ: John Wiley & Sons.

Evans, Liana. 2010. *Social Media Marketing*. Upper Saddle River, NJ: Que Publishing.

Eyler, David R. 1994. *The Home Business Bible*. Hoboken, NJ: John Wiley & Sons.

Farren, Carol E. 1999. *Planning and Managing Interior Projects*, 2nd ed. Kingston, MA: R.S. Means.

Farson, Richard. 2008. *The Power of Design*. Norcross, GA: Ostberg.

Fast, Julius. 1970. *Body Language*. New York: (Pocket Books)/Simon & Schuster.

Feather, Frank. 2000. *Future Consumer.com*. Toronto: Warwick.

Feldman, Melissa. 2012. *What Clients Want*. Bloomfield, CT: Finlay Printing.

Finnigan, Dan, and Marc Karasu. 2006. *Your Next Move: Success Strategies for Midcareer Professionals*. New York: Sterling Publishing.

Fisher, Lionel L. 1995. *On Your Own*. Englewood Cliffs, NJ: Prentice Hall.

Fisher, Roger, and William Ury. 1981. *Getting to Yes*. New York: Penguin Books.

Fisher, Thomas. 2010. *Ethics for Architects*. New York: Princeton Architectural Press.

Fishman, Stephen. 2011. *Working for Yourself*. Berkeley, CA: Nolo Press.

———. 2004. *Working for Yourself*, 5th ed. Berkeley, CA: Nolo Press.

———. 1996. *The Copyright Handbook*, 3rd ed. Berkeley, CA: Nolo Press.

Fletcher, Tana, and Julia Rockler. 2000. *Getting Publicity*. North Vancouver, BC, Canada: Self-Counsel Press.

Foote, Cameron S. 2002. *The Business Side of Creativity*. Revised ed. New York: W.W. Norton.

Forsyth, Patrick. 1999. *Marketing Professional Services*, 2nd ed. London: Kogan/Page.

Foster, Kari, Annette Stelmack, and Debbie Hindman. 2007. *Sustainable Residential Interiors*. Hoboken, NJ: John Wiley & Sons.

Fox, Vanessa. 2010. *Marketing in the Age of Google*. Hoboken, NJ: John Wiley & Sons.

Frederiksen, Lee W., and Aaron E. Taylor. 2010. *Spiraling Up*. Reston, VA: Hinge Research Institute.

Frey, Fred L., and Charles R. Stoner. 1995. *Strategic Planning for the New and Small Business*. Chicago, IL: Upstart Publishing.

Fria, Rick. 2005. *Successful RFPs in Construction*. New York: McGraw-Hill.

Friday, Stormy, and David G. Cotts. 1995. *Quality Facility Management*. Hoboken, NJ: John Wiley & Sons.

Fridson, Martin S. 1995. *Financial Statement Analysis*. Hoboken, NJ: John Wiley & Sons.

Friedman, Thomas L., and Michael Mandelbaum. 2011. *That Used to Be Us*. New York: Farrar, Straus and Giroux.

Frost, Susan E. 1995. *Blueprint for Marketing*, 2nd ed. Portland, OR: SEF Publications.

Gardella, Robert S. 2000. *The Harvard Business School Guide to Finding Your Next Job*. Boston: Harvard Business Reference.

Garner, Bryan A., ed. 2004. *Black's Law Dictionary*, 8th ed. St. Paul, MN: West Group.

———. 1999. *Black's Law Dictionary*, 7th ed. St. Paul, MN: West Group.

Getz, Lowell. 1997. *An Architect's Guide to Financial Management*. Washington, DC: AIA Press.

———. 1986. *Business Management in the Smaller Design Firm*. Newton, MA: Practice Management Associates.

Getz, Lowell, and Andrew Loebelson. 1983. *How to Profit in Contract Design*. New York: Interior Design Books.

Getz, Lowell, and Frank Stasiowski. 1984. *Financial Management for the Design Professional*. New York: Watson-Guptill.

Gerber, Michael E. 2005. *E Myth Mastery*. New York: Harper Business.

———. 1995. *The E Myth Revisited*. New York: Harper Business.

Gerbert, Philipp, Dirk Schneider, and Alex Birch. 2000. *The Age of E-tail*. Oxford, UK: Capstone Publishers.

Gilbert, Jill. 2004. *The Entrepreneur's Guide to Patents, Copyrights, Trademarks, Trade Secrets, and Licensing*. New York: Berkley Books.

Gitman, Lawrence J., and Carl McDaniel. 2003. *The Best of The Future of Business*. Mason, OH: Thomson.

Gitomer, Jeffrey H. 2011. *Social Boom!* Upper Saddle River, NJ: FT Press.

———. 1994. *The Sales Bible*. New York: William Morrow.

Gladwell, Malcolm. 2005. *Blink*. New York: Little, Brown.

———. 2000. *The Tipping Point*. New York: Back Bay Press.

Gomez-Mejia, Luis R., David B. Balkin, and Robert L. Cardy. 2005. *Management*, 2nd ed. New York: McGraw-Hill.

Gordon, Ian H. 1998. *Relationship Marketing*. Hoboken, NJ: John Wiley & Sons.

Graham, John W., and Wendy C. Havlick. 1994. *Mission Statements*. New York: Garland.

Grant, John. 2007. *The Green Marketing Manifesto*. West Sussex, UK: John Wiley & Sons.

Gray, John. 1999. *How to Get What You Want and Want What You Have*. New York: HarperCollins.

Greusel, David. 2002. *Architect's Essentials of Presentation Skills*. Hoboken, NJ: John Wiley & Sons.

Griessman, B. Eugene. 1994. *Time Tactics of Very Successful People*. New York: McGraw-Hill.

Groat, Linda, and David Wang. 2002. *Architectural Research Methods*. Hoboken, NJ: John Wiley & Sons.

Haldane, Bernard. 2000. *Haldane's Best Cover Letters for Professionals*. Manassas Park, VA: Impact.

Hale Associates, Inc. 1998. *Analysis of the Interior Design Profession*. Washington, DC: National Council for Interior Design Qualification.

Halligan, Brian, and Dharmesh Shah. 2010. *Inbound Marketing*. Hoboken, NJ: John Wiley & Sons.

Hamilton, D. Kirk, and David H. Watkins. 2009. *Evidence-Based Design for Multiple Building Types*. Hoboken, NJ: John Wiley & Sons.

Hanan, Mack, and Peter Karp. 1991. *Competing on Value*. New York: AMACOM.

Hansen, Jeffrey A. 1998. *Surviving Success*. Grants Pass, OR: Oasis Press.

Harding, Ford. 2006. *Creating Rainmakers*, 2nd ed. Holbrook, MA: Adams Media.

———. 1998. *Creating Rainmakers*. Holbrook, MA: Adams Media.

———. 1994. *Rain Making*. Holbrook, MA: Adams Media.

Harmon, Sharon Koomen, and Katherine E. Kennon. 2005. *The Code Guidebook for Interiors*, 3rd ed. Hoboken, NJ: John Wiley & Sons.

Harris, Cyril M. 2006. *Dictionary of Architecture and Construction*, 4th ed. New York: McGraw-Hill.

Harvard Business Essentials. 2006. *Marketer's Toolkit*. Cambridge, MA: Harvard Business School Press.

———. 2005. *Entrepreneur's Toolkit*. Cambridge, MA: Harvard Business School Press.

Hauser, Barbara R., ed. 1996. *Woman's Legal Guide*. Golden, CO: Fulcrum.

Haviland, David, ed. 1994. *The Architect's Handbook of Professional Practice* (Student Edition). Washington, DC: AIA Press.

Haylock, Christina Ford, and Len Muscarella. 1999. *Net Success*. Holbrook, MA: Adams Media.

Heim, Pat, and Susan K. Golant. 2005. *Hardball for Women*. Revised ed. New York: Plume.

———. 1995. *Smashing the Glass Ceiling*. New York: Fireside Books.

Heinecke, William E. (with Jonathan Marsh). 2000. *The Entrepreneur*. Singapore: John Wiley & Sons.

Helzel, Leo B., and friends. 1995. *A Goal Is a Dream with a Deadline*. New York: McGraw-Hill.

Henderson, Holly. 2012. *Becoming a Green Building Professional*. Hoboken, NJ: John Wiley & Sons.

Hiebing, Roman G., Jr., and Scott W. Cooper. 1999. *The One-Day Marketing Plan*, 2nd ed. Lincolnwood, IL: NTC Business Books.

Hinkelman, Edward G. 1997. *Canada Business*. San Rafael, CA: World Trade Press.

Hinze, Jimmie. 2001. *Construction Contracts*, 2nd ed. New York: McGraw-Hill.

Hirsch, Arlene S. 1996. *Love Your Work and Success Will Follow*. Hoboken, NJ: John Wiley & Sons.

Hoffman, Reid, and Ben Casnocha. 2012. *The Start-Up of You*. New York: Crown Publishing (Random House).

Holtz, Herman. 2000. *Getting Started in Sales Consulting*. Hoboken, NJ: John Wiley & Sons.

———. 1998. *The Consultant's Guide to Getting Business on the Internet*. Hoboken, NJ: John Wiley & Sons.

———. 1998. *Proven Proposal Strategies to Win More Business*. Chicago, IL: Upstart Publishing.

Hood, Jack B., Benjamin A. Harady, Jr., and Harold S. Lewis, Jr. 1999. *Worker's Compensation and Employee Protection Laws*. St. Paul, MN: West Publishing.

Hopkins, Tom. 2010. *Selling in Tough Times*. New York: Business Plus/Hachette Book Group.

Horn, Greg. 2006. *Living Green*. Topanga, CA: Freedom Press.

Horn, Sam. 2006. *Pop! Stand Out in Any Crowd*. New York: Perigee/Penguin.

Horngren, Charles T., George Foster, and Srikant M. Datar. 2000. *Cost Accounting*, 10th ed. Upper Saddle River, NJ: Prentice Hall.

Howard, Ronald A., and Clinton D. Korver. 2008. *Ethics (for the Real World)*. Boston: Harvard Business Press.

Howe, Neil, and William Strauss. 2000. *Millennials Rising: The Next Great Generation*. New York: Vintage Books/Random House.

Hyatt, Carole. 1998. *The Woman's New Selling Game*. New York: McGraw-Hill.

Interior Design Continuing Education Council (IDCEC). 2011. *Presenter's Guide for Interior Design Continuing Education*. Available at www.idcec.org.

Ittelson, Thomas. 1998. *Financial Statements*. Franklin Lakes, NJ: Career Press.

Ivancevich, John M., Peter Lorenzi, and Steven J. Skinner (with Philip B. Crosby). 1994. *Management*. Burr Ridge, IL: Irwin.

Jackson, Barbara J. 2004. *Construction Management Jump Start*. Alameda, CA: Sybex.

Jenkins, Michael D. 1999. *Starting and Operating a Business in the United States*. Palo Alto, CA: Running 'R' Media. (Includes a CD-ROM, with information on all 50 states.)

Jenks, Larry. 1995. *Architectural Office Standards and Practices*. New York: McGraw-Hill.

Jennings, Marianne M. 2006. *Business Ethics*, 5th ed. Mason, OH: Thomson.

———. 2006. *The Seven Signs of Ethical Collapse*. New York: St. Martin's Press.

Jentz, Gaylord A., Kenneth W. Clarkson, and Roger LeRoy Miller. 1987. *West's Business Law—Alternate UCC Comprehensive Edition*, 3rd ed. St. Paul, MN: West Publishing.

J. K. Lasser Institute. 1994. *How to Run a Small Business*, 7th ed. New York: McGraw-Hill.

Joel, Lewin G., III. 1996. *Every Employee's Guide to the Law*. New York: Pantheon Press.

Johnson, Allan G. 1995. *The Blackwell Dictionary of Sociology*. Cambridge, MA: Blackwell Reference.

Johnson, Lisa. 2006. *Mind Your X's and Y's*. New York: Free Press.

Johnson, Spencer. 1998. *Who Moved My Cheese?* New York: G.P. Putnam.

Jones, Gerre L. 1983. *How to Market Professional Design Services*, 2nd ed. New York: McGraw-Hill.

———. 1980. *Public Relations for the Design Professional*. New York: McGraw-Hill.

Jones, Katie. 1998. *Time Management*. New York: American Management Association.

Jones, Louise, ed. 2008. *Environmentally Responsible Design*. Hoboken, NJ: John Wiley & Sons.

Jones, Nancy L., with Phil Philcox. 2000. *The Women's Guide to Legal Issues*. Los Angeles, CA: Renaissance Books.

Kaderlan, Norman. 1991. *Designing Your Practice*. New York: McGraw-Hill.

Kanungo, Rabindra N., and Manuel Mendonca. 1996. *Ethical Dimensions of Leadership*. Thousand Oaks, CA: Sage Publications.

Karlen, Mark. 1993. *Space Planning Basics*. New York: Van Nostrand Reinhold.

Katzenbach, Jon R. 1998. *Teams at the Top*. Boston: Harvard Business School Press.

Keegan, Warren J., Sandra E. Moriarty, and Thomas R. Duncan. 1995. *Marketing*, 2nd ed. Englewood Cliffs, NJ: Prentice Hall.

Keller, Ed, and Jon Berry. 2003. *The Influentials*. New York: Free Press.

Kendall, Dick. 1995. *Nobody Told Me I'd Have to Sell*. New York: Birch Lane Press.

Kendall, Pat. 2000. *Jumpstart Your Online Job Search*. Rocklin, CA: Prima Publishers.

Kennedy, Joyce Lain. 1995. *Hook Up, Get Hired! The Internet Job Search Revolution*. Hoboken, NJ: John Wiley & Sons.

Kerzner, Harold. 2003. *Project Management*, 8th ed. Hoboken, NJ: John Wiley & Sons.

Kibert, Charles J. 2005. *Sustainable Construction*. Hoboken, NJ: John Wiley & Sons.

Klein, Rena M. 2010. *The Architect's Guide to Small Firm Management*. Hoboken, NJ: John Wiley & Sons.

Kliment, Stephen A. 1998. *Writing for Design Professionals*. New York: W.W. Norton.

———. 1977. *Creative Communications for a Successful Design Practice*. New York: Watson-Guptill.

Knackstedt, Mary. 2008. *Marketing and Client Relations*. Hoboken, NJ: John Wiley & Sons.

———. 2005. *The Interior Design Business Handbook*, 4th ed. Hoboken, NJ: John Wiley & Sons.

Knott, Mary Fisher. 2011. *Kitchen and Bath Design*. Hoboken, NJ: John Wiley & Sons.

Koren, David. 2005. *Architect's Essentials of Marketing*. Hoboken, NJ: John Wiley & Sons.

Kotler, Michael. 2000. *Marketing Management*. Millennium ed. Upper Saddle River, NJ: Prentice Hall.

Kotler, Philip, and Gary Armstrong. 1999. *Principles of Marketing*, 8th ed. Upper Saddle River, NJ: Prentice Hall.

Kotler, Phillip, and Nancy Lee. 2004. *Corporate Social Responsibility: Doing the Most Good for Your Company and Your Cause*. Hoboken, NJ: John Wiley & Sons.

Kotter, John P. 1996. *Leading Change*. Cambridge, MA: Harvard Business School Press.

Krannich, Ronald L., and Caryl Rae Krannich. 1994. *Dynamite Salary Negotiations*, 2nd ed. Manassas Park, VA: Impact Publications.

Kremer, John, and J. Daniel McComas. 1997. *High-Impact Marketing on a Low-Impact Budget*. Rocklin, CA: Rima Publishing.

Lakin, Alan. 1973. *How to Get Control of Your Time and Your Life*. New York, NY: Signet (Penguin Group).

Landes, William M., and Richard A. Posner. 2003. *Economic Structure of Intellectual Property Law*. Cambridge, MA: Belknap Press.

Laurie, Donald L. 2000. *The Real Work of Leaders*. Cambridge, MA: Perseus Publishing.

Lavington, Camilee (with Stephanie Losee). 1997. *You've Only Got Three Seconds*. New York: Doubleday.

Lawlor, Drue, and Michael A. Thomas. 2008. *Residential Design for Aging in Place*. Hoboken, NJ: John Wiley & Sons.

Lawson, Joseph W. R., II. 1998. *How to Develop an Employee Handbook*, 2nd ed. New York: American Management Association.

LeBoeuf, Michael. 1996. *The Perfect Business*. New York: Fireside.

Leider, Richard J. 1997. *The Power of Purpose*. San Francisco: Berrett-Koehler.

Leone, Bruno. 1995. *Ethics*. San Diego, CA: Greenhaven Press.

Levinson, Jay Conrad. 1998. *Guerrilla Marketing*, 3rd ed. Boston: Houghton Mifflin.

Levy, Justin R. 2010. *Facebook Marketing*, 2nd ed. Indianapolis, IN: Que.

Levy, Sidney M. 1994. *Project Management in Construction*, 2nd ed. New York: McGraw-Hill.

Lewin, Marsha D. 1995. *The Overnight Consultant*. Hoboken, NJ: John Wiley & Sons.

Lewis, James P. 1995. *Project Planning, Scheduling, and Control*. Revised ed. Chicago: Richard D. Irwin.

Liddle, Jeffrey L. 1981. "Malicious Terminations and Abusive Discharges: The Beginning of the End of Employment at Will." In *Employee Termination Handbook*. Englewood Cliffs, NJ: Executive Enterprises Publications.

Lientz, Bennet P., and Kathryn P. Rea. 1995. *Project Management for the 21st Century*. San Diego, CA: Academic Press.

Linton, Harold. 2000. *Portfolio Design*, 2nd ed. New York: W.W. Norton.

Llewellyn, A. Bronwyn, James P. Hendrix, and K. C. Golden. 2008. *Green Jobs*. Avon, MA: Adams Media.

Lloyd, Joan. 1992. *The Career Decisions Planner*. Hoboken, NJ: John Wiley & Sons.

Loebelson, Andrew. 1983. *How to Profit in Contract Design*. New York: Interior Design Books.

Lohmann, William T. 1992. *Construction Specifications: Managing the Review Process*. Boston: Butterworth Architecture.

Lovelock, Christopher H. 1996. *Services Marketing*, 3rd ed. Upper Saddle River, NJ: Prentice Hall.

Low, Robert. 2004. *Accounting and Finance for Small Business Made Easy*. Irvine, CA: Entrepreneur Press.

Lundy, James L. 1994. *Teams*. Chicago: Dartnell Press.

Macdonald, Keith M. 1995. *The Sociology of the Professions*. London: Sage Publications.

MacKay, Harvey. 1997. *Dig Your Well Before You're Thirsty*. New York: Currency/Doubleday.

MacKenzie, Alec. 1997. *The Time Trap*, 3rd ed. New York: American Management Association.

Maister, David H. 1993. *Managing the Professional Service Firm*. New York: Free Press.

Malburg, Christopher R. 1994. *The All-in-One Business Planning Guide*. Holbrook, MA: Bob Adams.

Mancuso, Joseph R. 2000. *Form Your Own Limited Liability Company*, 2nd ed. Berkeley, CA: Nolo Press. (The disc that is included with the book contains information for all 50 states.)

———. 2000. *Nolo's Quick LLC*. Berkeley, CA: Nolo Press.

———. 1996. *Mancuso's Small Business Resource Guide*. Naperville, IL: Sourcebooks.

———. 1993. *How to Prepare and Present a Business Plan*. New York: Fireside Books.

———. 1985. *How to Write a Winning Business Plan*. Englewood Cliffs, NJ: Prentice Hall.

Mann, Thorbjoern. 2004. *Time Management for Architects and Designers*. New York: W.W. Norton.

Marconi, Joe. 1999. *The Complete Guide to Publicity*. Lincolnwood, IL: NTC Business Books.

———. 1995. *Marketing Basics for Designers*. Hoboken, NJ: John Wiley & Sons.

Marshall, Gordon. 1998. *A Dictionary of Sociology*, 2nd ed. New York: Oxford University Press.

Marston, Cam. 2011. *Generational Sales Tactics That Work*. Hoboken, NJ: John Wiley & Sons.

Martin, Jane D., and Nancy Knoohuizen. 1995. *Marketing Basics for Designers*. Hoboken, NJ: John Wiley & Sons.

Martin, Jeanette S., and Lillian H. Chaney. 2012. *Global Business Etiquette: A Guide to International Communication and Customs*, 2nd ed. Santa Barbara, CA: Praeger.

Maslow, Abraham H. 2000. *The Maslow Business Reader*. Ed. Deborah C. Stephens. Hoboken, NJ: John Wiley & Sons.

———. 1998. *Maslow on Management*. Hoboken, NJ: John Wiley & Sons.

Maurer, Terri L., and Katie Weeks. 2010. *Interior Design in Practice: Case Studies of Successful Business Models*. Hoboken, NJ: John Wiley & Sons.

Maxwell, John C. 2002. *Your Road Map for Success*. Nashville, TN: Thomas Nelson.

Maxwell, John C., and Jim Dornan. 1997. *Becoming a Person of Influence*. Nashville, TN: Thomas Nelson.

Mayer, Jeffrey J. 1999. *Success Is a Journey: 7 Steps to Achieving Success in the Business of Life*. New York: McGraw-Hill.

McCarthy, E. Jerome, and William D. Perreault, Jr. 1993. *Basic Marketing*, 11th ed. Homewood, IL: Richard D. Irwin.

McGowan, Maryrose. 1996. *Specifying Interiors*. Hoboken, NJ: John Wiley & Sons.

McGuckin, Frances. 2005. *Business for Beginners*. Naperville, IL: Sourcebooks, Inc.

McKain, Scott. 2005. *What Customers Really Want*. Nashville, TN: Nelson Business.

McKenzie, Ronald A., and Bruce H. Schoumacher. 1992. *Successful Business Plans for Architects*. New York: McGraw-Hill.

McKinney, Anne. 1996. *Resumes and Cover Letters That Have Worked*. Fayetteville, NC: PREP Publishing.

Means, R. S. 2000. *Means Interior Cost Data 2001*. Kingston, MA: R.S. Means.

Meier, Hans W. 1978. *Construction Specifications Handbook*, 2nd ed. New York: Prentice Hall.

Meigs, Robert F., Mary A. Meigs, Mark Battner, and Ray Whittington. 1996. *Accounting: The Basis for Business Decisions*, 10th ed. New York: McGraw-Hill.

Mendler, Sandra F., and William Odell. 2000. *The HOK Guide to Sustainable Design*. Hoboken, NJ: John Wiley & Sons.

Miller, Roger LeRoy, and Gaylord A. Jentz. 2006. *Business Law Today: The Essentials*, 7th ed. Mason, OH: Thomson.

Mills, Harry. 2004. *The Rainmaker's Toolkit*. New York: AMACOM Press.

Mintzberg, Henry. 1994. *The Rise and Fall of Strategic Planning*. New York: Free Press.

Mintzberg, Henry, Bruce Ahlstand, and Joseph Lampel. 2005. *Strategy Bites Back*. Upper Saddle River, NJ: Pearson/Prentice Hall.

Mitton, Maureen. 2010. *Portfolios for Interior Designers*. Hoboken, NJ: John Wiley & Sons.

Mohammed, Rafi. 2005. *The Art of Pricing*. New York: Crown Business.

Mohr, Angie. 2005. *Managing Business Growth: Get a Grip on the Numbers That Count*. Bellingham, WA: Self-Counsel Press.

Molloy, John T. 1996. *The New Woman's Dress for Success Book*. New York: Time Warner Books.

———. 1988. *New Dress for Success*. New York: Time Warner Books.

Morgan, Jim. 1998. *Management for the Small Design Firm*. New York: Watson-Guptill.

———. 1984. *Marketing for the Small Design Firm*. New York: Watson-Guptill.

Morgenstern, Julie. 2004. *Making Work Work*. New York: Fireside Books.

Morrisey, George L. 1996. *Morrisey on Planning: A Guide to Long-Range Planning*. San Francisco: Jossey-Bass.

Morrison, Terri, Wayne A. Conway, and George A. Borden. 2006. *Kiss, Bow, or Shake Hands*, 2nd ed. Avon, MA: Adams Media.

Mose, Arlene K., John Jackson, and Gary Downs. 1997. *Day-to-Day Business Accounting*. Paramus, NJ: Prentice Hall.

Murphy, Tom. 2000. *Web Rules*. Chicago: Dearborn Financial Publishing.

Murray, Katherine. 1997. *PowerPoint 97*, 3rd ed. San Francisco: Sybex.

Nemich, Mary B., and Fred E. Jandt. 1999. *Cyberspace Resume Kit*. Indianapolis: JIST Publications.

Newton, Lisa H., and Maureen M. Ford, eds. 1996. *Taking Sides*, 4th ed. Guilford, CT: Dushkin Group.

Nierenberg, Gerard I. 1996. *The Art of Creative Thinking*. New York: Barnes & Noble Press.

Nierenberg, Gerard I., and Henry H. Calero. 2009. *The New Art of Negotiating*. Garden City Park, NY: Square One.

———. 1993. *How to Read a Person Like a Book*. New York: Barnes & Noble.

Oasis Press. 1997. *Smart Start Your Arizona Business*. Grants Pass, OR: Oasis Press. (Books are available for all 50 states.)

O'Leary, Arthur E. 1992. *Construction Administration in Architectural Practice*. New York: McGraw-Hill.

O'Shea, Tracy, and Jane LaLonde. 1998. *Sexual Harassment*. New York: St. Martin's Griffin.

Osterwalder, Alexander, and Yves Pigneur. 2010. *Business Model Generation*. Hoboken, NJ: John Wiley & Sons.

Oxford American College Dictionary. 2002. New York: Oxford University Press.

Pace, Elizabeth. 2009. *The X and Y of Buy*. Nashville, TN: Thomas Nelson.

Pachter, Barbara, and Marjorie Brody (with Betsy Anderson). 1995. *Complete Business Etiquette Handbook*. Englewood Cliffs, NJ: Prentice Hall.

Pack, Thomas. 1997. *10 Minute Guide to Business Research on the Net*. New York: Que/Macmillan.

Pakroo, Peri. 2010. *The Women's Small Business Start-Up Kit*. Berkeley, CA: Nolo Publishing.

Parker, Roger C. 2000. *Relationship Marketing on the Internet*. Holbrook, MA: Adams Media.

Parsons, Patricia J. 2004. *Ethics in Public Relations*. London: Kogan Press.

Patterson, Kerry, Joseph Grenny, Ron McMillan, and Al Switzler. 2002. *Crucial Conversations*. New York: McGraw-Hill.

Perkins Eastman Architects. 2007. *International Practice for Architects*. Hoboken, NJ: John Wiley & Sons.

Peters, Tom. 1999. *The Brand You 50*. New York: Knopf.

Petrocelli, William, and Barbara Kate Repa. 1999. *Sexual Harassment on the Job*, 4th ed. Berkeley, CA: Nolo Press.

Phillips, Patricia, and George Mair. 1997. *Know Your Rights: A Legal Handbook for Women Only*. New York: Macmillan.

Pickar, Roger L. 1991. *Marketing for Design Firms in the 1990s*. Washington, DC: American Institute of Architects.

Pile, John. 2009. *A History of Interior Design*, 3rd ed. Hoboken, NJ: John Wiley & Sons.

———. 2005. *A History of Interior Design*, 2nd ed. Hoboken, NJ: John Wiley & Sons.

Pinson, Linda. 2004. *Keeping the Books*, 6th ed. Chicago: Dearborn Trade Publishing.

Pinson, Linda, and Jerry Jinnett. 1998. *Keeping the Books*, 4th ed. Lincolnwood, IL: Upstart Publishing.

Pinto, Jeffrey K., and O. P. Kharbanda. 1995. *Successful Project Managers*. New York: Van Nostrand Reinhold.

Piotrowski, Christine M. 2011. *Problem Solving and Critical Thinking for Designers*. Hoboken, NJ: John Wiley & Sons.

———. 2009. *Becoming an Interior Designer*, 2nd ed. Hoboken, NJ: John Wiley & Sons.

———. 1992. *Interior Design Management: A Handbook for Owners and Managers*. Hoboken, NJ: John Wiley & Sons.

Piotrowski, Christine M., and Elizabeth A. Rogers. 2007. *Designing Commercial Interiors*, 2nd ed. Hoboken, NJ: John Wiley & Sons.

Plewa, Franklin J., Jr., and George T. Friedlob. 1995. *Understanding Cash Flow*. Hoboken, NJ: John Wiley & Sons.

Poage, Waller S. 2000. *The Building Professional's Guide to Contract Documents*, 3rd ed. Kingston, MA: R.S. Means.

———. 1987. *Plans, Specs, and Contracts for Building Professionals*. Kingston, MA: R.S. Means.

Popyk, Bob. 2000. *Here's My Card*. Los Angeles: Renaissance Books.

Post, Peggy, and Peter Post. 1999. *The Etiquette Advantage in Business*. New York: Harper & Row.

Preiser, Wolfgang F. E., Harvey Z. Rabinowitz, and Edward T. White. 1988. *Post-Occupancy Evaluation*. New York: Van Nostrand Reinhold.

Pressman, Andrew. 2006. *Professional Practice 101: A Compendium of Business and Management Strategies in Architecture*, 2nd ed. Hoboken, NJ: John Wiley & Sons.

Pressman, David. 1999. *Patent It Yourself*, 7th ed. Berkeley, CA: Nolo Press.

Putman, Anthony O. 1990. *Marketing Your Services*. Hoboken, NJ: John Wiley & Sons.

Quinn, Thomas M. 1999. *Quinn's Uniform Commercial Code Commentary and Law Digest*, 2nd ed. St. Paul, MN: West Group.

———. 1991. *Quinn's Uniform Commercial Code Commentary and Law Digest*. St. Paul, MN: West Group.

Rabb, Margaret Y. 1993. *The Presentation Design Book*, 2nd ed. Chapel Hill, NC: Ventana Press.

Rappoport, James E., Robert F. Cushman, and Karen Daroff. 1992. *Office Planning and Design Desk Reference*. Hoboken, NJ: John Wiley & Sons.

Ray, Paul H., and Sherry Ruth Anderson. 2000. *The Cultural Creatives*. New York: Three Rivers Press.

Reigle, Jack. 2011. *Positioning for Architecture and Design Firms*. Hoboken, NJ: John Wiley & Sons.

Reilly, Brian. 1997. *Create PowerPoint Presentations in a Weekend*. Rocklin, CA: Prima Publishing.

Reznikoff, S. C. 1989. *Specifications for Commercial Interiors*. Revised ed. New York: Watson-Guptill.

———. 1979. *Specifications for Commercial Interiors*. New York: Watson-Guptill.

Ries, Al, and Laura Ries. 2004. *The Origin of Brands*. New York: HarperCollins.

Ries, Al, and Jack Trout. 1993. *The 22 Immutable Laws of Marketing*. New York: Harper Business.

Roane, Susan. 1993. *The Secrets of Savvy Networking*. New York: Time Warner Books.

———. 1988. *How to Work a Room*. New York: Time Warner Books.

Roffer, Robin Fisher. 2002. *Make a Name for Yourself*. New York: Broadway Books.

Rogak, Lisa. 1997. *Smart Guide to Starting a Small Business*. Hoboken, NJ: John Wiley & Sons.

Rosen, Harold J. 1981. *Construction Specifications Writing*, 2nd ed. Hoboken, NJ: John Wiley & Sons.

Rouse, William B. 1994. *Best Laid Plans*. Englewood Cliffs, NJ: Prentice Hall.

Rubeling, Albert W., Jr. 1994. *How to Start and Operate Your Own Design Firm*. New York: McGraw-Hill.

———. 1986. *Positioning*. New York: Time Warner Books.

Rubin, Harriet. 1999. *Soloing: Realizing Your Life's Ambition*. New York: HarperCollins Business.

Sabath, Anne Marie. 2000. *Beyond Business Casual*. Franklin Lakes, NJ: Career Press.

Sack, Steven Mitchell. 1998. *The Working Woman's Legal Survival Guide*. Paramus, NJ: Prentice Hall.

Safko, Lon. 2012. *The Social Media Bible*, 3rd ed. Hoboken, NJ: John Wiley & Sons.

Sampson, Carol A. 1991. *Techniques for Estimating Materials Costs and Time for Interior Designers*. New York: Watson-Guptill.

Sandford, Carol. 2011. *The Responsible Business: Reimaging Sustainability and Success*. Hoboken, NJ: John Wiley & Sons.

Sandler, Corey, and Janice Keefe. 2005. *Performance Appraisals That Work*. Avon, MA: Adams Media.

Schatt, Stan, and Michele Lobl. 2012. *Paint Your Career Green*. Indianapolis, IN: JIST Works Publishing.

Schlesinger, Eric, and Susan Musich. 2000. *E-Job Hunting*. Indianapolis, IN: Sams/ Macmillan.

Schmidt, Jeff. 2000. *Disciplined Minds*. Lanham, UK: Rowman & Littlefield.

Schulhofer, Stephen J. 1998. *Unwanted Sex: The Culture of Intimidation and Failure of Law*. Cambridge, MA: Harvard University Press.

Schweich, Thomas A. 1998. *Protect Yourself from Business Lawsuits*. New York: Scribner.

Scott, David Meerman. 2010. *The New Rules of Marketing and Public Relations: How to Use Social Media, Blogs, News Releases, Online Video, and Viral Marketing to Reach Buyers Directly*. Hoboken, NJ: John Wiley & Sons.

Scott, Susan. 2002. *Fierce Conversations*. New York: Berkley Books.

Sheehy, Gail. 1995. *New Passages*. New York: Ballantine.

Sher, Barbara, with Barbara Smith. 1994. *I Could Do Anything if I Only Knew What It Was*. New York: Dell Publishing.

Shilling, Dana. 1998. *The Complete Guide to Human Resources and the Law*. Paramus, NJ: Prentice Hall.

Shonka, Mark, and Dan Kosch. 2002. *Beyond Selling Value*. Chicago: Dearborn Trade Publishing.

Siegel, Harry (with Alan Siegel). 1982. *A Guide to Business Principles and Practices for Interior Designers*. Revised ed. New York: Watson-Guptill.

Siegel, Joel G., and Jae K. Shim. 1995. *Accounting Handbook*, 2nd ed. Hauppauge, NY: Barron's.

Silber, Lee. 1998. *Time Management for the Creative Person*. New York: Three Rivers Press.

Silverman, George. 2001. *The Secrets of Word-of-Mouth Marketing*. New York: AMCOM.

Silverstein, Michael J., and Neil Fiske. 2005. *Trading Up*. New York: Penguin Group.

Simmons, H. Leslie. 1985. *The Specifications Writer's Handbook*. Hoboken, NJ: John Wiley & Sons.

Siress, Ruth Herrman (with Carolyn Riddle and Deborah Shouse). 1994. *Working Woman's Communications Survival Guide*. Englewood Cliffs, NJ: Prentice Hall.

Siropolis, Nicholas C. 1994. *Small Business Management. A Guide to Entrepreneurship*, 5th ed. Boston, MA: Houghton Mifflin.

Smith, Mari. 2011. *The New Relationship Marketing*. Hoboken, NJ: John Wiley & Sons.

Smith, Rob, Mark Speaker, and Mark Thompson. 2000. *The Complete Idiot's Guide to E-Commerce*. Indianapolis, IN: Que/Macmillan.

Snead, G. Lynne, and Joyce Wycoff. 1997. *To Do, Doing, Done*. New York: Fireside Books.

Stanley, Thomas J. 1993. *Networking with the Affluent*. New York: McGraw-Hill.

———. 1991. *Selling to the Affluent*. New York: McGraw-Hill.

Stasiowski, Frank. 2003. *Architect's Essentials of Winning Proposals*. Hoboken, NJ: John Wiley & Sons.

———. 2001. *Staying Small Successfully*, 2nd ed. Hoboken, NJ: John Wiley & Sons.

———. 1993. *Cash Management for the Design Firm*. Hoboken, NJ: John Wiley & Sons.

——— 1993. *Value Pricing for the Design Firm*. Hoboken, NJ: John Wiley & Sons.

———. 1985. *Negotiating Higher Design Fees*. New York: Watson-Guptill.

Stasiowski, Frank, and David Burstein. 1994. *Total Quality Project Management for the Design Firm*. Hoboken, NJ: John Wiley & Sons.

Steelcase, Inc. 1987. *Steelcase: The First 75 Years*. Grand Rapids, MI: Steelcase.

Steiner, George. 1997. *A Step-by-Step Guide to Strategic Planning*. New York: Free Press.

Steingold, Fred S. 2005. *The Employer's Legal Handbook*, 7th ed. Ed. Amy DelPo. Berkeley, CA: Nolo Press.

———. 2005. *Legal Guide for Starting and Running a Small Business*, 8th ed. Berkeley, CA: Nolo Press.

Stitt, Fred A., ed. 1986. *Design Office Management Handbook*. Santa Monica, CA: Arts and Architecture.

Stone, Brandford. 1975. *Uniform Commercial Code in a Nutshell*. St. Paul, MN: West Publishing.

Stone, Janet, and Jane Bachner. 1994. *Speaking Up*. Revised ed. New York: Carroll & Graf Publishers.

Sweet, Justin. 1985. *Legal Aspects of Architecture, Engineering, and the Construction Process*, 3rd ed. St. Paul, MN: West Publishing.

Talbot, Marianne. 2000. *Make Your Mission Statement Work*. Oxford, UK: How To Books.

Tate, Allen, and C. Ray Smith. 1986. *Interior Design in the 20th Century*. New York: Harper & Row.

Taylor, Jeff (with Doug Hardy). 2004. *Monster Careers*. New York: Penguin Group.

Thompson, Jo Anne Asher, ed. 1992. *ASID Professional Practice Manual*. New York: Watson-Guptill.

Thornhill, Matt, and John Marating. 2007. *Boomer Consumer*. Great Falls, VA: LINX Books.

Tingley, Judith C., and Lee E. Robert. 1999. *Gender Sell*. New York: Simon & Schuster.

Tracy, Brian. 2003. *Goals!* San Francisco: Berrett-Koehler.

———. 1993. *Maximum Achievement*. New York: Fireside Books.

Trevino, Linda K., and Katherine A. Nelson. 2011. *Managing Business Ethics*, 5th ed. Hoboken, NJ: John Wiley & Sons.

Trout, Jack, with Steve Rivkin. 2008. *Differentiate or Die*, 2nd ed. Hoboken, NJ: John Wiley & Sons.

Twitty-Villani, Teri. 1992. *Appearances Speak Louder Than Words*. Portland, OR: Voyager Press.

Underhill, Paco. 1999. *Why We Buy*. New York: Simon & Schuster.

Unerman, Sue, and Johnathan Salem Baskin. 2012. *Tell the Truth: Honesty Is Your Most Powerful Marketing Tool*. Dallas, TX: Ben Bella Books.

U.S. Green Building Council. 2006. *Commercial Interiors Reference Guide*, 3rd ed.

Veitch, Ronald M., Dianne R. Jackman, and Mary K. Dixon. 1990. *Professional Practice*. Winnipeg, MB: Peguis Publishers.

Viscott, David. 1985. *Taking Care of Business. A Psychiatrist's Guide for True Career Success*. New York: William Morrow.

Viscusi, Stephen. 2001. *On the Job*. New York: Three Rivers Press.

Wakita, Osamu A., and Richard M. Linde. 2002. *The Professional Practice of Architectural Working Drawings*, 3rd ed. Hoboken, NJ: John Wiley & Sons.

———. 1999. *The Professional Practice of Architectural Detailing*, 3rd ed. Hoboken, NJ: John Wiley & Sons.

Walsh, Ciaran. 1996. *Key Management Ratios*. London: F.T. Pitman.

Walters, Dottie, and Lilly Walters. 1997. *Speak and Grow Rich*. Revised ed. Paramus, NJ: Prentice Hall.

Wasserman, Barry, Patrick Sullivan, and Gregory Palermo. 2000. *Ethics and the Practice of Architecture*. Hoboken, NJ: John Wiley & Sons.

Weiss, Alan. 2002. *Value-Based Fees*. Hoboken, NJ: Jossey-Bass/Wiley.

Weiss, Donald H. 2000. *Fair, Square, and Legal*, 3rd ed. New York: American Management Association.

West's Encyclopedia of American Law. vol. 8. St. Paul, MN: West Publishing.

Wheatley, Margaret J. 1994. *Leadership and the New Science*. San Francisco: Berrett-Koehler.

Whitmore, Jacqueline. 2005. *Business Class: Etiquette Essentials for Success at Work*. New York: St. Martins Press.

Williams, David J. 1996. *Preparing for Project Management*. New York: American Society of Civil Engineers.

Williams, Jan R. 2000. Miller *GAAP Guide*. San Diego, CA: Harcourt Professional Publications.

Williams, Terrie (with Joe Cooney). 1994. *The Personal Touch*. New York: Time Warner Books.

Wilson, Robert F., and Adele Lewis. 2000. *Barron's Better Resumes for Executives and Professionals*, 4th ed. Hauppauge, NY: Barron's.

Windham, Laurie (with Ken Orton). 2000. *The Soul of the New Consumer*. New York: Allworth Press.

Woods, Mary N. 1999. *From Craft to Profession: The Practice of Architecture in Nineteenth-Century America*. Berkeley, CA: University of California Press.

Woodward, Cynthia A. 1990. *Human Resources Management for Design Professionals*. Washington, DC: AIA Press.

World Book Encyclopedia. 2000. vol. 17. Chicago: World Book.

World Commission on Environment and Development. 1987. *From One Earth to One World: An Overview*. Oxford: Oxford University Press.

Yohalem, Kathy C. 1997. *Thinking Out of the Box*. Hoboken, NJ: John Wiley & Sons.

Zeithaml, Valarie A., and Mary Jo Bitner. 1996. *Services Marketing*. New York: McGraw-Hill.

Zeithaml, Valarie A., Mary Jo Bitner, and Dwayne D. Gremler. 2009. *Services Marketing*, 5th ed. New York: McGraw-Hill.

Zikmund, William G. 1994. *Business Research Methods*, 4th ed. Fort Worth, TX: Dryden Press.

Ziglar, Zig. 2003. *Zig Ziglar's Secrets of Closing the Sale*. Updated ed. Grand Rapids, MI: Revell.

———. 1991. *Ziglar on Selling*. Nashville, TN: Thomas Nelson.

INTERNET RESOURCES

The reader should verify the site's reliability and usefulness. The author does not endorse any site other than those of the recognized interior design professional associations. Today, many other sites can be found relating to some of the associations, agencies, and organizations identified here. You may wish to carefully investigate these other sites by doing online searches.

Web site addresses were correct at the time of publication.

INTERIOR DESIGN PROFESSIONAL ASSOCIATIONS

These organizations are many of those most representative of professional interior designers or interior design professional interests. Note that a wide variety of publications and information is available on the practice of interior design at many of the professional association sites. In some cases, that information is only downloadable or available by members of the association.

American Academy of Health Care Designers (AAHID)
www.aahid.org

American Society of Interior Designers (ASID)
www.asid.org

Association of University Interior Designers
www.auid.org

British Institute of Interior Design
www.biid.org.uk

Council for Interior Design Accreditation (formally FIDER)
www.accredit-id.org

Institute of Store Planners
www.ispo.org

Interior Design Educators Council (IDEC)
www.idec.org

Interior Design Society (IDS)
www.interiordesignsociety.org

International Facility Management Association (IFMA)
www.ifma.org

International Federation of Interior Architects/Designers (IFI)
www.ifiworld.org

International Interior Design Association (IIDA)
www.iida.com

National Council for Interior Design Qualification (NCIDQ)
www.ncidq.org

CANADIAN ASSOCIATIONS

Association of Interior Designers of Nova Scotia (IDNS)
www.idns.ca

Association of Registered Interior Designers of New Brunswick (ARIDNB)
www.aridnb.ca

Association of Registered Interior Designers of Ontario (ARIDO)
www.arido.ca

Association Professionnelle des designers d'intérieur du Québec
www.apdiq.com

Interior Designers Association of Saskatchewan (IDAS)
www.idas.ca

Interior Designers Institute of British Columbia (IDIBC)
www.idibc.org

Interior Designers of Alberta
www.idalberta.com

Interior Designers of Canada (IDC)
www.interiordesigncanada.org

Professional Interior Designers Institute of Manitoba (PIDIM)
www.pidim.ca

ALLIED PROFESSIONAL ORGANIZATIONS, TRADE ASSOCIATIONS, AND RESOURCES

The following is a selected list of organizations and associations affiliated with the interior design and built environment industry and professions. A great deal of useful information can be downloaded from many of these sites.

American Hotel & Lodging Association
www.ahla.com

American Institute of Architects (AIA)
www.aia.org

American National Standards Institute (ANSI)
www.ansi.org

American Society for Testing and Materials (ASTM)
www.astm.org

American Society of Furniture Designers (ASFD)
www.asfd.com

American Society of Landscape Architects
www.asla.org

ARCOM Master Systems
www.arcomnet.com

Associated General Contractors of America
www.agc.org

Association of Professional Design Firms
www.apdf.org

British Contract Furnishing Association
www.thebcfa.com

Building Owners & Managers Association (BOMA)
www.boma.org

Business and Institutional Furniture Manufacturer's Association (BIFMA)
www.bifma.com

Business Design Center
www.thebcfa.com

Canada Green Building Council (CaGBC)
www.CaGBC.org

Center for Health Design
www.healthdesign.org

Center for Universal Design
www.design.ncsu.edu/cud

Color Marketing Group (CMG)
www.colormarketing.org

Construction Management Association of America
www.cmaanet.org

Construction Specifications Institute (CSI)
www.csinet.org

Contract Furniture Dealer Division

Independent Office Products and Furniture Dealers Association (formerly National Office Products Association)
www.iopfda.org

DIFFA National Office
www.diffa.org

Environmental Careers Organization
www.eco.org

Green Building Alliance
www.gbapgh.org

Harvard Design Magazine
www.gsd.harvard.edu/research/publications/hdm
Back issues of articles are available at the Harvard Graduate School of Design site.

Home Furnishings International Association
www.hfia.com

Hospitality Industry Network (NEWH)
www.newh.org

Illuminating Engineering Society of North America (IES)
www.iesna.org

Industrial Designers Society of America (IDSA)
www.idsa.org

InteriordesignPro
www.interiordesignpro.org
A Web site listing location for interior designers

International Association of Lighting Designers (IALD)
www.iald.org

International Code Council
www.iccsafe.org

International Furnishings and Design Association (IFDA)
www.ifda.com

Leadership in Energy and Environmental Design (LEED)
www.usgbc.org/leed

National Association of Home Builders
www.nahb.org

National Association of Schools of Art and Design (NASAD)
www.nasad.arts-accredit.org

National Association of Women Business Owners (NAWBO)
www.nawbo.org

National Council on Qualifications for Lighting Professionals (NCQLP)
www.ncqlp.org

National Fire Protection Association (NFPA)
www.nfpa.org

National Home Furnishings Association
www.nhfa.org

National Kitchen and Bath Association (NKBA)
www.nkba.org

National Restaurant Association
www.restaurant.org

National Trust for Historic Preservation
www.nationaltrust.org

NeoCon Trade Shows (Merchandise Mart Properties, Inc.)
www.merchandisemart.com

Organization of Black Designers (OBD)
www.core77.com/obd

Quebec Furniture Manufacturers Association
www.qfma.com

Retail Design Institute
www.retaildesigninstitute.org

Sweets Network—McGraw-Hill Construction
www.construction.com

Home page for the Sweets Catalog Files.
www.products.construction.com
Sweets product information site.

U.S. Green Building Council (USGBC)
www.usgbc.org

Whole Building Design Guidelines
www.wbdg.org

Other associations can be discovered by searching Google, Yahoo Business, or www.ipl.org/ref/AON. IPL is the Internet Public Library site.

HELPFUL GOVERNMENT AGENCY SITES

USA.gov
www.usa.gov
A portal to all U.S. government Web sites

Americans with Disabilities Act home page (Department of Justice)
www.ada.gov

Canada Revenue Agency
www.cra-arc.gc.ca
A portal for information on operating a small business in Canada

Environmental Protection Agency (EPA)
www.epa.gov

Equal Employment Opportunity Commission (EEOC)
www.eeoc.gov

Federal Trade Commission
www.ftc.gov

General Services Administration
www.gsa.gov

Library of Congress
www.loc.gov

Minority Business Development Agency
www.mbda.gov

Occupational Safety and Health Administration (OSHA) (Department of Labor)
www.osha.gov

U.S. Copyright Office
http://www.copyright.gov
Copies of the documents needed to register copyrights are available online.

U.S. Department of Commerce
www.doc.gov

U.S. Department of Justice
www.usdoj.gov

U.S. Department of Labor, Bureau of Labor Statistics
www.bls.gov

U.S. Internal Revenue Service
www.irs.gov
Most of the IRS forms and instruction booklets are available online.

U.S. Patent and Trademark Office
www.uspto.gov

U.S. Small Business Administration
www.sbaonline.sba.gov
A large amount of information for setting up and maintaining a small business is downloadable from the site.

GENERAL LEGAL RESOURCES

You can obtain specific information on legal requirements within your state by going to the home page for your state government (www.<statename>.gov). It will have links to the specific information you need.

Cornell Law School
www.law.cornell.edu
A very good site for a wide variety of federal and state laws. Other law school sites also provide legal information to the public.

National Conference of Commissioners on Uniform State Laws (NCCUSL)
www.nccusl.org

Nolo
www.nolo.com
A publisher of legal information on a wide variety of legal and business management topics.

GENERAL BUSINESS SITES

Allied Board of Trade, Inc.
www.alliedboardoftrade.com

American Institute of Certified Public Accountants
www.aicpa.org

American Management Association
www.amanet.org

American Society of Appraisers
www.appraisers.org
Some members specialize in business valuations.

American Women's Economic Development Corporation
www.awed.org

Directory of Associations
www.marketingsource.com

Dun & Bradstreet
www.dnb.com

Fuessler Group
www.fuessler.com
A publicity directory is available from this site for the A/E/C industry

Insurance Information Institute
www.iii.org
Insurance organization that promotes public understanding of insurance. Many insurance agencies and companies can be found on the Internet through searches on any business search engine.

John Wiley & Sons
www.wiley.com
Publisher of hundreds of interior design, architecture, and business topics books.

Lyon Mercantile Group
www.lyoncredit.com

National Small Business Association
www.nsba.net

National Society of Accountants
www.nsa.org

SCORE
www.score.org
A nonprofit organization dedicated to helping small businesses

Society for Marketing Professional Services
www.smps.org

Standard & Poor's Register of Corporations, Directors, and Executives
www.standardandpoors.com

Thomson Gale Research Company
www.gale.com
Publishers of e-research and educational publishing for libraries, schools, and businesses, including the *Encyclopedia of Associations*.

Toastmasters International
www.toastmasters.org

Ulrich's International Periodicals Directory
www.ulrichsweb.com
Extensive database, but not all magazines/periodicals are listed.

U.S. Hispanic Chamber of Commerce
www.ushcc.com

CAREER AND JOB INFORMATION

American Society of Interior Designers
www.asid.org

Career Resource for Interior Design Industry
www.interiordesignjobs.com

Careers in Interior Design
www.careersininteriordesign.com

International Interior Design Association
www.iida.org

Job-Job
www.job-e-job.com
Provides a listing of jobs available in architecture, interior design, and engineering.

Monster
www.monster.com
A popular job recruitment Web site for a wide variety of jobs.

U.S. Department of Labor, Bureau of Labor Statistics
www.bls.gov
Provides information on salary averages.